Writing Arguments

A Rhetoric with Readings

Eleventh Edition

Writing Arguments

A Rhetoric with Readings

Eleventh Edition

John D. Ramage
Arizona State University

John C. Bean
Seattle University

June Johnson
Seattle University

Pearson

330 Hudson Street, NY NY 10013

Director of English: Karon Bowers
Executive Producer and Publisher: Aron Keesbury
Development Editor: Steven Rigolosi
Marketing Manager: Nicholas Bolt
Program Manager: Rachel Harbour
Project Manager: Nathaniel J. Jones, SPi Global
Cover Designer: Pentagram
Cover Illustration: Christopher DeLorenzo
Manufacturing Buyer: Roy L. Pickering, Jr.
Printer/Binder: LSC Communications, Inc.
Cover Printer: Phoenix Color/Hagerstown

Acknowledgments of third-party content appear on pages 564–566, which constitute an extension of this copyright page.

Catalogue-in-Publishing Data is on file with the Library of Congress

1   18

Rental Edition ISBN 10:   0-134-75974-5
Rental Edition ISBN 13: 978-0-134-75974-6
A la Carte ISBN 10:   0-134-76096-4
A la Carte ISBN 13: 978-0-134-76096-4
Access Code Card ISBN 10:   0-134-80785-5
Access Code Card ISBN 13: 978-0-134-80785-0
Instructor Review Copy ISBN 10:   0-134-77059-5
Instructor Review Copy ISBN 13: 978-0-134-77059-8

Brief Contents

Detailed Contents

Public Health   461

Challenges in Education   477

Preface

Through ten editions, *Writing Arguments* has sustained its reputation as a leading college textbook in argumentation. By focusing on argument as a collaborative search for the best solutions to problems (as opposed to pro/con debate), *Writing Arguments* treats argument as a process of inquiry as well as a means of persuasion. Users and reviewers have consistently praised the book for teaching the critical thinking skills needed for writing arguments: how to analyze the occasion for an argument; how to analyze arguments rhetorically; how to ground an argument in the values and beliefs of the targeted audience; how to develop and elaborate an argument; and how to respond sensitively to objections and alternative views. We are pleased that in this eleventh edition, we have improved the text in key ways while retaining the text's signature strengths.

What's New in the Eleventh Edition?

Based on our continuing research into argumentation theory and pedagogy and on our own experiences as classroom teachers, we have made significant improvements in the eleventh edition that will increase students' understanding of the value of argument and help them negotiate the rhetorical divisiveness in today's world. Here are the major changes in the eleventh edition:

- **Use of Aristotle's "provisional truths" to address post-truth, post-fact challenges to argument.**   This edition directly engages the complexity of conducting reasoned argument in a public sphere that is often dominated by ideological camps, news echo chambers, and charges of fake news. A revised Chapter 1 uses Aristotle's view of probabilistic or provisional truths to carve out a working space for argument between unachievable certainty and nihilistic relativism. Chapter 1's view of argument as both truth-seeking and persuasion is carried consistently throughout the text. This edition directly tackles the challenges to reasoned argument posed by dominant ideological perspectives, siloed echo chambers, and a dependence on social media as a source of news.

- **A reordering, refocusing, and streamlining of chapters to create better pedagogical sequencing and coherence.**   The previous edition's Chapter 2, which focused on argument as inquiry combining summary writing and exploratory response, has been refocused and moved to Chapter 8. Previous Chapter 2 material on the genres of argument has now been placed in an expanded Chapter 7 on rhetorical analysis. This new sequencing allows students to focus first on understanding the principles of argument (Chapters 1-6) and then to switch to the critical thinking process of joining an argumentative conversation through reading and strong response. (See "Structure of the Text" later in this preface for further explanation.)

- **A new chapter on collaborative rhetoric as a bridge-building alternative to persuasion.**   Chapter 10, new to this edition, blends ideas from Rogerian communication with practices from conflict resolution to help prepare students for their roles in private, public, and professional life amidst clashing values and views. Explanations, guidelines, and exercises emphasize nonjudgmental listening, self-reflection, a search for common ground, and suggestions for encouraging ongoing problem-solving through learning, listening, and respectful use of language.

- **A substantially revised chapter on visual and multimodal arguments**. Chapter 9 on visual and multimodal rhetoric now includes a new example and guidelines for making persuasive videos as well as a new exercise to apply image analysis in the construction of visual arguments.

- **A revised chapter on rhetorical analysis.**   Chapter 7, "Analyzing Arguments Rhetorically," has been expanded by consolidating rhetorical instruction from several chapters into one chapter and linking it to the critical thinking skills required for joining an argumentative conversation.

- **Updated or streamlined examples and explanations throughout the text along with many new images.**   Instructors familiar with previous editions will find many new examples and explanations ranging from a new dialog in Chapter 1 to illustrate the difference between an argument and a quarrel to a streamlined appendix on logical fallacies at the end. New images, editorial cartoons, and graphics throughout the text highlight current issues such as legalizing marijuana, plastics in the ocean, graffiti in public places, a soda tax, cultural and religious diversity, refugees, travel bans, and cars' carbon footprints.

- **Two new student model essays, one illustrating APA style.**   One new student model essay evaluates gender bias in a high school dress code, and the other, illustrating APA style, explores the causes of math anxiety in children.

- **A handful of lively new professional readings in the rhetoric section of the text.**   New readings ask students to think about a ban on plastic bags, the social definition of adulthood, and the psychological effect of not recognizing ourselves in videos.

- **A thoroughly revised and updated anthology**.   The anthology features updated units as well as four entirely new units.

  - A new unit on self-driving cars explores the legal, economic, and societal repercussions of this new technological revolution in transportation.

  - A unit on the post-truth, post-fact era examines the difficulties of consuming news and evaluating the factual basis of news and scientific claims in the era of ideological siloes and of news as entertainment via social media.

  - A new unit on the public health crisis explores the personal and societal consequences of excessive consumption of sugar, the need to establish healthy eating habits in children, and the controversy over a soda tax.

  - A unit on challenges in education examines three areas of controversy: disciplinary policy in K-12 classrooms (restorative justice versus zero-tolerance); the voucher system and charter schools as alternatives to public school; and, at the college level, trigger warnings and divisive speakers on campus.

- An updated unit on sustainability examines the carbon tax and the environmental damage caused by the use and disposal of plastic bottles and plastic bags.
- The unit on immigration has been updated to explore the controversy over sanctuary cities and the American response to refugees.
- A brief argument classics unit offers some famous stylized historical arguments.

What Hasn't Changed? The Distinguishing Strengths of *Writing Arguments*

The eleventh edition of *Writing Arguments* preserves the text's signature strengths praised by students, instructors, and reviewers:

- **Argument as a collaborative search for "best solutions" rather than as pro-con debate.** Throughout the text, *Writing Arguments* emphasizes both the truth-seeking and persuasive dimensions of argument—a dialectic tension that requires empathic listening to all stakeholders in an argumentative conversation and the seeking of reasons that appeal to shared values and beliefs. For heated arguments with particularly clashing points of view, we show the value of Rogerian listening and, in this eleventh edition, point to collaborative rhetoric as a shift from making arguments to seeking deeper understanding and common ground as a way forward amid conflict.

- **Argument as a rhetorical act.** *Writing Arguments* teaches students to think rhetorically about argument: to understand the real-world occasions and contexts for argument, to analyze the targeted audience's underlying values and assumptions, to understand how evidence is selected and framed by an angle of vision, to appreciate the functions and constraints of genre, and to employ the classical appeals of *logos, pathos,* and *ethos.*

- **Argument as critical thinking.** When writing an argument, writers are forced to lay bare their thinking processes. Focusing on both reading and writing, *Writing Arguments* emphasizes the critical thinking that underlies reasoned argument: active questioning, empathic reading and listening, believing and doubting, asserting a contestable claim that pushes against alternative views, and supporting the claim with a logical structure of reasons and evidence—all while negotiating uncertainty and ambiguity.

- **Consistent grounding in argumentation theory.** To engage students in the kinds of critical and rhetorical thinking that argument demands, we draw on four major approaches to argumentation:
  - **The enthymeme as a rhetorical and logical structure.** This concept, especially useful for beginning writers, helps students "nutshell" an argument as a claim with one or more supporting *because* clauses. It also helps them see how real-world arguments are rooted in assumptions granted by the audience rather than in universal and unchanging principles.
  - **The three classical types of appeal—*logos, ethos,* and *pathos.*** These concepts help students place their arguments in a rhetorical context focusing on audience-based appeals; they also help students create an effective voice and style.

- **Toulmin's system of analyzing arguments.** Toulmin's system helps students see the complete, implicit structure that underlies an enthymeme and develop appropriate grounds and backing to support an argument's reasons and warrants, thus helping students tailor arguments to audiences. Toulmin analysis highlights the rhetorical, social, and dialectical nature of argument.
- **Stasis theory concerning types of claims.** This approach stresses the heuristic value of learning different patterns of support for different types of claims and often leads students to make surprisingly rich and full arguments.

- **Effective writing pedagogy.** This text combines explanations of argument with best practices from composition pedagogy, including exploratory writing, sequenced and scaffolded writing assignments, class-tested "For Writing and Discussion" tasks, and guidance through all stages of the writing process. To help students position themselves in an argumentative conversation, the text teaches the skills of "summary/strong response"—the ability to summarize a source author's argument and to respond to it thoughtfully. The moves of summary and strong response teach students to use their own critical and rhetorical thinking to find their own voice in a conversation.

- **Rhetorical approach to the research process.** *Writing Arguments* teaches students to think rhetorically about their sources and about the ways they might use these sources in their own arguments. Research coverage includes guidance for finding sources, reading and evaluating sources rhetorically, taking purposeful notes, integrating source material effectively (including rhetorical use of attributive tags), and citing sources using two academic citation systems: MLA (8th edition) and APA. The text's rhetorical treatment of plagiarism helps students understand the conventions of different genres and avoid unintentional plagiarism.

- **Extensive coverage of visual rhetoric.** Chapter 9 is devoted entirely to visual and multimodal rhetoric. Additionally, many chapters include an "Examining Visual Rhetoric" feature that connects visual rhetoric to the chapter's instructional content. The images that introduce each part of the text, as well as images incorporated throughout the text, provide opportunities for visual analysis. Many of the text's assignment options include visual or multimodal components, including advocacy posters or speeches supported with presentation slides.

- **Effective and engaging student and professional arguments.** The professional and student arguments, both written and visual, present voices in current social conversations, illustrate types of argument and argument strategies, and provide fodder to stimulate discussion, analysis, and writing.

Structure of the Text

Writing Arguments provides a coherent sequencing of instruction while giving instructors flexibility to reorder materials to suit their needs.

- Part One focuses on the principles of argument: an overview of argument as truth-seeking rather than pro-con debate (Chapter 1); the *logos* of argument including the enthymeme (Chapter 2); Toulmin's system for analyzing arguments (Chapter 3) and the selection and framing of evidence (Chapter 4); the rhetorical appeals of *ethos* and *pathos* (Chapter 5); and acknowledging and responding to alternative views (Chapter 6).

- Part Two shifts to the process of argument—helping students learn how to enter an argumentative conversation by summarizing what others have said and staking out their own position and claims. Chapter 7 consolidates instruction on rhetorical analysis to help students think rhetorically about an argumentative conversation. Chapter 8 focuses on argument as inquiry, teaching students the groundwork skills of believing and doubting, summarizing a source author's argument and speaking back to it with integrity.

- Part Three expands students' understanding of argument. Chapter 9 focuses on visual and multimodal argument. Chapter 10, new to the eleventh edition, teaches the powerful community-building skill of collaborative rhetoric as an alternative to argument. It focuses on mutual understanding rather than persuasion.

- Part Four (Chapters 11-15) introduces students to stasis theory, showing the typical structures and argumentative moves required for different claim types: definition, resemblance, causal, evaluation, and proposal arguments.

- Part Five (Chapters 16-18) focuses on research skill rooted in a rhetorical understanding of sources. It shows students how to use sources in support of an argument by evaluating, integrating, citing, and documenting them properly. An appendix on logical fallacies is a handy section where all the major informal fallacies are treated at once for easy reference.

- Part Six, the anthology, provides a rich and varied selection of professional arguments arranged into seven high-interest units, including self-driving cars, immigration, sustainability, education, public heath, and public media in an age of fake news and alternative facts. It also includes a unit on classic arguments. Many of the issues raised in the anthology are first raised in the rhetoric so that students' interest in the anthology topics will already be piqued.

Revel

Revel is an interactive learning environment that deeply engages students and prepares them for class. Media and assessment integrated directly within the authors' narrative lets students read, explore interactive content, and practice in one continuous learning path. Thanks to the dynamic reading experience in Revel, students come to class prepared to discuss, apply, and learn from instructors and from each other.

Learn more about Revel
http://www.pearson.com/revel

Supplements

Make more time for your students with instructor resources that offer effective learning assessments and classroom engagement. Pearson's partnership with educators does not end with the delivery of course materials; Pearson is there with you on the first day of class and beyond. A dedicated team of local Pearson representatives will work with you not only to choose course materials but also to integrate them into your class and assess their effectiveness. Our goal is your goal—to improve instruction with each semester.

Pearson is pleased to offer the following resources to qualified adopters of *Writing Arguments*. Several of these supplements are available to instantly download from Revel or on the Instructor Resource Center (IRC); please visit the IRC at www.pearsonhighered.com/irc to register for access.

- **INSTRUCTOR'S RESOURCE MANUAL,** by Hannah Tracy (Seattle University). Create a comprehensive roadmap for teaching classroom, online, or hybrid courses. Designed for new and experienced instructors, the Instructor's Resource Manual includes learning objectives, lecture and discussion suggestions, activities for in or out of class, research activities, participation activities, and suggested readings, series, and films as well as a Revel features section. Available within Revel and on the IRC.
- **POWERPOINT PRESENTATION.** Make lectures more enriching for students. The PowerPoint Presentation includes a full lecture outline and photos and figures from the textbook and Revel edition. Available on the IRC.

Acknowledgments

We are happy for this opportunity to give public thanks to the scholars, teachers, and students who have influenced our approach to composition and argument. For this edition, we owe special thanks to our long-time teammate and colleague at Seattle University, Hilary Hawley, who aided us in researching public controversies and finding timely, available readings on these issues. Hilary wrote the framing introductions, the headnotes, and the critical apparatus for many of the anthology units. Her experience teaching argument, especially he public controversies over sustainability, food, immigration, and health, shaped these units. We are also grateful to another of our Seattle University colleagues, Hannah Tracy, for writing the Instructor's Resource Manual, a task to which she brings her knowledge of argumentation and her experience teaching civic and academic argument. We thank Stephen Bean for his research on self-driving cars and on issues related to legalizing marijuana. Finally, we thank Kris Saknussemm and Janie Bube for their design contributions to several of the visual arguments in this edition.

We are particularly grateful to our talented students—Jesse Goncalves (argument on math anxiety), Hadley Reeder (argument on high school dress codes) and Camille Tabari (PSA video "It's a Toilet, Not a Trash Can")—who contributed to this edition their timely arguments built from their intellectual curiosity, ideas, personal experience, and research. Additionally, we are grateful to all our students whom we have been privileged to teach in our writing classes and to our other students who have enabled us to include their arguments in this text. Their insights and growth as writers have inspired our ongoing study of rhetoric and argumentation.

We thank too the many users of our texts who have given us encouragement about our successes and offered helpful suggestions for improvements. Particularly we thank the following scholars and teachers who reviewed the previous edition of *Writing Arguments* and whose valuable suggestions informed this new edition:

Max Hohner, Eastern Washington University

Jeff Kosse, Iowa Western Community College

Jeremy Meyer, Arizona State University

Jennifer Waters, Arizona State University

We wish to express our gratitude to our developmental editor Steven Rigolosi for his skill, patience, diligence, and deep knowledge of all phases of textbook production. Steve's ability to provide timely guidance throughout the production process made this edition possible.

As always, we thank our families, who ultimately make this work possible. John Bean thanks his wife, Kit, also a professional composition teacher, and his children Matthew, Andrew, Stephen, and Sarah, all of whom have grown to adulthood since he first began writing textbooks. Our lively conversations at family dinners, which now include spouses, partners, and grandchildren, have kept him engaged in arguments that matter about how to create a just, humane, and sustainable world. June Johnson thanks her husband, Kenneth Bube, a mathematics professor and researcher, and her daughter, Janie Bube. Ken and Janie have played major roles in the ongoing family analysis of argumentation in the public sphere on wide-ranging subjects. Janie's knowledge of environmental issues and digital design and Kenneth's of mathematical thinking and the public perception of science have broadened June's understanding of argument hotspots. They have also enabled her to meet the demands and challenges of continuing to infuse new ideas and material into this text in each revision.

John C. Bean

June Johnson

Writing Arguments

A Rhetoric with Readings

Eleventh Edition

PART ONE
Principles of Argument

Factory farming, the mass production of animals for meat on an industrial model, shown in this photo, is a network of controversial issues, including cruelty to animals, healthfulness of meat diets, disconnection of people from their food, strain on environmental resources, and economic effects on small farming.

1

Chapter 1
Argument: An Introduction

Learning Objectives

In this chapter you will learn to:

1.1 Explain common misconceptions about the meaning of *argument*.

1.2 Describe defining features of argument.

1.3 Understand the relationship of argument to the process of truth-seeking and inquiry.

This book is dedicated to the proposition that reasoned argument is essential for the functioning of democracies. By establishing a separation of powers and protecting individual rights, the U. S. Constitution places argument at the center of civic life. At every layer of democracy, government decisions about laws, regulations, right actions, and judicial outcomes depend on reasoned argument, which involves listening to multiple perspectives. As former Vice President Al Gore once put it, "Faith in the power of reason—the belief that free citizens can govern themselves wisely and fairly by resorting to logical debate on the basis of the best evidence available, instead of raw power—was and remains the central premise of American democracy."[1]

Yet, many public intellectuals, scholars, and journalists have written that we are now entering a *post-truth era*, where the "best evidence available" becomes unmoored from a shared understanding of reality. How citizens access information and how they think about public issues is increasingly complicated by the unregulated freedom of the Internet and the stresses of a globalized and ethnically and religiously diverse society. Many citizens now focus on the entertainment dimension of news or get their news from sources that match their own political leanings. One source's "news" may be another source's "fake news." In fact, the concept of argument is now entangled in post-truth confusions about what an argument is.

What, then, do we mean by *reasoned argument*, and why is it vital for coping with post-truth confusion? The meaning of reasoned argument will become clearer in this opening chapter and throughout this text. We hope your study of

---

[1] Al Gore, *Assault on Reason*. New York: Penguin, 2007, p. 2.

reasoned argument will lead you to value it as a student, citizen, and professional. We begin this chapter by debunking some common misconceptions about argument. We then examine three defining features of argument: It requires writers or speakers to justify their claims; it is both a product and a process; and it combines elements of truth-seeking and persuasion. Finally, we look closely at the tension between truth-seeking and persuasion to encourage you to use both of these processes in your approach to argument.

What Do We Mean by Argument?

1.1 Explain common misconceptions about the meaning of *argument*.

Let's begin by examining the inadequacies of two popular images of argument: fight and debate.

Argument Is Not a Fight or a Quarrel

To many, the word *argument* connotes anger and hostility, as when we say, "I just had a huge argument with my roommate," or "My mother and I argue all the time." We picture heated disagreement, rising pulse rates, and an urge to slam doors. Argument imagined as fight conjures images of shouting talk-show guests, flaming bloggers, or fist-banging speakers.

But to our way of thinking, argument doesn't imply anger. In fact, arguing is often pleasurable. It is a creative and productive activity that engages us at high levels of inquiry and critical thinking, often in conversation with people we like and respect. When you think about argument, we invite you to envision not a shouting match on cable news but rather a small group of reasonable people seeking the best solution to a problem. We will return to this image throughout the chapter.

Argument Is Not Pro-Con Debate

Another popular image of argument is debate—a presidential debate, perhaps, or a high school or college debate tournament. According to one popular dictionary, *debate* is "a formal contest of argumentation in which two opposing teams defend and attack a given proposition." Although formal debate can develop critical thinking, it has a key weakness: It can turn argument into a game of winners and losers rather than a process of cooperative inquiry.

For an illustration of this weakness, consider one of our former students, a champion high school debater who spent his senior year debating the issue of prison reform. Throughout the year he argued for and against propositions such as "The United States should build more prisons" and "Innovative alternatives to prison should replace prison sentences for most crimes." We asked him, "What do you personally think is the best way to reform prisons?" He replied, "I don't know. I haven't thought about what I would actually choose."

Here was a bright, articulate student who had studied prisons extensively for a year. Yet nothing in the atmosphere of pro-con debate had engaged him in truth-seeking inquiry. He could argue for and against a proposition, but he hadn't experienced the wrenching process of clarifying his own values and taking a personal stand. As we explain throughout this text, argument entails a desire for truth-seeking; it aims to find the best solutions to complex problems. We don't mean that arguers don't passionately support their own points of view or expose weaknesses in views they find faulty. Instead, we mean that their goal isn't to win a game but to find and promote the best belief or course of action.

Arguments Can Be Explicit or Implicit

Before we examine some of the defining features of argument, we should note also that arguments can be either explicit or implicit. *Explicit* arguments (either written or oral) directly state their contestable claims and support them with reasons and evidence. *Implicit* arguments, in contrast, may not look like arguments at all. They may be bumper stickers, billboards, posters, photographs, cartoons, vanity license plates, slogans on a T-shirt, advertisements, poems, or song lyrics. But like explicit arguments, they persuade their audience toward a certain point of view.

Consider the poster in Figure 1.1—part of one state's recent citizen campaign to legalize marijuana. The poster's comparative data about "annual deaths," its beautiful green marijuana leaves, and its cluster of peanuts make the implicit argument that marijuana is safe—even safer than peanuts.

The poster's intention is to persuade voters to approve the state initiative to legalize pot. But this poster is just one voice in a complex conversation. Does

Figure 1.1 An implicit argument favoring legalization of marijuana

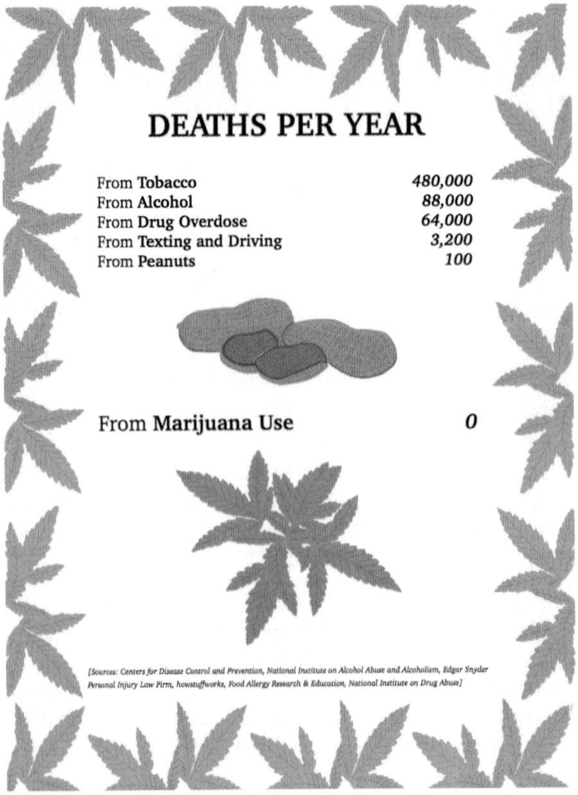

DEATHS PER YEAR

From **Tobacco**	480,000
From **Alcohol**	88,000
From **Drug Overdose**	64,000
From **Texting and Driving**	3,200
From **Peanuts**	100
From **Marijuana Use**	0

[Sources: Centers for Disease Control and Prevention, National Institute on Alcohol Abuse and Alcoholism, Edgar Snyder Personal Injury Law Firm, howstuffworks, Food Allergy Research & Education, National Institute on Drug Abuse]

marijuana have dangers that this poster makes invisible? Would children and adolescents have more access or less access to marijuana if the drug were legalized? Is marijuana a "gateway drug" to heroin and other, harder drugs? How would legalization of marijuana affect crime, drug trafficking, and prison populations? What would be the cultural consequences if marijuana became as socially acceptable as alcohol?

In contrast to the implicit argument made in Figure 1.1, consider the following explicit argument—a letter to the editor submitted by student writer Mike Overton. As an explicit argument, it states its claim directly and supports it with reasons and evidence.

An Explicit Argument Opposing Legalization of Marijuana

LETTER TO THE EDITOR BY STUDENT MIKE OVERTON

Proponents of legalizing marijuana claim that pot is a benign drug because it has a low risk of overdose and causes few deaths. Pot is even safer than peanuts, according to a recent pro-legalization poster. However, pot poses grave psychological risks, particularly to children and adolescents, that are masked if we focus only on death rate.

Several studies have shown adverse effects of marijuana on memory, decision making, and cognition. In one study, Duke University researchers examined IQ scores of individuals taken from childhood through age 38. They found a noticeable decline in the IQ scores of pot smokers compared with nonusers, with greater declines among those who smoked more. Daily pot smokers dropped, on average, eight IQ points.

There is also a clear link between pot usage and schizophrenia. Many studies have shown an increased risk of schizophrenia and psychosis from pot usage, particularly with regular use as an adolescent. Studies find that regular pot smokers who develop schizophrenia begin exhibiting symptoms of the disease earlier than nonusers, with the average diagnosis occurring 2.7 years earlier than for nonusers.

These are devastating mental illnesses that cut to the core of our well-being. We need to be sure our policies on marijuana don't ignore the documented mental health risks of pot, particularly to adolescents in the critical phase of brain development. I urge a "no" vote on legalizing marijuana in our state.

For Writing And Discussion

Implicit and Explicit Arguments

Any argument, whether implicit or explicit, tries to influence the audience's stance on an issue, with the goal of moving the audience toward the arguer's claim. Arguments work on us psychologically as well as cognitively, triggering emotions as well as thoughts and ideas. Each of the implicit arguments in Figures 1.2–1.4 makes a claim on its audience, trying to get viewers to adopt its position, perspective, belief, or point of view on an issue.

(continued)

Figure 1.2 Early 1970s cover of the controversial social protest magazine *Science for the People,* which has recently been revived

Figure 1.3 Image from website promoting education in prisons (HTTP://WWW.PRISONEDUCATION.COM/)

Figure 1.4 Cartoon on social etiquette and digital media *(continued)*

"Do you John promise that your schedule, please put your iPhone away, will never be more important than your times together?"

Individual task:

For each argument, answer the following questions:

1. Observe each argument carefully and then describe it for someone who hasn't seen it.
2. What conversation do you think each argument joins? What is the issue or controversy? What is at stake? (Sometimes "insider knowledge" might be required to understand the argument. In such cases, explain to an outsider the needed background information or cultural context.)
3. What is the argument's claim? That is, what value, perspective, belief, or position does the argument ask its viewers to adopt?
4. What is an opposing or alternative view? What views is the argument pushing against?
5. How do the visual details of each argument contribute to the persuasive effect?
6. Convert the implicit argument into an explicit argument by stating its claim and supporting reasons in words. How do implicit and explicit arguments work differently on the brains or hearts of the audience?

Group task:

Working in pairs or as a class, share your answers with classmates.

The Defining Features of Argument

1.2 Describe defining features of argument.

We now examine arguments in more detail. (Unless we say otherwise, by *argument* we mean explicit arguments that attempt to supply reasons and evidence to support their claims.) This section examines three defining features of such arguments.

Argument Requires Justification of Its Claims

To begin defining argument, let's turn to a humble but universal area of disagreement: the conflict between new housemates over house rules. In what way and in what circumstances do such conflicts constitute arguments?

AVERY: (*grabbing his backpack by the door*) See you. I'm heading for class.

DANIEL: (*loudly and rapidly*) Wait. What about picking up your garbage all over the living room?—that pizza box, those cans, and all those papers. I think you even spilled Coke on the rug.

AVERY: Hey, get off my case. I'll clean it up tonight.

With this exchange, we have the start of a quarrel, not an argument. If Daniel's anger picks up—suppose he says, "Hey, slobface, no way you're leaving this house without picking up your trash!"—then the quarrel will escalate into a fight.

But let's say that Daniel remains calm. The dialogue then takes this turn.

DANIEL: Come on, Avery. We had an agreement to keep the house clean.

Now we have the beginnings of an argument. Fleshed out, Daniel's reasoning goes like this: You should clean up your mess because we had an agreement to keep the house clean. The unstated assumption behind this argument is that people should live up to their agreements.

Now Avery has an opportunity to respond, either by advancing the argument or by stopping it cold. He could stop it cold by saying, "No, we never agreed to anything." This response pushes Avery's hapless housemates into a post-truth world where there is no agreement about reality. Unless stakeholders have a starting place grounded in mutually accepted evidence, no argument is possible. Their dispute can be decided only by power.

But suppose that Avery is a reasonable person of good will. He could advance the argument by responding this way:

AVERY: Yes, you are right that we had an agreement. But perhaps our agreement needs room for exceptions. I have a super-heavy day today.

Now a process of reasonable argument has emerged. Avery offers a reason for rushing from the house without cleaning up. In his mind his argument would go like this: "It is OK for me to wait until tonight to clean up my mess because I have a super-heavy day." He could provide evidence for his reason by explaining his heavy schedule (a group project for one course, a paper due in another, and his agreement with his boss to work overtime at his barista job throughout the afternoon). This reason makes sense to Avery, who is understandably immersed in his own perspective. However, it might not be persuasive to Daniel, who responds this way:

DANIEL: I appreciate your busy schedule, but I am planning to be at home all day, and I can't study in this mess. It is unfair for me to have to clean up your stuff.

Fleshed out, Daniel's argument goes like this: "It is not OK for you to leave trash in the living room, because your offer to clean your mess tonight doesn't override my right to enjoy a clean living space today." The dialogue now illustrates what is required for reasonable argument: (1) a set of two or more conflicting claims ("it is OK / is not OK to leave this mess until tonight") and (2) the attempt to justify the claims with reasons and evidence.

The first defining feature of argument, then, is the attempt to justify claims with reasons and evidence. Avery and Daniel now need to think further about how they can justify their claims. The disagreement between the housemates is not primarily about facts: Both disputants agree that they had established house rules about cleanliness, that Avery is facing a super-heavy day, and that Avery's mess disturbs Daniel. The dispute is rather about values and fairness—principles that are articulated in the unstated assumptions that undergird their reasons. Avery's assumption is that "unusual circumstances can temporarily suspend house rules." Daniel's assumption is that "a temporary suspension—to be acceptable—cannot treat other housemates unfairly." To justify his claim, therefore, Avery has to show not only that his day is super-heavy but also that his cleaning his mess at the end of the day isn't unfair to Daniel. To plan his argument, Avery needs to anticipate the questions his argument will raise in Daniel's mind: Will today's mess truly be a rare exception to our house rule, or is Avery a natural slob who will leave the house messy almost every day? What will be the state of the house and the quality of the living situation if each person simply makes his own exceptions to house rules? Will continuing to spill food and drinks on the carpet affect the return of the security deposit on the house rental?

In addition, Daniel needs to anticipate some of Avery's questions: Are temporary periods of messiness really unfair to Daniel? How much does Daniel's neat-freak personality get in the way of house harmony? Would some flexibility in house rules be a good thing? The attempt to justify their assumptions forces both Avery and Daniel to think about the degree of independence each demands when sharing a house.

As Avery and Daniel listen to each other's points of view (and begin realizing why their initial arguments have not persuaded their intended audience), we can appreciate one of the earliest meanings of the term *to argue*, which is "to clarify." As arguers clarify their own positions on an issue, they also begin to clarify their audience's position. Such clarification helps arguers see how they might accommodate their audience's views, perhaps by adjusting their own position or by developing reasons that appeal to their audience's values. Thus Avery might suggest something like this:

AVERY: Hey, Daniel, I can see why it is unfair to leave you with my mess. What if I offered you some kind of trade-off?

Fleshed out, Avery's argument now looks like this: "It is OK for me to wait until the end of the day to clean up my mess because I am willing to offer you a satisfactory trade-off." The offer of a trade-off immediately addresses Daniel's sense of being treated unfairly and might lead to negotiation on what this trade-off might be. Perhaps Avery agrees to do more of the cooking, or perhaps there are other areas of conflict that could become part of a trade-off bargain—noise levels, sleeping times, music preferences. Or perhaps Daniel, happy that Avery has offered a trade-off, says it isn't necessary: Daniel concedes that he can live with occasional messiness.

Whether or not Avery and Daniel can work out a best solution, the preceding scenario illustrates how the need to justify one's claims leads to a clarification of facts and values and to the process of negotiating solutions that might work for all stakeholders.

Argument Is Both a Process and a Product

As the preceding scenario revealed, argument can be viewed as a *process* in which two or more parties seek the best solution to a question or problem. Argument can also be viewed as a *product,* with each product being any person's contribution to the conversation at a given moment. In an informal discussion, the products are usually short pieces of conversation. In more formal settings, an orally delivered product might be a short, impromptu speech (say, during an open-mike discussion of a campus issue) or a longer, carefully prepared formal speech (as in a PowerPoint presentation at a business meeting or an argument at a public hearing for or against a proposed city project).

Similar conversations occur in writing. Roughly analogous to a small-group discussion is an exchange of the kind that occurs regularly online through informal chat groups or more formal blog sites. In an online discussion, participants have more thinking time to shape their messages than they do in a real-time oral discussion. Nevertheless, messages are usually short and informal, making it possible over the course of several days to see participants' ideas shift and evolve as conversants modify their initial views in response to others' views.

Roughly equivalent to a formal speech would be a formal written argument, which may take the form of an academic argument for a college course; a grant proposal; an online posting; a guest column for the op-ed* section of a newspaper; a legal brief; a letter to a member of Congress; or an article for an organizational newsletter, popular magazine, or professional journal. In each of these instances, the written argument (a product) enters a conversation (a process)—in this case, a conversation of readers, many of whom will carry on the conversation by writing their own responses or by discussing the writer's views with others. The goal of the community of writers and readers is to find the best solution to the problem or issue under discussion.

Argument Combines Truth-Seeking and Persuasion

In thinking about argument as a product, writers will find themselves continually moving back and forth between truth-seeking and persuasion—that is, between questions about the subject matter (What is the best solution to this problem?) and about audience (What do my readers already believe or value? What reasons and

---

* *Op-ed* stands for "opposite-editorial." It is the generic name in journalism for a signed argument that voices the writer's opinion on an issue, as opposed to a news story that is supposed to report events objectively, uncolored by the writer's personal views. Op-ed pieces appear in the editorial-opinion section of newspapers, which generally features editorials by the resident staff, opinion pieces by syndicated columnists, and letters to the editor from readers. The term *op-ed* is often extended to syndicated columns appearing in newsmagazines, advocacy websites, and online news services.

evidence will most persuade them?). Writers weave back and forth, alternately absorbed in the subject of their argument and in the audience for that argument.

Neither of the two focuses is ever completely out of mind, but their relative importance shifts during different phases of the development of an argument. Moreover, different rhetorical situations place different emphases on truth-seeking versus persuasion. We can thus place arguments on a continuum that measures the degree of attention a writer gives to subject matter versus audience. (See Figure 1.5.) At the full truth-seeking (left) end of the continuum might be an exploratory piece that lays out several alternative approaches to a problem and weighs the strengths and weaknesses of each with no concern for persuasion. At the other (persuasion) end of the continuum would be outright propaganda, such as a political adver-tisement that reduces a complex issue to sound bites and distorts an opponent's position through out-of-context quotations or misleading use of data. (At its most blatant, propaganda obliterates truth-seeking; it will use any tool, including bogus evidence, distorted assertions, and outright lies, to win over an audience.) In the middle ranges of the continuum, writers shift their focuses back and forth between inquiry and persuasion but with varying degrees of emphasis.

As an example of a writer focusing primarily on truth-seeking, consider the case of Kathleen, who, in her college argument course, addressed the definitional ques-tion "Is American Sign Language (ASL) a 'foreign language' for purposes of meeting the university's foreign language requirement?" Kathleen had taken two years of ASL at a community college. When she transferred to a four-year college, the chair of the foreign languages department would not allow her ASL coursework to count toward Kathleen's foreign language requirement. "ASL isn't a language," the chair said summarily. "It's not equivalent to learning French, German, or Japanese."

Kathleen disagreed, so she immersed herself in developing her argument. While doing research, she focused almost entirely on the subject matter, searching for what linguists, neurologists, cognitive psychologists, and sociologists have said about the language of deaf people. Immersed in her subject matter, she was only tacitly concerned with her audience, whom she thought of primarily as her classmates and the professor of her argument class—people who were friendly to her views and interested in her experiences with the deaf community. She wrote a well-documented paper, citing several scholarly articles, that made a good case to her classmates (and the professor) that ASL is indeed a distinct language.

Proud of the A she received on her paper, Kathleen decided for a subsequent assignment to write a second paper on ASL—but this time aiming it directly at the chair of the foreign languages department and petitioning her to accept ASL proficiency for the foreign language requirement. Now her writing task fell closer to the persuasive end of our continuum. Kathleen once again immersed herself in

Figure 1.5 Continuum of arguments from truth-seeking to persuasion

Truth Seeking				Persuasion
Exploratory essay	Delayed thesis argument	Classical argument	One-sided argument	Outright propaganda
Essay examining all sides of an issue and possibly not arriving at a conclusive answer	Argument as inquiry; asking audience to think out the issue with the writer	Argument, aimed at a neutral or skeptical audience, that shows awareness of different views	Argument aimed at a friendly audience (often for fundraising or calls to action)	Aggressive onesided argument that simply delivers a message

research, but this time she focused not on subject matter (whether ASL is a distinct language) but on audience. She researched the history of the foreign language requirement at her college and discovered some of the politics behind it (the foreign language requirement had been dropped in the 1970s and reinstituted in the 1990s, partly—a math professor told her—to boost enrollments in foreign language courses). She also interviewed foreign language teachers to find out what they knew and didn't know about ASL. She discovered that many teachers thought ASL was "easy to learn," so that accepting ASL would give students a Mickey Mouse way to avoid the rigors of a "real" foreign language class. Additionally, she learned that foreign language teachers valued immersing students in a foreign culture; in fact, the foreign language requirement was part of her college's effort to create a multicultural curriculum.

This increased understanding of her target audience helped Kathleen reconceptualize her argument. Her claim that ASL is a real language (the subject of her first paper) became only one section of her second paper, much condensed and abridged. She added sections showing the difficulty of learning ASL (to counter her audience's belief that learning ASL is easy), showing how the deaf community forms a distinct culture with its own customs and literature (to show how ASL would meet the goals of multiculturalism), and showing that the number of transfer students with ASL credits would be negligibly small (to allay fears that accepting ASL would threaten enrollments in language classes). She ended her argument with an appeal to her college's public emphasis (declared boldly in its mission statement) on eradicating social injustice and reaching out to the oppressed. She described the isolation of deaf people in a world where almost no hearing people learn ASL, and she argued that the deaf community on her campus could be integrated more fully into campus life if more students could talk with them. Thus the ideas included in her new argument—the reasons selected, the evidence used, the arrangement and tone—all were determined by her primary focus on persuasion.

Our point, then, is that all along the continuum, writers attempt both to seek truth and to persuade, but not necessarily with equal balance. Kathleen could not have written her second paper, aimed specifically at persuading the chair of the foreign languages department, if she hadn't first immersed herself in truth-seeking research that convinced her that ASL is indeed a distinct language. Note that we are not saying that Kathleen's second argument was better than her first. Both arguments fulfilled their purposes and met the needs of their intended audiences. Both involved truth-seeking and persuasion, but the first focused primarily on subject matter whereas the second focused primarily on audience.

Argument and the Problem of Truth in the 21st Century

1.3 Understand the relationship of argument to the process of truth-seeking and inquiry.

The tension that we have just examined between truth-seeking and persuasion raises an ancient issue in the field of argument: Is the arguer's first obligation to truth or to winning the argument? And just what is the nature of the truth to which arguers are supposed to be obligated?

Early Greek rhetoricians and philosophers—particularly the Sophists, Socrates, Plato, and Aristotle—all wrestled with this tension. In Plato's *Dialogues*, these questions were at the heart of Socrates' disagreement with the Sophists. The Sophists were professional rhetoricians who specialized in training orators to win arguments. Socrates, who valued truth-seeking over persuasion and believed that truth could be discovered through philosophic inquiry, opposed the Sophists. For Socrates (and Plato), Truth resided in the ideal world of forms, and through philosophic rigor humans could transcend the changing, shadowlike world of everyday reality to perceive the world of universals where Truth, Beauty, and Goodness resided. Through his method of questioning, Socrates would gradually peel away layer after layer of false views until Truth was revealed. The good person's duty, Socrates believed, was not to win an argument but to pursue this higher Truth. Socrates and Plato distrusted professional rhetoricians because these professionals were interested only in the power and wealth that came from persuading audiences to the orator's views. In contrast, Plato's pupil Aristotle maintained Plato's commitment to ethical living but valued rhetoric as a way of reaching conclusions or what he called "probable truth" in the realm of everyday living—the best answers available to people who were willing to think deeply and argue reasonably about a problem. Aristotle taught rhetoric and argument as collective inquiry in search of new understanding—probable truths and best solutions supported persuasively by reasons and evidence that could be shared and agreed upon.

Let's apply these perspectives to a modern example. Suppose your community is divided over the issue of raising environmental standards versus keeping open a job-producing factory that doesn't meet new guidelines for waste discharge. In a dispute between jobs and the environment, which is the best course? The Sophists would train you to argue any side of this issue on behalf of any lobbying group willing to pay for your services. This relativism and willingness to manipulate language led over time to the term *sophistry* being associated with trickery in argument. If, however, you applied Aristotle's practical concern for "probable truth," you would be inspired to listen to all sides of the dispute, peel away unsatisfactory arguments through reasonable inquiry, and commit yourself to a course of action that you have come to believe is the best for as many stakeholders as possible.

In sum, Plato was concerned with absolute truths residing in the spiritual world of forms, while Aristotle valued rhetoric's focus on probable truths in our messy human world. Aristotle's view is thus close to that expressed by Al Gore at the beginning of this chapter. Aristotle and Gore would agree that truth—the search for best solutions—is messy and complicated and needs to be negotiated in an ongoing spirit of argument. Every day we face complex questions with multiple stakeholders. Do sanctuary cities make citizens safer, as many sheriffs and police departments argue, or do they shelter criminals and endanger citizens, as some people contend? Should all controversial speakers be allowed to speak on college campuses, or should universities carefully monitor and restrict these public forums? There are no simple or clear-cut answers to these questions, but one thing is certain: People can't carry on productive argument if they retreat to siloed echo chambers where they encounter only those views with which they already agree. Daniel the neat freak has to encounter Avery the slob; otherwise, no growth is possible. Argument works only if we are willing to question and clarify our own positions and engage in dialogue with those stakeholders with whom we disagree.

This truth-seeking approach to argument helps us combat various traps that we may fall into. A first trap is that we might become intellectually lazy, failing to question easily found or sensationalist information and views. We might succumb to "desirability bias"[2]–the tendency to accept information that "we want to believe." Or we might cling to what political scientist Morgan Marietti calls "sacred values"[3]—religious or secular beliefs that are so central to our worldviews and identities that we accept them as absolute, unquestionable, and inviolable. For example, for some persons a woman's right to control her own body is a sacred value; for others, an unborn fetus's right to life is a sacred value. Because we hesitate to question our sacred values, our emotional adherence to them can create a network of beliefs that interpret the world for us. Emerging from our own siloed echo chambers is the best way to seek a shareable reality in what otherwise might seem a post-truth world. However, as we have seen, truth-seeking takes intellectual work and ethical commitment. To restore the value of argument as truth-seeking, we must accept the world as pluralistic, recognizing that others may not value what we value.

If we accept this pluralistic view of the world, do we then endorse the Sophists' radical relativism, freeing us to argue any side of any issue? Or do we doggedly pursue some modern equivalent of Aristotle's "probable truth"?

If your own sympathies are with argument as truth-seeking, then you must admit to a view of truth that is tentative, cautious, and conflicted, and you must embrace argument as process. In the 21st century, truth-seeking does not mean finding the "right answer" to a disputed question, but neither does it mean a valueless relativism in which all answers are equally good. Seeking truth means taking responsibility for determining the "best answer" or "best solution" to the question; it means considering the good of the entire community when taking into consideration the interests of all stakeholders. It means making hard decisions in the face of uncertainty. Viewed in this way, argument cannot "prove" your claim, but only make a reasonable case for it. Even though argument can't provide certainty, learning to argue effectively has deep value for society and democracy: It helps communities settle conflicts in a rational and humane way by finding, through the exchange of ideas, the best solutions to problems without resorting to violence.

For Writing and Discussion

Role-Playing Arguments

On any given day, the media provide evidence of the complexity of living in a pluralistic culture. Issues that could be readily decided in a completely homogeneous culture raise questions in a society that has fewer shared assumptions. Choose one of the following cases as the subject for a "simulation game" in which class members present the points of view of the people involved.

---

[2] Ben Tappin, Leslie van der Leer, and Ryan McKay define "desirability bias" in their op-ed piece, "Your Opinion Is Set in Stone." *The New York Times*, May 28, 2017, SR 8.

[3] Morgan Marietta, "From My Cold, Dead Hands: Democratic Consequences of Sacred Rhetoric." *The Journal of Politics* Vol. 70, No. 3, July 2008.

Case 1 : Political Asylum for a German Family Seeking the Right to Homeschool Their Children

In 2010 an Evangelical Christian family from Germany, Uwe and Hannelore Romeike and their five children, moved to the United States seeking asylum from political persecution. At the U.S. immigration hearings, the couple argued that if they remained in Germany their decision to homeschool their children would result in fines, possible arrest, and even forced separation from their children. German law forbids homeschooling on the grounds that failure to attend recognized schools will create "parallel societies" whose members will fail to integrate into Germany's open and pluralistic culture. In early 2011, a U.S. federal immigration judge granted political asylum to the family, denouncing the German government's policy against home-schooling. He called it "utterly repellent to everything we believe as Americans." However, in 2013 the Sixth Circuit Court unanimously overturned the original decision and revoked the family's status as political refugees. Stating that the United States cannot give political asylum to every victim of perceived unfairness in another country's laws, the court declared that Germany's ban on homeschooling did not constitute political persecution. The decision led to international debate about the role of homeschooling in a pluralistic society and about the definition of political persecution. In the United States, the Homeschooling Legal Defense Association urged that the case be heard by the United States Supreme Court and sponsored a petition drive supporting the Romeike family.

Your task:

Imagine a public hearing on this issue where all stakeholders are invited to present their points of view. The U.S. Immigration website offers the following definition of refugee status:

> Refugee status or asylum may be granted to people who have been persecuted or fear they will be persecuted on account of race, religion, nationality, and/or membership in a particular social group or political opinion.

Your goal isn't to make your own decision about this case but rather to bring to imaginative life all the viewpoints on the controversy. Hold a mock public hearing in which classmates play the following roles: (a) A U.S. parent advocating homeschooling; (b) a U.S. teacher's union representative opposing homeschooling; (c) an attorney arguing that the Romeike family meets the criteria for "refugee status"; (d) an attorney arguing that the Romeike family does not meet the criteria for refugee status; (e) a German citizen supporting the German law against homeschooling; (f) a Romeike parent arguing that the family would be persecuted if the family returned to Germany; (g) other roles that are relevant to this case.

Case 2 : HPV Vaccines for Sixth Grade Girls (and Boys)

In 2007 the pharmaceutical company Merck developed a vaccine against the sexually trans-mitted HPV virus (human papillomavirus), some strains of which can cause cervical cancer as well as genital warts. The company launched an extensive television campaign promoting the vaccine (which would bring substantial profits to Merck) and advised that girls should get the vaccine before they reach puberty. Following recommendations from doctors and medical researchers, several states passed laws mandating that the HPV vaccine for girls be included among the other vaccinations required of all children for entry into the sixth or seventh grades (depending on the state). These laws sparked public debate about the bene-fits versus potential adverse effects of vaccines, and about the state's versus parents' role in determining what vaccines a child should get.

(continued)

Your task:

Imagine a public hearing addressing what your state's laws should be concerning HPV vaccinations for prepubescent children. Your goal isn't to make your own decision about this case but rather to bring to imaginative life all the viewpoints in the controversy. Hold a mock hearing in which classmates play the following roles: (a) a cancer specialist who supports mandatory HPV vaccination for girls; (b) a public health specialist who supports expanding the requirement to include boys; (c) a skeptical person concerned about the potential adverse effects of vaccines in general; (d) a religiously conservative parent who believes in abstinence and monogamy and opposes the cultural message of the HPV vaccination.

Conclusion

In this chapter we explored the complexities of argument, showing that argument is not a fight or win-lose debate but rather a process of rational inquiry in search of the best solution to a problem shared by stakeholders. Good argument requires justification of its claim, is both a process and product, and combines truth-seeking with persuasion. We also showed that argument does not seek absolute truth (in Plato's and Socrates' sense) but messy probable truth (in Aristotle's sense). The best defense against the post-truth doubts that make argument impossible is to emerge from siloed echo chambers in order to seek views different from your own, and to treat these views respectfully. Although like the Sophists you can use the skills of argument to support any side of any issue, we hope you won't. We hope that, like Aristotle, you will use argument for inquiry and discovery and that you will consequently find yourself, on at least some occasions, changing your position on an issue while writing a rough draft (a sure sign that the process of arguing has complicated your views).

At the deepest level, we believe that the skills of reason and inquiry developed through writing arguments can help you get a clearer sense of who you are. If our culture sets you adrift in pluralism, argument can help you take a stand, based on truth-seeking, listening, and reasoning. In this text we will not tell you what position to take on any given issue. But as a responsible being, you will often need to take a stand, to define yourself, to say, "Here are the reasons that choice A is better than choice B, not just for me but for you also." If this text helps you base your commitments and actions on reasonable grounds, then it will be successful.

Chapter 2
The Core of an Argument

A Claim with Reasons

Learning Objectives

In this chapter you will learn to:

2.1 Describe the key elements of classical argument.

2.2 Explain the rhetorical appeals of *logos, ethos*, and *pathos.*

2.3 Distinguish between issue and information questions and between genuine and pseudo-arguments.

2.4 Describe the basic frame of an argument.

In Chapter 1 we explained that argument is best viewed not as a quarrel or as a pro-con debate, but rather as a conversation of reasonable stakeholders seeking the best solution to a shared problem or issue. As a conversation of stakeholders, argument is both a process and a product. The rest of Part One provides an overview of the parts of an argument along with the general principles that make arguments effective. This chapter focuses on the core of an argument, which is a structure of claim, reasons, and evidence. The remaining chapters of Part One cover the same territory with more elaboration and detail.

The Classical Structure of Argument

2.1 **Describe the key elements of classical argument.**

The core of an argument can best be understood by connecting it to the ancient pattern of classical argument revealed in the persuasive speeches of ancient Greek and Roman orators. Formalized by the Roman rhetoricians Cicero and Quintilian, the parts of the argument speech even had special names: the *exordium*, in which the speaker gets the audience's attention; the *narratio*, which provides needed background; the *propositio*, which is the speaker's claim or thesis; the *partitio*, which forecasts the main parts of the speech; the *confirmatio,* which presents the speaker's arguments supporting the claim; the *confutatio,* which summarizes and rebuts opposing views; and the *peroratio,* which concludes the speech by summing up the argument, calling for action, and leaving a strong, lasting impression. (Of course, you don't need to remember these tongue-twisting Latin terms. We cite them only to assure you that in writing a classical argument, you are joining a time-honored tradition that links back to the origins of democracy.)

Let's go over the same territory again using more contemporary terms. Figure 2.1 provides an organization plan showing the structure of a classical argument, which typically includes these sections:

- *The introduction.* Writers of classical argument typically begin by connecting the audience to the issue by showing how it arises out of a current event or by using an illustrative story, memorable scene, or startling statistic—something that grabs the audience's attention. They continue the introduction by focusing the issue—often by stating it directly as a question or by briefly

Figure 2.1 Organization plan for an argument with classical structure

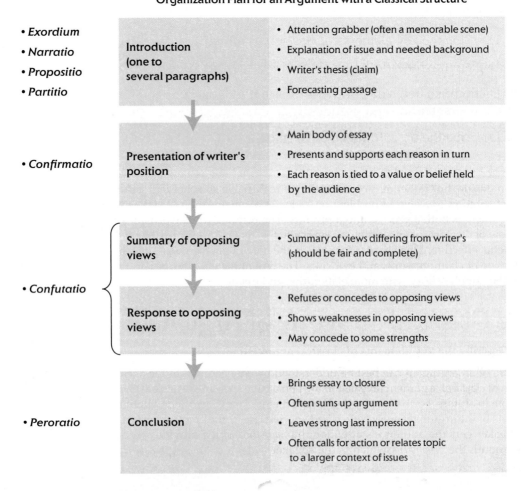

Organization Plan for an Argument with a Classical Structure

• *Exordium* • *Narratio* • *Propositio* • *Partitio*	**Introduction** **(one to** **several paragraphs)**	• Attention grabber (often a memorable scene) • Explanation of issue and needed background • Writer's thesis (claim) • Forecasting passage
• *Confirmatio*	**Presentation of writer's** **position**	• Main body of essay • Presents and supports each reason in turn • Each reason is tied to a value or belief held by the audience
• *Confutatio*	**Summary of opposing** **views**	• Summary of views differing from writer's (should be fair and complete)
	Response to opposing **views**	• Refutes or concedes to opposing views • Shows weaknesses in opposing views • May concede to some strengths
• *Peroratio*	**Conclusion**	• Brings essay to closure • Often sums up argument • Leaves strong last impression • Often calls for action or relates topic to a larger context of issues

summarizing opposing views—and providing needed background and context. They conclude the introduction by presenting their claim (thesis statement) and forecasting the argument's structure.

- *The presentation of the writer's position.* The presentation of the writer's own position is usually the longest part of a classical argument. Here writers present the reasons and evidence supporting their claims, typically choosing reasons that tie into their audience's values, beliefs, and assumptions. Usually each reason is developed in its own paragraph or sequence of paragraphs. When a paragraph introduces a new reason, writers state the reason directly and then support it with evidence or a chain of ideas. Along the way, writers guide their readers with appropriate transitions.

- *The summary and critique of alternative views.* When summarizing and responding to opposing views, writers have several options. If there are several opposing arguments, writers may summarize all of them together and then compose a single response, or they may summarize and respond to each argument in turn. As we explain in Chapter 6, writers may respond to opposing views either by refuting them or by conceding to their strengths and shifting to a different field of values.

- *The conclusion.* Finally, in their conclusion, writers sum up their argument, often restating the stakes in the argument and calling for some kind of action, thereby creating a sense of closure and leaving a strong final impression.

In this organization, the body of a classical argument has two major sections—one presenting the writer's own position and the other summarizing and responding to alternative views. The organization plan in Figure 2.1, and the discussion that follows, have the writer's own position coming first, but it is possible to reverse that order.

For all its strengths, an argument with a classical structure may not always be your most persuasive strategy. In some cases, you may be more effective by delaying your thesis, by ignoring alternative views altogether, or by showing great sympathy for opposing views (see Chapter 6). In some cases, in fact, it may be better to abandon argument altogether and simply enter into a empathic conversation with others to bridge the gaps between opposing points of view (see Chapter 10 on collaborative rhetoric as an alternative to classical argument). In most cases, however, the classical structure is a useful planning tool. By calling for a thesis statement and a forecasting statement in the introduction, it helps you see the whole of your argument in miniature. And by requiring you to summarize and consider opposing views, the classical structure alerts you to the limits of your position and to the need for further reasons and evidence. As we will show, the classical structure is particularly persuasive when you address a neutral or undecided audience.

Classical Appeals and the Rhetorical Triangle

2.2   **Explain the rhetorical appeals of *logos*, *ethos*, and *pathos*.**

Besides developing a template or structure for an argument, classical rhetoricians analyzed the ways that effective speeches persuaded their audiences. They identified three kinds of persuasive appeals, which they called *logos*, *ethos*, and

Figure 2.2 The rhetorical triangle

Message
LOGOS: *How can I make the argument internally consistent and logical? How can I find the best reasons and support them with the best evidence?*

Audience
PATHOS: *How can I make the reader open to my message? How can I best appeal to my reader's values and interests? How can I engage my reader emotionally and imaginatively?*

Writer or Speaker
ETHOS: *How can I present myself effectively? How can I enhance my credibility and trustworthiness?*

pathos. These appeals can be understood within a rhetorical context illustrated by a triangle with points labeled *message, writer or speaker,* and *audience* (Figure 2.2). Effective arguments pay attention to all three points on this *rhetorical triangle.*

As Figure 2.2 shows, each point on the triangle corresponds to one of the three persuasive appeals:

- *Logos* (Greek for "word") focuses attention on the quality of the message—that is, on the internal consistency and clarity of the argument itself and on the logic of its reasons and support. The impact of *logos* on an audience is referred to as its *logical appeal.*

- *Ethos* (Greek for "character") focuses attention on the writer's (or speaker's) character as it is projected in the message. It refers to the writer's credibility. *Ethos* is often conveyed through the writer's investment in his or her claim; through the fairness with which the writer considers alternative views; through the tone and style of the message; and even through the message's professional appearance on paper or screen, including correct grammar, flawless proofreading, and appropriate formats for citations and bibliography. In some cases, *ethos* is also a function of the writer's reputation for honesty and expertise independent of the message. The impact of *ethos* on an audience is referred to as the *ethical appeal* or *appeal from credibility.*

- *Pathos* (Greek for "suffering" or "experience") focuses attention on the values and beliefs of the intended audience. It is often associated with emotional appeal. But *pathos* appeals more specifically to an audience's imaginative sympathies—their capacity to feel and see what the writer feels and sees. Thus, when we turn the abstractions of logical discourse into a tangible and immediate story, we are making a pathetic appeal. Whereas appeals to *logos* and *ethos* can further an audience's intellectual assent to our claim, appeals to *pathos* engage the imagination and feelings, moving the audience to a deeper appreciation of the argument's significance.

A related rhetorical concept, connected to the appeals of *logos*, *ethos*, and *pathos*, is that of *kairos*, from the Greek word for "right time," "season," or "opportunity." This concept suggests that for an argument to be persuasive, its timing must be effectively chosen and its tone and structure in right proportion or measure. You may have had the experience of composing a contentious e-mail and then hesitating before clicking the "send" button. Is this the right moment to send this message? Is my audience ready to hear what I'm saying? Would my views be better received if I waited for a couple of days? If I send this message now, should I change its tone and content? *Kairos* refers to this attentiveness to the unfolding of time. We will return to this concept in Chapter 5, when we consider *ethos* and *pathos* in more depth.

Given this background on the classical appeals, let's turn now to *logos*—the logic and structure of arguments.

Issue Questions as the Origins of Argument

2.3   Distinguish between issue and information questions and between genuine and pseudo-arguments.

At the heart of any argument is an *issue*, which we can define as a controversial topic area (such as legalizing marijuana or building a wall between Mexico and the United States) that gives rise to differing points of view and conflicting claims. A writer can usually focus an issue by asking an issue question that invites alternative answers. Within any complex issue—for example, the issue of abortion—there are usually a number of separate issue questions: What governmental restrictions should be placed on abortion? Should the federal government authorize Medicaid payments for abortions? When does a fetus become a human person? (At conception? At three months? At birth?) What would be the consequences of expanding or limiting a woman's right to an abortion? (One person might stress that legalized abortion leads to greater freedom for women. Another person might respond that it lessens a society's respect for human life.)

Difference between an Issue Question and an Information Question

Of course, not all questions are issue questions that can be answered reasonably in differing ways. Some questions ask for information rather than for arguments. Rhetoricians have traditionally distinguished between *explication*, which is writing that sets out to inform or explain, and *argumentation*, which sets out to change a reader's mind. The following example illustrates the difference between an issue question and an information question:

Issue question: Should health insurance policies be required to cover contraceptives? (Reasonable persons can disagree.)

Information question: How does the teenage pregnancy rate in the United States compare with the rate in Sweden? (Reasonable persons assume that a "right answer" to this question is available.)

Although the difference between the two kinds of questions may seem simple, the distinction can become blurry. Suppose we asked "Why is the teenage pregnancy rate in Sweden lower than in the United States?" Although this might seem to be an informative question with a right answer, we can also imagine disagreement. One writer might emphasize Sweden's practical, secular sex-education courses, leading to more consistent use of contraceptives among Swedish teenagers. Another writer might point to the higher use of birth-control pills among teenage girls in Sweden (partly a result of Sweden's generous national health program) and to less reliance on condoms for preventing unwanted pregnancy. Another might argue that moral decay in the United States or a breakdown of the traditional family is responsible for the higher teenage pregnancy rate in the United States. Thus, what initially looks like a simple information question becomes an issue question.

How to Identify an Issue Question

You can generally tell whether a question is an information question or an issue question by determining whether your purpose is (1) to explain or teach something to your audience or (2) to change their minds about something. Often the same question can be an information question in one context and an issue question in another. Let's look at the following examples:

- *How does a diesel engine work?* (This is an information question because reasonable people who know about diesel engines will agree on how they work. This question would be posed by an audience of new learners asking experts for an explanation.)

- *Why is a diesel engine more fuel efficient than a gasoline engine?* (This also seems to be an information question because experts will probably agree on the answer. Once again, the audience seems to be new learners, perhaps students in an automotive class.)

- *What is the most cost-effective way to produce diesel fuel from crude oil?* (This could be an information question if experts agree and you are addressing new learners. But if you are addressing engineers and one engineer says process X is the most cost-effective and another engineer argues for process Y, then the question is an issue question.)

- *Should the present highway tax on diesel fuel be increased?* (This is certainly an issue question. One person says yes; another says no; another offers a compromise.)

For Writing and Discussion

Information Questions Versus Issue Questions

Working as a class or in small groups, decide which of the following questions are information questions and which are issue questions. Many of them could be either, depending on the rhetorical context. For those questions, create hypothetical contexts to show your reasoning.

1. What percentage of public schools in the United States are failing?
2. Which causes more traffic accidents, drunk driving or texting while driving?
3. What is the effect on children of playing first-person-shooter video games?
4. What effect will the advent of self-driving cars have on truck drivers?
5. Should people get rid of their land lines and have only cell phones?

Difference between a Genuine Argument and a Pseudo-Argument

Although every argument is sparked by an issue question with alternative answers, not every dispute over answers constitutes a rational argument. Rational arguments require three additional factors: (1) reasonable participants who operate within the conventions of reasonable behavior; (2) potentially sharable assumptions that can serve as a starting place or foundation for the argument; (3) confidence that evidence used in an argument is verifiable. Lacking these conditions, disagreements remain stalled at the level of pseudo-arguments. Let's look at each of these conditions in turn.

PSEUDO-ARGUMENTS CAUSED BY UNREASONABLE BEHAVIOR Reasonable behavior in argument assumes the possibility of growth and change; disputants may modify their views as they acknowledge strengths in an alternative view or weaknesses in their own. Such growth becomes impossible—and argument degenerates to pseudo-argument—when disputants are so rigidly committed to their positions that they can't imagine alternative views. Consider the case of the true believer and the fanatical skeptic.

From one perspective, true believers are admirable persons, guided by unwavering values and beliefs. True believers stand on solid rock, unwilling to compromise their principles or bend to the prevailing winds. But from another perspective, true believers can seem rigidly fixed, incapable of growth or change. In Chapter 1, we mentioned that arguers can cling to *sacred values*—either religious or secular principles that they consider absolute, inviolable, indisputable. When true believers from two clashing belief systems—each with its own set of sacred values—try to engage in dialogue with each other, a truth-seeking exchange of views becomes difficult. They talk past each other; dialogue is replaced by monologue from within isolated silos. Once true believers push each other's buttons on global warming, guns, health care, taxes, political correctness, or some other issue, each disputant resorts to an endless replaying of the same prepackaged arguments based on absolute principles. Disagreeing with a true believer is like ordering the surf to quiet down. The only response is another crashing wave.

In contrast to the true believer, the fanatical skeptic dismisses the possibility of ever believing anything. Skeptics often demand proof where no proof is possible. So what if the sun has risen every day of recorded history? That's no proof that it will rise tomorrow. Short of absolute proof, which never exists, fanatical skeptics accept nothing. In a world where the most we can hope for is increased audience adherence to our ideas, the skeptic demands an ironclad, logical demonstration of our claim's rightness.

PSEUDO-ARGUMENTS CAUSED BY LACK OF SHARED ASSUMPTIONS   As we have seen, reasonable argument degenerates to pseudo-argument when there is no possibility for listening, learning, growth, or change. In this section, we look more closely at a cause of unreasonableness in argument: lack of shared assumptions.

A lack of shared assumptions necessarily dooms arguments about purely personal opinions—for example, someone's claim that opera is boring or that pizza tastes better than nachos. Of course, a pizza-versus-nachos argument might be possible if the disputants assume a shared criterion about nutrition. For example, a nutritionist could argue that a vegetable-laden pizza is better than nachos because pizza provides more balanced nutrients per calorie than nachos do. But if one of the disputants responds, "Nah, nachos are better than pizza because nachos taste better," then he makes a different assumption—"My sense of taste is better than your sense of taste." This is a wholly personal standard, an assumption that others are unable to share.

Lack of shared assumptions can also doom arguments when the disputants have different ideologies, as we saw in the discussion of true believers. *Ideology* is an academic word for belief systems or worldviews. We all have our own ideologies. We all look at the world through a lens shaped by our life's experiences. Our beliefs and values are shaped by our family background, our friends, our culture, our particular time in history, our race or ethnicity, our gender or sexual orientation, our social class, our religion, our education, and so forth. Because we tend to think that our particular lens for looking at the world is natural and universal rather than specific to ourselves, we must be aware that persons who disagree with us may not share our deepest assumptions and beliefs.

This lack of shared assumptions is evident in many disputes concerning politics or religion. For example, consider differences over how to interpret the Bible within communities identifying as Christian. Some Christian groups choose a straightforward, literal interpretation of the Bible as God's inerrant word, sometimes quoting Biblical passages as "proof texts" to support their stand on civic issues. Others believe the Bible is divinely inspired, meant to lead humans to a relationship with God, but transmitted through human authors. Other groups tend to read the Bible metaphorically or mythically, focusing on the paradoxes, historical contexts, and interpretive complexities of the Bible. Still other Christian groups read it as an ethical call for social justice. Members of these different Christian groups may not be able to argue rationally about, say, evolution or gay marriage because they have very different ways of reading Biblical passages and invoking the Bible's authority. Similarly, within other religious traditions, believers may also differ about the meaning and applicability of their sacred texts to scientific issues and social problems.

Similar disagreements about assumptions occur in the political arena as well. Our point is that certain religious or political beliefs or texts cannot be evoked for evidence or authority when an audience does not assume the belief's truth or does not agree on the way that a given text should be read or interpreted.

PSEUDO-ARGUMENTS CAUSED BY LACK OF CONFIDENCE IN EVIDENCE
Finally, pseudo-arguments arise when disputants can't agree about the trustworthiness of particular evidence or about the possibility of trustworthy evidence existing at all, as if all facts are relative—an especially troublesome problem in

an era where many have raised concerns about "fake news" and "alternative facts." Reasonable arguments must be grounded in evidence that can be verified and trusted. Sometimes unethical writers invent facts and data to create propaganda, advance a conspiracy theory, or make money from the sale of fake stories. Scientific fraud has also occasionally occurred wherein scientists have fudged their data or even made up data to support a claim. Tabloids and fringe news sites are notorious for spreading fake news, often in their attention-grabbing but bizarre headlines ("Farmer shoots 23-pound grasshopper").

For disputants with different ideologies, pseudo-arguments may even occur with issues grounded in science. Liberals may distrust scientific data about the safety of genetically modified organisms, whereas conservatives may distrust the scientific data about climate change. Genuine argument can emerge only when all sides of the dispute agree that any given evidence derives from verifiable facts or data. We don't mean that reasonable disputants must use the same facts: Arguers necessarily and always select and frame their evidence to support their points (see the discussion of *angle of vision* in Chapter 4). But no matter what evidence is chosen, disputants must agree that the evidence is verifiable—that it is real news or evidence, not fake news or evidence.

For Writing and Discussion

Reasonable Arguments Versus Pseudo-Arguments

Individual task:

Which of the following questions will lead to reasonable arguments, and which will lead only to pseudo-arguments? Explain your reasoning.

1. Are the *Star Wars* films good science fiction?
2. Is it ethically justifiable to capture dolphins or orca whales and train them for human entertainment?
3. Should cities subsidize professional sports venues?
4. Is this abstract oil painting created by a monkey smearing paint on a canvas a true work of art?
5. Are nose rings and tongue studs attractive?

Group task:

Working in pairs, small groups, or as a class, share your reasoning about these questions with classmates.

Frame of an Argument: A Claim Supported by Reasons

2.4   Describe the basic frame of an argument.

We said earlier that an argument originates in an *issue question*, which by definition is any question that provokes disagreement about the best answer. When you write an argument, your task is to take a position on the issue and to support it with reasons and evidence. The *claim* of your essay is the position you want your audience to accept. To put it another way, your claim is your essay's *thesis state-ment*, a one-sentence summary answer to your issue question. Your task, then, is to make a claim and support it with reasons.

What Is a Reason?

A *reason* (also called a *premise*) is a claim used to support another claim. In speaking or writing, a reason is usually linked to the claim with a connecting word such as *because, since, for, so, thus, consequently,* or *therefore,* indicating that the claim follows logically from the reason.

Let us take an example of a controversial issue that frequently gets reported in the news—the public debate over keeping large sea mammals such as dolphins, porpoises, and orcas (killer whales) in captivity in marine parks where they entertain large crowds with their performances. This issue has many dimensions, including safety concerns for both the animals and their human trainers, as well as moral, scientific, legal, and economic concerns. Popular documentary films have heightened the public's awareness of the dangers of captivity to both the animals and the humans who work with them. For example, *The Cove* (2009) exposes the gory dolphin hunts in Japan in which fishermen kill dolphins en masse, capturing some for display in shows around the world. *Blackfish* (2013) tells the history of the orca Tilikum, who in 2010 killed his trainer, Dawn Blancheau, at SeaWorld in Orlando, Florida. The death of Tilikum in 2017 resparked public debates about treatment of marine animals in captivity. Recently a flurry of legal efforts to release the captive orca Lolita back into the wild has also contributed to the larger battle among advocacy, governmental, scientific, and commercial groups over the value of marine parks.

In one of our recent classes, students heatedly debated the ethics of capturing wild dolphins and training them to perform in marine parks. One student cited his sister's internship at SeaWorld San Diego, where she worked on sea mammal rescue and rehabilitation, one of the marine park's worthy projects. In response, another student mentioned the millions of dollars these marine parks make on their dolphin and orca shows as well as on the stuffed animals, toys, magnets, T-shirts, and hundreds of other lucrative marine park souvenirs. Here are the frameworks the class developed for two alternative positions on this public issue:

One View

CLAIM: The public should not support marine parks.

REASON 1: Marine parks inhumanely separate dolphins and orcas from their natural habitats.

REASON 2: The education these parks claim to offer about marine mammals is just a series of artificial, exploitive tricks taught through behavior modification.

REASON 3: These parks are operated by big business with the goal of making large profits.

REASON 4: Marine parks encourage artificial breeding programs and cruel hunts and captures.

REASON 5: Marine parks promote an attitude of human dominance over animals.

Alternative View

CLAIM: The public should continue to enjoy marine parks.

REASON 1: These parks observe accreditation standards for animal welfare, health, and nutrition.

REASON 2: These marine parks enable scientists and veterinarians to study animal behavior in ways not possible with field studies in the wild.

REASON 3: These marine parks provide environmental education and memorable entertainment.

REASON 4: Marine parks use some of their profits to support research, conservation, and rescue and rehabilitation programs.

REASON 5: In their training of dolphins and orcas, these marine parks reinforce natural behaviors, exercise the animals' intelligence, and promote beneficial bonding with humans.

Formulating a list of reasons in this way breaks your argumentative task into a series of subtasks. It gives you a frame for building your argument in parts. In this example, the frame for the argument opposing commercial use of sea mammals suggests five different lines of reasoning a writer might pursue. You might use all five reasons or select only two or three, depending on which reasons would most persuade the intended audience. Each line of reasoning would be developed in its own separate section of the argument. For example, you might begin one section of your argument with the following sentence: "The public should not support marine parks because they teach dolphins and orcas clownish tricks and artificial behaviors, which they pass off as 'education' about these animals." You would then provide examples of the tricks that dolphins and orcas are taught, explain how these stunts contrast with their natural behaviors, and offer examples of erroneous facts or information provided by commercial marine parks. You might also need to support the underlying assumption that it is good to acquire *real knowledge* about sea mammals in the wild. You would then proceed in the same manner for each separate section of your argument.

To summarize: The frame of an argument consists of the claim (the essay's thesis statement), which is supported by one or more reasons, which are in turn supported by evidence or sequences of further reasons.

For Writing and Discussion

Using Images to Support an Argument

In Chapter 1, we discussed the way that images and photographs can make implicit arguments. This exercise asks you to consider how images can shape or enhance an argument. Imagine that your task is to argue why a nonprofit group in your city should (or should not) offer as a fund-raising prize a trip to Sea-World in Orlando, Florida; San Antonio, Texas; or San Diego, California. Examine the photographs of orcas in Figures 2.3 and 2.4 and describe the implicit argument that each photo seems to make about these whales. How might one or both of these photos be used to support an argument for or against the prize trip to Sea-World? What reasons for going (or not going) to SeaWorld are implied by each photo? Briefly sketch out your argument and explain your choice of the photograph(s) that support your position.

Figure 2.3 Orca performance at a marine park

Figure 2.4 Orcas breaching

Expressing Reasons in *Because* Clauses

Chances are that when you were a child, the word *because* contained magical explanatory powers. (*I don't want that kind of butter on my toast! Why? Because. Because why? Just because.*) Somehow *because* seemed decisive. It persuaded people to accept your view of the world; it changed people's minds. Later, as you got older, you discovered that *because* only introduced your arguments and that it was the reasons following *because* that made the difference. Still, *because* introduced you to the powers potentially residing in the adult world of logic.

This childhood power of *because* perhaps explains why *because* clauses are the most common way of linking reasons to a claim. For example:

> The public should not support marine parks because these parks inhumanely separate dolphins and orcas from their natural habitats.

Of course, there are also many other ways to express the logical connection between a reason and a claim. Our language is rich in ways of stating *because* relationships:

- Marine parks inhumanely separate dolphins and orcas from their natural habitats. Therefore, the public should not support marine parks.

- Marine parks inhumanely separate dolphins and orcas from their natural habitats, so the public should not support these parks.

- One reason that the public should not support marine animal parks is that these parks inhumanely separate dolphins and orcas from their natural habitats.

- My argument that the public should not support marine animal parks is grounded on evidence that these parks inhumanely separate dolphins and orcas from their natural habitats.

Even though logical relationships can be stated in various ways, writing out one or more *because* clauses seems to be the most succinct and manageable way to clarify an argument for yourself. We therefore suggest that at some time in the writing process, you create a *working thesis statement* that summarizes your main reasons as *because* clauses attached to your claim.*

When you compose your own working thesis statement depends largely on your writing process. Some writers like to plan their whole argument from the start and compose their working thesis statements with *because* clauses before they write their rough drafts. Others discover their arguments as they write. Some writers use a combination of both techniques. For these writers, an extended working thesis statement is something they might write halfway through the composing process as a way of ordering their argument when various branches seem to be growing out of control. Or they might compose a working thesis

---

* A working thesis statement opposing the commercial use of captured dolphins and orcas might look like this: The public should not support marine parks because marine parks inhumanely separate dolphins and orcas from their natural habitats; because marine parks are mainly big businesses driven by profit; because marine parks create inaccurate and incomplete educational information about dolphins and orcas; because marine parks encourage inhumane breeding programs, hunts, and captures; and because marine parks promote an attitude of human dominance over animals. You probably would not put a bulky thesis statement like this into your essay; rather, a working thesis statement is a behind-the-scenes way of summarizing your argument so that you can see it fully and clearly.

statement after they've written a complete first draft as a way of checking the essay's unity.

The act of writing your extended thesis statement can be simultaneously frustrating and thought provoking. Composing *because* clauses can be a powerful discovery tool, causing you to think of many different kinds of arguments to support your claim. But it is often difficult to wrestle your ideas into the *because* clause shape, which may seem overly tidy for the complex network of ideas you are working with. Nevertheless, trying to summarize your argument as a single claim with reasons should help you see more clearly the emerging shape of your argument.

For Writing and Discussion

Developing Claims and Reasons

Try this group exercise to help you see how writing *because* clauses can be a discovery procedure. Divide into small groups. Each group member should contribute an issue with potentially opposing claims. While thinking of your issue, imagine a person who might disagree with you about it. This person will become your audience. Discussing each group member's issue in turn, help each member develop a claim supported by several reasons that might appeal to the imagined audience. Express each reason as a *because* clause. Then write out the working thesis statement for each person's argument by attaching the *because* clauses to the claim. Finally, try to create *because* clauses in support of an alternative claim for each issue. Each group should select two or three working thesis statements to present to the class.

Conclusion

This chapter introduced you to the structure of classical argument, to the rhetorical triangle (message, writer or speaker, and audience), and to the classical appeals of *logos*, *ethos*, and *pathos*. It also showed how arguments originate in issue questions, how issue questions differ from information questions, and how reasonable arguments differ from pseudo-arguments. The frame of an argument is a claim supported by reasons. As you generate reasons to support your own arguments, it is often helpful to articulate them as *because* clauses attached to the claim.

In the next chapter we will see how to support a reason by examining its logical structure, uncovering its unstated assumptions, and planning a strategy of development.

Writing Assignment

An Issue Question and Working Thesis Statements

Decide on an issue and a claim for a classical argument that you would like to write. Also imagine a reader who might be skeptical of your claim. Write a one-sentence question that summarizes the controversial issue that your claim addresses. Then draft a working thesis statement for your proposed argument. Organize the thesis as a claim with bulleted *because* clauses for reasons. You should have at least two reasons, but it is okay to have three or four. Also include an opposing thesis statement—that is, a claim with *because* clauses for an alternative position on your issue. Think of this opposing argument as your imagined reader's starting position.

Unless you have previously done research on an issue, it is probably best to choose an issue based on your personal experiences and observations. For example, you might consider issues related to your college or high school life, your work life, your experiences in clubs or family life, your prospective career, and so forth. (Part Two of this text introduces you to research-based argument.) As you think about your claim and *because* clauses for this assignment, take comfort in the fact that you are in a very early stage of the writing process: the brainstorming stage. Writers almost always discover new ideas when they write a first draft. As they take their writing project through multiple drafts and share their drafts with readers, their views may change substantially. In fact, honest writers can change positions on an issue by discovering that a counter-argument is stronger than their own. Thus the working thesis statement that you submit for this assignment may evolve when you begin to draft your essay.

Below, as well as in Chapters 3 and 4, we follow the process of student writer Carmen Tieu as she constructs an argument on violent video games. During a class discussion, Carmen mentioned a psychology professor who described playing violent video games as gendered behavior (overwhelmingly male). The professor indicated his dislike for such games, pointing to their antisocial, dehumanizing values. In class, Carmen described her own enjoyment of violent video games—particularly first-person-shooter games—and reported the pleasure that she derived from beating boys at Halo 2 and 3. Her classmates were interested in her ideas. She knew that she wanted to write an argument on this issue. The following is Carmen's submission for this assignment.

Carmen's Issue Question and Working Thesis Statements

Issue Question: Should girls be encouraged to play first-person-shooter video games?
My claim: First-person-shooter (FPS) video games are great activities for girls,
- because they empower girls when they beat guys at their own game.
- because they equip girls with skills that free them from feminine stereotypes.
- because they give girls a different way of bonding with males.
- because they give girls new insights into a male subculture.
Opposing claim: First-person-shooter games are a bad activity for anyone, especially girls,
- because they promote antisocial values such as indiscriminate killing.
- because they amplify the bad, macho side of male stereotypes.
- because they waste valuable time that could be spent on something constructive.
- because FPS games could encourage women to see themselves as objects.

Chapter 3
The Logical Structure of Arguments
Logos

Learning Objectives

In this chapter you will learn to:

3.1 Explain the logical structure of argument in terms of claim, reason, and assumption granted by the audience.

3.2 Use the Toulmin system to describe an argument's logical structure.

3.3 Use the Toulmin system to generate ideas for your argument and test it for completeness.

In Chapter 2 you learned that the core of an argument is a claim supported by reasons and that these reasons can often be stated as *because* clauses attached to a claim. In this chapter, we examine the logical structure of arguments in more depth.

An Overview of *Logos*: What Do We Mean by the "Logical Structure" of an Argument?

3.1 **Explain the logical structure of argument in terms of claim, reason, and assumption granted by the audience.**

As you will recall from our discussion of the rhetorical triangle, *logos* refers to the strength of an argument's support and its internal consistency. *Logos* is the argument's logical structure. But what do we mean by "logical structure"?

Formal Logic Versus Real-World Logic

First of all, what we *don't* mean by logical structure is the kind of precise certainty you get in a philosophy class in formal logic. Logic classes deal with symbolic assertions that are universal and unchanging, such as "If all *p*s are *q*s and if *r* is a *p*, then *r* is a *q*." This statement is logically certain so long as *p*, *q*, and *r* are pure abstractions. But in the real world, *p*, *q*, and *r* turn into actual things, and the relationships among them suddenly become fuzzy. For example, *p* might be a class of actions called "Sexual Harassment," while *q* could be the class called "Actions That Justify Getting Fired from One's Job." If *r* is the class "Telling Off-Color Stories," then the logic of our *p–q–r* statement suggests that telling off-color stories (*r*) is an instance of sexual harassment (*p*), which in turn is an action justifying getting fired from one's job (*q*).

Now, most of us would agree that sexual harassment is a serious offense that might well justify getting fired. In turn, we might agree that telling off-color stories, if the jokes are sufficiently raunchy and are inflicted on an unwilling audience, constitutes sexual harassment. But few of us would want to say categorically that all people who tell off-color stories are harassing their listeners and ought to be fired. Most of us would want to know the particulars of the case before making a final judgment.

In the real world, then, it is difficult to say that *r*s are always *p*s or that every instance of a *p* results in *q*. That is why we discourage students from using the word *prove* in claims they write for arguments (as in "This paper will prove that euthanasia is wrong"). Real-world arguments seldom *prove* anything. They can only make a good case for something, a case that is more or less strong, more or less probable. Often the best you can hope for is to strengthen the resolve of those who agree with you or weaken the resistance of those who oppose you.

The Role of Assumptions

A key difference, then, between formal logic and real-world argument is that real-world arguments are not grounded in abstract, universal statements. Rather, as we shall see, they must be grounded in beliefs, assumptions, or values granted by the audience. A second important difference is that in real-world arguments, these beliefs, assumptions, or values are often unstated. So long as writer and audience share the same assumptions, it's fine to leave them unstated. But if these underlying assumptions aren't shared, the writer has a problem.

To illustrate the nature of this problem, suppose that you are an environmentalist opposed to the use of plastic bags in grocery stores. You have several reasons for opposing these bags, one of which is their role in polluting the oceans. You express this reason in a *because* clause as follows:

> States should ban plastic bags from grocery stores because banning bags will reduce plastic pollution in the ocean.

On the face of it, this is a plausible argument, but it depends on the audience's accepting the writer's assumption that it is good to reduce plastic pollution in the ocean. In other words, you might agree that plastics are polluting the ocean, but unless you also believe that this pollution is significantly harming the oceans, you might not automatically agree that plastic bags should be banned from grocery stores. What if you believe that pollution-caused damage to the ocean is not as severe as proponents claim? What if you believe that plastic bags account for only a small percentage of plastic pollution in the oceans? What if you believe that the harm to the oceans is outweighed by the environmental benefits of plastic bags, which are reusable, recyclable, and more ecofriendly to produce and transport than paper bags? What if you believe that harm to the oceans might soon be reduced by scientific advances in creating biodegradable plastics or in developing microorganisms that "eat" plastics? If these were your beliefs, the argument wouldn't work for you because you would reject its underlying assumption that plastic pollution is significantly harmful. To make this line of reasoning persuasive, the writer would have to provide evidence not only that plastic bags are polluting the ocean but also that this pollution is harmful enough to justify a ban.

The Core of an Argument: The Enthymeme

The previous core argument ("States should ban plastic bags from grocery stores because banning bags will reduce plastic pollution in the ocean") is an incomplete logical structure called an *enthymeme*. Its persuasiveness depends on an underlying assumption or belief that the audience must accept. To complete the enthymeme and make it effective, the audience must willingly supply a missing premise—in this case, that plastic pollution of the oceans is significantly harmful. The Greek philosopher Aristotle showed how successful enthymemes root the speaker's argument in assumptions, beliefs, or values held by the audience. The word *enthymeme* comes from the Greek *en* (meaning "in") and *thumos* (meaning "mind"). Listeners or readers must have in mind an assumption, belief, or value that lets them willingly supply the missing premise. If the audience is unwilling to supply the missing premise, then the argument fails. Our point is that successful arguments depend both on what the arguer says and on what the audience already has "in mind."

To clarify the concept of enthymeme, let's go over this same territory again, this time more slowly, examining what we mean by "incomplete logical structure." The sentence "States should ban plastic bags from grocery stores because banning bags will reduce plastic pollution in the ocean" is an enthymeme. It combines a claim (States should ban plastic bags from grocery stores) with a reason expressed as a *because* clause (because banning bags will reduce plastic pollution in the ocean). To render this enthymeme logically complete, the audience must willingly supply a missing assumption—that plastic pollution is harmful enough to the oceans to justify a ban on plastic bags. If your audience accepts this assumption, then you have a starting place on which to build an effective argument. If your audience doesn't accept this assumption, then you must supply another argument to support it, and so on until you find common ground with your audience.

To sum up:

1. Claims are supported with reasons. You can usually state a reason as a *because* clause attached to a claim.

2. A *because* clause attached to a claim is an incomplete logical structure called an enthymeme. To create a complete logical structure from an enthymeme, the underlying assumption (or assumptions) must be articulated.

3. To serve as an effective starting point for the argument, this underlying assumption should be a belief, value, or principle that the audience grants.

Let's illustrate this structure by putting the previous example into schematic form.

ENTHYMEME

CLAIM: States should ban plastic bags from grocery stores

REASON: because banning plastic bags will reduce plastic pollution in the ocean.

Audience must supply this assumption ——————→

UNDERLYING ASSUMPTION
Plastic pollution in the ocean is harmful enough to justify a ban.

The Power of Audience-Based Reasons

Aristotle's concept of the enthymeme focuses on the writer's need to create what we can now call "audience-based reasons" as opposed to "writer-based reasons." A reason that is persuasive to you as a writer might not be persuasive to your audience. Finding audience-based reasons means finding arguments effectively anchored within your audience's beliefs and values.

To illustrate the difference between an audience-based reason and a writer-based reason, suppose that you are a vegetarian persuaded mainly by ethical arguments against causing needless suffering to animals. Suppose further that you want to persuade others to become vegetarians or at least to reduce their consumption of meat. Your "writer-based reason" for vegetarianism could be stated as follows:

> You should become a vegetarian because doing so will help reduce the needless suffering of animals.

The underlying assumption here is that it is wrong to cause the suffering of animals. This writer-based reason might also be an audience-based reason for persons who are wrestling with the moral dimension of animal suffering. But this assumption might not resonate with people who have made their own peace with eating meat. How might you use audience-based reasons to appeal to these meat-eaters? Here are two more possible enthymemes:

> You should become a vegetarian because doing so may help you lower your cholesterol.
> You should become a vegetarian because doing so will significantly lower your carbon footprint.

These arguments hook into the assumption that it is good to lower one's cholesterol (health values) or that it is good to lower one's carbon footprint (environmental values). All three of the arguments—whether based on ethics, health, or the environment—might further the practice of vegetarianism or at least reduce the amount of meat consumed, but they won't appeal equally to all audiences. From the perspective of logic alone, all three arguments are equally sound. But they will affect different audiences differently.

For Writing and Discussion

Identifying Underlying Assumptions and Choosing Audience-Based Reasons

Part 1 Working individually or in small groups, identify the unstated assumption that the audience must supply in order to make the following enthymemes persuasive.

Example

> **Enthymeme:** Rabbits make good pets because they are gentle.
> **Underlying assumption:** Gentle animals make good pets.

1. We shouldn't elect Joe as committee chair because he is too bossy.
2. The federal government should institute a carbon tax because doing so will reduce U.S. production of greenhouse gases.
3. The federal government should not institute a carbon tax because doing so will damage the economy.
4. We should strengthen the Endangered Species Act because doing so will preserve genetic diversity on the planet.
5. The Endangered Species Act is too stringent because it severely restricts the rights of property owners.

Part 2 For each of the following items, decide which of the two reasons offered would be more persuasive to the specified audience. How might the reason not chosen be effective for a different kind of audience? Explain your reasoning.

1. Audience: people who advocate a pass/fail grading system on the grounds that the present grading system is too competitive
   a. We should keep the present grading system because it prepares people for the dog-eat-dog pressures of the business world.
   b. We should keep the present grading system because it tells students that certain standards of excellence must be met if individuals are to reach their full potential.
2. Audience: environmentalists
   a. We should support fracking for natural gas because doing so will help reduce our dependence on foreign sources of oil.
   b. We should support fracking for natural gas because doing so will provide a greener "bridge fuel" that will give us time to develop better renewable technologies.
3. Audience: proponents of preventing illegal immigration into the United States by building a wall between the United States and Mexico
   a. U.S. citizens should oppose building the wall because doing so promotes a racist image of America.
   b. U.S. citizens should oppose building the wall because doing so may end up giving control of the Rio Grande river to Mexico.

Adopting a Language for Describing Arguments: The Toulmin System

3.2   Use the Toulmin system to describe an argument's logical structure.

Understanding a new field usually requires you to learn a new vocabulary. For example, if you were taking biology for the first time, you'd have to learn hundreds and hundreds of new terms. Luckily, the field of argument requires us to learn a mere handful of new terms. A particularly useful set of argument terms, one we'll be using occasionally throughout this text, comes from philosopher

Stephen Toulmin. In the 1950s, Toulmin rejected the prevailing models of argument based on formal logic in favor of a very audience-based courtroom model.

Toulmin's courtroom model differs from formal logic in that it assumes that (1) all assertions and assumptions are contestable by "opposing counsel" and that (2) all final "verdicts" about the persuasiveness of the opposing arguments will be rendered by a neutral third party, a judge, or a jury. As writers, keeping in mind the "opposing counsel" forces us to anticipate counterarguments and to question our assumptions. Keeping in mind the judge and jury reminds us to answer opposing arguments fully and without rancor, and to present positive reasons for supporting our case as well as negative reasons for disbelieving the opposing case. Above all else, Toulmin's model reminds us not to construct an argument that appeals only to those who already agree with us. In short, it helps arguers tailor arguments to their audiences.

The system we use for analyzing arguments combines Toulmin's language with Aristotle's concept of the enthymeme. It builds on the system you have already been practicing. We simply need to add a few key terms from Toulmin. The first term is Toulmin's *warrant*, the name we will now use for the underlying assumption that turns an enthymeme into a complete, logical structure as shown below.

Toulmin derives his term *warrant* from the concept of "warranty" or "guarantee." The warrant is the value, belief, or principle that the audience has to hold if the soundness of the argument is to be guaranteed or warranted. We sometimes make similar use of this word in ordinary language when we say "That is an unwarranted conclusion," meaning one has leaped from information about a situation to a conclusion about that situation without any sort of general principle to justify or "warrant" that move. Thus the warrant—once accepted by the audience—"guarantees" the soundness of the argument.

ENTHYMEME

CLAIM: States should ban plastic bags from grocery stores

REASON: because banning plastic bags will reduce plastic pollution in the ocean.

Audience must supply this warrant ⟶

WARRANT

Plastic pollution in the ocean is harmful enough to justify a ban.

But arguments need more than claims, reasons, and warrants. These are simply one-sentence statements—the frame of an argument, not a developed argument. To give body and weight to our arguments and make them convincing, we need what Toulmin calls *grounds* and *backing*. Let's start with grounds. Grounds are the supporting evidence that causes an audience to accept your reason. Grounds are facts, data, statistics, causal links, testimony, examples, anecdotes—the blood and muscle that flesh out the skeletal frame of your enthymeme. Toulmin suggests that grounds are "what you have to go on" in an argument—the stuff you can point to and present before a jury. Here is how grounds fit into our emerging argument schema:

> **ENTHYMEME**
>
> CLAIM: States should ban plastic bags from grocery stores
>
> REASON: because banning plastic bags will reduce plastic pollution in the ocean.

Grounds support the reason

> **GROUNDS**
>
> Evidence that a substantial percentage of thrown-away plastic bags end up as ocean pollution and could be reduced with bans:
>
> - According to the Earth Policy Institute, 100 billion plastic bags pass through the hands of U.S. consumers each year.
> - Plastic bags that don't end up in landfills often float into the oceans from river and stream pollution.
> - According to Ocean Crusaders, plastic bags are the most prevalent man-made thing that sailors see in the ocean.
> - A scientific study in 2014 estimated that there are 269,000 metric tons of plastic and 5.25 trillion plastic particles on the ocean's surface.
> - Plastics float on the surface, where they are concentrated by ocean currents. *National Geographic* has documented the "Pacific trash vortex"—a floating garbage patch the size of Texas.
> - Bans, which are becoming acceptable to consumers as shown by states and cities that have recently instituted bans on plastic grocery bags, have cut down on plastic bags in landfills and coastal areas.

In many cases, successful arguments require just these three components: a claim, a reason, and grounds. If the audience already accepts the unstated assumption behind the reason (the warrant), then the warrant can safely remain in the background, unstated and unexamined. But if there is a chance that the audience will question or doubt the warrant, then the writer needs to back it up by providing an argument in its support. *Backing* is the argument that supports the warrant. It may require as little as one or two sentences or as much as a major section in your argument. Its goal is to persuade the audience to accept the warrant. Here is how *backing* is added to our schema:

> **WARRANT**
>
> Plastic pollution in the ocean is harmful enough to justify a ban.

Backing supports the warrant

> **BACKING**
>
> Arguments that plastics, especially plastic bags, are significantly harmful to the oceans:
>
> - Plastics cause great harm to marine life (sea turtles eat plastic bags, which look like jellyfish; birds and surface-feeding fish ingest small pieces of plastic, which often results in death or starvation).
> - Toxins absorbed from digesting plastic work their way up the food chain, including into the fish we eat, jeopardizing food safety.
> - Plastic particles unbalance the ecosystem; for example, some ocean insect species breed more quickly where plastics are floating.
> - *National Geographic News* reports a study showing that "degrading plastics are leaching potentially toxic chemicals such as bisphenol A into the seas, possibly threatening ocean animals, and us."

Toulmin's system next asks us to imagine how a resistant audience would try to refute our argument. Specifically, an adversarial audience might challenge our reason and grounds by arguing that plastic bags are not polluting the oceans or that the pollution is not extensive. The adversary might also attack our warrant

ENTHYMEME

CLAIM: States should ban plastic bags from grocery stores

REASON: because banning plastic bags will reduce plastic pollution in the ocean.

GROUNDS

Evidence that a substantial percentage of thrown-away plastic bags end up as ocean pollution:

- According to the Earth Policy Institute, 100 billion plastic bags pass through the hands of U.S. consumers each year.
- Plastic bags that don't end up in landfills often float into the oceans from river and stream pollu-tion.
- According to Ocean Crusaders, plastic bags are the most prevalent man-made thing that sailors see in the ocean.
- A scientific study in 2014 estimated that there are 269,000 metric tons of plastic and 5.25 trillion plastic particles on the ocean's surface.
- Plastics float on the surface, where they are con-centrated by ocean currents. *National Geographic* has documented the "Pacific trash vortex"—a floating garbage patch the size of Texas.
- Bans, which are becoming acceptable to consumers as shown by states and cities that have recently instituted bans on plastic grocery bags, have cut down on plastic bags in landfills and coastal areas.

Writer must anticipate these attacks from skeptics

POSSIBLE CONDITIONS OF REBUTTAL

A skeptic can attack the reason and grounds:

- Arguments that plastic bags from grocery stores comprise only a small proportion of plastic pollution in the ocean (far greater damage comes from plastic bottles, Styrofoam pellets, and floating fish nets)
- Arguments that the pollution is not extensive
- Arguments that banning plastic bags would eliminate all the ecological and consumer benefits of plastic bags
- Arguments that plastic bags are more eco-friendly to produce than paper bags and are completely recyclable
- Arguments that plastic bags are reusable, are better than paper for storing moist products, and save on use of plastic wrapping
- Arguments that bans don't work and that other polices would be more effective at tackling this problem, such as placing higher fees on plastic bags or implementing intensive recycling campaigns

WARRANT

Plastic pollution in the ocean is harmful enough to justify a ban.

BACKING

Arguments that plastics, especially plastic bags, are significantly harmful to the oceans:

- Plastics cause great harm to marine life (sea turtles eat plastic bags, which look like jellyfish; birds and surface-feeding fish ingest small pieces of plastic, which often results in death or starvation).
- Toxins absorbed from digesting plastic work their way up the food chain, including into the fish we eat, jeopardizing food safety.
- Plastic particles unbalance the ecosystem; for example, some ocean insect species breed more quickly where plastics are floating.
- *National Geographic News* reports a study showing that "degrading plastics are leaching potentially toxic chemicals such as bisphenol A into the seas, possibly threatening ocean animals, and us."

POSSIBLE CONDITIONS OF REBUTTAL

A skeptic could attack the warrant and backing:

- Arguments that data about harm to sea life are primarily anecdotal and amplified by photographs appealing to *pathos*
- Argument conceding that some harm is done to the ocean, but research has not yet documented the extent of the danger to marine life
- Arguments that ocean damage is not severe enough to justify a ban, especially when balanced against the ecological benefits of plastic bags
- Arguments that the problem of ocean pollution might soon be solved by science, which is on track to devise biological methods to "eat plastic" or to make plastic more biodegradable

and backing by arguing that the harm caused by plastic pollution is not significant enough to justify a ban on plastic bags. These rebuttal strategies are outlined in the right-hand column of our schema:

As this example shows, adversarial readers can question an argument's reasons and grounds, or its warrant and backing, or sometimes both. Conditions of rebuttal remind writers to look at their arguments from the perspective of skeptics.

The use of a Toulmin schema to plan an argument strategy can also be illustrated in the issue we examined in the last chapter—whether the public should support marine parks that use trained captive orcas and dolphins for public entertainment. In the following example, the writer argues that the public should not support these parks because they inhumanely separate dolphins and orcas from their natural habitat.

Writer must anticipate these attacks from skeptics

ENTHYMEME

CLAIM: The public should not support marine parks

REASON: because marine parks inhumanely separate dolphins and orcas from their natural habitat.

"POSSIBLE CONDITIONS OF REBUTTAL

A skeptic can attack the reason and grounds":

• Argument that these programs must observe strict accreditation standards for animal welfare, health, and education

• Marine parks exercise dolphins' and orcas' intelligence and abilities and build on their natural behaviors.

• Many dolphins and orcas have been bred in captivity, so they aren't "wild."

• The education and entertainment provided by marine parks promote public concern for dolphins and orcas.

GROUNDS

Evidence and arguments showing the inhumane difference between the wild environment of dolphins and orcas and their environment in captivity:

• In the wild, dolphins swim in pods in the open oceans, dolphins around forty miles a day, and orcas around sixty miles a day, whereas marine park tanks provide only a fraction of that space.

• Evidence that the echoes from concrete pools, music of dolphin shows, and the applause and noise of audiences are stressful and harmful

• Statistics about the excessive number of performances or about the levels of stress hormones produced in dolphins

WARRANT

It is wrong to separate wild animals from their natural habitats.

BACKING

Arguments showing why it is unwise, unethical, or otherwise wrong to separate wild animals from their natural environments:

• Examples of wild animals (those in aquariums and zoos) that do not thrive in artificially constructed environments, that don't live long, or that suffer psychological stress from confinement

• An ecological argument about the beauty of animals in the wild and the complexity of the natural webs of which animals are a part

• A philosophical argument that humans shouldn't treat animals as instruments for their own enjoyment or profit

"POSSIBLE CONDITIONS OF REBUTTAL

A skeptic can attack the warrant and backing.

• The natural habitat is not always the best environment for wild animals.

• Captivity may actually preserve some species.

• Scientists have been able to conduct valuable studies of dolphins and learn more about orcas in captivity, which would have been impossible in the wild.

Toulmin's final term, used to limit the force of a claim and indicate the degree of its probable truth, is *qualifier*. The qualifier reminds us that real-world arguments almost never prove a claim. We may say things such as *very likely, probably,* or *maybe* to indicate the strength of the claim we are willing to draw from our grounds and warrant. Thus, if there are exceptions to your warrant or if your grounds are not very strong, you may have to qualify your claim. For example, you might say, "States should ban plastic bags from grocery stores because banning plastic bags would be a small first step toward reducing plastic pollution of the oceans" or "Except for limited cases of scientific research, dolphins and orcas should not be held in captivity." In our future displays of the Toulmin scheme we will omit the qualifiers, but you should always remember that no argument is 100 percent conclusive.

For Writing and Discussion

Developing Enthymemes with the Toulmin Schema

Working individually or in small groups, imagine that you have to write arguments developing the five enthymemes listed in the first For Class Discussion exercise in this chapter. Use the Toulmin schema to help you determine what you need to consider when developing each enthymeme. We suggest that you try a four-box diagram structure as a way of visualizing the schema. We have applied the Toulmin schema to the first enthymeme: "We shouldn't elect Joe as committee chair because he is too bossy."

ENTHYMEME

CLAIM We shouldn't elect Joe as committee chair

REASON because he is too bossy.

GROUNDS

Evidence of Joe's bossiness:

- Examples of the way he dominates meetings—doesn't call on people, talks too much
- Testimony about his bossiness from people who have served with him on committees
- Anecdotes about his abrasive style

CONDITIONS OF REBUTTAL

Attacking the reason and grounds:

Evidence that Joe is not bossy or is only occasionally bossy:

- Counterevidence showing his collaborative style
- Testimony from people who have liked Joe as a leader and claim he isn't bossy; testimony about his cooperativeness and kindness
- Testimony that anecdotes about Joe's bossiness aren't typical

WARRANT

Bossy people make bad committee chairs.

BACKING

Problems caused by bossy committee chairs:

- Bossy people don't inspire cooperation and enthusiam.
- Bossy people make others angry.
- Bossy people tend to make bad decisions because they don't incorporate advice from others.

CONDITIONS OF REBUTTAL

Attacking the warrant and backing:

- Arguments that bossiness can be a good trait
  - Sometimes bossy people make good chairpersons.
  - This committee needs a bossy person who can make decisions and get things done.
- Argument that Joe has other traits of good leadership that outweigh his bossiness

Using Toulmin's Schema to Plan and Test Your Argument

3.3 Use the Toulmin system to generate ideas for your argument and test it for completeness.

So far we have seen that a claim, a reason, and a warrant form the frame for a line of reasoning in an argument. Most of the words in an argument, however, are devoted to grounds and backing.

Hypothetical Example: Cheerleaders as Athletes

For an illustration of how a writer can use the Toulmin schema to generate ideas for an argument, consider the following case. In April 2005, the Texas House of Representatives passed a bill banning "sexually suggestive" cheerleading. Across the nation, evening TV comedians poked fun at the bill, while newspaper editorialists debated its wisdom and constitutionality. In one of our classes, however, several students, including one who had earned a high school varsity letter in competitive cheerleading, defended the bill by contending that provocative dance moves hurt the athletic image of cheerleading. In the following example, which draws on ideas developed in class discussion, we create a hypothetical student writer (we'll call her Chandale) who argues in defense of the Texas bill. Chandale's argument is based on the following enthymeme:

> The bill banning suggestive dancing for high school cheerleaders is a good law because it promotes a view of female cheerleaders as athletes.

Chandale used the Toulmin schema to brainstorm ideas for developing her argument. Here are her notes:

Chandale's Planning Notes Using the Toulmin Schema

Enthymeme: The bill banning suggestive dancing for high school cheerleaders is a good law because it promotes a view of female cheerleaders as athletes.

Grounds: First, I've got to use evidence to show that cheerleaders are athletes.

- Cheerleaders at my high school are carefully chosen for their stamina and skill after exhausting two-week tryouts.
- We begin all practices with a mile run and an hour of warm-up exercises—we are also expected to work out on our own for at least an hour on weekends and on days without practice.
- We learned competitive routines and stunts consisting of lifts, tosses, flips, catches, and gymnastic moves. This requires athletic ability! We'd practice these stunts for hours each week.
- Throughout the year cheerleaders have to attend practices, camps, and workshops to learn new routines and stunts.
- Our squad competed in competitions around the state.
- Competitive cheerleading is a growing movement across the country—the University of Maryland has made it a varsity sport for women.
- Skimpy uniforms and suggestive dance moves destroy the image of cheerleaders as athletes by making women eye candy (for example, the Dallas Cowboys cheerleaders).

Warrant: It is a good thing to view female cheerleaders as athletes.

Backing: Now I need to make the case that it is good to see cheerleaders as athletes rather than as eye candy.

- Athletic competition builds self-esteem, independence, and a powerful sense of achievement. It also contributes to health, strength, and conditioning.
- Competitive cheerleading is one of the few sports where teams are made up of both men and women. (Why is this good? Should I use this?)
- The suggestive dance moves turn women into sex objects whose function is to be gazed at by men, which suggests that women's value is based on their beauty and sex appeal.
- We are talking about HIGH SCHOOL cheerleading—it is a very bad early influence on girls to model themselves on Dallas Cowboys cheerleaders or sexy videos of rock stars.
- Junior-high girls want to do what senior-high girls do—suggestive dance moves promote sexuality way too early.

Conditions of Rebuttal: Would anybody try to rebut my reasons and grounds that cheerleading is an athletic activity?

- No. I think it is obvious that cheerleading is an athletic activity once they see my evidence.
- However, they might not think of cheerleading as a sport. They might say that the University of Maryland just declared it a sport as a cheap way to meet Title IX federal rules to have more women's sports. I'll have to make sure that I show that cheerleading is really a sport.
- They also might say that competitive cheerleading shouldn't be encouraged because it is too dangerous—lots of serious injuries, including paralysis, have been caused by mistakes in doing flips, lifts, and tosses. If I include this, maybe I could say that other sports are dangerous also, and it is in fact danger that makes this sport so exciting.

Would anyone doubt my warrant and backing that it is good to see female cheerleaders as athletes?

- Yes, all those people who laughed at the Texas legislature think that people are being too prudish and that banning suggestive dance moves violates free expression. I'll need to make my case that it is bad for young girls to see themselves as sex objects too early.

The information that Chandale lists under "grounds" is what she sees as the facts of the case—the hard data she will use as evidence to support her contention that cheerleading is an athletic activity. The following paragraph shows how this argument might look in a more formally written format.

First Part of Chandale's Argument

Although evening TV comedians have made fun of the Texas legislature's desire to ban "suggestive" dance moves from cheerleading routines, I applaud this bill because it promotes a healthy view of female cheerleaders as athletes rather than showgirls. I was lucky enough to attend a high school

Summarizes opposing view

States her claim

(continued)

For grounds, uses personal experience details to show that cheerleading is an athletic activity

where cheerleading is a sport, and I earned a varsity letter as a cheerleader. To get on my high school's cheerleading squad, students have to go through an exhausting two-week tryout of workouts and instruction in the basic routines; then they are chosen based on their stamina and skill. Once on the squad, cheerleaders begin all practices with a mile run and an hour of grueling warm-up exercises, and they are expected to exercise on their own on weekends. As a result of this regimen, cheerleaders achieve and maintain a top level of physical fitness. In addition, to get on the squad, students must be able to do handstands, cartwheels, handsprings, high jumps, and splits. Each year the squad builds up to its complex routines and stunts consisting of lifts, tosses, flips, catches, and gymnastic moves that only trained athletes can do. In tough competitions at the regional and state levels, the cheerleading squad demonstrates its athletic talent. This view of cheerleading as a competitive sport is also spreading to colleges. As reported recently in a number of newspapers, the University of Maryland has made cheerleading a varsity sport, and many other universities are following suit. Athletic performance of this caliber is a far cry from the sexy dancing that many high school girls often associate with cheerleading. By banning suggestive dancing in cheerleading routines, the Texas legislature creates an opportunity for schools to emphasize the athleticism of cheerleading.

Provides more grounds by showing emerging views of cheerleading as a competitive sport

As you can see, Chandale has plenty of evidence for arguing that competitive cheerleading is an athletic activity quite different from sexy dancing. But how effective is this argument as it stands? Is Chandale's argument complete? The Toulmin schema encourages writers to include—if needed for the intended audience—explicit support for their warrants as well as attention to conditions for rebuttal. Because the overwhelming national response to the Texas law was ridicule at the perceived prudishness of the legislators, Chandale decided to expand her argument as follows:

Continuation of Chandale's Argument

Supplies warrant: It is good to see cheerleaders as athletic and bad to see them as sex objects

Supplies backing: Shows benefits that come from seeing cheerleaders as athletes

Anticipates an objection

This emphasis on cheerleaders as athletes rather than sexy dancers is good for girls. The erotic dance moves that many high school cheerleaders now incorporate into their routines show that they are emulating the Dallas Cowboys cheerleaders or pop stars in music videos. Our already sexually saturated culture (think of the suggestive clothing marketed to little girls) pushes girls and women to measure their value by their beauty and sex appeal. It would be far healthier, both physically and psychologically, if high school cheerleaders were identified as athletes. For women and men both, competitive cheerleading can build self-esteem, pride in teamwork, and a powerful sense of achievement, as well as promote health, strength, and fitness.

Some people might object to competitive cheerleading by saying that cheerleading isn't really a sport. Some have accused the University of Maryland of making cheerleading a varsity sport only as a cheap way of meeting Title IX requirements. But anyone who has watched competitive cheerleading, and imagined what it would be like to be thrown high into the air, knows instinctively that this is a sport indeed. In fact, other persons might object to competitive cheerleading because it is too dangerous, with potential for very severe injuries, including paralysis. Obviously the sport is dangerous—but so are many sports, including football, gymnastics, diving, and trampoline. The danger and difficulty of the sport are part of its appeal. Part of what can make cheerleaders as athletes better role models for girls than cheerleaders as erotic dancers is the courage and training needed for success. Of course, the Texas legislators might not have had athleticism in mind when they banned suggestive dancing. They might only have been promoting their vision of morality. But at stake are the role models we set for young girls. I'll pick an athlete over a Dallas Cowboys cheerleader every time.

Responds to objection by supplying more evidence that cheerleading is a sport; in fact, it is a dangerous sport

Sums up by returning to claim

Our example suggests how a writer can use the Toulmin schema to generate ideas for an argument. For evidence, Chandale draws primarily on her personal experiences as a cheerleader/athlete and on her knowledge of popular culture. She also draws on her reading of several newspaper articles about the University of Maryland making cheerleading a varsity sport. (In an academic paper rather than a newspaper editorial, she would need to document these sources through formal citations.) Although many arguments depend on research, many can be supported wholly or in part by your own personal experiences, so don't neglect the wealth of evidence from your own life when searching for data. (Chapter 4 provides a more detailed discussion of evidence in arguments.)

Extended Student Example: Girls and Violent Video Games

Let's look at one more example of how the Toulmin system can help you generate ideas for your argument. In this case, we will look at a complete example from student writer Carmen Tieu, whose evolving argument about girls and violent video games was introduced in the last chapter. Carmen's assignment was to write a "supporting reasons" argument, which is a shortened form of the classical argument described at the beginning of Chapter 2. It has all the features of a classical argument except for the requirement to summarize and rebut opposing views. In planning her argument, Carmen decided to use four lines of reasoning, as shown in her *because* clauses listed at the end of Chapter 2. She began by creating a basic Toulmin frame for each reason:

Carmen's Toulmin Frames

My claim: Playing first-person-shooter (FPS) video games is good for girls

1. **Reason:** because playing FPS games empowers girls when they beat guys at their own game. **Warrant:** It is good for girls to feel empowered.
2. **Reason:** because playing FPS games equips girls with skills that free them from feminine stereotypes. **Warrant:** It is good for girls to be freed from feminine stereotypes.
3. **Reason:** because playing FPS games gives girls a different way of bonding with males. **Warrant:** It is good for girls to find a different way of bonding with males.

4. **Reason:** because playing FPS games gives girls new insights into a male subculture. **Warrant:** It is good for girls to get new insights into a male subculture.

As Carmen began drafting her essay, she was confident she could support her first three lines of reasoning. For reason 1 she could use evidence (grounds) from personal experience to show how she learned to beat guys at video games. She could also support her warrant by showing how beating guys made her feel empowered. For reason 2, she decided that she primarily needed to support her warrant (backing). It is obvious that playing FPS games breaks feminine stereotypes. What she had to show was why it was good or valuable to be freed from feminine stereotypes. Reason 3, she felt, needed support for both the reason and the warrant. She had to show how these games gave her a different way of bonding with males (grounds) and then why this different way was a good thing (backing). Carmen felt that her reason 4 was the most complex. Here are her more detailed planning notes for reason 4:

Carmen's Planning Notes for Reason 4

Enthymeme: First-person-shooter (FPS) video games are great activities for girls because playing these games gives girls new insights into male subculture.

Grounds: I've got to show the insights into male subculture I gained.

- The guys who play these video games are intensely competitive.
  - They can play for hours without stopping—intense concentration.
  - They don't multitask—no small talk during the games; total focus on playing.
  - They take delight in winning at all costs—they boast with every kill; they call each other losers.

- They often seem homophobic or misogynist.

  - They put each other down by calling opponents "faggot" and "wussy," or other similar names that are totally obscene.
  - They associate victory with being macho.

Warrant: It is beneficial for a girl to get these insights into male subculture.

Backing: How can I show these benefits?

- It was a good learning experience to see how girls' way of bonding is very different from that of guys; girls tend to be nicer to one another rather than insulting one another. Although I enjoy winning at FPS games, as a girl I feel alienated from this male subculture.
- The game atmosphere tends to bring out these homophobic traits; guys don't talk this way as much when they are doing other things.
- This experience helped me see why men may progress faster than women in a competitive business environment—men seem programmed to crush one another, and they devote enormous energy to the process.
- What else can I say? I need to think about this further.

Based on these planning notes, Carmen's composed argument went through several drafts. Here is her final version.

Student Essay

Why Violent Video Games Are Good for Girls

Carmen Tieu

It is ten o'clock P.M., game time. My entire family knows by now that when I am home on Saturday nights, ten P.M. is my gaming night when I play my favorite first-person-shooter (FPS) games, usually *Halo 3*, on Xbox Live. Seated in my mobile chair in front of my family's 42-inch flat screen HDTV, I log onto Xbox Live. A small message in the bottom of the screen appears with the words "Kr1pL3r is online," alerting me that one of my male friends is online and already playing. As the game loads, I send Kr1pL3r a game invite, and he joins me in the pre-game room lobby.

In the game room lobby, all the players who will be participating in the match are chatting aggressively with each other: "Oh man, we're gonna own you guys so bad." When a member of the opposing team notices my gamer tag, "embracingapathy," he begins to insult me by calling me various degrading, gay-associated names: "Embracing apa-what? Man, it sounds so emo. Are you some fag? I bet you want me so bad. You're gonna get owned!" Players always assume from my gamer tag that I am a gay male, never a female. The possibility that I am a girl is the last thing on their minds. Of course, they are right that girls seldom play first-person-shooter games. Girls are socialized into activities that promote togetherness and talk, not high-intensity competition involving fantasized shooting and killing. The violent nature of the games tends to repulse girls. Opponents of violent video games typically hold that these games are so graphically violent that they will influence players to become amoral and sadistic. Feminists also argue that violent video games often objectify women by portraying them as sexualized toys for men's gratification. Although I understand these objections, I argue that playing first-person-shooter games can actually be good for girls.

First, playing FPS games gives girls the chance to beat guys at their own game. When I first began playing *Halo 2*, I was horrible. My male friends constantly put me down for my lack of skills, constantly telling me that I was awful, "but for a girl, you're good." But it didn't take much practice until I learned to operate the two joysticks with precision and with quick instinctual reactions. While guys and girls can play many physical games together, such as basketball or touch football, guys will always have the advantage because on average they are taller, faster, and stronger than females. However, when it comes to video games, girls can compete equally because physical strength isn't required, just quick reaction time and manual dexterity—skills that women possess in abundance. The adrenaline rush that I receive from beating a bunch of testosterone-driven guys at something they supposedly excel at is empowering and exciting; I especially savor the look of horror on their faces when I completely destroy them.

(continued)

Side annotations:

Title makes persuasive claim

Attention-grabbing scene

Continues scene and provides more background

Sums up opposing views

States claim

States first reason

For grounds, uses personal narrative to show how she can beat guys

Briefly backs warrant by showing the good feeling of empowerment

States second reason

Because female video gamers are so rare, playing shooter games allows girls to be freed from feminine stereotypes and increases their confidence. Our culture generally portrays females as caring, nonviolent, and motherly beings who are not supposed to enjoy FPS games with their war themes and violent killings. I am in no way rejecting these traditional female values because I myself am a compassionate, tree-hugging vegan. But I also like to break these stereotypes. Playing video games offers a great way for females to break the social mold of only doing "girly" things and introduces them to something that males commonly enjoy. Playing video games with sexist males has also helped me become more outspoken. Psychologically, I can stand up to aggressive males because I know that I can beat them at their own game. The confidence I've gotten from excelling at shooter games may have even carried over into the academic arena because I am majoring in chemical engineering and have no fear whatsoever of intruding into the male-dominated territory of math and science. Knowing that I can beat all the guys in my engineering classes at *Halo* gives me that little extra confidence boost during exams and labs.

Details focus on backing for warrant: It is good for girls to be freed from feminine stereotypes

Provides third reason

Another reason for girls to play FPS games is that it gives us a different way of bonding with guys. Once when I was discussing my latest *Halo 3* matches with one of my regular male friends, a guy whom I didn't know turned around and said, "You play *Halo*? Wow, you just earned my respect." Although I was annoyed that this guy apparently didn't respect women in general, it is apparent that guys will talk to me differently now that I can play video games. From a guy's perspective I can also appreciate why males find video games so addicting. You get joy from perfecting your skills so that your high-angle grenade kills become a thing of beauty. While all of these skills may seem trivial to some, the acknowledgment of my skills from other players leaves me with a perverse sense of pride in knowing that I played the game better than everyone else. Since I have started playing, I have also noticed that it is much easier to talk to males about lots of different subjects. Talking video games with guys is a great ice-breaker that leads to different kinds of friendships outside the realm of romance and dating.

Uses a narrative example for grounds; shows how FPS games give her a different way of bonding with males

Backing for warrant: This new kind of bonding is good

Provides final reason

Finally, playing violent video games can be valuable for girls because it gives them insights into a disturbing part of male subculture. When the testosterone starts kicking in, guys become blatantly homophobic and misogynistic. Any player, regardless of gender, who cannot play well (as measured by having a high number of kills and a low number of deaths) is made fun of by being called gay, a girl, or worse. Even when some guys finally meet a female player, they will also insult her by calling her a lesbian or an ugly fat chick who has no life. Their insults towards the girl will dramatically increase if she beats them because they feel so humiliated. In their eyes, playing worse than a girl is embarrassing because girls are supposed to be inept at FPS games. Whenever I play *Halo* better than my male friends, they often comment on how "it makes no sense that we're getting owned by Carmen."

Provides grounds: gives examples of what she learned about male subculture

When males act like such sexist jerks it causes one to question if they are always like this. My answer is no because I know, firsthand, that when guys like that are having one-on-one conversations with a female, they show a softer side, and the macho side goes away. They don't talk about how girls

Provides backing for warrant: Shows value of learning about male subculture while keeping separate from it should stay in the kitchen and make them dinner, but rather how they think it is cool that they share a fun, common interest with a girl. But when they are in a group of males their fake, offensive macho side comes out. I find this phenomenon troubling because it shows a real problem in the way boys are socialized. To be a real "man" around other guys, they have to put down women and gays in activities involving aggressive behavior where men are supposed to excel. But they don't become macho and aggressive in activities like reading and writing, which they think of as feminine. I've always known that guys are more physically aggressive than women, but until I started playing violent video games I had never realized how this aggression is related to misogyny and homophobia. Perhaps these traits aren't deeply ingrained in men but come out primarily in a competitive male environment. Whatever the cause, it is an ugly phenomenon, and I'm glad that I learned more about it. Beating guys at FPS games has made me a more confident woman while being more aware of gender differences in the way men and women are socialized. I joined the guys in playing *Halo,* but I didn't join their subculture of ridiculing women and gays.

Sums up why her playing FPS games is valuable

The Thesis-Governed "Self-Announcing" Structure of Classical Argument

Like the complete classical argument explained at the beginning of Chapter 2, Carmen's supporting-reasons argument has a thesis-governed structure in which she states her claim near the end of the introduction, begins body paragraphs with clearly stated reasons, and uses effective transitions throughout to keep her reader on track. This kind of tightly organized structure is sometimes called a *self-announcing* or *closed-form* structure because the writer states his or her claim before beginning the body of the argument and forecasts the structure that is to follow. In contrast, an *unfolding* or *open-form* structure often doesn't give away the writer's position until late in the essay. (We discuss delayed-thesis arguments in Chapter 6.) A general rule of thumb for arguments using more than one line of reasoning is to place your most important or most interesting reason last, where it will have the greatest impact on your readers.

In writing a self-announcing argument, students often ask how much of the argument to summarize in the thesis statement. Consider Carmen's options:

- She might announce only her claim:

   Playing first-person-shooter games can be good for girls.

- She might forecast a series of parallel reasons:

   There are several reasons that playing first-person-shooter games can be good for girls.

- She might forecast the actual number of reasons:

   I will present four reasons that playing first-person-shooter games can be good for girls.

- Or she might forecast the whole argument by including her *because* clauses with her claim:

Playing first-person-shooter games can be good for girls because it lets girls feel empowered by beating guys at their own game, because it frees girls from feminine stereotypes, because it gives girls a different way of bonding with guys, and because it gives girls new insights into a male subculture.

This last thesis statement forecasts not only the claim, but also the supporting reasons that will serve as topic sentences for key paragraphs throughout the body of the paper.

No formula can tell you precisely how much of your argument to forecast in the introduction. However, these suggestions can guide you: In writing a self-announcing argument, forecast only what is needed for clarity. In short arguments, readers often need only your claim. In longer arguments, however, or in especially complex arguments, readers appreciate your forecasting the complete structure of the argument (claim with reasons). Also, as we explain in later chapters, the directness of classical argument is not always the best way to reach all audiences. On many occasions more open-form or delayed-thesis approaches are more effective.

For Writing and Discussion

Reasons, Warrants, and Conditions of Rebuttal

Individual task:

1. Choose one of the following reasons. Then write a passage that provides grounds to support the reason. Use details from personal experience or imagine plausible, hypothetical details.
   a. Web surfing or checking social media can be harmful to college students because it wastes study time.
   b. Getting one's news from social media undermines informed citizenship because social media tend to sensationalize news events.
   c. The university's decision to raise parking fees for solo drivers is a good environmental plan because it encourages students to use public transportation.
2. Now create an argument to support the warrant for the reason you chose in task 1. The warrants for each of the arguments are stated below.
   a. Support this warrant: Wasting study time is harmful for college students.
   b. Support this warrant: Sensationalizing of the news is harmful to citizens' understanding.
   c. Support this warrant: It is good for the environment to encourage students to use public transportation.

Group task:
Working in pairs, small groups, or as a class, share your strategies for supporting your chosen reason and warrant.

Conclusion

Chapters 2 and 3 have provided an anatomy of argument. They have shown that the core of an argument is a claim with reasons that usually can be summarized in one or more *because* clauses attached to the claim. Often, it is as important to articulate and support the underlying assumptions in your argument (warrants) as it is to support the stated reasons because a successful argument should be rooted in your audience's beliefs and values. To plan an audience-based argument strategy, arguers can use the Toulmin schema to help them discover grounds, warrants, and backing for their arguments and test them through conditions of rebuttal.

A Note on the Informal Fallacies

The Toulmin system explained in this chapter is a response to the problem of uncertainty or inconclusiveness in real-world arguments, where we have to deal with probability as opposed to the certainty of formal logic. In the real world, we seldom encounter arguments that are absolutely conclusive. We can say that an argument is more or less "persuasive" or "non-persuasive" to certain audiences but not that it proves its case conclusively.

Another response to the problem of conclusiveness is the class of reasoning problems known as the informal fallacies. (You have probably heard of at least some of them with their exotic, Latinate, or sometimes funny names—hasty generalization, *post hoc ergo propter hoc*, slippery slope, or poisoning the well.) They are called "informal" because, like the Toulmin system, they don't focus on the form of the syllogism.* Although the fallacies are not useful for helping writers plan and test their own arguments, they can often help us name what is uncertain or illogically seductive in someone else's argument. They function as a compendium of the ways that flawed arguments can nevertheless seem persuasive on the surface. To provide flexibility in the way that informal fallacies can be integrated into a course, we have placed them all together in a convenient appendix at the end of the text.

Writing Assignment

Plan of an Argument's Details

This assignment asks you to return to the working thesis statement that you created for the brief writing assignment in Chapter 2. From that thesis statement extract one of your enthymemes (your claim with one of your *because* clauses). Write out the warrant for your enthymeme. Then use the Toulmin schema to brainstorm the details you might use (grounds, backing, conditions of rebuttal) to convert your enthymeme into a fleshed-out argument. Use as your model Chandale's planning notes or Carmen's planning notes earlier in this chapter. Note that this is a process-oriented brainstorming task aimed at helping you generate ideas for an argument in progress. You may end up changing your ideas substantially as you compose the actual argument. (An assignment to write a complete "supporting reasons" argument like Carmen's comes at the end of the next chapter, which explains the uses of evidence.)

---

* A **syllogism** is a three-part logical structure containing a major premise, a minor premise, and a conclusion. If the syllogism is worded in a valid, correct way and if the premises are both true, then the conclusion must necessarily be true.
Major premise: All men are mortal.
Minor premise: Socrates is a man.
Conclusion: Socrates is mortal.

Chapter 4
Using Evidence Effectively

Learning Objectives

In this chapter you will learn to:

4.1 Explain the different kinds of evidence

4.2 Make your evidence persuasive by using the STAR criteria and other strategies

4.3 Understand evidence rhetorically by explaining how the selection and framing of evidence reveal an angle of vision

In Chapters 2 and 3 we introduced the concept of *logos*—the logical structure of reasons and evidence in an argument—and showed how an effective argument advances the writer's claim by linking its supporting reasons to one or more assumptions, beliefs, or values held by the intended audience. In this chapter, we turn to the uses of evidence in argument. By *evidence*, we mean all the verifiable data and information a writer might use as support for an argument. In Toulmin's terms, evidence is part of the *grounds* or *backing* of an argument in support of reasons or warrants. By understanding evidence rhetorically, you will better understand how to use evidence ethically, responsibly, and persuasively in your own arguments.

Kinds of Evidence

4.1 Explain the different kinds of evidence.

You have numerous options for the kinds of evidence you can use in an argument, including personal experience, observations, interviews, questionnaires, field or laboratory research, or findings derived from researching primary or secondary sources found in libraries, databases, or the web. Carmen Tieu's argument in Chapter 3 is based on personal experience. More commonly, college arguments require library and Internet research—skills we teach in Part Two (Entering an

Argumentative Conversation") and Part Five ("The Researched Argument"). This chapter focuses more basically on how evidence functions rhetorically in an argument and how it is selected and framed.

We begin by categorizing and evaluating different kinds of evidence, illustrating how each might be incorporated into an argument.

DATA FROM PERSONAL EXPERIENCE   One powerful kind of evidence comes from personal experience.

Example	Strengths and Limitations
Despite recent criticism that Ritalin is overprescribed for hyperactivity and attention deficit disorder, it can often seem like a miracle drug. My little brother is a perfect example. Before he was given Ritalin, he was a terror in school . . . . [Tell the "before" and "after" story of your little brother.]	• Personal-experience examples help readers identify with the writer; they show the writer's personal connection to the issue. • Vivid stories capture the imagination and appeal to *pathos*. • Skeptics may sometimes argue that personal-experience examples are insufficient (the writer is guilty of hasty generalization), not typical, or not adequately scientific or verifiable.

DATA FROM OBSERVATION OR FIELD RESEARCH   You can also develop evidence by personally observing a phenomenon or by doing your own field research.

Example	Strengths and Limitations
The intersection at Fifth and Montgomery is particularly dangerous because pedestrians almost never find a comfortable break in the heavy flow of cars. On April 29, I watched fifty-seven pedestrians cross the street. Not once did cars driving in either direction on Fifth Avenue stop before the pedestrian stepped off the sidewalk to cross Montgomery Street. [Continue with observed data about danger.]	• Field research imparts a sense of scientific credibility. • Observations and field research increase typicality by expanding the database beyond a single example. • Observation and field research enhance the *ethos* of the writer as personally invested and reasonable. • Skeptics may point to flaws in how observations were conducted, showing how data are insufficient, inaccurate, or nontypical.

DATA FROM INTERVIEWS, QUESTIONNAIRES, AND SURVEYS   You can also gather data by interviewing stakeholders in a controversy, creating questionnaires, or conducting surveys. (See Chapter 16 for advice on how to conduct this kind of field research.)

Example	Strengths and Limitations
Another reason to ban laptops from classrooms is the extent to which laptop users disturb other students. In a questionnaire that I distributed to fifty students in my residence hall, a surprising 60 percent said that they are annoyed by fellow students checking Instagram, sending e-mail, paying their bills, or surfing the Web while pretending to take notes in class. Additionally, I interviewed five students who gave me specific examples of how these distractions interfere with learning. [Report the examples.]	• Interviews, questionnaires, and surveys enhance the sufficiency and typicality of evidence by expanding the database beyond the experiences of one person. • Quantitative data from questionnaires and surveys often increase the argument's scientific feel. • Surveys and questionnaires often uncover local or recent data not available in published research. • Interviews can provide engaging personal stories, thus enhancing *pathos*. • Skeptics can raise doubts about research methodology, questionnaire design, or typicality of interview subjects.

DATA FROM LIBRARY OR INTERNET RESEARCH   For many arguments, evidence is derived from reading, particularly from library or Internet research. Part Five of this text helps you conduct effective research and incorporate research sources into your arguments.

Example	Strengths and Limitations
The belief that a high-carbohydrate, low-fat diet is the best way to lose weight has been challenged by research conducted by Walter Willett and his colleagues in the department of nutrition at the Harvard School of Public Health. Willett's research suggests that complex carbohydrates such as pasta and potatoes spike glucose levels, increasing the risk of diabetes. Additionally, some fats—especially monounsaturated and polyunsaturated fats found in nuts, fish, and most vegetable oils—help lower "bad" cholesterol levels (45).*	• Researched evidence is often powerful, especially when sources speak with verifiable authority/expertise on their subjects and are respected by your audience; writers can spotlight the source's credentials through attributive tags (see Chapter 17). • Researched data may take the form of facts, examples, quotations, summaries of research studies, and so forth. • Skeptics might doubt the accuracy of facts, the credentials of a source, or the research design of a study. They might also cite studies with different results. • Skeptics might raise doubts about sufficiency, typicality, or relevance of your research data.

TESTIMONY   Writers frequently use testimony when direct data are either unavailable or highly technical or complex. Testimonial evidence can come from research or from interviews.

Example	Strengths and Limitations
Although the Swedish economist Bjorn Lomborg claims that acid rain is not a significant problem, many environmentalists disagree. According to David Bellamany, president of the Conservation Foundation, "Acid rain does kill forests and people around the world, and it's still doing so in the most polluted places, such as Russia" (qtd. in *BBC News*).	• By itself, testimony is generally less persuasive than direct data. • Persuasiveness can be increased if the source has impressive credentials, which the writer can convey through attributive tags introducing the testimony (see Chapter 17). • Skeptics might undermine testimonial evidence by questioning the source's credentials, showing the source's bias, or quoting a countersource.

STATISTICAL DATA   Many contemporary arguments rely heavily on statistical data, often supplemented by graphics such as tables, pie charts, and graphs. (See Chapter 9 for a discussion of the use of graphics in argument.)

Example	Strengths and Limitations
After graduating from college, millennials aren't leaving their parents' homes the way college graduates used to. According to the U.S. Census Bureau's 2015 American Community Survey, 34.1 percent of people between the ages of eighteen and thirty-four lived in their parents' households, with the percentage even higher in states with high real-estate costs.	• Statistics can provide powerful snapshots of aggregate data from a wide database. • Statistics are often used in conjunction with graphics. • Statistics can be calculated and displayed in different ways to achieve different rhetorical effects, so the reader must be wary. • Skeptics might question statistical methods, research design, and interpretation of data.

HYPOTHETICAL EXAMPLES, CASES, AND SCENARIOS   Arguments occasionally use hypothetical examples, cases, or scenarios, particularly to illustrate conjectured consequences of an event or to test philosophical hypotheses.

---

*Parenthetical citations in this example and the next follow the MLA documentation system. See Chapter 18 for a full discussion of how to cite and document sources.

Example	Strengths and Limitations
Consider what might happen if we continue to use biotech soybeans that are resistant to herbicides. The resistant gene, through cross-pollination, might be transferred to an ordinary weed, creating an out-of-control superweed that herbicides couldn't kill. Such a superweed could be an ecological disaster.	• Scenarios have strong imaginative appeal. • Scenarios are persuasive only if they seem plausible. • A scenario narrative often conveys a sense of "inevitability" even if the actual scenario is unlikely; hence, the rhetorical effect may be illogical. • Skeptics might show the implausibility of the scenario or offer an alternative scenario.

REASONED SEQUENCE OF IDEAS   Sometimes arguments are supported with a reasoned sequence of ideas rather than with concrete facts or other forms of empirical evidence. The writer's goal is to support a point through a logical progression of ideas. Such arguments are conceptual, supported by linked ideas, rather than evidential. This kind of support occurs frequently in arguments and is often intermingled with evidential support.

Example	Strengths and Limitations
Embryonic stem cell research, despite its promise in fighting diseases, may have negative social consequences. This research encourages us to place embryos in the category of mere cellular matter that can be manipulated at will. Currently we reduce animals to this category when we genetically alter them for human purposes, such as engineering pigs to grow more human-like heart valves for use in transplants. Using human embryos in the same way—as material that can be altered and destroyed at will—may benefit society materially, but this quest for greater knowledge and control involves a reclassifying of embryos that could potentially lead to a devaluing of human life.	• These sequences are often used in causal arguments to show how causes are linked to effects or in definitional or values arguments to show links among ideas. • A sequence of ideas has great potential to clarify values and show the belief structure on which a claim is founded. • A sequence of ideas can sketch out ideas and connections that would otherwise remain latent. • The effectiveness of this type of evidence depends on the audience's acceptance of each link in the sequence of ideas. • Skeptics might raise objections at any link in the sequence, often by pointing to different values or outlining different consequences.

The Persuasive Use of Evidence

4.2   Make your evidence persuasive by using the STAR criteria and other strategies.

We turn now from kinds of evidence to strategies for making evidence as convincing and persuasive as possible. Consider a target audience of educated, reasonable, and careful readers who approach an issue with healthy skepticism, open-minded but cautious. What demands would such readers make on a writer's use of evidence? To answer that question, let's look at some general principles for using evidence persuasively.

Apply the STAR Criteria to Evidence

Our open-minded but skeptical audience would expect the evidence to meet what rhetorician Richard Fulkerson calls the STAR criteria:[*]

---

[*]Richard Fulkerson, *Teaching the Argument in Writing* (Urbana, IL: National Council of Teachers of English, 1996), 44–53. In this section, we are indebted to Fulkerson's discussion.

Sufficiency: Is there enough evidence?

Typicality: Is the chosen evidence representative and typical?

Accuracy: Is the evidence accurate and up-to-date?

Relevance: Is the evidence relevant to the claim?

Let's examine each in turn.

SUFFICIENCY OF EVIDENCE   How much evidence you need is a function of your rhetorical context. In a court trial, opposing attorneys often agree to waive evidence for points that aren't in doubt in order to concentrate on contested points. The more contested a claim or the more skeptical your audience, the more evidence you may need to present. On the one hand, if you provide too little evidence you may be accused of *hasty generalization* (see Appendix), a reasoning fallacy in which you make a sweeping conclusion based on only one or two instances. On the other hand, if you provide too much evidence your argument may become overly long and tedious. You can guard against having too little or too much evidence by appropriately qualifying the claim your evidence supports.

> **Strong claim:** Working full-time seriously harms a student's grade point average (much data needed—probably a combination of examples and statistical studies).
> **Qualified claim:** Working full-time often harms a student's grade point average (a few representative examples may be enough).

TYPICALITY OF EVIDENCE   If readers are to trust your evidence, they need to be confident that you have chosen typical and representative cases rather than extreme or outlier cases. Suppose that you want to argue that students can successfully work full-time while going to college full-time. You cite the case of your friend Pam, who earned a straight-A grade point average while working forty hours per week as a night receptionist in a small hotel. Your audience might doubt the typicality of Pam's case because a night receptionist can often use work hours for studying. What about more typical jobs, they'll ask, where you can't study while you work?

ACCURACY OF EVIDENCE   Evidence can't be used ethically unless it is accurate and up-to-date, and it can't be persuasive unless the audience believes in the credibility of the writer's sources. This criterion is particularly important in an era of "fake news" and "alternative facts." Arguers need to evaluate their sources, analyzing where each source might be placed on the continuum from "truth-seeking" to "persuasion" (see Figure 1.5). Ethical arguers must also develop an eye and ear for identifying reliable sources of data, distinguishing, for example, between widely respected news and public affairs sites and potential fake news sites. Later in this section, we illustrate our own fact-checking search to ensure the accuracy of a piece of evidence, explaining how we tracked down the original source for a piece of data cited in a *The New Yorker* article.

RELEVANCE OF EVIDENCE   Finally, evidence will be persuasive only if the reader considers it relevant to what is at stake in the dispute. Consider the following student argument: "I deserve an A in this course because I worked exceptionally hard." The student then cites substantial evidence of how hard he worked—a log of study hours, copies of multiple drafts of papers, testimony from friends, and so forth. But what is at stake here is the underlying assumption (warrant) that grades should be based on effort, not quality of work. The student provides ample evidence to support the reason ("I worked exceptionally hard"), but this evidence is irrelevant to the warrant ("People who work exceptionally hard deserve an A"). Although some instructors may give partial credit for effort, the criterion for grades is usually the quality of the student's performance, not the student's time spent studying.

Establish a Trustworthy *Ethos*

Besides supplying evidence that meets the STAR criteria, you can make your evidence more persuasive by being fair, honest, and open to uncertainty (the appeal to *ethos*—see Chapter 5). To establish your readers' confidence, you must first tell them the source of your evidence. If your evidence comes from personal experience or observation, your prose needs to make that clear. If your evidence comes from others (for example, through interviews or library/Internet research), you must indicate these sources through attributive tags (phrases like "according to T. Alvarez" or "as stated by a recent EPA report"). For academic papers, you must also cite and document your sources using an appropriate style for in-text citations and concluding bibliography. (Part Five of this text explains how to find, use, and cite research sources.) Finally, you need to be fair in the way you select evidence from your research sources. For example, it is unethical to take quotations out of context or to write an unfair summary that oversimplifies or distorts a source author's intended meaning.

Be Mindful of a Source's Distance from Original Data

When you support an argument through library/Internet research, you often encounter sources that report evidence from a second- or third-hand perspective. You need to imagine where your source author found the information that you now want to use in your own argument. How might you trace the process that led from the original data to your source author's use of it? Let's take as an example a passage from an article on the minimum wage by James Surowiecki writing for *The New Yorker.* (You can read the full article in Chapter 8.) Because the source is a magazine article rather than an academic paper, it contains no footnotes or bibliography, but the author nevertheless uses attributive tags to identify his main sources. Here is a passage from the article:

Passage from "The Pay Is Too Damn Low" by James Surowiecki

[O]ver the past three decades, the U.S. economy has done a poor job of creating good middle-class jobs; five of the six fastest-growing job categories today pay less than the median wage. That's why, as a recent study by the economists John Schmitt and Janelle Jones has shown, low-wage workers are older and better educated than ever. More important, more of them are relying on their paychecks not for pin money or to pay for Friday-night dates but, rather, to support families.

Attributive tag (cites this study as his source)

Purported factual statement that we are examining

Much of Surowiecki's argument for increasing the minimum wage depends on evidence that low-wage workers are "older and better educated than ever." But we might ask: How does Surowiecki know about the age and education of low-wage workers? Why should we trust him? Using an attributive tag, he identifies his source as a recent study by economists John Schmitt and Janelle Jones. We conducted a Google search and quickly located the source: a working paper titled "Low-Wage Workers Are Older and Better Educated than Ever," dated April 2012. The paper was published by the Center for Economic and Policy Research, which, according to its Web site, is a nonprofit, nonpartisan research center aimed at providing factual economic data for public policy makers. So where did Schmitt and Jones get their data? They cite statistical tables compiled by the *Current Population Survey*, which is a joint effort of the Census Bureau and the Bureau of Labor Statistics. Based on these original data, Schmitt and Jones constructed two graphs showing shifts in the distribution of low-wage workers by age and then by education from 1971 to 2011. One of these graphs shows that in 1979, 26 percent of low-wage jobs were held by teenagers, but by 2011 only 12 percent of low-wage jobs were held by teenagers. (You can see this graph in Figure 8.3). In contrast, Schmitt and Jones's second graph shows that in 1979 only 25 percent of low-wage job holders had completed at least some college, but by 2011, 43 percent had completed some college.

Let's summarize the process we have just traced. The original data came from government statistics collected by the Census Bureau and the Bureau of Labor Statistics. Schmitt and Jones then converted these data into detailed graphs. Surowiecki then summarized the graphs' message into a single sentence. If you were to cite Surowiecki as your source of this same information ("low-wage workers are older and better educated than ever"), you would be depending on a chain of trust stretching from the original data through Schmitt and Jones and Surowiecki to you.

Of course, you can't be expected to trace all your research-gathered evidence back to the original data, but you need to imagine that it is possible to do so. The closer you can get to the original data, the more trustworthy your evidence. Unfortunately, fact-checkers employed by news sources or nonprofit organizations often discover that purportedly accurate information cannot be traced back to a credible original source. They might show that the information is not factual at all, that it is derived from flawed or discredited studies, that it has been distorted unfairly, or that it is purposely invented fake news in the service of propaganda. Politifact.com, a nationally respected fact-checker, uses a "truth-o-meter" to rank purported evidential statements along a scale from "True" to "False," with the most egregiously false statements earning their famous "[Liar, Liar] Pants-on-Fire" award. To develop a respected *ethos*, you need to develop your own internal truth-o-meter by being aware of a source's distance from the original data and by occasionally tracing a piece of evidence back to its origins.

Rhetorical Understanding of Evidence

4.3   Understand evidence rhetorically by explaining how the selection and framing of evidence reveal an angle of vision.

In the previous section we presented some principles for persuasive use of evidence. We now ask you to look more closely at the rhetorical context in which evidence operates.

Angle of Vision and the Selection and Framing of Evidence

When we enter the argumentative arena, we arrive as complex, whole persons, not as disembodied computers that reach claims through a value-free calculus. We enter with our own ideologies, beliefs, values, and guiding assumptions as formed by our particular lived lives. These differences help explain why one person's terrorist might be another person's freedom fighter, or why a handgun in a drawer might be one person's defense against intruders and another person's accident waiting to happen. In writing about guns, a believer in Second Amendment rights is apt to cite evidence that having a gun can stop a violent intruder or prevent a rape. Conversely, proponents of gun control are apt to cite evidence about accidental deaths or suicides. In an argument, evidence is always selected to further the arguer's claim and is never simply an inert, neutral "fact."

These guiding beliefs and values work together to create a writer's *angle of vision*: a perspective, bias, lens, filter, frame, or screen that helps determine what a writer sees or doesn't see. This angle of vision makes certain items stand out in a field of data while other items become invisible. The angle of vision both determines and reveals the writer's view of which data are important and significant, and which data are trivial and can be ignored.

To help you better understand the concepts of selection and framing, we offer the following exercise based on different angles of vision regarding Uber, the ride-sharing company. Wildly popular in many cities, Uber has been accused of unfair or unsafe business practices causing dilemmas for city governments, regulatory agencies, insurance companies, and customers who want to avoid supporting socially irresponsible companies.

Suppose that your city has scheduled a public hearing on whether Uber needs stricter government regulations—either for public safety or for ensuring fair business practices. The following pieces of data and evidence are available to the people who plan to attend the hearing.

- Uber has provided income opportunity for over 1 million drivers.
- Customers generally love Uber for the ease of its rider experience. The rider is automatically billed through the mobile app without the need to pull out a credit card or pay a tip.
- Some Uber drivers have complained of low pay and stressful work conditions. Uber data show that 11 percent of Uber drivers quit within a month, and about half quit within a year.
- Uber classifies its drivers as independent contractors rather than employees. Therefore, Uber doesn't have to provide health insurance, overtime pay, and other benefits.
- As independent contractors, Uber drivers have the freedom to work any hours they wish, and they accept only the riders and destinations they choose.
- In San Francisco, an Uber driver who was watching his Uber app for a potential rider struck a six-year-old girl in a crosswalk. The parents sued Uber, but Uber lawyers claimed that the company bore no responsibility for the accident because the driver was an independent contractor and was not carrying a rider.
- Uber stores every user's ride-history data. If your Uber app is running, Uber can also track your location even if you aren't requesting an Uber

ride. Uber has been accused of using its tracking data to dig up dirt on journalists who are critical of Uber and to spy on Uber's rivals.

- Several independent studies have shown that a rollout of Uber in new areas is frequently associated with a decrease in drunk driving incidents.

- Several American cities have reported instances of Uber drivers sexually assaulting passengers. Two lawsuits in California accuse Uber of misleading customers about the quality of their background checks for drivers. As part of the suits, district attorneys cited findings that twenty-five Uber drivers in San Francisco and Los Angeles had criminal records.

- An Australian report found that Uber is less risky than a taxi because both passengers and drivers have profiles that can be checked before pickup. Unlike taxi services, Uber provides an online record of who the driver is.

- Taxicab drivers and union leaders complain that Uber's "surge pricing" policies are unfair to both regulated taxi companies and to customers. During low demand times, Uber is cheaper than taxis; during surge times, customers are often surprised by a bill that is higher than what a taxi company would charge.

- One union leader for taxi drivers said: "Either the city should deregulate us [taxis] completely, like them [Uber] . . . or regulate them at least closer to us, and let there be fair business competition."

For Writing and Discussion

Creating Contrasting Angles of Vision

Individual task:

Drawing on data that you select from the above list, compose two short speeches, one supporting the current Uber business model and one calling for more government regulation of Uber. Be ready to explain how you selected and framed data to create a pro-Uber angle of vision in one speech and an anti-Uber angle of vision in the other. How do data highlighted in one of your speeches become "less seen" or even "unseen" in the other?

Group task:

Working in pairs or as a whole class, share your speeches with classmates. Then, after you have shared examples, explain the approaches that different classmates employed. What principle of selection was used? If arguers included evidence contrary to their positions, how did they handle it, respond to it, minimize its importance, or otherwise channel its rhetorical effect?

Examining Visual Arguments

Angle of Vision

Angle of vision can be conveyed visually as well as verbally. The photos in Figures 4.1 and 4.2 display different angles of vision toward graffiti or street art, a controversial subject worldwide that affects urban dwellers' and tourists' experience of public spaces. Suppose you are writing a short blurb advertising city sights for a free travel magazine available at rental car agencies, hotels, and train stations. Which image

Figure 4.1 Urban site with graffiti

(Pearson Asset Library)

Figure 4.2 Urban site with graffiti

(Source: June Johnson)

would you include with your magazine blurb? Why? Now suppose that you are blogging against graffiti and street art, perhaps urging city residents to support tougher enforcement of laws against graffiti, which you see as vandalism. Which image would you choose? Why?

Analyze the features of the two photographs to explain how they are constructed to create alternative angles of vision on graffiti.

Rhetorical Strategies for Framing Evidence

What we hope you learned from the preceding exercises is that an arguer consciously selects evidence from a wide field of data and then frames these data through rhetorical strategies that emphasize some data, minimize other data, and guide the reader's response. Now that you have a basic idea of what it means to frame evidence, here are some strategies you can use to guide what the reader sees and feels.

STRATEGIES FOR FRAMING EVIDENCE

- **Controlling the space given to supporting versus contrary evidence.** Depending on your audience and purpose, you can devote most of your space to supporting evidence and minimal space to contrary evidence (or omit it entirely). Thus, people arguing in favor of Uber's current business model may have used the pro-Uber evidence from the list while omitting (or summarizing very briefly) the negative data about Uber.

- **Emphasizing a detailed story versus presenting a lot of facts and statistics.** Often, you can choose to support a point with a memorable individual case or with aggregate data such as statistics or lists of facts. A memorable story can have a strongly persuasive effect. For example, to argue for more government regulation of Uber, you might tell the harrowing story of the parents who sued Uber when a distracted Uber driver killed their daughter in a crosswalk. In contrast, a supporter of Uber might tell stories of happy Uber customers using the Uber app instead of standing on a corner trying to hail a taxi.

    A different strategy is to use aggregate data such as facts and statistics rather than narratives. For example, a pro-regulation (anti-Uber) argument might use graphs to show how Uber has cut into the revenue stream of taxi companies, or it might use comparative data about the way different cities, states, or governments have tried to regulate ride-sharing companies like Uber and Lyft. In contrast, a pro-Uber argument might use data showing the cost savings of using uber rather than taxis.

    Each method has its own strengths and weaknesses. The narrative story often has a powerful rhetorical effect, but it is always open to the charge that it is an insufficient or nonrepresentative example. Vivid anecdotes make for engaging reading, but by themselves they may not be compelling logically. In contrast, aggregate data, often used in scholarly publications, can provide more compelling, logical evidence but sometimes make the prose wonkish and dense.

- **Providing contextual and interpretive comments when presenting data.** When citing data, you can add brief contextual or interpretive comments that act as lenses over the readers' eyes to help them see the data from your perspective. Suppose you want to support Uber, but you also want to admit that the Uber business model creates new problems. You could make these problems seem inconsequential with this sentence: "It is true that Uber has had occasional start-up problems, but that is to be expected whenever free enterprise creates a better business model." That sentence identifies Uber with creative free enterprise while minimizing Uber's problems as "typical" of all start-ups. An Uber supporter might also spin Uber positively through an interpretive analogy that positions Uber as "modern" and taxis as obsolete: "Protecting taxi companies by regulating Uber is like protecting stagecoaches by regulating trains."

- **Putting contrary evidence in subordinate positions.**   Just as a photographer can emphasize or deemphasize an object by placing it in the center or the background of a photograph, you can place a piece of data in a subordinate or main clause of a sentence. Note how the structure of the following sentences changes the writer's angle of vision:

  - "Although Uber drivers sometimes complain of stressful work conditions and low pay, they are free as independent contractors to work any hours they wish and accept only the riders and destinations they choose." (negative data in subordinate clause deemphasizes it)

  - "Although Uber drivers are free to work any times they wish and to accept only the rides and destinations they choose, drivers' complaints about low pay and high stress are frequent." (negative data in main clause emphasizes it).

- **Choosing labels and names that guide the reader's response to data.**   One of the most subtle ways to control your readers' response to data is to choose labels and names that prompt them to see the issue as you do. If you like Uber, you might call its business model "creative entrepreneurship," praising Uber for destroying the old, clunky regulations on taxis. In contrast, if you dislike Uber, you might call it a "dangerously unregulated predator" that steals fares from hardworking taxi drivers. The labels you choose, along with the connotations of the words you select, urge your reader to share your angle of vision.

- **Using images (photographs, drawings, other graphics) to guide the reader's response to data.**   Another strategy for moving your audience toward your angle of vision is to include a photograph, drawing, or other graphic that portrays a contested issue from your perspective. Supporters of Uber might include an up-close photograph of an Uber app showing the location of the approaching driver. Anti-Uber images might depict taxi drivers participating in a protest demonstration. (See Chapter 9 for a complete discussion of using visuals in argument.)

- **Revealing the value system that determines the writer's selection and framing of data.**   Ultimately, how you select and frame evidence is linked to the system of values that organizes your argument. If you admire Uber, you probably favor technological innovation and the "creative destruction" (of older business models) made possible by free markets. You might want government to require background checks for Uber drivers, but in general you likely want the government to stay out of the free market. If you don't admire Uber, you probably favor more government regulation aimed at ensuring consumer safety, enhancing workers' rights, and protecting consumers against fraud or false advertising. You may also have doubts about the sharing economy, which may benefit consumers but may have long-range negative effects on workers. If you are targeting an audience that shares your assumptions, you can frame your selected data by stating explicitly the values that guide your argument.

Strategies for Framing Statistical Evidence

Numbers and statistical data can be framed in so many ways that this category of evidence deserves a much closer look. By recognizing how writers frame numbers to support the story they want to tell, you will always be aware that other stories are also possible. Ethical use of numbers means that you use reputable sources for your basic data, that you don't invent or distort numbers to suit your own purposes, and that you don't ignore alternative points of view. Here are some of the choices you can make when framing statistical data:

- **Numbers versus percentages.**   You can alter the rhetorical effect of a statistic by choosing between numbers and percentages. If your uncle reports a $5,000 drop in his retirement account, that sounds scary. It sounds much less scary if he reports a 1 percent drop. You can apply this framing option directly to the Uber case. To emphasize the danger of sexual assault by an Uber driver, you can say that in a given year eight persons filed sexual assault suits against Uber. This use of numbers emphasizes each reported case. To minimize this statistic, you could report it as a percentage of the total number of Uber rides within the United States in a given year. When reported as a percentage, the sexual assault rate by Uber drivers is a tiny fraction of 1 percent.

- **Median versus mean.**   Another way to alter the rhetorical effect of numbers is to choose between the median and the mean. The *mean* is the average of all numbers in a list. The *median* is the middle number when all the numbers are arranged in order from high to low. In 2016 the mean annual income of retirees aged 70–74 in the United States was $38,000—not a large amount of income, but enough to live on comfortably if the retirees owned their own home. However, retirees' median income in 2016 was only $23,000, a figure that points to a much more unequal income distribution among older Americans. This median figure means that half of the retired persons in this age bracket had annual incomes of $23,000 or less—close to poverty level. The much higher mean income indicates that some retired Americans are very wealthy. This wealth raises the average of all incomes (the mean) but doesn't affect the median.

- **Unadjusted versus adjusted numbers.**   Suppose your boss tells you that you are getting a 5 percent raise. You might be happy—unless inflation rates are running at 6 percent. Economic data can be hard to interpret across time unless the dollar amounts are adjusted for inflation. This same problem occurs in other areas. For example, comparing grade point averages of college graduates in 1970 versus 2016 means little unless one can somehow adjust the numbers for grade inflation.

- **Interval sizes on graphs.**   Whenever you draw a line graph, you can manipulate a curve's slope (angle) by the intervals you choose on the vertical axis. If you want to make a graph showing that Earth's average temperature has increased by 1.5 degrees Fahrenheit since 1850, the curve will look steep if you choose ½ degree intervals on the vertical axis. However, if you choose five-degree intervals, the curve will look almost flat. You can see this difference by comparing graphs produced by climate scientists (where global warming is made to "pop out") versus those produced by climate skeptics (where global warming is made to seem nonexistent). For more on graphic display of data, see Chapter 9.

For Class Discussion

Using Strategies to Frame Statistical Evidence

A proposal to build a publicly funded sports stadium in a major American city yielded a wide range of statistical arguments. All of the following statements are reasonably faithful to the same facts:

- The stadium would be paid for by raising the sales tax from 8.2 percent to 8.3 percent for a twenty-year period.
- The sales tax increase is one-tenth of 1 percent.
- The sales tax increase represents an average of $7.50 per person per year—about the price of a special coffee drink and a pastry.
- The sales tax increase represents $750 per five-person family over the twenty-year period in which the higher tax is in effect.
- For a family building a new home in this city, this tax will increase building costs by $200.
- This is a $250 million tax increase for city residents.

How would you describe the costs of the proposed sports stadium if you opposed the proposal?
How would you describe the costs if you supported the proposal?

Creating a Plan for Gathering Evidence

As you begin contemplating an argument, you can use the following checklist to help you think of possible sources for evidence.

A CHECKLIST FOR BRAINSTORMING SOURCES OF EVIDENCE

- What personal experiences have you had with this issue? What details from your life or the lives of your friends, acquaintances, or relatives might serve as examples or other kinds of evidence?

- What observational studies would be relevant to this issue?

- Which people could you interview to provide insights or expert knowledge on this issue?

- Which questions about your issue could be researched with a survey or questionnaire?

- What useful information on this issue might encyclopedias or specialized reference works in your university library provide?

- What evidence might you seek on this issue using licensed databases to search for relevant articles from magazines, newspapers, and scholarly journals?

- How might an Internet search help you research this issue?

- What evidence might you find on this issue from reliable statistical resources such as the U.S. Census Bureau, the Centers for Disease Control, or the website USA.gov? (For more information on the last four points, see Chapter 16.)

Conclusion

Effective use of evidence is an essential skill for arguers. In this chapter we showed you various kinds of evidence ranging from personal experience to library/Internet research. We then discussed ways you can make your evidence persuasive by applying the STAR criteria, developing a trustworthy *ethos*, and being mindful of a secondary source's distance from the original data. We next examined how a writer's angle of vision influences his or her selection and framing of evidence. Finally, we described framing strategies for emphasizing, de-emphasizing, and guiding your reader's response to evidence.

Writing Assignment

A Supporting-Reasons Argument

Write an argument that uses at least two reasons to support your claim and appropriate evidence to develop your reasons. Your argument should include the features of a classical argument described at the beginning of Chapter 2 except that you can omit the section on summarizing and responding to opposing views, which we will cover in Chapter 6. This assignment builds on the brief writing assignments in Chapter 2 (create a thesis statement for an argument) and Chapter 3 (brainstorm support for one of your enthymemes using the Toulmin schema). Like a complete classical argument, a supporting-reasons argument has a thesis-governed structure in which you state your claim at the end of the introduction, begin body paragraphs with clearly stated reasons, and use effective transitions throughout to keep your reader on track. In developing your own argument, place your most important, persuasive, or interesting reason last, where it will have the greatest impact on your readers. A model for a supporting-reasons argument is Carmen Tieu's "Why Violent Video Games Are Good for Girls" in Chapter 3.

Chapter 5
Moving Your Audience
Ethos, Pathos, and Kairos

Learning Objectives

In this chapter you will learn to:

5.1 Explain how the classical appeals of *logos*, *ethos*, and *pathos* work together to move your audience.

5.2 Create effective appeals to *ethos*.

5.3 Create effective appeals to *pathos*.

5.4 Be mindful of *kairos* or the "timeliness" of your argument.

5.5 Explain how images make visual appeals to *logos*, *ethos*, *pathos*, and *kairos*.

5.6 Explain how audience-based reasons appeal to *logos*, *ethos*, *pathos*, and *kairos*.

In Chapters 3 and 4 we focused on *logos*—the logical structure of reasons and evidence in argument. Even though we have treated *logos* in its own chapters, an effective arguer's concern for *logos* is always connected to *ethos* and *pathos* (see the rhetorical triangle in Figure 2.2) and always considers the *kairos*, or timeliness of the argument. This chapter explains how arguers can create effective appeals from *ethos*, *pathos*, and *kairos*. It also explains the crucial role played by concrete language, examples, narrative stories, and use of images in enhancing ethical and emotional appeals. We conclude by showing how audience-based reasons enhance *logos* while also appealing to *ethos* and *pathos*.

Logos, *Ethos*, and *Pathos* as Persuasive Appeals: An Overview

5.1 Explain how the classical appeals of *logos*, *ethos*, and *pathos* work together to move your audience.

At first, one may be tempted to think of *logos*, *ethos*, and *pathos* as "ingredients" in an essay, like spices you add to a casserole. But a more appropriate metaphor might be that of different lamps and filters used on theater spotlights to vary lighting effects on a stage. Thus, if you switch on a *pathos* lamp (possibly through using more concrete language or vivid examples), the resulting image will engage the audience's sympathy and emotions more deeply. If you overlay an *ethos* filter (perhaps by adopting a different tone toward your audience), the projected image of the writer as a person will be subtly altered. If you switch on a *logos* lamp (by adding, say, more data for evidence), you will draw the reader's attention to the logical appeal of the argument. Depending on how you modulate the lamps and filters, you shape and color your readers' perception of you and your argument.

Our metaphor is imperfect, of course, but our point is that *logos*, *ethos*, and *pathos* work together to create an impact on the reader. Consider, for example, the different impacts of the following arguments, all having roughly the same logical appeal.

1. People should adopt a vegetarian diet because doing so will help prevent the cruelty to animals caused by factory farming.

2. If you are planning to eat chicken tonight, please consider how much that chicken suffered so that you could have a tender and juicy meal. Commercial growers cram the chickens so tightly together into cages that they never walk on their own legs, see sunshine, or flap their wings. In fact, their beaks must be cut off to keep them from pecking each other's eyes out. One way to prevent such suffering is for more people to become vegetarians.

3. People who eat meat are no better than sadists who torture other sentient creatures to enhance their own pleasure. Unless you enjoy sadistic tyranny over others, you have only one choice: Become a vegetarian.

4. People committed to justice might consider the extent to which our love of eating meat requires the agony of animals. A visit to a modern chicken factory—where chickens live their entire lives in tiny, darkened coops without room to spread their wings—might raise doubts about our right to inflict such suffering on sentient creatures. Indeed, such a visit might persuade us that vegetarianism is a more just alternative.

Each argument has roughly the same logical core:

But the impact of each argument varies. The difference between arguments 1 and 2, most of our students report, is the greater emotional power of argument 2. Whereas argument 1 refers only to the abstraction "cruelty to animals," argument 2 paints a vivid picture of chickens with their beaks cut off to prevent their pecking each other blind. Argument 2 makes a stronger appeal to *pathos* (not necessarily a stronger argument), stirring feelings by appealing simultaneously to the heart and to the head.

ENTHYMEME

CLAIM: People should adopt a vegetarian diet

REASON: because doing so will help prevent the cruelty to animals caused by factory farming.

GROUNDS

- Evidence of suffering in commercial chicken farms, where chickens are crammed together and lash out at one another

- Evidence that only widespread adoption of vegetarianism will end factory farming

WARRANT

If we have an alternative to making animals suffer, we should use it.

The difference between arguments 1 and 3 concerns both *ethos* and *pathos*. Argument 3 appeals to the emotions through highly charged words such as *torture, sadists,* and *tyranny.* But argument 3 also draws attention to its writer, and most of our students report not liking that writer very much. His stance is self-righteous and insulting. In contrast, argument 4's author establishes a more positive *ethos.* He establishes rapport by assuming his audience is committed to justice and by qualifying his argument with the conditional term *might.* He also invites sympathy for the chickens' plight—an appeal to *pathos*—by offering a specific description of chickens crammed into tiny coops.

Which of these arguments is best? The answer depends on the intended audience. Arguments 1 and 4 seem aimed at receptive audiences reasonably open to exploration of the issue, whereas arguments 2 and 3 seem designed to shock complacent audiences or to rally a group of true believers. Even argument 3, which is too abusive to be effective in most instances, might work as a rallying speech at a convention of animal liberation activists.

Our point thus far is that *logos, ethos,* and *pathos* are different aspects of the same whole, different lenses for intensifying or softening the light beam you project onto the screen. Every choice you make as a writer affects in some way each of the three appeals. The rest of this chapter examines these choices in more detail.

How to Create an Effective *Ethos*: The Appeal to Credibility

5.2   Create effective appeals to *ethos.*

The ancient Greek and Roman rhetoricians recognized that an argument would be more persuasive if the audience trusted the speaker. Aristotle argued that such trust resides within the speech itself, not in the speaker's prior reputation. Speakers project their credibility through their manner and delivery, their tone, their word choice, their use of trustworthy evidence, and the sympathy and fairness with which they treat alternative views. Aristotle called the impact of the speaker's credibility the appeal from *ethos*. How does a writer create credibility? We suggest four ways:

- **Be knowledgeable about your issue.** The first way to gain credibility is to *be* credible—that is, to argue from a strong base of knowledge, to have at hand the examples, personal experiences, statistics, and other empirical data needed to make a sound case. If you have done your homework, you will command the attention of most audiences.

- **Be fair.** Besides being knowledgeable about your issue, you need to demonstrate fairness and courtesy to alternative views. Because true argument can occur only where people may reasonably disagree with one another, your *ethos* will be strengthened if you demonstrate that you understand and empathize with other points of view. There are times when you may appropriately scorn an opposing view. But these times are rare, and they mostly occur when you address audiences predisposed to your view. Demonstrating empathy to alternative views is generally the best strategy.

- **Build a bridge to your audience.** A third means of establishing credibility—building a bridge to your audience—has been treated at length in our earlier discussions of audience-based reasons. By grounding your argument in shared values and assumptions, you demonstrate your goodwill and enhance your image as a trustworthy person respectful of your audience's views. We mention audience-based reasons here to show how this aspect of *logos*—finding the reasons that are most rooted in the audience's values—also affects your *ethos* as a person respectful of your readers' views.

- **Demonstrate professionalism.** Finally, you can enhance your *ethos* by the professionalism revealed in your manuscript itself. Appropriate style, careful editing and proofreading, accurate documentation, and adherence to the genre conventions expected by your audience all contribute to the image of the person behind the writing. If your manuscript is sloppy, marred by spelling or grammatical errors, or inattentive to the tone and style of the expected genre, your credibility will be damaged.

How to Create *Pathos*: The Appeal to Beliefs and Emotions

5.3   Create effective appeals to *pathos*.

Before the federal government outlawed unsolicited telephone marketing, newspapers published flurries of articles complaining about annoying telemarketers. Within this context, a United Parcel Service worker, Bobbi Buchanan, wanted to create sympathy for telemarketers. She wrote a *New York Times* op-ed piece entitled "Don't Hang Up, That's My Mom Calling," which begins as follows:

> To those Americans who have signed up for the new national do-not-call list, my mother [a telemarketer] is a pest . . . . To others, she's just another anonymous voice on the other end of the line. But to those who know her, she's someone struggling to make a buck, to feed herself and pay her utilities.

The op-ed continues with a heartwarming description of Buchanan's mother, LaVerne. Buchanan's rhetorical aim is to transform the reader's anonymous, depersonalized image of telemarketers into the concrete image of her mother: a "hardworking, first generation American; the daughter of a Pittsburgh steelworker; survivor of the Great Depression; the widow of a World War II veteran; a mother of seven, grandmother of eight, great-grandmother of three . . . ." The intended effect is to alter our view of telemarketers through the positive emotions triggered by our identification with LaVerne.

By urging readers to think of "my mother, LaVerne" instead of an anonymous telemarketer, Buchanan illustrates the power of *pathos,* an appeal to the reader's emotions. Arguers create pathetic appeals whenever they connect their claims to readers' values, thus triggering positive or negative emotions depending on whether these values are affirmed or transgressed. Pro-life proponents appeal to *pathos* when they graphically describe the dismemberment of a fetus during an abortion. Proponents of improved women's health and status in Africa appeal to *pathos* when they describe the helplessness of wives forced to have unprotected sex with husbands likely infected with HIV. Opponents of oil exploration in the Arctic National Wildlife Refuge (ANWR) appeal to *pathos* when they lovingly describe the calving grounds of caribou.

Are such appeals legitimate? Our answer is yes, if they intensify and deepen our response to an issue rather than divert our attention from it. Because understanding is a matter of feeling as well as perceiving, *pathos* can give access to nonlogical, but not necessarily nonrational, ways of knowing. *Pathos* helps us see what is deeply at stake in an issue, what matters to the whole person. Appeals to *pathos* help readers walk in the writer's shoes. That is why arguments are often improved through the use of stories that make issues come alive or sensory details that allow us to see, feel, and taste the reality of a problem.

Appeals to *pathos* become illegitimate, we believe, when they confuse an issue rather than clarify it. Consider the case of a student who argues that Professor Jones ought to raise his grade from a D to a C, lest he lose his scholarship and be forced to leave college, shattering the dreams of his dear old grandmother. To the extent that students' grades should be based on performance or effort, the student's image of the dear old grandmother is an illegitimate appeal to *pathos* because it diverts the reader from rational criteria to irrational criteria. The weeping grandmother may provide a legitimate motive for the student to study harder but not for the professor to change a grade.

Although it is difficult to classify all the ways that writers can create appeals from *pathos,* we will focus on four strategies: concrete language; specific examples and illustrations; narratives; and connotations of words, metaphors, and analogies. Each of these strategies lends presence to an argument by creating immediacy and emotional impact.

Use Concrete Language

Concrete language—one of the chief ways that writers achieve voice—can increase the liveliness, interest level, and personality of a writer's prose. When used in argument, concrete language typically heightens *pathos.* For example, consider the differences between the first and second drafts of the following student argument:

FIRST DRAFT

> People who prefer driving a car to taking a bus think that taking the bus will increase the stress of the daily commute. Just the opposite is true. Not being able to find a parking spot when in a hurry to be at work or school can cause a person stress. Taking the bus gives a person time to read or sleep, etc. It could be used as a mental break.

SECOND DRAFT (CONCRETE LANGUAGE ADDED)

> Taking the bus can be more relaxing than driving a car. Having someone else behind the wheel gives people time to chat with friends or study for an exam. They can check Instagram and Twitter, send text messages, doze off, read their favorite news website, or get lost in a novel rather than foam at the mouth looking for a parking space.

In this revision, specific details enliven the prose by creating images that evoke positive feelings. Who wouldn't want some free time to doze off or to get lost in a novel?

Use Specific Examples and Illustrations

Specific examples and illustrations serve two purposes in an argument: They provide evidence that supports your reasons; simultaneously, they give your argument presence and emotional resonance. Note the flatness of the following draft arguing for the value of multicultural studies in a university core curriculum:

FIRST DRAFT

> Another advantage of a multicultural education is that it will help us see our own culture in a broader perspective. If all we know is our own heritage, we might not be inclined to see anything bad about this heritage because we won't know anything else. But if we study other heritages, we can see the costs and benefits of our own heritage.

Now note the increase in presence and emotional resonance when the writer adds a specific example:

SECOND DRAFT (EXAMPLE ADDED)

> Another advantage of multicultural education is that it raises questions about traditional Western values. For example, owning private property (such as buying your own home) is part of the American dream. However, in studying the beliefs of American Indians, students are confronted with a very different view of private property. When the U.S. government sought to buy land in the Pacific Northwest from Chief Sealth, he is alleged to have replied:

> The president in Washington sends words that he wishes to buy our land. But how can you buy or sell the sky? The land? The idea is strange to us. If we do not own the freshness of the air and the sparkle of the water, how can you buy them? [. . .] We are part of the earth and it is part of us. [. . .] This we know: The earth does not belong to man, man belongs to the earth.
>
> Our class was shocked by the contrast between traditional Western views of property and Chief Sealth's views. One of our best class discussions was initiated by this quotation from Chief Sealth. Had we not been exposed to a view from another culture, we would have never been led to question the "rightness" of Western values.

The writer begins his revision by evoking a traditional Western view of private property, which he then questions by shifting to Chief Sealth's vision of land as open, endless, and unobtainable as the sky. Through the use of a specific example, the writer brings to life his previously abstract point about the benefit of multicultural education.

Use Narratives

A particularly powerful way to evoke *pathos* is to tell a story that either leads into your claim or embodies it implicitly and that appeals to your readers' feelings and imagination. Brief narratives—whether true or hypothetical—are particularly effective as opening attention grabbers for an argument. To illustrate how an introductory narrative (either a story or a brief scene) can create appeals to *pathos*, consider the following first paragraph to an argument opposing jet skis:

> I dove off the dock into the lake, and as I approached the surface I could see the sun shining through the water. As my head popped out, I located my cousin a few feet away in a rowboat waiting to escort me as I, a twelve-year-old girl, attempted to swim across the mile-wide, pristine lake and back to our dock. I made it, and that glorious summer day is one of my most precious memories. Today, however, no one would dare attempt that swim. Jet skis have taken over this small lake where I spent many summers with my grandparents. Dozens of whining jet skis crisscross the lake, ruining it for swimming, fishing, canoeing, rowboating, and even water-skiing. More stringent state laws are needed to control jet skiing because it interferes with other uses of lakes and is currently very dangerous.

This narrative makes a case for a particular point of view toward jet skis by winning our identification with the writer's experience. She invites us to relive that experience with her while she also taps into our own treasured memories of summer experiences that have been destroyed by change.

Opening narratives to evoke *pathos* can be powerfully effective, but they are also risky. If they are too private, too self-indulgent, too sentimental, or even too dramatic and forceful, they can backfire. If you have doubts about an opening narrative, read it to a sample audience before using it in your final draft.

Use Words, Metaphors, and Analogies with Appropriate Connotations

Another way of appealing to *pathos* is to select words, metaphors, or analogies with connotations that match your aim. We have already described this strategy in our discussion of the "framing" of evidence in Chapter 4. By using words with particular connotations, a writer guides readers to see the issue through the writer's angle of vision. Thus, if you want to create positive feelings about a recent city council decision, you can call it "bold and decisive"; if you want to create negative feelings, you can call it "short-sighted and autocratic." Similarly, writers can use favorable or unfavorable metaphors and analogies to evoke different imaginative or emotional responses. A tax bill might be viewed as a "potentially fatal poison pill" or as "unpleasant but necessary economic medicine." In each of these cases, the words create an emotional as well as intellectual response.

For Writing and Discussion

Incorporating Appeals to *Pathos*

Outside class, rewrite the introduction to one of your previous papers (or a current draft) to include more appeals to *pathos*. Use any of the strategies for giving your argument presence: concrete language, specific examples, narratives, metaphors, analogies, and connotative words. Bring both your original and your rewritten introductions to class. In pairs or in groups, discuss the comparative effectiveness of these introductions in trying to reach your intended audience.

Kairos: The Timeliness and Fitness of Arguments

5.4   Be mindful of *kairos* or the "timeliness" of your argument.

To increase your argument's effectiveness, you need to consider not only its appeals to *logos*, *ethos*, and *pathos*, but also its *kairos*—that is, its timing, its appropriateness for the occasion. *Kairos* is one of those wonderful words adopted from another language (in this case, ancient Greek) that is impossible to define, yet powerful in what it represents. In Greek, *kairos* means "right time," "season," or "opportunity." It differs subtly from the ordinary Greek word for time, *chronos*, the root of our words "chronology" and "chronometer." You can measure *chronos* by looking at your watch, but you measure *kairos* by sensing the opportune time through psychological attentiveness to situation and meaning. To think *kairotically* is to be attuned to the total context of a situation in order to act in the right way at the right moment. By analogy, consider a skilled base runner who senses the right moment to steal second, a wise teacher who senses the right moment to praise or critique a student's performance, or a successful psychotherapist who senses the right moment to talk rather than listen in a counseling session. *Kairos* reminds us that a rhetorical situation is not stable and fixed, but evolves as events unfold or as audiences experience the psychological ebbs and flows of attention and care. Here are some examples that illustrate the range of insights contained by the term *kairos:*

- If you write a letter to the editor of a newspaper or post a response to a blog, you usually have a one- or two-day window before a current event becomes "old news" and is no longer interesting. An out-of-date response will go unread, not because it is poorly written or argued but because it misses its *kairotic* moment. (Similar instances of lost timeliness occur in class discussions: On how many occasions have you wanted to contribute an idea to class discussion, but the professor doesn't acknowledge your raised hand? When you finally are called on, the *kairotic* moment has passed.)

- Bobbi Buchanan's "Don't Hang Up, That's My Mom Calling," which we used earlier in this chapter to illustrate *pathos*, could have been written only during a brief historical period when telemarketing was being publicly debated. Moreover, it could have been written only late in that period, after numerous writers had attacked telemarketers. The piece was published in *The New York Times* because the editor received it at the right *kairotic* moment.

- A sociology major is writing a senior capstone paper as a graduation requirement. The due date for the paper is fixed, so the timing of the paper isn't at issue. But *kairos* is still relevant. It urges the student to consider what is appropriate for such a paper. What is the "right way" to produce a sociology paper at this moment in the history of the discipline? Currently, what are leading-edge versus trailing-edge questions in sociology? What theorists are now in vogue? What research methods would most impress a judging committee? How would a good capstone paper written in 2019 differ from one written a decade earlier?

As you can see from these examples, *kairos* concerns a whole range of questions connected to the timing, fitness, appropriateness, and proportions of a message within an evolving rhetorical context. There are no rules to help you determine the *kairotic* moment for your argument, but being attuned to *kairos* will help you "read" your audience and rhetorical situation in a dynamic way.

Often you can establish the *kairos* of your argument in the opening sentences of your introduction. An introduction might mention a recent news event, political speech, legislative bill, or current societal problem that the audience may have experienced, thereby using awareness of *kairos* to connect with the audience's interests, knowledge, and experience. Elsewhere in your argument, attention to *kairos* can infuse currency and immediacy by establishing the stakes in the argument and enlisting the audience's concern. For example, if you are going to argue that your university's policy on laptops in the classroom is too restrictive, you might enhance your argument by mentioning several recent editorials in your campus newspaper on this subject. If you are going to argue for increased urban gardening in your city, you might cite a recent TED talk on successful experiments with urban gardening. If you are creating a text that includes images, you might also establish *kairos* through a photograph or cartoon that signals appropriate currency. Thinking about *kairos* helps you focus on the public conversation your argument is joining and on your audience's interests, knowledge, and values.

For Writing and Discussion

Analyzing an Argument from the Perspectives of *Logos, Ethos, Pathos,* and *Kairos*

Your instructor will select an argument for analysis. Working in small groups or as a class, analyze the assigned argument first from the perspective of *kairos* and then from the perspectives of *logos, ethos,* and *pathos.*

1. As you analyze the argument from the perspective of *kairos,* consider the following questions:
   a. What is the motivating occasion for this argument? That is, what causes this writer to put pen to paper or fingers to keyboard?
   b. What conversation is the writer joining? Who are the other voices in this conversation? What are these voices saying that compels the writer to add his or her own voice? How was the stage set to create the *kairotic* moment for this argument?
   c. Who is the writer's intended audience and why?
   d. What is the writer's purpose? Toward what view or action is the writer trying to persuade his or her audience?
   e. To what extent can various features of the argument be explained by your understanding of its *kairotic* moment?
2. Now analyze the same argument for its appeals to *logos, ethos,* and *pathos.* How successful is this argument in achieving its writer's purpose?

Using Images to Appeal to *Logos, Ethos, Pathos,* and *Kairos*

5.5 **Explain how images make visual appeals to *logos, ethos, pathos,* and *kairos.***

One of the most powerful ways to move your audience is to use photos or other images that can appeal to *logos, ethos, pathos,* and *kairos* in one glance. (Chapter 9 focuses exclusively on visual rhetoric—the persuasive power of images.) Although many written arguments do not lend themselves to visual illustrations, we suggest that when you construct arguments you consider the potential of visual support. Imagine that your argument is to be delivered as a PowerPoint presentation or appear in a newspaper, in a magazine, or on a website where space will be provided for one or two visuals. What photographs or drawings might help persuade your audience toward your perspective?

When images work well, they make particularly powerful appeals to *pathos* analogous to the verbal strategies of concrete language, specific illustrations, narratives, and connotative words. The challenge in using visuals is to find material that is straightforward enough to be understood without elaborate explanations, that is timely and relevant, and that clearly adds impact to a specific part of your argument. As an example, suppose you are writing an argument supporting fund-raising efforts to help a developing country that has recently experienced a natural catastrophe. To add a powerful appeal to *pathos,* you might consider incorporating into your argument the photograph shown in Figure 5.1 of the devastation and personal loss caused by Typhoon Haiyan in the Philippines in 2013. A photograph such as this one can evoke a strong emotional and imaginative response as well as make viewers think.

For Writing and Discussion

Analyzing Images as Appeals to *Pathos*

Individual task:

Use the following questions to analyze the photo in Figure 5.1.

1. How would you describe the emotional/imaginative impact of Figure 5.1? What specific details of the photo create its appeal to *pathos*?
2. Many disaster-relief photos seek to convey the magnitude of the destruction and suffering, sometimes shockingly, by depicting destroyed buildings, mangled bodies, and images of human misery. How is your response to Figure 5.1 similar to or different from your response to commonly encountered close-up photographs of grief-stricken victims or to distance shots of widespread destruction? To what extent is Figure 5.1's story—told from the perspective of a child—different from the more typical photographs of destroyed buildings or anguished faces?
3. After searching the web for other photos taken after Typhoon Haiyan, write a rationale for why you would, or would not, choose this photo to accompany a proposal argument appealing for support for people in this region of the Philippines.

Group task:

Share your individual analysis and rationale with others in your class.

Figure 5.1 Photo after Typhoon Haiyan in the Philippines

Examining Visual Arguments

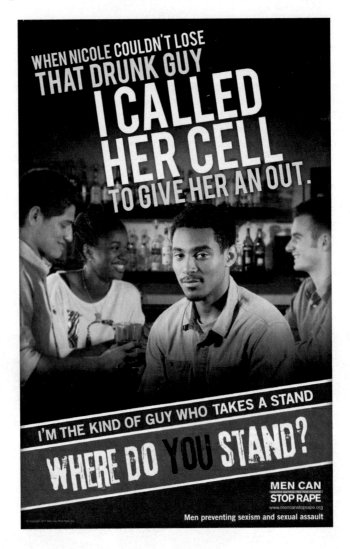

Logos, Ethos, Pathos, and *Kairos*

Efforts to combat sexual assault and date rape on college campuses have figured prominently in public conversation recently, with discussions booming on the websites of newly formed organizations and stories of rallies on university campuses appearing on news sites. As this advocacy poster shows, the need to bolster bystander intervention is a critical piece in addressing this problem.

How does this advocacy poster attempt to move its audience? Analyze the poster's visual and verbal appeals to *logos, ethos, pathos,* and *kairos.*

How Audience-Based Reasons Appeal to *Logos*, *Ethos*, *Pathos*, and *Kairos*

5.6 **Explain how audience-based reasons appeal to *logos*, *ethos*, *pathos*, and *kairos*.**

We conclude this chapter by returning to the concept of audience-based reasons that we introduced in Chapter 3. Audience-based reasons enhance *logos* because they build on underlying assumptions (warrants) that the audience is likely to accept. But they also enhance *ethos*, *pathos*, and *kairos* by helping the audience identify with the writer, by appealing to shared beliefs and values, and by conveying a shared sense of an issue's timeliness. To consider the needs of your audience, you can ask yourself the questions in Table 5.1.

To see how a concern for audience-based reasons can enhance *ethos* and *pathos*, we ask you to role play a student in the following hypothetical scenario. Interested in a career in public health, you are a nursing major who has done

Table 5.1 Questions for Analyzing Your Audience

What to Ask	Why to Ask It
1. *Who is your audience?*	Your answer will help you think about audience-based reasons.
	▪ Are you writing to a single person, a committee, or the general readership of a newspaper, magazine, blog, and so forth?
	▪ Are your readers academics, professionals, other students, general citizens, or people with specialized background and interests?
	▪ Can you expect your audience to be politically and culturally liberal, middle of the road, conservative, or a mixture of these groups?
	▪ What are the religious views of your audience?
	▪ How do you picture your audience in terms of social class, ethnicity, gender, sexual orientation, gender identity, age, and cultural identity?
	▪ To what extent does your audience share your own interests and cultural position? Are you writing to insiders or to outsiders with regard to your own values and beliefs?
2. *How much does your audience know or care about your issue?*	Your answer can especially affect your introduction and conclusion.
	▪ Do your readers need background on your issue, or are they already in the conversation?
	▪ If you are writing to specific decision makers, are they currently aware of the problem you are addressing? If not, how can you get their attention?
	▪ Does your audience care about your issue? If not, how can you get them to care?
3. *What is your audience's current attitude toward your issue?*	Your answer will help you decide the structure and tone of your argument.
	▪ Are your readers already supportive of your position? Undecided? Skeptical? Strongly opposed?
	▪ What points of view other than your own will your audience be weighing?
4. *What will be your audience's likely objections to your argument?*	Your answer will help determine the content of your argument and will alert you to extra research you may need to conduct.
	▪ What weaknesses will audience members find in your argument?
	▪ What aspects of your position will be most threatening to your audience and why?
5. *What values, beliefs, or assumptions about the world do you and your audience share?*	Your answer will help you find common ground with your audience.
	▪ How are your basic assumptions, values, or beliefs different from your audience's?
	▪ Despite different points of view on this issue, where can you find common ground with your audience?
	▪ How might you use common ground to build bridges to your audience?

research on the obesity crisis in the United States. You have also researched the role of sugary soda and energy drinks in promoting heart disease and diabetes. Recently health advocates in your city have teamed with preschool education advocates to persuade the city council to propose a soda tax. Revenue from the tax would be used to improve the city's preschool programs. Your city council points to nationwide precedents for soda taxes, citing Philadelphia; Berkeley, California; and Cook County, Illinois, which includes Chicago. Other cities, such as Seattle, are on the verge of creating such a tax. The tax being proposed in your city would raise the price of a twelve-pack of soda by four dollars; the price of a large fountain soda at a fast-food restaurant would go up 35 cents.

As you can expect, the proposed tax is controversial. Opponents include the beverage industry, grocery store owners, fast-food restaurants, truck drivers (who deliver soda to the stores), and citizens who oppose the government's telling private citizens what they should or should not buy. Proponents include health advocates and education advocates. Medical and nursing associations point to the long-range health benefits of reducing consumption of sugary drinks. Meanwhile, education advocates point to the value of improved and extended preschool programs made possible by revenue from the soda tax.

Your school's student nurse association is scheduling a meeting next week to produce an advocacy piece in favor of the soda tax. Here is your dilemma: You are opposed to the soda tax, not from the perspective of business owners but from the perspective of disproportionate costs to lower-income city residents. What bothers you is the fact that the soda tax is regressive, meaning that it will hit low-income consumers harder than wealthier consumers. Will you have enough courage to speak out at the nursing association meeting? After all, your anti-tax stance will be unpopular among other nursing students, even though it might be applauded by business owners, truck drivers, and the beverage industry.

As you think about your upcoming speech, you formulate your audience-based problem like this:

> **Problem:** How can I create an argument rooted in shared values with my fellow nursing students? How can I reduce my audience's fear that I am becoming an advocate for the beverage industry? How can I make the case that I share my audience's goals of reducing sugar consumption and improving preschool education? How can I show that these goals might be accomplished in a fairer way?

Possible bridge-building strategies:

- Show that I support the health goals of our nursing association—to fight obesity-related diseases by reducing consumption of sugary drinks.
- Show that I support the educational goals made reachable by revenue from the tax. This revenue will make improved preschool education available for all children in the city.
- Stress that both my audience and I share a concern for the welfare of the poorest citizens, who will be hit hardest by the tax.
- Make the case that the tax will eat up a higher proportion of poor people's income than wealthier people's income. Research shows that poorer people buy more soda than wealthy people. Paying an extra four dollars for a 12-pack of soda puts a substantial strain on a poor family's budget. (Wealthy people

often choose diet soda or get their sugar fix from syrups in their espresso coffee drinks). The cost of improving the city's preschools will thus be borne disproportionately by the poor.

- Show that the values underlying the tax are incoherent: If the tax truly reduces consumption of soda (the goal of health advocates), then it will not generate enough revenue to achieve the goals of the education advocates. In sum, the goals of one set of tax proponents are in conflict with the goals of the other set of proponents.

- Show that the goal of reducing sugar consumption might be better achieved through an aggressive educational campaign. Putting a "sin tax" on soda won't be as effective in the long run as raising public awareness about healthy diets and the danger of wasted calories.

- Show that the goal of improving preschool education can be achieved by establishing a fairer tax that puts a higher burden on wealthier people who can afford it.

These thinking notes allow you to develop the following plan for your argument:
Our nursing association should take a courageous stand against the soda tax

- because a soda tax places a disproportionate burden on low-income consumers. (*WARRANT: Taxes that primarily burden low-income consumers are unfair.*)

- because preschool revenue can be raised by a more equitable tax that burdens the wealthy more than the poor. (*WARRANT: It is fair for wealthier people to pay a greater proportion of their income on taxes than the poor.*)

- because an educational campaign may be more effective than a soda tax in changing long-range diet behaviors. (*WARRANT: If alternative solutions can be applied to a problem, the one promoting long-range change is better.*)

As this plan shows, your strategy is to seek reasons whose warrants your audience will accept. Even though you oppose the soda tax, your argument differs significantly from the pro-business arguments mounted by the beverage industry. Whereas their arguments are aimed at undecided voters, your argument is aimed specifically at supporters of the tax. You can hope to persuade them only if you can build bridges to them with audience-based reasons and appeals to shared values.

For Writing and Discussion

Planning an Audience-Based Argumentative Strategy

Individual task:

1. Choose one of the following cases and plan an audience-based argumentative strategy. Follow the thinking process used by the writer of the anti-soda tax argument: (1) state several problems that the writer must solve to reach the audience, and (2) develop possible solutions to those problems.

   a. An argument for the right of software companies to continue making and selling violent video games: Aim the argument at parents who oppose their children playing these games.

(continued)

 b. An argument to reverse grade inflation by limiting the number of As and Bs a professor can give in a course: Aim the argument at students who fear getting lower grades.
 c. An argument supporting the legalization of cocaine: Aim the argument at readers of *Reader's Digest*, a conservative magazine that supports the current war on drugs.

Group task:

Share your planning notes with other members of your class, and discuss how your sketched argument would make appeals to *ethos* and *pathos* as well as to *logos*.

Conclusion

In this chapter, we explored ways that writers can strengthen the persuasiveness of their arguments by creating appeals to *ethos* and *pathos*, by being attentive to *kairos*, by thinking visually, and by building bridges to their readers through audience-based reasons. Arguments are more persuasive if readers trust the writer's credibility and if the argument appeals to readers' hearts and imaginations as well as to their intellects. Attentiveness to *kairos* keeps the writer attuned to the dynamics of a rhetorical situation in order to create the right message at the right time. Sometimes images such as drawings or photographs may reinforce the argument by evoking strong emotional responses, thus enhancing *pathos*. Finally, all these appeals come together when the writer explicitly focuses on finding audience-based reasons.

Writing Assignment

Revising a Draft for *Ethos*, *Pathos*, and Audience-Based Reasons

Part 1:

Choose an argument that you have previously written or that you are currently drafting. Revise the argument with explicit focus on increasing its appeals to *logos, ethos, pathos,* and *kairos* via audience-based reasons and other strategies. Consider especially how you might improve *ethos* by building bridges to the audience or improve *pathos* through concrete language, specific examples, metaphors, or connotations of words. Finally, consider the extent to which your reasons are audience-based.

Or

Create a multimodal argument by adding effective photographs or images to an argument that you have previously written or are currently drafting that could be enhanced with effective photographs or images. Revise your argument to include these images, perhaps creating a desktop-published document that wraps text around visuals chosen to enhance *pathos*. Other multimodal possibilities include transforming your argument into a speech supported by PowerPoint images (see Chapter 15, into a poster argument (see Chapter 9), or even into a podcast that includes music.

Part 2:

Attach to your revision or transformed project a reflective letter explaining the choices you made in revising your original argument or in transforming it using a multimodal approach. Describe for your instructor the changes or transformations you made, and explain how or why your new version enhances your argument's effectiveness at moving its audience.

Chapter 6
Responding to Objections and Alternative Views

Learning Objectives

In this chapter, you will learn to:

6.1 Explain the differences between one-sided, multisided, and delayed-thesis arguments.

6.2 Determine the degree of your audience's resistance to your views in order to shape the content, structure, and tone of your argument.

6.3 Use one-sided argument to appeal to supportive audiences.

6.4 Use classical argument to appeal to neutral or undecided audiences, using refutation and concession.

6.5 Consider using delayed- thesis argument to appeal to resistant audiences.

Chapter 5 discussed strategies for moving your audience through appeals to *ethos, pathos,* and *kairos.* In this chapter we examine strategies for addressing opposing or alternative views—whether to omit them, refute them, concede to them, or incorporate them through compromise and conciliation.

One-Sided, Multisided, and Delayed-Thesis Arguments

6.1 **Explain the differences between one-sided, multisided, and delayed-thesis arguments.**

Arguments can be one-sided, multisided, or delayed thesis:

- **A one-sided argument** presents only the writer's position on the issue without summarizing and responding to alternative viewpoints.
- **A multisided argument** presents the writer's position, but it also summarizes and responds to possible objections and alternative views.
- **A delayed thesis argument** has a strong component of inquiry in which writers present themselves as uncertain and invite resistant readers to become partners in the dialogue. By keeping the question open (and not presenting the writer's own view until later), the writer considers and values multiple perspectives. However, if an issue is heatedly contested, it may be fruitful to move beyond argument altogether and to use instead the listening and negotiating strategies of collaborative rhetoric explained in Chapter 10.

One-sided and multisided arguments often take an adversarial stance in that writers regard alternative views as flawed or wrong and support their own claims with a strongly persuasive intent. Although multisided arguments can be adversarial, they can also be made to feel conciliatory and dialogic, depending on the way the writer introduces and responds to alternative views.

At issue, then, is the writer's treatment of alternative views. Does the writer omit them (a one-sided argument), summarize them in order to rebut them (an adversarial kind of multisided argument), or summarize them in order to acknowledge their validity, value, and force (a more dialogic kind of multisided argument)? Each of these approaches can be appropriate for certain occasions, depending on your purpose, your confidence in your own stance, and your audience's resistance to your views.

How can you determine the kind of argument that would be most effective in a given case? As a general rule, if an issue is highly contested, one-sided arguments tend to strengthen the convictions of those who are already in the writer's camp but alienate those who aren't. In contrast, for those initially opposed to a writer's claim, a multisided argument shows that the writer has considered other views and thus reduces some initial hostility.

An especially interesting effect can occur with neutral or undecided audiences. In the short run, one-sided arguments are often persuasive to a neutral audience, but in the long run, multisided arguments have more staying power. Neutral audiences who have heard only one side of an issue tend to change their minds when they hear alternative arguments. By anticipating and rebutting opposing views, a multisided argument diminishes the surprise and force of subsequent counterarguments. If we move from neutral to highly resistant audiences, adversarial approaches—even multisided ones—are seldom effective because they increase hostility and harden the differences between writer and reader. In such cases, a delayed thesis argument can be helpful. When conflict is emotionally heated, we may even choose to turn from argument to collabortive rhetoric, where we simply listen to those with whom we disagree in an effort to open up channels of communication and consensual problem-solving. These collaborative, dialogic approaches have the best chance of establishing common ground for inquiry and consensus (see Chapter 10).

In the rest of this chapter we will show you how your choice of writing one-sided, multisided, or delayed-thesis arguments is a function of how you perceive your audience's resistance to your views, your level of confidence in your own views, and your purpose—to persuade your audience or open up dialogue.

Determining Your Audience's Resistance to Your Views

6.2   Determine the degree of your audience's resistance to your views in order to shape the content, structure, and tone of your argument.

When you write an argument, you must always consider your audience's point of view. One way to imagine your relationship to your audience is to place it on a scale of resistance ranging from strong support of your position to strong opposition (Figure 6.1). At the "Accord" end of this scale are like-minded people who basically agree with your position on the issue. At the "Resistance" end are those who strongly disagree with you, perhaps unconditionally, because their values, beliefs, or assumptions sharply differ from your own. Between "Accord" and "Resistance" lies a range of opinions. Close to your position will be those leaning in your direction but with less conviction than you have. Close to the resistance position will be those basically opposed to your view but willing to listen to your argument and perhaps willing to acknowledge some of its strengths. In the middle are those undecided people who are still sorting out their feelings, seeking additional information, and weighing the strengths and weaknesses of alternative views.

Seldom, however, will you encounter an issue in which the range of disagreement follows a simple line from accord to resistance. Often, resistant views fall into different categories so that no single line of argument appeals to all those whose views are different from your own. You thus have to identify not only your audience's resistance to your ideas but also the causes of that resistance.

Consider, for example, the issues surrounding publicly financed sports stadiums. In one city, a ballot initiative asked citizens to agree to an increase in sales taxes to build a new re-tractable-roof stadium for its baseball team. Supporters of the initiative faced a complex array of resisting views (Figure 6.2). Opponents of the initiative could be placed into four categories. Some simply had no interest

---

Figure 6.1 Scale of resistance

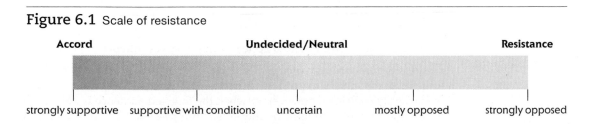

Figure 6.2 Scale of resistance, baseball stadium issue

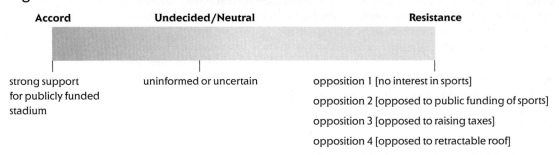

Accord	Undecided/Neutral	Resistance

strong support
for publicly funded
stadium

uninformed or uncertain

opposition 1 [no interest in sports]

opposition 2 [opposed to public funding of sports]

opposition 3 [opposed to raising taxes]

opposition 4 [opposed to retractable roof]

in sports, cared nothing about baseball, and saw no benefit in building a huge, publicly financed sports facility. Another group loved baseball and followed the home team passionately, but was philosophically opposed to subsidizing rich players and owners with taxpayer money. This group argued that the whole sports industry needed to be restructured so that stadiums were paid for out of sports revenues. Still another group was opposed to tax hikes in general. That group focused on two principles: (1) reducing the size of government and (2) using tax revenues only for essential services. Finally, another powerful group supported baseball and supported the notion of public funding of a new stadium but opposed the kind of retractable-roof stadium specified in the initiative. This group wanted an old-fashioned, open-air stadium like Baltimore's Camden Yards or Cleveland's Progressive Field.

Writers supporting the initiative found it impossible to address all of these resisting audiences at once. If supporters of the initiative wanted to persuade those uninterested in sports, they could stress the spinoff benefits of a new ball-park (for example, the new ballpark would attract tourist revenue, renovate a deteriorating downtown neighborhood, create jobs, make sports lovers more likely to vote for public subsidies of the arts, and so forth). But these arguments would be irrelevant to those who wanted an open-air stadium, who opposed tax hikes categorically, or who objected to public subsidies for millionaires.

The baseball stadium example illustrates the difficulty of adapting your argument to your audience's position on the scale of resistance. Still, doing so is important because you need a stable vision of your audience before you can create audience-based reasons that appeal to your audience's values, assumptions, and beliefs. In the next sections, we show how you can adjust your arguing strategy depending on whether your audience is supportive, neutral, or hostile.

Appealing to a Supportive Audience: One-Sided Argument

6.3 Use one-sided argument to appeal to supportive audiences.

One-sided arguments may occur early in an argumentative conversation when a writer's aim is merely to put forth a new or different point of view. When an issue is highly contested, however, or when the targeted audience is indifferent, one-sided arguments are used mainly to stir the passions of supporters or to inspire the apathetic—for example, to convert belief into action by inspiring a party member to contribute to a senator's campaign or a bored office worker to sign up for a change-your-life weekend seminar.

Typically, appeals to a supportive audience are structured as one-sided arguments that either ignore opposing views or reduce them to "enemy" stereotypes. Filled with motivational language, these arguments list the benefits that will follow from the reader's donations to the cause and the horrors just around the corner if the other side wins. One of the authors of this text received a fund-raising letter from an environmental lobbying group declaring, "It's crunch time for the polluters and their pals on Capitol Hill." The "corporate polluters" and "anti-environment politicians," the letter continues, have "stepped up efforts to roll back our environmental protections—relying on large campaign contributions, slick PR firms, and well-heeled lobbyists to get the job done before November's election." This letter makes the reader feel like part of an in-group of good guys fighting the big business "polluters." Nothing in the letter examines environmental issues from business's perspective or attempts to examine alternative views fairly. Because the intended audience already believes in the cause, nothing in the letter invites readers to consider the issues more thoroughly. Rather, the letter's goal is to solidify support, increase the fervor of belief, and inspire action. Most appeal arguments make it easy to act, ending with an 800 phone number to call, a website to visit, an online petition to sign, or a congressperson's address to write to.

Appealing to a Neutral or Undecided Audience: Classical Argument

6.4 **Use classical argument to appeal to neutral or undecided audiences, using refutation and concession.**

The in-group appeals that motivate an already supportive audience can repel a neutral or undecided audience. Because undecided audiences are like jurors weighing all sides of an issue, they distrust one-sided arguments that caricature other views. Generally the best strategy for appealing to undecided audiences is the classically structured argument described in Chapter 2.

What characterizes the classical argument is the writer's willingness to summarize opposing views fairly and to respond to them openly—either by trying to refute them or by conceding to their strengths and then shifting to a different field of values. Let's look at these strategies in more depth.

Summarizing Opposing Views

The first step toward responding to opposing views in a classical argument is to summarize them fairly. Follow the *principle of charity*, which obliges you to avoid loaded, biased, or "straw man" summaries that oversimplify or distort opposing arguments, making them easy to knock over.

Consider the difference between an unfair and a fair summary of an argument. In the following example, a hypothetical supporter of genetically engineered foods intends to refute the argument of organic-food advocate Lisa Turner, who opposes all forms of biotechnology.

UNFAIR SUMMARY OF TURNER'S ARGUMENT

In a biased article lacking scientific understanding of biotechnology, natural-foods huckster Lisa Turner parrots the health food industry's party line that genetically altered crops are Frankenstein's monsters run amok. She ignorantly claims that consumption of biotech foods will lead to worldwide destruction, disease, and death, ignoring the wealth of scientific literature showing that genetically modified foods are safe. Her misinformed attacks are scare tactics aimed at selling consumers on overpriced "health food" products to be purchased at boutique organic-food stores.

FAIR SUMMARY OF TURNER'S ARGUMENT

In an article appearing in a nutrition magazine, health-food advocate Lisa Turner warns readers that much of our food today is genetically modified using gene-level techniques that differ completely from ordinary crossbreeding. She argues that the potential, unforeseen, harmful consequences of genetic engineering offset the possible benefits of increasing the food supply, reducing the use of pesticides, and boosting the nutritional value of foods. Turner asserts that genetic engineering is imprecise, untested, unpredictable, irreversible, and also uncontrollable because of animals, insects, and winds.

In the unfair summary, the writer distorts and oversimplifies Turner's argument, creating a straw man argument that is easy to knock over because it doesn't make the opponent's best case. In contrast, the fair summary follows the principle of charity, allowing the strength of the opposing view to come through clearly.

For Writing and Discussion

Distinguishing Fair from Unfair Summaries

Individual task:

Use the following questions to analyze the differences between the two summaries of Lisa Turner's article.

1. What makes the first summary unfair? Explain.
2. In the unfair summary, what strategies does the writer use to make the opposing view seem weak and flawed? In the fair summary, how is the opposing view made strong and clear?
3. In the unfair summary, how does the writer attack Turner's motives and credentials? This attack is sometimes called an *ad hominem* argument ("against the person"—see the Appendix for a definition of this reasoning fallacy) because it attacks the arguer rather than the argument. How does the writer treat Turner differently in the fair summary?
4. Do you agree with our view that arguments are more persuasive if the writer summarizes opposing views fairly rather than unfairly? Why or why not?

Group task:

As a group, write a fair and an unfair summary of an argument that your instructor gives you, using the strategies you analyzed in the Turner examples.

Refuting Opposing Views

Once you have summarized opposing views, you can either refute them or concede to their strengths. In refuting an opposing view, you attempt to convince readers that its argument is logically flawed, inadequately supported, or based on erroneous assumptions. In refuting an argument, you can rebut (1) the writer's stated reason and grounds, (2) the writer's warrant and backing, or (3) both. Put in less specialized language, you can rebut a writer's reasons and evidence or the writer's underlying assumptions. Suppose, for example, that you wanted to refute this hypothetical argument from a writer we'll call Jason Jones:

> Students should limit the number of internships they take because internships are time-consuming.

We can clarify the structure of this argument by showing it in Toulmin terms:

ENTHYMEME

CLAIM: Students should limit the number of internships they take

REASON: because internships are time-consuming.

WARRANT
Time-consuming internships are bad for students.

One way to refute this argument is to rebut the stated reason that internships are time-consuming. Your rebuttal might go something like this:

> I disagree with Jones' argument that internships are time-consuming. In fact, organizations and businesses are usually very upfront, realistic, and flexible in the weekly hours that they ask of students. The examples that Jones cites of overly demanding internships are exceptions. Furthermore, these internships have since been retailored to students' schedules. [The writer could then provide examples of effective, limited-time internships.]

Or you could concede that internships are time-consuming but rebut the argument's warrant that a time-consuming internship is bad for students:

> I agree that internships take sizable chunks of students' time, but investment in real-world work environments is a worthwhile use of students' time. Through this investment, students clarify their professional goals, log work experience, and gain references. Without interning in these work environments, students would miss important career preparation.

Let's now illustrate these strategies in a more complex situation. Consider the controversy inspired by a *New York Times Magazine* article titled "Recycling Is Garbage." Its author, John Tierney, argued that recycling is not environmentally sound and that it is cheaper to bury garbage in a landfill than to recycle it. Tierney argued that recycling wastes money; he provided evidence that "every time a sanitation department crew picks up a load of bottles and cans from the curb, New York City loses money." In Toulmin's terms, one of Tierney's arguments is structured as shown below.

ENTHYMEME

CLAIM: Recycling is bad policy

REASON: because it costs more to recycle material than to bury it in a landfill.

GROUNDS

• Evidence of the high cost of recycling [Tierney says it costs New York City $200 more per ton for recyclables than trash.]

WARRANT

We should dispose of garbage in the least expensive way.

A number of environmentalists responded angrily to Tierney's argument, challenging either his reason, his warrant, or both. Those refuting the reason offered counterevidence showing that recycling isn't as expensive as Tierney claimed. Those refuting the warrant said that even if the costs of recycling are higher than the costs of burying wastes in a landfill, recycling still benefits the environment by reducing the amount of virgin materials taken from nature. These critics, in effect, offered a new warrant: Conserving the world's resources is an important goal of garbage disposal.

Strategies for Rebutting Evidence

Whether you are rebutting an argument's reasons or its warrant, you will frequently need to question a writer's use of evidence. Here are some strategies you can use:

- **Deny the accuracy of the data.** Arguers can disagree about the facts of a case. If you have reasons to doubt a writer's facts, call them into question.
- **Cite counterexamples and countertestimony.** You can often rebut an argument based on examples or testimony by citing counterexamples or countertestimony that denies the conclusiveness of the original data.
- **Cast doubt on the representativeness or sufficiency of examples.** Examples are powerful only if they are believed to be representative and sufficient. Many environmentalists complained that John Tierney's attack on recycling was based too largely on data from New York City and that it didn't accurately take into account the more positive experiences of other cities and states. When data from outside New York City were examined, the cost-effectiveness and positive environmental impact of recycling seemed more apparent.

- **Cast doubt on the relevance or recency of the examples, statistics, or testimony.** The best evidence is up-to-date. In a rapidly changing universe, data that are even a few years out-of-date are often ineffective. For example, as the demand for recycled goods increases, the cost of recycling will be reduced. Out-of-date statistics will skew any argument about the cost of recycling.

- **Question the credibility of an authority.** If an opposing argument is based on testimony, you can undermine its persuasiveness if you show that a person being cited lacks current or relevant expertise in the field. (This approach is different from the *ad hominem* fallacy discussed in the Appendix because it doesn't attack the personal character of the authority but rather the authority's expertise on a specific matter.)

- **Question the accuracy or context of quotations.** Evidence based on testimony is frequently distorted by being either misquoted or taken out of context. Often scientists qualify their findings heavily, but the popular media omit these qualifications. You can thus attack the use of a quotation by putting it in its original context or by explaining how scientists qualified their findings in the original source.

- **Question the way statistical data were produced or interpreted.** Chapter 4 provides fuller treatment of how to question statistics. In general, you can rebut statistical evidence by calling into account how the data were gathered, treated mathematically, or interpreted. It can make a big difference, for example, whether you cite numbers or percentages or whether you choose large or small increments for the axes of graphs.

Conceding to Opposing Views

In writing a classical argument, a writer must sometimes concede to an opposing argument rather than refute it. Sometimes you encounter portions of an argument that you simply can't refute. For example, suppose that you are a libertarian who supports the legalization of hard drugs such as cocaine and heroin. Adversaries argue that legalizing hard drugs will increase the number of drug users and addicts. You might dispute the size of their numbers, but you reluctantly agree that they are right. Your strategy is thus not to refute the opposing argument but to concede to it by admitting that legalization of hard drugs will promote heroin and cocaine addiction. Having made that concession, your task is then to show that the benefits of drug legalization, such as a reduction in crime and fewer people serving time in America's prisons, still outweigh the costs you've just conceded.

As this example shows, the strategy of a concession argument is to switch from the field of values employed by the writer you disagree with to a different field of values more favorable to your position. You don't try to refute the writer's stated reason and grounds (by arguing that legalization will *not* lead to increased drug usage and addiction) or the writer's warrant (by arguing that increased drug use and addiction is not a problem). Rather, you shift the argument to a new field of values by introducing a new warrant, one that you think your audience can share (that the benefits of legalization outweigh the costs of increased addiction). To the extent that opponents of legalization share your desire to stop drug-related crime, shifting to this new field of values is a good strategy. Although it may seem that you weaken your own position by conceding to an opposing argument, you may actually strengthen it by increasing your credibility and gaining your audience's goodwill. Moreover, conceding to one part of an opposing argument doesn't mean that you won't refute other parts of that argument.

Example of a Student Essay Using Refutation Strategy

The following essay by student writer Trudie Makens grew out of her research into the issue of raising the minimum wage to a living wage. Trudie's essay illustrates how a classical argument appealing to a neutral or even mildly resistant audience engages with alternative views. Note the use of both concession and rebuttal strategies. (Trudie's in-text parenthetical citations and her Works Cited list follow the MLA documentation style explained in Chapter 18.)

Student Essay

Bringing Dignity to Workers: Make the Minimum Wage a Living Wage

Trudie Makens

Uses personal example to illustrate problems of low-wage workers

Having worked as a busser in a pizza restaurant, a part-time barista, and a server at a dumpling café, I have worked a number of minimum-wage jobs. My coworkers have ranged from students like myself to single parents and primary providers for their families. As a student, I have always had my parents as a safety net protecting me from financial hardship. However, my coworkers whose only income is their minimum wage endured financial hardships daily. I witnessed one of my coworkers, Maria, lose her home trying to balance supporting her two children and paying her rent. At work, Maria would describe her anxiety as she bounced from relative to relative, straining her family relations and image of herself as an able provider. Without a living wage or the government's providing social insurance programs to ensure financial security for all citizens, families like Maria's are locked into poverty.

Thesis statement

Raising the federal minimum wage to a livable standard is an important and necessary step to eradicate poverty and ensure dignified living for individuals and families.

Forecasts rebuttal of three opposing views raised by Saltsman

Yet some argue that a higher federal minimum wage will do more harm than good. Michael Saltsman, the research director of the Employment Policy Institute, elaborates the pro-business objections to a minimum wage in several op-ed pieces published in national print or online newspapers. Saltsman primarily makes three arguments against raising the minimum wage. Each of them, I contend, is weak or flawed.

Summarizes Saltsman's first objection to minimum wage

First, Saltsman warns that raising the minimum wage will force businesses to cut jobs. In order to maintain profit and to keep prices low, Saltsman argues, businesses will pay for a higher wage by slashing the number of workers. Worse, businesses may cut entire departments in favor of automation, such as having fast-food customers order their meals from computer touch screens. Saltsman's argument, however, depends on older studies

Rebuts argument by citing more recent research

that, according to University of California economist Michael Reich, are "fundamentally flawed" (Maclay). In a study published in 2010, Reich and his coauthors find that these earlier studies fail to account for all the critical variables besides wages that influence employment levels. By comparing employment levels between states with higher versus lower minimum-wage levels, Reich and his colleagues provide empirical evidence that raising the minimum wage produces no "adverse employment effects" (954).

Saltsman's second objection to a higher minimum wage is that it targets the wrong people and thus won't reduce overall poverty levels. According to Saltsman, a majority of people living in poverty are unemployed while a majority of minimum-wage workers are from households above the poverty line. Although Saltsman may be correct that a higher minimum wage won't help a jobless person, he ignores the benefits of a living wage to the working poor who would be lifted out of poverty. Moreover, a higher minimum wage might itself stimulate jobs because minimum-wage workers with more money in their pockets are apt to spend it, increasing demand for goods.

Finally, Saltsman argues that the minimum wage is less effective at reducing poverty than the Earned Income Tax Credit, which boosts the income of low-wage workers while not giving any income boost to workers who are already above the poverty level. However, the Earned Income Tax Credit, like the minimum wage, does nothing for the jobless poor. Moreover, the Earned Income Tax Credit puts the burden of poverty relief on taxpayers rather than employers and corporate shareholders, doing little to shift the economy in an equitable direction. We need both an increased minimum wage and the Earned Income Tax Credit.

It seems clear that to combat poverty, the United States needs a many-pronged effort, with a hike in the minimum wage being only one of the prongs. Although a higher minimum wage will not by itself eliminate poverty, it will certainly help. It needs to be combined with investments in infrastructure to create jobs, with affordable higher education, with better job training, and with other safety-net systems such as those in place in Europe to give dignity to all citizens. Rather than our government and market system prioritizing corporations and profit, the rights and dignity of workers should be held foremost important. Raising the minimum wage to a living wage will help change the structure of a market system that often exploits workers.

Summarizes Saltsman's second objection

Concedes that higher minimum wage won't help jobless, but shifts to other benefits that Saltsman ignores

5

Summarizes Saltsman's last argument

Rebuts this argument by showing weaknesses in the Earned Income Tax Credit approach

Uses conclusion to summarize additional measures (besides higher minimum wage) to combat poverty

Works Cited

Maclay, Kathleen. "Minimum Wage Hikes Don't Eliminate Jobs, Study Finds." *UC Berkeley News Center*, 1 Dec. 2010, news.berkeley.edu/2010/12/01/minimumwagejobs.

Reich, Michael, et al. "Minimum Wage Effects Across State Borders: Estimates Using Contiguous Counties." *Review of Economics and Statistics*, vol. 92, no. 4, 2010, pp. 945–64.

Saltsman, Michael. "The Wrong Way to Reduce Poverty." *USA Today*, 20 Sept. 2013, www.usatoday.com/story/opinion/2013/09/20/minimum-wages-poverty-column/2839003.

---. "To Help the Poor, Move Beyond 'Minimum' Gestures." *The Huffington Post*, 26 Apr. 2013, updated 26 June 2013, www.huffingtonpost.com/michael-saltsman/earned-income-tax-credit-minimum-wage_b_3165459.html.

For Writing and Class Discussion

Refutation Strategies

Individually or in groups, examine each of the following arguments, imagining how the claim and reason could be fleshed out with grounds and backing. Then attempt to refute each argument. Suggest ways to rebut the reason, or the warrant, or both, or to concede to the argument and then switch to a different field of values.

a. The criminal justice system should reduce sentences for low-level, nonviolent offenders because this change will save taxpayers' money.

b. Majoring in engineering is better than majoring in music because engineers make more money than musicians.

c. The SAT exam for college entrance should not be required by colleges and universities because high-school grades are a better predictor of student success than SAT scores.

d. The United States should build more nuclear reactors because nuclear reactors will provide substantial electrical energy without emitting greenhouse gases.

e. People should be allowed to own handguns because owning handguns helps them protect their homes against potentially violent intruders.

Appealing to a Resistant Audience: Delayed-Thesis Argument

6.5 Consider using delayed-thesis argument to appeal to resistant audiences.

Whereas classical argument is effective for neutral or undecided audiences, it is often less effective for audiences strongly opposed to the writer's views. Because resistant audiences hold values, assumptions, or beliefs widely different from the writer's, they are often unswayed by classical argument, which attacks their worldview too directly. Unlike a classical argument, a delayed-thesis argument assumes either an initial exploratory approach to a subject or an approach that focuses on shared values, evoking sympathy for the audience's views. With some issues, you may want to convey that you are still thinking out your position, finding your way through a thicket of alternative views and the complexities of the issue. On other issues, you might simply want to focus first on shared values. Under these rhetorical conditions, a delayed-thesis argument enables you to establish initial rapport with your audience. Instead of declaring a claim and reasons early in the argument, you may work your way slowly to your claim, often delaying your thesis until the end.

Let's look at an example of a delayed-thesis argument, examining its form and its emotional impact. (For another example of a delayed-thesis argument, see Ellen Goodman's "Womb for Rent—for a Price" in Chapter 7.) The following essay, by British journalist Alexander Chancellor, appeared in the conservative British magazine *The Spectator*:

Oh, How I Will Miss the Plastic Bag

Alexander Chancellor

It has taken years, but finally England has joined the rest of the United Kingdom and other countries around the world in declaring war on the plastic carrier bag. This week for the first time English supermarkets are being forbidden by law to give plastic bags away for free. From now on they will have to charge 5p for every one of them. It is the beginning of the end. The plastic bag is heading for oblivion. The most useful shopping tool of the last half-century will soon, I imagine, be extinct.

It seems only appropriate at this point to say how wonderful plastic bags have been. They are the most useful carriers ever invented—strong, light, capacious, and absurdly cheap to produce. Life without them will never be so easy again. In future, anyone wanting to buy a few things from the supermarket on the way home from work will have to remember to take a reusable shopping bag out with him in the morning. Anyone stocking up with food at the weekend will have to set out with a supply of his own bags in the car. I already try to do this, but usually forget. Oh, how I will miss the plastic bag.

But the remarkable thing is that the end of the plastic bag, when it happens, will not have been an imposition from above but a fulfilment of the popular will. A consultation exercise carried out eight years ago found, for example, that 90 percent of Londoners were in favor of banning plastic bags altogether. Ninety percent of Londoners wanted to abolish one of the greatest conveniences of their everyday lives! Who can say that people are always selfish?

The popularity of the new measure against plastic bags, the docile acceptance of having to pay for something that always used to be free, is evidence of how responsive people can be to campaigns for the wider public good. The campaign against smoking has been successful, too, but smoking kills individuals, which is rather different. Plastic bags just threaten the world.

That threat, however, is impressive. The statistics are enough to alarm anyone. Hitherto in Britain, billions of plastic bags have been given to shoppers each year, and they have all got thrown away. About 60,000 tons of them have ended up in landfills, where they can take more than 400 years to decompose—a process that promotes climate change by releasing carbon dioxide into the atmosphere.

Throughout the world, between 500 and 1,000 billion plastic bags are thought to be consumed annually, more than a million a minute. And those that don't reach landfill sites get blown about on the wind from the North Pole to the South, littering every continent and polluting every sea.

Those floating out at sea have a devastating effect on marine life. Turtles eat them, thinking they are jellyfish, and die in consequence. Altogether, more than 100,000 mammals, including whales and seals, and up to one million seabirds are thought to be killed each year from eating or getting tangled up in plastic. And like the poignant photograph of a dead child on a beach in Turkey that got the campaign to admit refugees to Britain going, it took a distressing image to spark the revolution against plastic bags.

Marginal annotations:

Title shows fondness for plastic bags

Provides context and explains new law requiring stores to charge for plastic bags

Establishes rapport with audience by praising the usefulness of plastic bags

Elaborates his shared view with the audience—the value of plastic bags

Surprises reader by acknowledging that British citizens, not the government, voted to ban the bags

Credits the ban to the unselfishness of people, who put the environment ahead of convenience

Provides evidence of the environmental damage caused by discarded plastic bags

Provides more evidence of the damage caused to oceans and marine life

Shows the dramatic power of a visual image to turn citizens against plastic bags

It was the sight of some albatross chicks dying from eating plastic on a beach in Devon that eight years ago upset Rebecca Hosking, a BBC camerawoman, so much that she persuaded shopkeepers in her hometown of Modbury to give up plastic bags altogether, thus launching the campaign of which we are seeing the results today.

States his thesis: Plastic bags "are not a good thing"

Discarded plastic bags may occasionally have their uses. I am told that in some parts of Africa there has developed a cottage industry in which people turn them into hats. But on the whole I have to say that even I am convinced that they are not a good thing. So I will try not to mourn them. I will stock up on sturdy canvas bags and try to remember to take them with me to the supermarket. Or maybe I should do the sensible thing and start getting my groceries delivered to my home instead.

If Chancellor had chosen to write a classical argument, he might have declared his position in the first paragraph, perhaps with a thesis statement like this:

> The forthcoming British ban on plastic bags is a good thing because the ban will help reduce the plastic pollution of oceans and other environmental damage caused by discarded bags.

He would have then presented his evidence about environmental damage caused by plastic bags, particularly to marine life. Near the end of his argument, he might have summarized an opposing view ("Of course, many people like plastic bags . . . "), conceded that the plastic bags had many uses, but then switched to another field of values: "However, the environmental harm caused by pollution outweighs the benefits to consumers." Organized as a classical argument, Chancellor's essay would use a Toulmin schema similar to our plastic bag example in Chapter 3.

But Chancellor delays stating his thesis until the last paragraph and instead begins his argument with what looks like a lament for the loss of the plastic bag—"the most useful shopping tool of the last half-century." As a cultural conservative writing for a conservative British magazine, he imagines his readers being angry at the government for banning these wonderful plastic bags. He assumes that his readers will expect him to oppose the ban on plastic bags, viewing the ban as an example of an overreaching liberal government. But instead he surprises them halfway through by supporting the ban.

His delayed thesis structure allows him to bring in a second argument in favor of the ban—an argument praising the unselfishness of British citizens who voted overwhelmingly to go against their own selfish interests. The actor in this happy story is not an overreaching liberal government but rather the average British citizen, whose unselfishness is made more vivid by the writer's and readers' shared love of the plastic bag. The title of the essay and the opening paragraphs give readers a chance to identify first with their beloved plastic bags and then second with the unselfishness of good people acting to save the world. Whereas the classical argument can often seem to divide stakeholders into pro and con camps, Chancellor's delayed-thesis approach unites writer and readers as unselfish, good people placing the needs of the world above themselves. Conservatives' grumbles against an overreaching government dissolve into warm feelings about being unselfish and doing good for the world.

Writing a Delayed-Thesis Argument

Clearly, where you place your claim can affect your argument's impact on its audience. We should note, however, that a delayed-thesis argument is not simply a classical argument turned upside down. Instead, it promotes empathy for the audience's views, inviting rather than compelling them toward the writer's stance. It places value on enriching and complicating the discussion by exploring different perspectives. It entails some risk to the writer because it leaves space only at the end of the argument for developing the writer's claim. Moreover, it can backfire in a confusing way if the writer simply seems to change positions without explanation. When done well, however, it may lead the writer and readers to a deeper understanding of the issue, provide clarification, and promote further discussion. Although there is no set form, the organization plan in Figure 6.3 shows characteristic elements often found in delayed-thesis arguments.

Figure 6.3 Organizational plan for a delayed-thesis argument

Organization Plan for a Delayed-Thesis Argument

Introduction	• Establish the problem under discussion and (when appropriate) the occasion that makes the issue timely (*kairos*).
Option 1: Truth-seeking exploration of issue*	• Explore the problem from multiple perspectives, showing the validity of different views • Show how you are wrestling with the problem • For a good portion of the argument, keep the problem open, building some suspense about what your thesis will be
Option 2: Establishment of shared values**	• Focus on values or beliefs that you share with the resistant audience • Show openness and sympathy toward your audience's view of the issue
Delayed thesis and support	• Present your thesis-claim later in the argument • If you present your thesis at the end, it should grow out of reasons and evidence presented earlier • If you present your thesis in the middle, then support it with reasons and evidence
Conclusion	• Leave a last impression favoring your thesis

*This exploratory approach is illustrated by Ellen Goodman's "Womb for Rent—For a Price" in Chapter 7.

**The shared values approach is illustrated by Alexander Chancellor's "Oh How I Will Miss the Plastic Bag" in this chapter.

Conclusion

This chapter explained strategies for addressing alternative views. When intending to engage supportive audiences in a cause, writers often compose one-sided arguments. Neutral or undecided audiences generally respond most favorably to classical argument, which uses strong reasons in support of its claim while openly summarizing alternative views and responding to them through rebuttal or concession. Strongly resistant audiences, who might not be persuaded by classical argument, may be reached more effectively through a delayed-thesis argument that begins with openness toward opposing views.

Writing Assignment
A Classical Argument or a Delayed Thesis Argument

Option 1: A Classical Argument

Write a classical argument following the explanation in Section 2.1 at the beginning of Chapter 2 and using the guidelines for developing such an argument throughout Chapters 2–6. Consider carefully how you will handle alternative views in your argument, based on your awareness of your audience's degree of resistance to your claim and reasons. How will you rebut opposing views? Where will you concede to them? Depending on your instructor's preferences, this argument could be on a new issue, or it could be a final stage of an argument in progress. For an example of a classical argument, see "The Dangers of Digital Distraction" by Lauren Shinozuka (below). Note how Lauren uses research to show that she is joining a larger public conversation on her generation's use of digital technology.

Option 2: A Delayed-Thesis Argument

If you imagine a strongly resistant audience, write a delayed-thesis argument following the model of either Alexander Chancellor in this chapter or of Ellen Goodman in Chapter 7.

Reading

The following essay, by student writer Lauren Shinozuka, illustrates a classical argument. This essay grew out of Lauren's own wrestling with her immersion in social media. She decided to persuade her peers to see the problem her way with the goal that they will join her in new awareness and new habits.

Student Essay
The Dangers of Digital Distractedness
Lauren Shinozuka

We are the Net Generation, the Facebook Generation—digital natives. Cultural critics praise us for our digital skills, our facility with multimedia, and our ability to interact electronically with others through collaboration and co-creation. But at what cost? If we are honest, the following antisocial scene is familiar. You are sitting at a table with friends, and then you hear various pings and look up to see every one of your friends with squinted eyes, checking social media apps and text messages, scrolling away on their phones and furiously punching a reply. What kind of togetherness is this? We seem to feel some urgency or need to know what the world wants from us in that moment, prompting us to check our smartphones every six and a half minutes a day. Although we may seem to be skillfully interactive technologically, I argue that our behavior represents dependence, even addiction, that has deep, pervasive consequences. It harms us by promoting an unproductive habit of multitasking, by dehumanizing our relationships, and by encouraging a distorted self-image.

I can hear my peers immediately rejecting these claims as too extreme and too critical, and I acknowledge that a good case can be made for our digital savvy and the benefits that it brings. Armed with smartphones and laptops, we believe we are masters of technology because we can access so much information easily and immediately. Thanks to our cell phones, all of our friends are only a mere click or swipe away for starting a conversation or sending an invitation to meet up. I also have to admit that our digital knowledge gives us on-the-job advantages. At my part-time job at a high-end retail store, I constantly use a mobile point-of-sale system to ring up customers for fast and easy "on-the-spot checkout," receiving compliments for my competence. With my comfort with the company's technology, I can troubleshoot easily and help other employees. Because technology facilitates much of what we do and keeps us plugged into the rest of the world, I recognize that it can be difficult to see the negative aspects of our relationship to digital technology, but it is time for serious self-examination.

In college, we tell ourselves that multitasking with technology helps us use our time wisely, but in actuality we become even less productive. I notice that while I study, I feel the need to stop every five or ten minutes to check my phone, or log onto a website and allow myself to get distracted before going back to my task. These momentary distractions eat away at my time; when I sit down to write a paper at 9 P.M. I am often startled to find that it is suddenly 12 A.M. and I have less than a page written. We Millennials think we are so cutting edge with our multitasking, yet we get little done with our time. We submerge ourselves into a technological bubble consisting of laptops and music and cell phones, convinced that by arming ourselves with these tools, we can really do it all. In actuality, as writer John Hamilton explains in his report for National Public Radio, our brains cannot "focus on more than one thing at a time." Hamilton cites MIT neuroscientist Earl Miller, who says that our minds are "not paying attention to . . . two things simultaneously, but switching between them very rapidly"; thus, multitasking in itself is a myth. Furthermore, as we continue to overload our brains with multiple tasks, we also begin to reshape our thought processes. Technology—the Internet in particular—helps us avoid the hard work of concentration and contemplation. In the article "Is Google Making Us Stupid?" nonfiction business and technology writer Nicholas Carr describes this way we take in and distribute information as a "swiftly moving stream

(continued)

of particles." We skim rather than read; we rapidly switch tasks rather than truly multitask. I recognize this superficial way of operating in the world in my own behavior. I often turn to Google for an immediate answer to a question I have: Who's the current Speaker of the House? How many ounces are in a cup? Then I click on the first link I see, and more often than not, I see the little subheading that states, "You've visited this page X times." I realize my mental instincts tell me that it's much easier to Google an answer multiple times rather than just *learn* the information. Because I constantly overindulge in my technology, I have engrained the habits of skimming streams of information, constantly bouncing from one task to another, but never stopping to bask in its depths.

Our obsession with technology and social media not only reshapes the way we think, but also fosters a type of false superficial friendship with people we barely know, dehumanizing the kinds of relationships we have. Since coming to college, I've made hundreds of new Facebook friends and attracted dozens of new followers on Twitter. To be fair, a number of these people are truly my good friends, but most of these "friendships" came from a one-time meeting at a party or a class I had with them during my sophomore year. Although some will insist on the vital role social media plays in keeping them connected to distant family and friends, we need to address more directly the extent and pervasive effects of our more common arbitrary cyber friendships. Last summer, while I taught a program at a local elementary school, I would occasionally post a Facebook status of something funny that happened that day, or a picture of my class. Back home later for a short vacation, I ran into a girl from high school whom I hadn't seen in four years and barely knew then. When we stopped to chat, she asked me all about my summer program, and she commented that all my students were so cute! After our chat, I left feeling perturbed and uneasy. Immediately, I thought she was so "creepy," but I realized that ultimately I chose to share my life with the rest of the world. Speaking about these digital relationships, Sherry Turkle, MIT professor and author of *Alone Together: Why We Expect More from Technology and Less from Each Other*, labels our behavior "a Goldilocks effect": "We can't get enough of one another if we can use technology to keep one another at distances we can control: not too close, not too far, just right." That moment when my distant "friend" reached out to me about my summer felt so disturbing because she crossed that Goldilocks line through a personal face-to-face conversation. I am embarrassed to say that I was comfortable only when she was one of the masses; I didn't want to engage in a true interpersonal connection.

5   This lack of intimacy through false relationships leads to the creation of a distorted identity. We begin to form a social identity through our conscious decisions of what we choose to share with the rest of the digital world. We want to post pretty pictures that will garner us a number of "likes," and we want to tweet something witty or profound so others will retweet us. When I began to reevaluate my own social media identity, I found that I consciously try to word my Facebook status in order for people to find it

funny, and I'm obsessed with editing my pictures with the right filters to achieve that hipster artist effect. I realized that I was interpreting my own life experiences in such a way that I would seem interesting or entertaining to all of my "friends," as if I were performing for an audience I was trying to please. That image of myself is dishonest: It conveys the person I want people to think I am, not the real me.

We see this willful self-distortion in a growing trend called "catfishing": an Internet phenomenon where one person creates a false online identity to engage in a romantic relationship with another person physically far removed. Instead of using his or her own photo, the "catfisher" substitutes photos of attractive, talented people to create a false identity. A documentary named for this phenomenon, *Catfish*, features these long-distance lovers traveling across the country for a chance to meet the person who is really on the other side of the screen. Often that person's appearance and even gender and motives are strikingly at odds with the self-portrayal. While it is easy for us to judge negatively these extreme cases of catfishing, Molly McHugh, writer for *Digital Trends*, points out what she calls the "slippery slope of catfishdom." These cases may seem extreme, but to an extent, all of us who embrace social media are indeed "catfish" as well. We succumb to what McHugh calls the "aspirational beast" of social media, bending the truth online to some degree in order to portray the self that we want to be. With our growing reliance on social media and technology, the tendency for our romantic relationships to blend into our digital selves becomes even more prevalent. When we continue to mix this intimate, personal self with the demands and desires of social media, we produce tragic, ill-formed identities that no longer resemble our true selves.

Of course, we may draw a sharp distinction between our own digital dependence and the growing number of young users who are actual technological addicts. (According to Carolyn Gregoire's *Huffington Post* article, there is now an inpatient Internet rehabilitation center designed specifically for true addicts.) However, our own participation in the more widespread digital craze remains a serious problem too. Yet by taking the first step of making the unconscious conscious, I believe we can combat the digital damage in our lives. I have begun by taking several steps. I purposefully put my phone across the table so I physically need to get up to check it; I let myself binge-check all my social media apps only once, just before going to bed, rather than ten times a day, and I have stopped trying to take pictures of every pretty meal I consume or sunset I see because I know that those are my own special moments, not some glamorous, envy-inducing image I want to project. I have begun to avoid friends who find their phones more interesting than the immediate world around them, and this new company has made it easier to break away from my own addiction. I am trying to rehumanize my friendships, and I am finding solace in deep reading once more without the distractions of cell phone vibrations. I invite members of my generation to join me, so we can be together, no longer alone together.

(continued)

Works Cited

Carr, Nicholas. "Is Google Making Us Stupid? What the Internet Is Doing to Our Brains." *The Atlantic*, July-Aug. 2008, www.theatlantic.com/magazine/archive/2008/07/is-google-making-us-stupid/306868.

Gregoire, Carolyn. "Welcome to Internet Rehab." *The Huffington Post*, 25 Sept. 2013, updated 25 Oct. 2013, www.huffingtonpost.com/2013/09/25/this-is-where-people-are-_n_3976240.html.

Hamilton, John. "Think You're Multitasking? Think Again." *National Public Radio*, 2 Oct. 2008, www.npr.org/templates/story/story.php?storyId=95256794.

McHugh, Molly. "It's Catfishing Season! How to Tell Lovers from Liars Online, and More." *Digital Trends*, 23 Aug. 2013, www.digitaltrends.com/web/its-catfishing-season-how-to-tell-lovers-from-liars-online-and-more.

Turkle, Sherry. "The Flight from Conversation." *The New York Times*, 21 Apr. 2012, www.nytimes.com/2012/04/22/opinion/sunday/the-flight-from-conversation.html.

Critiquing "The Dangers of Digital Distractedness"

1. How does Lauren Shinozuka establish the *kairos* of her argument? In what ways does she use *pathos* to reach her primary audience of Millennials?

2. What is her claim? What reasons does she use to support her claim?

3. What evidence does Lauren employ to support her reasons? What pieces of evidence do you find especially effective?

4. Where has Lauren anticipated resistance to her argument and how has she responded to opposing views?

5. If you were discussing the issue of digital distractedness with Lauren, what ideas would you contribute to further support, complicate, or refute her argument?

PART TWO
Entering an Argumentative Conversation

7 Analyzing Arguments Rhetorically

8 Argument as Inquiry: Reading, Summarizing, Responding

Across the country, protests like this one are raising awareness of the poverty-level wages of fast-food workers, who are not represented by unions and who often depend on public assistance such as food stamps to get by every month. While protestors argue for a minimum wage of $15 per hour, opponents argue that raising the minimum wage would increase food prices and reduce the number of jobs. If you were making a brochure or poster in favor of an increased minimum wage for fast-food workers, how effective would this realistic, low-key photo be in raising sympathy for the cause? Chapter 8 explores the issue of a living wage for unskilled workers.

Chapter 7

Analyzing Arguments Rhetorically

Learning Objectives

In this chapter you will learn to:

7.1 Explain what it means to think rhetorically about texts.

7.2 Reconstruct a source text's rhetorical context by analyzing the text's author, purpose, motivating occasion, audience, genre, and angle of vision.

7.3 Ask questions that promote rhetorical thinking.

7.4 Conduct a rhetorical analysis of a source text.

In Part One of this textbook, we explained the principles of argument—identifying an issue, making a claim, supporting the claim with reasons and evidence (and perhaps supporting the underlying warrants also), summarizing and responding to opposing views, and paying attention to the rhetorical appeals of *logos*, *ethos*, and *pathos*.

In Part Two we shift attention to the critical thinking skills you will need when, as a researcher and a reader of arguments, you begin exploring a new issue. By emphasizing exploration and inquiry, Part Two focuses on the truth-seeking aim of argument as the entry point into a new issue.

To engage thoughtfully in inquiry, you need to analyze arguments rhetorically—that is, to examine an argument closely to understand the author's purpose and intended audience, to evaluate the author's choices, and to determine what makes the argument effective or ineffective for its targeted audience. A rhetorical analysis identifies the text under scrutiny, summarizes its main ideas, presents some key points about the text's rhetorical strategies for persuading its audience, and elaborates on these points.

Becoming skilled at analyzing arguments rhetorically will have multiple payoffs for you. This skill helps you become an inquisitive, truth-seeking reader. It also plays a major role in helping you construct your own arguments. Particularly, analyzing sources rhetorically helps you determine the reliability of the evidence you might draw from other sources while also helping you summarize and respond to opposing views. In this chapter, we explain what it means to think "rhetorically" about other people's arguments (and your own). Chapter 8 then teaches you to apply rhetorical thinking to an actual issue; there, you will draw on your own critical skills to summarize other stakeholders' arguments, analyze their strengths and weaknesses, and begin formulating your own stance.

Thinking Rhetorically about a Text

7.1   Explain what it means to think rhetorically about texts.

To become an effective reader of arguments and to construct effective arguments yourself, you need to think of all arguments as voices in ongoing conversations about issues. Invested stakeholders construct arguments in order to move their audiences to see the issues their way. To understand these arguments fully, you need to think about them rhetorically.

Let's look more closely at what we mean by "thinking rhetorically." At the broadest level, *rhetoric* is the study of how human beings use language and other symbols to influence the attitudes, beliefs, and actions of others. In a narrower sense, rhetoric is the art of making messages persuasive. Perhaps the most famous definition comes from Aristotle, who defined rhetoric as "the ability to see, in any particular case, all the available means of persuasion."

Thinking rhetorically means determining what "available means of persuasion" a writer is using in a particular argument. You can do this by getting inside an argument, listening carefully to what the writer is arguing, and determining *how* this argument has been constructed to reach its audience. To think rhetorically, you should imagine stakeholders as real persons who were motivated to write by some occasion and to achieve some real purpose.

Reconstructing a Text's Rhetorical Context

7.2   Reconstruct a source text's rhetorical context by analyzing the text's author, purpose, motivating occasion, audience, genre, and angle of vision.

To enter an argumentative conversation, you need to think rhetorically about each stakeholder's argument. A first step in doing so is to reconstruct the text's rhetorical context by asking questions about the author and then about the author's purpose, motivating occasion, audience, genre, and angle of vision. Let's look at each of these in turn.

Author, Motivating Occasion, and Purpose

The first three questions you should ask about a source text are these:

- Who is the author?
- What motivates the author to write?
- What is the author's purpose?

Imagine answering these questions about something you are writing. If you see yourself simply as a student acting out school roles, you might answer the questions this way: "I am a first-year college student. My motivating occasion is an assignment from my professor. My purpose is to get a good grade." But to see yourself rhetorically, it is better to put yourself in a plausible real-world situation: "I am a first-year student concerned about global warming. My motivating occasion is my anger at our school's environmental action task force for not endorsing nuclear power. My purpose is to persuade this group that using nuclear power is the best way to reduce our nation's carbon footprint." In real life, writers are motivated to write because some occasion prompts them to do so. In most cases, the writer's purpose is to bring about some desirable change in the targeted audience's actions, beliefs, or views.

If you are in a face-to-face argumentative conversation (say, on a committee), you will know most of the stakeholders and the roles they play. But if you are uncovering the conversation yourself through research, you may have difficulty imagining the author of, say, a blog post or a magazine article as a real person writing for a real purpose sparked by a real occasion. The following list identifies some of the categories of real-world people who are apt to write arguments about civic issues.

Typical Stakeholders in Argumentative Discussion of Civic Issues

- **Lobbyists and advocacy groups.** Lobbyists and advocacy groups commit themselves to a cause, often with passion, and produce avidly partisan arguments aimed at persuading voters, legislators, government agencies, and other decision makers. They often maintain advocacy websites; buy advertising space in newspapers, magazines, and online; and lobby legislators face to face.

- **Legislators, political candidates, and government officials.** Whenever new laws, regulations, or government policies are proposed, staffers do research and write arguments recommending positions on an issue. Often these arguments are available on the web.

- **Business professionals and labor union leaders.** Business spokespeople often address public issues in ways that support corporate or business interests. In contrast, labor union officials support wage structures or working conditions favorable to workers.

- **Lawyers and judges.** Lawyers write briefs supporting their clients' cases or file "friend-of-the-court" briefs aimed at influencing a judge's decision. Also, judges write opinions explaining their decisions on a case.

- **Journalists, syndicated columnists, and media commentators.** Many controversial issues attract the attention of media commentators (journalists, columnists, bloggers, political cartoonists) who write editorials, blogs, or op-ed pieces on the issue or produce editorial cartoons, filtering their arguments through the perspective of their own political views.

- **Professional freelance or staff writers.** Some of the most thoughtful analyses of public issues are composed by freelance or staff writers for public forum magazines such as *Atlantic Monthly* or *The National Review* or for online news sites or blogs such as *The Daily Kos* or *The Drudge Report*. These can range from in-depth background pieces to arguments with a highly persuasive aim. (See Chapter 16, Table 16.3.)

- **Think tank members.** Because many of today's political, economic, and social issues are very complex, policy makers and commentators often rely on research institutions or think tanks to supply statistical studies and in-depth investigation of problems. These think tanks range across the political spectrum from conservative or libertarian to centrist or liberal (see Chapter 16, Table 16.3).

- **Scholars and academics.** College professors play a public role through their scholarly research, contributing data, studies, and analyses to public debates. Scholarly research differs substantially from advocacy argument in that scholarly research is a systematic attempt to arrive at the best answers to questions based on the full examination of relevant data. Scholarly research is usually published in refereed academic journals rather than in popular magazines.

- **Documentary filmmakers.** Testifying to the growing popularity of film and its power to involve people in issues, documentary filmmakers often embed their point of view into their dramatic storytelling to create persuasive arguments on public issues. The global film industry is adding international perspectives as well.

- **Citizens and students.** Engaged citizens influence social policy through e-mails to legislators, letters to the editor, contributions to advocacy websites, guest editorials for newspapers, blogs, and speeches in public forums. Students also write for university communities, present their work at undergraduate research conferences, and influence public opinion by writing to political leaders and decision makers.

Audience

Effective argument depends on the writer's rhetorical understanding of audience. A writer's analysis of a targeted audience often includes demographic data (income, geographic region, typical occupations), political ideology (liberal, centrist, libertarian, conservative, populist), and what scholars call *intersectional positioning* (race, class, gender, ethnicity, sexual orientation, gender identity), and other factors. The writer's goal is to walk in his or her audience's shoes, to see where they are coming from, to understand their values, assumptions, and beliefs. Although writers of arguments occasionally preach to the choir (that is, address people who already agree with them), they usually want to reach people who hold alternative views or are otherwise skeptical of the writer's position. As we saw throughout Part One, effective arguers try to base their arguments on *audience-based reasons* that appeal to the targeted audience's underlying beliefs, values, and assumptions.

Genre

Genres, or types of writing, emerge from specific social contexts and represent social actions. Think of these genres, for example: billboard ads, infomercials, product reviews, and letters to the editor. The term *genre* refers to recurring categories of writing that follow certain conventions of style, structure, approach to subject matter, and document design. The genre of any given argument helps determine its length, tone, sentence complexity, level of informality or formality, use of visuals, kinds of evidence, and the presence or absence of documentation.

Consider, for example, the difference between a tweet and a letter to the editor. Both genres are short (a tweet is limited to 140 characters, a letter to about 200 words). The initial audience for a tweet are the tweeter's followers; the size of the audience depends on the number of followers and on the number of those who retweet the message to their own followers. (During his presidential candidacy, Donald Trump—a master user of Twitter—was able to reach millions of potential voters in seconds.) Because a tweet is self-published with no editor or fact checker, the reader must be especially wary. A tweet's shortness allows no space for a complete argument, only for an opinion or claim. In contrast, letters to the editor have quite different features. The audience for a letter are those newspaper subscribers who follow the editorial pages. Unlike tweets, letters to the editor are just long enough to allow a mini-argument, letting writers support their claims with brief reference to reasons and evidence. Also, unlike a tweet, there is some editorial review of a letter because editors must read many competing submissions for the limited space and choose letters that contribute something valuable to a conversation.

The concept of genre creates strong reader expectations, placing specific demands on writers. Genres are social practices that arise out of particular social needs and conditions. How you write any given grant proposal, op-ed piece, bumper sticker, or academic argument depends on the structure and style of hundreds of previous grant applications, op-ed pieces, bumper stickers, or academic articles written before yours. Table 7.1 identifies some of the important genres of argument that you will encounter as part of an argumentative conversation.

In addition to these commonly encountered print genres, arguments are also carried on in multimedia genres such as advocacy advertisements, advocacy websites, political cartoons, PowerPoint speeches, and documentary films. See Chapter 16, Table 16.1 for a rhetorical overview of sources across a range of genres.

Angle of Vision

Angle of vision, as we explained in Chapter 4, refers to the way that writers frame an issue through their own ideological perspective. Rhetoricians often use an optical metaphor: A writer looks at an issue through a lens that colors or filters the subject matter in a certain way. This lens causes the writer to select certain details while omitting others or to choose words with connotations that reflect the writer's view (whether to say, for example, "greedy capitalist" or "job creator"). A writer's angle of vision is persuasive because it controls what the reader "sees." Unless readers are rhetorically savvy, they can lose awareness that they are seeing the writer's subject matter through a lens that both reveals and conceals.

Closely connected to angle of vision is a writer's degree of advocacy along the continuum from "truth seeking" to "persuasion" (see Chapter 1, Figure 1.5). The more writers are trying to persuade readers toward their view, the more the reader has to recognize angle of vision at work. When doing research, for example, you should be aware of the angle of vision taken by many media outlets themselves—journals, magazines, newspapers, blogs, and websites—that may be associated with a political ideology. It is important to know, for example, whether an article you are reading came from *Mother Jones* (a liberal magazine), *National Review* (a conservative magazine), or *infowars.com* (an alt-right site often associated with "fake news"). For an overview of the angle of vision of many media outlets, see Chapter 16, Figure 16.3).

Table 7.1 Frequently Encountered Genres of Argument

Genre	Explanation and Examples	Stylistic Features
Newspaper editorials and op-ed pieces	• Published on the editorial or op-ed ("opposite-editorial") pages • Editorials promote the views of the newspaper's owners/editors • Op-ed pieces, usually written by professional columnists or guest writers, range in bias from ultraconservative to socialist (see Figure 17.3 in Chapter 17) • Often written in response to political events or social problems in the news	• Usually short (500–1,000 words) • Vary from explicit thesis-driven arguments to implicit arguments with stylistic flair • Have a journalistic style (short paragraphs) without detailed evidence • Sources are usually not documented
Blogs and postings to chat rooms and electronic bulletin boards	• Web-published commentaries, usually on specific topics and often intended to influence public opinion • Blogs (weblogs) are gaining influence as alternative commentaries to the established media	• Often blend styles of journalism, personal narrative, and formal argument • Often difficult to determine identity and credentials of blogger
Magazine articles	• Reflect a wide range of perspectives • Usually written by staff writers or freelancers • Appear in public-affairs magazines such as *National Review* or *The Progressive* or in niche magazines for special-interest groups such as *Rolling Stone* (popular culture), *Minority Business Entrepreneur* (business), or *The Advocate* (gay and lesbian issues) • Often reflect the magazine's political point of view	• Often provide hyperlinks to related sites on the web • Frequently include narrative elements rather than explicit thesis-and-reasons organization • Often provide well-researched coverage of various perspectives on a public issue
Articles in scholarly journals	• Peer-reviewed articles published by nonprofit academic journals subsidized by universities or scholarly societies • Characterized by scrupulous attention to completeness and accuracy in treatment of data	• Usually employ a formal academic style • Include academic documentation and bibliographies • May reflect the biases, methods, and strategies associated with a specific school of thought or theory within a discipline

Asking Questions That Promote Rhetorical Thinking

7.3 Ask questions that promote rhetorical thinking.

At an operational level, seeing arguments rhetorically means posing certain kinds of questions that uncover the rhetorical context and position of each stakeholder in the conversation. When you hear or read someone else's argument (let's call this argument a "source" written by a "source author"), you need to ask rhetorically focused questions about the source author's argument. If you seek answers to the list of questions shown in Table 7.2, you will be thinking rhetorically about arguments. Although a rhetorical analysis will not include answers to all these questions, using some of these questions in your thinking stages can give you a thorough understanding of the argument while helping you generate insights for your own rhetorical analysis essay.

Table 7.2 Questions for Rhetorical Analysis

What to Focus on	Questions to Ask	Applying These Questions
The *kairotic* moment and writer's motivating occasion	• What motivated the writer to produce this piece? • What social, cultural, political, legal, or economic conversations does this argument join?	• Is the writer responding to a bill pending in Congress, a speech by a political leader, or a local event that provoked controversy? • Is the writer addressing cultural trends such as the impact of science or technology on values?
Rhetorical context: Writer's purpose and audience	• What is the writer's purpose? • Who is the intended audience? • What assumptions, values, and beliefs would readers have to hold to find this argument persuasive? • How well does the text suit its particular audience and purpose?	• Is the writer trying to change readers' views by offering a new interpretation of a phenomenon, calling readers to action, or trying to muster votes or inspire further investigations? • Does the audience share a political or religious orientation with the writer?
Rhetorical context: Writer's identity and angle of vision	• Who is the writer and what is his or her profession, background, and expertise? • How does the writer's personal history, education, ethnicity, age, class, sexual orientation, gender identity, and political leaning influence the angle of vision? • What is emphasized and what is omitted in this text? • How much does the writer's angle of vision dominate the text?	• Is the writer a scholar, researcher, scientist, policy maker, politician, professional journalist, or citizen blogger? • Is the writer affiliated with conservative or liberal, religious or lay publications? • Is the writer advocating a stance or adopting a more inquiry-based mode? • What points of view and pieces of evidence are "not seen" by this writer?
Rhetorical context: Genre	• What is the argument's original genre? • What is the original medium of publication? How do the genre and the argument's place of publication influence its content, structure, and style?	• How popular or scholarly, informal or formal is this genre? • Does the genre allow for in-depth or only sketchy coverage of an issue?
Logos of the argument	• What is the argument's claim, either explicitly stated or implied? • What are the main reasons in support of the claim? Are the reasons audience-based? • How effective is the writer's use of evidence? How is the argument supported and developed? • How well has the argument recognized and responded to alternative views?	• Is the core of the argument clear and soundly developed? Or do readers have to unearth or reconstruct the argument? • Is the argument one-sided, multisided, or delayed-thesis? • Does the argument depend on assumptions the audience may not share? • What evidence does the writer employ? Does this evidence meet the STAR criteria?
Ethos of the argument	• What *ethos* does the writer project? • How does the writer try to seem credible and trustworthy to the intended audience? • How knowledgeable does the writer seem in recognizing opposing or alternative views, and how fairly does the writer respond to them?	• If you are impressed or won over by this writer, what has earned your respect? • If you are filled with doubts or skepticism, what has caused you to question this writer? • How important is the character of the writer in this argument?
Pathos of the argument	• How effective is the writer in using audience-based reasons? • How does the writer use concrete language, word choice, narrative, examples, and analogies to tap readers' emotions, values, and imaginations?	• What examples, connotative language, and uses of narrative or analogy stand out for you in this argument? • Does this argument rely heavily on appeals to *pathos*? Or is it more brainy and logical?
Writer's style	• How do the writer's language choices and sentence length and complexity contribute to the impact of the argument? • How well does the writer's tone (attitude toward the subject) suit the argument?	• How readable is this argument? • Is the argument formal, scholarly, journalistic, informal, or casual? • Is the tone serious, mocking, humorous, exhortational, confessional, urgent, or something else?

Table 7.2 Continued

What to Focus on	Questions to Ask	Applying These Questions
Design and visual elements	• How do design elements—layout, font sizes and styles, and use of color—influence the effect of the argument? (See Chapter 9 for a detailed discussion of these elements.) • How do graphics and images contribute to the persuasiveness of the argument?	• Do design features contribute to the logical or the emotional/imaginative appeals of the argument? • How would this argument benefit from visuals and graphics or some different document design?
Overall persuasiveness of the argument	• What features of this argument contribute most to making it persuasive or not persuasive for its target audience and for you yourself? • How would this argument be received by different audiences? • What features contribute to the rhetorical complexity of this argument? • What is particularly memorable, disturbing, or problematic about this argument? • What does this argument contribute to its *kairotic* moment and the argumentative controversy of which it is a part?	• Are appeals to *pathos* legitimate and suitable? Do the quality and quantity of the evidence help build a strong case, or do they fall short? • What specifically would count as a strength for the target audience? • If you differ from the target audience, how do you differ and where does the argument derail for you? • What gaps, contradictions, or unanswered questions are you left with? • How does this argument indicate that it is engaged in a public conversation? How does it "talk" to other arguments you have read on this issue?

For Writing and Discussion

Practicing Rhetorical Analysis

In the following exercise, consider the strategies used by two different writers to persuade their audiences to act to stop climate change. The first is from the opening paragraphs of an editorial in the magazine *Creation Care: A Christian Environmental Quarterly.* The second is from the website of the Sierra Club, an environmental action group.

Individual task:

Read the following passages carefully, and then write out your exploratory answers to the questions that follow. Refer to Table 7.2, "Questions for Rhetorical Analysis," to help you examine how these texts' key features contribute to their impact on readers.

Passage 1

As I sit down to write this column, one thing keeps coming to me over and over: "Now is the time; now is the time."

In the New Testament the word used for this type of time is *kairos.* It means "right or opportune moment." It is contrasted with *chronos,* or chronological time as measured in seconds, days, months, or years. In the New Testament *kairos* is usually associated with decisive action that brings about deliverance or salvation.

The reason the phrase, "Now is the time" kept coming to me over and over is that I was thinking of how to describe our current climate change moment.

The world has been plodding along in chronological time on the problem of climate change since around 1988. No more.

(continued)

Simply put: the problem of climate change has entered *kairos* time; its *kairos* moment has arrived. How long will it endure? Until the time of decisive action to bring about deliverance comes—or, more ominously, until the time when the opportunity for decisive action has passed us by. Which will we choose? Because we do have a choice.

—Rev. Jim Ball, Ph.D., "It's *Kairos* Time for Climate Change: Time to Act," *Creation Care: A Christian Environmental Quarterly* (Summer 2008), 28.

Passage 2

[Another action that Americans must take to combat global warming is to transition] to a clean-energy economy in a just and equitable way. Global warming is among the greatest challenges of our time, but also presents extraordinary opportunities to harness home-grown clean energy sources and encourage technological innovation. These bold shifts toward a clean energy future can create hundreds of thousands of new jobs and generate billions of dollars in capital investment. But in order to maximize these benefits across all sectors of our society, comprehensive global warming legislation must auction emission allowances to polluters and use these public assets for public benefit programs.

Such programs include financial assistance to help low and moderate-income consumers and workers offset higher energy costs as well as programs that assist with adaptation efforts in communities vulnerable to the effects of climate change. Revenue generated from emissions allowances should also aid the expansion of renewable and efficient energy technologies that quickly, cleanly, cheaply, and safely reduce our dependence on fossil fuels and curb global warming. Lastly, it is absolutely vital that comprehensive global warming legislation not preempt state authority to cut greenhouse gas emissions more aggressively than mandated by federal legislation.

—Sierra Club, "Global Warming Policy Solutions," 2008, http://www.sierraclub.org/

1. How do the strategies of persuasion differ in these two passages? Explain these differences in terms of targeted audience, original genre, writer's purpose, and writer's angle of vision.
2. How would you describe the relationship between *logos* and *pathos* in each text?
3. How would you describe the writer's style in each?
4. How effective would either argument be for readers outside the intended audience?

Group task:

Share your responses to the above questions with class members. Explain your points with specific examples from the texts.

Conducting a Rhetorical Analysis of a Source Text

7.4 Conduct a rhetorical analysis of a source text.

To illustrate rhetorical analysis, we will analyze two articles on reproductive technology, a subject that continues to generate arguments in the public sphere. (The first article is in this section; the second is in the student example at the end of this chapter.) By *reproductive technology* we mean scientific advances in the treatment of infertility, such as egg and sperm donation, artificial insemination, in vitro fertilization, and surrogate motherhood. Our first article, written over a decade ago, springs from the early and increasing popularity of these technological options.

Our second article—to be used in our later student example—responds to the recent globalization of this technology.

At this point, please read the first article, "Egg Heads" by Kathryn Jean Lopez (immediately following), and then proceed to the discussion questions that follow. Lopez's article was originally published in the conservative news commentary magazine *National Review*.

Egg Heads

KATHRYN JEAN LOPEZ

Filling the waiting room to capacity and spilling over into a nearby conference room, a group of young women listen closely and follow the instructions: Complete the forms and return them, with the clipboard, to the receptionist. It's all just as in any medical office. Then they move downstairs, where the doctor briefs them. "Everything will be pretty much normal," she explains. "Women complain of skin irritation in the local area of injection and bloating. You also might be a little emotional. But, basically, it's really bad PMS."

This is not just another medical office. On a steamy night in July, these girls in their twenties are attending an orientation session for potential egg donors at a New Jersey fertility clinic specializing in in-vitro fertilization. Within the walls of IVF New Jersey and at least two hundred other clinics throughout the United States, young women answer the call to give "the gift of life" to infertile couples. Egg donation is a quietly expanding industry, changing the way we look at the family, young women's bodies, and human life itself.

It is not a pleasant way to make money. Unlike sperm donation, which is over in less than an hour, egg donation takes the donor some 56 hours and includes a battery of tests, ultrasound, self-administered injections, and retrieval. Once a donor is accepted into a program, she is given hormones to stimulate the ovaries, changing the number of eggs matured from the usual one per month up to as many as fifty. A doctor then surgically removes the eggs from the donor's ovary and fertilizes them with the designated sperm.

Although most programs require potential donors to undergo a series of medical tests and counseling, there is little indication that most of the young women know what they are getting themselves into. They risk bleeding, infection, and scarring. When too many eggs are matured in one cycle, it can damage the ovaries and leave the donor with weeks of abdominal pain. (At worst, complications may leave her dead.) Longer term, the possibility of early menopause raises the prospect of future regret. There is also some evidence of a connection between the fertility drugs used in the process and ovarian cancer.

But it's good money—and getting better. New York's Brooklyn IVF raised its "donor compensation" from $2,500 to $5,000 per cycle earlier this year in order to keep pace with St. Barnabas Medical Center in nearby Livingston, New Jersey. It's a bidding war. "It's obvious why we had to do it," says Susan Lobel, Brooklyn IVF's assistant director. Most New York–area IVF programs have followed suit.   5

Some infertile couples and independent brokers are offering even more for "reproductive material." The International Fertility Center in Indianapolis, Indiana, for instance, places ads in the *Daily Princetonian* offering Princeton girls as much as $35,000 per cycle. The National Fertility Registry, which, like many egg brokerages, features an online catalogue for couples to browse in, advertises $35,000 to $50,000 for Ivy League eggs. While donors are normally paid a flat fee per cycle, there have been reports of higher payments to donors who produce more eggs.

College girls are the perfect donors. Younger eggs are likelier to be healthy, and the girls themselves frequently need money—college girls have long been susceptible to classified ads offering to pay them for acting as guinea pigs in medical research. One 1998 graduate of the University of Colorado set up her own website to market her eggs. She had watched a television show on egg donation and figured it "seemed like a good thing to do"—especially since she had spent her money during the past year to help secure a country music record deal. "Egg donation would help me with my school and music expenses while helping an infertile couple with a family." Classified ads scattered throughout cyberspace feature similar offers.

The market for "reproductive material" has been developing for a long time. It was twenty years ago this summer that the first test-tube baby, Louise Brown, was born. By 1995, when the latest tally was taken by the Centers for Disease Control, 15 percent of mothers in this country had made use of some form of assisted-reproduction technology in conceiving their children. (More recently, women past menopause have begun to make use of this technology.) In 1991 the American Society for Reproductive Medicine was aware of 63 IVF programs offering egg donation. That number had jumped to 189 by 1995 (the latest year for which numbers are available).

Defenders argue that it's only right that women are "compensated" for the inconvenience of egg donation. Brooklyn IVF's Dr. Lobel argues, "If it is unethical to accept payment for loving your neighbor, then we'll have to stop paying baby-sitters." As long as donors know the risks, says Glenn McGee of the University of Pennsylvania's Center for Bioethics, this transaction is only "a slightly macabre version of adoption."

10   Not everyone is enthusiastic about the "progress." Egg donation "represents another rather large step into turning procreation into manufacturing," says the University of Chicago's Leon Kass. "It's the dehumanization of procreation." And as in manufacturing, there is quality control. "People don't want to say the word any more, but there is a strong eugenics issue inherent in the notion that you can have the best eggs your money can buy," observes sociology professor Barbara Katz Rothman of the City University of New York.

The demand side of the market comes mostly from career-minded baby-boomers, the frontierswomen of feminism, who thought they could "have it all." Indeed they *can* have it all—with a little help from some younger eggs. (Ironically, feminists are also among its strongest critics; *The Nation*'s Katha Pollitt has pointed out that in egg donation and surrogacy, once you remove the "delusion that they are making babies for other women," all you have left is "reproductive prostitution.")

Unfortunately, the future looks bright for the egg market. Earlier this year, a woman in Atlanta gave birth to twins after she was implanted with frozen donor eggs. The same technology has also been successful in Italy. This is just what the egg market needed, since it avoids the necessity of coordinating donors' cycles with recipients' cycles. Soon, not only will infertile couples be able to choose from a wider variety of donor offerings, but in some cases donors won't even be needed.

Young women will be able to freeze their own eggs and have them thawed and fertilized once they are ready for the intrusion of children in their lives.

There are human ovaries sitting in a freezer in Fairfax, Virginia. The Genetics and IVF Institute offers to cut out and remove young women's ovaries and cryopreserve the egg-containing tissue for future implantation. Although the technology was originally designed to give the hope of fertility to young women undergoing treatment for cancer, it is now starting to attract the healthy. "Women can wait to have children until they are well established in their careers and getting a little bored, sometime in their forties or fifties," explains Professor Rothman. "Basically, motherhood is being reduced to a good leisure-time activity."

Early this summer, headlines were made in Britain, where the payment of egg donors is forbidden, when an infertile couple traveled to a California clinic where the woman could be inseminated with an experimental hybrid egg. The egg was a combination of the recipient's and a donor's eggs. The clinic in question gets its eggs from a Beverly Hills brokerage, the Center for Surrogate Parenting and Egg Donation, run by Karen Synesiou and Bill Handel, a radio shock-jock in Los Angeles. Miss Synesiou recently told the London *Sunday Times* that she is "interested in redefining the family. That's why I came to work here."

The redefinition is already well under way. Consider the case of Jaycee Buz-   15
zanca. After John and Luanne Buzzanca had tried for years to have a child, an embryo was created for them, using sperm and an egg from anonymous donors, and implanted in a surrogate mother. In March 1995, one month before the baby was born, John filed for divorce. Luanne wanted child support from John, but he refused—after all, he's not the father. Luanne argued that John is Jaycee's father legally. At this point the surrogate mother, who had agreed to carry a baby for a stable two-parent household, decided to sue for custody.

Jaycee was dubbed "Nobody's Child" by the media when a California judge ruled that John was not the legal father nor Luanne the legal mother (neither one was genetically related to Jaycee, and Luanne had not even borne her). Enter Erin Davidson, the egg donor, who claims the egg was used without her permission. Not to be left out, the sperm donor jumped into the ring, saying that his sperm was used without his permission, a claim he later dropped. In March of this year, an appeals court gave Luanne custody and decided that John is the legal father, making him responsible for child support. By contracting for a medical procedure resulting in the birth of a child, the court ruled, a couple incurs "the legal status of parenthood." (John lost an appeal in May.) For Jaycee's first three years on earth, these people have been wrangling over who her parents are.

In another case, William Kane left his girlfriend, Deborah Hect, 15 vials of sperm before he killed himself in a Las Vegas hotel in 1991. His two adult children (represented by their mother, his ex-wife) contested Miss Hect's claim of ownership. A settlement agreement on Kane's will was eventually reached, giving his children 80 percent of his estate and Miss Hect 20 percent. Hence she was allowed three vials of his sperm. When she did not succeed in conceiving on the first two tries, she filed a petition for the other 12 vials. She won, and the judge who ruled in her favor wrote, "Neither this court nor the decedent's adult children possess reason or right to prevent Hect from implementing decedent's pre-eminent interest in realizing his 'fundamental right' to procreate with the woman of his choice." One day, donors may not even have to have lived. Researchers are experimenting with using aborted female fetuses as a source of donor eggs.

And the market continues to zip along. For overseas couples looking for donor eggs, Bill Handel has the scenario worked out. The couple would mail him frozen sperm of their choice (presumably from the recipient husband); his clinic would use it to fertilize donor eggs, chosen from its catalogue of offerings, and reply back within a month with a frozen embryo ready for implantation. (Although the sperm does not yet arrive by mail, Handel has sent out embryos to at least one hundred international customers.) As for the young women at the New Jersey clinic, they are visibly upset by one aspect of the egg-donation process: they can't have sexual intercourse for several weeks after the retrieval. For making babies, of course, it's already obsolete.

For Writing and Discussion

Identifying Rhetorical Features

Working in groups or as a class, develop responses to the following questions:

1. How does Lopez appeal to *logos*? What is her main claim, and what are her reasons?
2. What does she use for evidence? What ideas would you have to include in a short summary of "Egg Heads"?
3. What appeals to *pathos* does Lopez make in this argument? How well are these suited to the conservative readers of the *National Review*?
4. How would you characterize Lopez's *ethos*? Does she seem knowledgeable and credible? Does she seem fair to stakeholders in this controversy?
5. Choose an additional focus from the "Questions for Rhetorical Analysis" (Table 7.2) to apply to "Egg Heads." How does this question expand your understanding of Lopez's argument?
6. What strikes you as problematic, memorable, or disturbing in this argument?

Our Own Rhetorical Analysis of "Egg Heads"

Now that you have identified some of the rhetorical features of "Egg Heads," we offer our own notes for a rhetorical analysis of this argument.

RHETORICAL CONTEXT   As we began our analysis, we reconstructed the rhetorical context in which "Egg Heads" was published. In the late 1990s, a furious debate about egg donation rippled through college and public newspapers, popular journalism, websites, and scholarly commentary. This debate had been kicked off by several couples placing ads in the newspapers of the country's most prestigious colleges, offering up to $50,000 for the eggs of brilliant, attractive, athletic college women. Coinciding with these consumer demands, advances in reproductive technology provided an increasing number of complex techniques to surmount the problem of infertility, including fertilizing eggs in petri dishes and implanting them into women through surgical procedures. These procedures could use either a couple's own eggs and sperm or donated eggs and sperm. All these social and medical factors created the *kairotic* moment for Lopez's article and motivated her to protest the increasing use of these procedures. (Egg donation, concerns for the long-term health of egg donors, surrogate motherhood, and the potential dehumanizing of commercial reproduction continue to be troubling and unresolved controversies across many genres, as you will see when you read Ellen

Goodman's op-ed piece at the end of this chapter and student Zachary Stumps's rhetorical analysis of it.)

GENRE AND WRITER   When we considered the genre and writer of this article and its place of publication, we noted that this article appeared in the *National Review*, which describes itself as "America's most widely read and influential magazine and website for Republican/conservative news, commentary, and opinion." It reaches "an affluent, educated, and highly responsive audience of corporate and government leaders, the financial elite, educators, journalists, community and association leaders, as well as engaged activists all across America" (http://www.nationalreview.com). According to our Internet search, Kathryn Jean Lopez is known nationally for her conservative journalistic writing on social and political issues. Currently the editor-at-large of *National Review Online*, she has also published in *The Wall Street Journal*, the *New York Post*, and the *Washington Times*. This information told us that in her article "Egg Heads," Lopez is definitely on home territory, aiming her article at a conservative audience.

LOGOS   Turning to the *logos* of Lopez's argument, we decided that the logical structure of Lopez's argument is clear throughout the article. Her claim is that egg donation and its associated reproductive advances have harmful, long-reaching consequences for society. Basically, she argues that egg donation and reproductive technology represent bad scientific developments for society because they are potentially harmful to the long-range health of egg donors and because they lead to an unnatural dehumanizing of human sexuality. She states a version of this last point at the end of the second paragraph: "Egg donation is a quietly expanding industry, changing the way we look at the family, young women's bodies, and human life itself."

The body of her article elaborates on each of these reasons. In developing her reason that egg donation endangers egg donors, Lopez lists the risks but doesn't supply supporting evidence about the frequency of these problems: damage to the ovaries, persistent pain, early menopause, possible ovarian cancer, and even death. She supports her claim about "the expanding industry" by showing how the procedures have become commercialized. To show the popularity of these procedures as well as their commercial value, she quotes a variety of experts such as directors of in vitro clinics, fertility centers, bioethicists, and the American Society for Reproductive Medicine. She also cleverly bolsters her own case by showing that even liberal cultural critics agree with her views about the big ethical questions raised by the reproductive-technology business. In addition to quoting experts, Lopez has sprinkled impressive numbers and vivid examples throughout the body of her argument; these numbers and examples give her argument momentum as it progresses from the potential harm to young egg donors to a number of case studies that depict increasingly disturbing ethical problems.

PATHOS   Much of the impact of this argument, we noted, comes from Lopez's appeals to *pathos*. By describing in detail the waiting rooms for egg donors at fertility clinics, Lopez relies heavily on pathetic appeals to move her audience to see the physical and social dangers of egg donation. She conveys the growing commercialism of reproductive technology by giving readers an inside look at the egg-donation process as these young college women embark on the multistep process of donating their eggs. These young women, she suggests in her title "Egg Heads," are largely unaware of the potential physical dangers to themselves and of the ethical implications and consequences of their acts. She asserts that they are driven largely by the desire for money. Lopez also appeals to *pathos* in her choice of emotionally loaded and often cynical language, which creates an angle of vision opposing reproductive technology: "turning procreation into manufacturing"; "reproductive prostitution"; "the intrusion of children in their lives"; "motherhood . . . reduced to a good leisure-time activity"; "aborted female fetuses as a source of donor eggs"; and intercourse as an "obsolete" way to make babies.

AUDIENCE Despite Lopez's success at spotlighting serious medical and ethical questions, her lack of attention to alternative views and the alarmism of her language caused us to wonder: Who might find this argument persuasive, and who would challenge it? What is noticeably missing from Lopez's argument—and apparently from her worldview—is the perspective of infertile couples hoping for a baby. Pursuing our question, we decided that a provocative feature of this argument—one worthy of deeper analysis—is the disparity between how well this argument is suited to its target audience and yet how unpersuasive it is for readers who do not share the assumptions, values, and beliefs of this primary audience.

To Lopez's credit, she has attuned her reasons to the values and concerns of her conservative readers of the *National Review*, who believe in traditional families, gender differences, and gender roles. Opposed to feminism as they understand it, this audience sanctions careers for women only if women put their families first. Lopez's choice of evidence and her orchestration of it are intended to play to her audience's fears that science has fallen into the hands of those who have little regard for the sanctity of the family or traditional motherhood. For example, in playing strongly to the values of her conservative readers, Lopez belabors the physical, social, and ethical dangers of egg donation, mentioning worst-case scenarios; however, these appeals to *pathos* will most likely strike other readers who do some investigating into reproductive technology as overblown. She emphasizes the commercialism of the process as her argument moves from college girls as egg donors to a number of sensationalist case studies that depict intensifying ethical and legal ambiguity. In other words, both the *logos* and the *pathos* of her argument skillfully focus on details that tap her target audience's values and beliefs, feeding that audience's fears and revulsion.

USE OF EVIDENCE For a broader or skeptical audience, the alarmism of Lopez's appeals to *pathos*, her use of atypical evidence, and her distortion of the facts weaken the *logos* and *ethos* of her argument. First, Lopez's use of evidence fails to measure up to the STAR criteria (that evidence should be sufficient, typical, accurate, and relevant). She characterizes all egg donors as young women seeking money. But she provides little evidence that egg donors are only out to make a buck. She also paints these young women as shortsighted, uninformed, and foolish. As a gap in her evidence, she neglects to examine the potential for long-term health consequences to egg donors. Lopez would rather toss out threats and criticize the young women than really explore this issue. Lopez also weakens her *ethos* by not considering the young women who may be motivated, at least in part, by compassion for couples who can't conceive on their own.

Lopez also misrepresents the people who are using egg donation, placing them all into two groups: (1) wealthy couples eugenically seeking designer babies with preordered special traits and (2) feminist career women. She directs much of her criticism toward this latter group: "The demand side of the market comes mostly from career-minded baby-boomers, the frontierswomen of feminism, who thought they could 'have it all.'" However, readers who do a little research on their own, as we did, will learn that infertility affects one in seven couples; that it is often a male and a female problem, sometimes caused by an incompatibility between the man's and the woman's reproductive material; and that most couples who take the big step of investing in these expensive efforts to have a baby have been trying to get pregnant for a number of years. Rather than being casual about having children, they are often deeply desirous of children and depressed about their inability to conceive. In addition, far from being the sure thing and quick fix that Lopez suggests, reproductive technology has a success rate of only 50 percent overall and involves a huge investment of time, money, and physical discomfort for women receiving donor eggs.

Another way that Lopez violates the STAR criteria is her choice of extreme cases. For readers outside her target audience, her argument appears riddled with straw man and slippery-slope fallacies. (See the Appendix, "Informal Fallacies.") Her examples become more bizarre as her tone becomes more hysterical. Here are some specific instances of extreme, atypical cases:

- her focus on career women casually and selfishly using the service of young egg donors
- the notorious case of Jaycee Buzzanca, dubbed "Nobody's Child" because her adoptive parents who commissioned her creation divorced before she was born
- the legal contest between a dead man's teen girlfriend and his ex-wife and adult children over his vials of sperm
- the idea of taking eggs from aborted female fetuses

By keeping invisible the vast majority of ordinary couples who go to fertility clinics out of last-hope desperation, Lopez uses extreme cases to create a "brave new world" intended to evoke a vehement rejection of these reproductive advances. Skeptical readers would offer the alternative view of the sad, ordinary couples of all ages sitting week after week in fertility clinics, hoping to conceive a child through the "miracle" of these reproductive advances and grateful to the young women who have contributed their eggs.

CONCLUDING POINTS   In short, we concluded that Lopez's angle of vision, although effectively in sync with her conservative readers of the *National Review,* exaggerates and distorts her case against these reproductive advances. Lopez's traditional values and slanting of the evidence undermine her *ethos,* limit the value of this argument for a wider audience, and compel that audience to seek out alternative sources for a more complete view of egg donation.

Conclusion

This chapter explained how to think rhetorically about texts. The first step is to reconstruct a text's rhetorical context by focusing on the author, the author's motivating occasion and purpose, the targeted audience, the text's genre, and its angle of vision. We also explained how to apply a list of questions to a text to help you conduct a rhetorical analysis. To analyze a text rhetorically means to determine how it works: what effect it has on readers and how it achieves or fails to achieve its persuasiveness through appeals to *logos, ethos,* and *pathos.*

The following writing assignment includes a student's rhetorical analysis of another article about reproductive technology. In Chapter 8, we provide more detailed instruction on how to summarize and respond to source texts.

Writing Assignment
A Rhetorical Analysis

Write a thesis-driven rhetorical analysis essay in which you examine the rhetorical effectiveness of an argument specified by your instructor. Unless otherwise stated, direct your analysis to an audience of your classmates. In your introduction, establish the argumentative conversation to which this argument is contributing. Briefly summarize the argument and present your thesis highlighting the rhetorical features of the argument that you find central to its effectiveness or ineffectiveness. Zachary Stumps's analysis of Ellen Goodman's "Womb for Rent" (reproduced at the end of this chapter) is an example of this assignment.

Generating Ideas for Your Rhetorical Analysis

To develop ideas for your essay, you might follow these steps:

Step	How to Do It
Familiarize yourself with the article you are analyzing.	Read the article several times. Divide it into sections to understand its structure.
Place the article in its rhetorical context.	Reconstruct the article's rhetorical context following the advice in this chapter. Use the list of questions in Table 7.2, "Questions for Rhetorical Analysis."
Summarize the article.	If you have never written a summary before, you can find specific instruction in Chapter 8.
Reread the article, identifying "hot spots."	Note hot spots in the article—points that impress you, disturb you, confuse you, or puzzle you.
Use the list of questions in Table 7.2, "Questions for Rhetorical Analysis"	Choose several of these questions and freewrite responses to them.
From your notes and freewriting, identify the focus for your analysis.	Choose several features of the article that you find particularly important and that you want to discuss in depth in your essay. Identify points that will bring something new to your readers and that will help them see this article with new understanding. You may want to list your ideas and then look for ways to group them together around main points.
Write a thesis statement for your essay.	Articulate your important points in one or two sentences, setting up these points clearly for your audience.

In finding a meaningful focus for your rhetorical analysis essay, you will need to create a focusing thesis statement that avoids wishy-washy formulas such as, "This argument has some strengths and some weaknesses." To avoid a vapid thesis statement, focus on the complexity of the argument, the writer's strategies for persuading the target audience, and the features that might impede its persuasiveness for skeptics. The best thesis statements articulate how their writers see the inner workings of these arguments as well as the arguments' contributions to their public conversations. For example:

> Lopez's angle of vision, although effectively in sync with her conservative readers of the *National Review*, exaggerates and distorts her case against certain reproductive advances, weakening her *ethos* and the value of her argument for a wider audience. [This is the thesis we would use if we were writing a stand-alone essay on the Lopez article.]

To make your rhetorical analysis of your article persuasive, you will need to develop each of the points stated or implied in your thesis statement using textual evidence, including short quotations. Your essay should show how you have listened carefully to the argument you are analyzing, summarized it fairly, and probed it deeply.

Organizing Your Rhetorical Analysis

The organization plan in Figure 7.1 provides a possible structure for your rhetorical analysis.

Figure 7.1 Organizational plan for a rhetorical analysis of an argument

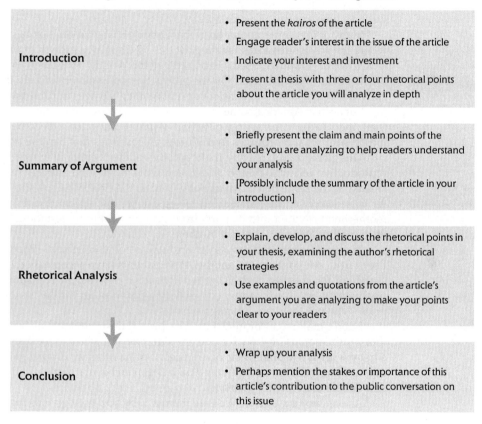

Organization Plan for a Rhetorical Analysis of an Argument

Introduction
- Present the *kairos* of the article
- Engage reader's interest in the issue of the article
- Indicate your interest and investment
- Present a thesis with three or four rhetorical points about the article you will analyze in depth

Summary of Argument
- Briefly present the claim and main points of the article you are analyzing to help readers understand your analysis
- [Possibly include the summary of the article in your introduction]

Rhetorical Analysis
- Explain, develop, and discuss the rhetorical points in your thesis, examining the author's rhetorical strategies
- Use examples and quotations from the article's argument you are analyzing to make your points clear to your readers

Conclusion
- Wrap up your analysis
- Perhaps mention the stakes or importance of this article's contribution to the public conversation on this issue

Readings

Our first reading is by Pulitzer Prize–winning columnist, author, and speaker Ellen Goodman. In our second reading, student Zachary Stumps analyzes Goodman's op-ed piece rhetorically.

Womb for Rent

ELLEN GOODMAN

By now we all have a story about a job outsourced beyond our reach in the global economy. My own favorite is about the California publisher who hired two reporters in India to cover the Pasadena city government. Really.

There are times as well when the offshoring of jobs takes on a quite literal meaning. When the labor we are talking about is, well, labor.

In the last few months we've had a full nursery of international stories about surrogate mothers. Hundreds of couples are crossing borders in search of lower-cost ways to fill the family business. In turn, there's a new coterie of international workers who are gestating for a living.

Many of the stories about the globalization of baby production begin in India, where the government seems to regard this as, literally, a growth industry. In the little town of Anand, dubbed "The Cradle of the World," 45 women were recently on the books of a local clinic. For the production and delivery of a child, they will earn $5,000 to $7,000, a decade's worth of women's wages in rural India.

5   But even in America, some women, including Army wives, are supplementing their income by contracting out their wombs. They have become surrogate mothers for wealthy couples from European countries that ban the practice.

This globalization of baby-making comes at the peculiar intersection of a high reproductive technology and a low-tech work force. The biotech business was created in the same petri dish as Baby Louise, the first IVF baby. But since then, we've seen conception outsourced to egg donors and sperm donors. We've had motherhood divided into its parts from genetic mother to gestational mother to birth mother and now contract mother.

We've also seen the growth of an international economy. Frozen sperm is flown from one continent to another. And patients have become medical tourists, searching for cheaper health care whether it's a new hip in Thailand or an IVF treatment in South Africa that comes with a photo safari thrown in for the same price. Why not then rent a foreign womb?

I don't make light of infertility. The primal desire to have a child underlies this multinational Creation, Inc. On one side, couples who choose surrogacy want a baby with at least half their own genes. On the other side, surrogate mothers, who are rarely implanted with their own eggs, can believe that the child they bear and deliver is not really theirs.

As one woman put it, "We give them a baby and they give us much-needed money. It's good for them and for us." A surrogate in Anand used the money to buy a heart operation for her son. Another raised a dowry for her daughter. And before we talk about the "exploitation" of the pregnant woman, consider her alternative in Anand: a job crushing glass in a factory for $25 a month.

10   Nevertheless, there is—and there should be—something uncomfortable about a free-market approach to baby-making. It's easier to accept surrogacy when it's a gift from one woman to another. But we rarely see a rich woman become a surrogate for a poor family. Indeed, in Third World countries, some women sign these contracts with a fingerprint because they are illiterate.

For that matter, we have not yet had stories about the contract workers for whom pregnancy was a dangerous occupation, but we will. What obligation does a family that simply contracted for a child have to its birth mother? What control do—should—contractors have over their "employees'" lives while incubating "their" children? What will we tell the offspring of this international trade?

"National boundaries are coming down," says bioethicist Lori Andrews, "but we can't stop human emotions. We are expanding families and don't even have terms to deal with it."

It's the commercialism that is troubling. Some things we cannot sell no matter how good "the deal." We cannot, for example, sell ourselves into slavery. We cannot sell our children. But the surrogacy business comes perilously close to both of these deals. And international surrogacy tips the scales.

So, these borders we are crossing are not just geographic ones. They are ethical ones. Today the global economy sends everyone in search of the cheaper deal as if that were the single common good. But in the biological search, humanity is sacrificed to the economy and the person becomes the product. And, step by step, we come to a stunning place in our ancient creation story. It's called the marketplace.

Critiquing "Womb for Rent"

1. What is Goodman's main claim and what are her reasons? In other words, what ideas would you have to include in a short summary?

2. What appeals to *pathos* does Goodman make in this argument? How do these appeals function in the argument?

3. Choose an additional focus from Table 7.2, "Questions for Rhetorical Analysis," to apply to "Womb for Rent." How does this question affect your perspective on Goodman's argument?

4. What strikes you as problematic, memorable, or disturbing in this argument?

Our second reading shows how student writer Zachary Stumps analyzed the Ellen Goodman article.

Student Essay

A Rhetorical Analysis Of Ellen Goodman's "Womb For Rent"

Zachary Stumps

With her op-ed piece "Womb for Rent," published in the *Seattle Times* (and earlier in *The Washington Post*), syndicated columnist Ellen Goodman enters the murky debate about reproductive technology gone global. Because Americans are outsourcing everything else, "Why not then rent a foreign womb?" she asks. Goodman, a Pulitzer Prize–winning columnist for the Washington Post Writers Group, is known for helping readers understand

Introduction provides context and poses issue to be addressed

Provides background on Goodman

(continued)

the "tumult of social change and its impact on families," and for shattering "the mold of men writing exclusively about politics" ("Ellen Goodman"). This op-ed piece continues her tradition of examining social change from the perspective of family issues.

Summarizes the op-ed piece

Goodman launches her short piece by asserting that one of the most recent and consequential "jobs" to be outsourced is having babies. She explains how the "globalization of baby production" is thriving because it brings together the reproductive desires of people in developed countries and the bodily resources of women in developing countries such as India. Briefly tracing how both reproductive technology and medical tourism have taken advantage of global possibilities, Goodman acknowledges that the thousands of dollars Indian women earn by carrying the babies of foreign couples represent a much larger income than these women could earn in any other available jobs.

After appearing to legitimize this global exchange, however, Goodman shifts to her ethical concerns by raising some moral questions that she says are not being addressed in this trade. She concludes with a full statement of her claim that this global surrogacy is encroaching on human respect and dignity, exploiting business-based science, and turning babies into products.

Thesis paragraph

In this piece, Goodman's delay of her thesis has several rhetorical benefits: It gives Goodman space to present the perspective of poor women, enhanced by her appeals to *pathos*, and it invites readers to join her journey into the complex contexts of this issue. However, this strategy is also risky because it limits the development of her own argument.

Develops first point 5 in thesis: use of *pathos* in exploring perspective of poor women

Instead of presenting her thesis up front, Goodman devotes much of the first part of her argument to looking at this issue from the perspective of foreign surrogate mothers. Using the strategies of *pathos* to evoke sympathy for these women, she creates a compassionate and progressive-minded argument that highlights the benefits to foreign surrogate mothers. She cites factual evidence showing that the average job for a woman in Anand, India, yields a tiny "$25 a month" gotten through the hard work of "crushing glass in a factory," compared to the "$5,000 to $7,000" made carrying a baby to term. To carry a baby to term for a foreign couple represents "a decade's worth of women's wages in rural India." Deepening readers' understanding of these women, Goodman cites one woman who used her earnings to finance her son's heart operation and another who paid for her daughter's dowry. In her fair presentation of these women, Goodman both builds her own positive *ethos* and adds a dialogic dimension to her argument by helping readers walk in the shoes of impoverished surrogate mothers.

Develops second point in thesis: the complex contexts of this issue—outsourcing and medical tourism

The second rhetorical benefit of Goodman's delayed thesis is that she invites readers to explore this complex issue of global surrogacy with her before she declares her own view. To help readers understand and think through this issue, she relates it to two other familiar global topics: outsourcing and medical tourism. First, she introduces foreign surrogacy as one of the latest forms of outsourcing: "This globalization of baby-making comes at the peculiar intersection of a high reproductive technology and a low-tech work force." Presenting these women as workers, she explains that women in India are getting paid for "the production and delivery of a child" that is analogous to the production and delivery of sneakers or bicycle parts. Goodman also sets this phenomenon in the context of global medical tourism. If people can pursue lower-cost treatment for illnesses and health conditions in other countries, why shouldn't an infertile couple seeking to start a family not also have such access to these more affordable and newly available means? This reasoning provides a foundation for readers to begin understanding the many layers of the issue.

The result of Goodman's delayed-thesis strategy is that the first two-thirds of this piece seem to justify outsourcing surrogate motherhood. Only after reading the whole op-ed piece can readers see clearly that Goodman has been dropping hints about her view all along through her choice of words. Although she clearly sees how outsourcing surrogacy can help poor women economically, her use of market language such as "production," "delivery," and "labor" carry a double meaning. On first reading of this op-ed piece, readers don't know if Goodman's punning is meant to be catchy and entertaining or serves another purpose. This other purpose becomes clear in the last third of the article when Goodman forthrightly asserts her criticism of the commercialism of the global marketplace that promotes worldwide searching for a "cheaper deal": "humanity is sacrificed to the economy and the person becomes the product." This is a bold and big claim, but does the final third of her article support it?

Shows how the delayed-thesis structure creates two perspectives in conflict

In the final five paragraphs of this op-ed piece, Goodman begins to develop the rational basis of her argument; however, the brevity of the op-ed genre and her choice not to state her view openly initially have left Goodman with little space to develop her own claim. The result is that she presents some profound ideas very quickly. Some of the ethically complex ideas she introduces but doesn't explore much are these:

Restates the third point in his thesis: lack of space limits development of Goodman's argument

- The idea that there are ethical limits on what can be "sold"
- The idea that surrogate motherhood might be a "dangerous occupation"
- The idea that children born from this "international trade" may be confused about their identities.

Goodman simply has not left herself enough space to develop these issues and perhaps leaves readers with questions rather than with changed views. I am particularly struck by several questions. Why have European countries banned surrogacy in developing countries, and why has the United States not banned this practice? Does Goodman intend to argue that the United States should follow Europe's lead? She could explore more how this business of finding illiterate women to bear children for the wealthy continues to exploit third-world citizens much as sex tourism exploits women in the very same countries. It seems to perpetuate a tendency for the developed world to regard developing countries as poor places of lawlessness where practices outlawed in the rest of the world (e.g., child prostitution, slave-like working conditions) are somehow tolerable. Goodman could have developed her argument more to state explicitly that a woman who accepts payment for bearing a baby becomes an indentured servant to

Discusses examples of ideas raised by Goodman but not developed

(continued)

the family. Yet another way to think of this issue is to see that the old saying of "a bun in the oven" is more literal than metaphorical when a woman uses her womb as a factory to produce children, a body business not too dissimilar to the commercialism of prostitution. Goodman teases readers by mentioning these complex problems without producing an argument.

Conclusion   10

Still, although Goodman does not expand her criticism of outsourced surrogate motherhood or explore the issues of human dignity and rights, this argument does introduce the debate on surrogacy in the global marketplace, raise awareness, and begin to direct the conversation toward a productive end of seeking a responsible, healthy, and ethical future. Her op-ed piece lures readers into contemplating deep, perplexing ethical and economic problems, and it lays a foundation for readers to create an informed view of this issue.

Works Cited

Uses MLA format to list sources cited in the essay

"Ellen Goodman." *Washingtonpost.com*, www.washingtonpost.com/wp-srv/post/writersgroup/biogoodman.htm. Accessed 8 Apr. 2016.

Goodman, Ellen. "Womb for Rent." *The Washington Post*, 11 Apr. 2008, p. B6.

Chapter 8
Argument as Inquiry
Reading, Summarizing, and Speaking Back

Learning Objectives

In this chapter, you will learn to:

8.1 Use exploratory strategies to find an engaging issue.

8.2 Summarize a stakeholder's argument as an entry into the issue.

8.3 Respond to a stakeholder's argument through believing, doubting, and dialectic thinking.

8.4 Delay closure by thinking dialectically.

This chapter, like the preceding one, focuses on the inquiring or truth-seeking aim of argument. Truth-seeking is an antidote to locking ourselves up in echo chambers of like-minded individuals who have little interest in other people's views because they believe they already know the truth. Dismayed by these echo chambers, cultural critic Matt Miller recently posed the questions: "Is it possible in America today to convince anyone of anything he doesn't already believe? . . . [A]re there enough places where this mingling of minds occurs to sustain a democracy?"*

Miller's "mingling of minds" is essential for the truth-seeking process to work. Argument as truth-seeking depends on the willingness of stakeholders to listen to one another and to change their views in the face of new reasons and evidence. We value the insight of rhetorician Wayne Booth, who proposes that when we enter an argumentative conversation, we should not ask first "How can I change your mind?" but rather "When should I change my mind?"**

Argument as truth-seeking is not easy because argumentative conversations always entail disagreements. Whenever you argue, you necessarily bring your

---

*Matt Miller, "Is Persuasion Dead?" *The New York Times*, 4 June 2005, A29.
**Wayne Booth raised these questions in a featured session with Peter Elbow titled "Blind Skepticism vs. the Rhetoric of Assent: Implications for Rhetoric, Argument, and Teaching," presented at the CCCC annual convention, Chicago, Illinois, March 2002.

view into tension with some alternative view: *"Although some stakeholders think X, I am arguing Y."* Your view on an issue (which you will need to support with your own reasons and evidence) pushes against an alternative view (which you must be able to summarize fairly). When you first begin exploring an issue, you may not know where you stand on the issue, and even if you do know, you should be willing to change your mind as your research takes you deeper into the issue. To participate thoughtfully in this inquiry process, you need two high-level skills: (1) the ability to summarize each stakeholder's view as you encounter it and (2) the ability to formulate your own thoughtful response to that view. Eventually this exploratory process of summary and response can help you stake out your own claim in the conversation and determine your best means of supporting it.

This chapter teaches you these summary/response skills. After presenting strategies to help you discover an engaging issue, we show you how to summarize a stakeholder's argument and then respond to it through believing, doubting, and dialectic thinking. To illustrate argument as inquiry, we follow the thinking process of student writer Trudie Makens as she explores the problem of whether fast-food workers and other low-wage laborers should be paid a "living wage" of $15 per hour.

Finding Issues to Explore

8.1 Use exploratory strategies to find an engaging issue.

Your engagement with a controversial issue might be sparked by personal experience, by conversations with others, or by something you listen to, see, or read. Sometimes you will be confused about the issue, unable to take a stand. At other times, you will have a visceral gut reaction that causes you to take an immediate position, even though you haven't thought through the issue in depth. At the start of the arguing process, the confused or puzzled position is often the stronger one because it promotes inquiry as truth-seeking. If you start with a firm stand, you might be less disposed to uncover your issue's complexity and let your position evolve. In this section we examine some strategies you can use to find issues worth exploring.

Do Some Initial Brainstorming

As a first step, make an inventory of issues that interest you. Many of the ideas you develop may become subject matter for arguments that you will write later in this course. The strategies suggested in Table 8.1 (Brainstorming Issues to Explore) will help you generate a productive list.

Once you've made a list, add to it as new ideas strike you and return to it each time you are given a new argumentative assignment.

Be Open to the Issues All Around You

We are surrounded by argumentative issues. You'll start noticing them everywhere once you get attuned to them. You will be invited into argumentative conversations by posters, bumper stickers, tweets, blog sites, newspaper editorial pages, magazine articles, the sports section, movie reviews, and song lyrics. When you read or listen, watch for "hot spots"—passages or moments that evoke strong agreement,

Table 8.1 Brainstorming Issues to Explore

What You Can Do	How It Works
Make an inventory of the communities to which you belong. Consider classroom communities; clubs and organizations; residence hall, apartment, neighborhood, or family communities; church/synagogue or work communities; communities related to your hobbies or avocations; your city, state, region, nation, and world communities.	Because arguments arise out of disagreements within communities, you can often think of issues for argument by beginning with a list of the communities to which you belong.
Identify controversies within those communities. Think both big and small: • Big issue in world community: What is the best way to prevent destruction of rain forests? • Small issue in residence-hall community: Should quiet hours be enforced?	To stimulate thinking, use prompts such as these: • People in this community frequently disagree about _____. • Within my work community, Person X believes _____; however, this view troubles me because _____. • In a recent residence-hall meeting, I didn't know where I stood on _____. • The situation at _____ could be improved if _____.
Narrow your list to a handful of problematic issues for which you don't have a position; share it with classmates. Identify a few issues that you would like to explore more deeply. When you share your list with classmates, add their list of issues to yours.	Sharing your list with classmates stimulates more thinking and encourages conversations. The more you explore your views with others, the more ideas you will develop. Good writing grows out of good talking.
Brainstorm a network of related issues. Any given issue is always embedded in a network of other issues. To see how open-ended and fluid an argumentative conversation can be, try connecting one of your issues to a network of other issues, including subissues and side issues.	Brainstorm questions that compel you to look at an issue in a variety of ways. For example, if you explored the controversy over whether states should legalize marijuana (see Chapter 1), you might generate these questions about related issues: • Is marijuana a gateway drug toward cocaine or heroin? • How will legalizing marijuana affect the black market in drugs? • What should be the role of government in regulating the safety and potency of cannabis, including both inhaled and edible versions? • What has been the experience of states that have already legalized marijuana?

disagreement, or confusion. As an illustration of how arguments are all around us, try the following exercise on the issue of a living wage for low-wage workers.

Explore Ideas by Freewriting

Freewriting is useful at any stage of the writing process. When you freewrite, you put fingers to keyboard (or pen to paper) and write rapidly *nonstop*, usually five to ten minutes at a stretch, without worrying about structure, grammar, or correctness. Your goal is to generate as many ideas as possible without stopping to edit your work. If you can't think of anything to say, write "relax" or "I'm stuck" over and over until new ideas emerge. Here is Trudie Makens's freewrite in response to the protest photo that introduces Part 2.

Figure 8.1 Full-page ad opposed to raising the minimum wage for fast-food workers

For Writing and Discussion

Responding to Visual Arguments About a Living Wage

Suppose, in your initial search for a controversial issue, you encounter visual texts related to raising the minimum wage for fast-food workers: photos of protestors, newspaper ads, cartoons, graphics, and other forms of visual arguments (See Figures 8.1–8.3; see also the protest photo introducing Part 2, just before Chapter 7). Working individually or in small groups, generate exploratory responses to these questions:

1. What claim is each of these visual texts making?
2. What background information about the problems of minimum-wage workers do these visual texts assume?
3. What network of issues do these visual texts suggest?
4. What puzzling questions do these visual texts raise for you?

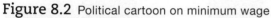

Figure 8.2 Political cartoon on minimum wage

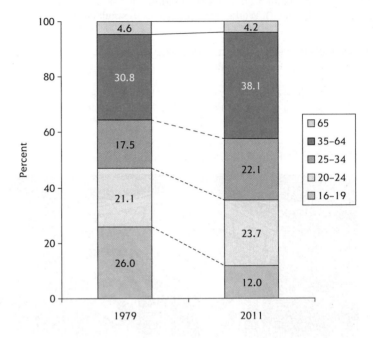

Figure 8.3 Graph offering employment statistics relevant to minimum wage controversy

Adapted from Schmitt, John, and Janelle Jones, "Low-Wage Workers Are Older and Better Educated than Ever." Center for Economic and Policy Research. April 2012.

TRUDIE'S FREEWRITE

Working in the food and service industry as a busser, I relate to the people in the picture wearing union T-shirts and arguing for a $15/hour minimum wage. It's hard to live off of minimum wage, and if it weren't for my tips, I wouldn't be able to pay some of my bills. And that is with help from my parents because I am a college student. I can't imagine what it would be like for full-time workers in the fast-food industry where orders are taken via counter. I remember when I worked counter service jobs, as a barista and at a dumpling café, no one ever tipped. They didn't feel like they needed to because it was not formal wait service. My work, and my coworkers' work, was not valued. What some people don't realize is that whether you are working at McDonald's or in an upscale restaurant, you are still working hard to provide good service. If anything, it is harder to work jobs like McDonald's where customers are dismissive and don't value the service they are receiving. Think, relax. Why do people not value the work of fast-food and counter service workers? Because it is considered unskilled labor? A lot of the people I have worked with didn't have the time or money to go to college because they were burdened with the financial strains of having children or caring for sick or elderly relatives. I remember my coworker Maria who was always stressed out because she couldn't pay her rent and had a child to support. A living wage would help people who haven't been lucky enough to inherit wealth to pull themselves out of poverty. And it wouldn't hurt corporations like McDonald's to live with a little less profit.

Explore Ideas by Idea Mapping

Another good technique for exploring ideas is *idea mapping*. To make an idea map, draw a circle in the center of a page and write some trigger idea (a broad topic, a question, or working thesis statement) in the center of the circle. Then record your ideas on branches and subbranches extending from the center circle. As long as you pursue one train of thought, keep recording your ideas on that branch. But when that line of thinking gives out, start a new branch. Often your thoughts will jump back and forth between branches. That's a major advantage of "picturing" your thoughts; you can see them as part of an emerging design rather than as strings of unrelated ideas.

Idea maps usually generate more ideas, though less well-developed ones, than freewrites. Figure 8.4 shows an idea map that Trudie Makens created on the issue of the minimum wage after class discussion of the visual texts in Figures 8.1–8.3.

Explore Ideas by Playing the Believing and Doubting Game

The believing and doubting game, a critical-thinking strategy developed by rhetorician Peter Elbow that systematically stretches your thinking, is an excellent way to imagine views different from your own and to anticipate responses to those views.

- *As a believer, your role is to be wholly sympathetic to an idea.* You must listen carefully to the idea and suspend all disbelief. You must identify all the ways in which the idea may appeal to different audiences and all the reasons for believing the idea. The believing game can be difficult, even frightening, if you are asked to believe an idea that strikes you as false or threatening.

Figure 8.4 Trudie's idea map

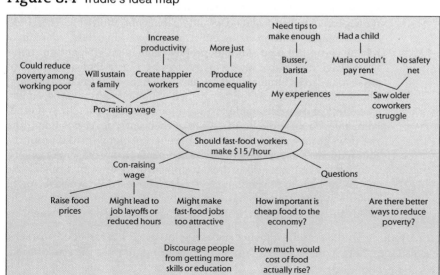

- *As a doubter, your role is to be judgmental and critical, finding fault with an idea.* The doubting game is the opposite of the believing game. You do your best to find counterexamples and inconsistencies that undermine the idea you are examining. Again, it can be threatening to doubt ideas that you instinctively want to believe.

When you play the believing and doubting game with an assertion, simply write two different chunks, one chunk arguing for the assertion (the believing game) and one chunk opposing it (the doubting game). Freewrite both chunks, letting your ideas flow without censoring them. Or, alternatively, make an idea map with believing and doubting branches. Here is how Trudie Makens played the believing and doubting game with the assertion "Fast-food workers should be paid $15 per hour."

Trudie's Believing and Doubting Game

Believing: I doubt anyone strives to become a full-time fast-food worker, but many people become stuck in those jobs and can't advance because they don't have a college education or because there are no better jobs available. Sometimes the workers are college students, so an increase in minimum pay would help them not accrue so much debt and perhaps have more time to study because they wouldn't have to work so many hours. But the real benefit would come to the uneducated, unskilled fast-food worker whose financial situation has led him or her to the fast-food job. The current minimum wage is barely livable. If fast-food workers were to receive $15 per hour, there is far more of a chance for them to support themselves and their family comfortably without the stress of poverty. Even if full-time fast-food workers do not go on to get more skills or go to college, it becomes more likely their children will be able to go to college if the fast-food worker is receiving a higher wage. Thus, the cycle of poverty as it is inherited generationally is, at least mildly, disrupted.

Doubting: If a $15 per hour minimum wage were to be implemented, the fast-food corporations would have to find ways to compensate for the loss of profits. The most obvious way would be to raise food prices. If prices were to rise, fast food would no longer be affordable. This could have damaging and reversing effects on the working class, which may rely on cheap fast food. Another problem is that the $15 per hour minimum wage may encourage workers to stay put in their jobs and not strive for a career. Student workers may no longer see the benefit of going into debt to get a degree and be satisfied with their current fast-food job. The effect of more desirable fast-food jobs may put pressure on other companies to raise the hourly wage of their entry-level positions. The rise in wage may, again, have the ripple effect of higher-priced products, thus reducing sales and forcing these companies to lay off some workers. No matter what scenario is dreamt up, it would seem that raising the minimum wage to $15 per hour, even if just for fast-food workers, might have damaging effects on the economy that would diminish any benefits or advantages that theoretically come from receiving a higher wage.

Although Trudie sees the injustice of paying low wages to fast-food workers, she also sees that paying such workers $15 per hour might raise the cost of food, reduce the number of jobs available, or have other negative consequences. Playing the believing and doubting game has helped her articulate the dilemma and see the issue in more complex terms.

For Writing and Discussion
Playing the Believing and Doubting Game

Individual task:

Choose one or more of the following controversial claims and play the believing and doubting game with it, through either freewriting or idea mapping.

1. A student should report a fellow student who is cheating on an exam or plagiarizing an essay.
2. Federal law should forbid the purchase of assault weapons or other firearms with high-capacity magazines.
3. Athletes should be allowed to take steroids and human growth hormone under a doctor's supervision.
4. Illegal immigrants already living in the United States should be granted amnesty and placed on a fast track to U.S. citizenship.
5. Respond to a claim from a controversial reading in your class.

Group task:

Working in pairs, in small groups, or as a class, share your results with classmates.

Summarizing a Stakeholder's Argument

8.2   **Summarize a stakeholder's argument as an entry into the issue.**

When you research an issue, you will encounter the conflicting views of many different stakeholders. You will eventually push against some of these stakeholders with your own claim and reasons (*"Although Jones and Lopez argue X, I argue Y"*). But you may also be in full or partial agreement with other stakeholders, drawing on them for support or evidence. In either case, you have to understand thoroughly the sources you are engaging with.

One way to show this understanding is to summarize a stakeholder's argument in your own words. A summary (also called an *abstract*, a *précis*, or a *synopsis*) presents only a text's major points and eliminates supporting details. Summaries can be any length, depending on the writer's purpose, but usually they range from several sentences to one or two paragraphs. To maintain your own credibility, your summary should be as neutral and fair to that piece as possible.

To explain how to write a summary, we will continue with our example of raising the minimum wage. The following article, "The Pay Is Too Damn Low," appeared in *The New Yorker*, a magazine with a liberal perspective. It was written by James Surowiecki, an American journalist who writes the "Financial Page" column for *The New Yorker*. Please read this article carefully in preparation for the exercises and examples that follow.

The Pay Is Too Damn Low

JAMES SUROWIECKI

A few weeks ago, Washington, D.C., passed a living-wage bill designed to make Walmart pay its workers a minimum of $12.50 an hour. Then President Obama called on Congress to raise the federal minimum wage (which is currently $7.25 an hour). McDonald's was widely derided for releasing a budget to help its employees plan financially, since that only underscored how brutally hard it is to live on a McDonald's wage. And last week fast-food workers across the country staged walkouts, calling for an increase in their pay to fifteen dollars an hour. Low-wage earners have long been the hardest workers to organize and the easiest to ignore. Now they're front-page news.

The workers' grievances are simple: low wages, few (if any) benefits, and little full-time work. In inflation-adjusted terms, the minimum wage, though higher than it was a decade ago, is still well below its 1968 peak (when it was worth about $10.70 an hour in today's dollars), and it's still poverty-level pay. To make matters worse, most fast-food and retail work is part time, and the weak job market has eroded what little bargaining power low-wage workers had: their earnings actually fell between 2009 and last year, according to the National Employment Law Project.

5   Still, the reason this has become a big political issue is not that the jobs have changed; it's that the people doing the jobs have. Historically, low-wage work tended to be done either by the young or by women looking for part-time jobs to supplement family income. As the historian Bethany Moreton has shown, Walmart in its early days sought explicitly to hire underemployed married women. Fast-food workforces, meanwhile, were dominated by teenagers. Now, though, plenty of family breadwinners are stuck in these jobs. That's because, over the past three decades, the U.S. economy has done a poor job of creating good middle-class jobs; five of the six fastest-growing job categories today pay less than the median wage. That's why, as a recent study by the economists John Schmitt and Janelle Jones has shown, low-wage workers are older and better educated than ever. More important, more of them are relying on their paychecks not for pin money or to pay for Friday-night dates but, rather, to support families. Forty years ago, there was no expectation that fast-food or discount-retail jobs would provide a living wage, because these were not jobs that, in the main, adult heads of household did. Today, low-wage workers provide 46 percent of their family's income. It is that change which is driving the demand for higher pay.

The situation is the result of a tectonic shift in the American economy. In 1960, the country's biggest employer, General Motors, was also its most profitable company and one of its best-paying. It had high profit margins and real pricing power, even as it was paying its workers union wages. And it was not alone: firms such as Ford, Standard Oil, and Bethlehem Steel employed huge numbers of well-paid workers while earning big profits. Today, the country's biggest employers are retailers and fast-food chains, almost all of which have built their businesses on low pay—they've striven to keep wages down and unions out—and low prices.

This complicates things, in part because of the nature of these businesses. They make plenty of money, but most have slim profit margins: Walmart and

Target earn between three and four cents on the dollar; a typical McDonald's franchise restaurant earns around six cents on the dollar before taxes, according to an analysis from Janney Capital Markets. In fact, the combined profits of all the major retailers, restaurant chains, and supermarkets in the Fortune 500 are smaller than the profits of Apple alone. Yet Apple employs just 76,000 people, while the retailers, supermarkets, and restaurant chains employ 5.6 million. The grim truth of those numbers is that low wages are a big part of why these companies are able to stay profitable while offering low prices. Congress is currently considering a bill increasing the minimum wage to $10.10 over the next three years. That's an increase that the companies can easily tolerate, and it would make a significant difference in the lives of low-wage workers. But that's still a long way from turning these jobs into the kind of employment that can support a middle-class family. If you want to accomplish that, you have to change the entire way these companies do business. Above all, you have to get consumers to accept significantly higher, and steadily rising, prices. After decades in which we've grown used to cheap stuff, that won't be easy.

Realistically, then, a higher minimum wage can be only part of the solution. We also need to expand the Earned Income Tax Credit and strengthen the social-insurance system, including child care and health care (the advent of Obamacare will help in this regard). Fast-food jobs in Germany and the Netherlands aren't much better-paid than in the United States, but a stronger safety net makes workers much better off. We also need many more of the "middle-class jobs" we're always hearing about. A recent McKinsey report suggested that the government should invest almost a trillion dollars over the next five years in repairing and upgrading the national infrastructure, which seems like a good place to start. And we really need the economy as a whole to grow faster, because that would both increase the supply of good jobs and improve the bargaining power of low-wage workers. As Jared Bernstein, an economist at the Center for Budget and Policy Priorities told me, "The best friend that low-wage workers have is a strong economy and a tight job market." It isn't enough to make bad jobs better. We need to create better jobs.

Thinking Steps for Writing a Summary

To help you write an effective summary, we recommend the following steps:

Step 1: *Read the argument for general meaning.* Don't judge it. Put your objections aside; just follow the writer's meaning, trying to see the issue from the writer's perspective. Try to adopt the writer's values and belief system. Walk in the writer's shoes.

Step 2: *Reread the article slowly, writing brief* does *and* says *statements for each paragraph (or group of closely connected paragraphs).* A *does* statement identifies a paragraph's function, such as "summarizes an opposing view," "introduces a supporting reason," "gives an example," or "uses statistics to support the previous point." A *says* statement summarizes a paragraph's content. Your challenge in writing *says* statements is to identify the main idea in each paragraph and translate that idea into your own words, most likely condensing it at the same time. This process may be easier with an academic article that uses long, developed paragraphs headed by clear topic sentences than with more informal, journalistic articles that use shorter, less developed paragraphs. What follows are *does* and *says* statements for the first three paragraphs of Surowiecki's article:

Does/Says Analysis of Surowiecki's Article

Paragraph 1: *Does:* Gives examples of recent news stories about protests of low-wage workers. *Says:* Hard-to-organize, low-wage earners are now in the news demanding an increase in the minimum wage.

Paragraph 2: *Does:* Provides details about the workers' grievances. *Says*: A weakening job market combined with low wages, lack of benefits, and mainly part-time hours keeps low-wage workers at poverty levels.

Paragraph 3: *Does:* Explains the changing demographics of those who hold low-wage jobs. *Says*: In the past, minimum-wage jobs were held primarily by teenagers or by women desiring part-time work to supplement family incomes, but today many primary breadwinners depend on minimum-wage jobs to support a family.

For Writing and Discussion

Does/Says Statements

Working individually or in small groups, write *does* and *says* statements for the remaining paragraphs of Surowiecki's article.

Step 3: *Examine your* does *and* says *statements to determine the major sections of the argument.* Create a list of the major points (and subpoints) that must appear in a summary in order to represent that argument accurately. If you are visually oriented, you may prefer to make a diagram, flowchart, or scratch outline of the sections of Surowiecki's argument.

Step 4: *Turn your list, outline, flowchart, or diagram into a prose summary.* Typically, writers do this in one of two ways. Some start by joining all their *says* statements into a lengthy paragraph-by-paragraph summary and then prune it and streamline it. They combine ideas into sentences and then revise those sentences to make them clearer and more tightly structured. Others start with a one-sentence summary of the argument's thesis and major supporting reasons and then flesh it out with more supporting ideas. Your goal is to be as neutral and objective as possible by keeping your own response to the writer's ideas out of your summary. To be fair to the writer, you also need to cover all the writer's main points and give them the same emphasis as in the original article.

Step 5: *Revise your summary until it is the desired length and is sufficiently clear, concise, and complete.* Your goal is to spend your words wisely, making every word count. In a summary of several hundred words, you will often need transitions to indicate structure and create a coherent flow of ideas: "Surowiecki's second point is that . . . " or "Surowiecki concludes by . . . ."

However, don't waste words with meaningless transitions such as "Surowiecki goes on to say . . . ." When you incorporate a summary into your own essay, you must distinguish the author's views from your own by using *attributive tags* (expressions such as "Surowiecki asserts" or "according to Surowiecki"). You must also put any directly borrowed wording in quotation marks. Finally, you must cite the original author using appropriate conventions for documenting sources.

Examples of Summaries

What follows are two summaries of Surowiecki's article—a one-paragraph version and a one-sentence version—by student writer Trudie Makens. Trudie's one-paragraph version illustrates the MLA documentation system, with complete bibliographic information placed in a Works Cited list at the end of the paper. The in-text citations do not have page numbers because the work cited is from a web source. See Chapter 18 for a complete explanation of the MLA and APA documentation systems.

TRUDIE'S ONE-PARAGRAPH SUMMARY OF SUROWIECKI'S ARGUMENT

In his *The New Yorker* article "The Pay Is Too Damn Low," James Surowiecki analyzes the grievances of workers at fast-food franchises, Walmart, or Target. In the past, it didn't matter that these jobs were low-pay, part-time, and without benefits because they were held mainly by teenagers or married women seeking to supplement a husband's wages. But today, says Surowiecki, a growing number of primary breadwinners rely on these poverty-level wages to support families. The problem stems from a "tectonic shift in the American economy." While in 1960, "firms such as Ford, Standard Oil, and Bethlehem Steel employed huge numbers of well-paid workers while earning big profits," nowadays America's biggest employers are fast-food and retail companies with low profit margins. These companies depend on low-wage workers to keep prices cheap for the American consumer. Paying living wages to workers would completely change the business model, resulting in steadily rising prices. According to Surowiecki, raising the minimum wage is only one tool for fighting poverty. America also needs to create a social insurance system like that of Germany or the Netherlands. Surowiecki calls for an increase in the Earned Income Tax Credit, universal health insurance, affordable child care, and investment of almost a trillion dollars in infrastructure to create good middle-class jobs.

Works Cited

Surowiecki, James. "The Pay Is Too Damn Low." *The New Yorker*, 12 Aug. 2013, www.newyorker.com/magazine/2013/08/12/the-pay-is-too-damn-low.

TRUDIE'S ONE-SENTENCE SUMMARY OF SUROWIECKI'S ARGUMENT

In his *The New Yorker* article, "The Pay Is Too Damn Low," James Surowiecki argues that raising the minimum wage is only a partial solution to the problem of poverty and needs to be supplemented with a European-style social security network including an increase in the Earned Income Tax Credit, universal health insurance, affordable child care, and investment of almost a trillion dollars in infrastructure to create good middle-class jobs.

Responding to a Stakeholder's Argument

8.3 **Respond to a stakeholder's argument through believing, doubting, and dialectic thinking.**

Once you have summarized an argument, you need to respond to it in thoughtful ways that go beyond simple agreement ("I like it"), disagreement ("I don't like it"), or partial agreement ("It has good parts and bad parts"). To help you resist these simple responses, we urge you to follow the spirit of the believing and doubting game, which will stretch your critical thinking in powerful ways.

Practicing Believing: Willing Your Own Acceptance of the Writer's Views

A powerful strategy for reading an argument rhetorically is to will yourself to "believe" a stakeholder's argument even if you tend to doubt it. When you read to believe an argument, you practice what psychologist Carl Rogers calls *empathic listening*. Empathic listening requires that you see the world through the author's eyes, temporarily adopt the author's beliefs and values, and suspend your skepticism and biases in order to hear what the author is saying.

Although writing an accurate summary of an argument shows that you have listened to it effectively and understood it, summary writing by itself doesn't mean that you have actively tried to enter the writer's worldview. Rhetorician Peter Elbow reminds us that before we doubt a text, we should try to "dwell with" and "dwell in" the writer's ideas—play the believing game—in order to "earn" our right to criticize.* He asserts, and we agree, that this use of the believing game to engage with strange, threatening, or unfamiliar views can lead to a deeper understanding and may provide a new vantage point on our own knowledge, assumptions, and values. To believe a writer and dwell with his or her ideas, find places in the text that resonate positively for you, look for values and beliefs you hold in common (however few), and search for personal experiences and values that affirm his or her argument.

Practicing Doubting: Willing Your Own Resistance to the Writer's Views

After willing yourself to believe an argument, will yourself to doubt it. Turn your mental energies toward raising objections, asking questions, expressing skepticism, and withholding your assent. When you read as a doubter, you question the writer's logic, the writer's evidence and assumptions, and the writer's strategies for developing the argument. You also think about what is *not* in the argument by noting what the author has glossed over, left unexplained, or left out entirely. You

---

*Peter Elbow, "Bringing the Rhetoric of Assent and the Believing Game Together—Into the Classroom," *College English*, 67.4 (March 2005), 389.

add a new layer of marginal notes, articulating what is bothering you, demanding proof, doubting evidence, and challenging the author's assumptions and values. Writing your own notes helps you read a text actively, bringing your own voice into conversation with the author.

For Writing and Discussion

Raising Doubts About Surowiecki's Argument

Return now to Surowiecki's article and read it skeptically. Raise questions, offer objections, and express doubts. Then, working as a class or in small groups, list all the doubts you have about Surowiecki's argument.

Now that you have doubted Surowiecki's article, compare your questions and doubts to some raised by Trudie Makens.

Trudie's Doubts about Surowiecki's Article

- In his second paragraph, Surowiecki outlines three workers' grievances: "low wages, few (if any) benefits, and little full-time work." But increasing the minimum wage addresses only one of the grievances. A higher minimum wage might make it less likely for a worker to receive benefits or obtain full-time rather than part-time work. Moreover, with a higher wage, large companies may try to maintain profits by cutting jobs.
- Surowiecki asserts that large retailers and fast-food companies would absorb the cost of a higher minimum wage by raising prices on consumer goods. But if low-wage workers are also consumers, won't higher prices on previously cheap products defeat the benefits of a higher wage?
- Though he ends his article by calling for a multifaceted solution to poverty, he does so without offering a way to accomplish this goal. Where would the money come from in order to expand the Earned Income Tax Credit, strengthen the United States' current social insurance system, or invest in infrastructure? Further, how would the United States effectively implement and sustain these nationwide social programs without upsetting the already delicate economy?
- In his article, Surowiecki mentions several studies, but there is no way to tell if these are widely respected studies or controversial ones. Would other studies, for example, conclude that low-wage workers today are responsible for 46 percent of their family's income?

These are only some of the objections that might be raised against Surowiecki's argument. The point here is that doubting as well as believing is a key part of the exploratory process and purpose. *Believing* takes you into the views of others so that you can expand your views and perhaps see them differently and modify or even change them. *Doubting* helps protect you from becoming overpowered by others' arguments and teaches you to stand back, consider, and weigh points carefully. It also leads you to new questions and points you might want to explore further.

Thinking Dialectically

8.4   Delay closure by thinking dialectically.

This chapter's final strategy—thinking dialectically to bring texts into conversation with one another—encompasses all the previous strategies and can have a powerful effect on your growth as a thinker and arguer. The term *dialectic* is associated with the German philosopher Georg Wilhelm Friedrich Hegel, who postulated that each thesis prompts an opposing thesis (which he calls an "antithesis") and that the conflict between these views can lead thinkers to a new claim (a "synthesis") that incorporates aspects of both views. Dialectic thinking is the philosophical underpinning of the believing and doubting game, pushing us toward new and better ideas. As Peter Elbow puts it, "Because it's so hard to let go of an idea we are holding (or more to the point, an idea that's holding us), our best hope for leverage in learning to doubt such ideas is *to take on different ideas.*"*

This is why expert thinkers actively seek out alternative views—not to shout them down but to listen to them. If you were an arbitrator, you wouldn't settle a dispute between A and B on the basis of A's testimony only. You would also insist on hearing B's side of the story (and perhaps also C's and D's if they are stakeholders in the dispute). Dialectic thinking means playing ideas against one another, creating a tension that forces you to keep expanding your perspective. It helps you achieve the "mingling of minds" that we discussed in the introduction to this chapter.

As you listen to differing views, try to identify sources of disagreement among arguers, which often fall into two categories: (1) disagreement about the facts or truths of the case and (2) disagreement about underlying values, beliefs, or assumptions. We saw these disagreements in Chapter 1 in the conversation about legalizing marijuana. At the level of fact and truth, disputants disagreed about whether marijuana was a dangerous drug. At the level of values, disputants disagreed on their vision of a good society. As you try to determine your own position on an issue, consider what research you might have to do to resolve questions of fact or truth; also try to articulate your own underlying values, beliefs, and assumptions.

As you consider multiple points of view on an issue, try using the questions in Table 8.2 to promote dialectic thinking:

Responding to questions like these—either through class discussion or through exploratory writing—can help you work your way into a public controversy. Earlier in this chapter you read James Surowiecki's article expressing liberal support for raising the minimum wage and enacting other government measures

---

*Peter Elbow, "Bringing the Rhetoric of Assent and the Believing Game Together—Into the Classroom," *College English* 67.4 (March 2005), 390.

Table 8.2 Questions to Promote Dialectic Thinking

1. What would writer A say to writer B?
2. After I read writer A, I thought _____; however, after I read writer B, my thinking on this issue had changed in these ways: _____.
3. To what extent do writer A and writer B disagree about facts and interpretations of facts?
4. To what extent do writer A and writer B disagree about underlying beliefs, assumptions, and values?
5. Can I find any areas of agreement, including shared values and beliefs, between writer A and writer B?
6. What new, significant questions do these texts raise for me?
7. After I have wrestled with the ideas in these two texts, what are my current views on this issue?

to help the poor. Now consider an article expressing a quite different point of view, an opinion piece appearing in *The Huffington Post* written by Michael Saltsman, the research director at the Employment Policies Institute—a pro-business, free-market think tank opposed to raising the minimum wage. We ask you to read the article and then use the questions in Table 8.2 to stimulate dialectic thinking about Surowiecki versus Saltsman.

For Writing and Discussion

Practicing Dialectic Thinking with Two Articles

Individual task:
Freewrite your responses to the questions in Table 8.2, in which Surowiecki is writer A and Saltsman is writer B.

Group task:
Working as a class or in small groups, share your responses to the two articles, guided by the dialectic questions.

To Help the Poor, Move Beyond "Minimum" Gestures

MICHAEL SALTSMAN

Actor and director Ben Affleck made news this week with the announcement that he'll spend five days living on just $1.50—the U.S.-dollar daily equivalent of extreme poverty, according to the Global Poverty Project.

Affleck's heart is in the right place, but his actions won't provide a measurable benefit for people who actually live in poverty. On that score, Affleck's actions are not unlike a series of recently-introduced proposals to raise the federal minimum wage—well-intentioned but ultimately empty gestures that will do little to raise poor families out of poverty.

For poverty-reducing policies to benefit the poor, the benefits first have to be properly targeted to people living in poverty. On this count, a higher minimum wage fails miserably. Census Bureau data shows that over 60 percent of people living below the poverty line don't work. They don't need a raise—they need a job.

Among those who do earn the minimum wage, a majority actually don't live in poverty. According to a forthcoming Employment Policies Institute analysis of Census Bureau data, over half of those covered by President Obama's $9 proposal live in households with income at least twice the poverty level—and one-third are in households with an income three times or greater than the poverty level.

5   That's because nearly 60 percent of affected employees aren't single earners, according to the EPI report—they're living in households where a parent or a spouse often earns an income far above the minimum. (The average family income of this group is $50,789.) By contrast, we found that only 9 percent of people covered by President Obama's $9 minimum wage are single parents with children.

It's for reasons like these that the majority of academic research shows little connection between a higher minimum wage and reductions in poverty. For instance, economists from American and Cornell Universities examined data from the 28 states that raised their minimum wages between 2003 and 2007, and found no associated reductions in poverty.

Of course, poor targeting isn't the only problem. The vast majority of economic research—including 85 percent of the most credible studies from the last two decades—finds that job loss for the least-skilled employees follows on the heels of minimum wage hikes.

That's why better-targeted policies like the Earned Income Tax Credit (EITC) deserve the support of politicians and public figures who want to do something about poverty. It's been empirically proven to boost employment and incomes, without the unintended consequences of a wage hike. Accounting for the EITC, the full-time hourly wage for many minimum wage earners is already above the $9 figure that President Obama has proposed.

Three Ways to Foster Dialectic Thinking

In this concluding section, we suggest three ways to stimulate and sustain the process of dialectic thinking: Effective discussions (in class, over coffee, or online); a reading log in which you make texts speak to one another; or a formal exploratory essay. We'll look briefly at each in turn.

EFFECTIVE DISCUSSIONS   Good, rich talk is one of the most powerful ways to stimulate dialectic thinking and foster a "mingling of minds." The key is to keep these discussions from becoming shouting matches or bully pulpits for those who like to dominate the airtime. Discussions are most productive if people are willing to express different points of view or to role-play those views for the purpose of advancing the conversation. Try Rogerian listening, in which you summarize someone else's position before you offer your own, different position. (See Chapter 10 for more explanation of Rogerian listening.) Probe deeply to discover whether disagreements are primarily about facts and evidence or about underlying values and beliefs. Be respectful of others' views, but don't hesitate to point out where you see problems or weaknesses. Good discussions can occur in class, in late-night coffee shops, or in online chat rooms or on discussion boards.

READING LOGS   In our classes, we require students to keep reading logs or journals in which they use freewriting and idea mapping to explore their ideas as they encounter multiple perspectives on an issue. One part of a journal or reading log should include summaries of each article you read. Another part should focus on your own dialectic thinking as you interact with your sources while you are reading them. Adapt the questions in Table 8.2 for promoting dialectic thinking.

A FORMAL EXPLORATORY ESSAY   A formal exploratory essay tells the story of an intellectual journey. It is both a way of promoting dialectical thinking and a way of narrating one's struggle to negotiate multiple views. The keys to writing successful exploratory essays are: (1) choosing an issue to explore on which you don't yet have an answer or position (or on which you are open to changing your mind); (2) wrestling with an issue or problem by resisting quick, simple answers and by exploring diverse perspectives; and (3) letting your thinking evolve and your own stance on the issue grow out of this exploration.

Exploratory essays can be powerful thinking and writing experiences in their own right, but they can also be a valuable precursor to a formal argument. Many instructors assign a formal exploratory paper as the first stage of a course research project—what we might call a "thesis-seeking" stage. (The second stage is a formal argument that converts your exploratory thinking into a hierarchically organized argument using reasons and evidence to support your claim.) Although often used as part of a research project, exploratory essays can also be low-stakes reflective pieces narrating the evolution of a writer's thinking.

An exploratory essay includes these thinking moves and parts:

- The essay is opened and driven by the writer's issue question or research problem—not a thesis.
- The introduction to the essay presents the question and shows why it interests the writer, why it is significant, and why it is problematic rather than clear-cut or easy to resolve.
- The body of the essay shows the writer's inquiry process. It demonstrates how the writer has kept the question open, sincerely wrestled with different views on the question, accepted uncertainty and ambiguity, and possibly redefined the question in the midst of reading and reflecting on multiple perspectives.
- The body of the essay includes summaries of the different views or sources that the writer explored and often includes believing and doubting responses to them.
- In the essay's conclusion, the writer may clarify his or her thinking and discover a thesis to be developed and supported in a subsequent argument. But the conclusion can also remain open because the writer may not have discovered his or her own position on the issue and may acknowledge the need or desire for more exploration.

One of the writing assignment options for this chapter is a formal exploratory paper. Trudie Makens's exploratory essay at the end of this chapter shows how she explored different voices in the controversy over raising the minimum wage to $15 per hour.

Conclusion

This chapter has focused on inquiry as a way to enrich your reading and writing of arguments. It offered four main strategies for deep reading: (1) use a variety of questions and prompts to find an issue to explore; (2) demonstrate careful listening by summarizing a stakeholder's argument; (3) respond to the argument through believing, doubting, and dialectic thinking; and (4) practice various methods for sustaining dialectic thinking. This chapter has also explained how to summarize an article and incorporate summaries into your own writing, using attributive tags to distinguish the ideas you are summarizing from your own ideas. Finally, it has offered the exploratory essay as a way to encourage wrestling with multiple perspectives rather than seeking early closure.

Writing Assignment

An Argument Summary or a Formal Exploratory Essay

Option 1: An Argument Summary

Write a 250-word summary of an argument selected by your instructor. Then write a one-sentence summary of the same argument. Use as models Trudie Makens's summaries of James Surowiecki's argument on raising the minimum wage earlier in this chapter.

Option 2: A Formal Exploratory Essay

Write an exploratory essay in which you narrate in first-person, chronological order the evolution through time of your thinking about an issue or problem. Rather than state a thesis or claim, begin with a question or problem. Then describe your inquiry process as you worked your way through sources or different views. Follow the guidelines for an exploratory paper shown in Figure 8.5. When you cite the sources you have considered, be sure to use attributive tags so that the reader can distinguish between your own ideas and those of the sources you have summarized. If you use research sources, use MLA documentation for citing ideas and quotations and for creating a Works Cited at the end of your essay (see Chapter 18).

Explanation and Organization

An exploratory essay could grow out of class discussion, course readings, fieldwork and interviews, or simply the writer's role-playing of alternative views. In all cases, the purpose of an exploratory paper is not to state and defend a thesis. Instead, its purpose is to think dialectically about multiple perspectives, narrating the evolution through time of the writer's thought process. Many students are inspired by the open, "behind-the-scenes" feel of an exploratory essay. They enjoy taking readers on the same intellectual and emotional journey they have just traveled.

Figure 8.5 Organization plan for an exploratory essay

Introduction (one to several paragraphs)	• Establish that your question is complex, problematic, and significant. • Show why you are interested in it. • Present relevant background on your issue. Begin with your question or build up to it, using it to end your introductory section.
Body section 1: First view or source	• Introduce your first source and show why you started with it. • Provide rhetorical context and information about it. • Summarize the source's content and argument. • Offer your response to this source, including both believing and doubting points. • Talk about what this source contributes to your understanding of your question: What did you learn? What value does this source have for you? What is missing from this source that you want to consider? Where do you want to go from here?
Body section 2: Second view or source	• Repeat the process with a new source selected to advance the inquiry. • Explain why you selected this source (to find an alternative view, pursue a subquestion, find more data, and so forth). • Summarize the source's argument. • Respond to the source's ideas. Look for points of agreement and disagreement with other sources. • Show how your cumulative reading of sources is shaping your thinking or leading to more questions.
Body sections 3, 4, 5, etc.	• Continue exploring views or sources.
Conclusion	• Wrap up your intellectual journey and explain where you are now in your thinking and how your understanding of your problem has changed. • Present your current answer to your question based on all that you have learned so far, or explain why you still can't answer your question, or explain what research you might pursue further.

Reading

What follows is Trudie Makens's exploratory essay on the subject of raising the minimum wage. Her research begins with the articles by Surowiecki and Saltsman that you have already read and discussed. She then moves off in her own direction.

Student Essay

Should Fast-Food Workers Be Paid $15 per Hour?

Trudie Makens

Having worked as a busser in a pizza restaurant, a part-time barista, and a server at a dumpling café, I was immediately attracted to our class discussions of minimum wage, sparked by recent protests of fast-food workers demanding pay of $15 per hour. My first job as a barista exposed me to the harsh reality of living on today's existing minimum wage as I witnessed my coworker Maria lose her home because she couldn't pay rent and support her kids at the same time. As a single mother of two, Maria had to bounce from relative to relative, which put a strain on her family relations, her image of herself as an able provider, and her children. I am lucky because, as a student, I am blessed to have my family operate as a safety net for me. If I am ever short on a bill or get sick or hurt, my parents will assist me financially. Many of the individuals I have worked with do not have that same safety net. These individuals are often older and have children or are beginning a family. Understanding the hardships of minimum-wage jobs, I entered our class discussions in support of the $15/hour demand because this pay rate would give workers a living wage. However, despite my personal affinities with these workers, I also understood that raising the minimum wage might have negative consequences for our economy. I wanted to explore this issue in more depth so I decided to pose my research question as "Should fast-food workers be paid a living wage of $15 per hour?"

My exploration began with an article that our instructor assigned to the whole class: "The Pay Is Too Damn Low" by James Surowiecki from *The New Yorker*. In the past, according to Surowiecki, it didn't matter that jobs at Walmart, Target, or fast-food franchises were low-pay, part-time, and without benefits because they were held mainly by teenagers or married women seeking to supplement a husband's wages. But today, says Surowiecki, a growing number of primary breadwinners rely on these poverty-level wages to support families. The problem stems from a "tectonic shift in the American economy." While in 1960, "firms such as Ford, Standard Oil, and Bethlehem Steel employed huge numbers of well-paid workers while earning big profits," nowadays America's biggest employers are fast-food and retail companies with low profit margins. While Surowiecki acknowledges that these retail companies and food franchises depend on low-wage

Title as question indicates an exploratory purposec

Introduction identifies the issue, explains the writer's interest in it, and acknowledges its complexity

Writer states her research question

Writer identifies her first source

Writer summarizes the article

workers to keep prices cheap for the American consumer, he still supports increasing the minimum wage but sees it as only one tool for fighting poverty. He argues that America also needs to create a European-style safety-net system and calls for an increase in the Earned Income Tax Credit, universal health insurance, affordable child care, and investment of almost a trillion dollars in infrastructure to create good middle-class jobs.

Surowiecki's concluding remarks about a safety net system resonated with me. I understood that what protected me from a financial crisis was my family acting as a safety net. The government, Surowiecki argues, should perform the same function for low-wage earners through such programs as child care and health care. He points to Germany and the Netherlands, arguing the stronger safety net put in place for workers by these European governments provides a better economic and social situation for low-wage workers, even though they are paid around the same amount as U.S. low-wage workers. Surowiecki also addressed some of my concerns regarding the economic consequences of implementing a living wage. Even though some low-wage jobs might be eliminated and food costs might go up, government investment in infrastructure might create more high-paying, middle-class jobs, resulting in a net benefit. But I still wasn't convinced or completely satisfied. How exactly would the government raise the money for a redesigned social insurance system? Would the country accept the needed higher taxes? While Surowiecki had convinced me that the government had an important role to play in creating the conditions for a living wage, I still was unclear on how the government could effectively do so without having a negative impact on the economy.

I wanted to know more about raising the minimum wage from the business perspective, so I Googled "living wage" and found an anti-minimum wage article from Michael Saltsman, the research director of the Employment Policy Institute. The opinion piece was published online in *The Huffington Post* and entitled "To Help the Poor, Move Beyond 'Minimum' Gestures." I also found a full-page ad from the same conservative institute depicting a robot doing the work of a fast-food employee. Saltsman believes that despite the good intentions of living-wage proponents, a higher federal minimum wage will do more harm than good. Within his piece, Saltsman equates the symbolic value of Ben Affleck's pledge to live five days on $1.50, "the U.S.-dollar equivalent of extreme poverty," to proposals for a higher federal minimum wage. Both, according to Saltsman, are "ultimately empty gestures" that do little to lift families out of poverty. What the poor need, Saltsman asserts, is "not a raise" but a job. Saltsman claims that over "60% of people living below the poverty line don't work," and those who do earn a minimum wage don't live in households whose total wages are below the poverty line. Even if a member of the working poor were to receive a living wage, Saltsman argues, "job loss for the least-skilled employees follows on the heels of a minimum wage hike." What helps to reduce poverty, according to Saltsman, is not a higher minimum wage but the Earned Income Tax Credit, "empirically proven to boost employment and incomes" and thus providing "a measurable difference for the poor."

(continued)

Writer shows how this article has advanced her thinking by strengthening her previous mention of "safety nets"

Writer includes doubting points by identifying problems not resolved in first source

Writer shows rhetorical thinking by purposely seeking an argument from a business perspective; she identifies the author's conservative credentials and summarizes his argument

Writer summarizes second source

Writer includes both 5
believing and doubt-
ing points

Writer shows dia-
lectic thinking by
comparing and con-
trasting views of first
two sources

Writer again seeks
sources purposefully;
she shows how she
found the source and
places it in rhetorical
context

Writer summarizes
the article

Writer shows how
the pro-business
sources have com-
plicated her initial
tentative position

Writer uses believing
and doubting
strategies to think
dialectically, looking
for a synthesis

Prior to reading Saltsman, I had not fully considered the potential that workers would be laid off because it would be cheaper for businesses to use robots or other automation than to employ higher-wage workers. Though Saltsman got me thinking about the dangers of job displacement, I wasn't convinced by his argument that an increased minimum wage would primarily benefit people who didn't need it, such as teenagers or second earners in an already middle-class family. I could see that an increased minimum wage wouldn't help the 60 percent of the poor who are unemployed, but I also realized that the Earned Income Tax Credit wouldn't help the unemployed either because it goes only to poor people who report income. (I Googled "earned income tax credit" just to make sure I understood how it works by giving a boost of income to poor but working tax filers.) Though Saltsman persuaded me to consider the negative economic consequences of a living wage, I wasn't convinced the living wage was entirely ineffective. I thought back to Surowiecki who, unlike Saltsman, saw a living wage as one component in a larger solution to reduce poverty. Both recommended an expanded Earned Income Tax Credit, but Surowiecki went further and also encouraged a stronger social-insurance system in addition to a higher minimum wage. Neither article persuaded me the living wage was either fully beneficial or fully injurious. To clarify my position, I needed to do more research.

I wanted another economist's perspective, so I typed "economic impact and living wage" into ProQuest, an interdisciplinary research database. One of the articles that caught my attention was "Living Wage: Some Gain, Neediest Lose Out." The article was an interview with labor economist Richard Toikka by author Charles Oliver featured in *Investor's Business Daily*, a conservative financial newspaper focused on stock and bond investments. In the interview, Oliver prompts Toikka to discuss the unintended consequences of a higher minimum wage. Toikka asserts that in order to absorb the cost of a higher wage, companies seek to hire higher-skilled workers who require less training, and thus cost the company less money. With a higher wage offered, Toikka argues, more high-skilled workers, such as college students, seek these jobs, increasing "the competition low-skilled workers face." Thus an increased minimum wage reduces the number of low-skilled jobs available. Toikka also makes the same argument as Saltsman, concluding that the benefits of a higher wage don't go towards the families who need it, but instead to second-earners who aren't living below the poverty line. Toikka cites a survey among labor economists asked to rate the efficiency of anti-poverty measures, and "69% said living wages weren't at all efficient in meeting the needs of poor families." The more efficient way to combat poverty, Toikka argues, is not a living wage but an expansion of the Earned Income Tax Credit.

Putting Oliver/Toikka in conversation with Saltsman, I began to understand and heed the warnings of both economists. Though well-intentioned, increasing the minimum wage by itself is not apt to reduce poverty and would ultimately injure the poor rather than helping them. If a living wage does lead to heightened competition and employers slashing jobs, then perhaps a living wage is ineffective and therefore should be abandoned in favor of the Earned Income Tax Credit. So far, all the articles agreed the Earned Income Tax Credit is a good way to reduce poverty, even though it too benefits only those with jobs. Even so, I couldn't help but think that abandoning a living wage was a concession to a flawed economic system that doesn't value the working poor or impoverished, unemployed people enough. I thought back to Surowiecki when he praised Germany and the Netherlands for providing a strong social-insurance system that serves as a safety net for those in low-wage jobs. If Europe can ensure dignity and security to its citizens, then why can't the United States? Although 69 percent of labor economists say that a living wage is an inefficient way to alleviate poverty, we don't know what they would say if the government also invested in infrastructure to create well-paying jobs. Right now, it seems from my readings, that the current market doesn't value low-wage workers. What is valued in our economy is capital, profit, and cheap goods, all of which come at the expense of millions of workers. Is the structure of the economy where wealth is unequally distributed and workers are exploited really inevitable? Or is it an economic trend that can be reversed? I wanted to believe the latter, so I returned to ProQuest to find another article addressing the economic impact of a living wage but from a pro-labor perspective.

> Writer purposefully seeks a different perspective

In my search, I found an article entitled "The Task Rabbit Economy," authored by Robert Kuttner and published in the progressive magazine *The American Prospect*. Kuttner begins by describing a successful San Francisco company whose website matches people who have an odd job they need done with people who will do the work for a fee. The company, named Task Rabbit, is like an online temp agency that operates by having would-be workers bid against one another, driving the price down for their labor. Kuttner argues that Task Rabbit's business model, which produces cheap labor, is analogous to our current economy, where workers have lost "bargaining power" and work has become casual and unstable (46). Kuttner argues that this low-wage economy has produced less economic growth, less prosperity, and more unemployment than earlier eras when there was more job stability and higher wages. According to Kuttner, the claim made by labor economists that a higher minimum wage leaves low-skilled workers without a job ignores how an unregulated labor market has allowed corporations to "weaken labor . . . and extract abnormal profits" (47). Kuttner draws on the economy of Sweden to provide an example where a living wage, full employment, and a "deliberate effort to narrow wage gaps" has been implemented effectively (48). What's more, Kuttner addresses the concern of rising prices by citing a Demos study that found raising wages so retail workers "earned at least $25,000 a year" only cost large retailers "1 percent of their $2.17 trillion annual sales" (52). Kuttner closes his article by emphasizing that "organized labor" is what will change the labor market, using both collective bargaining and "political force" (55).

> Writer identifies next source and places it in rhetorical context

> Writer summarizes the article

Kuttner's article moved me in a way that Oliver/Toikka and Saltsman's pieces could not. Instead of accepting an economic system where low-wage workers are exploited for stockholder profits and cheap goods, Kuttner criticizes the labor market for its failure to value workers. Kuttner acknowledges that a higher minimum wage will upset the present economy, but he argues that the present economic system isn't inevitable but rather the result of large employers choosing to value capital over people in the absence of strong governmental policies protecting labor and the

> Writer shows how this source has advanced and solidified her own thinking

(continued)

poor. Moreover, Kuttner's article illuminates the inefficiency of our economy. The studies Kuttner references reveal that the United States was better off in the years after World War II, when jobs were stable, plentiful, and paid a living wage. Most of all, I appreciated Kuttner's concluding call to action, and his assurance that such action will not lead to economic suicide but instead create the "dynamic, supple, and innovative" economy our nation strives for. According to Kuttner, we can choose to allow the market to continue unregulated, or, through organizing workers, we can push towards policies that value people—their rights, health, and dignity. As I read Kuttner, I wondered what current labor movements are in existence today and the progress they are making in their fight to gain rights and a living wage. I again turned to ProQuest.

My search handed me a long list of results, but I found one article that provided a relevant look into a labor campaign organized by Walmart sales associates. Titled "Job Insecurity," the article was written by Kevin Clarke and published in the Catholic magazine *America*. Clarke begins by introducing William Fletcher, a twenty-three-year-old retail sales associate at Walmart. According to Fletcher, he loves his job and "working with the public" but, he says, he and other employees constantly struggle with "low wages, chaotic scheduling, and insensitive management." Both Fletcher and Clarke wonder why being a retail sales associate for Walmart warrants not receiving enough to "have a home, have health insurance, have all the basic things in life." In order to improve his working conditions, Fletcher joined Organization United for Respect at Walmart, or OUR Walmart. OUR Walmart, Clarke states, is "part of an emerging labor phenomenon of non-union activism against Walmart and other powerful, profitable U.S. corporations that maintain large, low-paid work forces." Walmart, according to both Fletcher and Clarke, is a trend-setting company. If labor conditions improve at Walmart, other companies could follow suit. The organization draws from the tactics of "community organizing and the civil rights movement." Unfortunately, Clarke states, Walmart management continues to thwart protests or walkouts. Despite obstacles, OUR Walmart persists, marking a major moment in the contemporary labor movement. The article ends with Clarke's appeal to the Catholic social justice tradition of solidarity with the poor. He notes that Walmart sales associates depend on government support programs such as food stamps and housing assistance. He reminds his readers that our continual search for the cheapest goods makes us partially guilty of the exploitation of workers. He urges us to shop conscientiously and thoughtfully.

I reached the end of the article feeling shocked. I was amazed that Walmart could dismiss the demands of OUR Walmart. Clarke states the owners of Walmart, the Walton family, possess "48% of Walmart stock and [are] the richest family on earth, with over $107 billion in net worth." Hearing numbers like these confirmed my forming conviction that the unregulated labor market dangerously exploits workers in order to gain cheap labor, cheap goods, and bloated profits. What's more, Walmart actively tries to scare workers from organizing—threatening to take away their jobs. Though there is much more to read and learn about the growing labor movement in the United States, Clarke's article, as well as Surowiecki,

Writer again shows purposeful search for next source

10

Writer identifies next source and places it in rhetorical context

Writer pulls together the results of her dialectic thinking, which has resulted in a synthesis

Saltsman, Oliver/Toikka, and Kuttner's pieces, allowed me to round out my position on a higher minimum wage. As I end my exploratory paper, I understand that a living wage is possible and should be provided to service workers as a basic human right. But it also needs to be supplemented with the kinds of social insurance systems stressed by Surowiecki and Kuttner.

Works Cited

Clarke, Kevin. "Job Insecurity." *America*, 18 Feb. 2013, americamagazine .org/issue/article/job-insecurity.

Kuttner, Robert. "The Task Rabbit Economy." *The American Prospect*, 24 Sept. 2013, pp. 45-55.

Oliver, Charles. "Living Wage: Some Gain, Neediest Lose Out." *Investor's Business Daily*, 5 Sept. 2000. *ProQuest*, 10 Jan. 2014, search.proquest .com/docview/1026806044/fulltext/DA48476F0F254E4CPQ/1?accou ntid=10226.

Saltsman, Michael. "To Help the Poor, Move Beyond 'Minimum' Gestures." *The Huffington Post*, 26 Apr. 2013, updated 26 June 2013, www .huffingtonpost.com/michael-saltsman/earned-income-tax-credit-minimum-wage_b_3165459.html.

Surowiecki, James. "The Pay Is Too Damn Low." *The New Yorker*, 12 Aug. 2013, www.newyorker.com/magazine/2013/08/12/ the-pay-is-too-damn-low.

PART THREE
Expanding Our Understanding of Argument

Increasingly, countries are employing hydraulic fracturing (called fracking), which extracts natural gas from deeply buried shale, to meet their energy needs. Burning natural gas is cleaner than burning gasoline, oil, and coal and emits less carbon dioxide. However, each fracking site uses millions of gallons of water, leaves contaminated waste water, and often emits methane. Also environmentalists fear that fracking may contaminate aquifers. This photo depicts anti-fracking views in a protest near Manchester, England, in January 2014. To what extent does the garb of the protestors make effective appeals to *logos* and *pathos* to turn viewers against fracking?

Chapter 9
Making Visual and Multimodal Arguments

Learning Objectives

In this chapter you will learn to:

9.1 Explain the visual design elements in multimodal arguments.

9.2 Analyze the compositional features of photographs and drawings rhetorically.

9.3 Explain the genres of multimodal argument.

9.4 Construct your own multimodal arguments.

9.5 Use information graphics rhetorically in arguments.

This chapter focuses on the rhetorical persuasiveness of images, either by themselves or in combination with words to create multimodal arguments. A **multimodal** argument is an argument that combines two or more modes of communication, such as words (written or spoken), images, sounds, or numerical graphics. The term *multimodal* is derived from "multi" (many) and "modal" (modes or modalities of communication). Multimodal arguments most commonly combine words with images (as in posters or print ads), but other combinations are also possible: spoken text and sounds (as in a podcast), sounds and images (as in a photographic slide show set to music), or words and graphics (as in a PowerPoint slide featuring words and a pie chart). Advocacy videos typically combine three modes (words, images, and music and other sounds).

To appreciate the power of multimodal arguments, consider Figure 9.1—a photo of demonstrators protesting a federal travel ban on persons from certain Muslim-majority countries. The photograph contains several layers of multimodal arguments. The protest itself is a multimodal argument in which the protestors shout slogans, sing chants, and wave banners emphasizing the value of cultural and religious diversity. In this photograph, the poster carried by one of

Figure 9.1 A multimodal argument about cultural and religious diversity

the protestors is also a multimodal argument combining words ("We the people are greater than fear"—set in different type sizes for rhetorical effect) with the drawing of a Muslim woman wearing the American flag as a hijab. The poster visually identifies and welcomes the Muslim woman as an American whose flag hijab is just as legitimate as a flag cowboy hat or a flag T-shirt.

The poster in Figure 9.1 makes use of all three classical appeals. It appeals to *logos* by arguing that this woman is one of the "us" in "we the people" (highlighted in bold capital letters) based on the constitutional claim that the United States is a nation of diverse peoples. It appeals to *pathos* by taking a patriotic symbol beloved by Americans (the flag) and associating it with groups of people whom the government has labeled as a threat. It also appeals to *ethos* by showing citizens courageously protesting and rejecting fear. The striking multimodal poster and the surrounding protesters in the photo create a memorable social and political argument.

Understanding Visual Design Elements in Multimodal Argument

9.1   Explain the visual design elements in multimodal arguments.

To understand how visual images can produce an argument, you need to understand the design elements that work together to create a visual text. In this section we explain and illustrate the four basic components of visual design: use of type, use of space and layout, use of color, and use of images and graphics.

Use of Type

Type is an important visual element of written arguments. Variations in type, such as size, **boldface**, *italics*, <u>underlining</u>, or ALL CAPS, can direct a reader's attention to an argument's structure and highlight main points. In arguments designed specifically for visual impact, such as posters or advocacy advertisements, type is often used in eye-catching and meaningful ways.

In choosing type, you need to consider the typeface or font style, the size of the type, and formatting options. The main typefaces or fonts are classified as serif, sans serif, and specialty type. *Serif* type has little extensions on the letters, as on the bottom of the letter "p" in "type." (This text is set in serif type.) *Sans serif* type lacks these extensions. *Specialty type* includes script fonts and special symbols.

In addition to font style, type comes in different sizes. It is measured in points, with 1 point equal to 1/72 of an inch. Most text-based arguments consisting mainly of body text are set in 10- to 12-point type, while more image-based arguments may use a mixture of type sizes that interact with the images for persuasive effect. Table 9.1 shows examples of type styles, as well as their typical uses.

The following basic principles for choosing type for visual arguments can help you achieve the three key goals of readability, visual appeal, and suitability.

PRINCIPLES FOR CHOOSING TYPE FOR VISUAL ARGUMENTS

1. If you are creating a poster or advocacy advertisement, you will need to decide how much of your argument will be displayed in words and how much in images. For longer passages of text that must be easy on the eyes, choose *body* or *text type* (serif). For titles, headings, and slogans, *display type* (sans serif) or specialty fonts can be effective.

2. Make type functional and appealing by using only two or three font styles per document.

3. Use consistent patterns of type (similar type styles, sizes, and formats) to indicate relationships among similar items or different levels of importance.

4. Choose type to project a specific impression (a structured combination of serif and sans serif type to create a formal, serious, or businesslike impression; sans serif and specialty type to create a casual, informal, or playful impression).

Besides these general principles, rhetorical considerations of genre and audience expectations should govern decisions about type. Text-based arguments in scholarly publications generally use plain, conservative fonts with little variation,

Table 9.1 Examples and Uses of Type Styles

Type Style	Font Name	Example	Use
Serif fonts	Times New Roman Palatino Garamond	Use type wisely. Use type wisely. Use type wisely.	Easy to read; good for long documents; good for *body type*, or the main verbal parts of a document
Sans serif fonts	Arial Calibri	Use type wisely. Use type wisely.	Tiring to read for long stretches; good for *display type* such as headings, titles, and slogans
Specialty fonts	Papyrus Lucida Calligraphy	Use type wisely. Use type wisely.	Difficult to read for long stretches; effective when used sparingly for playful or decorative effect

whereas text-based arguments in popular magazines may use more variations in font style and size, especially in headings and opening leads. Visual arguments such as posters, fliers, and advocacy ads exploit the aesthetic potential of type.

Use of Space and Layout

A second component of visual design is layout, which is critical for creating the visual appeal of an argument and for conveying meaning. Even visual arguments that are mainly textual should use space very purposefully. By spacing and layout we mean all of the following elements:

- Page size and type of paper
- Proportion of text to white space
- Proportion of text to image(s) and graphics
- Arrangement of text on page (space, margins, columns, length of paragraphs, spaces between lines and paragraphs, justification of margins)
- Use of highlighting elements such as bulleted lists, tables, sidebars, and boxes
- Use of headings and other means of breaking text into visual elements

In arguments that don't use visuals directly, the writer's primary visual concern is document design, in which the writer tries to meet the conventions of a genre and the expectations of the intended audience. For example, Jesse Goncalves's researched argument in Chapter 13 is designed to meet the document conventions of the American Psychological Association (APA). That paper uses a plain, conventional typeface (for easy reading); double spacing and one-inch margins (to leave room for editorial marking and notations); and a special title page, headers, and page number locations (to meet the expectations of readers familiar with APA documents, which all look exactly the same).

But in moving from verbal-only arguments to visual arguments that use visual elements for direct persuasive effect—for example, posters, fliers, or advocacy ads—creative use of layout is vital. Here are some ideas to help you think about the layout of a visual argument.

PRINCIPLES FOR LAYING OUT PARTS OF A VISUAL TEXT

1. Choose a layout that avoids clutter and confusion by limiting how much text and how many visual items you put on a page.
2. Focus on using layout to create coherence and meaning.
3. Develop an ordering or structuring principle that clarifies the relationships among the parts.
4. Use layout and spacing to indicate the importance of items and to emphasize key ideas. Because Western readers read from left to right and top to bottom, top and center are positions that readily draw readers' eyes.

AN ANALYSIS OF A MULTIMODAL ARGUMENT USING TYPE AND SPATIAL ELEMENTS   To illustrate the persuasive power of type and layout, we ask you to consider Figure 9.2, which reproduces a public affairs ad sponsored by the Ad Council and an advocacy organization, StopBullying.gov. This advocacy piece, which is part of an ongoing campaign to curtail bullying among young people, is aimed at parents, urging them to encourage their children to actively oppose bullying.

Figure 9.2 Anti-bullying public affairs ad

This ad demonstrates how the use of type can create powerful visual effects that combine with the words to convey its argument. The ad's creators chose to use lettering—rather than a photograph or a drawing—to illustrate bullying. The type style, presentation of the letters, and words themselves create a strange rhetorical effect—simultaneously personal and impersonal—that draws viewers into the ad more than an image would. The type style and font make strong appeals to *pathos* through the blend of the shocking abusive language and disturbing lettering style. The words "dumb," "piece," and "trash" are all harshly derogatory. The direct address to the viewer in the word "you" conveys that bullying is an attack, sometimes verbal and often physical.

Note how the blurring of the message in the large bold type makes a visual statement about the act of bullying, how bullying is perceived, and the psychological damage it causes. These large, heavy, blurred letters convey multiple messages. Bullying can be crude and forceful, but it is often carried on covertly where authority figures cannot see or stop it. The lettering itself bullies the viewers while at the same time reinforcing the idea that not everyone is aware of bullying. The blurring of these letters also suggests that bullying washes out the personhood of its victims. In addition, the ad makes it look as though these dark letters have smudged and stained the yellow background, suggesting that bullying also harms society.

The layout of this ad also contributes to its *logos* and *ethos*. The shock of reading the bold message propels readers to the black sidebar in the ad's lower right side, where the message in smaller type interprets and explains the message of the blurred letters. The text speaks directly to parents' unawareness of the hostility in their kids' environment and makes an urgent appeal to parental responsibility. While the lettering and layout convey the causal reasons behind the need for action, the message in the smaller letters states the proposal claim: Instruct your kids how to become more than passive observers of bullying: "Teach your kids to be more than a bystander." In addition to delivering a strong message, this ad conveys a positive *ethos* by demonstrating knowledge of the problem and directing readers to authoritative sources of information that will help them engage with this serious social issue.

Use of Color

A third important element of visual design is use of color, which can contribute significantly to an argument's visual appeal by moving readers emotionally and imaginatively. In considering color in visual arguments, writers are especially controlled by genre conventions. For example, academic arguments make minimal use of color, whereas popular magazines often use color lavishly. The appeal and the associations of colors for specific audiences are also important. For instance, the psychedelic colors of 1960s rock concert posters would probably not be effective in poster arguments directed toward conservative voters.

Sometimes the color choices in visual arguments mean having no color at all—for example, the use of a black-and-white image instead of a color image. As you will see in our discussions of color throughout this chapter, makers of visual arguments need to decide whether color will be primarily decorative (using colors to create visual appeal), functional (for example, using colors to indicate relationships), realistic (using colors like a documentary photo), emotional (for example, using colors that are soothing, exciting, or disturbing), or some intentional combination of these.

Use of Images and Graphics

The fourth design element includes images and graphics, which can powerfully condense information into striking and memorable visuals; clarify ideas; and add depth, liveliness, and emotion to your arguments. Keep in mind this important point when using images: A few simple images may be more powerful than complicated and numerous images. Other key considerations are (1) how you intend an image to work in your argument (for example, to convey an idea, illustrate a point, or evoke an emotional response) and (2) how you will establish the relationship between the image or graphic and the verbal text.

Because using images and graphics effectively can be especially challenging, we devote the rest of this chapter to explaining how you can incorporate images and graphics into visual arguments. We discuss the use of photographs and drawings in the next main section of the chapter, and we examine the use of quantitative graphics in the chapter's final section.

AN ANALYSIS OF A MULTIMODAL ARGUMENT USING ALL THE DESIGN COMPONENTS   Before we discuss the use of images and graphics in detail, we illustrate how all four of the design components—use of type, layout, color, and images—can reinforce and support one another to achieve a rhetorical effect in a multimodal argument as shown in the advocacy ad in Figure 9.3. Because the intricacies of copyright law restrict our reproduction of advertisements in

Figure 9.3 Advocacy ad: Morementum

Morementum provides care, training, and specialized equipment for injured vets.
Your donation can help a hero find a new horizon.

this textbook, we commissioned an ad team to create this advocacy piece for a fictitious organization, "Morementum." This ad is intended for publication in a regional magazine or in the ad insert of a major regional newspaper. It highlights the design features of image, color, and layout, with type used to interpret and reinforce the message delivered by the other features.

Let's examine the ad in more detail. The layout highlights the connection between the wheel-chair-bound person in the lower-left center of the ad, the scene he is viewing, and readers who take in the whole scene. The text in the band of color at the top ("Mobility is more than an app") arouses curiosity and plays on words: For many people, mobility *is* an app—simply touch Uber or Lyft on your smartphone. However, the words "more than" suggest that this ad looks more deeply at the idea of "mobility." What is at stake, as the "story" of the ad makes clear, is a different kind of dependence and independence. The ad's story is suggested by the text in smaller print at the bottom of the ad, which leads readers to reconsider the person in the wheelchair: "Morementum provides care, training, and specialized equipment for injured vets." The next line of text further interprets the African American man as a military hero and clarifies the purpose of the ad: to elicit donations to help these vets enlarge their options and expand their quality of life It says, "Your donation can help a hero find a new horizon."

This advocacy ad works on readers by blending three themes—the hope for mobility and independence in the face of disability; a subtle patriotic appeal; and the symbolic meaning of "new horizons"—to convey how people's support of Morementum can empower veterans with disabilities to help themselves. These themes are portrayed through various visual strategies. The focus on one figure—a man in a wheelchair on a boardwalk—underscores the fact that he has maneuvered himself to the spot on his own. He sits in the kind of athletic wheelchair used in basketball games, and his special leather gloves highlight his ability to roll this wheelchair himself, emphasizing his desire to be independent, active, and mobile. He is out and about on a nice day, listening to music and taking photos of the attractive view from the side of the lake. This equipment has opened up activities for him.

The man's identity as a veteran is further developed by the ad's color scheme, which is both realistic and symbolic in its subtle patriotism. The white lettering on a red background relates well with the deep blue of the man's shirt and the white of his shorts, framing the ad in America's colors: red, white, and blue. Finally, the symbolism of horizons infuses this whole advocacy ad. For the photo of the scene itself, the ad designers positioned the camera behind the man in the wheelchair so that the scene includes the disabled veteran but also reaches outward to the view that the man sees, compelling readers to consider the whole scene. The fact that the man takes up much of the foreground makes him central to the ad's message. However, the camera's position behind the man also forces readers' gaze out to what the man sees, converting the disabled veteran from a particular individual into an "every veteran."

Note that the man is looking off to the horizon on the other side of the lake. Even the industrial pier with refueling and loading stations for boats and the buildings in the distance across the lake have a subtle symbolism: This is not a resort or vacation setting, but rather a place for jobs and productive activity. The brightness of the scene and the deep aqua color of the water combined with the man's engagement with the scene capture the sense of hope and new possibilities inherent in the concept of horizon. The text itself ties the whole ad together. The organization's title, "Morementum," encompasses the concept of

For Writing and Discussion

Analyzing an Advocacy Ad

Individual Task

Using your knowledge of type, layout, color, and image, analyze the Buzzed Driving advocacy ad sponsored by the Ad Council and the National Highway and Traffic Safety Administration in Figure 9.4. The following questions can guide your response:

1. What story does this ad tell? What is the ad's core argument?

Figure 9.4 Advocacy ad against drunk driving

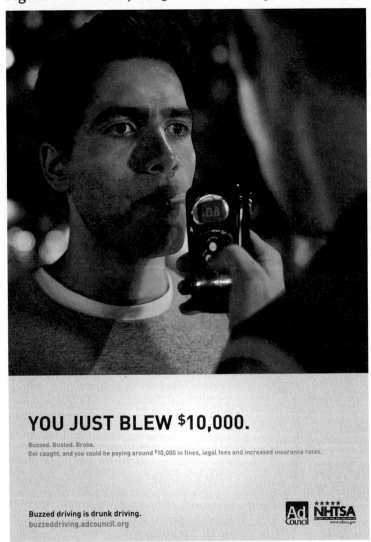

2. How does this ad use type, layout, image, and color for persuasive effect?
   - Layout and Image: Does the image convey an idea, illustrate a point, or evoke an emotional response? Why do you think the ad designer chose to give spatial preference to the image?
   - Color: Is the use of color in this ad decorative, realistic, aesthetic, or some combination of these? Explain. How does the use of color contribute to the ad's message?
   - Type: What is the relationship between the image and the type? Look at the words and ideas in each line of type. What is the effect of using different font sizes?

3. How does this ad appeal to *logos, ethos,* and *pathos?*

Group Task:

Working in pairs or as a class, share your analysis of this multimodal advocacy ad. Consider alternative designs for ads warning against driving under the influence of alcohol. What other images, layouts, use of type, and color might be effective in conveying the same message as this ad?

momentum—moving—and the altering of "momentum" to include the word "more" suggests a reaching forward to a better and bigger life, not one restricted by disability. It also asks readers to participate by adding something "more" to these veterans' lives through awareness, concern, and donations.

The rhetorical design choices in the construction of this advocacy ad explain its positive effect on readers. The ad portrays an upbeat scene of a veteran enjoying his ability to get around on a city boardwalk to experience the nice weather and lake view. The image, layout, and color scheme work in conjunction with the positive words "help," "hero," and "new horizon." The tagline of the piece— "MOREMENTUM. THE DIFFERENCE IS US"—continues the positive feelings by encouraging readers to contribute money so that more veterans can find pleasure in life and move forward.

The Compositional Features of Photographs and Drawings

9.2 Analyze the compositional features of photographs and drawings rhetorically.

Now that we have introduced you to the four major elements of visual design— type, layout, color, and images—we turn to an in-depth discussion of photographic images and drawings. Used with great shrewdness in most product advertisements, photos and drawings can be employed with equal shrewdness in posters, fliers, advocacy ads, and websites. When an image is created specifically for the purpose of advancing an argument, almost nothing is left to chance. Although such images are often made to seem spontaneous and "natural," they are almost always composed. That is, designers consciously select the details of staging and composition. They also use camera techniques (filters, camera angle, lighting) and digital or chemical development techniques (airbrushing, merging of images) to control the message.

Even news photography can have a composed feel. For example, public officials often try to control the effect of photographs by creating "photo opps" (photographing opportunities), wherein reporters are allowed to photograph an event only during certain times and only from certain angles. Political photographs appearing in newspapers often come from press releases officially approved by the politician's staff.

To analyze a photograph or drawing, or to create visual images to include with your own arguments, you need to think both about the composition of the image and about the camera's relationship to the subject. Because drawings produce a perspective on a scene analogous to that of a camera, you can apply design considerations for photographs to drawings as well. The following list can guide your analysis of any persuasive image.

Compositional Features to Examine in Photos and Drawings

- **Type of photograph or drawing:** Is the image documentary-like (representing a real event), fiction-like (intending to tell a story or dramatize a scene), or conceptual (illustrating or symbolizing an idea or theme)? The photo of factory farming at the start of Part 1, the photo of the protest for higher wages for fast-food workers at the start of Part 2, and the photo of the anti-fracking march at the start of Part 3 are documentary photos capturing real events in action.

- In contrast, the cartoonish drawing of the fly in the health poster in Figure 9.5 is both a fictional narrative telling a story and a conceptual drawing illustrating a concept. The vaping ad at the start of Part 4 is yet another type of drawing. The drawing of a woman's face, showing her perfect make-up, healthy skin, and vapor-wreathed lips, tries to persuade us visually that vaping is safer and healthier than smoking cigarettes.

- **Distance from the subject:** Is the image a close-up, medium shot, or long shot? Close-ups tend to increase the image's intensity and suggest its importance; long shots tend to blend the subject into the background. The photo of the fast-food containers spilling out of the garbage can and scattered on the ground (at the start of Part 5) is intensified by the close-up shot without background. In contrast, the medium shot of the boy holding the toy he has found in the wreckage caused by Typhoon Haiyan (Figure 5.1) focuses on both the boy and his surroundings. While the photo captures the magnitude of the disaster, it also shows the child's interests and his attempt to recover some of his past life.

- **Image orientation and camera angle:** Is the camera (or artist) positioned in front of or behind the subject? Is the camera positioned below the subject, looking up (a low-angle shot)? Or is it above the subject, looking down (a high-angle shot)? Front-view shots (for example, the photo of the fracking protestor at the start of Part 3) tend to emphasize the persons being photographed. In contrast, rear-view shots often emphasize the scene or setting. A low-angle perspective tends to make the subject look superior and powerful, whereas a high-angle perspective can reduce the size—and by implication, the importance—of the subject. A level angle tends to imply equality.

- **Point of view:** Does the camera or artist stand outside the scene and create an objective effect? Or is the camera or artist inside the scene as if the photographer or artist is an actor in the scene, creating a subjective effect?

Figure 9.5 Health poster from the War Department in World War II

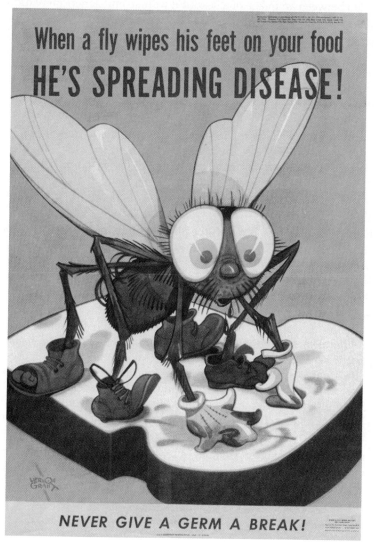

- **Use of color:** Is the image in color or in black and white? Is this choice determined by the restrictions of the medium (such as images designed to run in black-and-white in newspapers), or is it the choice of the photographer or artist? Are the colors realistic or muted? Have special filters been used (for example, a photo made to look old through the use of brown tints)? Are bright colors intended to be catchy, attractive, dominant, or disturbing?

- **Compositional special effects:** Is the entire image clear and realistic? Is any portion of it blurred? Is it blended with other realistic or nonrealistic images (for example, a car ad that blends a city and a desert; a body lotion ad that merges a woman and a cactus)? Is the image an imitation of some other famous image such as a classic painting (as in parodies)? The image of the Muslim woman wearing the American flag (Figure 9.1) as a hijab makes a visual association between an image of a beautiful woman and American patriotism.

- **Juxtaposition of images:** Are several different images juxtaposed (that is, placed closed together or side by side), suggesting relationships between them? Juxtaposition can suggest sequential or causal relationships, or it can metaphorically transfer the identity of a nearby image or background to the subject (as when a bath soap is associated with a meadow). Juxtaposition of images is frequently used to shape viewers' perceptions of political figures, as when political figures are photographed with patriotic monuments.

- **Manipulation of images:** Are staged images made to appear real, natural, or documentary-like? Are images altered with airbrushing? Are the images a series of composites of a number of images (for instance, using images of different women's bodies to create one perfect model in an ad or film)? Are images *cropped* for emphasis? That is, has any part of the original photo been cut out? If so, what is left out? Are images downsized or enlarged?

- **Settings, furnishings, props:** Is the photo or drawing an outdoor scene or an indoor scene? What is in the background and foreground? What furnishings and props (such as furniture, objects in a room, pets, and landscape features) help create the scene? What social associations of class, race, and gender are attached to these settings and props?

- **Characters, roles, actions:** Does the photo or drawing tell a story? Are the people in the scene models? Are the models instrumental (acting out real-life roles), or are they decorative (extra and included for visual or sex appeal)? What are the people's facial expressions, gestures, and poses? What are the figures' spatial relationships? (Who is in the foreground, center, and background? Who is large and prominent?) What social relationships are implied by these poses and positions? In the "Morementum" advocacy ad in Figure 9.3, the solitary man in the wheelchair enjoying the view from the wooden boardwalk tells the story of hoped-for independence.

- **Presentation of images:** Are images separated from one another in a larger composition or connected to one another? Are the images large in proportion to written text? How are images labeled, if at all? How does the text relate to the image(s)? Does the image illustrate the text? Does the text explain or comment on the image?

An Analysis of a Multimedia Video Argument Using Words, Images, and Music

To show you how to analyze a multimodal argument with images and text, let's examine a student advocacy video, "It's a Toilet, Not a Trash Can," made for a first-year inquiry seminar on water and citizenship. Eight stills from this advocacy video are shown in Figures 9.6–9.13. The assignment asked students to construct an advocacy video addressing a public problem related to water, inviting them to explore questions such as: What should responsible citizens know about where their water comes from, where it goes, and what it costs? How should we manage water to be certain that it is clean, safe, and available? How do we allot available water to different stakeholders such as households, industry, agriculture, and recreation? For this assignment, students were asked to construct a video to encourage a specific audience to act responsibly in their water usage. Having taken a class trip to a local wastewater treatment plant, the students in this class became aware of how nonbiodegradable trash enters the wastewater system instead of going to a landfill or a recycling plant. One group of students chose to attack one cause of this problem: the casual flushing of trash items down residence hall toilets.

This video uses humorous exaggeration to underscore its serious point. The video begins with scenes from a windy fall day, with different groups of students returning to a residence hall with what seem to be full grocery bags. Students walk and talk with friends, take the residence hall elevator, and walk down their hallway toward their rooms (Figures 9.6 and 9.7). At this point, the advocacy video spins off into hyperbole (exaggeration) and absurdity. Some students, instead of carrying groceries in their shopping bags, have been carrying garbage, which they proceed to dump into the toilet (Figure 9.8). The humorous shock value of this action is intensified through close-ups of a large amount of garbage emptied into the toilet (Figures 9.9 and 9.11). Interspersed between action scenes are a few verbal text screens that explain the problem of trash in the sewage system and drive home the costs of the problem (such as the verbal text screen in Figure 9.10). The final screens use text to state the video's message explicitly (Figures 9.12 and 9.13).

As the story builds intensity, this advocacy video combines appeals to *pathos*, *ethos*, and *logos*. The appeals to *pathos* begin with the simple, fast-paced, haunting instrumental music that plays in the background throughout the video; the music is both pleasant and somewhat disturbing, the kind that lingers in the mind. Student viewers can also easily relate to the characters in the video (a quality of *pathos*) in that the student actors wear ordinary clothing and the residence hall

Figure 9.6 Students carrying plastic bags into a residence hall elevator

Figure 9.7 Students in residence hallway carrying the same bags

Figure 9.8 Student dumping garbage in residence hall toilet

Figure 9.9 Garbage filling the toilet

Figure 9.10 Screen explaining why this trash is harmful

"Tampons and other commonly flushed products including wipes and condoms cannot be broken down in the sewage System."
Tara Johnson (EPA)

Figure 9.11 Hand adding more garbage to the toilet

Figure 9.12 Screen stating the absurdity of the actions in the video

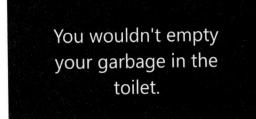

You wouldn't empty your garbage in the toilet.

Figure 9.13 Final screen with tagline that summarizes the advocacy video's point

It's a toilet, not a trash can.

elevator and hallway are so generic that they could be found anywhere in the country. Once the surprise of the garbage dumping starts, the mild shock and humor stir different kinds of emotions. Viewers can no longer predict where the video is going. The dumping of garbage into the toilet is so puzzling and so over the top that it elicits both laughs and gasps from the audience. Close-ups of toilets filled with floating bottles and garbage are ridiculously distressing.

In addition to appeals to *pathos*, the video includes appeals to *logos* through the interspersed text-based screens (stark in their white type on a black background) that explain the harm done by trash in the sewage system. Several of these screens also appeal to *ethos* by citing facts from authorities such as the Environmental Protection Agency (as in Figure 9.10) and the Clean Watersheds Needs Survey (not shown in the sequence of still photos), which explain the burden and cost of garbage in wastewater treatment plants. In fact, all kinds of items—pieces of clothing and plastic, combs, condoms, sanitary products, diapers, even dollar bills—find their way into these treatment systems and need to be fished out. The message conveyed by the video emerges from the actions portrayed and confronts readers directly in the final screens. The video does not state its proposal claim initially because the creators of the video did not want viewers to dismiss the claim outright or arouse defensiveness. The final tagline ("It's a toilet, not a trash can") plays on viewers' emotions through its memorable, catchy alliteration ("toilet" and "trash can"). This line just might come to mind the next time someone is about to drop a piece of trash in the toilet.

For Writing and Discussion

Thinking Rhetorically about Photos

Working individually or in groups, imagine that you have been asked to compose a brochure that either supports or opposes a state proposal to ban the use of plastic bags in grocery stores. Your task is to choose two to four of the following images for your brochure. First analyze the composition of the images. Then explain which ones you would choose to achieve the most persuasive impact in your brochure. How would you arrange these images?

1. Study the six images in Figures 9.14 through 9.19, and then answer the following questions:
    a. What camera techniques and composition features do you see in each photo or image? For each image, consider the list of compositional features earlier in this chapter.
    b. What do you think is the dominant impression of each photo? In other words, what is each photo's implicit argument?
2. Once you have analyzed the images, decide which are the most striking or memorable and try to reach consensus about your choices for a rhetorically effective brochure.
3. Sometimes designers and ad creators choose cartoonish images to deliver their arguments. How might you use a cartoon drawing in your brochure? For ideas, you might consider the cartoon fly in the War Department's health poster in Figure 9.5.

Figure 9.14 Photo of plastic bags blowing in a forest

Figure 9.15 Photo of dump with plastic bags and seagulls

Figure 9.16 Photo of a shopper carrying purchases in plastic bags

Figure 9.17 Photo of children picking up plastic bags in a forest

(continued)

Figure 9.18 Photo of a plastic bag tangled in flowers

Figure 9.19 Photo of plastic bags packed for recycling

The Genres of Multimodal Argument

9.3 Explain the genres of multimodal argument.

In some cases, multimodal texts are primarily written text with inserted photographs or drawings that enhance the *logos* or *pathos* of the argument. For example, a verbal argument promoting help for AIDS victims in Africa might be accompanied by a photograph of a dying mother and child. In contrast, in some multimodal genres the visual design carries most of the argumentative weight; verbal text is used primarily for labeling, for focusing the argument's claim, or for commenting on the images. In this section, we describe a variety of multimodal genres that rely primarily on visual elements.

Posters and Fliers

To persuade audiences, an arguer might create a poster or flier to rally support for a cause. For example, during World War II, posters asked Americans to invest in war bonds and urged women to join the workforce in order to free men for active combat. During the Vietnam War, famous posters used slogans such as "Make Love, Not War" or "Girls say yes to boys who say no" to increase national resistance to the war.

The hallmark of an effective poster is the way it uses a visual-verbal text to focus and encode a complex meaning, often with one or more striking images. These images are often symbolic—for example, using children to symbolize family and home, a soaring bird to symbolize freedom, or three firefighters raising the American flag over the World Trade Center rubble on September 11, 2001, to symbolize American heroism, patriotism, and resistance to terrorism. These symbols derive potency from the values they share with their target audience. Posters tend to use words sparingly, either as slogans or as short, memorable

Figure 9.20 Poster for *The Humble Assessment*

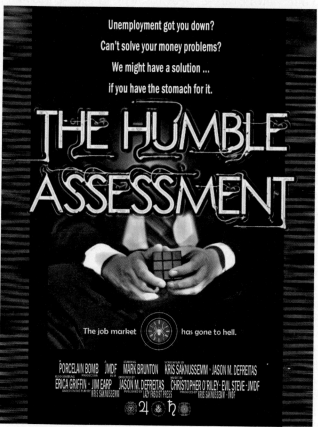

directives. This concise verbal text augments the message encoded in an eye-catching, dominant image.

As an example of a contemporary poster urging people to see a recent independent film, consider *The Humble Assessment* poster in Figure 9.20. Because this film is new and unknown, the poster must arouse curiosity and elicit interest. In this poster, the text creates the context—the competitive job market and the financial anxieties of applicants. The poster shows a man in a business suit, white shirt, and tie in a sitting position, possibly waiting for an interview. However, the poster leaves viewers with many questions: Is the man sitting on a chair or cramped into a coffin-like space? Why doesn't the man have a head? Why is he playing with a Rubik's cube? Why do his hands look tense? Why are the clock's hands replaced by a spider whose eight legs point to a bewildering number of time possibilities? Why are the clock with the spider and the line "The job market has gone to hell" placed between the man's knees? How do the wavering letters of the film's title contribute to the claustrophobic, unsettling impression produced by the text and image? How does the use of the words "stomach for it," "you," "we," and "gone to hell" both draw viewers in and put them on edge? "Assessment" means a judgment of value. What does that word have to do with "humble," and why would a job interview be called "an assessment"? In short, this film poster uses text and image to pique curiosity and suggest disturbing content in this absurdist, surreal postmodern depiction of the demoralizing and dehumanizing corporate job market.

Public Affairs Advocacy Advertisements

Public affairs advocacy advertisements share with posters an emphasis on visual elements, but they are designed specifically for publication in newspapers and magazines (and are often reproduced on websites). In their persuasive strategies, they are very similar to product advertisements. Public affairs advocacy ads are usually sponsored by a corporation or an advocacy organization, often are part of a particular campaign with a theme, and have a more immediate and defined target audience than posters do. Designed as condensed arguments aimed at influencing public opinion on civic issues, these ads are characterized by their brevity, audience-based appeals, and succinct, "sound bite" style. Often, in order to put forth their claim and reasons clearly and concisely, they employ headings and subheadings, bulleted lists, different sizes and styles of type, and a clever, pleasing layout on the page. They usually have an attention-getting slogan or headline such as "MORE KIDS ARE GETTING BRAIN CANCER. WHY?" or "STOP THE TAX REVOLT JUGGERNAUT!" And they usually include a call to action, such as a donation, a letter of protest to legislators, or an invitation to join the advocacy group.

The balance between verbal and visual elements in an advocacy advertisement varies. Some advocacy ads are verbal only, with visual concerns focused on document design (for example, an "open letter" from the president of a corporation appearing as a full-page newspaper ad). Other advocacy ads are primarily visual, using images and other design elements with the same shrewdness as advertisements.

This text reproduces a variety of public affairs advocacy ads across chapters. We have already examined the anti-bullying ad in Figure 9.2, the anti-drunk driving ad in Figure 9.4, and the fictionalized Morementum ad in Figure 9.3. These ads use text and images in different ways to present their messages. Although it is designed more like a poster than an advocacy ad, the World War II health warning about the spread of germs (Figure 9.5) uses a humorous cartoon drawing to accompany its alarming message about the dangers of infectious disease.

As another example of a public affairs advocacy ad, consider the ad featuring a coat hanger at the beginning of Chapter 15. This ad attempts to raise fears about the negative consequences of the pro-life movement's campaign against abortion. As you can see, this ad is dominated by one stark image: a question mark formed by the hook of a coat hanger. The shape of the hook draws the reader's eye to the concentrated type centered below it. The hook carries most of the weight of the argument. Simple, bold, and harsh, the image of the hanger taps readers' cultural knowledge and evokes the dangerous scenario of illegal abortions performed crudely by nonmedical people in the dark backstreets of cities. The ad wants viewers to think of the dangerous last resorts to which desperate women would have to turn if they could not obtain abortions legally. Also consider the hanger itself. It is in the shape of a question mark, thereby suggesting a question about what will happen if abortions are made illegal. The coat hanger itself provides the ad's disturbing answer to the printed question—desperate women will go to backstreet abortionists who use coat hangers as abortion tools.

Cartoons

An especially charged kind of visual argument is the editorial or political cartoon and its extended forms, the comic strip and the graphic novel. Here we focus on political cartoons, which are often mini-narratives portraying an issue dramatically, compactly, and humorously, through images and a few well-chosen words that dramatize conflicts and problems. Using caricature, exaggeration, and distortion, a cartoonist distills an issue down to an image that boldly reveals the cartoonist's perspective on the issue. The purpose of political cartoons is usually satirical, often criticizing some groups of people or ideas while delighting and inspiring those who agree with the cartoonist's viewpoint. Because they are so condensed and are often connected to current affairs, political cartoons are particularly dependent on the audience's background knowledge of cultural and political events. When political cartoons work well, their perceptive combination of images and words flashes a brilliant, clarifying light or opens a new lens on an issue, often giving readers a shock of insight.

As an example, note the cartoon by Milt Priggee in Figure 9.22. The setting of the cartoon envisions a humorous blend of prehistoric and contemporary times. This cartoon responds to recent scientific discussions of the creation and development of the universe and the age of the Earth. (Note the mention of dark matter, which is an energy-mass concept from physics and astronomy.) However, the main story of the cartoon connects the dinosaur characters with the behavior of people today who go about walking and tweeting, oblivious to everything around them, including dangerous environments. Thus, the cartoon links discussions of evolution to discussions of the contemporary obsession with smartphones and social media.

For Writing and Discussion

Analyzing Posters Rhetorically

Working individually or in groups, examine the the poster shown in Figure 9.21, which shows a photo of an attractive girl behind the line "HEATHER'S LIFE ENDED TOO SOON." This poster, which appears on the TxtResponsibly.org website, reaches out to young drivers and their parents, using both images and text.

   a. What visual features of this poster immediately attract your attention? What principles for the effective use of type, layout, color, and image does this ad exemplify?
   b. What is this ad's core argument?
   c. Why did Heather's parents choose a large photo of her? How does that photo work with the other photo of a mangled car?
   d. How does the frankness of the text and the size and use of color lettering combine to convey the ad's message?
   e. How would you design a poster warning against texting while driving? Consider the use of type, layout, and image; the core of its argument; and its appeals to *ethos*, *pathos*, and *kairos*.

(continued)

Figure 9.21 Poster argument warning against texting while driving

Figure 9.22 Tweeting and evolution cartoon

For Writing and Discussion

Analyzing Cartoons

Cartoons can provide insight into how the public is lining up on issues. Choose a current issue such as healthcare reform, use of drones, immigration policy, tax policy, or identity theft. Then, using an online cartoon index such as Daryl Cagle's Professional Cartoonists Index (www.cagle.com) or a web search of your own, find several cartoons that capture different perspectives on your issue.

1. What is the mini-narrative in each cartoon? What is the main claim? How are caricature, exaggeration, and/or distortion used in each cartoon?
2. How is *kairos*, or timeliness, important to each cartoon?

Websites

So far we have only hinted at how the World Wide Web has accelerated the use of visual images in argument. Multimodal websites exhibit the web's complex mix of text and image, a mix that has changed the way many writers think of argument. For example, the home page of an advocacy site often has many features of a poster argument, with hypertext links to galleries of images on the one hand and to verbal arguments on the other. These verbal arguments themselves often contain photographs, drawings, and graphics. The strategies discussed in this chapter for analyzing and interpreting visual texts also apply to websites.

Because the web is such an important tool in research, we have placed our main discussion of websites in Chapter 16. In that chapter you will find detailed explanations for reading, analyzing, and evaluating websites.

Advocacy Videos

Advocacy videos, often posted on YouTube, are perhaps the most influential of all multimodal arguments. Whether professionally made or quickly planned and produced by amateurs using video production software, advocacy videos allow powerful combinations of sounds, images, and verbal text (either as spoken dialogue, as voice-overs, or as inserted written text). Advocacy websites (and their parallel Facebook, Twitter, or Instagram sites) frequently link to advocacy videos. Earlier in this chapter, we described and analyzed a student advocacy video, "It's a Toilet, Not a Trash Can," and reproduced stills from the video. In the next section we offer guidelines for constructing your own advocacy video.

Constructing Your Own Multimodal Arguments

9.4   **Construct your own multimodal arguments.**

The most common multimodal arguments you are likely to create are posters, fliers, public affairs advocacy ads, and advocacy videos. The following guidelines will help you apply your understanding of visual elements to the construction of your own multimodal arguments.

Guidelines for Creating the Visual Elements in Posters, Fliers, and Advocacy Ads

1. **Genre:** Determine where this visual argument is going to appear (on a bulletin board, circulated as a flier, on one page of a magazine or newspaper, or on a website).

2. **Audience-based appeals:** Determine who your target audience is.
   - What values and background knowledge regarding your issue can you assume that your audience has?
   - What specifically do you want your audience to think or do after reading your visual argument?
   - If you are promoting a specific course of action (sign a petition, send money, vote for or against a bill, attend a meeting), how can you make that request clear and direct?

3. **Core of your argument:** Determine what clear claim and reasons will form the core of your argument; decide whether this claim and these reasons will be explicitly stated or implicit in your visuals and slogans.
   - How much verbal text will you use?
   - If the core of your argument will be largely implicit, how can you make it readily apparent and clear for your audience?

4. **Visual design:** What visual design and layout will grab your audience's attention and be persuasive?

   - How can font sizes and styles, layout, and color be used in this argument to create a strong impression?
   - What balance and harmony can you create between the visual and verbal elements of your argument? Will your verbal elements be a slogan, express the core of the argument, or summarize and comment on the image(s)?

5. **Use of images:** If your argument lends itself to images, what photo or drawing would support your claim or have emotional appeal? (If you want to use more than one image, be careful that you don't clutter your page and confuse your message. Simplicity and clarity are important.)

   - What image would be memorable and meaningful to your audience? Which would be more effective: a photo or a drawing?
   - Will your image(s) be used to provide evidence for your claim, illustrate a main idea, evoke emotions, or enhance your credibility and authority?

Guidelines for Creating Video Arguments

1. **Rhetorical situation:** Consider your purpose and audience, your core argument, and the effect you want your video to have on your targeted audience.

   - What is your core argument?
   - Are you imagining a sympathetic, neutral, or opposing audience?
   - How do you plan to appeal to *logos*, *ethos*, and *pathos*?
   - What role will you assume? Will you stay behind the scenes or appear in the video?
   - Does your rhetorical purpose call for one point of view or multiple points of view to move your audience toward your view?

2. **Use of a storyboard to map out scenes:** Storyboards (rough sketch drawings of intended scenes) are like graphic organizers that help you plan your video scene by scene. When creating a storyboard, you plan the scenes you will use to tell a story and plan the camera angles you will use to create the visual narrative.

   - How will you organize individual shots?
   - How will you use camera angles to create a narrative story?
   - How would zooming, fading, or rapid cuts to a different angle help you create transitions between scenes?

3. **Priority on visual elements:** Audiences of video texts expect to be engaged visually at all times.

   - How will your sequence of scenes convey your message visually? Consider using different camera angles—establishing shots (medium or long shots), point-of-view shots (through a character's eyes), and reaction shots (close-ups of faces)—to tell a story.
   - While keeping priority on images, how might you use words to help readers interpret images? Consider using captions, inserted text screens, or voice-overs.
   - Have you paced your video effectively so that it leaves your audience neither confused nor bored?

4. **Incorporation of effective verbal and written text:** You can incorporate verbal text into a video through spoken dialogue, voice-overs, or printed text inserted as captions or as separate screens. Video technology allows for more versatile text options than just about any other multimodal form.

- How might spoken or written text underscore the intended rhetorical effect of images by emphasizing main points and highlighting important information?
- If you use voice-overs, how will you avoid using monotonous or uninteresting visuals as filler during stretches of spoken text?
- If you insert written text, how will you make your points vivid and clear, avoiding both text density and vagueness?

5. **Use of musical elements and other sound options:** Sound options can underscore important rhetorical goals with auditory effects. Sound or the choice of silence can have a subtle but powerful impact on the viewers of a video text.

- Have you matched sound effects to the meaning and rhetorical effect you want to achieve? Consider how you will use music, background sounds (street noise, café buzz, bird chirps, sudden silence), and voice qualities (accent, pitch, emotional emphasis).
- If you have used separate microphones, are they well placed? Is the sound too soft or too loud? Is voice audible rather than muffled?

For Writing and Discussion

Developing Ideas for an Advocacy Ad or Poster Argument

This exercise asks you to do the thinking and planning for an advocacy ad, poster argument, or advocacy video for your college or university campus. Working individually, in small groups, or as a class, choose an issue that is controversial on your campus (or in your town or city), and follow the Guidelines for Creating Visual Arguments or the Guidelines for Creating Advocacy Videos to envision the view you want to advocate on that issue. For an advocacy video, map your argument as scenes using a storyboard. What might the core of your argument be? Who is your target audience? Are you representing a group, club, or other organization? What image(s) might be effective in attracting and moving your audience? Possible issues might be commuter parking; poor conditions in the computer lab; student reluctance to use the counseling center; problems with residence hall life; financial aid programs; intramural sports; ways to improve orientation programs for new students; work-study programs; travel-abroad opportunities; or new initiatives such as study groups for big lecture courses or new service-learning opportunities.

Using Information Graphics in Arguments

9.5 Use information graphics rhetorically in arguments.

Besides images in the form of photographs and drawings, writers often use quantitative graphics to support number-based arguments. In Chapter 4 we introduced the use of quantitative data in arguments, showing how stakeholders can use numbers for evidence, often framing those numbers to support their angle of vision. Using spreadsheet and presentation programs, today's writers often create and import quantitative graphics into their documents. These visuals—such as tables, pie charts, and line graphs or bar graphs—can have great rhetorical power by using numbers to tell a story at a glance. In this section, we show you how to make numbers speak with quantitative graphics. We also show you how to analyze graphics, incorporate them into your text, and reference them effectively.

How Tables Contain a Variety of Stories

Data used in arguments usually have their origins in raw numbers collected from surveys, questionnaires, observational studies, scientific experiments, and so forth. Through a series of calculations, the numbers are combined, sorted, and arranged in a meaningful fashion, often in detailed tables. Some of the tables published by the U.S. Census Bureau, for example, stretch across dozens of pages. The denser the table, the more its use is restricted to statistical experts who pore over the data to analyze and interpret them. More useful to the public are shorter tables contained on one or two pages that report data at a higher level of abstraction.

Consider, for example, Table 9.2, which reproduces data from a more detailed table published by the U.S. Energy Information Administration. This table shows the amount of energy consumed in the United States during selected years from 1950 to 2016 from specified primary sources such as coal, natural gas, nuclear power, wind, or the sun (solar energy).

Take a few moments to peruse the table and be certain you know how to read it. You read tables in two directions: from top to bottom and from left to

Table 9.2 U.S. Primary Energy Consumption by Source, 1950 to 2016 (Quadrillion BTUs)

| | Fossil Fuels | | | | Nuclear Energy | Renewable Sources | | | | | | | |
	Coal	Natural Gas	Petro-leum	Total	Nuclear Electric Power	Hydro-Electric Power	Geo-Thermal	Solar	Wind	Bio-mass	Total	Grand Total*
1950	12.35	5.97	13.32	31.63	0.00	1.42	-	-	-	1.56	2.98	34.62
1955	11.17	9.00	17.26	37.41	0.00	1.36	-	-	-	1.42	2.78	40.21
1960	9.84	12.39	19.92	42.14	0.01	1.61	-	-	-	1.32	2.93	45.09
1965	11.58	15.77	23.25	50.58	0.04	2.06	-	-	-	1.34	3.40	54.02
1970	12.27	21.80	29.52	63.52	0.24	2.63	0.01	-	-	1.43	4.07	67.84
1975	12.66	19.95	32.73	65.36	1.90	3.16	0.03	-	-	1.50	4.69	71.97
1980	15.42	20.24	34.21	69.83	2.74	2.90	0.05	-	-	2.48	5.43	78.07
1985	17.48	17.70	30.93	66.09	4.08	2.97	0.10	-	-	3.02	6.08	76.39
1990	19.17	19.60	33.55	72.33	6.10	3.05	0.17	0.06	0.03	2.74	6.04	84.48
1995	20.09	22.67	34.44	77.26	7.08	3.21	0.15	0.07	0.03	3.10	6.56	91.03
2000	22.58	23.82	38.27	84.74	7.86	2.81	0.16	0.06	0.06	3.01	6.10	98.82
2005	22.80	22.57	40.30	85.71	8.16	2.70	0.18	0.06	0.18	3.11	6.23	100.19
2010	20.83	24.58	35.49	80.89	8.43	2.54	0.21	0.09	0.92	4.27	8.03	97.45
2015	15.55	28.20	35.60	79.33	8.34	2.32	0.21	0.43	1.78	4.73	9.47	97.37
2016	14.23	28.42	35.94	78.57	8.42	2.48	0.23	0.59	2.11	4.76	10.16	97.40

*Note: Grand totals may not sum exactly due to rounding.

right. Always begin with the title, which tells you what the table contains by including elements from the table's vertical and horizontal dimensions and by indicating the table's unit(s) of measure. In Table 9.2, the unit of measure is a quadrillion British thermal units (BTU). (A *quadrillion* is one million billions—that is, a 1 followed by 15 zeros. A BTU is the amount of energy needed to raise the temperature of one pound of water one degree Fahrenheit.) In Table 9.2, the vertical dimension shows years (every fifth year from 1950 to 2015, plus 2016). The horizontal dimension shows various sources of energy. The highest level of this horizontal dimension identifies the three primary energy sources: fossil fuels, nuclear energy, and renewable sources. Fossil fuels and renewable sources are then further divided into subcategories.

To make sure you know how to read the table, pick a couple of rows at random and explain what each number means. For example, the 1970 row shows that in 1970 Americans consumed 12.27 quadrillion BTUs of energy from coal, 21.8 quadrillion BTUs from natural gas, and 29.52 quadrillion BTUs from petroleum for a total of 63.52 quadrillion BTUs of fossil fuel energy. That same year, Americans used .24 quadrillion BTUs from nuclear energy and a total of 4.07 quadrillion BTUs from renewable energy. Renewable energy in 1970 was limited to hydropower (2.63 quadrillion BTUs), geothermal (.01 quadrillion BTUs) and biomass (1.43 quadrillion BTUs). (In 1970, *biomass* meant primarily the burning of wood and charcoal; in more recent years it has included the use of biofuels such as ethanol.) The total U.S. consumption of energy from that year—obtained by adding fossil fuels, nuclear energy, and renewable sources—is shown in the far right column: 67.84 quadrillion BTUs.

Now that you know how to read the table, examine it carefully to identify the kinds of questions it raises and stories it tells. What does the table show us, for example, about trends in total energy consumption in the United States? Is our use of natural gas increasing or decreasing? How about our use of nuclear energy or solar energy? In addition to looking just at the numbers on the table, you could convert numbers to percentages. For example, in any given year, what percent of total energy consumption came from renewable sources versus fossil fuels? Table 9.2 can also initiate interesting causal questions: In 2005, Americans consumed 22.8 quadrillion BTUs of coal energy. But by 2016 that number dropped to 14.23 quadrillion BTUs. Why has the use of coal declined? (Some people attribute the decline to anti-coal environmental regulations imposed by the Obama administration. Others attribute the decline to cheap natural gas made possible by fracking.)

Using a Graph to Tell a Story

Table 9.2 has many embedded energy stories, but you must tease them out from the dense columns of numbers. If you want to make a story pop out for readers, you can convert it to a graph. Three common types of graphs are bar graphs, pie charts, and line graphs.

BAR GRAPHS   Bar graphs use bars of varying length, extending either horizontally or vertically, to contrast two or more quantities. As with any graphic presentation, you must create a comprehensive title. In the case of bar graphs, titles tell readers what is being compared. Most bar graphs also have *legends*, which explain what the different features on the graph represent. Bars are typically distinguished from one another by use of different colors, shades, or patterns of crosshatching.

Making Visual and Multimodal Arguments **183**

Figure 9.23 U.S. consumption of energy from coal and natural gas, 2005 and 2016 (quadrillion BTUs)

SOURCE: United States Energy Information Agency

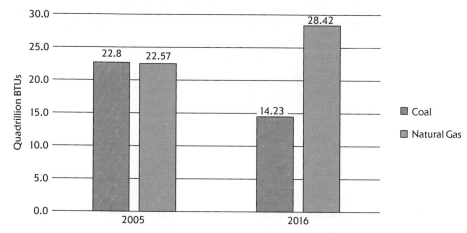

Bar graphs can help readers make quick comparisons. Suppose you want to link the recent decline in coal consumption to increased use of natural gas. You could tell this story at a glance with a bar graph, as in Figure 9.23. The first set of bars shows that in 2005 Americans used almost equal amounts of coal and natural gas. However, in the second set of bars (2016), the bar for coal has shrunk significantly while the bar for natural gas has grown.

PIE CHARTS   Another vivid kind of graph is a pie chart or circle graph, which depicts different percentages of a total (the pie) in the form of slices. Pie charts are often used to show how a whole is divided up into parts. For example, suppose that you wanted your readers to notice the percentage of U.S. energy consumption that came from each of the primary sectors in 2016. You could use a pie chart to make that percentage quickly visible through a pie chart like the one shown in Figure 9.24, which is based on the data in Table 9.2 As you can see, a pie chart shows at a glance how the whole of something is divided into segments. In this case there are only three segments.

A general note: The effectiveness of pie charts diminishes as you add more slices. In most cases, a pie chart becomes ineffective if you include more the five or six slices.

LINE GRAPHS   Another powerful quantitative graphic is a line graph, which converts numerical data into a series of points on a grid and then connects them to create flat, rising, or falling lines. The result is a picture of the relationship between the variables represented on the horizontal and vertical axes. By convention, the horizontal axis of a line graph contains the predictable, known variable, which has no surprises—what researchers call the *independent variable*. The vertical axis contains the unpredictable variable (what researchers call the *dependent variable*), which tells the graph's story.

Imagine that you want to create a line graph that compares use of energy sources that emit greenhouse gases with those that don't. Greenhouse-gas-emitting sources include both fossil fuels and biomass fuels. (Although biomass

Figure 9.24 Consumption of energy by percentage from fossil fuel, nuclear, and renewal sources, 2016

SOURCE: United States Energy Information Agency.

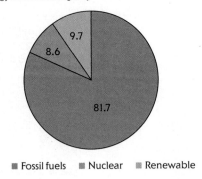

■ Fossil fuels   ■ Nuclear   ■ Renewable

fuels such as wood and ethanol are listed in Table 9.2 as "renewable energy sources," they nevertheless emit greenhouse gases.) The energy sources that don't emit greenhouse gases are nuclear, hydroelectric, geothermal, solar, and wind. Using a spreadsheet you can move the biomass data from the "renewable energy" data and add it to the fossil fuel data. You can then add the nuclear power data into the remaining renewable sources data. You can then use the spreadsheet to create a line graph that compares these two variables over time (see Figure 9.25).

Figure 9.25 U.S. energy consumption from greenhouse-gas-emitting sources versus zero emission sources, 1950–2016 (quadrillion BTUs)

NOTE: "Greenhouse-gas-emitting" sources of energy are fossil fuels and biomass fuels. "Zero emission" sources of energy are nuclear, geothermal, hydroelectric, solar, and wind power.

SOURCE: United States Energy Information Agency

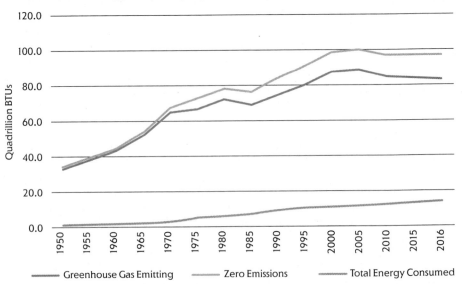

To determine what this graph is telling you, you need to clarify what's represented on the two axes. The horizontal axis lists years from 1950 to 2016 while the vertical axis shows the amount of energy consumed in any given year as measured in quadrillion BTUs. The graph's "story" is shown in the three lines: The top line (in gray) shows the total amount of energy consumed in a given year; the blue line below it represents the amount consumed from greenhouse-gas-emitting sources, and the red line represents energy consumed from zero-emission sources. The good news in this graph is that U.S. energy consumption appears to have peaked around 2005 and then declined slightly despite increases in population. Another piece of good news is that the consumption of zero-emission sources is slowly increasing while the use of greenhouse-gas-emitting sources is slowly decreasing. The bad news is that the gap between them is still huge.

Incorporating Graphics into Your Argument

Today, writers working with quantitative data usually use graphing software that automatically creates tables, graphs, or charts from data entered into the cells of a spreadsheet. For college papers, some instructors may allow you to make your graphs with pencil and ruler and paste them into your document. The following suggestions will be helpful as you think about the best ways to incorporate graphics into your argument.

DESIGNING THE GRAPHIC   When you design your graphic, your goal is to have a specific rhetorical effect on your readers, not to demonstrate all the bells and whistles available on your software. Adding extraneous data to the graph or chart, or using such features as a three-dimensional effect, can often distract from your graph's story. Keep the graphic as uncluttered and simple as possible, and design it so that it reinforces the point you are making.

NUMBERING, LABELING, AND TITLING THE GRAPHIC   In newspapers and popular magazines, writers often include graphics in boxes or sidebars without specifically referring to them in the text itself. However, in academic and professional workplace writing, graphics are always labeled, numbered, titled, and referred to directly in the text. By convention, tables are listed as "Tables," whereas line graphs, bar graphs, pie charts, and any other kinds of drawings or photographs are labeled as "Figures." Suppose you create a document that includes four graphics—a table, a bar graph, a pie chart, and a photograph. The table would be labeled as Table 1. The others would be labeled as Figure 1, Figure 2, and Figure 3.

In addition to numbering and labeling, every graphic needs a comprehensive title that explains fully what information is being displayed. In a line graph showing changes over time, for example, a typical title will identify the information on both the horizontal and vertical axes (including the years covered). Bar graphs may also include a legend explaining how the bars are coded. When you import the graphic into your own text, be consistent in where you place the title—either above the graphic or below it.

Look again at the tables and figures in this chapter and compare their titles to the information in the graphics.

Figure 9.26 Example of a student text with a referenced graph

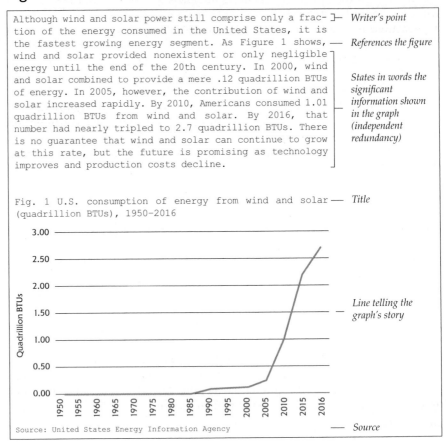

Although wind and solar power still comprise only a frac-]— *Writer's point*
tion of the energy consumed in the United States, it is
the fastest growing energy segment. As Figure 1 shows, —— *References the figure*
wind and solar provided nonexistent or only negligible
energy until the end of the 20th century. In 2000, wind
and solar combined to provide a mere .12 quadrillion BTUs   *States in words the*
of energy. In 2005, however, the contribution of wind and   *significant*
solar increased rapidly. By 2010, Americans consumed 1.01   *information shown*
quadrillion BTUs from wind and solar. By 2016, that   *in the graph*
number had nearly tripled to 2.7 quadrillion BTUs. There   *(independent*
is no guarantee that wind and solar can continue to grow   *redundancy)*
at this rate, but the future is promising as technology
improves and production costs decline.

Fig. 1 U.S. consumption of energy from wind and solar —— *Title*
(quadrillion BTUs), 1950–2016

Line telling the
graph's story

Source: United States Energy Information Agency   —— *Source*

REFERENCING THE GRAPHIC IN YOUR TEXT   Academic and professional
writers follow a referencing convention called *independent redundancy*. The general rule is this: The graphic should be understandable without the text; the text should be understandable without the graphic; the text should repeat the most important information in the graphic. Figure 9.26 provides an example.

A Note on How Graphics Frame Data Rhetorically

Note that graphs are designed to tell a story hidden in a much larger set of data. Any graph necessarily selects some data from a larger set and omits other data. Because no graph can tell the whole story, it always frames its designer's selected data for rhetorical emphasis. The graph shown in the student example in Figure 9.26 (called Figure 1 in the example) tells a true story about the rapid increase in the use of wind and solar energy. But that graph doesn't tell the whole story. One of the things it omits is the gap between solar and wind production and the total energy needs of the United States. A graph telling this larger story appears in Figure 9.27.

Figure 9.27 Total U.S. energy consumption versus consumption of energy from wind and solar (quadrillion BTUs), 1950–2016

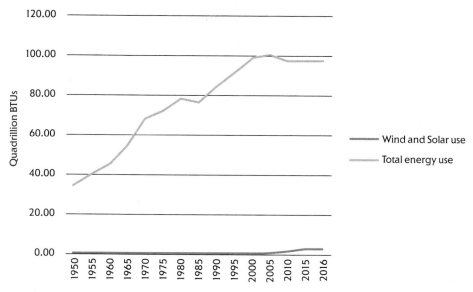

This graph no longer emphasizes the steep upward slope of solar and wind power usage. Rather, it emphasizes the huge difference between the total energy consumed in the United States and the comparatively tiny amount of wind and solar usage. Note that the vertical axis in Figure 9.27 goes from 0 to 120 quadrillion BTUs in increments of 20, while the same axis in the student graph in Figure 9.26 goes from 0 to 3 in increments of .5. The result in Figure 9.27 is to flatten out the wind/solar line until it is almost a straight, horizontal line. Both of these graphs (Figures 9.26 and 9.27) accurately use the original data in Table 9.2. Both are "true," but they tell different stories.

Conclusion

In this chapter we have explained the challenge and power of using visuals to create multimodal arguments. We have examined the components of visual design—use of type, layout, color, and images—and have shown how these components can be used for persuasive effect in arguments. We have also described the argumentative genres that depend on effective use of visuals—posters and fliers, advocacy advertisements, videos, cartoons, and websites—and invited you to produce your own multimodal argument. Finally, we showed you that graphics can tell a numeric story in a focused and dramatic way. Specifically, we explained the functions of tables, bar graphs, pie charts, and line graphs, showed you how to reference graphics and incorporate them into your own prose, and noted how graphs frame data rhetorically to tell a story but never the whole story.

Writing Assignment
A Visual Argument Rhetorical Analysis, a Visual Argument, or a Short Argument Using Quantitative Data

Option 1:
Writing a Rhetorical Analysis of a Visual Argument
Write a thesis-driven rhetorical analysis essay in which you examine the rhetorical effectiveness of a visual argument, either one of the visual arguments in this text or one specified by your instructor. Unless otherwise stated, direct your analysis to an audience of your classmates. In your introduction, establish the argumentative conversation to which this argument is contributing. Briefly summarize the argument and describe the visual text. Present your thesis, highlighting two or more rhetorical features of the argument—such as the way the argument appeals to *logos, ethos,* and *pathos*—that you find central to the effectiveness or ineffectiveness of this argument. To develop and support your own points, you will need to include visual features and details (such as color, design, camera angle, framing, and special effects) as well as short quotations from any verbal parts of the argument.

Option 2:
Multimodal Assignment: A Public Affairs Advocacy Ad, a Poster Argument, or an Advocacy Video
Working with the idea of an advocacy ad or poster argument that you explored in the For Writing and Discussion activity earlier in this chapter, use the visual design principles throughout the chapter; your understanding of visual argument and its genres; the Guidelines for Creating the Visual Elements in Posters, Fliers, and Advocacy Ads; the Guidelines for Creating Video Arguments; and your own creativity to produce a visual argument that can be displayed on your campus or in your town or city and/or posted somewhere on the web. Consider whether you will use photos or drawings. Try out the draft of your advocacy ad, poster, or video argument on people who are part of your target audience. Based on these individuals' suggestions for improving the clarity and impact of this visual argument, prepare a final version of your multimodal argument.

Option 3:
Multimodal Assignment: Cartoon
Choose a controversial issue important to you and create a single-frame political cartoon that presents your perspective on the issue in a memorable way. Use the cartoon strategies of mini-narrative, caricature, exaggeration, distortion, and the interaction between image and text.

Option 4:
A Short Argument Using a Quantitative Graphic
Write a short argument of one to two paragraphs that tells a story based on data you select from Table 9.2 or from some other table provided by your instructor or located by you. Include in your argument at least one quantitative graphic (table, line graph, bar graph, pie chart), which should be labeled and referenced according to standard conventions. Use as a model the short piece shown in Figure 9.26.

Chapter 10
An Alternative to Argument
Collaborative Rhetoric

Learning Objectives

In this chapter, you will learn to:

10.1 Explain the appropriateness and usefulness of collaborative rhetoric.

10.2 Explain the principles of collaborative rhetoric.

10.3 Prepare for collaborative rhetoric through reflective writing and discussion.

10.4 Write an open letter that demonstrates collaborative rhetoric by addressing and listening to someone who disagrees with you on an emotionally laden issue in order to open channels of communication and promote problem solving.

In Chapter 6, we introduced you to one-sided, multisided, and delayed-thesis arguments as strategies for persuading audiences with different degrees of resistance to your views. However, many argumentative situations you will encounter will not be conducive to persuasion.

In this chapter, we broaden your understanding of argument to include communication that does not seek to persuade but rather to promote listening. Simply put, sometimes situations are too populated by strongly divergent perspectives to make classical argument fruitful. In some situations, the lack of shareable assumptions or the commitment to religious or secular sacred values (principles that people believe are absolute—see Chapter 1) make persuading others to accept your views unrealistic. In such situations, simply listening to differing points of view can be powerful. Such listening can enlarge everyone's perspectives and move a community of stakeholders toward problem solving.

This chapter focuses on rhetorical situations in which speakers and writers face emotionally laden issues with substantial disagreement among stakeholders. The most hopeful strategy is to switch from argument toward communication that listens, seeks clarification and understanding, and explores common ground. People facing emotionally laden issues often find opposing perspectives highly threatening. At stake for all involved are our deep-seated values, strong emotions, and even our identities. To change our positions on some issues, we may think, is to change who we are. Therefore, instead of argument that seeks to change people's views, the goal of communication shifts to listening to one another, opening channels of exchange, and seeking mutual growth in perspectives.

As this chapter shows, the principles of collaborative rhetoric can be helpful in emotional situations perceived as threatening—situations that you will often encounter in your personal, academic, professional, and civic life. This chapter focuses on both discussion and written communication as means of collaborative rhetoric. It concludes by explaining how to write an *open letter* as collaborative rhetoric to someone with whom you disagree.

The Appropriateness and Usefulness of Collaborative Rhetoric

10.1 Explain the appropriateness and usefulness of collaborative rhetoric.

Much public communication today is mired in cross-purpose exchanges between people who don't "hear" opposing views. Stakeholders, who often have their emotions and identities entangled in issues and are wedded to their own sacred values, may not be willing to stop expressing their own views long enough to listen to other views. You will recognize situations like the following that involve clashing views and values.

- In one city community that has a "green belt" with a creek running through it, the question of land development has become an emotional issue. One group of people wants to widen and pave a path through the woods, turning this "wild" area into a park for all city residents. Another group opposes this development, believing that it will increase the volume of traffic in the neighborhood and disrupt the bird sanctuary. Several community meetings have ended in angry expressions of these clashing values, with some adamant about increasing accessibility to the public and others defending community safety and environmental preservation.

- Across the country, opinions of Planned Parenthood vary greatly. Some people view Planned Parenthood as an important healthcare provider and community service for women's overall health needs. They note that Planned Parenthood provides screenings for breast and cervical cancer, tests and treatment for STDs, and contraception. Others view Planned Parenthood mainly as an organization that provides abortions. Here, commitment to healthcare as a public good (including the right to preventive care) clashes with sacred pro-life values.

- A group of white students at a university don't see how their attitudes, words, and actions have made students from underrepresented minorities feel inferior and unwelcome. The white students point to the increase in acceptance of students from underrepresented groups as progress toward social justice. However, members of these underrepresented groups cite the insensitive remarks of roommates and racial judgments in classrooms as negatively affecting the climate of the university.

Impasses like these meet us at every turn in our public lives, and we could also find similar substantial disagreements in our personal lives.

Scholars who study political communication have demonstrated that our positions on conflicted issues are powerfully influenced by our emotions. In such situations, where our values and identities are at stake, we are unlikely to be persuaded by logical arguments. In the words of social psychologist Jonathan Haidt, "You can't change people's minds by utterly refuting their arguments."[1] So what kind of alternative communication is possible?

An approach that has been developed by scholars, professionals, and organizations across disciplines focuses on *collaborative rhetoric* rather than adversarial argument. The goal of collaborative rhetoric in speech and writing is to open dialogue by listening to others' perspectives in order to increase mutual understanding and enlarge vision. Collaborative rhetoric also promotes seeking common ground by identifying places where parties might find agreement. For example, pro-choice and pro-life advocates may never agree on a woman's right to an abortion, but they may share common ground in wanting to reduce teenage pregnancy. In other words, there is room for conversation, if not for agreement. In this sense, collaborative rhetoric shares the principles important to argument as truth-seeking, where arguers build bridges to their audience and seek audience-based reasons. However, relinquishing persuasion as a goal, collaborative rhetoric finds value simply in continuing the conversation, keeping channels of communication open in a search for a more complex view of the problem and provisional solutions.

The Principles of Collaborative Rhetoric

10.2 Explain the principles of collaborative rhetoric.

Current understanding of collaborative rhetoric has emerged from a convergence of many disciplines and organizations: rhetoric and composition scholars studying Rogerian communication based on the work of psychotherapist Carl Rogers; practitioners of intergroup dialogue who seek to promote social justice; leaders in nonviolent communication; leaders in conflict resolution such as the Harvard Negotiation Project and the Compassionate Listening Project; and feminist scholars such as Krista Ratcliffe, who focus on rhetorical listening as a means of ethical growth. All of these approaches teach constructive communication practices suited to situations of high emotional investment, friction, and difference. While many of these theorists emphasize face-to-face oral communication, others explore how collaborative rhetoric can involve reading and writing. Despite the different work these theorists and practitioners do, they all subscribe to four main

---

[1] *The Righteous Mind: Why Good People Are Divided by Politics and Religion.* Vintage, 2012, p. 57.

principles: nonjudgmental listening; identifying how values, emotions, and identities are involved; seeking common ground; and promoting openness to ongoing communication and change. We will explain each in turn.

Practicing Nonjudgmental Listening

The most important component of collaborative rhetoric is *nonjudgmental listening*: a commitment to listening to others' views for the purpose of simply understanding other perspectives. Because people are often threatened by other perspectives, the starting place must be an attitude of listening without judging and evaluating. As the manual for the Compassionate Listening Project states, "Everyone has a partial truth, and we must listen to, discern, and acknowledge this partial truth in everyone—particularly those with whom we disagree."[2] To help us appreciate each other's truths, to achieve the other's "frame of reference," Carl Rogers focuses on "empathic listening" between listeners to create a context "in which I see how the problem appears to you, as well as to me, and you see how it appears to me, as well as to you."[3] All proponents of collaborative rhetoric would agree with the Harvard Negotiation Project writers Douglas Stone, Bruce Patton, and Sheila Heen, who believe that the biggest attitudinal change with collaborative rhetoric is the shift from a *message-delivery stance* (speaking to tell others what we think, to prove a point, and to shape them to match our vision) to a *learning stance* (seeking to understand the other person's point of view, to initiate sharing conversations, and to learn from one another).[4]

To demonstrate that you are listening nonjudgmentally, with understanding and empathy, Rogerian scholars emphasize the importance of the *say back* practice, which obligates a listener to summarize a previous speaker's views fairly and accurately before speaking his or her own views. The *say back* principle is comforting to all participants because it ensures that all speakers are being listened to and understood.

Identifying Values, Emotions, and Identities

Not only does collaborative rhetoric ask us to acknowledge the validity of others' feelings and views, it also asks us to reflect on our own values, emotions, and identities. Because conflicts threaten us on multiple levels, we need to use the reflective process to get in touch with our own emotional investments in issues. In situations of high threat and tension, it is important for speakers and writers to take stock of the attitudes they are bringing to the conflict.

To truly listen, we must acknowledge our own feelings. As Stone, Patton, and Heen say, "What is the story we are telling ourselves that is giving rise to how we feel?" We must recognize how our own identities are involved in the conflict.

[2*] Carol Hwoschinsky. *Listening with the Heart: A Guide for Compassionate Listening*. 3rd Ed. Compassionate Listening Project, p. xii.

[3] Rogers, *On Becoming a Person: A Therapist's View of Psychotherapy*. Houghton Mifflin, 1961, p. 336.

[4] We are indebted to the approaches explained in Douglas Stone, Bruce Patton, and Sheila Heen's, *Difficult Conversations: How to Discuss What Matters Most*, 10th Anniversary Ed., Penguin, 2010. This book, an outgrowth of the Harvard Negotiation Project, has had years of success in helping people who are in business, professional, and personal conflicts communicate to improve their relationships and the quality of their lives.

What is at stake for us? Why are we threatened by the other's perspective? What role do our past experiences and self-interest play in our interpretations of the issue and of others' views?

The powerful growth-promoting potential of this reflective practice, which tasks us to look inward honestly, is enhanced by its outward direction of listening to—and understanding—someone else's threatening view. We are invited to enlarge our own view, to role-play new perspectives, to turn walls into windows. Collaborative rhetoric urges writers to play Peter Elbow's "believing game," where the writer must try to see from the perspective of someone who holds unwelcome ideas. (See our discussion of the believing and doubting game in Chapter 8.) This living within an unappealing idea (Elbow calls it "dwelling in") often compels writers to articulate their own values and to achieve a new understanding of them. Collaborative rhetoric thus promotes a writer's self-examination, exploration of multiple perspectives on a problem, and a willingness to consider change. This double process of reflection and exploration can in turn lead to a change of mind or at least to a deeper understanding of a problem.

Seeking Common Ground

Collaborative rhetoric also involves seeking common ground through sharing perspectives in dialogic exchange. In focusing on conversation and addressing a problem of mutual concern, speakers/writers need to discover areas of agreement between their perspectives and their audience's positions and to highlight areas of agreement. We have stressed this search for common ground in earlier chapters in our discussions of truth-seeking and audience-based reasons. But in classical argument, the goal is to use these audience-based reasons to further a claim. In collaborative rhetoric, the goal is simply to put multiple perspectives side by side and in conversation, with the goal of creating a foundation for ongoing conversation and problem solving.

For example, suppose that you are an environmentalist in conversation with a pro-oil-and-coal advocate with a "Drill, baby, drill" bumper sticker. Do you share any common ground that might reduce tension and establish conditions for continued conversation and problem solving? Collaborative rhetoric urges you first to summarize the other person's position empathically. You need to walk in that person's shoes, understanding his or her concern for the jobs of oil workers, coal miners, highway construction workers, and owners of local gas stations. You must also appreciate that this person views fracking as an engineering wonder that recovers natural gas and promotes energy independence. Finally, you must feel this person's anger at the way government regulations stifle energy production and at the hypocrisy of environmentalists who drive cars and fly on airplanes.

Once you understand these views, your own reflective practice urges you to find (or grow toward) some common ground. Perhaps you might show this person that you too value people's jobs, that you agree with the importance of energy independence (so that we don't have to import foreign oil), that you appreciate recent advances in safe drilling technology, and that you are disturbed by people who deny our country's vast energy needs. You also agree that it is unrealistic to pretend that we can dispense with our fossil fuel needs overnight. Your effort to understand your audience's views and to build bridges between you and your audience will encourage dialogue and make your audience more likely to listen when you offer your perspective.

Promoting Openness to Ongoing Communication and Change

Finally, collaborative rhetoric emphasizes negotiation and mutual openness to change. It aims to keep the conversation going. Contrary to adversarial argument, which rebuts opposing views and seeks to win others over, collaborative rhetoric takes what Stone, Patton, and Heen call an "And Stance"—the ability to hold different views in mind without pressuring any parties to give up their views. According to Stone, Patton, and Heen, instead of feeling forced to choose between these two stories, we can use the And Stance to recognize the complexity of the world and "embrace both" stories.[5] Think in terms of learning and opportunity, not pressure. The act of listening, seeking to understand, and being heard yourself will often lead to an enlarged vision that reflects the input of both perspectives.

Consequently, collaborative rhetoric often does result in changed perspectives. We feel as if we have "grown" into a new perspective without persuasive pushing on either side, which is often threatening. As Peter Elbow says in reference to the believing game, sometimes ideas hold onto us too tightly, and we can let go only by entering into the perspective of those who think differently. From the vantage point of the other, we gain a fresh perspective on our own position. For scholar-teacher Krista Ratcliffe, who uses the terms "rhetorical listening" and "standing under" other perspectives (instead of simply "understanding"), collaborative rhetoric opens up awareness so we can "consciously integrat[e] this information into our world views and decision making."[6] As psychologists note, the experience of feeling heard, understood, and respected can often result in change. Indeed, collaborative rhetoric has potential to bring about change in both parties. Thus, we see how collaborative rhetoric becomes a foundation for further discussion and for problem solving.

All four of these principles concentrate on reducing antagonism toward those with different beliefs, initiating steps in understanding, cultivating mutual respect, and encouraging further problem-solving—in short, nurturing conditions for future exchanges. Collaborative rhetoric is appropriate and possible whenever speakers or writers seek to open up dialogue with people who hold quite different views and are themselves willing to work toward a bigger picture, a synthesis of views, or at least future exchanges.

For Writing and Discussion

Listening Empathically and Seeking Common Ground

The heated national debate over travel bans on immigrants and refugees from Muslim-majority countries is highlighted in the photos shown in Figures 10.1–10.3. The debate taps into deep-seated emotions of fear, anger, patriotism, and frustration. Should the United States take stringent measures to reduce the flow of immigrants and refugees into the United States, or should it rely on the already existing vetting process? Should the United States target travelers from specific countries? What will be the consequences to immigrants and refugees who already have family members residing in the United States? How do travel bans conflict with the premise of the United States as a nation of immigrants?

---

[5] Douglas Stone, Bruce Patton, and Sheila Heen, *Difficult Conversations: How to Discuss What Matters Most*, 10th Anniversary Ed., Penguin, 2010, pp. 39-40.

[6] Krista Ratcliffe, *Rhetorical Listening: Identification, Gender, Whiteness*. Carbondale, Southern Illinois University Press, p. 29.

Individual Task:

From the three photos, choose one that represents the position on immigration with which you most dis-agree. Then imagine that you are conducting a collaborative discussion with the people in the photo (or the people who made the banners or signs) and follow these thinking and writing steps:

1. What feelings and values of your own are bound up in your views on U.S. immigration policies? What aspects of your identity does this issue touch? Where might you feel threatened by this issue and the controversies it has spawned? Explore your own values and personal investment.
2. Employing nonjudgmental listening and the *say back practice*, summarize the views you think the people in your chosen photo hold. Write your summary in fair, neutral language that indicates your understanding and that would make your summary acceptable to the people with whom you disagree.
3. Finally, write a common-grounds paragraph in which you go beyond summary to show your respectful understanding of the values held by these people. Consider how these views might be valid. Demon-strate your empathy, and add an example of your own that shows how your views and those of the people in the photo could intersect.

Group Task:

As you share your summaries and common-grounds paragraphs with members of your class, role-play the people in the photo with whom the writer is trying to seek common values and a basis for collaborative prob-lem solving. From your assumed role, comment on how well the writer has understood and identified with your views and values.

Figure 10.1 Immigration ban protest

Figure 10.2 Immigration ban protest

Figure 10.3 Immigration ban protest

Preparing for Collaborative Rhetoric Through Reflective Writing and Discussion

10.3 **Prepare for collaborative rhetoric through reflective writing and discussion.**

We now turn to steps you can take to learn and feel comfortable with this mode of communication and to put the principles of collaborative rhetoric into practice.

Preparing for Collaborative Rhetoric Through Reflective Writing

Reflective writing can develop your understanding of your personal communication style, a step that can be important for your growth as a collaborative thinker, speaker, and writer. Because collaborative rhetoric seeks to promote growth in all parties, reflective writing, which is a quiet, introspective, and exploratory activity, can play a vital role in preparing speakers and writers to participate in collaborative rhetoric. Reflective writing can help you understand what you as a communicator bring to situations where major disagreement is involved. For example, you might reflect on how you usually behave in the midst of these difficult conversations. The following questions can serve as a preliminary self-inventory to prompt reflective writing.

REFLECTIVE SELF-INVENTORY OF COMMUNICATION HABITS

1. How would you assess your ability to listen in situations involving conflict?
2. In the midst of conflict, do you clam up, seek to escape, or jump in when you find yourself feeling threatened by a conversation? Think of an example.
3. When have you felt the need to speak out forcefully to defend your views? When have you listened calmly and nonjudgmentally to others' perspectives?
4. Can you remember a time when you changed your views as a result of listening to someone else? If so, how did your change come about?

Achieving self-awareness about how you tend to listen can help you prepare for conversations or group discussions where nonjudgmental listening is critical.

You might also employ reflective writing to prepare to enter a specific situation where you need to use collaborative rhetoric. Think of this reflective writing, most likely freewriting or short informal writing, as a valuable opportunity for you to explore your personal relationship with the controversial issue and with the people who disagree with you. Take stock of your past experiences, your feelings, your values, your identity, and your investment in the issue. For example, after reading a controversial article that you know your class will be discussing, you might write a reflection that enables you to probe and pour out your responses. Your reflection might even be a short narrative. Or you might try freewriting about your own investment in an issue before you conduct library research on it. The following questions may help you discover and reflect on what matters to you in this issue and why.

REFLECTING ON YOUR PERSONAL ENGAGEMENT IN AN ISSUE

1. How do thinking about this issue and hearing what others think about it make you feel?
2. Why do you think you feel concerned, bothered, anxious, or angry?
3. Can you identify the values you hold that are engaged in this conflict?
4. What aspects of your identity are involved in this conflict? What is particularly threatening to you?

The reflective writing that you do might be entirely for yourself, or your instructor might assign it as a preparation for a collaborative discussion or a lead-in to formal writing. Either way, it can help you achieve more self-understanding, which will in turn make you a more effective participant in collaborative rhetoric.

Practicing Collaborative Rhetoric in Discussion

For most of us, collaborative rhetoric challenges our inclinations, our habits, our past communication backgrounds, and our contemporary culture. It also steps outside our experience of formal argumentation. Therefore, it is useful to practice collaborative rhetoric principles, sometimes as incremental steps. This practice could take the form of trying out nonjudgmental listening when you listen to a friend or to a controversial campus speaker. It could entail making a conscious effort to seek out common ground with someone who challenges your views, or it could simply involve imagining respectful, unemotional ways to state your own views to people who disagree with you. These examples represent components of collaborative rhetoric. Practicing them can be useful in helping you develop communication skills for use in volatile situations.

The following exercise involving group listening and discussion calls on collaborative rhetoric practices.

For Writing and Discussion

Conducting a Collaborative Rhetoric Discussion

This oral and written exercise allows you to practice the principles of collaborative rhetoric, emphasizing nonjudgmental listening to your classmates' views on a controversial short YouTube video or article. Your instructor will show a controversial short YouTube video presenting an argument or assign an argumentative article on a controversial topic. Because the argument made in the video or reading will be controversial, you and your classmates will have widely different responses, so your challenge will be to listen and speak carefully and respectfully. After engaging with the video or article, follow these steps:

1. Individually freewrite for ten minutes your response to the video or article. What emotions, values, or aspects of your identity does this video or article engage? How do these relate to your response to the video or article? In what way is your identity involved in this issue? How might you feel threatened by the video or article's perspective? This personal reflection will deepen your contribution to the discussion.
2. As a class, conduct a collaborative discussion by following these steps.
   a. After someone in the class identifies a main problem at stake in this video or article, summarizes its argument, including its purpose and main points, this person starts the class discussion by offering a comment either praising or criticizing the video or article or agreeing or disagreeing with its perspective. This contribution (and others) could comment on the key points of the video or

(continued)

article's argument; its appeals to *logos, ethos, or pathos*; its effectiveness for its intended audience; its achievement of its purpose; or any other important or troubling aspect.

b. Each successive speaker begins by summarizing the comments of the person who spoke just before him or her. Modeling the *say back* rule, you cannot proceed to add your own comment to the discussion until the speaker before you has accepted your summary of his or her views as accurate and fair. If the person does not accept your summary, then you must try again and rephrase your statements so that that speaker will accept your summary.

Example:

Toni thinks that Annie Leonard's video against bottled water is not effective. She believes it is one-sided because it neglects to mention situations in which the only clean water is bottled water. (summary of previous speaker)

I agree that Toni has identified a weakness in this advocacy video. I think we need to consider how Leonard's choice of a target audience—people in developed countries, such as the United States, who drink a huge amount of bottled water when they have access to clean water from the tap—has substantially shaped the argument and tone of the video. (second speaker's new contribution to the discussion)

c. Each successive speaker should summarize the contribution of the person before, but this person could also loop back to summarize an earlier comment and respond to that.

d. Instead of mostly building on earlier comments, a more likely response is a clashing view, which needs to be toned down and shaped into an *And Stance* response.

Example:

I can see the importance of praising GetLit.org for opening up the world of artistic expression and activist art to young people. I am concerned, though, about the way this organization might promote the misunderstanding that all creative expression has to be activist and angry.

e. The collaborative discussion of the class's responses to the video or article proceeds until everyone has had a chance to try the dual roles of summarizer and contributor. The best comments—even while they disagree—exhibit a spirit of collaboration and seek to keep the conversation open. They might relate to, build on, find congruence with, or respectfully diverge from the points made by the preceding speaker. It is assumed that responses to the video or article will differ widely.

3. The final part of this exercise entails writing a reflection in response to these questions:
   a. To what extent has the the collaborative discussion clarified an issue or problem or reached a synthesized perspective?
   b. How has the collaborative discussion of this video or article enlarged your perspective of its issue?
   c. What was challenging for you about participating in a collaborative discussion?

Writing an Open Letter as Collaborative Rhetoric

10.4 Write an open letter that demonstrates collaborative rhetoric by addressing and listening to someone who disagrees with you on an emotionally laden issue in order to open channels of communication and promote problem solving.

The main setting for collaborative rhetoric in writing is two parties in conversation. Most practitioners of collaborative rhetoric focus on face-to-face conversations between disputants with the aim of reducing emotional threat and fear by abandoning the desire to persuade. The goal is to take the *And Stance*, wherein your view and the other person's view are both on the table for validation and respect. Rogerian psychotherapy, nonviolent communication workshops, and many negotiation processes are all rooted in this approach.

When we move from speaking to writing, it is easy to imagine this kind of face-to-face conversation carried on in real-time chat rooms or even by text or e-mail (although you lose all the important cues of body language, facial expressions, and tone of voice, though emojis can help). It is harder to imagine collaborative rhetoric in a stand-alone longer essay going in just one direction—from writer to reader/audience. However, the genre of the personal letter is quite conducive to collaborative rhetoric. The personal letter can also be converted into an "open letter" that can be read by a larger audience. In that case, the writer addresses a particular person but understands that a larger audience will also read this letter, including many people who agree with the person the writer is addressing in the letter. We now show you an example of an open letter written as collaborative rhetoric and then provide further instructions on how to write a letter like this yourself.

How do you find an issue and an audience for practicing collaborative rhetoric? In a classroom setting, a common way is for students to select an issue of their choice and then find an argument that strongly opposes their own stance on the issue. In the following example of an open letter written as collaborative rhetoric, student writer Colleen Fontana responds to an article written by Robert A. Levy, a senior fellow for constitutional studies at the Cato Institute, a libertarian think tank. In this open letter, Colleen conducts a collaborative discussion directed toward solving the problem of gun violence.[7] Annotations in the margins indicate how Colleen is practicing collaborative rhetoric principles.

Student Essay

An Open Letter to Robert Levy in Response to His Article "They Never Learn"

Colleen Fontana

Dear Robert Levy,

My recent interest in preventing gun violence led me to find your article "They Never Learn" in *The American Spectator* about the mass shooting at Virginia Tech in 2007. I was struck by the similarities between that incident and the recent shooting in Tucson, Arizona, where a young man gunned down U.S. Representative Gabrielle Giffords and nineteen others in a supermarket parking lot. Although your article came several years before this Arizona incident, we can see that gun violence remains an enduring issue. I have long struggled with the question of how we can reduce gun-related violence without detracting from an individual's right to own a gun. Your article shed new light on this question for me.

(continued)

Writer addresses the audience

Writer identifies the problem, shows its current timeliness (*kairos*), and establishes a cordial relationship with the audience

---

[7] We are indebted to Doug Brent for his insight that Rogerian communication can take the form of a letter addressed to the author of an article that a reader finds disturbing. See "Rogerian Rhetoric: Ethical Growth Through Alternative Forms of Argumentation." In *Argument Revisited; Argument Redefined,* eds. Barbara Emmel, Paula Resch, and Deborah Tenney (Thousand Oaks, CA: Sage, 1996), p. 81.

In neutral, fair terms, the writer demonstrates nonjudgmental listening as she summarizes the audience's previous argument without evaluation

Your article stresses the need for something different from our nation's current gun policies. You assert that the solution lies not in stricter gun control policies, but rather in "liberalized laws." According to you, Mr. Levy, it was primarily the existence of anti-gun laws on the Virginia Tech campus that prevented an armed citizen from saving the victims of the 2007 shooting. You comment that "gun control does not work. It just prevents weaker people from defending themselves against stronger predators." Your article gives detailed examples of studies that have substantiated that stricter gun laws have not resulted in lower murder rates. You also cite evidence that fewer crimes are likely to happen if the victim brandishes a gun, even if he or she never fires it. According to your article, stricter gun laws are doing nothing to help society, and your solution lies in relaxed laws, allowing more responsible citizens to carry concealed weapons.

Common ground: Writer identifies common values that she shares with her audience; she demonstrates empathic listening; she imagines instances where the audience's values make the most sense

Living on a college campus myself, I identify immediately with your concern for preventing school shootings. I appreciate that you are concerned with the safety of the students and the public, and I agree that there exists a need for greater safety on school campuses. I also agree that current gun laws are not effective, as is shown by the number of gun-related deaths that happen annually. Even though such laws exist, they are not likely to stop "crazed fanatics undeterred by laws against murder," as you say, from committing certain crimes. I particularly agree with you when you discuss the right of self-defense. I struggle with laws that forbid carrying a gun because I believe in the right of self-defense. As you mentioned in your article, instances do occur in which civilians carrying guns have the ability to save themselves and others. Although I have not experienced this situation personally, I have read of brave acts of self-defense and intervention. For example, my research turned up an article by John Pierce on *MonachusLex.com*, "It Takes a Gun to Stop a Gunman." In this article Pierce describes an occurrence in Richmond, Virginia, in July of 2009 where a store owner and several customers were saved from an armed robber by a civilian in the store who happened to be carrying a firearm. Even though Pierce is a long-time gun rights advocate and an NRA-certified instructor, the points he brought up were striking. If that civilian hadn't been carrying a gun in that store on that day, then everyone in the store might have been killed by the robber. This realization resonates with me. I imagine myself in that store, and I know I would have been quite grateful that he was carrying a weapon that saved my life. Reading this story has forced me to think of the responsibility many gun-owning citizens must feel—a responsibility to protect not only themselves but those around them as well. A similar event happened recently in New York where a person attempting to rob a jewelry shop was shot by the owner in an act of self-defense. His neighbors regard him as a hero (Kilgannon).

Writer moves respectfully to an And Stance. She presents her own questions and differing perspectives on the problem. Note her tone of negotiation and her willingness to engage in further discussion

While I agree with you that self-defense is an important right and that armed citizens can sometimes prevent the death of innocent people, I wonder whether the possibility of allowing more guns in public through liberalized gun laws is the best solution. Is there a chance more guns in the hands of more people would foster a more danger-prone climate both from accidents and from sudden fits of rage? I was surprised to learn from a recent *New York Times* article by Charles M. Blow that for every ten people in America there are nine guns. Among major nations, according to a U.N. study, we have both the highest ratio of guns to people and the highest incidence of violence. If liberalizing gun ownership will lead to even more guns, then my concern is that there will be a higher chance of children finding a loaded gun in a parent's bed stand or of deaths caused by gang warfare or from momentary rage in an escalating fight between neighbors. Such danger could also exist on school campuses if guns were allowed. On a campus where drinking nurtures the party scene, I worry that rowdy people waving a gun perhaps as a joke might turn a party into a tragedy. Do you have any ideas, Mr. Levy, for reducing gun accidents or irresponsible use of firearms if they are widely available?

I found your point about owning a firearm for self-defense really thought provoking. But even if Virginia Tech had allowed guns on campus, what are the odds that an armed student or teacher would have been at the right place at the right time with an actual chance of shooting the gunman? Only in the movies are good guys and heroes *always* on the spot and capable of taking the right action to protect potential victims. Although I can really see your point about using handguns for self-defense, I don't think self-defense can be used as a justification for assault weapons or automatic weapons with large clips. If guns were freely allowed on campuses, perhaps massacres such as the one at Virginia Tech might occur more often. Or is there a way to allow people to carry concealed handguns on campus but still to forbid rifles, shotguns, or other weapons more useful for massacres than for self-defense?

After reading your article I have more understanding of the arguments in favor of guns, and I continue to ponder the ethical and practical issues of gun control versus the right to self-defense. You have underscored for me the importance of our continuing to seek means of preventing these terrible massacres from happening in our nation's schools. You have also opened my eyes to the fact that no amount of enforcement of gun laws can deter determined people from using guns to harm others. I am not sure, however, that your proposal to eliminate gun-control laws is the best solution, and I am hoping that you might be willing to consider some of my reasons for fearing guns, especially assault weapons and automatic weapons that can be fired like machine guns. Perhaps we could both agree that pursuing responsible gun ownership is a step in the right direction so that we reduce the number of accidents, keep guns away from children, and reduce access to guns capable of unleashing mass murder. I am hopeful that with our common concern over the current ineffectiveness of gun laws and the desire for safety in our schools, we can find a reasonable solution while still preserving the human right of self-defense.

Sincerely,

Colleen Fontana

5

Writer expresses a second concern, one that Levy did not mention: assault weapons

Writer concludes her letter with a reiteration of the mutual concerns she shares with her audience; she acknowledges how her perspectives have been widened by Levy's views; she seeks to keep the channel of communication open; and she expresses interest in further problem solving

Works Cited

Blow, Charles M. "Obama's Gun Play." *The New York Times*, 21 Jan. 2011, www.nytimes.com/2011/01/22/opinion/22blow.html?_r=0.

Kilgannon, Cory. "After Shooting, Merchant Is Hero of Arthur Avenue." *The New York Times*, 12 Feb. 2011, www.nytimes.com/2011/02/18/nyregion/18arthur.html.

Levy, Robert A. "They Never Learn." *The American Spectator*, 25 Apr. 2007, spectator.org/articles/45477/they-never-learn.

Pierce, John. "It Takes a Gun to Stop a Gunman." *MonachusLex.com*, 15 July 2009, monachuslex.com/?p=262.

As Figure 10.4 shows, the open letter usually begins with context, a respectful address to the audience, and an expression of the problem of mutual concern. It adopts and maintains a *learning stance* by beginning with an empathic summary of the reader's view on the issue and then tries to articulate the writer's and reader's common ground of shared values or beliefs. Both the summary and the common grounds section allow you to hear the other story. The entire letter must be a *learning conversation*, not a *message-delivery* one. Ideally, the letter will help

Figure 10.4 Organization plan for an open letter as collaborative rhetoric

Introduction	• Address the audience and identify the problem that you and your audience want to solve. • Possibly show the timeliness (*kairos*) of the problem. • Try to establish a friendly or cordial relationship with the audience. • Possibly include information that shows your familiarity with the audience.
Summary of the Audience's Views	• Summarize the audience's views in a fair and neutral way that the audience would accept. • Show that you understand the audience's position. • Also show an understanding of, and respect for, the audience's values and beliefs; the goal of this "saying back" (Rogers' term) is to summarize these views in a way that will be entirely acceptable to the audience.
Common Ground	• Identify common ground you share with your audience. • Demonstrate your growth through empathic consideration of views that you would otherwise find threatening or unwelcome. • Show understanding of the audience's views by "indwelling" with them and perhaps by extending them to other situations through new examples. • Show how your views have been enlarged by empathic listening to the audience's ideas.
Contribution of New Points to the Negotiation	• Respectfully propose your own way of looking at this issue. • Through a respectful and inquiring tone, encourage the audience to listen and work with you to solve the problem.
Conclusion	• Possibly propose a synthesis of the two positions, discuss how both parties gain from an enlarged vision, or invite the audience to ongoing negotiation.

you loosen your hold on your own perspectives (how else will you grow?) while inviting readers to loosen theirs.

The *And Stance* enables you to fully engage with another view without compromising your values. In keeping with the And Stance, the open letter also has room for your own views, but it presents these views as "both/and" rather than "either/or." The conclusion of the open letter should demonstrate how sharing perspectives has enlarged your view of the problem as you have seen it through another's eyes. Remember that you don't have to abandon your values, but you do need to acknowledge that no one has the total perspective, the whole story. The concluding section of the letter should invite the audience to continue the conversation by writing back (or perhaps by meeting up somewhere for face-to-face conversation).

Using collaborative rhetoric requires writers (and speakers) to use language carefully, respectfully, and provisionally. Therefore, throughout the whole letter your language should be exploratory and negotiating. You are sharing, inviting, and considering. You are saying, "Let's share our perspectives and think this problem out together." Because you must stay in this listening/learning/loosening mode while focusing on collaboration and ongoing dialogue about a problem, you use a different vocabulary and sentence structure than you do when you argue. You are suggesting, offering, inviting, proposing, and encouraging your audience to consider the perspective that you are bringing to this conversation. You stay in this mode by asking questions, using language that is more tentative and provisional than you would if you were arguing. For example, collaborative rhetoric often uses what psychotherapists call "I statements" that avoid blaming the other party.

> **Blaming statement:** Your pro-oil views are destroying the earth.
>
> **I statement:** When I think of how much we all drive our cars, I fear that the earth is at risk.

In addition to "I" statements, you can focus on word choices that don't imply anger or blame and that ask questions rather than make strong assertions. You can offer your own view along with examples to support it, but you must treat these as points of consideration, not as rebuttals to the other party. Your sign-off in your letter must maintain a *learning stance*, keeping the door open for future dialogue.

The following guidelines can help you engage in collaborative rhetoric by preparing you to assume a *learning stance* rather than an argumentative stance. These guidelines can serve as reminders in situations that involve either speaking or writing. We suggest you focus on them in writing your open letter as collaborative rhetoric.

Guidelines for Practicing Collaborative Rhetoric

1. Demonstrate nonjudgmental listening.
   - Assume a *learning stance*, giving space and time to the other party's expression of ideas.
   - Employ the Rogerian *say back* rule by accurately summarizing what you have heard from or read by the other party.
   - Ask questions but resist all evaluations.
   - Show a desire to understand the other's position logically and emotionally.

2. Reflect on the way your own values, feelings, and identity are involved.
   - Identify either in your own mind or by articulating orally or on paper your own investment in the issue.
   - What is potentially threatening to you in this issue? What emotions does this issue arouse in you? What values does it tap?
   - How is your identity involved?

3. Seek common ground in a problem-solving spirit.
   - What similarities can you find between your views and that of the other party?
   - Under what conditions can you imagine the other party's perspective making sense to you?
   - How can you show that you have seen the issue sympathetically from the other party's perspective or *frame of reference*?
   - Can you add examples of your own to the other party's position?

4. Practice the *And Stance* and open channels for mutual change and further conversation.
   - What points of your own do you want to contribute to the discussion? Ask questions about particularly difficult points of disagreement and lay your view side-by-side rather than falling into assertive *message-delivery mode*.
   - How have your views been influenced by those of the other party?
   - What can you integrate into your own perspective?
   - How can you imagine steps toward problem-solving and further exchanges?

Conclusion

This chapter explained how collaborative rhetoric offers an alternative mode of communication to the persuasive purpose of classical argument. Collaborative rhetoric is appropriate in rhetorical situations involving pronounced disagreement and potential threat to values, feelings, and identities. This chapter has discussed how collaborative rhetoric seeks to reduce threat; promote active, non-judgmental listening; seek common ground; and open ongoing, problem-solving discussion. Finally, the suggestions for preparing for and practicing collaborative rhetoric, the explanation of the open letter as collaborative rhetoric, and the Guidelines for Practicing Collaborative Rhetoric have offered you direction in participating in this kind of communication.

Writing Assignment

An Open Letter as Collaborative Rhetoric

Write an open letter employing collaborative rhetoric addressed to a specific person, either someone you know, someone you have heard deliver a speech, or the author of an article that has disturbed you. As you generate ideas for your letter, take stock of what you know about your own feelings and values on the issue on which you and your audience disagree. Think about your audience and summarize the person's views in a way that your audience would find satisfactory. Demonstrate nonjudgmental listening as you adopt a learning stance. As you explore what your audience values and believes in, also explore how your own values differ. Where do you agree with your audience? Under what conditions would you find your audience's values acceptable? How might the *And Stance* serve you? Follow the suggestions in the Guidelines for Practicing Collaborative Rhetoric in your open letter. Can you envision a synthesis of views, or depending on the distance between your views and your audience's, your goal may be simply to put your different perspectives into conversation, to encourage mutual listening, and to open up a discussion.

Imagine that your letter will be printed in a newspaper, so keep in mind that a larger audience beyond the person addressed in the letter will read it. In addition to Colleen Fontana's open letter on gun issues, we offer an additional example, Monica Allen's "An Open Letter to Christopher Eide in Response to His Article 'High-Performing Charter Schools Can Close the Opportunity Gap'" as a reading. Your instructor may ask you to attach a reflective response in which you describe how your experience of writing collaborative rhetoric in your open letter differed from your experience of writing classical arguments.

Reading

Student writer Monica Allen wrote her open letter as collaborative rhetoric as part of her larger research project to understand the stakes involved in her state's expansion of charter schools. Her instructor asked her to provide a Works Cited list to document all the sources she draws on in the letter.

Student Essay

An Open Letter to Christopher Eide in Response to His Article "High-Performing Charter Schools Can Close the Opportunity Gap"

Monica Allen

Dear Mr. Eide,

I want to thank you for your article "High-Performing Charter Schools Can Close the Opportunity Gap," which contributes to the national conversation about the role of charter schools in education reform. Like you, I am concerned about whether publicly funded, privately run charter schools can provide innovative new approaches to increase the quality of education for minority and economically disadvantaged students. I have been wrestling with the claims that charter schools can help reduce this troubling opportunity gap. Your helpful article has deepened my understanding of charter schools and has given me much to think about.

Your article proposes legislation specifically designed to create high-performing, effective charter schools. What is most exciting in your article is your suggestion that this legislation has the potential to close the opportunity gap. Citing the Stanford Center for Research on Education (CREDO) study and national charter efforts like the Knowledge is Power Program (KIPP), which focus on achievement gains for low-income students in some charter schools, you believe that increased charter education will enable our

(continued)

nation to better educate academically underserved students. Ultimately, you want to look beyond the inconsistent results charter schools have historically shown nationwide and urge our state to focus its charter-school innovation on improving opportunities for its students suffering most from the opportunity gap.

Your encouraging article speaks to the belief I share with you that the highest priority in educational innovation needs to be closing the opportunity gap. As education researcher Sean Reardon has shown in "The Widening Income Achievement Gap," the differences in opportunities and outcomes between low- and high-income background students have continued to widen throughout the past three decades. Clearly, we are in desperate need of more and better educational improvement. I share your concern that charter schools, focusing on the wrong objectives, could become a force that widens, rather than narrows, the opportunity gap. I particularly appreciate your commitment to concentrating reform efforts where they are needed most—with students from low-income backgrounds who are disproportionately left behind in traditional public schools. As an English Language Learning (ELL) tutor and teacher, I am encouraged that the CREDO study you cite indicates that some charter schools produce better gains for ELL students than do traditional public schools. I am grateful that you advocate for underserved students, such as English Language Learners, and am now much more interested in understanding the charter movement because of your conviction that it can address our most pressing educational issue.

Your article also answers some of my prior concerns about charter schools, making me more open to charter education. In particular, I have been wary of the inconsistent performance of charter schools nationwide, and so I appreciate that you support rigorous legislation to hold charter schools accountable to the highest standards possible. Your article also helped dispel some of my concerns that charter schools tend to serve disproportionately higher-income students and thereby segregate our schools into high-income charters and low-income traditional public schools. It led me to do more research about charter schools' student demographics and to find that there are many examples of charters serving primarily low-income groups of students. Finally, I appreciated your article's urgency. I, too, believe that the needs of disproportionally poorly educated, low-income students today make this issue a pressing one that calls for immediate action.

5 Because your article awakened me to the social benefits that charter schools can provide, I'd like to share with you four reservations in the hopes that, together, people like us who hold different perspectives on charter schools can learn from one another and better close our education opportunity gap.

First, I share your belief that charter schools offer needed opportunities to be education laboratories—places whose freedom from bureaucracy enables them to test out new strategies that can inform widespread practices. However, are charter schools really experimental? Adamant charter school supporter and Columbia University researcher Priscilla Wohlstetter writes that despite her belief in the prospects of charter schools generally, "most [charter schools] do little to tap the potential of unique, innovative strategies. For all the hype, charters typically borrow familiar classroom strategies (back-to-basics, project-based learning, college prep) from private and traditional public schools." I share Wohlstetter's concern that while the education laboratory concept has popularized charter schools, research demonstrates they have not functioned as such in our education system. Though I am encouraged by your commitment to highly regulated charter schools, I am unsure whether state legislation that regulates only based on the test results of charter-school students really ensures that charters deliver what they intend to. Perhaps we should explore other means to measure innovation to ensure that the investment of public funds in charter schools results in gains for the education system as a whole, in part by demonstrating that charter schools can teach us how to teach better. That would be a partnership between public and charter education that I believe we all hope to see.

A second question I have is whether charter schools will make innovative learning more accessible to students who are traditionally underserved. While the CREDO study you cite shows some promising results, Jean Allen, head of the Center for Education Reform, has questioned the conclusiveness of the data (Sanchez). Indeed, researchers across the board believe that the jury is very much still out on the question of whether charter-school students really learn as much as traditional public-school students, which is why the National Alliance for Public Charter Schools and Harvard University just started afresh with a comprehensive study last fall. I am concerned that we may be implementing a system that has yet to be effectively tested. I do think the anecdotal evidence you cite about KIPP schools is extremely exciting and deserves public attention, because KIPP schools serve a majority of low-income student populations *and* are outperforming traditional public schools near them. But shouldn't we also consider that KIPP schools rely heavily on significant private donations and are unique among charters in this way? To me, it makes sense that KIPP schools outperform other local schools when their operating budgets are 30–50 percent higher (Di Carlo). Could we agree that the results of this disparity in school funding call for more investigation?

I also have a third, more fundamental question with respect to charter schools. I wonder whether in the enthusiasm to innovate our schools, we will lose sight of that which makes American education innovative at its core—its commitment to democratic education. I am concerned that charter schools focusing on low-income student bodies might contribute to the nondemocratic socioeconomic and ethnic segregation of our schools. I believe that the segregation of schools into the haves and have-nots is one of the largest issues facing our national education system. Could charter schools that concentrate on serving low-income and traditionally underserved ethnic groups unintentionally widen the gap? Along with education activist and writer Jonathan Kozol (Cody), I fear that charter schools with names like "Black Success Academy" and "The African-American Academy for Leadership and Enterprise" divert attention from what really needs to be attended to—the de-segregating of our already divided schools and our school funding along lines of race and socioeconomic status. While I, like you, want us to do everything we can immediately to improve the chances for underserved students, I am most interested in focusing our efforts on

(continued)

equalizing our schools' demographics and budgets. How can charters and traditional public schools work together to do this?

Finally, Mr. Eide, I also wonder whether privatizing education will ultimately be in the best interest of students on the low spectrum of the opportunity gap. Public education promises public responsibility to educate each of its students for successful vocational and civic lives. Right now, you and I both know that the American public has not been living up to that responsibility. How can we do better? I am concerned that privatizing education removes not only the public investment in education (namely, tax dollars) from public hands, but also diminishes our sense of responsibility and capacity to be a nation that educates all its citizens. I wonder whether, in the long run, the students who stand to lose the most from the public's loss of responsibility to educate all are those who are the most vulnerable. How can charter and traditional schools work together to build public confidence in the civic power of education?

Because my own home state will soon be instituting new charter schools, I am thankful for having read your article. Clearly, people who hold different views about the potential of charter schools have much to learn from one another. I hope to see my home state pioneer cutting-edge methods for charter-school regulation and to build relationships between charter- and public-school communities so that the existence of charter schools in our state has a large-scale impact. I am very glad to have read your article and to know that many advocates of charter schools are committed to equalizing opportunity in education.

Regards,

Monica Allen

Works Cited

Cody, Anthony. "Confronting the Inequality Juggernaut: A Q&A with Jonathan Kozol." *Education Week: Teacher*, 18 July 2011, blogs.edweek.org/teachers/living-in-dialogue/2011/07/time_to_get_off_our_knees_why.html.

Di Carlo, Matthew. "Controversial Consensus on KIPP Charter Schools." *Albert Shanker Institute*, 12 Mar. 2013, www.shankerinstitute.org/blog/controversial-consensus-kipp-charter-schools.

Eide, Christopher. "High-Performing Charter Schools Can Close the Opportunity Gap." *The Seattle Times*, 11 July 2012, www.seattletimes.com/opinion/high-performing-charter-schools-can-close-the-opportunity-gap.

Reardon, Sean F. "The Widening Income Achievement Gap." *Educational Leadership*, vol. 70, no. 8, 2013, pp. 10-16.

Sanchez, Claudio. "The Charter School vs. Public School Debate Continues." *NPR Education*, 16 July 2013, www.npr.org/2013/07/16/201109021/the-charter-school-vs-public-school-debate-continues.

Wohlstetter, Priscilla. "The Debate Must Move On: Charter Schools Are Here to Stay." *WNYC: School Book*, 9 Dec. 2013, www.wnyc.org/story/charter-schools-are-here-stay-now-lets-have-useful-conversation-about-them.

Thinking Critically About "an Open Letter to Christopher Eide in Response to His Article 'High-Performing Charter Schools Can Close the Opportunity Gap'"

1. How does Monica Allen establish a context and a collaborative tone and purpose in the opening of her letter?

2. How does Monica's summary indicate that she has listened nonjudgmentally to Christopher Eide's perspective?

3. Where does Monica indicate that she is engaged in problem-solving with Eide and seeking to find common ground (that is, points of agreement with him)?

4. The bulk of Monica's open letter indicates that her views differ substantially from Eide's. In the face of these diverging perspectives, how does she employ the *And Stance* and avoid assuming a *message-delivery* manner? What specific examples do you see of her careful choice of language and sentence structure?

5. How well does the close of Monica's letter demonstrate an enlarged perspective and maintain open channels for future communication?

PART FOUR
Arguments in Depth: Types of Claims

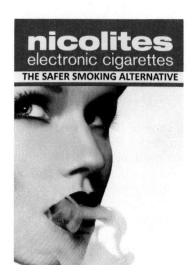

This advertisement for Nicolites is one voice in the public controversy over e-cigarettes. The ad claims that e-cigarettes are safer than regular cigarettes but chooses to use the word "smoking" rather than the more sanitized word "vaping." The vapor from e-cigarettes usually has nicotine (and may have added flavors or aromas) but not the tar that cigarettes have. However, as the discussion in Chapter 11 shows, the safety, healthfulness, and advisability of e-cigarettes are hotly debated. Think about the strategies from Chapter 9 on analyzing visual texts. How do the words and images in this ad work together to make positive claims about e-cigarettes?

Chapter 11
An Introduction to the Types of Claims

Learning Objectives

In this chapter you will learn to:

11.1 Identify different claim types and their characteristic patterns of development.

11.2 Use strategies based on claim types to help focus an argument, generate ideas for it, and structure it persuasively.

11.3 Be mindful of how different claim types work together in hybrid arguments.

In Parts One, Two, and Three of this text, we showed how argument entails both inquiry and persuasion. We explained strategies for creating a compelling structure of reasons and evidence for your arguments (*logos*), for linking your arguments to the beliefs and values of your audience (*pathos*), and for establishing your credibility and trustfulness (*ethos*). We also showed you how to think about arguments rhetorically, how to do a rhetorical analysis of both verbal and visual texts, and how to use collaborative rhetoric as an alterative to classical argument.

Now, in Part Four, we examine arguments in depth by explaining five types of claims. Each type has its own characteristic patterns of development and support. Because almost all arguments use one or more of these types of claims as "moves" or building blocks, knowing how to develop each claim type will advance your skills in argument. The claims we examine in Part Four are related to an ancient rhetorical concept called *stasis*, from a Greek term meaning "stand," as in "to take a stand on something." There are many competing theories of stasis, so no two rhetoricians discuss stasis in exactly the same way. In Part Four, we present a version of stasis theory based on five types of claims. Studying these claim types will increase your flexibility and sophistication as an arguer.

The Types of Claims and Their Typical Patterns of Development

11.1 Identify different claim types and their characteristic patterns of development.

To appreciate what a study of claim types can do, imagine one of those heated but frustrating arguments in which the question at issue keeps shifting. Everyone talks at cross-purposes, with each speaker's point unconnected to the previous speaker's. Suppose your heated discussion is about the use of steroids. You might get such a discussion back on track if you say: "Hold it for a moment. What are we actually arguing about here? Are we arguing about whether steroids are a health risk or whether steroids should be banned from sports? These are two different issues. We can't debate both at once." Whether you recognize it or not, you are applying the concept of claim types to focus the argument.

To understand how claim types work, let's return to the concept of stasis. A stasis is an issue or question that focuses a point of disagreement. You and your audience may agree on the answer to question A and so have nothing to argue about. Likewise, you may agree on the answer to question B. But on question C you disagree. Question C constitutes a stasis where you and your audience diverge. It is the place where disagreement begins, where as an arguer you take a stand against another view. Thus you and your audience may agree that steroids, if used carefully under a physician's supervision, pose few long-term health risks but still disagree on whether steroids should be banned from sports. This last issue constitutes a stasis, the point where you and your audience part company.

Rhetoricians have discovered that the kinds of questions that divide people have classifiable patterns. In this text we identify five broad types of claims—each type originating in a different kind of question. Table 11.1 gives you an overview of these five types of claims, each of which is developed in more detail in

Table 11.1 Five Types of Claims about Truth or Value

Claim Type and Generic Question	Examples of Issue Questions	Typical Methods for Structuring an Argument
Claims about Truth (Reality or the Way Things Are)		
Definitional arguments: *In what category does this thing belong?* (Chapter 12)	• Is solitary confinement cruel and unusual punishment? • Is a skilled video game player an athlete?	• Create a definition that establishes criteria for the category. • Use examples to show how the contested case meets the criteria.
Resemblance arguments: *To what is this thing similar?* (Chapter 12)	• Is requiring someone to buy medical insurance like requiring him or her to buy car insurance? • Is addiction to sugar like addiction to tobacco?	• Let the analogy or precedent itself create the desired rhetorical effect. [or] • Elaborate on the relevant similarities between the given case and the analogy or precedent.
Causal arguments: *What are the causes or consequences of this phenomenon?* (Chapter 13)	• What are the causes of bee colony collapse disorder? • What might be the consequences of raising the minimum wage to a living wage?	• Explain the links in a causal chain going from cause to effect, or summarize experimental studies showing cause or consequence.

(Continued)

Claim Type and Generic Question	Examples of Issue Questions	Typical Methods for Structuring an Argument
Claims About Values		
Evaluation and ethical arguments: *What is the worth or value of this thing?* (Chapter 14)	• Is talk therapy a good approach for treating anxiety? • Is it ethical to use reproductive technology to make "designer babies"?	• Establish the criteria for a "good" or "ethical" member of this class or category. • Use examples to show how the contested case meets the criteria.
Proposal arguments: *What action should we take?* (Chapter 15)	• Should medical insurance policies be required to cover contraception? • Should the federal government enact a carbon tax?	• Make the problem vivid. • Explain your solution. • Justify your solution by showing how it is motivated by principle, by good consequences, or by resemblance to a previous action that the audience approves of.

subsequent chapters. It also shows you a typical structure for each type of argument. Note that the first three claim types concern questions of truth or reality, whereas the last two concern questions of value. You'll appreciate the significance of this distinction as you proceed through this chapter.

For Writing and Discussion

Identifying Types of Claims

Working as a class or in small groups, read the following questions and decide which claim type is represented by each. Sometimes there are several different ways to classify a claim, so if you believe that the question fits two categories, explain your reasoning.

1. Should the U.S. president be authorized to employ weaponized drones to kill terrorists?
2. Is taking Adderall to increase concentration on an exam a form of cheating?
3. What would be the economic consequences of a carbon tax aimed at reducing carbon emissions?
4. Is burning the U.S. flag an act of free speech?
5. Is the war on drugs really like fighting an actual war?
6. How effective is acupuncture in reducing morning sickness?
7. Is acupuncture quackery or real medicine?
8. Should universities ban the use of calculators during calculus exams?
9. Does the rodeo sport of riding bucking horses or bulls constitute cruelty to animals?
10. Why are couples who live together before marriage more likely to divorce than couples who don't live together before marriage?

Using Claim Types to Focus an Argument and Generate Ideas: An Example

11.2 Use strategies based on claim types to help focus an argument, generate ideas for it, and structure it persuasively.

Having provided an overview of the types of claims, we now show you some of the benefits of this knowledge. First of all, understanding claim types will help you focus an argument by asking you to determine what's at stake between you and your audience. Where do you and your audience agree and disagree? What are the questions at issue? Second, it will help you generate ideas for your argument by suggesting the kinds of reasons, examples, and evidence you'll need.

To illustrate, let's take the recent public controversy about e-cigarettes, which use a battery-powered heating element to vaporize the liquid in a small cartridge. The user inhales the vapor (an act often called "vaping"). Cartridges can be purchased containing various amounts of nicotine or no nicotine at all; flavored liquids (such as apple cinnamon or peach cobbler) are also available. Although there is debate about whether the vapors from e-cigarettes are harmful, everyone agrees that the nicotine-laced liquid itself is poisonous if ingested in its liquid form. In the absence of federal regulations, many states and cities have enacted their own laws about e-cigarettes, often treating them exactly as if they were real cigarettes—banning them from bars, restaurants, and other public places; forbidding their sale to minors; and restricting the ways they can be advertised.

Let's now take the hypothetical case of a city debating a policy on e-cigarettes. Imagine three different writers. Writer 1 wants to ban e-cigarettes, making them subject to the same restrictions as real cigarettes. Writer 2 wants to promote e-cigarettes as a preferred alternative to real cigarettes. Writer 3, a libertarian opposed to the nanny state, wants no restrictions on e-cigarettes other than forbidding sale of nicotine cartridges to minors and making sure that the liquid-containing cartridges are childproof. Let's consider how familiarity with claim types can help each writer generate ideas for his or her argument.

Writer 1: Ban E-Cigarettes

Writer 1, who believes that e-cigarettes are harmful, imagines a somewhat live-and-let-live audience inclined to take no action against e-cigarettes. Her goal is to portray e-cigarettes negatively in order to persuade this audience that e-cigarettes should be banned.

- **Definition argument:** Because regular cigarettes are already banned in public places, Writer 1 wants to place e-cigarettes in the same category as real cigarettes. For part of her argument she can use a definitional strategy, showing that e-cigarettes and regular cigarettes belong in the same category because both deliver nicotine extracted from tobacco leaves. She can argue that the differences between regular cigarettes and e-cigarettes, such as one producing smoke and the other vapor, are superficial. What makes them the same is the delivery of nicotine.

- **Resemblance argument:** Using a resemblance strategy, Writer 1 can also show how e-cigarettes are designed to look like regular cigarettes and make smoking look cool again. You can blow "smoke" rings with the exhaled vapor, just as you can with real tobacco smoke.

- **Causal argument:** To increase her negative portrayal of e-cigarettes, Writer 1 can also use a causal strategy. She can argue that e-cigarettes will hook children and teenagers on real cigarettes. She can show how flavored vapors such as "bubble gum" or "pancake" seem marketed to children and how the availability of cartridges that combine flavored vapors with nicotine give Big Tobacco a new way to create the next generation of nicotine addicts.

- **Evaluation argument:** Here Writer 1 will have to summarize and rebut counterviews that e-cigarettes are a good replacement for regular cigarettes.

Supporters will say the e-cigarettes are better than regular cigarettes because e-cigarettes contain fewer carcinogens (cancer-causing agents) and are thus safer. Writer 1 will need to argue that the negative aspects of e-cigarettes—nicotine addiction and the enticement of children toward smoking—outweigh their increased safety. She can also argue that the propellant ingredients in the cartridges have not yet been proven safe, and she can refer to research showing that the liquid itself is extremely poisonous if ingested directly.

- **Proposal argument:** The city council should ban e-cigarettes.

This example shows that writers often need to argue issues of reality and truth in order to make claims about values. In this case, Writer 1's proposal claim to ban e-cigarettes is based on reasons that are themselves derived from definition, resemblance, and cause: "E-cigarettes should be banned because they contain the same tobacco-derived nicotine as real cigarettes (definition), because they are advertised to make smoking look cool again (resemblance), and because they will hook kids on smoking (cause)."

Writer 2: Promote E-Cigarettes as a Preferred Alternative to Real Cigarettes

Writer 2 shares with his audience a belief that cigarettes are harmful and that smoking should be banned. However, he wants to emphasize the benefits of e-cigarettes to people who already smoke. Like Writer 1, he can use the five claim types to generate strategies for his argument.

- **Definition argument:** To portray e-cigarettes more positively, Writer 2 can make the definitional claim that e-cigarettes are *not* the same as real cigarettes and thus belong in a different category. He can argue that the essential trait of real cigarettes is cancer-causing tar derived from the combustion of tobacco leaves. It is the danger of the tar and secondhand smoke, not the nicotine, that gave rise to the anti-smoking movement in the first place. By arguing that the delivery of nicotine is a superficial rather than essential criterion for defining cigarettes, Writer 2 can show that e-cigarettes' absence of tar and secondhand smoke makes them essentially different from real cigarettes.

- **Resemblance argument:** Using a resemblance strategy, Writer 2 can show that although e-cigarettes are essentially different from real cigarettes, the two have pleasing similarities. Vaping provides the same physical and social pleasures as does smoking, but without the harm to self and others.

- **Causal argument:** Writer 2 can also portray e-cigarettes positively through the causal argument that they can save current smokers' lives by converting them from a dangerous way of getting nicotine to a less dangerous way of getting nicotine. Without condoning nicotine addiction, Writer 2 can point to the positive health consequences of getting a nicotine hit without the carcinogens. Writer 2 can also argue that e-cigarettes can help people stop smoking because vapers can gradually reduce the nicotine content in the cartridges they purchase.

- **Evaluation argument:** Here Writer 2 can claim that e-cigarettes are better than real cigarettes by arguing that the health benefits of no smoke and no tar outweigh the drawbacks of an addiction to nicotine, which in itself causes little health risk.

- **Proposal argument:** E-cigarettes should be promoted as a safe alternative to real cigarettes.

Writer 3: Place No Restrictions on E-Cigarettes

Writer 3 is a libertarian who dislikes nanny-state restrictions on our individual freedoms. She wants to argue that the only restrictions on e-cigarettes should be federally mandated childproofing of the cartridges, truth-in-labeling requirements about what the cartridges contain, and banning sales of nicotine-containing cartridges to minors.

- **Definition argument:** Writer 3, like Writer 2, can argue that e-cigarettes are in a different category from regular cigarettes. Unlike regular cigarettes, e-cigarettes present no proven dangers either to self or to others through secondhand smoke.

- **Resemblance argument:** To celebrate the libertarian endorsement of individual freedom, Writer 3 can show the resemblance between taking a pleasurable hit on an e-cigarette and other pleasures frowned upon by the nanny state—drinking sugary sodas, buying a Big Mac, or owning a muscle car.

- **Causal argument:** Whereas Writer 2 argues that e-cigarettes are safer than regular cigarettes, Writer 3 can argue that nobody has demonstrated any firsthand or secondhand health hazards for e-cigarettes. She can make the additional causal argument that government wants to treat e-cigarettes like regular cigarettes so that they can tax them heavily to produce "sin-tax" revenue. She can also argue that nanny-state regulations lead to the loss of personal freedoms and the shutting down of free enterprise.

- **Evaluation argument:** Writer 3 can argue that people should be free to make their own evaluations of e-cigarettes.

- **Proposal argument:** The city should place no restrictions on sales of e-cigarettes to adults.

Hybrid Arguments: How Claim Types Work Together in Arguments

11.3 Be mindful of how different claim types work together in hybrid arguments.

As the e-cigarette example shows, hybrid arguments can be built from different claim types. A writer might develop a proposal argument with a causal subargument in one section, a resemblance subargument in another section, and an evaluation subargument in still another section. Although the overarching proposal argument follows the typical structure of a proposal, each of the subsections follows a typical structure for its own claim type.

Some Examples of Hybrid Arguments

The following examples show how these combinations of claim types can play out in actual arguments. (For more examples of hybrid arguments, see Chapter 15, Tables 15.1 and 15.2, where we explain how lower-order claims about reality and truth can support higher-order claims about values.)

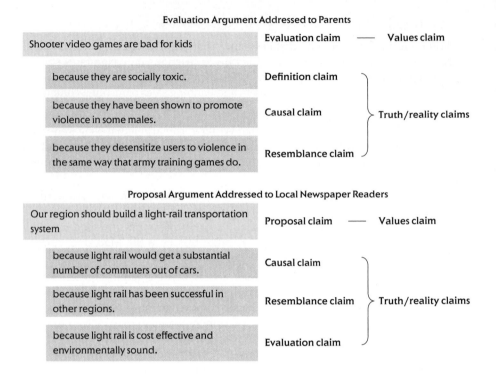

Evaluation Argument Addressed to Parents

Shooter video games are bad for kids	Evaluation claim —— Values claim
because they are socially toxic.	Definition claim
because they have been shown to promote violence in some males.	Causal claim
because they desensitize users to violence in the same way that army training games do.	Resemblance claim

Truth/reality claims (Definition claim, Causal claim, Resemblance claim)

Proposal Argument Addressed to Local Newspaper Readers

Our region should build a light-rail transportation system	Proposal claim —— Values claim
because light rail would get a substantial number of commuters out of cars.	Causal claim
because light rail has been successful in other regions.	Resemblance claim
because light rail is cost effective and environmentally sound.	Evaluation claim

Truth/reality claims (Causal claim, Resemblance claim, Evaluation claim)

For Writing and Discussion
Exploring Different Claim Types and Audiences

Individual task:

Choose one of the following issues and role-play one of the suggested authorial purposes. Write out your exploratory ideas for how you might use several of the claim types (definition, resemblance, cause, evaluation, proposal) to develop your argument. Use our example arguments about e-cigarettes as your models. Imagine an audience skeptical of your chosen position.

1. Carbon footprint: You want (do not want) the Environmental Protection Agency to regulate the amount of carbon dioxide that power plants can emit.
2. Gun restrictions: You want (do not want) the federal government to ban assault rifles and high-volume ammunition cartridges.
3. Diet: You want your classmates to adopt (or not to adopt) the paleo diet.
4. Minimum wage: You want (do not want) your city or state to adopt as its minimum wage a living wage of $15 per hour.
5. Some other issue that you think will be reasonably familiar to your classmates.

Group task:

Share with classmates your initial efforts to use the claim types to help generate ideas. What worked for you and what didn't? Where was it useful to think of the category in which something belonged (definition)? For example, is carbon dioxide a "pollutant," a "poison," or a "harmless and natural chemical compound"? Where was it helpful to think about resemblance? Is a paleo diet like a caveman's diet? How about cause and effect? What will be the consequences of raising the minimum wage? How did your thinking about issues of truth or reality help you develop evaluation or proposal claims?

An Extended Example of a Hybrid Argument

As the previous examples illustrate, different claim types often serve as building blocks for larger arguments. We ask you now to consider a more extended example. Read the following argument from *Outside Magazine* aimed at enthusiasts of outdoor sports such as hiking, camping, mountain climbing, skiing, biking, and distance running. The magazine's readers are often health-conscious consumers of multivitamins and other dietary supplements such as minerals, fish oils, herbals, botanicals, enzymes, antioxidants, amino acids, and other substances often ingested as tablets, capsules, powders, energy drinks, or energy bars. In this startling article, the writer uses recent scientific studies to make the evaluation claim that these supplements are either "useless" or "worse than useless." Notice how this overall evaluation claim is supported by claims from definition, resemblance, and cause.

Your Daily Multivitamin May Be Hurting You

ALEX HUTCHINSON

In June, at this year's European College of Sport Science conference in Barcelona, Mari Carmen Gomez-Cabrera, a physiologist at the University of Valencia and one of the world's leading experts on antioxidants, was debating the merits of supplements with two top researchers. For more than 90 minutes they went back and forth, parsing the accumulated evidence in front of a packed auditorium. Finally, Gomez-Cabrera landed on a provocative question that summarized her position.

Introduces the **evaluation** *issue "Are supplements good/bad?"*

The debate, she explained, isn't whether supplements are good or bad for athletes. Rather, it's "are they useless, or are they worse than useless?"

Restates **evaluation** *issue with implied claim: Supplements are either useless or worse than useless*

The question may come as a shock to the more than half of Americans who take some sort of dietary supplement—a vast catch-all term that includes everything from vitamins and minerals to herbal remedies to exotic performance boosters like deer-antler spray and glutamine. It's no surprise that the purported muscle-building supplements make unproven claims and may come with hazardous side effects. But in the past few years, Gomez-Cabrera and a growing number of researchers have come to believe that even respectable mainstream supplements such as vitamins C and E suffer from the same basic flaw: few apparent benefits and increasing evidence of negative effects. For example, in July's issue of the *Journal of Physiology,* researchers discovered that resveratrol, an antioxidant in red wine, actually limited the positive effects of cardiovascular exercise—like an increased VO2 max—when taken daily in high concentrations. In July, scientists at the Fred Hutchinson Cancer Research Center found that men with high levels of the omega-3 fatty acid DHA in their blood, often from fish-oil supplements, had a significantly greater risk of prostate cancer.

Further develops **evaluation claim:** *Supplements are bad because they make unproven claims and because they may come with hazardous side effects*

Uses **causal arguments** *to illustrate bad side effects*

According to Pieter Cohen, a professor at Harvard Medical School, there are really only two types of sports supplements: those that are safe but don't work, and those that might work but have side effects, especially at higher than normal levels. "If any supplement, no matter how beneficial, has a pharmaceutical effect, it's also got a downside," he says. "There's no way to get around that basic principle."

Definition claim: Supplements belong to one of two categories: (1) safe but don't work or (2) work but have bad side effects

Most supplements stay firmly in the first category. Taking a daily multivitamin, Cohen emphasizes, won't harm you, but it usually won't help either, which is why major health organizations such as the American Heart Association and the American College of Sports Medicine don't recommend supplements to healthy people.

Develops **definition** *argument by showing how supplements fit first category of being safe but useless* 5

It's not that vitamins and minerals aren't important. If you don't get enough vitamin C, you can get scurvy; without enough iron, you can become anemic; and if you live far enough north to see Russia from your backyard, you may need some extra vitamin D. But all three of these substances have also been linked to negative effects at high doses. Same goes for prolonged use of other common supplements such as vitamin E and calcium. In short, unless tests have shown that you're low in a particular vitamin or mineral, there's no evidence to suggest that you should take a daily supplement.

Causal argument showing bad side effects (places supplements in second category of being harmful)

That rule also applies if you're an athlete who takes supplements because, say, you assume your training requires an antioxidant boost to speed recovery. Gomez-Cabrera and her colleagues at the University of Valencia have shown that antioxidant supplements suppress the oxidative stress that signals your body to adapt and get stronger. The result: regular use of something seemingly innocuous such as vitamin C can actually block gains in endurance-boosting mitochondria.

Causal argument showing still more bad side effects

The balance between risk and return also works in subtler ways, as Wen-Bin Chiou, a psychologist at National Sun Yatsen University in Taiwan, has shown in a series of experiments on a phenomenon called the licensing effect. As part of a battery of tests, subjects were asked to take a pill; half were told the pill was a multivitamin, while the other half were told it was a placebo. In truth, they were all placebos.

Causal argument from psychology showing different bad effect: People who take supplements feel they are healthier and thus actually act in less healthy ways

In subsequent tests, the subjects who thought they'd taken a vitamin consistently behaved in less healthy ways. When asked to try out a pedometer, they were more likely to choose a shorter walking route; at lunch, they chose less healthy food. In follow-up studies, Chiou has also discovered that smokers who think they've been given a vitamin smoke more, and people who are given a weight-loss supplement are less likely to stick to their diet. The same thing happens when you go to the gym or eat a plate of spinach. The difference is that exercise and vegetables have real benefits, so you've still got a chance to come out ahead. If you take a pill with no benefits, the best you can do is break even.

Brief resemblance argument: Taking a vitamin is NOT like eating spinach or going to the gym

Which brings us back to Gomez-Cabrera in Barcelona. She, of all people, has enormous respect for the powers of micronutrients such as antioxidants—she has devoted her life to studying them. "But if you eat enough fruits and vegetables, five servings a day," she says, "I don't think you need anything else." And if you're not eating like that, then taking a pill isn't a solution. In fact, it may be part of the problem.

Conclusion

As this editorial demonstrates, awareness of different kinds of claims can help you increase your flexibility and effectiveness as an arguer. In the following chapters, we discuss each of the claim types in more detail, showing how they work and how you can develop skills and strategies for supporting each type of claim.

Chapter 12
Definition and Resemblance Arguments

Learning Objectives

In this chapter, you will learn to:

12.1 Explain what is at stake in arguments about definition and resemblance.

12.2 Explain four types of categorical arguments.

12.3 Explain the criteria-match structure of categorical arguments based on definition.

12.4 Use criteria-match reasoning to generate ideas for your own definition argument.

12.5 Write your own definition argument.

Arguments about definition or resemblance concern disputes about what category something belongs to, either directly by definition or indirectly or metaphorically through comparison or resemblance. They are among the most common argument types you will encounter.

Case 1: In What Category Does My Wad of Gum (Wrapped in Mustard-Stained Tissue) Belong?

This cartoon by Rina Piccolo poses a definitional issue. The ethically motivated hero of this cartoon, trying valiantly to do the right thing, ponders the criteria for each bin. Is her wad of tissue-wrapped gum "just plain old garbage"? Or is it perhaps "organic waste"? (The answer depends on how you define "garbage" versus "organic waste.") While pointing to the challenges of classifying waste, the cartoon gently mocks the bureaucratic mind that invents all these categories and then has to define them. In the wonderful way that cartoons can work, the cartoon's categorical choices can even define human actors. As long as the woman stands pondering, she defines herself as a "concerned environmentalist." But the next person might define herself as an environmental scoffer by chucking the wad of gum into the "no conscience" bin or the "climate change denier/polluter" bin. This cartoon both mocks environmentalists and honors the definitional difficulties of defining and sorting different kinds of waste.

Case 2: Is a Frozen Embryo a Person or Property?

An infertile couple conceived several embryos in a test tube and then froze the fertilized embryos for future use. During the couple's divorce, they disagreed about the disposition of the embryos. The woman wanted to use the frozen embryos to try to get pregnant, and the man wanted to destroy them. When the courts were asked to decide what should be done with the embryos, several questions of definition arose: Should the frozen embryos be categorized as "persons," thus becoming analogous to children in custody disputes? Or should they be divided up as "property," with the man getting half and the woman getting the other half? Or should a new legal category be created for them that regards them as more than property but less than actual persons? The judge decided that frozen embryos "are not, strictly speaking, either 'persons' or 'property,' but occupy an interim category that entitles them to special respect because of their potential for human life."*

What Is at Stake in an Argument about Definition and Resemblance?

12.1 Explain what is at stake in arguments about definition and resemblance.

Definition and resemblance arguments occur whenever a community disagrees about the category a particular person, thing, act, or phenomenon should be placed in or identified with. Here are some examples:

Issues Involving Categories

Question	Does this specific phenomenon . . .	. . . belong to (or is it similar to) this category?
Is atmospheric carbon dioxide a pollutant?	Atmospheric carbon dioxide	Pollutant
For purposes of our state's tax on candy, is a cough drop "candy" or an "over-the-counter drug"?	Cough drop	Candy (or over-the-counter drug)
Is women's obsession with thinness today similar in effect to women's footbinding in ancient China?	Women's obsession with thinness	Footbinding in ancient China

* See Vincent F. Stempel, "Procreative Rights in Assisted Reproductive Technology: Why the Angst?" *Albany Law Review* 62 (1999), 1187.

Much is at stake when we place things into categories because the category that something belongs to can have real consequences. Naming the category that something belongs to makes an implicit mini-argument.

Consequences Resulting from Categorical Claims

To appreciate the consequences of categorical claims, consider the competing categories proposed for whales in the international controversy over commercial whaling. What category does a whale belong to? Some arguers might say that "whales are sacred animals," implying that their intelligence, beauty, grace, and power mean they should never be killed. Others might argue that "whales are a renewable food resource" like tuna, crabs, cattle, and chickens. This category implies that we can harvest whales for food the same way we harvest tuna for tuna fish sandwiches or cows for beef. Still others might argue that "whales are an endangered species"—a category that argues for the preservation of whale stocks but not necessarily for a ban on controlled hunting of individual whales. Each of these whaling arguments places whales in a separate, different category that implicitly urges the reader to adopt that category's perspective on whaling.

Significant consequences can also result from resemblance claims. Consider the way that media analysts tried to make sense of the September 11, 2001, terrorist attacks on the World Trade Center and the Pentagon by comparing them to different kinds of previous events. Some commentators said, "The September 11 attacks are like Timothy McVeigh's bombing of the Alfred P. Murrah Federal Building in Oklahoma City in 1995"—an argument that framed the terrorists as criminals who must be brought to justice. Others said, "The September 11 attacks are like the 1941 Japanese attack on Pearl Harbor"—an argument suggesting that the United States should declare war on some yet-to-be-defined enemy. Still others said, "The September 11 attacks are like an occasionally disastrous earthquake or an epidemic," arguing that terrorists will exist as long as the right conditions breed them and that it is useless to fight them using the strategies of conventional war. Under this analogy, the "war on terror" is a metaphorical war like the "war on poverty" or the "war against cancer." Clearly, each of these resemblance claims had high-stakes consequences. In 2001, the Pearl Harbor claim prevailed, and the United States went to war, first in Afghanistan and then in Iraq. Many critics of these wars continue to say that war is an inappropriate strategy for fighting the "disease of terrorism."

The Rule of Justice: Things in the Same Category Should Be Treated the Same Way

As you can see, the category we place something into—either directly through definition or indirectly through comparison—can have significant implications for people's actions or beliefs. To ensure fairness, philosophers refer to the *rule of justice*, which states that "beings in the same essential category should be treated in the same way." For example, the problem of how the courts should treat the users or sellers of marijuana depends on the category marijuana belongs to. Marijuana might be placed in the same category as tobacco and alcohol, in which case the possession and sale of marijuana would be legal but subject to regulation and taxes. Or marijuana could be placed in the same category as meth, cocaine, and heroin; in this case, it would be an illegal drug subject to criminal prosecution. Some states have placed marijuana in the same category as penicillin and insulin, making it a legal drug so long as it is obtained from a licensed dispensary with a doctor's prescription. Many states are not happy with any of these categories and are trying to define marijuana in some fourth way.

To take another example, suppose your professor says that absence from an exam can be excused for emergencies only. How would you define "emergency"? Clearly, if you broke your leg on the morning of an exam, you would be excused. But is attending your grandmother's funeral or your best friend's wedding an "emergency"? How about missing an exam because your car wouldn't start? Although your interests might be best served by a broad definition of emergency, your professor might prefer a narrow definition, which would permit fewer exceptions.

The rule of justice becomes especially hard to apply when we consider contested cases marked by growth or slow change through time. At what point does a child become an adult? When does a binge drinker become an alcoholic, an Internet poker player a compulsive gambler, or a fetus a human person? Although we may be able arbitrarily to choose a particular point and declare that "adult" means someone at least eighteen years old or that "human person" means a fetus at conception, at three months, or at birth, in the everyday world the distinction between child and adult, between fetus and person, between Friday-night poker playing and compulsive gambling seems an evolution, not a sudden and definitive step. Nevertheless, our language requires an abrupt shift between categories. In short, applying the rule of justice often requires us to adopt a digital approach to reality (switches are either on or off, either a fetus is a human person or it is not), whereas our sense of life is more analogical (there are numerous gradations between on and off; there are countless shades of gray between black and white).

As we can see from the preceding examples, the promise of language to structure what psychologist William James called "the buzz and confusion of the world" into an orderly set of categories turns out to be elusive. In most category debates, an argument, not a quick trip to the dictionary, is required to settle the matter.

For Writing and Discussion

Applying the Rule of Justice

Suppose your landlord decides to institute a "no pets" rule. The rule of justice requires that all pets have to go—not just your neighbor's barking dog, but also Mrs. Brown's cat, the kids' hamster downstairs, and your own pet tarantula. That is, all these animals have to go, unless you can argue that some of them are not "pets" for purposes of the landlord's "no pets" rule.

1. Working in small groups or as a class, define pets by establishing the criteria an animal would have to meet to be included in the category "pets." Consider your landlord's "no pets" rule as the cultural context for your definition.

2. Based on your criteria, which of the following animals is definitely a pet that would have to be removed from the apartment? Based on your criteria, which animals could you exclude from the "no pets" rule? How would you make your argument to your landlord?

   - a German shepherd
   - a small housecat
   - a tiny, well-trained lapdog
   - a gerbil in a cage
   - a canary
   - a tank of tropical fish
   - a tarantula

Types of Categorical Arguments

12.2 Explain four types of categorical arguments

Categorical arguments assert that a disputed phenomenon is (or is not) either a member of a certain category or is like a certain category. Such arguments can be divided into four kinds:

1. **Simple categorical arguments**, in which there is no dispute about the definition of the category.

2. **Definition arguments**, in which there is a dispute about the boundaries of the category and hence its definition.

3. **Resemblance arguments by analogy**, in which the writer uses metaphor or other figurative language to link the phenomenon to a certain category.

4. **Resemblance arguments by precedent**, in which the arguer claims that one phenomenon or situation is similar to another phenomenon or situation.

Let's look at each in turn.

Simple Categorical Arguments

A categorical argument is "simple" if there is no disagreement about the definition of the category into which a person, event, or phenomenon is placed. For example, if you make the claim that "Joe is bossy," you are placing him in the category of "bossy people." In this case, you assume that you and the audience agree on what "bossy" means. Your dispute is simply whether Joe meets the criteria for "bossy." To support your claim, you would provide examples of his bossiness (his poor listening skills, his shouting at people, his making decisions without asking the committee). Similarly, if you want to make the simple categorical claim that "low-carb diets are dangerous," you would need to provide evidence of this danger (scientific studies, testimony from doctors, anecdotes). The dispute in this case is about low-carb diets, not about the definition of "dangerous." To rebut a simple categorical claim, you would provide counterevidence to show that the person, event, or phenomenon does not meet the criteria for the category.

For Writing and Discussion

Supporting and Rebutting Simple Categorical Claims

Working individually or in small groups, consider how you would support the following simple categorical claims. What examples or other data would convince readers that the specified case fits within the named category? Then discuss ways you might rebut each claim.

1. Bottled water is environmentally unfriendly. [That is, bottled water belongs in the category of "environmentally unfriendly substances."]
2. Macklemore is a pure rapper.
3. Americans today are obsessed with their appearance. [That is, Americans belong in the category of "people obsessed with their appearance."]
4. Competitive cheerleading is physically risky.
5. Dinosaurs were warm-blooded.

Definition Arguments

Simple categorical arguments morph into definition arguments whenever stakeholders disagree about the boundaries of a category. In the previous exercise, suppose that you had said about Macklemore, "Well, that depends on how you define 'pure rapper.'" The need to define the term "pure rapper" adds a new layer of complexity to your arguments about Macklemore. You are disputing not only specifics about Macklemore but also the definition of "pure rapper" itself.

Full-blown definition arguments occur, then, when the disputants don't agree on the definition of the category into which a person, event, or phenomenon is placed. Consider, for example, the environmental controversy over the definition of *wetland*. Section 404 of the federal Clean Water Act provides for federal protection of wetlands, but it leaves the task of defining *wetland* to administrative agencies and the courts. Currently, about 5 percent of the land surface of the contiguous forty-eight states is potentially affected by the wetlands provision, and 75 percent of this land is privately owned. Efforts to define *wetland* have created a battleground between pro-environment and pro-development or property-rights groups. Farmers, homeowners, and developers often want a narrow definition of wetlands so that more property is available for commercial or private use. Environmentalists favor a broad definition in order to protect different habitat types and maintain the environmental safeguards that wetlands provide (including control of water pollution, spawning grounds for aquatic species, and flood-water containment).

The problem is that defining *wetland* is tricky. For example, one federal regulation defines a wetland as any area that has a saturated ground surface for twenty-one consecutive days during the year. But how would you apply this law to a pine flatwood ecosystem that was wet for ten days this year but thirty days last year? And how should the courts react to lawsuits claiming that the regulation itself is either too broad or too narrow? One can see why the wetlands controversy provides hefty incomes for lawyers and congressional lobbyists.

As we will explain in more detail later in this chapter, definition arguments require a *criteria-match structure* in which the arguer must first define the category term by specifying the criteria that must be met for something to be placed in that category. The writer then shows that the disputed person, event, or phenomenon matches those criteria.

Resemblance Argument Using Analogy

Whereas definition arguments claim that a particular phenomenon belongs to a certain category, resemblance arguments simply compare one thing to another. A common kind of resemblance argument uses *analogies*—imaginative comparisons often with subtle persuasive effects. If you don't like your new boss, you can say that she's like a Marine drill sergeant or the cowardly captain of a sinking ship. Each of these analogies suggests a different category in which to place your boss, clarifying the nature of your dislike while conveying an emotional charge. The arguer's intention is to transfer the audience's understanding of (or feelings about) the second thing back to the first. The risk of resemblance arguments is that the differences between the two things being compared are often so significant that the argument collapses under close examination.

Sometimes, as in the "My boss is like a Marine drill sergeant" example, arguers use short, undeveloped analogies for quick rhetorical effect. At other times, arguers develop extended analogies that carry a substantial portion of the argument. As an example of an extended analogy, consider the following excerpt from a professor's argument opposing a proposal to require a writing proficiency exam for graduation. In the following portion of his argument, the professor compares development of writing skills to the development of physical fitness.

> A writing proficiency exam gives the wrong symbolic messages about writing. It suggests that writing is simply a skill, rather than an active way of thinking and learning. It suggests that once a student demonstrates proficiency, then he or she doesn't need to do any more writing.
>
> Imagine two universities concerned with the physical fitness of their students. One university requires a junior-level physical-fitness exam in which students must run a mile in less than 10 minutes, a fitness level it considers minimally competent. Students at this university see the physical-fitness exam as a one-time hurdle. As many as 70 percent of them can pass the exam with no practice; another 10–20 percent need a few months' training; and a few hopeless couch potatoes must go through exhaustive remediation. After passing the exam, any student can settle back into a routine of TV and potato chips having been certified as "physically fit."
>
> The second university, however, believing in true physical fitness for its students, is not interested in minimal competency. Consequently, it creates programs in which its students must take a one-credit physical-fitness course each term for the entire four years of the undergraduate curriculum. There is little doubt which university will have the more physically fit students. At the second university, fitness becomes a way of life, with everyone developing his or her full potential. Similarly, if we want to improve our students' writing abilities, we should require writing in every course throughout the curriculum.

Thus analogies have the power to get an audience's attention like virtually no other persuasive strategy. But seldom are they sufficient in themselves to provide full understanding. At some point, with every analogy, you need to ask yourself, "How far can I legitimately go with this? At what point are the similarities between the two things I am comparing going to be overwhelmed by their dissimilarities?" Analogies are useful attention-getting devices, but they can conceal and distort as well as clarify.

For Writing and Discussion

Developing Analogies

The following exercise will help you clarify how analogies function in the context of arguments. Working individually or in small groups, think of two analogies for each of the following topics. One analogy should urge readers toward a positive view of the topic; the other should urge a negative view. Write each of your analogies in the following one-sentence format:

      _____ is like _____: A, B, C . . . (in which the first term is the contested topic being discussed; the second term is the analogy; and A, B, and C are the points of comparison).

(continued)

Example

- **Topic:** Cramming for an exam
- **Negative analogy:** Cramming for an exam is like pumping iron for ten hours straight to prepare for a weight-lifting contest: exhausting and counterproductive.
- **Positive analogy:** Cramming for an exam is like carbohydrate loading before a big race: It gives your brain a full supply of facts and concepts, all fresh in your mind.
- **Topics:**

  1. Checking social media constantly
  2. Building a wall to secure U.S. borders
  3. Using steroids to increase athletic performance
  4. Paying college athletes
  5. Eating at fast-food restaurants

Resemblance Arguments Using Precedent

Another kind of resemblance argument uses precedent for its persuasive force. An argument by precedent tries to show that a current situation is like a past situation and that therefore a similar action or decision should be taken or reached. You can refute a precedence argument by showing that the present situation differs substantially from the past situation.

Precedence arguments are very common. For example, during the debate about healthcare reform in the first year of Barack Obama's presidency, supporters of a single-payer, "Medicare-for-all" system pointed to Canada as a successful precedent. According to supporters, a single-payer system was successful in Canada; it would therefore also be successful in the United States. But opponents also used the Canadian precedent to attack a single-payer system. They pointed to problems in the Canadian system as a reason to reject a Medicare-for-all system in the United States.

A good example of an extended precedence argument can be found in an article entitled "The Perils of Ignoring History: Big Tobacco Played Dirty and Millions Died. How Similar Is Big Food?"* The authors' goal is to place "Big Food" in the same category as "Big Tobacco." The authors argue that the food-processing industry is trying to avoid government regulations by employing the same "dirty tricks" used earlier by Big Tobacco. The authors show how Big Tobacco hired lobbyists to fight regulation, how it created clever advertising to make cigarette smoking seem cool, and how it sponsored its own research to cast doubt on data linking nicotine to lung cancer or asthma to secondhand smoke. The researchers argue that Big Food is now doing the same thing. Through lobbying efforts, coordinated lawsuits, and public-relations campaigns, Big Food resists labeling ingredients in food products, casts doubt on scientific evidence about possible carcinogens (cancer-causing agents) in processed foods, and uses advertising to create a local, "family farm" image for Big Food. The researchers use this precedence argument to call for stricter government oversight of Big Food.

---

* Kelly D. Brownell and Kenneth E. Warner, "The Perils of Ignoring History: Big Tobacco Played Dirty and Millions Died. How Similar Is Big Food?" *The Milbank Quarterly* 87.1 (2009), 259–294.

For Writing and Discussion

Using Claims of Precedent

Consider the following claims of precedent, and evaluate how effective you think each precedent might be in establishing the claim. How would you develop the argument? How would you cast doubt on it?

1. To increase alumni giving to our university, we should put more funding into our football program. When University X went to postseason bowls for three years in a row, alumni donations to building programs and academics increased by 30 percent. We can expect the same increases here.
2. Postwar democracy can be created successfully in Afghanistan because it was created successfully in Germany and Japan following World War II.
3. Euthanasia laws work successfully in the Netherlands. Therefore they will work successfully in the United States.

Examining Visual Arguments

Claim about Category (Definition)

This cartoon, by political cartoonist Randy Bish of the *Pittsburgh Tribune Review,* creates a visual pun that makes a categorical argument against heroin. How does Bish's rendering of the letter "r" make a categorical claim? What is that claim? How effective do you find this cartoon in highlighting the seductive danger of heroin?

The Criteria-Match Structure of Definition Arguments

12.3 Explain the criteria-match structure of categorical arguments based on definition.

Of the four types of categorical arguments explained in the previous section, definition arguments require the fullest range of argumentative skills. For the rest of this chapter, we'll explain more fully the argumentative moves required to write your own definition argument.

Overview of Criteria-Match Structure

Definition arguments usually have a two-part structure: (1) a definition part that tries to establish the boundaries of the category and (2) a match part that argues whether a given case meets that definition. To describe this structure, we use the term *criteria-match*. Here are two examples:

> **Definition issue:** In a divorce proceeding, is a frozen embryo a "person" rather than "property"?
>
> **Criteria part:** What criteria must "a person" meet?
>
> **Match part:** Does a frozen embryo meet these criteria?
>
> **Definition issue:** Is this thirty-acre parcel of land near Swan Lake a "wetland"?
>
> **Criteria part:** What criteria must a wetland meet?
>
> **Match part:** Does this parcel of land meet these criteria?

To show how a definition issue can be developed into a claim with supporting reasons, let's look more closely at a third example:

> **Definition issue:** For purposes of my feeling good about buying my next pair of running shoes, is the Hercules Shoe Company a socially responsible company?
>
> **Criteria part:** What criteria must a company meet to be deemed "socially responsible"?
>
> **Match part:** Does the Hercules Shoe Company meet these criteria?

Let's suppose you work for a consumer information group that wishes to encourage patronage of socially responsible companies and the boycott of socially irresponsible companies. Your group's first task is to define *socially responsible company*. After much discussion and research, your group establishes three criteria that a company must meet to be considered socially responsible:

> *Your definition:* A company is socially responsible if it (1) avoids polluting the environment, (2) sells goods or services that contribute to the community's well-being, and (3) treats its workers justly.

The criteria section of your argument would explain and illustrate these criteria.

The match part of the argument would then try to persuade readers that a specific company does or does not meet the criteria. A typical thesis statement might be as follows:

> *Your thesis statement:* Although the Hercules Shoe Company is nonpolluting and provides a socially useful product, it is not a socially responsible company because it treats workers unjustly.

Toulmin Framework for a Definition Argument

Here is how the core of the preceding Hercules definition argument could be displayed in Toulmin terms. Note how the reason and grounds constitute the match argument while the warrant and backing constitute the criterion argument.

Toulmin Analysis of the Hercules Shoe Company Argument

ENTHYMEME

CLAIM The Hercules Shoe Company is not a socially responsible company

REASON because it treats workers unjustly.

GROUNDS

Evidence of unjust treatment:

- Evidence that the company manufactures its shoes in East Asian sweatshops

- Evidence of the inhumane conditions in these shops

- Evidence of hardships imposed on displaced American workers

CONDITIONS OF REBUTTAL

Attacking reasons and grounds

- Possible countervidence that the shops maintain humane working conditions

- Possible questioning of statistical data about hardships on displaced workers

WARRANT

Socially responsible companies treat workers justly.

BACKING

- Arguments showing that just treatment of workers is right in principle and also benefits society

- Arguments that capitalism helps society as a whole only if workers achieve a reasonable standard of living, have time for leisure, and are not exploited

CONDITIONS OF REBUTTAL

Attacking warrant and backing

Justice needs to be considered from an emerging nation's standpoint:

- The wages paid to workers are low by American standards but are above average by East Asian standards.

- Displacement of American workers is part of the necessary adjustment of adapting to a global economy and does not mean that a company is unjust.

As this Toulmin schema illustrates, the warrant and backing constitute the criteria section of the argument by stating and defending "just treatment of workers" as a criterion for a socially responsible company. The reason and grounds constitute the match section of the argument by arguing that the Hercules Shoe Company does not treat its workers justly. How much emphasis you need to place on justifying each criterion and supporting each match depends on your audience's initial beliefs. The conditions of rebuttal help you imagine alternative views and see places where opposing views need to be acknowledged and rebutted.

For Writing and Discussion

Identifying Criteria and Match Issues

Consider the following definition claims. Working individually or in small groups, identify the criteria issue and the match issue for each of the following claims.

Definition issue: A Honda assembled in Ohio is (is not) an American-made car.
Criteria part: What criteria must an "American-made car" meet?
Match part: Does a Honda assembled in Ohio meet these criteria?
Claims:

1. American Sign Language is (is not) a "foreign language" for purposes of a college graduation requirement.
2. The violence in *Grand Theft Auto* is (is not) constitutionally protected free speech.
3. Bungee jumping from a crane is (is not) a "carnival amusement ride" subject to state safety inspections.
4. For purposes of a state sales tax on "candy," a Twinkie is (is not) candy.
5. A skilled video game player is (is not) a true athlete.

Creating Criteria Using Aristotelian Definition

When creating criteria for a category, you can often follow the pattern of *Aristotelian definition*. The Aristotelian definitional strategy, regularly used in dictionaries, defines a term by placing it within the next larger class or category and then showing the specific attributes that distinguish the term from other terms within the same category. For example, according to a legal dictionary, *robbery* is "the felonious taking of property" (next larger category) that differs from other acts of theft because it seizes property "through violence or intimidation." Legal dictionaries often provide specific examples to show the boundaries of the term. Here is one example:

> There is no robbery unless force or fear is used to overcome resistance. Thus, surreptitiously picking a man's pocket or snatching something from him without resistance on his part is *larceny*, but not robbery.

Many states specify degrees of robbery with increasingly heavy penalties. For example, *armed robbery* involves the use of a weapon to threaten the victim. In all cases, *robbery* is distinguished from the lesser crime of *larceny*, in which no force or intimidation is involved.

As you can see, an Aristotelian definition of a term identifies specific attributes or criteria that enable you to distinguish it from other members of the next larger class. We created an Aristotelian definition in our example about socially responsible companies. A socially responsible company, we said, is any company (next larger class) that meets three criteria: (1) it doesn't pollute the environment;

(2) it creates goods or services that promote the community's well-being; and (3) it treats its workers justly.

In constructing Aristotelian definitions, you may find it useful to employ the concepts of accidental, necessary, and sufficient criteria.

- An *accidental criterion* is a usual but not essential feature of a concept. For example, armed robbers frequently wear masks, but wearing a mask is an accidental criterion because it has no bearing on the definition of *robbery*. In our example about socially responsible companies, "makes regular contributions to charities" might be an accidental criterion; most socially responsible companies contribute to charities, but some do not. And many socially irresponsible companies also contribute to charities—often as a public-relations ploy.

- A *necessary criterion* is an attribute that *must* be present for something to belong to the category being defined. To be guilty of robbery rather than larceny, a thief must have used direct force or intimidation. The use of force is thus a necessary criterion for robbery. However, for a robbery to occur, another criterion must also be met: The robber must also take property from the victim.

- *Sufficient criteria* are all the criteria that must be present for something to belong to the category being defined. Together, the use of force plus the taking of property are *sufficient criteria* for an act to be classified as robbery.

Consider again our defining criteria for a "socially responsible" company: (1) the company must avoid polluting the environment; (2) the company must create goods or services that contribute to the community's well-being; and (3) the company must treat its workers justly. In this definition, each criterion is necessary, but none of the criteria alone is sufficient. In other words, to be defined as socially responsible, a company must meet all three criteria at once, as the word *and* signals. It is not enough for a company to be nonpolluting (a necessary but not sufficient criterion); if that company makes a shoddy product or treats its workers unjustly, it fails to meet the other necessary criteria and can't be deemed socially responsible. Because no one criterion by itself is sufficient, the company must meet all three criteria together before it can be deemed socially responsible.

In contrast, consider the following definition of *sexual harassment* as established by the U.S. Equal Employment Opportunity Commission in its 1980 guidelines:

> Unwelcome sexual advances, requests for sexual favors, and other verbal or physical conduct of a sexual nature constitute sexual harassment when (1) submission to such conduct is made either explicitly or implicitly a term or condition of an individual's employment, (2) submission to or rejection of such conduct by an individual is used as the basis for employment decisions affecting such individual, or (3) such conduct has the purpose or effect of unreasonably interfering with an individual's work performance or creating an intimidating, hostile, or offensive working environment.*

Here each of these criteria is sufficient. If just one criterion is met, the act constitutes sexual harassment.

---

* Quoted in Stephanie Riger, "Gender Dilemmas in Sexual Harassment Policies and Procedures," *American Psychologist* 46 (May 1991), 497–505.

For Writing and Discussion

Working with Criteria

Working individually or in small groups, try to determine whether each of the following is a necessary criterion, a sufficient criterion, an accidental criterion, or no criterion for defining the indicated concept. Be prepared to explain your reasoning and to account for differences in points of view.

Criterion	Concept to Be Defined
Presence of gills	Fish
Profane and obscene language	R-rated movie
Line endings that form a rhyming pattern	Poem
Disciplining a child by spanking	Child abuse
Diet that excludes meat	Vegetarian
Killing another human being	Murder
Good sex life	Happy marriage

Creating Criteria Using an Operational Definition

In some rhetorical situations, particularly those arising in the physical and social sciences, writers need precise *operational definitions* that can be measured empirically and are not subject to problems of context and conflicting values and beliefs. A social scientist studying the effects of television on aggression in children needs a precise, measurable definition of *aggression*. Typically, the scientist might measure "aggression" by counting the number of blows a child gives to an inflatable bobo doll over a fifteen-minute period when other play options are available. In our wetlands example, a federal authority created an operational definition of *wetland:* a wetland is a parcel of land that has a saturated ground surface for twenty-one consecutive days during the year.

Such operational definitions are useful because they are precisely measurable, but they are also limited because they omit criteria that may be unmeasurable but important. Thus, we might ask whether it is adequate to define an *honors student* as someone with a 3.8 GPA or higher or a *successful sex-education program* as one that results in a 25 percent reduction in teenage pregnancies. What important aspects of an honors student or a successful sex-education program are not considered in these operational definitions?

Conducting the Match Part of a Definition Argument

In conducting a match argument, you need to supply examples and other evidence showing that your contested case does (does not) meet the criteria you established in your definition. In essence, you support the match part of your argument in much the same way you would support a simple categorical claim.

For example, if you were developing the argument that the Hercules Shoe Company is not socially responsible because it treats its workers unjustly, your match section would provide evidence of this injustice. You might supply data about the percentage of shoes produced in East Asia, about the low wages paid to these workers, and about the working conditions in these factories. You might also describe the suffering of displaced American workers when Hercules closed its American factories and moved operations to Asia, where the labor is non-union and cheap. The match section should also summarize and respond to opposing views.

Idea-Generating Strategies for Creating Your Own Criteria-Match Argument

12.4 Use criteria-match reasoning to generate ideas for your own definition argument.

In constructing criteria to define your contested term, you can either research how others have defined your term or make your own definitions. If you use the first strategy, you turn to standard or specialized dictionaries, judicial opinions, or expert testimony to establish a definition based on the authority of others. The second strategy is to use your own critical thinking to make your own definition, thereby defining the contested term yourself. This section explains these approaches in more detail.

Strategy 1: Research How Others Have Defined the Term

When you take this approach, you search for authoritative definitions acceptable to your audience yet favorable to your case. When the state of Washington tried to initiate a new sales tax on candy, lawyers and legislators wrestled with a definition. They finally created the following statute, which is available to the public on a government website:

What Is the Definition of Candy?

"Candy" is a preparation of sugar, honey, or other natural or artificial sweeteners combined with chocolate, fruits, nuts, or other ingredients or flavorings in the form of bars, drops, or pieces. Candy does not require refrigeration, and does not include flour as an ingredient.

"Natural or artificial sweeteners" include, but are not limited to, high fructose corn syrup, dextrose, invert sugar, sucrose, fructose, sucralose, saccharin, aspartame, stevia, fruit juice concentrates, molasses, evaporated cane juice, and rice syrup.

"Flour" includes any flour made from a grain, such as wheat flour, rice flour, and corn flour.

Items that require "refrigeration," either before or after opening, are not candy. For example, popsicles, ice cream bars, and fruits in sweetened syrups are not candy.

This definition made it easy for state officials to exclude from the "candy tax" any snack food that contained flour. Thus Twinkies, Fruit Loops cereal, and chocolate-covered pretzels were exempt from the tax. But considerable debate occurred over cough drops and halvah (a traditional dessert in India and Mediterranean countries). The state decided to exclude cough drops if the package contained a "drug facts" panel and a list of active ingredients. (Such cough drops were then classified as "over-the-counter drugs.") Halvah made with nut-butter was taxed as candy but not halvah made with flour.

Turning to established definitions is thus a first step for many definition arguments. Common sources of these definitions are specialized dictionaries, such as *Black's Law Dictionary*, which form a standard part of the reference holdings of any library. Other sources of specialized definitions are state and federal appellate court decisions, legislative and administrative statutes, and scholarly articles examining a given definition conflict. Lawyers use this research strategy exhaustively in preparing court briefs. They begin by looking at the actual text of laws as passed by legislatures or written by administrative authorities. Then they look at all the court cases in which the laws have been tested and examine the ways courts have refined legal definitions and applied them to specific cases. Using these refined definitions, lawyers then apply them to their own case at hand.

If your research uncovers definitions that seem ambiguous or otherwise unfavorable to your case, you can sometimes appeal to the "original intentions" of those who defined the term. For example, if a scientist is dissatisfied with definitions of *wetlands* based on consecutive days of saturated ground surface, she might proceed as follows: "The original intention of Congress in passing the Clean Water Act was to preserve the environment." What Congress intended, she could then claim, was to prevent development of those wetland areas that provide crucial habitat for wildlife or that inhibit water pollution. She could then propose an alternative definition based on criteria other than consecutive days of ground saturation.

Strategy 2: Create Your Own Extended Definition*

Often, however, you need to create your own definition of the contested term. An effective strategy is to establish initial criteria for your contested term by thinking of hypothetical cases that obviously fit the category you are trying to define and then altering one or more variables until the hypothetical case obviously doesn't fit the category. You can then test and refine your criteria by applying them to borderline cases. For example, suppose you work at a homeless shelter where you overhear your clients discuss an incident that strikes you as potential "police brutality." You wonder whether you should write to your local paper to bring attention to the incident.

---

* The defining strategies and collaborative exercises in this section are based on the work of George Hillocks and his research associates at the University of Chicago. See George Hillocks Jr., Elizabeth A. Kahn, and Larry R. Johannessen, "Teaching Defining Strategies as a Mode of Inquiry: Some Effects on Student Writing," *Research in the Teaching of English* 17 (October 1983), 275–84. See also Larry R. Johannessen, Elizabeth A. Kahn, and Carolyn Calhoun Walter, *Designing and Sequencing Prewriting Activities* (Urbana, IL: NCTE, 1982).

A Possible Case of Police Brutality

Two police officers confront an inebriated homeless man who is shouting obscenities on a street corner. The officers tell the man to quiet down and move on, but he keeps shouting obscenities. When the officers attempt to put the man into the police car, he resists and takes a wild swing at one of the officers. As eyewitnesses later testified, this officer shouted obscenities back at the drunk man, pinned his arms behind his back in order to handcuff him, and lifted him forcefully by the arms. The man screamed in pain and was later discovered to have a dislocated shoulder. Is this officer guilty of police brutality?

To your way of thinking, this officer seems guilty: An inebriated man is too uncoordinated to be a threat in a fight, and two police officers ought to be able to arrest him without dislocating his shoulder. But a friend argues that because the man took a swing at the officer, the police were justified in using force. The dislocated shoulder was simply an accidental result of using justified force.

To make your case, you need to develop a definition of "police brutality." You can begin by creating a hypothetical case that is obviously an instance of police brutality:

A Clear Case of Police Brutality

A police officer confronts a drunk man shouting obscenities and begins hitting him in the face with his police baton. [*This is an obvious incidence of police brutality because the officer intentionally tries to hurt the drunk man without justification; hitting him with the baton is not necessary for making an arrest or getting the man into the police car.*]

You could then vary the hypothetical case until it is clearly *not* an instance of police brutality.

Cases That Are Clearly Not Police Brutality

Case 1:

The police officer handcuffs the drunk man, who, in being helped into the police car, accidentally slips on the curb and dislocates his arm while falling. [*Here the injury occurs accidentally; the police officer does not act intentionally and is not negligent.*]

Case 2:

The police officer confronts an armed robber fleeing from a scene and tackles him from behind, wrestling the gun away from him. In this struggle, the officer pins the robber's arm behind his back with such force that the robber's shoulder is dislocated. [*Here aggressive use of force is justified because the robber was armed, dangerous, and resisting arrest.*]

Using these hypothetical cases, you decide that the defining criteria for police brutality are (1) *intention* and (2) use of *excessive force*—that is, force beyond what was required by the immediate situation. After more contemplation, you are convinced that the officer was guilty of police brutality and have a clearer idea of how to make your argument. Here is how you might write the "match" part of your argument:

Match Argument Using Your Definition

If we define police brutality as the *intentional* use of *excessive* force, then the police officer is guilty. His action was intentional because he was purposefully responding to the homeless man's drunken swing and was angry enough to be shouting obscenities back at the drunk (according to eyewitnesses). Second, he used excessive force in applying the handcuffs. A drunk man taking a wild swing hardly poses a serious danger to two police officers. Putting handcuffs on the drunk may have been justified, but lifting the man's arm violently enough to dislocate a shoulder indicates excessive force. The officer lifted the man's arms violently not because he needed to but because he was angry, and acting out of anger is no justification for that violence. In fact, we can charge police officers with police brutality precisely to protect us from being victims of police anger. It is the job of the court system to punish us, not the police's job. Because this officer acted intentionally and applied excessive force out of anger, he should be charged with police brutality.

The strategy we have demonstrated—developing criteria by imagining hypothetical cases that clearly do and do not belong to the contested category—gives you a systematic procedure for developing your own definition for your argument.

For Writing and Discussion

Developing a Definition

Individual task:

1. Suppose you want to define the concept of courage. In each of the following cases, decide whether the person in question is acting courageously or not. In each instance explain your reasoning.
   a. A neighbor rushes into a burning house to rescue a child from certain death and emerges, coughing and choking, with the child in his arms. Is the neighbor courageous?
   b. A firefighter rushes into a burning house to rescue a child from certain death and emerges with the child in her arms. The firefighter is wearing protective clothing and a gas mask. When a newspaper reporter calls her courageous, she says, "Hey, this is my job." Is the firefighter courageous?
   c. A teenager rushes into a burning house to recover a memento given to him by his girlfriend, the first love of his life. Is the teenager courageous?
   d. A parent rushes into a burning house to save a trapped child. The fire marshal tells the parent to wait because there is no chance that the child can be reached from the first floor. The fire marshal wants to try cutting a hole in the roof to reach the child. The parent rushes into the house anyway and is burned to death. Was the parent courageous?
2. Now formulate your own definition of a "courageous act." Use the following format: "An act would be considered courageous if it meets the following criteria: [you specify]."
3. Finally, apply your definition to the following case: An extreme sport enthusiast sets a record for a hang-gliding descent from a certain state's highest cliff. Is this record-setting descent a courageous act? Write a paragraph in which you argue that the descent is or is not courageous.

Group task:

Share the results from the individual task on courage. Then make up your own series of controversial cases, like those given previously for "courage," for one or more of the following concepts:

a. cruelty to animals

b. child abuse

c. true athlete

d. sexual harassment

e. free speech protected by the First Amendment

Finally, using the strategy of making up hypothetical cases that do and do not belong to each category, construct a definition of your chosen concept.

Writing Assignment: A Definition Argument

12.5 Write your own definition argument.

The assignment for this chapter focuses on definition disputes about categories. Write an essay in which you argue that a borderline or contested case fits (or does not fit) within a given category. In the opening of your essay, introduce the borderline case you will examine and pose your definition question. In the first part of your argument, define the boundaries of your category (criteria) by reporting a definition used by others or by developing your own extended definition. In the second part of your argument (the match), show how your borderline case meets (or doesn't meet) your definition criteria.

Exploring Ideas

Ideally, in writing this argument you will join an ongoing conversation about a definition issue that interests you. What cultural and social issues that concern you involve disputed definitions? In the public arena, you are likely to find numerous examples simply by looking through news stories—for example, the disputes about the definition of "torture" in interrogating terrorist suspects or about "freedom of religion" in debates about religious organizations having to pay for contraception in employees' health insurance. Often you can frame your own definition issues even if they aren't currently in the news. Is using TiVo to avoid TV commercials a form of theft? Is flag burning protected free speech? Is solitary confinement "cruel and unusual punishment"? Is Walmart a socially responsible company? Are voter ID laws racist?

If you have trouble discovering a local or national issue that interests you, you can create fascinating definition controversies among your classmates by asking whether certain borderline cases are "true" or "real" examples of some category: Are highly skilled video game players (race car drivers, synchronized swimmers, marbles players) true athletes? Is a gourmet chef (skilled furniture maker, tagger) a true artist? Is a chiropractor (acupuncturist, naturopathic physician) a "real doctor"? Working as a class or in small groups inside or outside class, create an argumentative discussion on one or more of these issues. Listen to the various voices in the controversy, and then write out your own argument.

You can also stimulate definition controversies by brainstorming borderline cases for such terms as *courage* (Is mountain climbing an act of courage?), *cruelty to animals* (Are rodeos [zoos, catch-and-release trout fishing, use of animals for medical research] guilty of cruelty to animals?), or *war crime* (Was the U.S. firebombing of Tokyo in World War II a war crime?).

As you explore your definition issue, try to determine how others have defined your category. If no stable definition emerges from your search, create your own definition by deciding what criteria must be met for a contested case to fit within your category. Try using the strategy for creating criteria that we discussed earlier in this chapter with reference to police brutality. Once you have determined your criteria, freewrite for five or ten minutes, exploring whether your contested case meets each of the criteria.

Identifying Your Audience and Determining What's at Stake

Before drafting your argument, identify your targeted audience and determine what's at stake. Consider your responses to the following questions:

- What audience are you targeting? What background do they need to understand your issue? How much do they already care about it?
- Before they read your argument, what stance on your issue do you imagine them holding? What change do you want to bring about in their views?
- What will they find new or surprising about your argument?
- What objections might they raise? What counterarguments or alternative points of view will you need to address?
- Why does your argument matter? Who might be threatened or made uncomfortable by your views? What is at stake?

Organizing a Definition Argument

As you compose a first draft of your essay, you may find it helpful to understand typical structures for definition arguments. There are two basic approaches, as shown in Figures 12.1 and 12.2. You can either discuss the criteria and the match separately or interweave the discussion.

Questioning and Critiquing a Definition Argument

A powerful way to stimulate global revision of a draft is to role-play a skeptical audience. The following questions will help you strengthen your own argument or rebut the definition arguments of others. In critiquing a definition argument, you need to appreciate its criteria-match structure because you can question the criteria argument, the match argument, or both.

Figure 12.1 Definition argument: Organization Plan 1

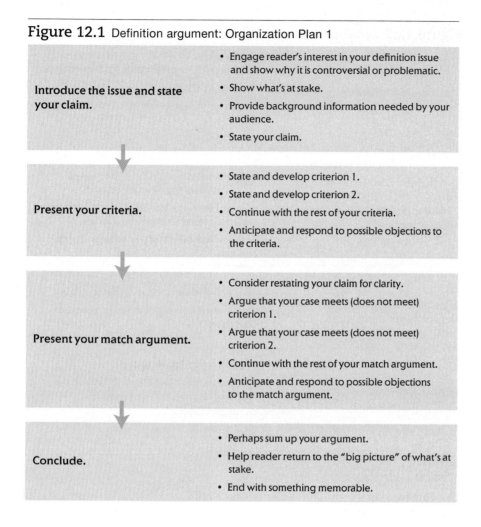

Introduce the issue and state your claim.

- Engage reader's interest in your definition issue and show why it is controversial or problematic.
- Show what's at stake.
- Provide background information needed by your audience.
- State your claim.

Present your criteria.

- State and develop criterion 1.
- State and develop criterion 2.
- Continue with the rest of your criteria.
- Anticipate and respond to possible objections to the criteria.

Present your match argument.

- Consider restating your claim for clarity.
- Argue that your case meets (does not meet) criterion 1.
- Argue that your case meets (does not meet) criterion 2.
- Continue with the rest of your match argument.
- Anticipate and respond to possible objections to the match argument.

Conclude.

- Perhaps sum up your argument.
- Help reader return to the "big picture" of what's at stake.
- End with something memorable.

Questioning Your Criteria

- Could a skeptic claim that your criteria are not the right ones? Could he or she offer different criteria or point out missing criteria?
- Could a skeptic point out possible bad consequences of accepting your criteria?
- Could a skeptic cite unusual circumstances that weaken your criteria?
- Could a skeptic point out bias or slant in your definition?

Questioning Your Match

- Could a skeptic argue that your examples or data don't meet the STAR criteria (see Chapter 4) for evidence?
- Could a skeptic point out counterexamples or alternative data that cast doubt on your argument?
- Could a skeptic reframe the way you have viewed your borderline case?

Figure 12.2 Definition argument: Organization Plan 2

Introduce the issue and state your claim.	• Engage reader's interest in your definition issue and show why it is problematic or controversial. • Show what's at stake. • Provide background information needed by your audience. • State your claim.
Present series of criterion-match arguments.	• State and develop criterion 1 and argue that your case meets (does not meet) the criterion. • State and develop criterion 2 and argue that your case meets (does not meet) the criterion. • Continue with the rest of your criterion-match arguments.
Respond to possible objections to your argument.	• Anticipate and summarize possible objections. • Respond to the objections through rebuttal or concession.
Conclude.	• Perhaps sum up your argument. • Help reader return to the "big picture" of what's at stake. • End with something memorable.

Readings

Our first reading, by student writer Arthur Knopf, grew out of his research into agricultural subsidies and the nutritional content of foods. It was written for the assignment in Learning Objective 12.5.

Student Essay

Is Milk a Health Food?

Arthur Knopf

If asked to name a typical health food, most of us would put milk high on our lists. We've all seen the "Got Milk?" ads with their milk-mustached celebrities or the dairy product campaigns entitled "Milk, It Does a Body Good" or "Body By Milk." These ads, featuring well-known athletes or trim celebrities, argue visually that milk helps you grow fit and strong. But if you define "health food" based on science rather than on marketing claims, and if you include in your definition of health food concerns for the planet as well as for individual bodies, then milk might not fit the category of health food at all.

My first criterion for a "health food" is that the food should have a scientifically supported health benefit with minimal risks. Based on the food pyramid from the United States Department of Agriculture (USDA), milk at first glance seems to fit this criterion. On the *MyPyramid* website the dairy group (milk, yogurt, cheese) is one of the essential components of a healthy diet (USDA). All elements of the milk group provide calcium, which is important for healthy bones and the prevention of osteoporosis. Dairy products also provide important vitamins. But the website entry under the dairy group specifies in a footnote, "Choose fat-free or low-fat milk, yogurt, and cheese." One cup of whole milk, according to the website, contains 70 more calories than a cup of skim milk (147 calories compared to 83). The extra 70 calories are potentially harmful saturated fats and sugar, linked to heart disease and obesity. We can say then that "nonfat milk" fits my first criterion for a health food, but that the rest of the milk group may not.

So how do dairy products in general get listed as essential ingredients on the food pyramid rather than just low-fat milk or yogurt? The answer to this question brings us to my second criterion for a health food: Potentially unhealthy aspects of the food should be widely disclosed, not hidden by marketing. Because we are bombarded daily by conflicting nutrition claims, many people turn to the U.S. government for neutral, unbiased information. But the place of dairy products on the USDA food pyramid may be itself a result of marketing. The USDA's mandate isn't directly to promote health, but rather to promote agriculture and to help farmers flourish economically. In recommending three servings of dairy products per day, the food pyramid serves the interests of dairy farmers by promoting the whole class of dairy products, not just skim milk. According to the Environmental Working Group's Farm Subsidy Primer, the USDA spent $4.8 billion in dairy subsidies between 1995 and 2009 ("Farm Subsidy Primer"). All these policies invest public dollars to create a steady consumption of dairy products and fundamentally depend on the premise that dairy products are good for us.

As we have seen, skim milk may be good for us, but dairy products in general are more problematic. When the fat in whole milk is removed to make skim milk, it is not thrown away. It is used to make high-calorie, high-fat products like cheese and ice cream. Revealing its true ambivalence to public nutrition, the USDA warns against saturated fats in its food pyramid site while simultaneously working with companies like Domino's Pizza to increase the amount of cheese in their products. According to *The New York Times* (Moss), the USDA helped Domino's create a pizza with 40 percent more cheese and paid for a $12 million ad campaign to promote it. *The New York Times* further writes that Americans now consume almost three times as much cheese as we did in 1970. At a time of a national obesity epidemic, the promotion of dairy products either directly or indirectly introduces high-calorie, high-saturated-fat foods into our diet while making many persons think they are eating healthfully.

Finally, I would like to suggest a third criterion for health food. A true health food should be good not only for our bodies but also for the earth. Milk, as it is currently produced in the United States, clearly does not meet this criterion. According to environmental writer Jim Motavalli, both "the front

5

(continued)

and rear ends of a cow" compete with coal plant smokestacks and vehicle tail-pipes as "iconic" causes of global warming and environmental degradation. Drawing on statistical sources from both the United Nations and the USDA, Motavalli states that livestock in the United States consumes 90 percent of the soy crop and more than 70 percent of the corn and grain crops—foods that could otherwise be used for people and could be grown in a more environmentally friendly way. Not only do cattle consume much of the world's grain supply, the need to clear space for grazing contributes to the destruction of rain forests. The other end of the cow, says Motavalli, is equally destructive. While chewing their cuds, cows directly emit methane gas (according to Motavalli, methane has a greenhouse effect 23 times more potent than carbon dioxide), and the concentration of their manure in factory farm sludge ponds produces ammonia, nitrous oxide, and additional methane. According to Motavalli, cows produce a staggering amount of manure ("five tons of waste for every U.S. citizen"), producing 18 percent of the world's greenhouse gases—more than all of the world's cars, trains, and planes. Motavalli also cites additional health risks posed by cows, including dangers of disease from unsafe processing of manure and from antibiotic-resistant bacteria (half of the world's antibiotics are given to cattle instead of humans).

In sum, there is no doubt that skim milk, along with low-fat yogurt and cheese, is a vital source of bone-building calcium and belongs on our list of health foods. But for most people, "milk" evokes dairy products in general, all of which we tend to associate with health. What we don't picture is the extra sugar and saturated fat in whole milk and cheese nor the environmental dangers of the dairy and livestock industries in general. From the perspective of the earth, perhaps dairy products should not be considered a health food at all.

Works Cited

"Farm Subsidy Primer." *Environmental Working Group,* farm.ewg.org/subsidyprimer.php. Accessed 8 Apr. 2018.

Moss, Michael. "While Warning About Fat, U.S. Pushes Cheese Sales." *The New York Times,* 6 Nov. 2010, www.nytimes.com/2010/11/07/us/07fat.html.

Motavalli, Jim. "The Meat of the Matter." *Orlando Weekly,* 31 July 2008, www.orlandoweekly.com/orlando/the-meat-of-the-matter/Content?oid=2273952.

U.S. Department of Agriculture, Center for Nutrition Policy and Promotion. *MyPyramid,* www.cnpp.usda.gov/mypyramid. Accessed 8 Apr. 2018.

Critiquing "Is Milk a Health Food?"

1. Identify the following features of Arthur's essay: (1) his implied definition of "health food"; (2) his criteria for determining whether a borderline case is a health food; (3) his match arguments showing whether milk fits each of the criteria.

2. Do you agree with Arthur's criterion that a true health food ought to be good for the planet as well as good for the body?

3. Based on Arthur's argument, do you think the inclusion of dairy products in the USDA's recommendations for a healthy diet is still justified? Visit the USDA's nutrition website, www.choosemyplate.gov. Would you suggest changes to these USDA recommendations? If so, what changes would you recommend and why?

The second reading, by student Alex Mullen, was also written for the definition assignment in Learning Objective 12.5. Alex's argument was stimulated by class discussions of property ownership in digital environments.

Student Essay

A Pirate But Not a Thief: What Does "Stealing" Mean in a Digital Environment?

Alex Mullen

I am a pirate. In the eyes of the law, I could face serious punishment in fines, up to thousands of dollars, or jail time for my crime. Legally, it matters very little that my crime is one perpetrated by millions of people every year (you yourself may be guilty of it) or that there are far worse offenders out there. But before we get out the noose and head for the yardarm, I think I ought to describe my crime. In my History of Film class we were asked to watch Jean Renoir's *La Grande Illusion*. Now, if you've spent any time searching for 1930s foreign films you will undoubtedly know what a pain it is to find them, and of the twenty or so films we watched for my class a grand total of three were available on streaming sites such as Netflix, Hulu, and YouTube. While there were several copies of this particular film at my university library, all had been checked out. I planned to make a journey to the fabled Scarecrow Video (one of the largest rental libraries in the United States), but time was running low at this point. Finally, I broke down and used a person-to-person torrent site to download the film illegally. In the end all the trouble was worthwhile, as *La Grande Illusion* remains one of the greatest films I have ever seen. After watching it several times and writing a brief paper, I deleted the film from my computer. Although I feel that my action was justifiable, many people think what I did was no better than shoplifting and that I am guilty of theft. As a film lover and aspiring filmmaker, I am conflicted on the issue of online piracy. Nevertheless, I contend that what I did wasn't stealing because I deprived no one of either property or profit.

Let's take a step back from online piracy and focus simply on what stealing is in its most basic form. In my mind, stealing is the unlawful taking of another's property or profits without permission. It is the underlying assumption about what makes stealing wrong that needs to be considered. In the case of property, stealing is wrong not because the thief has the property but because the original owner has been deprived of it. The owner's loss causes the wrong, not the thief's gain. To give an example in very simple

(continued)

terms, if you have a phone case and I make a copy of that case (as is quite possible with a 3D printer), you still possess the original case, so no harm has been done to you, the owner. However, suppose that you made your living by selling these phone cases. If I made exact duplicates with my 3-D printer and then sold these cases to others, then you could be deprived of profits that you might otherwise have received. Again, the wrong comes from the creator's loss and not the thief's gain.

Now let's focus on my particular example of online piracy. While I concede that piracy has the distinct potential to be stealing, I reject the accusation that all piracy is stealing. Based on the first part of my definition of stealing, my downloading *La Grande Illusion* deprived no consumer or creator of his or her copy of the film. This is why accusations that compare online piracy to shoplifting are false. In the case of shoplifting, the owner/creator has one fewer piece of merchandise to make a profit on; with online piracy, such loss does not occur because the original copy still exists.

However, the second part of my definition, which focuses on profits, still remains to be examined. Perhaps by downloading the film I have deprived the creators/owners of profits they would normally receive. Let me begin by saying that I never intended to purchase *La Grande Illusion*. While intention does not often register in legal matters, it does have a bearing on the type and degree of wrongdoing. Film-industry lawyers often argue that every time a film is pirated, the rightful owner is deprived of money because the pirate would have otherwise purchased the film. This claim, however, is fallacious because there is no way to show that these potential consumers would have purchased the film (I certainly wouldn't have). So while we may agree that some of these people would have purchased the film, it would be inaccurate to claim that in all cases piracy directly deprives creators of profit. I argue that what I did in the case of *La Grande Illusion* was more like borrowing than theft. Borrowing a film from a library (or renting it from a video store) has the same basic effect on the owner/creator as online piracy. That is, a library or video store purchases a copy and then loans it or rents it to others. Thus, many persons may not purchase a copy from the owner/creator because they can use this single public or commercial copy. Yet we do not consider borrowing or renting stealing even though it can have the same economic ramification as piracy. To go a step further, any time I borrow a film from a friend I cause the same outcome found so reprehensible in online piracy. In my case, instead of borrowing *La Grande Illusion* from an institution or business, I borrowed it from another individual via the Internet.

5 There is, of course, the counterargument that I could have rented the film from Scarecrow and thus stole profit from this film-rental store much loved by film buffs. While it is true that I did not benefit Scarecrow with my patronage (a fact that I partially regret because I do try to support Scarecrow as often as possible), it would be inaccurate to say that I stole from Scarecrow. I am under no obligation to supply them with profits. When I pay money to a rental organization, I am not paying for the film; I am paying for the service of being able to use their copy of the film for 24 hours. Had I purchased the film directly from the filmmaker, I would do the same harm to Scarecrow. Thus my not utilizing Scarecrow to obtain *La Grande Illusion* is not theft.

While I understand why the film industry (and also the music industry) views downloading from file-sharing torrent sites as piracy, their motives focus on preserving profits and blur the distinctions among buying, renting, and borrowing. If I owned a DVD version of a movie and loaned it to a friend, no one would object. But if I make the same movie available to a friend via a torrent or file-sharing site, I become a pirate subject to huge fines. The intention is the same; only the format changes. The problem stems from the hazy concept of "ownership" in a digital environment where physical copies are replaced by digital copies. Certainly, we pay to possess digital copies of films, music, and video games, but is this really the same as physical ownership? After all, I can lend, rent, or even sell a physical DVD, but such actions are impossible with digital copies without committing piracy. Our consumption of media is evolving rapidly, and while undoubtedly there will always be those who exploit these changes for personal gain, I feel we need to realize that our understanding of ownership, stealing, and illegal use must evolve along with these changes.

Critiquing "A Pirate But Not a Thief: What Does 'Stealing' Mean in a Digital Environment?"

1. Identify the following features of Alex's essay: (1) his definition of "stealing"; (2) his examples to illustrate the definition; (3) his match argument showing whether his downloading of the film fits each of the criteria; and (4) his summary of and responses to objections and opposing views.

2. Do you agree with Alex's contention that his downloading the film was an act of "borrowing" rather than "stealing"?

3. What do you see as the major strengths of Alex's argument? The major weaknesses?

4. Do you think that the laws about online piracy should be changed? At what point does online piracy clearly become stealing?

Our last reading is an op-ed piece from the *Los Angeles Times* by Mark Oppenheimer, a freelance author, journalist, and host of the podcast *Unorthodox*. The occasion for this piece was a pending bill in Connecticut to raise the age of legal marriage to eighteen. Oppenheimer notes the bewildering ways that "adulthood" is defined in different contexts and points out potential negative consequences of this definitional problem.

How Do We Define Adulthood?

MARK OPPENHEIMER

The legislature in my home state of Connecticut is considering a bill that would raise the age of legal marriage to 18. Right now, like 26 other states, Connecticut sets no minimum age: 16- and 17-year-olds can marry with parental consent, and younger children—15, 14, heck, 8 or 9—can marry with parental consent and a judge's approval. Between 2000 and 2014, there were 14 marriages in Connecticut involving 14-year-old girls.

As it happens, Connecticut is part of a trend. Eight states are considering similar bills, an explosion of interest due to the work of activist Fraidy Reiss, who entered into an arranged marriage with a fellow ultra-Orthodox Jew when she was 19, later divorced, and now runs a nonprofit called Unchained at Last.

Setting aside the merits of her movement—and I think there are many—the bill raises a larger question: Who counts as an adult? Our federal and state laws are an inconsistent patchwork of mixed messages. You can drive at 16 in most places, although not in New Jersey, where you have to be 17, or South Dakota, where you can get a license with some restrictions at 14 1/2. You can vote for president at 18, the same age at which you have to register for the draft. But if you are drafted at 18, you can't have a beer after a rough day of basic training—you have to wait until you're 21. Also at 18, you can buy a rifle or a shotgun from a licensed dealer—but not a handgun. For that, you have to wait until you're 21.

Want to change these laws? You can run for the House of Representatives at 25, the Senate at 30, the presidency at 35. You can be mayor of most cities at a far younger age, usually 18, which means you could theoretically run a town without being able to drink in its bars.

5   These inconsistencies aren't our countries' most pressing problem. But our culture's inability to agree on when adulthood begins contributes to some awfully infantile behavior, or at least our tolerance of it.

When the writer Charles Murray visited Middlebury College recently, students who disagreed with his views on race shouted him down, yelled obscenities, banged on windows, set off fire alarms and, after his talk, grabbed the hair of the professor who had debated against him. Some liberals said, in the students' defense, "They are children!" That's an odd way to think about adults old enough to vote and enlist in the Army, but perhaps a rational take on man-boys too young to drink.

We need to figure out who counts as an adult. It makes no sense to expect people to die for their country but not drink for their pleasure. By the same token, it's absurd to say that people who aren't old enough to vote are old enough to get married—if you can't vote for town government, you shouldn't be able to form your own household. There should be one age of majority when all of these rights are bestowed at once.

Of course, it's not easy to determine the right age. Research suggests that our brains don't reach cognitive maturity until we are well into our 20s—a strong argument for not letting 18-year-olds buy liquor or, for that matter, letting 18-year-olds drive cars or buy guns. Conversely, because 16-year-olds (and younger) can have babies, there's a good argument for letting them marry the babies' fathers, with the hope of creating stable families.

But the fact that any age of maturity we choose will necessarily seem arbitrary shouldn't blind us to the common-sense wisdom of having a uniform one. Eighteen—when most people are done with high school—seems as good an age as any.

10   If we raise the marriage age to 18, and lower the drinking age to 18—where it used to be in most states—then we'd have one meaningful age of majority for marriage, voting, drinking, and military service.

Not to mention signing contracts. "We don't allow children to enter into significant binding contracts before 18," said Derek Slap, a Democratic legislator from West Hartford who said he'll probably vote for the Connecticut marriage bill.

But what, I asked, about a couple of 17-year-olds who are truly in love? "Maybe once in a while Romeo and Juliet would have to cool their jets for a year," Slap said. "But I am OK with that."

Critiquing "How Do We Define Adulthood?"

1. Oppenheimer proposes an operational definition of adulthood: age 18. What reasons does he offer to support his claim?

2. Oppenheimer implies that there are problems with the operational definition of adulthood as age 18. What are some of these problems?

3. What other criteria besides age could be used to determine adulthood? How would you define adulthood if you couldn't specify an age?

4. If you had to vote on a single age for adulthood, would you agree with Oppenheimer that 18 is the best choice? Why or why not?

5. What is at stake in this argument?

Chapter 13
Causal Arguments

Learning Objectives

In this chapter you will learn to:

13.1 Explain and illustrate kinds of causal arguments.

13.2 Explain how different causal mechanisms function in cause/consequence arguments.

13.3 Understand key causal terms and avoid inductive fallacies in causal arguments.

13.4 Write your own cause or consequence argument.

We encounter causal issues all the time. What has caused the declining birth rate among teens in the United States? Why has kombucha become a popular drink among millennials? Why has there been a marked decline in the number of teenagers getting a driver's licence? Why are white teenage girls seven times as likely to smoke as African American teenage girls? Why do couples who live together before marriage have a higher divorce rate than those who don't? Why did fidget spinners become a fad?

In addition to asking causal questions like these, we pose consequence questions as well: What might be the consequences of installing stricter proof-of-citizenship requirements for voting? What might be the social and economic consequences of establishing public preschool programs? What have been the consequences of the smart phone on the social life of pre-teens and teens?

Often arguments about causes and consequences have important stakes because they shape our view of reality and influence government policies and individual decisions. This chapter explains how to wrestle responsibly with cause/consequence issues to produce effective causal arguments.

Case 1: What Causes Global Warming?

One of the early clues linking global warming to atmospheric carbon dioxide (CO_2) came from side-by-side comparisons of graphs plotting atmospheric carbon dioxide and global temperatures over time. These graphs show that increases in global temperature parallel increases in the percentage of carbon dioxide in the atmosphere. However, the graphs show only a correlation, or association, between increased carbon dioxide and higher average temperature. To argue that an increase in CO_2 could cause global warming, scientists needed to explain the links in a causal chain. They did so by comparing the earth to a greenhouse. Carbon dioxide, like glass in a greenhouse, lets some of the earth's heat radiate into space but also reflects some of the heat back to the earth. The higher the concentration of carbon dioxide, the more heat is reflected back to the earth.

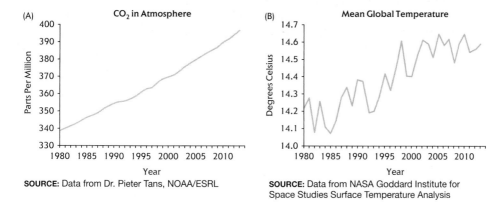

SOURCE: Data from Dr. Pieter Tans, NOAA/ESRL

SOURCE: Data from NASA Goddard Institute for Space Studies Surface Temperature Analysis

Case 2: What Has Caused the Change in the Rate of Teen Pregnancies in the United State in the Last Five Years?

Although the United States still has the highest rate of teen pregnancies among developed countries, studies show a decline in teen pregnancies since the early 1990s. What has caused this decline? Some economists point to the recession of 2007–2009 as a major cause, claiming that as the job market tightened, teens became afraid of not being able to get jobs when encumbered with babies. Other sources emphasize the role of parents in cautioning teens about irresponsible choices concerning sexual behavior and reproduction. A quite different explanation comes from a recent study by the National Bureau of Economic Research analyzing the impact of media images on viewers. This study has found a correlation between the decline in teen pregnancies and the watching of the MTV docudrama *16 and Pregnant* (which premiered in 2009) and its spinoff *Teen Moms*. While the Parents Television Council and other critics argue that these shows sensationalize and glamorize the lives of the teen moms, researchers, using Nielsen ratings and geographic data on viewership and data from Google Trends and Twitter, found that watching these shows "led to more searches and tweets regarding birth control and abortion, and ultimately led to a 5.7 percent reduction in teen births in the eighteen months" after *16 and Pregnant* first aired.[*] This study broadens social thinking on the use of reality TV and social media in promoting safe sex, as well as its potential value in addressing other social and health causes.

An Overview of Causal Arguments

13.1 Explain and illustrate kinds of causal arguments.

Typically, causal arguments try to show how one event brings about another. When causal investigation focuses on material objects—for example, one billiard ball striking another—the notion of causality appears fairly straightforward. But when humans become the focus of a causal argument, the nature of causality becomes more vexing. If we say that something happened to "cause" a person to act in a certain way, what do we mean? Do we mean that she was "forced" to act in a certain

---

[*] Melissa S. Kearney and Phillip B. Levine. "Media Influences on Social Outcomes: The Impact of MTV's *16 and Pregnant* on Teen Childbearing," NBER Working Paper No. 19795, National Bureau of Economic Research, January 2014.

way, thereby negating her free will (as in, an undiagnosed brain tumor caused her to act erratically), or do we mean more simply that she was "motivated" to act in a certain way (as in, her anger at her parents caused her to act erratically)? When we argue about causality in human beings, we must guard against confusing these two senses of "cause" or assuming that human behavior can be predicted or controlled in the same way that nonhuman behavior can. A rock dropped from a roof will always fall at thirty-two feet per second squared, and a rat zapped with electricity for turning left in a maze will always stop turning left. But if we raise interest rates, will consumers save more money? If so, how much money will they save? This is the sort of question that can be debated endlessly.

Kinds of Causal Arguments

Arguments about causality can take a variety of forms. Three typical kinds are speculations about possible causes, arguments for an unexpected or surprising cause, and predictions of consequences.

- **Speculations about possible causes.** Sometimes arguers speculate about possible causes of a phenomenon. For example, whenever a shooter opens fire on innocent bystanders (as in the 2015 mass killing at the Pulse gay nightclub in Orlando, Florida; the 2012 Sandy Hook Elementary School massacre in Connecticut; or the nearly fatal wounding of a Republican legislator practicing for a congressional baseball game in June 2017) social scientists, police investigators, terrorism specialists, and media commentators begin analyzing the causes. One of the most thoroughly studied and heavily debated shooting incidents occurred in 1999 when the nation was shocked by one of the first incidents of mass school shooting—the Columbine High School massacre in Littleton, Colorado, in which two male students opened fire on their classmates, killing thirteen people, wounding twenty-three others, and then shooting themselves. Figure 13.1 illustrates some of the proposed theories for the Columbine shootings. What was at stake was not only our desire to understand the sociocultural sources of school violence but also our desire

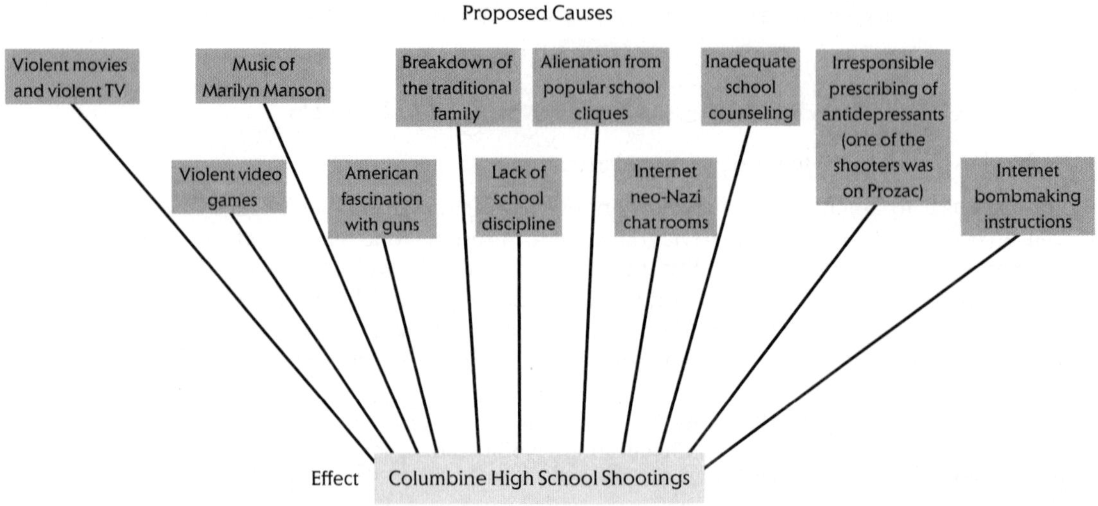

Figure 13.1 Speculation about possible causes: Columbine High School massacre

to institute policies to prevent future school shootings. If a primary cause is the availability of guns, then we might push for more stringent gun-control laws. But if the primary cause is the disintegration of the traditional family, the shooters' alienation from high-school cliques, or the dangerous side effects of antidepressant medications, then we might seek different solutions.

- **Arguments for an unexpected or surprising cause.** Besides sorting out possible causes of a phenomenon, sometimes arguers try to persuade readers to see the plausibility of an unexpected or surprising cause. This was the strategy used by syndicated columnist John Leo, who wanted readers to consider the role of violent video games as a contributing cause to the Columbine massacre.* After suggesting that the Littleton killings were partly choreographed on video-game models, Leo suggested the causal chain shown in Figure 13.2.

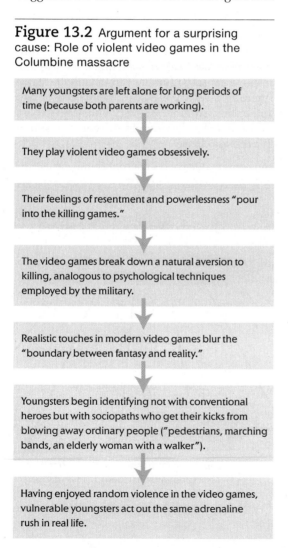

Figure 13.2 Argument for a surprising cause: Role of violent video games in the Columbine massacre

Many youngsters are left alone for long periods of time (because both parents are working).

They play violent video games obsessively.

Their feelings of resentment and powerlessness "pour into the killing games."

The video games break down a natural aversion to killing, analogous to psychological techniques employed by the military.

Realistic touches in modern video games blur the "boundary between fantasy and reality."

Youngsters begin identifying not with conventional heroes but with sociopaths who get their kicks from blowing away ordinary people ("pedestrians, marching bands, an elderly woman with a walker").

Having enjoyed random violence in the video games, vulnerable youngsters act out the same adrenaline rush in real life.

---

* John Leo, "Kill-for-Kicks Video Games Desensitizing Our Children," *Seattle Times*, 27 April 1999, B4.

- **Predictions of consequences.** Another frequently encountered kind of causal argument predicts the consequences of current, planned, or proposed actions or events. Consequence arguments have high stakes because we often judge actions on whether their benefits outweigh their costs. As we will see in Chapter 15, proposal arguments usually require writers to predict the consequences of a proposed action, conduct a cost/benefit analysis, and persuade readers that no unforeseen negative consequences will result. Just as a phenomenon can have multiple causes, it can also have multiple consequences. Figure 13.3 shows the consequence arguments considered by environmentalists who propose eliminating several dams on the Snake River in order to save salmon runs.

Toulmin Framework for a Causal Argument

Because causal arguments can involve lengthy or complex causal chains, they are often harder to summarize in *because* clauses than are other kinds of arguments. Likewise, they are not as likely to yield quick analysis through the Toulmin schema. Nevertheless, a causal argument can usually be stated as a claim with *because* clauses. Typically, a *because* clause pinpoints one or two key elements in the causal chain rather than summarize every link. John Leo's argument linking the Columbine massacre to violent video games could be summarized in the following claim with a *because* clause:

> Violent video games may have been a contributing cause to the Littleton massacre because playing these games can make random, sociopathic violence seem pleasurable.

Figure 13.3 Predictions of consequences: Eliminating dams on the Snake River

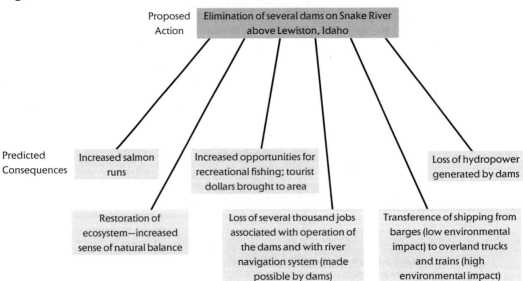

Once stated as an enthymeme, the argument can be analyzed using Toulmin's schema. It is easiest to apply Toulmin's schema to causal arguments if you think of the grounds as the observable phenomena at any point in the causal chain and the warrants as the shareable assumptions about causality.

Toulmin Analysis of the Violent Video Games Argument

ENTHYMEME

CLAIM Violent video games may have been a contributing cause to the Columbine school shooting

REASON because playing these games can make random, sociopathic violence seem pleasurable.

Qualifiers

GROUNDS

- Evidence that the killers, like many young people, played violent video games

- Evidence that the games are violent

- Evidence that the games involve random, sociopathic violence (not good guys versus bad guys) such as killing ordinary people—marching bands, little old ladies, etc.

- Evidence that young people derive pleasure from these games

CONDITIONS OF REBUTTAL

Attacking the reason and grounds

- Perhaps the killers didn't play violent video games.

- Perhaps the video games are no more violent than traditional kids' games such as cops and robbers.

- Perhaps the video games do not feature sociopathic killing.

WARRANT

If young people derive pleasure from random, sociopathic killing in video games, they can transfer this pleasure to real life, thus leading to the Columbine shooting.

BACKING

- Testimony from psychologists

- Evidence that violent video games desensitize people to violence

- Analogy to military training in which video games are used to "make killing a reflex action"

- Evidence that the distinction between fantasy and reality becomes especially blurred for unstable young people

CONDITIONS OF REBUTTAL

Attacking the warrant and backing

- Perhaps kids are fully capable of distinguishing fantasy from reality.

- Perhaps the games are just fun with no transference to real life.

- Perhaps the games are substantially different from military training games.

For Writing and Discussion

Developing Causal Chains

Individual task:

1. Create a causal chain to show how the item on the left could lead to the item on the right.

a. Invention of the automobile	Changes in sexual mores
b. Increased dependence on smartphones	New cultural trend toward "bailing" (abrupt canceling of social engagements)
c. Growth of social media as a source of news	The increasing polarization of politics in the United States
d. Millennials' desire for an urban lifestyle	Redesign of cities
e. Development of way to prevent rejections in transplant operations	Liberalization of euthanasia laws

2. For each of your causal chains, compose a claim with an attached *because* clause summarizing one or two key links in the causal chain—for example, "Millennials' desire for an urban lifestyle is spurring the redesign of cities because Millennials' car- and house-free habits are prompting developers to build new high-density urban communities that offer easy access to work and pleasure."

Group task:

Share your causal claim and *because* clause links with the other members of your class.

Two Methods for Arguing That One Event Causes Another

13.2 **Explain how different causal mechanisms function in cause/consequence arguments.**

One of the first things you need to do when preparing a causal argument is to note exactly what sort of causal relationship you are dealing with: a onetime phenomenon, a recurring phenomenon, or a puzzling trend. Here are some examples.

Kind of Phenomenon	Examples
Onetime phenomenon	• Volvo's 2017 decision to stop building gasoline-powered cars and move entirely to electric or hybrid vehicles • The election of Donald Trump as president of the United States • The 2017 collision of the *USS Fitzgerald* (a guided-missile destroyer) with a Philippine-flagged merchant vessel near Yokosuka, Japan
Recurring phenomenon	• Failure of teenagers to practice safe sex • Homelessness • Recidivism (tendency of former prisoners to return to crime after release from prison)
Puzzling trend	• Increase in the number of events counted as Olympic sports • Increase in opioid addiction (prescribed pain killer) in rural America • Declining populations of both bats and honeybees

With recurring phenomena or with trends, one has the luxury of being able to study multiple cases, often over time. You can interview people, make repeated observations, or study the conditions in which the puzzling phenomenon occurs.

But with a onetime occurrence, one's approach is more like that of a detective than a scientist. Because one can't repeat the event with different variables, one must rely only on the immediate evidence at hand, which can quickly disappear. Having briefly stated these words of caution, let's turn now to two main ways that you can argue that one event causes another.

First Method: Explain the Causal Mechanism Directly

The most convincing kind of causal argument identifies every link in the causal chain, showing how an initiating cause leads step by step to an observed effect. A causes B, which causes C, which causes D. In some cases, all you have to do is fill in the missing links. In other cases—when your assumptions about how one step leads to the next may seem questionable to your audience—you have to argue for the causal connection with more vigor.

A careful spelling out of each step in the causal chain is the technique used by science writer Robert S. Devine in the following passage from his article "The Trouble with Dams." Although the benefits of dams are widely understood (they produce pollution-free electricity while providing flood control, irrigation, barge transportation, and recreational boating), the negative effects are less commonly known and understood. In this article, Devine tries to persuade readers that dams have serious negative consequences. In the following passage, he explains how dams reduce salmon flows by slowing the migration of smolts (newly hatched, young salmon) to the sea.

Causal Argument Describing a Causal Chain

Such transformations lie at the heart of the ongoing environmental harm done by dams. Rivers are rivers because they flow, and the nature of their flows defines much of their character. When dams alter flows, they alter the essence of rivers.

Consider the erstwhile river behind Lower Granite (a dam on Idaho's Snake River). Although I was there in the springtime, when I looked at the water it was moving too slowly to merit the word "flow"—and Lower Granite Lake isn't even one of the region's enormous storage reservoirs, which bring currents to a virtual halt. In the past, spring snowmelt sent powerful currents down the Snake during April and May. Nowadays hydropower operators of the Columbia and Snake systems store the runoff behind the dams and release it during the winter, when demand—and the price—for electricity rises. Over the ages, however, many populations of salmon have adapted to the spring surge. The smolts used the strong flows to migrate, drifting downstream with the current. During the journey smolts' bodies undergo physiological changes that require them to reach salt water quickly. Before dams backed up the Snake, smolts coming down from Idaho got to the sea in six to twenty days; now it takes from sixty to ninety days, and few of the young salmon reach salt water in time. The emasculated current is the single largest reason that the number of wild adult salmon migrating up the Snake each year has crashed from predevelopment runs of 100,000–200,000 to what was projected to be 150–750 this year.*

This tightly constructed passage connects various causal chains to explain the decline of salmon runs.

---

* Robert S. Devine, "The Trouble with Dams," *Atlantic* (August 1995), 64–75. The example quotation is from page 70.

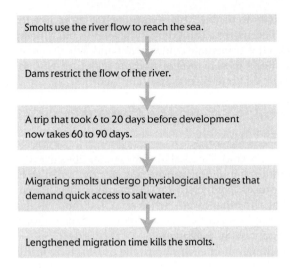

Describing each link in the causal chain—and making each link seem as plausible as possible—is the most persuasive means of convincing readers that a specific cause leads to a specific effect.

Second Method: Infer Causal Links Using Inductive Reasoning

If we can't explain a causal link directly, we often employ a reasoning strategy called *induction*. Through induction we infer a general conclusion based on a limited number of specific cases. For example, if on several occasions you got a headache after drinking red wine but not after drinking white wine, you would be likely to conclude inductively that red wine causes you to get headaches, although you can't explain directly how it does so. However, because there are almost always numerous variables involved, inductive reasoning leads to only probable truths, not certain truths.

THREE WAYS OF THINKING INDUCTIVELY   When your brain thinks inductively, it sorts through data looking for patterns of similarity and difference. In this section we explain three ways of thinking inductively: looking for a common element, looking for a single difference, and looking for correlations.

1. **Look for a common element.** One kind of inductive thinking sends you on a search for a common element that can explain recurrences of the same phenomenon. For example, psychologists attempting to understand the causes of anorexia have discovered that many anorexics (but not all) come from perfectionist, highly work-oriented homes that emphasize duty and responsibility. This common element is thus a suspected causal factor leading to anorexia.

2. **Look for a single difference.** Another approach is to look for a single difference that may explain the appearance of a new phenomenon. When infant death rates in the state of Washington shot up in July and August 1986, one event making these two months different stood out: increased radioactive fallout over Washington from the April Chernobyl nuclear meltdown in Ukraine. This single difference led some researchers to suspect radiation as a possible cause of the increase in infant deaths.

3. **Look for correlations.** Still another method of induction is correlation, which means that two events or phenomena tend to occur together but doesn't imply that one causes the other. For example, there is a correlation between nearsightedness and both intelligencesand academic achievement. (That is, in a given sample of nearsighted people and people with normal eyesight, the nearsighted group will have a somewhat higher average IQ score as well as higher academic rankings.) But the direction of causality isn't clear. It could be that high intelligence causes people to read more, thus ruining their eyes (high intelligence causes nearsightedness). Or it could be that nearsightedness causes people to read more, thus raising their academic achievement level and their IQ scores (nearsightedness causes high intelligence). Or it could be that some unknown phenomenon, perhaps a gene, is related to both nearsightedness and intelligence. So keep in mind that correlation is not causation—it simply suggests possible causation.

For Writing and Discussion

Developing Plausible Causal Chains Based on Correlations

Working individually or in small groups, develop plausible causal chains that may explain the relationship between the following pairs of phenomena:

a.	A person who registers a low stress level on an electrochemical stress meter	does daily meditation
b.	A binge drinker at college parties	has increased risk of becoming a perpetrator or victim of sexual violence
c.	A person who grew up in a house with two or more bathrooms	is likely to have higher SAT scores than a person who grew up in a one-bathroom home
d.	An area with an increased crime rate	also has an increased homelessness rate
e.	A member of the National Rifle Association	supports restrictions on immigration

Examining Visual Arguments

A Causal Claim

This billboard is part of a Texas campaign to fight sex trafficking. How do both the text and image in this billboard suggest links in a causal chain? Although this ad oversimplifies the complex issue of human trafficking, and some would say it represents only one view of sex workers, how do the words and the choice of images combine to make powerful appeals to both *logos* and *pathos*?

Key Terms and Inductive Fallacies in Causal Arguments

13.3 Understand key causal terms and avoid inductive fallacies in causal arguments.

Because causal arguments are often easier to conduct if writer and reader share a few specialized terms and concepts, this section explains key terms in causal reasoning and offers ways to avoid inductive fallacies.

A Glossary of Key Terms

- **The problem of oversimplified cause.** One of the great temptations is to look for *the* cause of something, as if a phenomenon has only one cause rather than multiple causes. For example, in recent years the number of persons in the United States sending out Christmas cards has declined substantially. Many commentators attribute the decline to the increasing use of Facebook, which keeps old friends in touch year-round, eliminating the need for holiday "family letters." But there may be other causes also, such as a decline in the number of nuclear families, fewer networks of long-term friends, or generational shifts away from older traditions. When you make a causal argument, be especially careful how you use words such as *all, most, some, the,* or *in part.* For example, to say that *all* the decline in Christmas cards is caused by Facebook is to make a universal statement about Facebook as *the* cause. An argument will be stronger and more accurate if the arguer makes a less sweeping statement: *Some* of the cause for the decline in Christmas cards can be attributed to Facebook. Arguers sometimes deliberately mix up these quantifiers to misrepresent and dismiss opposing views.

- **Immediate and remote causes.** Every causal chain extends backward indefinitely into the past. An *immediate cause* is the closest in time to the event being examined. Consider the causes for the release of nuclear contaminants around the Fukushima nuclear power plant following the 2011 earthquake off the coast of Japan. The immediate cause was loss of power to the water pumps that cooled the reactor's fuel rods, causing the rods to overheat and partially melt. A slightly less immediate cause (several days earlier) was the earthquake-produced tsunami that had swept away the diesel fuel tanks needed to run the backup generators. These immediate causes can be contrasted with a *remote cause*—in this case, a late-1960s design decision that used backup diesel generators to power the water pumps in case of an electrical power loss to the reactor facility. Still more remote causes were the economic and regulatory systems in the late 1960s that led to this particular design.

- **Precipitating and contributing causes.** These terms are similar to immediate and remote causes but don't designate a temporal link going into the past. Rather, they refer to a main cause emerging out of a background of subsidiary causes. For example, if a husband and wife decide to separate, the *precipitating cause* may be a stormy fight over money, after which one of the partners (or both) says, "I've had enough." In contrast, *contributing causes* would be all the background factors that are dooming the marriage: preoccupation with their careers, disagreement about priorities, in-law problems. Note that contributing causes and the precipitating cause all coexist at the same time.

- **Constraints.** Sometimes an effect occurs because some stabilizing factor—a *constraint*—is removed. In other words, the presence of a constraint may keep a certain effect from occurring. For example, in the marriage we have been discussing, the presence of children in the home may be a constraint against divorce. As soon as the children graduate from high school and leave home, the marriage may well dissolve.

- **Necessary and sufficient causes.** A *necessary cause* is one that has to be present for a given effect to occur. For example, fertility drugs are necessary to cause the conception of septuplets. Every couple who has septuplets must have used fertility drugs. In contrast, a *sufficient cause* is one that always produces or guarantees a given effect. Smoking more than a pack of cigarettes per day is sufficient to raise the cost of one's life insurance policy. This statement means that if you are a smoker, no matter how healthy you appear to be, life insurance companies will always place you in a higher risk bracket and charge you a higher premium. In some cases, a single cause can be both necessary and sufficient. For example, lack of ascorbic acid (Vitamin C) is both a necessary and a sufficient cause of scurvy. (Think of those old-time sailors who didn't eat fruit for months.) It is a necessary cause because you can't get scurvy any other way except through absence of ascorbic acid; it is a sufficient cause because the absence of ascorbic acid always causes scurvy.

Avoiding Common Inductive Fallacies That Can Lead to Wrong Conclusions

Largely because of its power, informal induction can often lead to wrong conclusions. You should be aware of two common fallacies of inductive reasoning that can tempt you into erroneous assumptions about causality. (Both fallacies are treated more fully in the Appendix.)

- *Post hoc* **fallacy:** The *post hoc, ergo propter hoc* fallacy ("after this, therefore because of this") mistakes sequence for cause. Just because event A regularly precedes event B doesn't mean that event A causes event B. The same reasoning that tells us that flipping a switch causes the light to go on can make us believe that low levels of radioactive fallout from the Chernobyl nuclear disaster caused a sudden rise in infant death rates in the state of Washington. The nuclear disaster clearly preceded the rise in death rates. But did it clearly *cause* it? Our point is that precedence alone is not proof of causality and that we are guilty of the *post hoc* fallacy whenever we are swayed to believe that one thing causes another just because it comes first.

- **Hasty generalization:** The *hasty generalization* fallacy occurs when you make a generalization based on too few cases or too little consideration of alternative explanations: You flip the switch, but the light bulb doesn't go on. You conclude—too hastily—that the light bulb has burned out. (Perhaps the power has gone off or the switch is broken.) How many trials does it take before you can make a justified generalization rather than a hasty generalization? It is difficult to say for sure.

Both the *post hoc* fallacy and the hasty generalization fallacy remind us that induction requires a leap from individual cases to a general principle and that it is always possible to leap too soon.

For Writing and Discussion

Brainstorming Causes and Constraints

The terms in the preceding glossary can be effective brainstorming tools for thinking of possible causes of an event. For the following events, try to think of as many causes as possible by brainstorming possible *immediate causes, remote causes, precipitating causes, contributing causes,* and *constraints*.

1. Working individually, make a list of different kinds of causes/constraints for one of the following:
   a. Your decision to attend your present college
   b. An important event in your life or your family (a job change, a major move, etc.)
   c. A personal opinion you hold that is not widely shared
2. Working as a group, make a list of different kinds of causes/constraints for one of the following:
   a. Why women's fashion and beauty magazines are the most frequently purchased magazines in college bookstores
   b. Why U.S. students consistently score below Asian and European students in academic achievement
   c. Why large supermarket chains are selling more organic food

Writing Assignment: A Causal Argument

13.4 Write your own cause or consequence argument.

Choose an issue about the causes or consequences of a trend, event, or other phenomenon. Write an argument that persuades an audience to accept your explanation of the causes or consequences of your chosen phenomenon. Within your essay you should examine alternative hypotheses or opposing views and explain your reasons for rejecting them. You can imagine your issue either as a puzzle or as a disagreement. If a puzzle, your task will be to create a convincing case for an audience that doesn't have an answer to your causal question already in mind. If a disagreement, your task will be more overtly persuasive because your goal will be to change your audience's views.

Exploring Ideas

Arguments about causes and consequences abound in public, professional, and personal life, so you shouldn't have difficulty finding a causal issue worth investigating and arguing.

Responding to his experiences as a junior-high math tutor, student writer Jesse Goncalves investigated the causes of math anxiety. He argued that math anxiety is primarily a learned behavior passed onto children from math-anxious parents and instructors (see the Readings at the end of this chapter). Student writer Carlos Macias, puzzled by the ease with which college students are issued credit cards, wrote a researched argument disentangling the factors leading young people to bury themselves in debt (see the Readings at the end of this chapter). Other students have focused on causal issues such as these: Why do kids join gangs? What are the consequences of mandatory drug testing (written by a student who has to take amphetamines for narcolepsy)? Why has the age of first marriage steadily increased since 1970?

If you have trouble finding a causal issue to write about, you can often create provocative controversies among your classmates through the following strategies:

- **Make a list of unusual likes and dislikes.** Think about unusual things that people like or dislike. You could summarize the conventional explanations that people give for an unusual pleasure or aversion and then argue for a surprising or unexpected cause. What attracts people to extreme sports? How do you explain the popularity of the paleo diet or of *Game of Thrones* or *The Walking Dead*?

- **Make a list of puzzling events or trends.** Another strategy is to make a list of puzzling phenomena and then try to explain their causes. Start with onetime events (a curriculum change at your school, the sudden popularity of a new app). Then list puzzling recurring events (failure of intelligent teenagers to practice safe sex). Finally, list some recent trends (growth of naturopathic medicine, increased interest in tattoos and piercing). Engage classmates in discussions of one or more of the items on your list. Look for places of disagreement as entry points into the conversation.

- **Explore contested or puzzling causes or consequences from your experience.** What causal issues or surprising consequences emerge from your participation in a group, club, sports team, internship, or job? Based on your experience, does having an internship during the academic year lead to a higher GPA or a lower GPA (or neither)? Based on your interviews with persons who have worked in assisted-living businesses, does animal therapy decrease depression in elderly residents? Based on your own experiences, what causes and consequences that others in this community might care about have you been inspired to explore?

- **Brainstorm consequences of a recent or proposed action.** Arguments about consequences are among the most interesting and important of causal disputes. If you can argue for an unanticipated consequence of a real or proposed action, whether good or bad, you can contribute importantly to the conversation. What might be the consequences, for example, of placing "green taxes" on coal-produced electricity; of legalizing marijuana; of overturning *Roe v. Wade* (which legalized abortion); or of requiring national public service for all young adults?

Identifying Your Audience and Determining What's at Stake

Before drafting your argument, identify your targeted audience and determine what's at stake. Consider your responses to the following questions:

- What audience are you targeting? What background do they need to understand your issue? How much do they already care about it?

- Before they read your argument, what stance on your issue do you imagine them holding? What change do you want to bring about in their views?

- What will they find new or surprising about your argument?

- What objections might they raise? What counterarguments or alternative points of view will you need to address?

- Why does your argument matter? Who might be threatened or made uncomfortable by your views? What is at stake?

Organizing a Causal Argument

At the outset, it is useful to know some of the standard ways that a causal argument can be organized. Later, you may decide on a different organizational pattern, but the standard ways shown in Figures 13.4, 13.5, and 13.6 will help you get started.

Figure 13.4 Argument explaining links in a causal chain

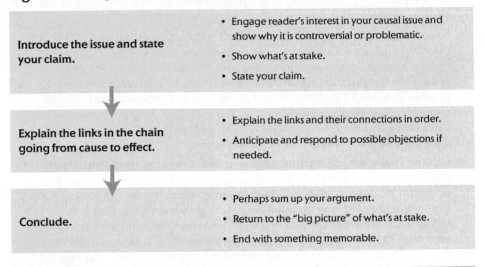

Introduce the issue and state your claim.	• Engage reader's interest in your causal issue and show why it is controversial or problematic. • Show what's at stake. • State your claim.
Explain the links in the chain going from cause to effect.	• Explain the links and their connections in order. • Anticipate and respond to possible objections if needed.
Conclude.	• Perhaps sum up your argument. • Return to the "big picture" of what's at stake. • End with something memorable.

Figure 13.5 Argument proposing multiple causes or consequences of a phenomenon

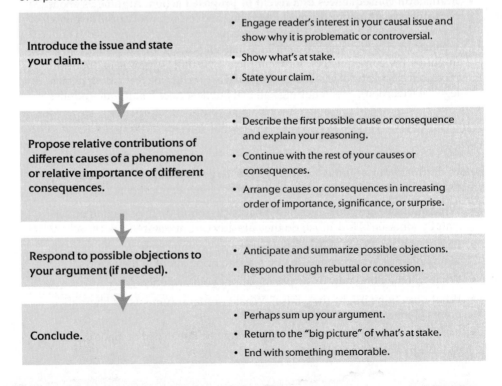

Introduce the issue and state your claim.	• Engage reader's interest in your causal issue and show why it is problematic or controversial. • Show what's at stake. • State your claim.
Propose relative contributions of different causes of a phenomenon or relative importance of different consequences.	• Describe the first possible cause or consequence and explain your reasoning. • Continue with the rest of your causes or consequences. • Arrange causes or consequences in increasing order of importance, significance, or surprise.
Respond to possible objections to your argument (if needed).	• Anticipate and summarize possible objections. • Respond through rebuttal or concession.
Conclude.	• Perhaps sum up your argument. • Return to the "big picture" of what's at stake. • End with something memorable.

Figure 13.6 Argument proposing a surprising cause or consequence

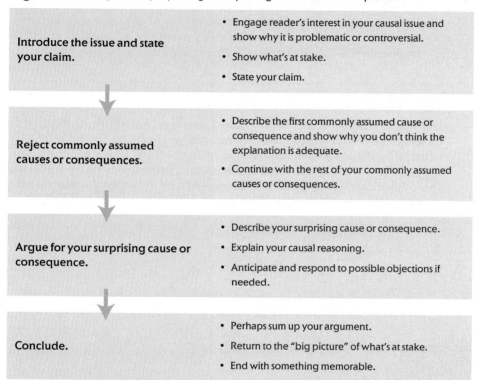

| Introduce the issue and state your claim. | • Engage reader's interest in your causal issue and show why it is problematic or controversial.
• Show what's at stake.
• State your claim. |

| Reject commonly assumed causes or consequences. | • Describe the first commonly assumed cause or consequence and show why you don't think the explanation is adequate.
• Continue with the rest of your commonly assumed causes or consequences. |

| Argue for your surprising cause or consequence. | • Describe your surprising cause or consequence.
• Explain your causal reasoning.
• Anticipate and respond to possible objections if needed. |

| Conclude. | • Perhaps sum up your argument.
• Return to the "big picture" of what's at stake.
• End with something memorable. |

Figures 13.5 and 13.6 are similar in that they examine numerous possible causes or consequences. Figure 13.5, however, tries to establish the relative importance of each cause or consequence, whereas Figure 13.6 aims at rejecting the causes or consequences normally assumed by the audience and argues for an unexpected, surprising cause or consequence. Figure 13.6 can also be used when your purpose is to change your audience's mind about a cause or consequence.

Questioning and Critiquing a Causal Argument

Knowing how to question and critique a causal argument will help you anticipate opposing views in order to strengthen your own. It will also help you rebut another person's causal argument. Here are some useful questions to ask:

- When you explain the links in a causal chain, can a skeptic point out weaknesses in any of the links?
- If you speculate about the causes of a phenomenon, could a skeptic argue for different causes or arrange your causes in a different order of importance?
- If you argue for a surprising cause or a surprising consequence of a phenomenon, could a skeptic point out alternative explanations that would undercut your argument?
- If your argument depends on inferences from data, could a skeptic question the way the data were gathered or interpreted? Could a skeptic claim that

the data aren't relevant (for example, research done with lab animals might not apply to humans)?

- If your causal argument depends on a correlation between one phenomenon and another, could a skeptic argue that the direction of causality should be reversed or that an unidentified, third phenomenon is the real cause?

Readings

Our first reading, by student writer Jesse Goncalves, was written in response to the assignment in this chapter. He became interested in the causes of math anxiety when he worked as a math tutor in a junior high school. Jesse's argument illustrates the format and documentation system for a paper following the guidelines of the American Psychological Association (APA). For further discussion of the APA documentation system, see Chapter 18.

What Causes Math Anxiety?

Jess Goncalves

October 18, 2018

What Causes Math Anxiety?

Why are so many people afraid of math? As an applied mathematics major, I did not realize the extent to which math can become inaccessible to those who fear it until I began working in a middle-school math classroom. Math anxiety is defined as "feelings of fear, apprehension, or dread that many people experience when they are in situations that require solving math problems" (Casad, Hale, & Wachs, 2015). After I learned about math anxiety, I quickly came to recognize the anxiety in many of my students, several of my college peers, and occasionally myself. Indeed, nearly half of all children in the United States develop moderate to severe math anxiety, a condition that often remains with them for the rest of their lives (Boaler, 2016). A great deal of research has been conducted on the causes of math anxiety over the past 50 years, and a wide variety of factors have been implicated. Contrary to the prevailing view that math anxiety is directly caused by a combination of genetics, institutional policies, and cultural forces, I argue that math anxiety may be best understood as a learned behavior that is passed on to children from math-anxious parents and teachers, leading to an intergenerational cycle of math anxiety.

Harkening back to the age-old question of nature versus nurture, many scholars have proposed and researched a connection between genetics and math anxiety, and some studies indicate that nature is indeed a strong predictor of a child's level of anxiety. A team of psychology researchers headed by Dr. Zhe Wang found that "[g]enetic factors accounted for roughly 40% of the variation in mathematical anxiety" when they studied 514 pairs of 12-year-old twins (2014). Dr. Wang and her co-authors argue that many of the same genetic factors that make people more likely to develop other anxieties also put them at a higher risk of developing math anxiety. They also note that biological factors such as dyscalculia, better known as mathematical dyslexia, are linked to poor math performance (Wang et al., 2014). Citing studies that implicate poor performance as both a cause and consequence of math anxiety, Dr. Wang contends that being genetically predisposed to struggle in math constitutes a predisposition towards math anxiety. Despite these findings, Dr. Wang does not side strongly with nature in the debate; her team discovered that "environmental factors independent of both general anxiety and math problem solving accounted for … 53% of the total variance" in math anxiety (2014). What,

WHAT CAUSES MATH ANXIETY?   3

then, are the factors that assume 53% responsibility for the epidemic of math anxiety?

Education policy is one environmental influence often cited as a cause of math anxiety. For example, Dr. Jo Boaler, a professor of mathematics education at Stanford University, condemns the frequency of timed testing as a major cause of math anxiety. She argues that "timed testing ... transforms children's brains, leading to an inevitable path of math anxiety and low math achievement" (2016). Timed testing is a policy problem due to mandated standardized testing. Moreover, as Dr. Boaler says, "some of the wording in the Common Core State Standards may point to an increased use of timed tests" (2016). Therefore, according to Dr. Boaler, education policy contributes substantially to the epidemic of math anxiety. Beyond policy, many cultural influences have also been accused of inducing math anxiety.

Perhaps the most often blamed and highly researched cultural cause of math anxiety is the unfounded stereotype that males are better at math than females. As Dr. Bettina Casad, a professor of psychology at University of Missouri–St. Louis, and her collaborators assert, "[C]ultural biases about the superiority of boys and men in math permeate our social consciousness" (2015). In a study of the interplay between these biases and math anxiety, Casad found that the "endorsement of math-gender stereotypes may be an antecedent for developing math anxiety for both boys and girls" (2015). Therefore, males and females alike who believe in men's mathematical superiority are at greater risk of developing math anxiety. Because "girls and women are more negatively impacted by cultural biases," a higher number of females suffer from math anxiety (Casad, Hale, & Wachs, 2015). However, the degree to which children are exposed to and influenced by math-gender stereotypes is primarily predicated on their parents and teachers.

While genetics, policy, and culture are all contributing causes of math anxiety, I argue that they do not contribute as significantly or directly as math-anxious parents and teachers. The instructors that shape children's relationships to math are foremost among the "environmental factors" responsible for math anxiety (Wang et al., 2014). Teachers also play a major role in determining the influence of education policies on children, as they are charged with the implementation of policy in their classrooms. Similarly, the extent to which math-gender stereotypes impact children depends in large part on their parents' and teachers' endorsement or rejection of those stereotypes. Thus, parents and teachers are the most immediate and significant causes of math anxiety, as they are the primary vehicles through which policy and culture exert influence.

When they frequently help with homework, math-anxious parents can instill math anxiety in their children by modeling negative attitudes towards math and promoting math-gender stereotypes. Parental homework help is normally correlated with improvement in students' performance; however, a team led by psychology researcher Dr. Erin Maloney found that when parents with math anxiety frequently helped with homework, their children's performance and level of math anxiety were negatively affected (2015). The correlation between parents' and children's math anxiety was present only when parents helped with homework, another indication that the anxiety is transmitted primarily through socialization rather than genetics. Maloney argues that math-anxious parents can cause their children to develop math anxiety because they "tend to believe that math is not useful and have low math self-efficacy and low motivation to succeed in math," so communicating their beliefs is "demotivating" to their children (2015). She also suggests that parents who are themselves afraid of failure in math "may be more likely to express negativity when their child is struggling, which in turn could cause their children to also learn to fear failing in mathematics and to avoid engaging in challenging situations" (Maloney et al., 2015). A separate study headed by Dr. Bettina Casad and colleagues supported Maloney's discovery that math-anxious parents often instill math anxiety in their children. Their results showed that "parents' anxiety plays a role in children's math anxiety, and the variables interact to predict several math education outcomes including math self-efficacy, math GPA, math behavioral intentions, math attitudes, and math devaluing" (2015). Casad also noted that math-anxious mothers are particularly prone to share their anxiety with their daughters, which she postulated is a result of these mothers endorsing math-gender stereotypes. Accordingly, Dr. Elizabeth Gunderson, a professor of psychology at Temple University, and her collaborators found that "parents' gender stereotypes bias their beliefs about their own child's math ability, and these beliefs affect children's own self-perceptions about math" (2012). So, while the endorsement of math-gender stereotypes can cause females and males alike to develop math anxiety, children generally learn to believe these stereotypes from math-anxious parents who have

WHAT CAUSES MATH ANXIETY? 5

themselves internalized the beliefs. In this way, through negative attitudes and biases, math anxiety is passed from one generation of parents to the next in a never-ending cycle. Unfortunately, children who do not receive homework help or who internalize stereotypes from a math-anxious parent, are still at risk of learning math anxiety from a teacher who suffers from the condition.

Perhaps even more influential than parents in the perpetuation of math anxiety are the many math-anxious elementary school teachers. An estimated 60% of elementary school teachers report having moderate to high levels of math anxiety (Bekdemir, 2010), which has been shown to affect instructional practices and classroom dynamics to the point where students perform worse and are at an increased risk of developing math anxiety themselves. Dr. Mehmet Bekdemir, an education researcher, speculates that math-anxious teachers gravitate towards elementary school to avoid teaching middle- or high-school math, however points out that elementary school is the time when children are most prone to developing math anxiety (2010). Dr. Kristin Hadley and Dr. Jim Dorward, both professors of teacher education, found that "teachers who were anxious about teaching mathematics tended to teach in a more traditional manner" (2011), meaning they adopted a conventional, by-the-book pedagogical style and declined to try more innovative strategies. This suggests that math-anxious teachers may be more likely to follow policies that increase students' math anxiety by encouraging traditional practices like frequent timed testing. They also may reject innovative new policies meant to reduce students' anxiety, such as accommodating different learning styles. As a result, the effect of education policy on children's math anxiety is mediated by teachers' levels of math anxiety. Teachers with math anxiety are also more likely to endorse and perpetuate math-gender stereotypes, and for their students, this translates directly to increased math anxiety (Casad, Hale, & Wachs, 2015). For instance, Dr. Elizabeth Gunderson found that in classrooms where teachers had high math anxiety, girls often came to endorse the stereotype that boys are better at math (2012). Therefore, through their instructional practices and biases, teachers with math anxiety put their students, some of whom will become the next generation of teachers, at an increased risk of developing math anxiety themselves. Luckily, individual parents and teachers can work to overcome math anxiety and thereby begin to break the cycle.

WHAT CAUSES MATH ANXIETY?   6

Because cultural forces and policy decisions work primarily through math-anxious parents and teachers to cause math anxiety in children, with genetics playing a subordinate role, addressing math anxiety in adults could greatly reduce the rate of math anxiety in future generations. Policy changes and cultural shifts are necessary to end the epidemic, but those transitions need to begin at the kitchen table and in front of the classroom, where parents and teachers must confront their own anxieties and math gender biases. I will certainly apply the lessons of this research to improve my own practice as a mentor, and perhaps one day as a teacher, to ensure that I do not perpetuate the cycle of math anxiety.

References

Bekdemir, M. (2010). The pre-service teachers' mathematics anxiety related to depth of negative experiences in mathematics classroom while they were students. *Educational Studies in Mathematics, 75*(3), 311–328.

Boaler, J. (2016). Timed tests and the development of math anxiety. *Education Week.* Retrieved from http://www.edweek.org/ew/articles/2012/07/03/36boaler.h31.html

Casad, B., Hale, P., & Wachs, F. (2015). Parent-child math anxiety and math-gender stereotypes predict adolescents' math education outcomes. *Frontiers in Psychology, 6,* 1597.

Gunderson, E. A., Ramirez, G., Levine, S. C., & Beilock, S. (2012). The role of parents and teachers in the development of gender-related math attitudes. *Sex Roles, 66,* 153-166.

Hadley, K., & Dorward, J. (2011). The relationship among elementary teachers' mathematics anxiety, mathematics instructional practices, and student mathematics achievement. *Journal of Curriculum and Instruction, 5*(2), 27–44.

Maloney, E., Ramirez, G., Gunderson, E., Levine, S., & Beilock, S. (2015). Intergenerational effects of parents' math anxiety on children's math achievement and anxiety. *Psychological Science, 26*(9), 1480-1488.

Wang, Z., Hart, S. A., Kovas, Y., Lukowski, S., Soden, B., Thompson, L. A., … & Petrill, S. A. (2014). Who is afraid of math? Two sources of genetic variance for mathematical anxiety. *Journal of Child Psychology and Psychiatry, 55,* 1056–1064.

Critiquing "What Causes Math Anxiety?"

1. In his research paper, Jesse's strategy is to present an unexpected cause of math anxiety. What unexpected cause or causes does Jesse argue for in this paper?

2. Which common explanations of math anxiety does Jesse summarize and explain? How effectively does Jesse use research evidence to persuade you that these causes contribute to math anxiety but aren't as important as Jesse's primary causes?

3. How effectively does Jesse support his claim that math anxious students are more likely to *learn* math anxiety from a math-anxious parent than to *inherit* math anxiety through the genes? What does he use as evidence? Are you persuaded by this evidence?

4. For Jesse, the most important cause of math anxiety is math-anxious elementary teachers. What causal chain does he propose? That is, what is it that math-anxious teachers say or do that passes on math anxiety to their students? How does Jesse use research evidence to make his case? Are you persuaded?

5. How would you characterize Jesse's use of *logos ethos*, and *pathos* in this essay?

Our second reading is from a blog by professional freelance writer and novelist Kris Saknussemm. It explores the surprising phenomenon that people have trouble recognizing themselves in moving pictures of themselves (videos), which should serve as mirrors. There seems to be no clear causal explanation for this counterintuitive observation that technological advancement might lead to a decline in self-recognition.

Mirror, Mirror on the Wall, Are We Really Here at All? Can *We* Tell?

KRIS SAKNUSSEMM

Does greater technological sophistication bring us closer to self-awareness—or does it distance us further? How odd, if increased intelligence in one sphere means a kind of basic blindness in another.

The mirror test was developed in 1970 by psychologist Gordon Gallup Jr. The goal of the test was to measure animals' capacity for self-recognition by marking animals with unscented dyes. Can an animal, watching itself move in the mirror, correlate the "marked" image in the mirror to the physical marking on its body? To date, these animals have passed the mirror test: orca whales, bottlenose dolphins, Asian elephants, chimpanzees, bonobos, orangutans, and Eurasian magpies. Humans, of course, can pass the mirror test, right? Well, here's the irony. With all our advances regarding image production and our exposure to visual information, our mental processing of images of ourselves seems to have led to disconnection and distance. Our perception seems to have failed to keep up or may have even stepped backward.

Take this example, which fascinated me. The groom was in his 50s, the bride in her 40s. The reception venue was an ordinary family home. I found the rambunctious grandchildren and the older folks swapping stories in the WD-40 garage a refreshing change to the high-priced, high-fashion wedding events I'd recently attended. The working-class house hummed with festivity . . . and then . . . the brother of the bride, who'd been videoing the activities, plugged his camera into the living-room TV.

Then the children stopped playing and gathered around. Within three minutes, all the Nerf ball hustle and bustle had ceased and everyone was engaged with the images on the screen. You may say that the people in attendance were in some way "hypnotized" by images of themselves. This is the Era of the Selfie, after all. You might imagine the people laughing at each other, or in some egotistical/self-esteem competition, checking out how much camera time they received relative to others. But what if something much more peculiar happened?

5   What I directly observed was people having trouble identifying themselves in the video. There was what the novelist Franz Kafka called a "strange uncertainty." I experienced this myself, despite the fact I was wearing a distinctive shirt. It got me doing research about technology, the human brain, and the culturally constructed sense of self.

In 1971, a Harvard University team of psychologists investigated auditory stimulation and response. The recording industry was at peak production. Radio had survived the onslaught of TV and remained the overall most pervasive form of information and entertainment delivery. Terms such as "noise pollution" were gaining currency. As a #1 song of the day said, "The air was full of sound."

Despite the level of auditory stimulation, test subjects demonstrated impressive capacity for subtle perceptions and distinctions. It appeared that the "more noise, the greater the ability to distinguish signal." We were getting smarter about sound. Good news. The famous "cocktail party effect" first identified by Colin Cherry in 1953 (whereby people have the selective-attention capability of hearing their name spoken in a crowded room) was in full evidence in Harvard's study. But by radical and paradoxical contrast, test subjects showed a remarkable confusion when listening to recordings of their own voices. It wasn't just that they didn't like the sound of their voices. They had perceptual trouble actually recognizing them.

Now, the deeper, related problem of visual recognition is supported by other studies. One of the largest treatment facilities in the United States, specializing in substance-abuse problems, introduced video into its rehabilitation program. The idea was to let people with alcohol issues openly indulge in drinking and then to videotape them. According to the program director, "We were working on the premise that when people were presented with hard evidence of how alcohol affected their behavior, they might reevaluate on a very personal level." The treatment center anticipated some shamed resistance. Instead, a significant percentage of participating patients did not express the expected degree of denial regarding their behavior—their issue was if it was really them in the video at all. This phenomenon of "nonrecognition" or severely delayed acceptance of recognition has been further demonstrated by one of America's most prominent security companies. When presented with CCTV images of themselves, people literally do not see themselves at first, not pushing their loaded carts toward the checkout stand nor talking with a friend by an apartment elevator. No cause for denial in these cases—just lack of connection—in a very fundamental way.

Perhaps we just want to see a different self? But there's something more at work than privately curated, idealized notions of ourselves, as younger or thinner.

10   Actually, as technology has introduced greater degrees of stimulation/information into our perceptual lives, humans may have become more adept at processing detail and sorting through information—with the important

exception of depictions of ourselves. In blunt terms, the more "mirrors," the less self-recognition. If more exposure leads us to less effective and accurate cognitive processing, do we need to rethink the interaction between apparent technological advance and actual human perception? If the more we see of ourselves the less we immediately recognize, there's a problem—maybe many.

Critiquing "Mirror, Mirror on the Wall, Are We Really Here at All? Can *We* Tell?"

1. Saknussemm points out a surprising consequence of our technological advances. The more we become sophisticated in producing and observing moving images of ourselves, the less we recognize ourselves in the videos. Have you ever had the experience of not quite recognizing yourself in a video? ("Hey, that doesn't look like me or sound like me.") How relevant and effective are the examples Saknussemm cites of this causal phenomenon?

2. How does does Saknussemm explain the cause of this phenomenon? What causal explanations does he consider but discount? What explanations do you propose?

3. Written as a blog, this piece has a speculative informal style that often includes abrupt and surprising transitions. How effective is this piece at arousing your own curiosity about our failure to recognize ourselves in videos? How would the piece be different if it were written in the genre of an academic research paper?

Our final reading has been chosen for its historical interest. Written by student Carlos Macias in 2008, it first appeared in the 8th edition of *Writing Arguments*. It examines the phenomenon of credit card debt among college students, showing how the lack of federal regulation on credit card companies led to exploitive practices that often mired students in unexpected debt. In 2009, Congress approved the Credit Card Act (signed into law by President Obama), which made many of these exploitive practices illegal. Students younger than 21 must now have a co-signer to receive a credit card—a requirement that has led to more extensive use of debit cards and a significant reduction in student credit card debt. Carlos's argument shows what it was like for college students before federal regulations reduced the aggressive practices of credit card companies.

Student Essay

"The Credit Card Company Made Me Do It!"—The Credit Card Industry's Role in Causing Student Debt

Carlos Macias

One day on spring break this year, I strolled into a Gap store. I found several items that I decided to buy. As I was checking out, the cute female clerk around my age, with perfect hair and makeup, asked if I wanted to open a GapCard to save 10 percent on all purchases I made at Gap, Banana

(continued)

Republic, and Old Navy that day. She said I would also earn points toward Gap gift certificates in the future. Since I shop at the Gap often enough, I decided to take her up on her offer. I filled out the form she handed me, and within seconds I—a jobless, indebted-from-student-loans, full-time college student with no substantial assets or income whatsoever—was offered a card with a $1000 credit line. Surprised by the speed at which I was approved and the amount that I was approved for, I decided to proceed to both Banana Republic and Old Navy that day to see if there was anything else I might be interested in getting (there was). By the end of the day, I had rung up nearly $200 in purchases.

I know my $200 shopping spree on credit is nothing compared to some of the horror stories I have heard from friends. One of my friends, a college sophomore, is carrying $2000 on a couple of different cards, a situation that is not unusual at all. The problem is that most students don't have the income to pay off their balances, so they become hooked into paying high interest rates and fees that enrich banks while exploiting students who have not yet learned how to exercise control on their spending habits.

Who is to blame for this situation? Many people might blame the students themselves, citing the importance of individual responsibility and proclaiming that no one forces students to use credit cards. But I put most of the blame directly on the credit card companies. Credit cards are enormously profitable; according to a *New York Times* article, the industry made $30 billion in pretax profits in 2003 alone (McGeehan). Hooking college students on credit cards is essential for this profit, not only because companies make a lot of money off the students themselves, but because hooking students on cards creates a habit that lasts a lifetime. Credit card companies' predatory lending practices—such as using exploitive advertising, using credit scoring to determine creditworthiness, disguising the real cost of credit, and taking advantage of U.S. government deregulation—are causing many unwitting college students to accumulate high levels of credit card debt.

First of all, credit card companies bombard students with highly sophisticated advertising. College students, typically, are in an odd "in-between" stage where they are not necessarily teens anymore, provided for by their parents, but neither are they fully adults, able to provide entirely for themselves. Many students feel the pressures from family, peers, and themselves to assume adult roles in terms of their dress and jobs, not relying on Mom or Dad for help. Card companies know about these pressures. Moreover, college students are easy to target because they are concentrated on campuses and generally consume the same media. I probably get several mailings a month offering me a preapproved credit card. These advertisements are filled with happy campus scenes featuring students wearing just the right clothes, carrying their books in just the right backpack, playing music on their iPods, or opening their laptop computers. They also appeal to students' desire to feel like responsible adults by emphasizing little emergencies that college students can relate to, such as car breakdowns on a road trip. These advertisements illustrate a point made by a team of researchers in an article entitled "Credit Cards as Lifestyle Facilitators": The authors explain how credit card companies want consumers to view credit cards as "lifestyle facilitators" that enable "lifestyle building" and "lifestyle signaling" (Bernthal et al.). Credit cards make it easy for students to live the lifestyle pictured in the credit card ads.

Another contributing cause of high credit card debt for college students is the method that credit card companies use to grant credit—through credit scoring that does not consider income. It was credit scoring that allowed me to get that quadruple-digit credit line at The Gap while already living in the red. The application I filled out never asked my income. Instead, the personal information I listed was used to pull up my credit score, which is based on records of outstanding debts and payment history. Credit scoring allows banks to grant credit cards based on a person's record of responsibility in paying bills rather than on income. According to finance guru Suze Orman, "Your FICO [credit] score is a great tool to size up how good you will be handling a new loan or credit card" (21). Admittedly, credit scoring has made the lending process as a whole much fairer, giving individuals such as minorities and women the chance to qualify for credit even if they have minimal incomes. But when credit card companies use credit scoring to determine college students' creditworthiness, many students are unprepared to handle a credit line that greatly exceeds their ability to pay based on income. In fact, the Center for Responsible Lending, a consumer advocacy organization in North Carolina, lobbied Congress in September 2003 to require credit card companies to secure proof of adequate income for college-age customers before approving credit card applications ("Credit & Prepaid Cards"). If Congress passed such legislation, credit card companies would not be able to as easily take advantage of college students who have not yet learned how to exercise control on their spending habits. They would have to offer students credit lines commensurate with their incomes. No wonder these companies vehemently opposed this legislation.

Yet another contributing cause of high levels of credit card debt is the high cost of having this debt, which credit card companies are especially talented at disguising. As credit card debt increases, card companies compound unpaid interest, adding it to the balance that must be repaid. If this balance is not repaid, they charge interest on unpaid interest. They add exorbitant fees for small slip-ups like making a late payment or exceeding the credit limit. While these costs are listed on statements when first added to the balance, they quickly vanish into the "New Balance" number on all subsequent statements, as if these fees were simply past purchases that have yet to be repaid. As the balance continues to grow, banks spike interest rates even higher. In his 2004 article "Soaring Interest Compounds Credit Card Pain for Millions," Patrick McGeehan describes a "new era of consumer credit, in which thousands of Americans are paying millions of dollars each month in fees that they did not expect . . . lenders are doubling or tripling interest rates with little warning or explanation." These rate hikes are usually tucked into the pages of fine print that come with credit cards, which many consumers are unable to fully read, let alone understand. Usually, a credit card company will offer a very low "teaser rate" that expires after several months. While this industry practice is commonly understood by consumers, many do not understand that credit card companies usually reserve the right to raise the rate at any time for almost any reason, causing debt levels to rise further.

5

(continued)

Admittedly, while individual consumers must be held accountable for any debt they accumulate and should understand compound and variable interest and fees, students' ignorance is welcomed by the credit card industry. To completely explain how the credit card industry has caused college students to amass high amounts of credit card debt, it is first necessary to explain how this vicious monster was let loose during banking deregulation over the past 30 years. In 1978, the Supreme Court opened the floodgates by ruling that the federal government could not set a cap on interest rates that banks charged for credit cards; that decision was to be left to the states. With Uncle Sam no longer protecting consumers, Delaware and South Dakota passed laws that removed caps on interest rates, in order to woo credit card companies to conduct nationwide business there (McGeehan). Since then, the credit card industry has become one of the most profitable industries ever. Credit card companies were given another sweet deal from the U.S. Supreme Court in 1996, when the Court deregulated fees. Since then, the average late fee has risen from $10 or less, to $39 (McGeehan). While a lot of fees and finance charges are avoidable if the student pays the balance in full, on time, every month, for college students who carry balances for whatever reason, these charges are tacked on, further adding to the principal on which they pay a high rate of compounded interest. Moreover, the U.S. government has refused to step in to regulate the practice of universal default, where a credit card company can raise the rate it charges if a consumer is late on an unrelated bill, like a utility payment. Even for someone who pays his or her bills in full, on time, 99 percent of the time, one bill-paying slip-up can cause an avalanche of fees and frustration, thanks to the credit card industry.

Credit card companies exploit college students' lack of financial savvy and security. It is no secret that most full-time college students are not independently wealthy; many have limited means. So why are these companies so willing to issue cards to poor college students? Profits, of course! If they made credit cards less available to struggling consumers such as college students, consumers would have a more difficult time racking up huge balances, plain and simple. It's funny that Citibank, one of the largest, most profitable credit card companies in the world, proudly exclaims "Live richly" in its advertisements. At the rate that it and other card companies collect interest and fees from their customers, a more appropriate slogan would be "Live poorly."

Works Cited

Bernthal, Matthew, et al. "Credit Cards as Lifestyle Facilitators." *Journal of Consumer Research,* vol. 32, no. 1, 2005, pp. 130–45.

"Credit & Prepaid Cards: Our Policy Positions." *Center for Responsible Lending,* www.responsiblelending.org/issues/credit-prepaid-cards/credit-prepaid-cards-policy. Accessed 18 June 2005.

McGeehan, Patrick. "Soaring Interest Compounds Credit Card Pain for Millions." *The New York Times,* 21 Nov. 2004, www.nytimes.com/2004/11/21/business/soaring-interest-compounds-credit-card-pain-for-millions.html.

Orman, Suze. *The Money Book for the Young, Fabulous, and Broke.* Riverhead, 2005.

Critiquing "The Credit Card Company Made Me Do It!"

1. How effective is Carlos's argument that the predatory practices of banks and credit card companies are the primary cause of credit card debt among college students? (See our introduction to Carlos's paper, which was written in 2008 before the signing of the federal Credit Card Act.)

2. The problems illustrated in Carlos's paper had received national attention for many years, but no legislation was passed until the 2009 Credit Card Act. This act has apparently been successful. According to ConsolidatedCredit. org, 46 percent of college students had a credit card in their name in 2005. By 2015, only 23 percent had credit cards. By 2015, only one in ten purchases by college students used credit cards. Instead, 42 percent of purchases used debit cards while 40 percent used cash. From the perspective of a college student, what are the advantages and disadvantages of a credit card versus a debit card?

3. Given the problems with credit card debt highlighted by Carlos, do you think federal regulations were necessary to protect college students? Or should the government stay out of the regulatory business and let individuals look out for themselves?

Chapter 14
Evaluation and Ethical Arguments

Learning Objectives

In this chapter you will learn to:

14.1 Explain and illustrate the difference between categorical and ethical evaluation arguments.

14.2 Conduct a categorical evaluation argument using a criteria-match strategy.

14.3 Conduct an ethical evaluation argument using principles or consequences.

14.4 Be mindful of common problems encountered in evaluation arguments.

14.5 Write your own categorical or ethical evaluation argument.

In our roles as citizens and professionals, we are continually expected to make evaluations and to persuade others to accept them. In this chapter, you will learn to conduct two kinds of evaluation arguments: categorical and ethical. Both have clarifying power to help us make difficult choices about good or bad, right or wrong.

Case 1: How Should We Evaluate the Film District 9?

In the film *District 9* (2009), directed by South African Neill Blomkamp and produced by Peter Jackson, a spaceship has stalled out over Johannesburg, South Africa, where it has hovered for several decades. Its starving alien passengers, derogatorily called "The Prawns" for their appearance, have been placed in what has become a crowded, militarized prison ghetto called District 9. As the film begins, South Africans have grown disgusted with and intolerantly fearful of the growing alien population, while corporate powers seek these aliens' technologically advanced bio-weapons. As this poster suggests—based on its "No Humans Allowed" sign, its ominous "You are not welcome here" slogan, and its barbed wire perimeter—the film includes graphic echoes of the racism of apartheid and disturbing depictions of xenophobia, abusive corporate powers, and mistreatment of refugees (the aliens). Nominated for numerous awards, *District 9* sparked heated evaluation arguments about whether it is a good film or a flawed film. Part of the debate focuses on what evaluative criteria to use—a decision that depends on the category into which the film should be placed. Should it be evaluated as a science-fiction film, as a corporate espionage thriller, or as a commentary on global social justice? Some critics, for example, have argued that *District 9* is not a great science-fiction film, but they have argued that it *is* a deeply provocative and moving commentary on social justice.

Case 2: What Is a "Good Organ" for a Transplant?
How Can an Ill Person Ethically Find an Organ Donor?

In the United States, some 117,000 sick people are waiting for an organ transplant. Some of these people have been waiting as long as six years, and some will die before they can find a donor. The problem of organ shortages raises two kinds of evaluation issues. First, doctors are reevaluating the criteria by which they judge a "good" organ—that is, a good lung, kidney, or liver suitable for transplanting. Formerly, people who were elderly or obese or who had engaged in risky behaviors or experienced heart failure or other medical conditions were not considered sources of good organs. Now doctors are reconsidering these sources as well as exploring the use of organs from pigs. Second, the shortage of organs for donation has raised numerous ethical issues: Is it ethical for people to bypass the national waiting list for organs by advertising on billboards and websites in search of a volunteer donor? Is it morally right for people to sell their organs? Is it right for patients and families to buy organs or in any way remunerate living organ donors? Some states are passing laws that allow some financial compensation to living organ donors.

An Overview of Categorical and Ethical Evaluation Arguments

14.1 Explain and illustrate the difference between categorical and ethical evaluation arguments.

In this chapter we explain strategies for conducting two different kinds of evaluation arguments. First, we examine categorical evaluations of the kind "Is this thing a good member of its class?"* (For example: Is Ramon a good leader?) In such an evaluation, the writer determines the extent to which a given something possesses the qualities or standards of its category or class. What are the traits of good leaders? Does Ramon possess these traits? Second, we examine ethical arguments of the kind "Is this action right (wrong)?" (For example: Was it right or wrong to drop atomic bombs on Hiroshima and Nagasaki in World War II?) In these arguments, the writer evaluates a given act from the perspective of some system of morality or ethics.

To see the difference between the two kinds of evaluations, consider the case of terrorists. From a nonethical standpoint, you could make a categorical evaluation by saying that certain people are "good terrorists" in that they fully realize the purpose of the class "terrorist": They cause great anguish and damage with a minimum of resources, and they bring much attention to their cause. In other words, they are good at what they do—terrorism. However, if we want to condemn terrorism on ethical grounds, we have to construct an ethical argument that terrorism is wrong. The ethical question is not whether a person fulfills the purposes of the class "terrorist," but rather whether it is wrong for such a class to exist. In the rest of this chapter, we explain categorical evaluations and ethical evaluations in more detail.

Constructing a Categorical Evaluation Argument

14.2 Conduct a categorical evaluation argument using a criteria-match strategy.

A categorical evaluation uses a criteria-match structure similar to the structure we examined in definition arguments (see Chapter 12).

---

*In addition to the term *good*, a number of other evaluative terms involve the same kind of thinking: *effective, successful, workable, excellent, valuable,* and so forth.

Criteria-Match Structure of Categorical Evaluations

A typical claim-with-reasons frame for an evaluation argument has the following criteria-match structure:

> This thing/phenomenon is/is not a good member of its class because it meets (fails to meet) criteria A, B, and C.

> *Claim:* This thing/phenomenon is (is not) a good member of its class.
> *Criteria:* The criteria for being a good member of this class are A, B, and C.
> *Match:* The thing/phenomenon meets (fails to meet) criteria A, B, and C.

The main conceptual difference between an evaluation argument and a definition argument is the nature of the contested category. In a definition argument, one argues whether a particular thing belongs within a certain category. (Is this

TOULMIN ANALYSIS OF THE FRACKING ARGUMENT SUPPORTING ENVIRONMENTAL SAFETY

ENTHYMEME

CLAIM Fracking is a good method for extracting natural gas from shale formations

REASON because it is environmentally safe.

GROUNDS

- Descriptions of safety measures employed by industry

- Descriptions of local, state, and federal regulations aimed at insuring safety

- Summaries of peer-reviewed studies and government studies showing the safety of fracking

- Refutation of anecdotal scare stories told by environmentalists

CONDITIONS OF REBUTTAL

Attacking the reason and grounds

Arguments that fracking is not environmentally safe

- Studies pointing to possible dangers such as contamination of aquifers, earthquakes, flaring of methane, and so forth

- Arguments that local, state, and federal regulations are too loose and unenforced

- Statistics about environmental costs in doing the fracking (huge amounts of required water, recovering contaminated water, use of carbon fuels to run the machinery, and so forth)

WARRANT

Environmental safety is an important criterion for evaluating a method of drilling for natural gas

BACKING

Arguments that safety must be a prime consideration of any business plan. One major accident could undermine public support of fracking. [Backing tries to counter the arguments of environmentalists that business interests put profit ahead of safety.]

CONDITIONS OF REBUTTAL

Attacking the warrant and backing

- Environmentalists will endorse the warrant, but may say that even if fracking is safe, it undermines the urgency of finding alternative energy sources.

- Business interests might want to loosen an insistence on absolute safety by acknowledging that some accidents are inevitable.

swampy area a *wetland*?) In an evaluation argument, we know what category something belongs to. For example, we know that this 2014 Nissan Leaf is a *used car*. For an evaluation argument, the question is whether this 2014 Nissan Leaf a *good used car*. Or, to place the question within a rhetorical context: Is this 2014 Nissan Leaf a *good used car for me to buy for commuting back and forth to campus*?

To illustrate the criteria-match structure of an evaluation argument, let's ask whether hydraulic fracturing (commonly called *fracking*) is a good means for extracting natural gas from shale formations. Supporters of fracking might say "yes," because fracking meets three major criteria:

- It is technologically efficient at extracting huge supplies of otherwise untappable natural gas.
- It is cost-effective.
- It is environmentally safe.

Opponents might make two counterarguments: First, they might claim that fracking is not environmentally safe. (Safety is a crucial criterion. Opponents argue that fracking doesn't meet this criterion.) Second, they might argue that fracking, by producing lots of relatively cheap natural gas, removes the urgency from efforts to convert the country to sources of renewable energy, such as the sun and the wind. Thus, fracking might be cost-effective (criterion 2) in the short run but disastrous in the long run. The following figure provides a Toulmin analysis of how proponents of fracking might develop their third reason: "Fracking is environmentally safe."

Developing Your Criteria

To help you develop your criteria, we suggest a three-step thinking process:

1. Place the thing you are evaluating in the smallest relevant category so that you don't compare apples to oranges.
2. Develop criteria for your evaluation based on the purpose or function of this category.
3. Determine the relative weight of your criteria.

Let's look at each of these steps in turn.

STEP 1: PLACE THE THING YOU ARE EVALUATING IN THE SMALLEST RELEVANT CATEGORY   Placing your contested thing in the smallest relevant category is a crucial first step. Suppose, for example, that you want one of your professors to write you a letter of recommendation for a summer job. The professor will need to know what kind of summer job you are applying for. Are you applying to become a camp counselor, a law-office intern, a retail sales clerk, or a tour guide at a wild animal park? Each of these jobs has different criteria for excellence.

To take a different example, suppose that you want to evaluate e-mail as a medium of correspondence. To create a stable context for your evaluation, you need to place e-mail in its smallest relevant category. You may choose to evaluate e-mail as a medium for business communication (by contrasting e-mail with direct personal contact, phone conversations, or postal mail), as a medium for staying in touch with high-school friends (in contrast, say, to text messaging,

Facebook or Instagram), or as a medium for carrying on a long-distance romance (in contrast, say, to old-fashioned love letters). Again, criteria will vary across these different categories.

By placing your contested thing in the smallest relevant class, you avoid the apples-and-oranges problem. That is, to give a fair evaluation of a perfectly good apple, you need to judge it under the class "apple" and not under the next larger class, "fruit," or a neighboring class such as "orange." To be even more precise, you may wish to evaluate your apple in the class "eating apple" as opposed to "pie apple" because the latter class is supposed to be tarter and the former class juicier and sweeter.

STEP 2: DEVELOP CRITERIA FOR YOUR EVALUATION BASED ON THE PURPOSE OR FUNCTIONS OF THIS CATEGORY   Suppose that the summer job you are applying for is tour guide at a wild animal park. The functions of a tour guide are to drive the tour buses, make people feel welcome, give them interesting information about the wild animals in the park, and make their visit pleasant. Criteria for a good tour guide would thus include reliability and responsibility, a friendly demeanor, good speaking skills, and knowledge of the kinds of animals in the wild animal park. In our e-mail example, suppose that you want to evaluate e-mail as a medium for business communication. The purpose of this class of communication is to provide a quick and reliable means of communication that increases efficiency, minimizes misunderstandings, and protects the confidentiality of internal communications. Based on these purposes, you might establish the following criteria:

> A good medium for business communication:
> * Is easy to use, quick, and reliable
> * Increases employee efficiency
> * Prevents misunderstandings
> * Maintains confidentiality where needed

STEP 3: DETERMINE THE RELATIVE WEIGHT OF YOUR CRITERIA   In some evaluations, all the criteria are equally important. However, sometimes a phenomenon to be evaluated is strong in one criterion but weak in another. This situation forces the evaluator to decide which criterion takes precedence. For example, the supervisor interviewing candidates for tour guide at the wild animal park may find one candidate who is very knowledgeable about the wildlife but doesn't have good speaking skills. The supervisor would need to decide which of these two criteria gets more weight.

Making Your Match Argument

Once you've established and weighed your criteria, you'll need to use examples and other evidence to show that the thing being evaluated meets or does not meet the criteria. For example, your professor could argue that you would be a good wildlife park tour guide because you have strong interpersonal skills (based on your work on a college orientation committee), that you have good speaking skills (based on a speech you gave in the professor's class), and that you have quite a bit of knowledge about animals and ecology (based on your major in environmental science).

In our e-mail example, you might establish the following working thesis:

> Despite its being easy to learn, quick, and reliable, e-mail is often not an effective medium for business communication because it reduces worker efficiency, leads to frequent misunderstandings, and often lacks confidentiality.

You could develop your last three points as follows:

- *E-mail reduces worker efficiency.* Although much important work can be done efficiently on e-mail, workers have to spend inordinate time separating important e-mail from noise (workplace announcements, annoying "reply all" strings, forwarded jokes, and so forth). You can use personal

Examining Visual Arguments

An Evaluation Claim

For many people, the polar bear has become the iconic image of the environmental repercussions of global warming. This photograph of a "polar bear" marching in a small-town parade creates a visual argument against climate change. This parade entry was sponsored by the Backbone Campaign, an environmental group that specializes in "artful activism," using visually arresting and often humorous costumes, papier mâché puppets, and other forms of art to advocate for progressive environmental policy. How effective is this visual argument as a small-town parade entry? Imagine that you are on a committee brainstorming for an "artful entry" into the small-town parade. What argument would you make in favor of a polar bear theme? How effective is this two-person polar bear costume?

anecdotes and research data to show how employees must sort through volumes of e-mail daily to sort out what messages need immediate attention. Managing e-mail eats into worker time (one research article says that the average worker devotes ten minutes of every working hour to reading and responding to e-mail).

- *E-mail leads to misunderstandings.* Because an e-mail message is often composed rapidly without revision, e-mail can cause people to state ideas imprecisely, to write something they would never say face to face, or to convey an unintended tone. You could give a personal example of a high-consequence misunderstanding caused by e-mail.

- *E-mail often lacks confidentiality.* You could provide anecdotal or research evidence of cases in which a person clicked on the "reply to all" button rather than the "reply" button, sending a message intended for one person to a whole group of people. Also, people sometimes forward e-mails without the sender's permission. Finally, e-mail messages are archived forever, so messages that you thought were deleted may show up years later in a lawsuit.

As these examples illustrate, the key to a successful match argument is to use sufficient examples and other evidence to show how your contested phenomenon meets or does not meet each of your criteria.

For Writing and Discussion

Developing Criteria and Match Arguments

The following small-group exercise can be accomplished in one or two class hours. It gives you a good model of the process you can go through in order to write your own categorical evaluation.

1. Choose a specific controversial person, thing, or event to evaluate. To help you think of ideas, try brainstorming controversial members of the following categories: *people* (athletes, political leaders, musicians); *technology* (new car features, phone apps); *media* (a social network, a TV program, a radio station); *government and world affairs* (an economic policy, a Supreme Court decision); *the arts* (a film, a book); *your college or university* (food service, an administrative policy); *the world of work* (a job, a company operation, a dress policy); or any other categories of your choice.

2. Place your controversial person or thing within the smallest relevant class, thus providing a rhetorical context for your argument and showing what is at stake. Do you want to evaluate Harvey's Hamburger Haven in the broad category of *restaurants,* in the narrow category of *hamburger joints,* or in a different narrow category such as *late-night study places*?

3. Make a list of the purpose or function of that class, and then list the criteria that a good member of that class would need to have in order to accomplish its purpose or function. (What is the purpose or function of a hamburger joint versus a late-night study place? What criteria for excellence can you derive from these purposes or functions?)

4. If necessary, rank your criteria from most to least important. (For a late-night study place, what is most important: good ambience, Wi-Fi availability, good coffee, or convenient location?)

5. Provide examples and other evidence to show how your contested something matches or does not match each of your criteria. (As a late-night study place, Carol's Coffee Closet beats out Harvey's Hamburger Haven. Although Harvey's Hamburger Haven has the most convenient location, Carol's Coffee Closet has Wi-Fi, an ambience conducive to studying, and excellent coffee.)

Constructing an Ethical Evaluation Argument

14.3 Conduct an ethical evaluation argument using principles or consequences.

A second kind of evaluation argument focuses on moral or ethical issues, which can often merge or overlap with categorical evaluations. For example, many apparently straightforward categorical evaluations can turn out to have an ethical dimension. Consider again the criteria for buying a car. Most people would base their evaluations on cost, safety, comfort, and so forth. But some people may feel morally obligated to buy the most fuel-efficient car, to buy an American car, or not to buy a car from a manufacturer whose labor policies they find morally repugnant. Depending on how large a role ethical considerations play in the evaluation, we may choose to call this an ethical argument based on moral considerations rather than a categorical evaluation based on the purposes of a class or category.

When we are faced with an ethical issue, we must move from arguments of good or bad to arguments of right or wrong. The terms *right* and *wrong* are clearly different from the terms *good* and *bad* when the latter terms mean, simply, "effective" (meets purposes of class, as in "This is a good laptop") or "ineffective" (fails to meet purposes of class, as in "This is a bad cookbook"). But *right* and *wrong* often also differ from what seems to be a moral use of the terms *good* and *bad*. We may say, for example, that sunshine is good because it brings pleasure and that cancer is bad because it brings pain and death, but that is not quite the same thing as saying that sunshine is "right" and cancer is "wrong." It is the problem of "right" and "wrong" that ethical arguments confront.

There are many schools of ethical thought—too many to cover in this brief overview—so we'll limit ourselves to two major systems: arguments from consequences and arguments from principles.

Consequences as the Base of Ethics

Perhaps the best-known example of evaluating acts according to their ethical consequences is *utilitarianism*, a down-to-earth philosophy that grew out of nineteenth-century British philosophers' concern to demystify ethics and make it work in the practical world. Jeremy Bentham, the originator of utilitarianism, developed the goal of the greatest good for the greatest number, or "greatest happiness," by which he meant the most pleasure for the least pain. John Stuart Mill, another British philosopher, built on Bentham's utilitarianism by using predicted consequences to determine the morality of a proposed action.

Mill's consequentialist approach allows you to readily assess a wide range of acts. You can apply the principle of *utility*—which says that an action is morally right if it produces a greater net value (benefits minus costs) than any available alternative action—to virtually any situation, and it will help you reach a decision. Obviously, however, it's not always easy to make the calculations called for by this approach because, like any prediction of the future, an estimate of consequences is conjectural. In particular, it's often very hard to assess the long-term consequences of any action. Too often, utilitarianism seduces us into a short-term analysis of a moral problem simply because long-term consequences are difficult to predict.

Principles as the Base of Ethics

Any ethical system based on principles will ultimately rest on moral tenets that we are duty bound to uphold, no matter what the consequences. (See our discussion of "sacred values" in Chapters 1 and 2.) Sometimes the moral tenets come from religious faith—for example, the Ten Commandments. At other times, however, the principles are derived from philosophical reasoning, as in the case of German philosopher Immanuel Kant. Kant held that no one should ever use another person as a means to his own ends and that everyone should always act as if his acts are the basis of universal law. In other words, Kant held that we are duty bound to respect other people's sanctity and to act in the same way that we would want all other people to act. The great advantage of such a system is its clarity and precision. We are never overwhelmed by a multiplicity of contradictory and difficult-to-quantify consequences; we simply make sure we are following (or not violating) the principles of our ethical system and proceed accordingly.

Example Ethical Arguments Examining Capital Punishment

To show you how to conduct an ethical argument, let's now apply these two strategies to the example of capital punishment. In general, you can conduct an ethical evaluation by using the frame for either a principles-based argument or a consequences-based argument or a combination of both.

- *Principles-Based Frame:* An act is right (wrong) because it follows (violates) principles A, B, and C.

- *Consequences-Based Frame:* An act is right (wrong) because it will lead to consequences A, B, and C, which are good (bad).

A principles-based argument looks at capital punishment through the lens of one or more guiding principles. Kant's principle that we are duty bound not to violate the sanctity of other human lives could lead to arguments opposing capital punishment. One might argue as follows:

> *Principles-based argument opposing capital punishment:* The death penalty is wrong because it violates the principle of the sanctity of human life.

You could support this principle either by summarizing Kant's argument that one should not violate the selfhood of another person or by pointing to certain religious systems such as Judeo-Christian ethics, where one is told "Vengeance is mine, says the Lord" and "Thou shalt not kill." To develop this argument further, you might examine two exceptions in which principles-based ethicists may allow killing—self-defense and war—and show how capital punishment does not fall into either category.

Principles-based arguments can also be developed to support capital punishment. You may be surprised to learn that Kant himself—despite his arguments for the sanctity of life—supported capital punishment. To make such an argument, Kant evoked a different principle about the suitability of the punishment to the crime:

> There is no sameness of kind between death and remaining alive even under the most miserable conditions, and consequently there is no equality between the crime and the retribution unless the criminal is judicially condemned and put to death.

Stated as an enthymeme, Kant's argument is as follows:

> *Principles-based argument supporting capital punishment:* Capital punishment is right because it follows the principle that punishments should be proportionate to the crime.

In developing this argument, Kant's burden would be to show why the principle of proportionate retribution outweighs the principle of the supreme worth of the individual. Our point is that a principles-based argument can be made both for and against capital punishment. The arguer's duty is to make clear what principle is being evoked and then to show why this principle is more important than opposing principles.

Unlike a principles-based argument, which appeals to certain guiding maxims or rules, a consequences-based argument looks at the consequences of a decision and measures the positive benefits against the negative costs. Here is the frame that an arguer might use to oppose capital punishment on the basis of negative consequences:

> *Consequences-based argument opposing capital punishment:* Capital punishment is wrong because it leads to the following negative consequences:

- The possibility of executing an innocent person
- The possibility that a murderer who may repent and be redeemed is denied that chance
- The excessive legal and political costs of trials and appeals
- The unfair distribution of executions so that one's chances of being put to death are much greater if one is a minority or is poor

To develop this argument, the reader would need to provide facts, statistics, and other evidence to support each of the stated reasons.

A different arguer might use a consequences-based approach to support capital punishment:

> *Consequences-based argument supporting capital punishment:* Capital punishment is right because it leads to the following positive consequences:

- It may deter violent crime and decrease the murder rate.
- It saves the cost of lifelong imprisonment.
- It stops criminals who are menaces to society from committing more murders.
- It helps grieving families reach closure and sends a message to victims' families that society recognizes their pain.

It should be evident, then, that adopting an ethical system doesn't lead to automatic answers to one's ethical dilemmas. A system offers a way of proceeding—a way of conducting an argument—but it doesn't relieve you of personal responsibility for thinking through your values and taking a stand. When you face an ethical dilemma, we encourage you to consider both the relevant principles and the possible consequences the dilemma entails. In many arguments, you can use both principles-based and consequences-based reasoning as long as irreconcilable contradictions don't present themselves.

For Writing and Discussion
Developing an Ethical Argument

Individual task:

Develop a frame for an ethical argument (based on principles, consequences, or both) for or against any two of the following actions. Use the previous examples on capital punishment as a model.

1. Eating meat
2. Using public transportation instead of owning a car
3. Legalizing assisted suicide for the terminally ill
4. Selling human organs
5. Allowing concealed weapons on college campuses

Group task:

Share your arguments with classmates.

Common Problems in Making Evaluation Arguments

14.4 Be mindful of common problems encountered in evaluation arguments.

When conducting evaluation arguments (whether categorical or ethical), writers can bump up against recurring problems that are unique to evaluation. In some cases, these problems complicate the establishment of criteria; in other cases, they complicate the match argument. Let's look briefly at some of these common problems.

- *The problem of standards—what is commonplace versus what is ideal:* In various forms, we experience the dilemma of the commonplace versus the ideal all the time. Is it fair to get a ticket for going seventy miles per hour on a sixty-five-mile-per-hour freeway when most of the drivers go seventy miles per hour or faster? (Does what is *commonplace*—going seventy—override what is *ideal*—obeying the law?) Is it better for high schools to pass out free contraceptives to students because students are having sex anyway (what's *commonplace*), or is it better not to pass them out in order to support abstinence (what's *ideal*)?

- *The problem of mitigating circumstances:* This problem occurs when an arguer claims that unusual circumstances should alter our usual standards of judgment. Ordinarily, it is fair for a teacher to reduce a grade if you turn in a paper late. But what if you were up all night taking care of a crying baby? Does that count as a *mitigating circumstance* to waive the ordinary criterion? When you argue for mitigating circumstances, you will likely assume an especially heavy burden of proof. People assume the rightness of usual standards of judgment unless there are compelling arguments for abnormal circumstances.

- *The problem of choosing between two goods or two bads:* Often an evaluation issue forces us between a rock and a hard place. Should we cut pay or eliminate jobs? Put our parents in a nursing home or let them stay at home, where they have become a danger to themselves? In such cases, one has to weigh conflicting criteria, knowing that the choices are too much alike—either both bad or both good.

- *The problem of seductive empirical measures:* The need to make high-stakes evaluations has led many people to seek quantifiable criteria that can be weighed mathematically. Thus we use grade point averages to select scholarship winners, student evaluation scores to decide merit pay for teachers, and judges' combined scores to evaluate figure skaters. In some cases, empirical measures can be quite acceptable, but they are often dangerous because they discount important nonquantifiable traits. The problem with empirical measures is that they seduce us into believing that complex judgments can be made mathematically, thus rescuing us from the messiness of alternative points of view and conflicting criteria.

- *The problem of cost:* A final problem in evaluation arguments is cost. Something may be the best possible member of its class, but if it costs too much, we have to go for second or third best. We can avoid this problem somewhat by placing items into different classes on the basis of cost. For example, a Mercedes will exceed a Kia on almost any criterion of quality, but if we can't afford more than a Kia, the comparison is pointless. It is better to compare a Mercedes to a Lexus and a Kia to an equivalent Ford. Whether costs are expressed in dollars, personal discomfort, moral repugnance, or some other terms, our final evaluation of an item must take cost into account.

Writing Assignment: An Evaluation or Ethical Argument

14.5 Write your own categorical or ethical evaluation argument.

Write an argument in which you try to change your readers' minds about the value, worth, or ethics of something. Choose a phenomenon to be evaluated that is controversial so that your readers are likely at first to disagree with your evaluation or at least to be surprised by it. Somewhere in your essay you should summarize alternative views and either refute them or concede to them (see Chapter 6).

Exploring Ideas

Evaluation issues are all around us. Think of disagreements about the value of a person, thing, action, or phenomenon within the various communities to which you belong—your dorm, home, or apartment community; your school community, including clubs or organizations; your academic community, including classes you are currently taking; your work community; and your city, state, national, and world communities. Once you have settled on a controversial thing to be evaluated, place it in its smallest relevant category, determine the purposes of that category, and develop your criteria. If you are making an ethical evaluation, consider your argument from the perspective of both principles and consequences.

Identifying Your Audience and Determining What's at Stake

Before drafting your argument, identify your targeted audience and determine what's at stake. Consider your responses to the following questions:

- What audience are you targeting? What background do they need to understand your issue? How much do they already care about it?

- Before they read your evaluation argument, what stance on your issue do you imagine them holding? What change do you want to bring about in their view?

- What will they find new or surprising about your argument?

- What objections might they raise? What counterarguments or alternative points of view will you need to address?

- Why does your evaluation matter? Who might be threatened or made uncomfortable by your views? What is at stake?

Organizing an Evaluation Argument

As you write a draft, you may find useful the prototypical structures for evaluation arguments shown in Figures 14.1 and 14.2. Of course, you can always alter these plans if another structure better fits your material.

Questioning and Critiquing a Categorical Evaluation Argument

Here is a list of questions you can use to critique a categorical evaluation argument:

- *Will a skeptic accept my criteria?* Many evaluative arguments are weak because the writers have simply assumed that readers will accept their criteria. Whenever your audience's acceptance of your criteria is in doubt, you will need to argue for your criteria explicitly.

- *Will a skeptic accept my general weighting of criteria?* Another vulnerable spot in an evaluation argument is the relative weight of the criteria. How much anyone weights a given criterion is usually a function of his or her own interests relative to your contested something. You should always ask whether some particular group might have good reasons for weighting the criteria differently.

- *Will a skeptic accept my criteria but reject my match argument?* The other major way of testing an evaluation argument is to anticipate how readers may object to your stated reasons and grounds. Will readers challenge you by showing that you have cherry-picked your examples and evidence? Will they provide counterexamples and counterevidence?

Figure 14.1 Organization plan 1: Criteria and match in separate sections

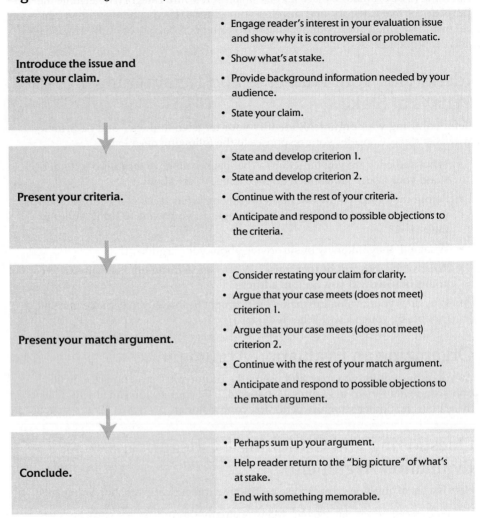

Introduce the issue and state your claim.	• Engage reader's interest in your evaluation issue and show why it is controversial or problematic. • Show what's at stake. • Provide background information needed by your audience. • State your claim.
Present your criteria.	• State and develop criterion 1. • State and develop criterion 2. • Continue with the rest of your criteria. • Anticipate and respond to possible objections to the criteria.
Present your match argument.	• Consider restating your claim for clarity. • Argue that your case meets (does not meet) criterion 1. • Argue that your case meets (does not meet) criterion 2. • Continue with the rest of your match argument. • Anticipate and respond to possible objections to the match argument.
Conclude.	• Perhaps sum up your argument. • Help reader return to the "big picture" of what's at stake. • End with something memorable.

Critiquing an Ethical Argument

Ethical arguments can be critiqued through appeals to consequences or principles. If an argument appeals primarily to principles, it can be vulnerable to a simple cost analysis. What are the costs of adhering to this principle? There will undoubtedly be some, or else there would be no real argument. If the argument is based strictly on consequences, we should ask whether it violates any rules or principles, particularly such commandments as the Golden Rule—"Do unto others as you would have others do unto you"—which most members of our audience adhere to. By failing to mention these alternative ways of thinking about ethical issues, we undercut not only our argument but our credibility as well.

Figure 14.2 Organization plan 2: Criteria and match interwoven

Introduce the issue and state your claim.	• Engage reader's interest in your evaluation issue and show why it is controversial or problematic. • Show what's at stake. • Provide background information needed by your audience. • State your claim.
Present series of criterion-match arguments.	• State and develop criterion 1 and argue that your case meets (does not meet) the criterion. • State and develop criterion 2 and argue that your case meets (does not meet) the criterion. • Continue with the rest of your criterion-match arguments.
Respond to possible objections to your argument.	• Anticipate and summarize possible objections. • Respond to the objections through rebuttal or concession.
Conclude.	• Perhaps sum up your argument. • Help reader return to the "big picture" of what's at stake. • End with something memorable.

Readings

Our first reading, by student writer Lorena Mendoza-Flores, critiques her former high school for the way it marginalizes Hispanic students. Lorena, a physics major in college, has changed the name of her high school and chosen not to reveal her home state.

Student Essay

Silenced and Invisible:
Problems of Hispanic Students at Valley High School

Lorena Mendoza-Flores

Every year, thousands of Mexican families come to the United States in order to escape economic hardships in Mexico and hope for better schools for their children. While many American schools try to accommodate immigrant

(continued)

---

non-native speakers, many immigrant families, according to case-study interviews, have increasingly negative perceptions of these attempts (Roessingh). There are action plans to bridge the gap between disadvantaged and advantaged students, yet Hispanic ESL (English as a Second Language) youth continue to perform considerably below that of other students (Good et al.). These problems pose the question: What is wrong with the way our schools treat Hispanic immigrants? Perhaps we could gain some understanding if we looked at a specific school—my own Valley High School in an agricultural region of [name of state]. Valley High School is a perfect example of a school with a growing Hispanic population, well-intentioned teachers, and hopes for Latino students' success that simply fall through. The failures at my school include inadequate ESL training for teachers, inadequate counseling for immigrant students, poor multicultural training for all teachers, and failure to value Hispanic identity and provide support for families.

Despite the fact that the Valley School District has 52 percent Hispanic students, a large percentage of whom have Spanish as their first language and parents who speak only Spanish, the staff at Valley High School is overwhelmingly white, with only one Hispanic teacher and only three or four teachers who speak Spanish. Even with a large number of ESL students, Valley High School has not hired teachers who are adequately trained in ESL. There is only one ESL teacher, who is responsible for all the ESL students. These students are assigned to regular classes and then go to the ESL classrooms for what is supposed to be extra support. When I've gone into the ESL classroom, I've found students surfing random sites online and the teacher, also the yearbook advisor, working on pages for the annual. Because I was senior editor of the yearbook, he was very open to talking to me about his students, always complaining that they didn't work hard enough even though I could see they weren't being given meaningful work. I was frustrated because it was obvious that the ESL classroom did not engage either the students or the teacher. The students' language progress remained stagnant, while the expectations of standardized testing became increasingly more demanding, dooming ESL students to failure.

Another problem is inadequate counseling for Hispanic students and inadequate methods of assessing their progress so they can be placed in the right classes. When immigrant students need help, teachers often recruit other students to address their needs. As a student mentor, I was called upon a few times to speak with students about their performance in class. In one particular situation, the math teacher called me in to talk to a student who had decided to drop out. The teacher was visibly concerned for the student's welfare but didn't have any means for understanding or addressing the student's issues. The student told me that he did not feel like he belonged at school. The lack of adequate counseling sent the message that immigrant students were not worth fighting for to stay in our school.

Additionally, when students enter the school, their skills in other coursework are not taken into consideration. All ESL students are placed in the basic math and English courses, and while they might move down, sometimes as far as being placed in special education classes, they're never moved up. A student's aptitude in math or science may never get recognized in the four years that he or she is in high school because the ESL students move as a single group and take just about all coursework together. Their status as ESL students becomes the sole determinant of their identity as a student within the school system, and they are not given the same considerations and levels of attention required to grow and develop academically. Personally, I have fallen victim to our school's overlooking of student progress. When I entered the Valley School District in 8th grade, I had already taken several years of algebra and tested far above other students in my grade. At my previous school in another district, I had surpassed the school's highest level of math. In fact, my 5th–7th grade math instructor had to find advanced online material for me so that I could keep progressing. Entering the Valley School District, however, I regressed two years. Even though I communicated to both my math teacher and the counselor that I was being placed too low and that the nearby high school had several higher-level courses, I was kept in the same class. The next year, I was shocked to see that two 8th grade white students were in my 9th grade geometry class; the system had catered to them while it had denied to me an acknowledgement of the same earned achievement. I felt dismissed because I was Hispanic.

A third problem is that outside of the ESL classroom, in the regular classroom settings, teachers are often untrained in how to create safe multicultural dialogue. One time in sociology my teacher asked the class why the Hispanic students were performing so much worse than white students. I tried to explain that our support was inadequate. I stated that since most Hispanic students came from immigrant backgrounds, our parents weren't able to help us maneuver through the school system. In doing our homework, we had no one to turn to, and if the instructions were unclear, we did not have access to a resource such as an English-speaking parent, something that many white students and faculty never even thought about when considering this gap in performance. When I started talking about these things, white students around the room started becoming upset. They argued that they were hard workers and didn't have their parents do their homework for them. Obviously, my point was not to dismiss their efforts but to emphasize that these are two different worlds we're living in. Coming from an immigrant background, I and my fellow Hispanic students undoubtedly had more obstacles to overcome every step of the way. What was most troubling about this situation was that at no point did my sociology teacher step up and defend the validity of my arguments. Teachers need to know how to facilitate these multicultural clashes by helping make injustices more visible rather than marginalizing someone for bringing up uncomfortable issues.

Finally, Valley High School does little to honor cultural identity or reach out to immigrant families. My senior year I was president of the International Club (the only club at our school that had lots of immigrant student participation). Without my consent, or that of the members, my advisor began a transition to convert the International Club into the InterAct club affiliated with the community's Rotaract Club (part of Rotary). While this new connection with the Rotary would provide more funding, the only club that was primarily made up of Hispanic members was now being taken over by one sponsored by an all-white organization. In this transition, our advisor had pre-elected leaders (also all white) to move it forward. By the time

(continued)

I graduated, the transition was well underway. In fact, on Cinco de Mayo, International Club's major event every year, our club members realized that our advisor didn't think this event was worth our time. As the only Mexican teacher, this advisor did not even advocate for the desires of our community. Ultimately, she turned her back on the members, and the following year InterAct became a primarily white club, just like every other club at school.

The loss of a club supporting Hispanic students is matched by failure to create a welcoming environment for Hispanic parents and families. When immigrant parents come to the school, they have to wait around until they can find a translator if they want to speak to a teacher or administrator. Usually this interpreter is another student, creating awkward moments for parents who don't want to discuss their children's problems in front of another student. The school occasionally does try to reach out to Hispanic parents by holding Hispanic Nights where all the events are held in Spanish. However, all the other school events are held only in English. Considering that the school population is more than half Hispanic, the absence of any interpreters makes it clear the school thinks of itself as white. In addition, there are no translators at larger school events such as academic award nights or sporting banquets. As a result, immigrant parents and families feel isolated from the school and unwelcomed.

Debate remains over the exact or best procedures for helping immigrant ESL students successfully integrate into schools, but what is not debated is that these students deserve equal opportunities to learn and grow. Just as any other students, immigrant students should meet the demanding academic standards needed for higher education, but first they must have adequate support. It is essential that schools support educational reforms that address the problem areas apparent at Valley High School. Particularly, schools need to hire qualified ESL instructors, provide adequate counseling for immigrant students, enable teachers to develop multicultural sensitivity and skills at handling ethnic conflict, and provide outreach to immigrant families while valuing their culture.

Works Cited

Good, Mary Ellen, et al. "Latino English Language Learners: Bridging Achievement and Cultural Gaps Between Schools and Families." *Journal of Latinos & Education*, vol. 9, no. 4, 2010, pp. 321–39.

Roessingh, Hetty. "The Teacher Is the Key: Building Trust in ESL High School Programs." *Canadian Modern Language Review*, vol. 62, no. 4, 2006, pp. 563–90.

Critiquing "Silenced and Invisible: Problems of Hispanic Students at Valley High School"

1. What criteria does Lorena Mendoza-Flores use to evaluate her high school's treatment of Hispanic students?

2. For evidence, Lorena uses primarily personal experiences, anecdotes, and observations. How effective do you find this evidence in developing the match part of her argument?

3. If Lorena were to identify the real name of her former high school and send the argument directly to the principal and to the city newspaper, how do you think it would be received?

4. How effectively does Lorena make appeals to *logos, ethos,* and *pathos?*

In our next reading, student writer Hadley Reeder, a major in environmental studies with a specialization in policy, politics, and justice, writes about her secondary interest, feminist issues and gender equality. From the vantage point of her college experience, she evaluates the inadequacy of her high school's dress code, particularly its unfairness toward female students.

Student Essay

A Defective and Detrimental Dress Code

Hadley Reeder

Most educational discussions of dress codes say that they are intended to create a positive and peaceful learning environment. A secondary purpose often mentioned is that dress codes level the social playing field for students. But to what extent are these purposes achieved? I suggest that a key dimension of dress code policies lies in their implementation and enforcement. While a quality learning environment and dress equality are important, they cannot be achieved without specifications for enforcement of the policy. From the expansive dress freedom of a university campus, I now see even more clearly the failure of my high school's dress-code policy. A good dress code in a public high school would state its requirements (acceptable and unacceptable items of clothing and accessories and styles) clearly, and most importantly it would outline an enforcement policy that would promote social justice. While my high school's dress code does clearly define what is and is not acceptable to wear at school and school events, it fails to explain how it will be enforced among its student body to avoid arbitrariness and gender discrimination and thus is socially unjust.

I don't think anyone would dispute that a high-school dress code should be clear in its specifications of what is or is not appropriate and allowed. The G___H__ High School Dress Code meets this criterion by identifying what is required of students. The policy states:

> DRESS CODE—On ALL days and at ALL school events: Do not wear clothing or accessories that present a health or safety hazard, damage school property, promote/display substances or actions illegal for high-school age students, promote/display weapons or violence, degrade others, have topics/images that are offensive, are inappropriate for the workplace, or disrupt the educational process in any way. Clothes must cover the midriff, cleavage, and undergarments. As students are standing, shorts and skirts need to go beyond the tips of the hands when arms are fully extended at their sides. No strapless tops. Faces need to be uncovered and visible. No bandanas. No clothing or accessories that are associated with gang affiliation.

(continued)

This code explicitly covers what can and cannot be worn in terms that apply across all genders and backgrounds of the high-school population. At the same time, it states when and where the dress code is to be followed. So far, so good.

However, neither the dress code nor the Student Handbook identifies the dress-code enforcers, the disciplinary action required, and how the dress code will be implemented to promote social justice. Are all faculty equally responsible for reporting violations of the code? Students can assume that GHHS staff has the power to enforce the dress code, but enforcement responsibility is not spelled out as it should be. For example, what happens when a student attends school wearing "an article of clothing that degrades others?" A male student in my senior English class wore a T-shirt featuring a half-naked woman multiple days throughout the school year without discipline. How is this T-shirt not "degrading to others" in the classroom? This instance clearly is an example of a violation of the GHHS Dress Code that went unenforced. In contrast, my Spanish teacher called me out into the hall in front of everyone to tell me my clothing was "inappropriate." I was wearing a white tank top that was apparently "too revealing," showing my bra straps and bralette. On the spot, she gave me the option to change my clothes (which I didn't have) or do detention, but neither option is listed in the dress code. I'm not sure which was more degrading—digging through the Lost and Found to find something semi-clean to wear or trying to return to class without everyone knowing what had happened. Interestingly enough, I had made it through the halls and three of my classes, and nobody had commented on my tank top. On another occasion, the female vice principal approached my friend, who was wearing a short dress, and said, "I like your dress, but I am unsure of the message you are sending to your peers." The vice principal did not ask her to change or enforce real consequences. Later I noticed the cheerleaders' skirts didn't follow the "going beyond the tips of the hands" rule. They are representatives of our school, so why didn't the rules apply to them? These examples illustrate the confusion over when the dress code policy is enforced and by whom. I think most educators and students would agree that a dress code is ineffective when a disparity in staff enforcement and favoring or discriminating against either gender occurs.

The social injustice of the arbitrariness and discriminatory effects of the GHHS Dress Code manifest most blatantly in the way that females are punished more frequently and harshly than their male peers. Simply put, the enforcing of the dress code against females interferes with their learning, forcing them to miss class. I suggest, though, that the social injustice touches deeper issues when it works on females' identity and self-esteem, playing into the bigger and even more important conversation about gender discrimination in our society. As Anna Kessel, athletic reporter and writer for *The Guardian* and *The Observer*, has noted, the female body has become a "public space" where people can critique, judge, and sexualize all they want (33). Because the female body is constantly "on display" in our culture, girls are held responsible for covering up and hiding their bodies to keep others from looking at them. My high school's dress code—and I would speculate, many other dress codes—directly fuels this societal perspective. I see the effect this message has on young girls with my Girls on the Run group, which I coach two days a week at Stevens Middle School. In this afterschool program, these third-grade through fifth-grade girls are much more conscious of their bodies than I was at their age. Some of the older girls do not like to wear shorts or tank tops when they run because they do not want to show that much skin. These young girls already have a fear of their own bodies, and this fear will be reinforced in their education at schools with dress codes similar to the dress code at GHHS. Dress codes like these are forcing females to conform to while male behaviors like sexual prowess, commenting on females' appearance, and pushing the rules are accepted or go unnoticed. Why is it that males often are not asked to comply with dress codes? Why do the rules not apply to them as often?

Students do need some limitations as to what they can and cannot wear to school. A school dress code helps them learn what is expected in professional work environments. Dress codes are an important part of the school environment and should diminish distractions and promote educational success. But is the code at GHHS accomplishing this goal? Without fair enforcement by school staff members to all students, I argue, this dress code fails in its goal. The room for arbitrary enforcement and discriminatory punishment, which falls heavily on females, sends the wrong message to our student body and will have long-term negative effects, as did the teacher who questioned my morality. Her words reminded me of the message society sends to women every day, that their bodies are a public space for judgment. Is this a message GHHS really wants to send our youth?

Work Cited

Kessel, Anna. *Eat Sweat Play*. Pan Macmillan, 2016.

Critiquing "A Detrimental and Defective Dress Code"

1. What criteria does Hadley Reeder use to evaluate her high school's dress code? What other criteria might be used?

2. Hadley hoped that the administrators of her former high school might read her argument. How persuasive do you think her criteria would be for this audience?

3. This argument relies mostly on evidence from personal experience. How does this evidence support Hadley's criteria? How might it be disputed? If she were to argue for an institutional change in the dress code, what other kinds of evidence could she enlist?

4. How persuasive do you find Hadley's causal reasoning that discrimination in dress codes has deeper personal and social repercussions for girls than it does for boys?

Our final readings represent two different ethical arguments emerging from recent research on therapeutic cloning at the Oregon Health and Sciences

University. The first article, by Judith Daar and Erez Aloni, appeared as an op-ed piece in the *Los Angeles Times*. Judith Daar, a professor of both law and medicine, is a member of the Ethics Committee of the American Society for Reproductive Medicine. Her co-author Erez Aloni is a professor at Whittier Law School. The second article appeared a year earlier in *National Review*. It was written by Catholic writer Samuel Aquila, the archbishop of the Archdiocese of Denver, Colorado.

Three Genetic Parents—For One Healthy Baby

JUDITH DAAR AND EREZ ALONI

Since January, a new California law allows for a child to have more than two legal parents. But children are still limited to two genetic parents. That could change soon, if the Food and Drug Administration approves human clinical trials for a technique known as mitochondrial replacement, which would enable a child to inherit DNA from three parents.

News of the pending application has caused a kind of panic not seen since Dolly the sheep was cloned, raising the possibility of a single genetic parent. But far from being the end of the human race as we know it, the technique might be a way to prevent hundreds of mitochondrial-linked diseases, which affect about one in 5,000 people.

The idea of multi-person reproductive collaborations is not new. Over the last several decades we have acclimated to various forms of assisted reproductive technologies. Indeed, in the U.S. about 75,000 infants are born each year to parents who enlist the aid of egg donors, sperm donors, or gestational carriers. These methods, however, still involve the "traditional" merger of DNA from one male and one female.

Mitochondrial replacement would alter this two-genetic-parent model by introducing a third set of DNA into the procreative process. The technique would enable women who carry harmful mutations in their mitochondria to have a child without those harmful mutations. As with all human reproduction, the child would carry a combination of genes from one male and one female. However, in this technique, the nucleus of the mother's egg would be injected into a "third parent's" nucleus-free egg containing healthy mitochondrial DNA. As a result, the child would inherit the characteristics of the original male and female but have healthy mitochondria from a third person.

5   Experiments employing the technique conducted on monkeys resulted in healthy offspring that did not carry the harmful mutation. Now, a team at Oregon Health and Sciences University is seeking approval from the FDA to begin human clinical trials.

It seems likely that, if it is proved safe and effective, mitochondrial replacement will eventually join the panoply of techniques facilitating the birth of healthy children through assisted conception. But it should be no surprise that the new technology is causing a furor.

The introduction of assisted reproductive technologies has followed a predictable pattern: initial panic followed by widespread condemnation, followed by gradual acceptance as a technique becomes more widespread. In the 1950s, when reports of pregnancies using donor sperm first appeared in medical journals, lawmakers declared the process "mechanical adultery" and sought its criminalization. Early reports of success with in vitro fertilization in the 1970s provoked editorials that decried the process as totally immoral. In the 1990s, the introduction of pre-implantation diagnosis of genetic diseases provoked allegations of a war on disabled individuals.

Today, detractors remain, but the methods have been embraced as the standard of care in reproductive medicine. Once a technique proves safe and effective, its ability to assist in the birth of healthy children generally paves the way for public approval.

For some, the introduction of a third genetic parent is alarming because the novel genetic configuration could be embedded in the child's DNA in perpetuity, with unknown implications for future generations. But the panic also rests in part on simple discomfort with upending the notion of genetic parenthood involving just two people.

A similar anxiety seized the public this year after California authorized judges   10
to recognize more than two people as a child's lawful parents. The law grew out of a horrendous situation in which the court's inability to recognize a third parent diverted a young child into foster care. Though it's hardly on par with the scientific breakthrough represented by mitochondrial replacement, the so-called three-parent law stirred deep fears about the durability of traditional family life in the modern era.

But the fears about three-parent possibilities—both genetic and legal—are likely to subside as people realize that they are aimed at one goal: the well-being of children. The California law orders judges to recognize three parents when not doing so "would otherwise be detrimental to the child." And mitochondrial replacement will be employed to avoid transmission of a heritable disease. If the "power of three" has the ability to improve a child's well-being, isn't that something worth embracing?

The "Therapeutic Cloning" of Human Embryos

SAMUEL AQUILA

Oscar Wilde's *The Picture of Dorian Gray* is the sort of timeless morality tale students read as an antidote, or at least an objection, to the hedonism that seems to follow naturally from youthful ideas about immortality.

The story is familiar to many: Dorian Gray is a narcissist who wishes that a portrait of him—his copy in paint—would age in his place. His wish comes true, and though his life is corrupted by a pursuit of pleasure, only his painted visage bears the effects. Dorian himself is visibly unscathed, though the novel's fatal climax exposes a soul rendered ugly by a life of egoistic debauchery.

The Picture of Dorian Gray took on a particular prescience yesterday. Scientists at Oregon Health and Science University reported a successful incidence of cloning, one that relied on the same method that researchers used 17 years ago to clone

(continued)

Dolly the sheep. This week, the cloned embryos were not sheep; they were human beings. The work is heralded as the success of "therapeutic cloning."

We will hear a lot about therapeutic cloning in the news this week. Researchers distinguish between "therapeutic cloning," which creates embryos in order to harvest their stem cells, and "reproductive cloning," which has the intention of a live birth. The Oregon researchers insist that theirs was not an act of "reproductive cloning."

5   But the distinction is spurious. *Both* types of cloning are reproductive. Both bring a new human being into existence. In fact, so-called therapeutic cloning is the more heinous because the process is intended to create life, exploit it, and then destroy it.

Consider what the cloning breakthrough means. Scientists have discovered how to create perfect human copies, to be used for the sole purpose of growing tissue in the effort to combat disease, and then these copies will be destroyed. From a scientific perspective, this breakthrough could solve, among other problems, that of tissue rejection or a delay that renders organ transplant unfeasible. From the standpoint of materialism, there has been no greater advance in regenerative medicine. Through therapeutic cloning, a person's health can be enhanced immeasurably—and only the copy, the embryo, will suffer the effects.

The problem is that the embryo is not merely a copy. The embryo is not an extension of the patient who donated the DNA, a cell bank to be utilized without consequence. The embryo, though genetically identical, is a new manifestation of human life, endowed by its very being with dignity. The embryo is a human being.

The humanity of the cloned embryo will be aggressively denied in the weeks to come. Though human life demonstrably begins at the embryonic stage of development, the created embryo will be presented as a collection of tissue, a biological tabula rasa from which organs can be grown. Scientists will seek more funding, and the Dickey Amendment, which prohibits federal funding for the creation of cloned embryos, will be attacked.

In 1968, Pope Paul VI warned in *Humanae Vitae* that the sexual revolution, beginning with a cultural acceptance of the contraceptive mentality, would lead to a wholesale denial of human dignity and the family. Now we are cloning embryos to destroy them. It will be only a matter of time before therapeutic cloning will cede to reproductive cloning. If we don't seriously contemplate the ethical consequences of therapeutic cloning now, eventually cloned human beings will be born in America.

10   The "progress" of therapeutic cloning will not be victimless. But the victims will be hidden from sight, tucked away in the dark like Dorian's decaying portrait.

The first class of victims, and the ones most pressing on our consciences, will be the embryos: brought into existence to be used, and then killed. If nurtured, as in a womb, these embryos would grow into fetuses, and then infants, and then children. They are, no matter their size, human beings. But because they are small and have no voice and offer such tremendous possibility, they will be ignored.

The embryos will be a class of human beings created only to be exploited and discarded.

The second class of victims will be the rest of us. We will be the ones remaining healthy and making progress and defeating disease—all by means of killing. We will be the ones who appear beautiful, while our souls embrace the most harrowing kind of social utilitarianism and darkness. If we ignore the problem, as we have done with contraception and abortion, we will only sink into a more violent depravity, like the one that befell vain Dorian Gray. We will be the ones whose portrait grows ever uglier, and who grow ever closer to madness.

Critiquing "Three Genetic Parents—For One Healthy Baby" and "The 'Therapeutic Cloning' of Human Embryos"

1. In "Three Genetic Parents—for One Healthy Baby," Daar and Aloni note that news coming from cloning research at Oregon Health and Science University "has caused a kind of panic not seen since Dolly the sheep was cloned." An example of this panic is the earlier *National Review* article by Archbishop Aquila. Summarize Aquila's objection to both therapeutic and reproductive cloning. What rhetorical strategies do Daar and Aloni use to counter the objections of those like Archbishop Aquila?

2. Identify in both articles examples of arguments from consequence and arguments from principle used either to support the authors' claims or to summarize opposing claims.

3. Aquila acknowledges the health benefits of therapeutic cloning, particularly its potential for curing or preventing certain diseases. He recognizes also that many people will consider therapeutic cloning a moral good because it produces good consequences. To make his case for the moral evil of cloning, he creates an analogy argument based on Oscar Wilde's novel *The Picture of Dorian Gray*. Explain how this analogy functions. What does Aquila compare to what?

Chapter 15
Proposal Arguments

Learning Objectives

In this chapter you will learn to:

15.1 Explain the special features and concerns of proposal arguments.

15.2 Use a problem-solution-justification structure to develop proposal arguments.

15.3 Use heuristic strategies to develop supporting reasons for your proposal argument.

15.4 Use words and images to create an advocacy poster or advertisement.

15.5 Write your own proposal argument.

Proposal arguments are essential for the workings of a free and open society. A proposal argument motivates its audience to recognize a problem and then proposes a solution to the problem. When effective, proposal arguments call an audience to action. Whether you are writing a grant proposal to seek funding for a research project, a practical proposal for remedying a problem at your workplace, or a policy proposal to address a national issue, proposal arguments are among the most important kinds of writing you will ever be called upon to produce.

Case 1: Should the Supreme Court Overturn *Roe v. Wade*?

Among the most heated debates in the United States is whether the due process and privacy protections of the Fourteenth Amendment can be extended to a woman's right to an abortion. The right-to-life movement has intensified its efforts to restrict access to abortions at the state level and to overturn *Roe v. Wade* in the U.S. Supreme Court. Meanwhile, pro-choice advocates such as Planned Parenthood have vigorously defended a woman's right to an abortion. Both sides make effective use of visual arguments. Right-to-life groups frequently use posters showing ultrasound images of unborn babies (often not using the word "fetus"). The poster in Figure 15.1, sponsored by Planned Parenthood, features a starkly black question mark that on second look is seen to be made from a coat hanger. It makes an implied proposal claim ("Abortion should remain legal") and supports it with a consequence argument: If abortions are outlawed, women will have abortions anyway—using coat hangers instead of medically safe procedures. The

Figure 15.1 Planned Parenthood poster

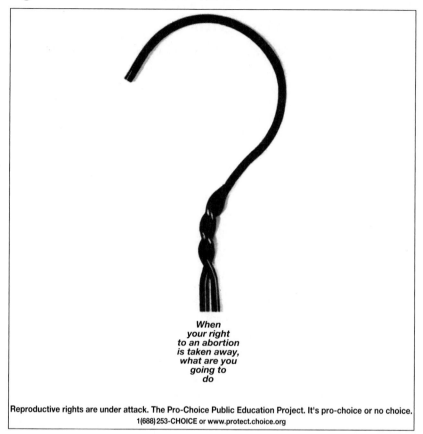

When
your right
to an abortion
is taken away,
what are you
going to
do

Reproductive rights are under attack. The Pro-Choice Public Education Project. It's pro-choice or no choice.
1(688)253-CHOICE or www.protect.choice.org

image of the coat hanger (reminiscent of horror stories about abortions prior to *Roe v. Wade*) appeals simultaneously to *logos* and *pathos*.

Case 2: How Should the United States Reduce the Carbon Footprint of Automobiles?

The concern for climate change—combined with the high price of gasoline—has increased the popularity of small, energy-efficient cars. Much debated among policy makers is the role that federal or state governments should play in further promoting a green transportation system. Some argue that the government should stay out of free markets, letting buyers decide for themselves what kinds of cars they want to buy. Others argue that free markets do not currently make gasoline consumers pay for the "externalities" (societal costs) of gasoline consumption—particularly the cost to the environment of emitting more carbon into the atmosphere. Concerned citizens have proposed dozens of ideas for reducing the carbon footprint of cars and trucks. Among the proposals are the following: placing a "green tax" on gasoline; requiring auto manufacturers to increase the fuel efficiency of their fleets; giving tax credits for buying a fuel-efficient car, particularly an electric car; increasing incentives for carpooling or taking public transportation; increasing the cost of parking; charging different gas prices at the pump (with higher prices for less fuel-efficient cars); retrofitting cars to burn natural gas; and rebuilding cities so that housing is closer to worksites.

The Special Features and Concerns of Proposal Arguments

15.1 Explain the special features and concerns of proposal arguments.

Although proposal arguments are the last type of argument we examine, they are among the most common arguments that you will encounter or be called on to write. The essence of proposal arguments is a call for action. In reading a proposal, the audience is enjoined to make a decision and then to act on it—to *do* something. Proposal arguments are sometimes called *should or ought* arguments because those helping verbs express the obligation to act. They typically have a three-part structure: (1) description of a problem, (2) proposed solution, and (3) justification for the proposed solution. In the justification section of your proposal argument, you develop *because* clauses of the kinds you have practiced throughout this text.

Practical Proposals Versus Policy Proposals

For instructional purposes, we distinguish between two kinds of proposal arguments—*practical proposals,* which propose an action to solve some kind of local or immediate problem, and *policy proposals,* which propose a broad plan of action to solve major social, economic, or political problems affecting the common good. A student's proposal to build bike paths on campus would be an example of a practical proposal. In contrast, an argument that the United States should abolish the income tax would be a policy proposal.

The primary difference is the narrowness versus breadth of the concern. Practical proposals are narrow, local, and concrete; they focus on the nuts and bolts of getting something done in the here and now. They are often concerned with the exact size of a piece of steel, the precise duties of a new person to be hired, or a close estimate of the cost of paint or computers to be purchased. Policy proposals, in contrast, are concerned with the broad outline and shape of a course of action, often on a regional, national, or even international issue. What government should do about overcrowding of prisons would be a problem addressed by policy proposals. How to improve the security alarm system for the county jail would be addressed by a practical proposal.

Learning to write both kinds of proposals is valuable. Researching and writing a policy proposal is an excellent way to practice the responsibilities of citizenship, which require the ability to understand complex issues and to weigh positive and negative consequences of policy choices. In your professional life, writing practical proposals may well be among your most important duties on the job. Effective proposal writing is the lifeblood of many companies and constitutes one of the most powerful ways you can identify and help solve problems.

Toulmin Framework for a Proposal Argument

The Toulmin schema is particularly useful for proposal arguments because it helps you support your proposal with reasons linked to your audience's beliefs, assumptions, and values. Suppose that your university is debating whether to banish fraternities and sororities. Suppose further that you are in favor of banishing the Greek system. One of your arguments is that eliminating the Greek system will improve your university's academic reputation. The following chart shows how you might use the Toulmin schema to make this line of reasoning as persuasive as possible.

Toulmin Analysis of the Greek System Argument

ENTHYMEME

CLAIM Our university should eliminate the Greek system

REASON because doing so will improve our university's academic reputation.

GROUNDS

Evidence that eliminating the Greek system will improve our academic reputation:

- Excessive party atmosphere of some Greek houses emphasizes social life rather than studying—we are known as a party school.

- Last year the average GPA of students in fraternities and sororities was lower than the GPA of non-Greek students.

- New pledges have so many house duties and initiation rites that their studies suffer.

- Many new students think about rush more than about the academic life.

WARRANT

It is good for our university to achieve a better academic reputation.

BACKING

- The school would attract more serious students, leading to increased prestige.

- Campus would be more academically focused and attract better faculty.

- Losing the "party-school" reputation would put us in better light for taxpayers and legislators.

- Students would graduate with more skills and knowledge.

CONDITIONS OF REBUTTAL
Attacking the reason and grounds

- Many of the best students are Greeks. Last year's highest-GPA award went to a sorority woman, and several other Greeks won prestigious graduate school scholarships.

- Statistics on grades are misleading. Many houses had a much higher average GPA than the university average. Total GPA was brought down by a few rowdy houses.

- Many other high-prestige universities have Greek systems.

- There are ways to tone down the party atmosphere on campus without abolishing the Greek system.

- Greeks contribute significantly to the community through service projects.

CONDITIONS OF REBUTTAL
Attacking the warrant and backing

- No one will argue that it is not good to have a strong academic reputation.

- However, skeptics may say that eliminating sororities and fraternities won't improve the university's academic reputation but will hurt its social life and its wide range of living options.

Special Concerns for Proposal Arguments

In their call for action, proposal arguments entail certain emphases and audience concerns that you don't generally face with other kinds of arguments. Let's look briefly at some of these special concerns.

- *The need for presence.* To persuade people to *act* on your proposal, particularly if the personal or financial cost of acting is high, you must give your argument presence as well as intellectual force. By *presence* we mean an argument's ability to grip your readers' hearts and imaginations as well as their intellects. You can give presence to an argument through appeals to *pathos,* such as effective use of details, provocative statistics, dialogue, illustrative narratives, and compelling examples that show the reader the seriousness of the problem you are addressing or the consequences of not acting on your proposal.

- *The need to overcome people's natural conservatism.* Another difficulty with proposals is the innate conservatism of all human beings, whatever their political persuasion, as suggested by the popular adage "If it ain't broke, don't fix it." The difficulty of proving that something needs fixing is compounded by the fact that frequently the status quo appears to be working. So, when writing a proposal, sometimes you can't argue that what we have is bad, but only that what we could have would be better. Often, then, a proposal argument will be based not on present evils but on the evils of lost potential. And getting an audience to accept lost potential may be difficult indeed, given the inherently abstract nature of potentiality.

- *The difficulty of predicting future consequences.* Most proposal makers will be forced to predict consequences of their proposed action. As the "law of unintended consequences" suggests, few major decisions lead neatly to their anticipated results without surprises along the way. So when we claim that our proposal will lead to good consequences, we can expect our audience to be skeptical.

- *The problem of evaluating consequences.* A final problem for proposal writers is the difficulty of evaluating consequences. In government and industry, managers often use a *cost-benefit analysis* to reduce all consequences to a single-scale comparison, usually money. Although this scale may work well in some circumstances, it can lead to grotesquely inappropriate conclusions in other situations. Just how does one balance the environmental benefits of a green tax on gasoline against the suffering of drivers who can't afford to get to work? Also, a benefit for one group often entails a cost for others. For example, a higher minimum wage will benefit low-wage workers at a cost to consumers, who must pay higher prices, or to other low-wage workers who get laid off.

These, then, are some of the general difficulties facing someone who sets out to write a proposal argument. Although these difficulties may seem daunting, the rest of this chapter offers strategies to help you overcome them and produce a successful proposal.

Developing a Proposal Argument

15.2 Use a problem-solution-justification structure to develop proposal arguments.

Writers of proposal arguments must focus on three main phases or stages of the argument: showing that a problem exists, explaining the proposed solution, and offering a justification.

Examining Visual Arguments

A Proposal Claim

This photo of a dead baby albatross on a Pacific island near an albatross nesting ground resembles the photos taken by environmental photographer Chris Jordan in his well-known 2009 exhibit entitled *Midway: Message from the Gyre*. The purpose of that exhibit was to draw attention to the effects of the increasing amount of ocean garbage on albatrosses, which mistake the garbage for food. How could this photo be used to generate concern and activism regarding this environmental problem? The colorful, plastic-filled carcass of the baby albatross creates a complex appeal to *pathos* in the way that it illustrates the problem. What verbal text would you use to interpret the photo's message and call people to action?

Convincing Your Readers That a Problem Exists

There is one argumentative strategy generic to all proposal arguments: calling your reader's attention to a problem. In some situations, your intended audience may already be aware of the problem and may have even asked for solutions. In such cases, you do not need to develop the problem extensively or motivate your audience to solve it. But in most situations, awakening your readers to the existence of a problem—a problem they may not have recognized before—is your first important challenge. You must give your problem presence through anecdotes, telling statistics, or other means that show readers how the problem affects people or otherwise has important stakes. Your goal is to gain your readers' intellectual assent to the depth, range, and potential seriousness of the problem and thereby motivate them to want to solve it.

Typically, the arguer develops the problem in one of two places: either (1) in the introduction prior to the presentation of the arguer's proposed solution or (2) in the body of the paper as the first main reason justifying the proposed solution.

In the second instance the writer's first *because* clause has the following structure: "We should do this action *because* it addresses a serious problem."

Here is how one student writer gave presence to a proposal, addressed to the chair of the mathematics department at her school, calling for redesign of the first-year calculus curriculum in order to slow its pace. She wants the chair to see the problem from her perspective.

Example Passage Giving Presence to a Problem

> I want to become a high-school math teacher. For me, the problem with introductory calculus is not its difficulty but its pace. My own experience in the Calculus 134 and 135 sequence last year showed me that it was not the learning of calculus that was difficult for me. I was able to catch on to the new concepts. My problem was that it went too fast. Just as I was assimilating new concepts and feeling the need to reinforce them, the class was on to a new topic before I had full mastery of the old concept.... Part of the reason for the fast pace is that calculus is a feeder course for computer science and engineering. If prospective engineering students can't learn calculus rapidly, they drop out of the program. The high dropout rate benefits the Engineering School because it uses the math course to weed out an overabundance of engineering majors. Thus the pace of the calculus course is geared to the needs of the engineering curriculum, not to the needs of someone like me, who wants to be a high-school mathematics teacher and who believes that my own difficulties with math—combined with my love for it—might make me an excellent math teacher.

By describing the fast pace of the math curriculum from the perspective of a future math teacher rather than an engineering student, this writer brings visibility to a problem. What before didn't look like a problem (it is good to weed out weak engineering majors) suddenly became a problem (it is bad to weed out future math teachers). Establishing herself as a serious student genuinely interested in learning calculus, she gave presence to the problem by calling attention to it in a new way.

Explaining the Proposed Solution: Showing the Specifics of Your Proposal

Having decided that there is a problem to be solved, you should lay out your thesis, which is a proposal for solving the problem. Your goal now is to stress the feasibility of your solution, including costs. The art of proposal making is the art of the possible. Certainly, not all proposals require elaborate descriptions of the implementation process. For example, if you are proposing that a local PTA chapter buy new tumbling mats for the junior-high gym classes, the procedures for buying the mats will probably be irrelevant. But in many arguments, the specifics of your proposal—the actual step-by-step methods of implementing it—may be instrumental in winning your audience's support.

You will also need to show how your proposal will solve the problem either partially or wholly. Sometimes you may first need to convince your reader that the problem is solvable and not something intractably rooted in "the way things are," such as earthquakes or jealousy. In other words, expect that some members of your audience will be skeptical about the ability of any proposal to solve the problem you are addressing. You may need, therefore, to "listen" to this point of view in your refutation section and to argue that your problem is at least partially solvable.

To persuade your audience that your proposal can work, you can follow any one of several approaches. A typical approach is to use a causal argument to show that your solution is feasible. Another approach is to use a resemblance argument to show how similar proposals have been successful elsewhere. Or, if similar things have failed in the past, you try to show how the present situation is different.

Offering a Justification: Convincing Your Readers That the Benefits of Your Proposal Outweigh the Costs

The justification phase of a proposal argument will need extensive development in some arguments and minimal development in others, again depending on your particular problem and the rhetorical context of your proposal. If your audience already acknowledges the seriousness of the problem you are addressing and has simply been waiting for the right solution to come along, then your argument will be successful, provided you can convince your audience that your solution will work and that it won't cost too much. Such arguments depend on the clarity of your proposal and the feasibility of its implementation.

But what if the costs are high? What if your readers don't think the problem is serious? What if they don't appreciate the benefits of solving the problem or the bad consequences of not solving it? In such cases you have to develop persuasive reasons for enacting your proposal. You may also have to determine who has the power to act on your proposal and apply arguments directly to that person's or agency's immediate interests. You need to know to whom or to what your power source is beholden or responsive. You must also know what values your power source holds that can be appealed to. In short, you're looking for the best pressure points.

Using Heuristic Strategies to Develop Supporting Reasons for Your Proposal

15.3 Use heuristic strategies to develop supporting reasons for your proposal argument.

To help you find supporting reasons for your proposal—the pressure points that will move your audience—we offer two heuristic strategies. (A *heuristic* is an exploratory problem-solving technique or invention aid that helps you generate ideas.) We call these heuristics the *claim types strategy* and the *stock issues strategy*.

The Claim Types Strategy

In Chapter 11 we explained how evaluation and proposal claims often use claims about category, cause, or resemblance for their supporting reasons. This fact leads to a powerful idea-generating strategy based on arguments from category (particularly from a category of actions that adhere to a certain principle), on arguments from consequences, or on arguments from resemblance. Table 15.1 illustrates this claim types strategy.

Before we give you some simple strategies for using this approach, let's illustrate it with another example.

Example

The United States should levy a "carbon tax" on carbon-based fuels

- because such a tax accords with the free-market principle that the price of a good should reflect the full cost of production (category/principle).
- because such a tax will accelerate the transition to cleaner fuels and thus help reduce global warming (cause/consequence).
- because this approach is similar to the market-based tax on sulfur emissions that helped solve the problem of acid rain (resemblance).

Note how each of these supporting reasons appeals to the value system of different kinds of voters. The writer argues that a carbon tax belongs to the category of things that use free market principles (particularly valued by conservative, pro-business voters); that it will lead to the good consequence of reducing global warming (valued particularly by environmentalists and others worried about climate change); and that it is similar to something that has already proved successful (the market-based approach to fighting acid rain, which has been applauded by both liberals and conservatives). The claim types strategy for generating ideas is easy to apply in practice. Table 15.2 shows you how.

Table 15.1 Explanation of Claim Types Strategy for Supporting a Proposal Claim

Claim Type	Generic Template	Example from Biotechnology Issue
Argument from principle or category	We should do this action - because doing so adheres to this good principle [or] - because this action belongs to this good category	We should support genetically modified foods - because doing so values scientific reason over emotion [or] - because genetically modified foods are safe [belong to the category of safe things]
Argument from consequences	- because this action will lead to these good consequences	- because biotech crops can reduce world hunger - because biotech crops can improve the environment by reducing use of pesticides
Argument from resemblance	- because this action has been done successfully elsewhere [or] - because this action is like this other good action	- because genetic modification is like natural crossbreeding that has been accelerated [or] - because genetic modification of food is like scientific advancements in medicine

Table 15.2 Suggestions for Applying the Claim Types Strategy to Your Proposal

Claim Type	Your Goal	Thinking Strategy
Argument from principle or category	Show how your proposed action follows a principle valued by your audience or belongs to a category valued by your audience.	Think of how your proposed action adheres to an audience-valued rule or principle or belongs to an audience-valued category (for example, "doing this action is kind, just, constitutional, appropriately restrained, safe, efficient, and so forth").
Argument from consequences	Show how your proposed action will lead to consequences valued by your audience.	Brainstorm consequences of your proposal and identify those that the audience will agree are good.
Argument from resemblance	Show how your proposed action has been done success- fully elsewhere or is like another action valued by your audience.	Find analogies that compare your proposed action to something the audience already values or find previous places or times that your proposed action (or something similar to it) has been done successfully.

The Stock Issues Strategy

Another effective heuristic for a proposal argument is to ask yourself a series of questions based on the stock issues strategy. For example, suppose you wanted to develop the following argument: "To solve the problem of students who won't take risks with their writing, the faculty should adopt a pass/fail method of grading in all writing courses." The stock issues strategy invites the writer to consider "stock" ways (that is, common, usual, frequently repeated ways) that such arguments can be conducted.

Stock issue 1: *Is there really a problem here that needs to be solved?* Is it really true that a large number of student writers won't take risks in their writing? Is this problem more serious than other writing problems, such as undeveloped ideas, lack of organization, and poor sentence structure? This stock issue invites the writer to convince her audience that a true problem exists. Conversely, an opponent of the proposal may argue that a true problem does not exist.

Stock issue 2: *Will the proposed solution really solve this problem?* Is it true that a pass/fail grading system will cause students to take more risks with their writing? Will more interesting, surprising, and creative essays result from pass/fail grading? Or will students simply put less effort into their writing? This stock issue prompts a supporter to demonstrate that the proposal will solve the problem; it also prompts the opponent to show that the proposal won't work.

Stock issue 3: *Can the problem be solved more simply, without disturbing the status quo?* An opponent of the proposal may agree that a problem exists and that the proposed solution might solve it. However, the opponent may say, "Are there not less radical ways to solve this problem? If we want more creative and risk-taking student essays, can't we just change our grading criteria so that we reward risky papers and penalize conventional ones?" This stock issue prompts supporters to show that *only* the proposed solution will solve the problem and that no minor tinkering with the status quo will be adequate. Conversely, opponents will argue that the problem can be solved without acting on the proposal.

For Writing and Discussion

Generating Ideas Using the Claim Types Strategy

Individual task:

Use the strategies of principle/category, consequence, and resemblance to create *because* clauses that support each of the following claims. Try to have at least one *because* clause for each of the claim types, but generate as many reasons as possible. Don't worry about whether any individual reason exactly fits the category. The purpose is to stimulate thinking, not fill in the slots.

Example

Congress should not pass gun-control laws (proposal claim)

- because the Second Amendment guarantees the right to own guns (principle or category).
- because owning a gun allows citizens to protect themselves, their homes, and their loved ones from intruders (consequence).
- because laws to ban guns will be as ineffective as laws to ban alcohol during Prohibition (resemblance).

Claims:

1. For graduation, colleges should require one course with an integrated community service component.
2. Restaurants should be required to post calorie counts and other ingredient information for all menu items.
3. Division-1 college athletes should receive salaries.
4. Alcohol should not be allowed on campus.
5. Parents should be heavily taxed for having more than two children.

Group task:

Share your efforts with classmates. Then, working in small groups or as a class, repeat the exercise, taking the opposite position on each issue.

Stock issue 4: *Is the proposed solution really practical? Does it stand a chance of actually being enacted?* Here an opponent to the proposal may agree that the proposal would work but contends that it involves pie-in-the-sky idealism. Nobody will vote to change the existing system so radically; therefore, it is a waste of our time to debate it. Following this prompt, supporters would have to argue that pass/fail grading is workable and that enough faculty members are in favor of it that the proposal is worth debating. Opponents may argue that the faculty is so traditional that pass/fail has no chance of being accepted, despite its merits.

Stock issue 5: *What will be the unforeseen positive and negative consequences of the proposal?* Suppose we do adopt a pass/fail system. What positive or negative consequences may occur that are different from our initial predictions? Using this prompt, an opponent may argue that pass/fail grading will reduce the effort put forth by students and that the long-range effect will be writing of even lower quality than we have now. Supporters would try to find positive consequences—perhaps a new love of writing for its own sake rather than for the sake of a grade.

For Writing and Discussion

Brainstorming Ideas for a Proposal

The following collaborative exercise takes you through the process of creating a proposal argument.

1. In small groups, identify and list several major problems facing students in your college or university.
2. Decide among yourselves which are the most important of these problems and rank them in order of importance.
3. Take your group's number-one problem and explore answers to the following questions. Group recorders should be prepared to present their group's answers to the class.
   a. Why is the problem a problem?
   b. For whom is the problem a problem?
   c. How will these people suffer if the problem is not solved? (Give specific examples.)
   d. Who has the power to solve the problem?
   e. Why hasn't the problem been solved up to this point?
   f. How can the problem be solved? (That is, create a proposal.)
   g. What are the probable benefits of acting on your proposal?
   h. What costs are associated with your proposal?
   i. Who will bear those costs?
   j. Why should this proposal be enacted?
   k. Why is it better than alternative proposals?
4. As a group, draft an outline for a proposal argument in which you
   a. describe the problem and its significance.
   b. propose your solution to the problem.
   c. justify your proposal by showing how the benefits of adopting that proposal outweigh the costs.
5. Recorders for each group should write their group's outline on the board and be prepared to explain it to the class.

Proposal Arguments as Advocacy Posters or Advertisements

15.4 Use words and images to create an advocacy poster or advertisement.

A frequently encountered kind of proposal argument is the one-page newspaper or magazine advertisement often purchased by advocacy groups to promote a cause. Such arguments also appear as web pages or as posters or fliers. These condensed advocacy arguments are marked by their bold, abbreviated, tightly planned format. The creators of these arguments know they must work fast to capture our attention, give presence to a problem, advocate a solution, and enlist our support. Advocacy advertisements frequently use photographs, images, or icons that appeal to a reader's emotions and imagination. In addition to images, they often use different type sizes and styles. Large-type text in these documents frequently takes the form of slogans or condensed thesis statements written in an arresting style.

To outline and justify their solutions, creators of advocacy ads often put main supporting reasons in bulleted lists and sometimes enclose carefully selected facts and quotations in boxed sidebars. To add an authoritative *ethos*, the arguments often include fine-print footnotes and bibliographies. (For more detailed discussion of how advocacy posters and advertisements use images and arrange text for rhetorical effect, see Chapter 9 on visual argument.)

Another prominent feature of these condensed, highly visual arguments is their appeal to the audience through a direct call for a course of action: for example, go to an advocacy website to find more information on how to support the cause; send an e-mail to a decision maker or political representative; vote for or against the proposition or the candidate; or donate money to a cause.

Figure 15.2 shows an example of a student-produced advocacy poster. Here, environmental studies student Janie Bube urges residents of her city to build rain gardens to help solve the problem of excess stormwater. At the top of this poster, Janie gives the problem presence by using a flood photo she took during her internship fieldwork. She then offers her proposed solution, made visually appealing by another of her own photos—a neighborhood rain garden. She offers three reasons to justify the creation of rain gardens, asserting why and how rain gardens work. The final lines of the poster send readers to a website for more information. The rhetorical effect of the text, image, and layout is to attract readers' attention, remind them of the problem, and push them toward adopting her proposed solution.

Writing Assignment: A Proposal Argument

15.5 Write your own proposal argument.

Option 1: A Practical Proposal Addressing a Local Problem Write a practical proposal offering a solution to a local problem. Your proposal should have three main sections: (1) description of the problem, (2) proposed solution, and (3) justification. Proposals are usually accompanied by a *letter of transmittal*—a one-page business letter that introduces the proposal to its intended audience and provides some needed background about the writer. Document design is important in practical proposals, which are aimed at busy people who have to make many decisions under time constraints. An effective design helps establish the writer's *ethos* as a quality-oriented professional and helps make the reading of the proposal as easy as possible. For a student example of a practical proposal, see Megan Johnson's argument at the end of this chapter.

Option 2: A Policy Proposal as a Guest Editorial Write a two- to three-page policy proposal suitable for publication as a feature editorial in a college or city newspaper, on an appropriate website, or in a publication associated with a particular group, such as a church newsletter or employee bulletin. The voice and style of your argument should be aimed at readers of your chosen publication or website. Your editorial should have the following features:

1. The identification of a problem (Persuade your audience that this is a genuine problem that needs solving; give it presence.)
2. A proposal for action that will help alleviate the problem
3. A justification of your solution (the reasons why your audience should accept your proposal and act on it)

Option 3: A Researched Argument Proposing Public Policy Write an eight- to twelve-page proposal argument as a formal research paper, using researched data for development and support. In business and professional life, this kind of research proposal is often called a *white paper*, which recommends a course of action internally within an organization or externally to a client or stakeholder. An example of a researched policy proposal is student writer Ivan Snook's "Flirting with Disaster: An Argument against Integrating Women into the Combat Arms" at the end of this chapter.

Option 4: Multimedia Project: A One-Page Advocacy Poster or Advertisement Using the strategies of visual argument discussed in Chapter 9 and earlier in this chapter, create a one-page advocacy advertisement urging action on a public issue. Your advertisement should be designed for publication in a newspaper or website or for distribution as a poster or flier. For an example of a student-produced advocacy poster, see Janie Bube's poster in Figure 15.2.

Figure 15.2 Student advocacy poster

Option 5: Multimedia Project: A Proposal Speech with Visual Aids Deliver a proposal argument as a prepared but extemporaneous speech of approximately five to eight minutes, supported with visual aids created on presentation software such as PowerPoint or Prezi. Your speech should present a problem, propose a solution, and justify the solution with reasons and evidence. Use visual aids to give presence to the problem and to enhance appeals to *logos*, *ethos*, and *pathos*. Good aids use visual strategies to create encapsulated visual arguments; they are not simply bullet point outlines of your speech. Sandy Wainscott's speech outline and selected PowerPoint slides (at the end of this chapter) illustrate this genre.

Exploring Ideas

Because *should or ought* issues are among the most common sources of arguments, you may already have ideas for proposal issues. To think of ideas for practical proposals, try making an idea map of local problems you would like to see solved. For initial spokes, try trigger words such as the following:

- Problems at my university (dorms, parking, registration system, financial aid, campus appearance, clubs, curriculum, intramural program, athletic teams)
- Problems in my city or town (dangerous intersections, ugly areas, inadequate lighting, parks, police policy, public transportation, schools)
- Problems at my place of work (office design, flow of customer traffic, merchandise display, company policies)
- Problems related to my future career, hobbies, recreational time, life as a consumer, life as a homeowner

If you can offer a solution to the problem you identify, you may make a valuable contribution to some phase of public life.

To find a topic for policy proposals, stay in touch with the news, which will keep you aware of current debates on regional and national issues. Also, visit the websites of your congressional representatives to see what issues they are currently investigating and debating. You might think of your policy proposal as a white paper for one of your legislators.

Once you have decided on a proposal issue, we recommend you explore it by trying one or more of the following activities:

- Explore ideas by using the claim types strategy.
- Explore ideas by using the stock issues strategy.
- Explore ideas using the eleven questions (3a–3k) in the For Writing and Discussion exercise, "Brainstorming Ideas for a Proposal."

Identifying Your Audience and Determining What's at Stake

Before drafting your argument, identify your targeted audience and determine what's at stake. Consider your responses to the following questions:

- What audience are you targeting? What background do they need to understand your problem? How much do they already care about it? How could you motivate them to care?
- After they read your argument, what stance do you imagine them holding? What change do you want to bring about in their view or their behavior?

- What will they find uncomfortable or threatening about your proposal? Particularly, what costs will they incur by acting on your proposal?
- What objections might they raise? What counterarguments or alternative solutions will you need to address?
- Why does your proposal matter? What is at stake?

Organizing a Proposal Argument

When you write your draft, you may find it helpful to have at hand an organization plan for a proposal argument. The plan in Figure 15.3 shows a typical structure for a proposal argument. In some cases, you may want to summarize and rebut opposing views before you present the justification for your own proposal.

Figure 15.3 Organization plan for a proposal argument

Introduce and develop the problem.	• Engage readers' interest in your problem. • Provide background, including previous attempts to solve the problem. • Give the problem "presence" by showing who is affected and what is at stake. • Argue that the problem is solvable (optional).
Present your proposed solution to the problem.	• First, state your proposal concisely to serve as your thesis statement or claim. • Then, explain the specifics of your proposal.
Justify your proposed solution through a series of supporting reasons.	• Restate your claim and forecast your supporting reasons. • Present and develop reason 1. • Present and develop reason 2. • Present and develop additional reasons.
Respond to objections or to alternative proposals.	• Anticipate and summarize possible objections or alternative ways to solve the problem. • Respond appropriately through rebuttal or concession.
Conclude.	• Sum up your argument and help readers return to the "big picture" of what's at stake. • Call readers to action. • End with something memorable.

Designing a One-Page Advocacy Poster or Advertisement

As an alternative to a traditional written argument, your instructor may ask you to create a one-page advocacy advertisement. The first stage of your invention process should be the same as that for a longer proposal argument. Choose a controversial public issue that needs immediate attention or a neglected issue about which you want to arouse public passion. As with a longer proposal argument, consider your audience in order to identify the values and beliefs on which you will base your appeal.

When you construct your argument, the limited space available demands efficiency in your choice of words and in your use of document design. Your goal is to have a memorable impact on your reader in order to promote the action you advocate. The following questions may help you design and revise your advocacy ad:

1. How could photos or other graphic elements establish and give presence to the problem?
2. How can type size, type style, and layout be used to present the core of your proposal, including the justifying reasons, in the most powerful way for the intended audience?
3. Can any part of this argument be presented as a memorable slogan or catch-phrase? What key phrases could highlight the parts or the main points of this argument?
4. How can document design clarify the course of action and the direct demand on the audience this argument is proposing?
5. How can use of color enhance the overall impact of your advocacy argument? (Note: One-page advertisements are expensive to reproduce in color, but you might make effective use of color if your advocacy ad were to appear as a poster or web page.)

Designing PowerPoint Slides or Other Visual Aids for a Speech

In designing visual aids, your goal is to increase the persuasive effect of your speech rather than to demonstrate your technical wizardry. A common mistake with PowerPoint presentations is to get enamored with the program's bells and whistles. If you find yourself thinking about special effects (animations, fade-outs, flashing letters) rather than about "at a glance" visual appeals to *logos or pathos*, you may be on the wrong track. Another common mistake is to use slides simply to project a bullet-point outline of your speech. Our best advice in designing slides is thus to "think visual argument."

In terms of visual argument, effective presentation slides can usually be placed in three design categories:

- Slides using images (photographs, drawings) to enhance *pathos* or to create a snapshot that visually clarifies a concept (*logos*)
- Slides using graphs or other visual displays of numbers to make numeric arguments
- Slides using bulleted (all-text) subpoints for evidence

All the strategies for visual arguments discussed in Chapter 9 and in this chapter under the heading "Proposal Arguments as Advocacy Posters or Advertisements" apply equally to presentation slides.

In most cases, the title of the slide should put into words the slide's *take-away point*. That is, the title should provide a verbal summary of the slide's visual argument. Most rhetoricians suggest that the title of a slide be a short sentence that makes a point rather than just a topic phrase.

Topic as Title (Weak)	Point as Title (Strong)
Coal and the Environment	Burning Coal Produces Dangerous Greenhouse Gases
The Effect of Money on Happiness	More Money Doesn't Mean More Happiness

Student writer Sandy Wainscott follows these principles in her speech and accompanying PowerPoint slides, shown in the reading at the end of this chapter.

Questioning and Critiquing a Proposal Argument

As we've suggested, proposal arguments need to overcome people's innate conservatism, the difficulty of anticipating all the consequences of a proposal, and so forth. What questions, then, can we ask about proposal arguments to help us anticipate these problems?

- *Will a skeptic deny that my problem is really a problem?* Be prepared for skeptics who aren't bothered by your problem, who see your problem as limited to a small group of people, or who think you are exaggerating.

- *Will a skeptic doubt the effectiveness of my solution?* A skeptic might agree that your problem is indeed important and worth solving but might not be convinced that your solution will work. For these skeptics, you'll need to provide evidence that your solution is feasible and workable. Also be prepared for skeptics who focus on the potential negative or unintended consequences of your proposed solution.

- *Will a skeptic think my proposal costs too much?* The most commonly asked question of any proposal is simply, "Do the benefits of enacting the proposal outweigh the costs?" Be wary of the (understandable) tendency to underestimate the costs and exaggerate the benefits of a proposal. Honesty will enhance your *ethos.*

- *Will a skeptic suggest counterproposals?* Once you've convinced readers that a problem exists, they are likely to suggest solutions different from yours. It makes sense to anticipate alternative solutions and to work out ways to argue why your solution is better. And who knows? You may end up liking the counterproposal better and changing your mind about what to propose!

Readings

Our first reading, by student writer Megan Johnson, is a practical proposal addressing the problem of an inequitable meal plan on her campus—one that she claims discriminates against women. As a practical proposal, it uses headings and other elements of document design aimed at giving it a finished and professional appearance. When sent to the intended audience, it is accompanied by a single-spaced letter of transmittal following the conventional format of a business letter.

Student Essay

A Practical Proposal

Megan Johnson

Ms. Jane Doe
Vice President for Budgeting and Finance
Certain University
Certain City
Certain State, Zip

Dear Ms. Doe:

Enclosed is a proposal that addresses our university's minimum meal-plan requirements for students living on campus. My proposal shows the problems associated with this requirement and suggests a workable solution for the university.

The enclosed proposal suggests a modest plan for allowing students to use their campus cards to purchase items off campus. Currently, students are required to purchase a minimum meal plan of $1,170, even though women eat less than men and often have to donate unspent meal funds back to the university. This proposal would give students the option to spend some of their meal plan money off campus. The benefits of my plan include more fairness to women students, fewer incentives toward binge eating, more opportunities for student bonding, and better relations with the nearby business community.

Through web research, I have discovered that other universities have systems in place similar to the one I am proposing. I hope that my proposal is received well and considered as a workable option. A change in the minimum meal-plan requirement might make our university a more desirable option for more prospective students as well as ultimately benefit the general welfare of the current student body.

Thank you for your time.

Sincerely,
Megan Johnson (Student)

A Proposal to Allow Off-Campus Purchases with a University Meal Card, Submitted by Megan Johnson (Student)

Problem

The problem with this university's required meal plan is that it is too large for many students, particularly women. For example, at the end of Winter Quarter, my final balance on my meal card was $268.50, all of which, except for $100, I had to donate back to the university. As the current system stands, students have to purchase a minimum meal plan for living on campus. The minimum meal plan totals $1,170 per quarter. During the academic year an amount of $100 may be rolled into the next quarter. At the end of the quarter any remaining funds, excluding the $100, will be removed from the meal plan. Therefore, if students do not spend the money on their meal plans, it will be wasted. As a woman, I am frustrated about having to decide whether to give my money back to the university or to use up my meal card by binge eating at the end of each quarter.

Proposed Solution

I propose that our university create a system in which students are able to use their campus meal plans at local businesses off campus such as local drug stores, grocery stores, and restaurants. As I will note later in this proposal, other universities have such a system, so the technical difficulties should be easy to solve. Basically, the card works as a debit card loaded with the amount of money the student places on the card. Local businesses would swipe a student's card the same way as the on-campus food service currently does, deducting the current charge against the amount still available on the card. It would probably be possible to limit the total number of dollars available for spending off campus.

Justification

My proposal would allow on-campus residential students to use some of their meal-plan money on groceries, on non-food related items such as toiletries, or on an occasional off-campus meal at a local restaurant. This proposal would resolve the problem of gender bias in the current system, promote opportunities for more bonding among students, and ultimately help create a healthier student body. Moreover, it would show the university's commitment to its students' welfare.

First of all, the current meal plan policy tends to discriminate against women. All students on campus are required to have a minimum meal plan, even though men and women have clearly different eating habits. Men tend to eat much more than women and frequently have to add money to their meal plans to get through the quarter. In contrast, many women, like myself, don't use up their prepaid amounts. For example, my friend James ran out of his meal plan by the eighth week of the quarter whereas my roommate Blaire had over $400 left on her card at the end of the quarter. She and I, like many other women, will have to donate our money back to the school. Therefore, women often feel cheated out of their money while men do not. It is discriminatory to require all students, regardless of gender, to have the same minimum meal plan. However, if the university is going to require all students to have the same minimum meal plan, then the university needs to give women more options to spend their money on things other than food purchased in the school dining halls.

In addition, my proposal would create more opportunities for bonding. For example, it would allow persons who love to cook, such as me, to use the residence-hall kitchens to create "home-cooked meals" for floormates, thus creating more friendships among students. Personally, I have had the pleasure of helping create such bonds among the women on my floor by cooking a "family dinner" in our floor's kitchen. The aroma of the roasted chicken and homemade mashed potatoes drew the students on the fifth floor into the lounge. After our shared dinner, it seemed as if the residents of our floor felt more comfortable being around one another in a more family-like way. I think that cooking on campus gives students a sense of comfort that they do not get when they go to the dining halls and have food pre-made for them. While I would love to cook dinner for my floor more often, the bottom line is that ingredients are too expensive to pay for on my regular credit card when I have already purchased from the university more food than I can eat. If the school were to implement a system where we could use a portion of our meal plans off campus, students would be able to buy groceries from local stores and to put to better use the kitchens already built into the residence halls.

In addition to creating closer bonds between students, an off-campus option for our meal cards would help women eat more healthfully. The current system promotes bad eating habits, causing women to overeat or even to binge in order to use up their extra meal plan money. For example, with the leftover money on my card at the end of Fall Quarter, I bought cases of energy drinks, which are filled with high-fructose corn syrup and other empty calories. As another example, my friend Amber purchases multiple meals such as pizza and a burger for dinner because

(continued)

she doesn't want to waste her money. Overeating is obviously unhealthy and could eventually lead to an increase in obesity or eating disorders. However, if students were able to use their meal card off campus, they could buy items such as shampoo or other toiletries, which would be more beneficial for women than overeating to avoid losing money.

Despite all these benefits of a new meal plan system, some administrators might be skeptical of the benefits and focus on the drawbacks instead. The biggest drawback is the potential loss of revenue to food services. As it is now, women help subsidize food costs for men. Without that subsidy, the food service might not be able to break even, forcing them to raise food costs for everyone. I don't have the financial expertise to know how to compute these costs. Clearly, however, other universities have thought about these issues and decided that allowing students to spend some of their food money off campus was a benefit worth providing for students. For example, the University of Texas, the University of Minnesota, and the University of Florida allow their meal cards to be used as debit cards at local businesses. As stated on their website, the University of Texas has a system called Bevo Bucks in which students can "purchase food, goods and services at participating locations, both on and off campus" by loading money onto their ID cards. Also, according to the University of Minnesota's website, students have a system called FlexDine connected to their ID cards. FlexDine gives students the "convenience … [to eat] at Papa John's for residence-hall residents." If other schools can implement off-campus use of dining cards, then the plan is feasible. It might also be possible to limit the number of dollars that could be spent each quarter off campus in order to assure a minimum level of revenue for the food service.

Even if my proposal would be costly in terms of lost revenue to the food service, the benefits of my plan might still outweigh the costs. A revised meal-card system might become a recruiting point for prospective students because they would feel as if the university is more personalized to fit the students' needs rather than just the university's needs. My proposal might help prospective students see how close the students at our university are and might draw more students to apply here. (Our website and view books could even include pictures of students cooking in the residence-hall kitchens or eating at a local restaurant.) Moreover, local off-campus businesses would welcome the opportunity for more student customers and might offer special promotions for students. A new meal-card system might even improve the relationship between the university and the surrounding community.

Based on all these reasons, I believe that the university community as a whole would benefit if my proposal were enacted. The new plan would be especially appreciated by women students, many of whom now subsidize the food costs of men. In addition, the new system would bring students closer together by encouraging more creative use of the residence-hall kitchens for community meals and by reducing the incentive toward binge eating at the end of each quarter. Finally, if other universities can use this system, then our university should be able to use it as well. Although the food service may lose money to local businesses, the university would ultimately benefit by creating a more flexible and attractive meal option—especially for women—and by showing administrative concern for student welfare.

Critiquing "A Proposal to Allow Off-Campus Purchases with a University Meal Card"

1. In your own words, summarize briefly the problem that Megan Johnson addresses, her proposed solution, and her justifying reasons.

2. Megan addresses her proposal to Ms. Jane Doe, an administrator who has the power to change policy. To what extent does Megan develop audience-based reasons that resonate with this audience of university administrators? How effectively does Megan anticipate and respond to objections her audience might raise?

3. How does Megan establish a positive *ethos* in this argument? To what extent does she appeal to *pathos* as well as *logos*?

4. How effective is Megan's proposal?

Our second reading, by student writer Ivan Snook, is a researched public policy proposal written in response to the option 3 assignment in Learning Objective 15.5. Snook's argument is based both on library and Internet research and on personal experience (he is a returning veteran who served as a Marine infantry soldier in Iraq). The kairotic moment for this paper (written in March 2014) was a January 2014 decision by the Obama administration to allow women to serve in the combat arms—a policy decision to which Snook objects. Snook's paper is formatted as a formal research paper using the documentation style of the Modern Language Association (MLA). A full explanation of this format is given in Chapter 18.

Ivan Snook

Dr. Johnson

Argumentative Writing

March 31, 2014

Flirting with Disaster: An Argument against Integrating

Women into the Combat Arms

In 2005 I was a rifleman for the elite 1st Reconnaissance Battalion in Iraq. My deployment was not all bad. When we returned to Camp Fallujah to repair our humvee we ate great chow, enjoyed good entertainment, and drank contraband vodka. I never had a girlfriend, though. I was too busy working in my all-male infantry unit. At the time I wished we had a few girls in the unit. What can I say? I wanted female companionship like the guys in noncombat jobs had. But I realized that women could never serve in the infantry because of the negative impact of boyfriend/girlfriend dramatics on unit morale, cohesiveness, and ultimately combat effectiveness.

However, America's civilian leadership recently moved towards integrating women into frontline combat arms units such as infantry, tanks, and artillery. In January 2014, Secretary of Defense Leon Panetta lifted the Pentagon's policy on all-male combat arms occupations. "The department's goal...is to ensure that the mission is met with the best qualified and most capable people, regardless of gender," he said. "I'm not talking about reducing the qualifications for the job—if they can meet the qualifications for the job, then they should have a right to serve" (qtd. in Michaels and Vanden Brook). President Obama expanded upon Panetta's sentiment by saying, "Every American can be proud *that our military will grow even stronger*, with our mothers, wives, sisters, and daughters playing a greater role in protecting this country we love" (qtd. in Michaels and Vanden Brook, emphasis mine.)

If this policy change will indeed strengthen our military, every American should support it. However, no one has specified how integrating women into the combat arms will strengthen our military. I wholeheartedly agree with integrationists who claim that women can meet the rigorous physical and mental requirements for frontline combat. Any CrossFit has at least half a dozen women more physically and mentally fit than some of my Marine brothers in arms. If those were the sole criteria by which we evaluate infantrymen, I would endorse integration. But, how an individual soldier affects the combat unit as a whole must be considered. The great military theorist Carl von Clausewitz coined the term "friction" to represent the "[c]ountless minor incidents . . . [that] combine to lower the general level of performance [of the military machine]." He continues, "We should bear in mind that none of its components is of one piece: each part is composed of individuals, every one of whom retains his potential of friction." Therefore, we must not judge individual soldiers only by their individual physical capabilities, but also by their impact on the unit as a whole.

Introducing women to previously all-male combat units means introducing the friction of romantic relationships. Petty jealousies and other dramatic relational issues combine to lower the general level of performance. In 1997, the nonprofit global policy think tank RAND Corporation studied how romantic relationships affect coed military units. The study reported that such relationships "sexualize" the work environment, making it "difficult for colleagues to regard one another as just coworkers. Thus, the cohesion of the unit is negatively affected" (Harrell and Miller 81). One respondent complained, "The [cafeteria] . . . at night looks more like a singles club or promenade deck than a cafeteria [for a military unit]." Another said, "I get tired of seeing a junior enlisted female and her boyfriend [at the cafeteria]. . . . This place is like high school all over again. Everyone is dating others. To me this is not the military. We are here to do a job not meet our spouse. Guys seem more worried about getting a girl than doing their job" (Harrell and Miller 81-82).

Integrationists claim the military's high level of discipline coupled with strict rules against fraternization will prevent romantic relationships. However, those strict rules have always been in place and have never worked. During the Gulf War, 5 percent of deployed women were sent home early due to pregnancy. The Navy sends home on average 10 percent of deployed female sailors for the same reason. The USS *Theodore Roosevelt*, one of America's largest aircraft carriers, lost 45 of its 300 female sailors to pregnancy leave and became one of the many U.S. Navy ships to earn the nickname "The Love Boat" (Browne 246). My point is not about morality. These statistics demonstrate that despite strict rules against fraternization, 18-to-25-year-olds succumb to their natural urges. What else should one expect when young adults are locked away on ship or deployed to Afghanistan for months at a time? It is analogous to locking the doors on a coed college dormitory for a year and making rules against sex. It is preposterous to expect 18-to-25-year-olds to work, live, and relax together in such close proximity and expect no romantic relationships to sprout.

These problems are more than just trifling lovers' quarrels. They affect a serious decline in performance and can lead to a total breakdown of command structure. In 2005, Brian Kates of the *New York Daily News* visited Camp Bucca, a military prison in Southern Iraq, which he described as a drunken "out-of-control frat party." "In front of a cheering male audience, two young women wearing only bras and panties threw themselves into a mud-filled plastic kiddie pool and rolled around in a wild wrestling match." Sergeant Emil Ganim, who refereed the match, said other non-commissioned officers "had been lending out their rooms for soldiers to have sex." These were not just young privates, either. A witness told investigators that a drunken first sergeant and master sergeant, two high-ranking non-commissioned officers, were in attendance (Kates). Although Camp Bucca was far away from any actual fighting, it is safe to assume similar sexual antics and command-structure breakdowns will occur in coed frontline combat units, whose members confront their own mortality on a daily basis.

Still, Camp Bucca is not the worst-case scenario. The military is currently battling an epidemic of rape and sexual assault. A study conducted by the Department of Veterans' Affairs reported that one-third of female veterans say they were victims of rape or attempted rape. A third of those claim they were raped multiple times, and 14 percent claim they were gang raped (Browne). Introducing females to frontline combat units will only exacerbate the problem. Dr. David Grossman, one of the world's foremost experts on human aggression and the psychology of combat, has explained how combat stress affects the human sex drive. He analogizes the human body's ability to cope with stress to a bathtub: It can hold only so much water before overflowing. When our body overflows with stress, the midbrain releases hormones causing a fight-or-flight response, often followed by a dramatic change in hunger and sex drive. Grossman writes, "Some people lose their appetite for food in response to stress, but many have an enhanced craving to eat. In the same way, some individuals can lose their sex drive in response to great stress, but other people experience a tremendous sex drive, especially after a combat situation in which they were triumphant" (275). Frontline combat is fueled by stress hormones, and the potential for a woman to be sexually assaulted is very high. An inter-unit sexual assault costs the unit two soldiers: the victim is typically transferred to a new unit, the assaulter is sent to prison. Replacing two comrades integrated in a tight-knit unit with two new recruits is a difficult blow to a unit's esprit de corps and trust members have in one another. Thus, to put at risk a female soldier's sexual well-being is to also put at risk her unit's combat ability.

Rather than respond to the physiological realities of preparing for and engaging in combat, integrationists such as CNN's Maren Leed deflect to a false analogy connecting integration of women to past arguments against integrating minorities and homosexuals. Regarding minorities, race is a social construct, not a biological difference. Whereas the military somewhat successfully trained its men to not act on racial prejudices, it is improbable that 18-to-25-year-old men can be trained not to be sexually attracted to women. Regarding homosexuals, one homosexual has little effect on a group of heterosexuals, but one female can have a significant impact on a large group of heterosexual men driven by stress hormones.

Another integrationist argument is that changes in modern warfare already put women in combat. They say modern warfare is "asymmetric" and attacks can come from anywhere. It is true that women have served in combat in Afghanistan and Iraq, but integrationists erroneously believe the nature of warfare has evolved beyond traditional frontlines. Every American military engagement since World War II has been a limited war, but that does not mean all future wars will be. The wars our military must prepare to fight are global conflicts where combat troops face well-armed and well-trained enemies on traditional frontlines.

Perhaps the most important argument made by integrationists, and one to which I am sympathetic, concerns fairness and equity. It is extremely difficult to be promoted to general without infantry training. Some may say the Army should change its promotion policy, but this would harm overall morale. Frontline troops more enthusiastically follow leaders who are sharing, or have at one time shared, the toils and dangers of war. Thus, high-ranking female officers hit a glass ceiling because no such experience is available to them. However, there is an alternative to break through this glass ceiling without making all combat units coed. The U.S. Army National Guard consists of every imaginable combat-arms occupation. If these occupations were opened to aspiring female soldiers, those women would have access to the necessary experience for advancement to the military's upper echelon and have the option of transferring from the National Guard to active duty. General John Vessey began his illustrious career in the National Guard infantry and was later selected as Chairman of the Joint Chiefs of Staff. This compromise would give women the opportunity to get infantry training while still protecting our active-duty frontline infantry units from the unnecessary friction caused by romantic relationships.

Although some outsiders call terms like friction, morale, and unit cohesion mere buzzwords, to the Marines they mean life or death. Coed infantry is a parlous experiment with too much at stake. The restriction against women joining the infantry must be reinstated before the policy becomes entrenched and the negative side effects of romantic relationships deteriorate our fighting ability. I fully support gender equality, and I am proud of the brave women in the Marines, Army, Navy, and Air Force who have sacrificed so much defending this country I love. But when one considers the ultimate mission of the military, which is to win wars, we must not risk losing the cohesion of combat units when there is no exigent reason to do so except for the sake of expanding military career opportunities for women.

Works Cited

Browne, Kingsley. *Co-Ed Combat: The New Evidence That Women Shouldn't Fight the Nation's Wars.* Sentinel, 2007.

Snook 6

Clausewitz, Carl von. *On War.* Translated by Michael Howard and
Peter Paret, Princeton UP, 1984.

Grossman, David. *On Combat: The Psychology and Physiology of
Deadly Conflict in War and in Peace.* 3rd ed., Warrior Science, 2008.

Harrell, Margaret C., and Laura L. Miller. "New Opportunities
for Military Women: Effects Upon Readiness, Cohesion, and
Morale." *RAND Corporation,* 1 Jan. 1997, www.rand.org/pubs/
monograph_reports/MR896.html.

Kates, Brian. "Out of Control at Camp Crazy! Female Soldiers Dress
Down & Get Dirty for Mud Romps." *New York Daily News,* 6 Feb.
2005, www.nydailynews.com/archives/news/control-camp-crazy-
female-soldiers-dress-dirty-mud-romps-g-s-wild-article-1.590262.

Leed, Maren. "Will Infantry Men Accept Women as Peers?"
CNN, 26 Jan. 2013, www.cnn.com/2013/01/25/opinion/
leed-women-in-infantry.

Michaels, Jim, and Tom Vanden Brook. "Women, Men Must
Meet Same Combat Standards in Military." *USA Today,* 25 Jan.
2013, www.usatoday.com/story/news/world/2013/01/24/
women-in-combat-briefing/1861887.

Critiquing "Flirting with Disaster: An Argument against Integrating Women into the Combat Arms"

1. What is Ivan Snook's core argument for not integrating women into the combat arms? What evidence does he provide in support of his argument? Do you find that evidence persuasive?

2. What opposing or alternative views does Snook summarize? How effectively does Snook respond to these views?

3. Snook offers as a counterproposal a way that women could get infantry training (for purposes of career advancement) without the need to make all infantry units coed. How effective do you find his counterproposal?

4. How effective is Snook's use of audience-based reasons? How would you evaluate his overall appeal to *logos, ethos,* and *pathos*?

Our third reading, from the Save-Bees.org website, is a one-page paid advocacy advertisement. Working in conjunction with other environmental organizations such as Beyond Pesticides, the Center for Food Safety, and Pesticide Action Network, the Save the Bees organization advocates a moratorium on pesticides that are killing off bees. The website itself demonstrates how the Internet can be used for education and advocacy. It solicits support for a petition directed to the U.S. Environmental Protection Agency calling for an immediate discontinuation in the use of certain toxic chemicals deadly to bees. On the web, this advocacy ad shows a list of organizations in support of this moratorium.

Bees can't wait 5 *more* years.

And neither can we.

Honey bees, native bees and other pollinators are responsible for 1 out of every 3 bites of food we eat. Bees pollinate 71 of the 100 crops that make up 90% of the world's food supply. Many fruits and vegetables, including apples, blueberries, strawberries, carrots and broccoli, as well as almonds and coffee, rely on bees. These beneficial insects are critical to maintaining our diverse food supply.

Honey bee populations have been in alarming decline since 2006. Widespread use of a new class of toxic pesticides, neonicotinoids, is a significant contributing factor. In addition to killing bees outright, research has shown that even low levels of these dangerous pesticides impair bees' ability to learn, to find their way back to the hive, to collect food, to produce new queens, and to mount an effective immune response.

This week, 15 countries are imposing a two-year restriction on the use of several of these chemicals. Meanwhile, the United States is **stalling**.

The U.S. Environmental Protection Agency estimates it will be **2018, 5 years from now,** before it makes a decision on this deadly class of pesticides.

Bees can't wait 5 more years – they are dying now. The U.S. Environmental Protection Agency has the power and responsibility to protect our pollinators. Our nation's food system depends on it.

HELP PROTECT FOOD CHOICES

❀ **Save-Bees.org**

Critiquing the Save the Bees Advocacy Ad

1. How does this advocacy advertisement give presence to the problem with bees?

2. What solution does the ad propose for helping the bees? Why hasn't this solution already been adopted? What action does the ad ask readers to take?

3. What reasons and evidence does this advocacy ad provide to persuade readers to take action? How effective is this evidence?

4. How does this proposal argument appeal to personal interest as well as environmental values? How do appeals to *logos, ethos,* and *pathos* work together in this advocacy piece?

Our fourth reading, by student Sandy Wainscott, illustrates option 5 in Learning Objective 15.5. It is a proposal speech supported by visual aids. We have reproduced Sandy's outline for her speech, along with her scripts for the introduction and conclusion. (Although she delivered the body of the speech extemporaneously from her outline, she scripted the introduction and conclusion to reduce nervousness.) We have also reproduced four of her ten PowerPoint slides in Figure 15.4. She used these four slides to introduce each of the four main points shown on the outline. Note how she has constructed her slides as visual arguments supporting a main point (stated in the slide title).

Student Essay

Why McDonald's Should Sell Meat and Veggie Pies: A Proposal to End Subsidies for Cheap Meat

Sandy Wainscott

Script for Introduction: McDonald's hamburgers are popular because they're satisfying and pretty darn cheap. But I will argue that the hamburger is cheap because the American taxpayer subsidizes the cost of meat. Uncle Sam pays agribusiness to grow feed corn while not requiring agribusiness to pay the full cost for water or for cleaning up the environmental damage caused by cattle production. If meat producers had to recover the true cost of their product, the cost of meat would be substantially higher, but there would be offsetting benefits: a healthier environment, happier lives for cows and chickens, and healthier diets for all of us.

1. Meat is relatively cheap partly because taxpayers help feed the cows.
   a. U.S. taxpayers give farmers money to grow feed corn, which is fed to cows.
   b. U.S. taxpayers provide farmers with cheap water.

2. Cheap meat threatens health.
   a. Factory-style farms significantly reduce effectiveness of antibiotics.
   b. Antibiotic-resistant pathogens are potentially huge killers.
   c. Factory farms are likely sources of new swine and bird flus.
   d. Meat-related food poisoning harms millions of people per year and causes thousands of deaths.

3. Cheap meat hurts the environment.
   a. Factory farms create 130 times more sewage than humans.
   b. Animal farming contributes more to global warming than all forms of human transportation combined.
   c. Farming uses much of the world's land and water.

4. Cheap meat requires cruelty to animals.
   a. Ninety-eight percent of egg-laying hens in the United States spend their entire lives in stacked cubicle cages with 9-inch sides.
   b. Cruel conditions also exist for pigs and cows.

Script for Conclusion: If we stop providing taxpayer subsidies to farmers and require farmers to pay for the pollution they cause, the cost of meat would be much higher—but with great benefits to our health and to our environment. A restaurant like McDonald's would likely adjust its menus. McDonald's would move the burger off its 99-cent menu and replace it with something like a meat pie, a similarly warm, quick, and satisfying choice, but with a lower proportion of meat than a burger. In a fair market, we should have to pay more for a hamburger than for a meat pie or a stir fry. But we would have the benefit of a healthier Earth.

Figure 15.4 Sandy's PowerPoint slides used to introduce main points

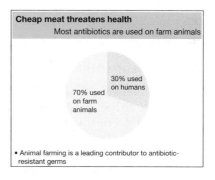

Critiquing "Why McDonald's Should Sell Meat and Veggie Pies: A Proposal to End Subsidies for Cheap Meat"

1. Although it is common to design PowerPoint slides that use topics and bullets to reproduce the speaker's outline, most public speaking experts prefer the approach that Sandy takes in this speech. She uses photographs, drawings, and graphics to create a visual argument that reinforces rather than simply reproduces the verbal message of her speech. How do her slides operate visually to create arguments from both *logos* and *pathos*?

2. Note that the top heading of each slide is a complete sentence making a point rather than a topic phrase without a subject and verb. For example, the top-left slide in Figure 15.4 might have had the heading "Cheap Meat" or "Role of Subsidies." Do you agree with most experts, who would say that the complete-sentence version ("Meat is relatively cheap because taxpayers help feed the cows") is more effective? Why or why not?

3. How effective do you find Sandy's speech?

Our final reading appeared in *The Wall Street Journal* on February 19, 2011. The authors are both professors of entomology at Wageningen University in the Netherlands. In 2007, Marcel Dicke was awarded the NWO-Spinoza award, often called the Dutch Nobel Prize. He gives speeches (summaries of which are available on the web) arguing that humans should eat insects rather than meat as one solution to the environmental degradation caused by the meat industry. Coauthor Arnold Van Huis coordinates a research consortium of scientists investigating the nutritional value of insects. He also gives cooking classes featuring bug recipes.

The Six-Legged Meat of the Future

MARCEL DICKE AND ARNOLD VAN HUIS

At the London restaurant Archipelago, diners can order the $11 Baby Bee Brulee: a creamy custard topped with a crunchy little bee. In New York, the Mexican restaurant Toloache offers $11 chapulines tacos: two tacos stuffed with Oaxacan-style dried grasshoppers.

Could beetles, dragonfly larvae, and water bug caviar be the meat of the future? As the global population booms and demand strains the world's supply of meat, there's a growing need for alternate animal proteins. Insects are high in protein, B vitamins and minerals like iron and zinc, and they're low in fat. Insects are easier to raise than livestock, and they produce less waste. Insects are abundant. Of all the known animal species, 80% walk on six legs; over 1,000 edible species have been identified. And the taste? It's often described as "nutty."

Worms, crickets, dung beetles—to most people they're just creepy crawlers. To Brooklyn painter and art professor Marc Dennis, they're yummy ingredients for his Bug Dinners.

The vast majority of the developing world already eats insects. In Laos and Thailand, weaver-ant pupae are a highly prized and nutritious delicacy. They are prepared with shallots, lettuce, chilies, lime, and spices and served with sticky rice. Further back in history, the ancient Romans considered beetle larvae to be gourmet fare, and the Old Testament mentions eating crickets and grasshoppers. In the 20th century, the Japanese emperor Hirohito's favorite meal was a mixture of cooked rice, canned wasps (including larvae, pupae, and adults), soy sauce, and sugar.

5   Will Westerners ever take to insects as food? It's possible. We are entomologists at Wageningen University, and we started promoting insects as food in the Netherlands in the 1990s. Many people laughed—and cringed—at first, but interest gradually became more serious. In 2006 we created a "Wageningen—City of Insects" science festival to promote the idea of eating bugs; it attracted more than 20,000 visitors.

Over the past two years, three Dutch insect-raising companies, which normally produce feed for animals in zoos, have set up special production lines to raise locusts and mealworms for human consumption. Now those insects are sold, freeze-dried, in

two-dozen retail food outlets that cater to restaurants. A few restaurants in the Netherlands have already placed insects on the menu, with locusts and mealworms (beetle larvae) usually among the dishes.

Insects have a reputation for being dirty and carrying diseases—yet less than 0.5% of all known insect species are harmful to people, farm animals, or crop plants. When raised under hygienic conditions—eating bugs straight out of the backyard generally isn't recommended—many insects are perfectly safe to eat.

Meanwhile, our food needs are on the rise. The human population is expected to grow from six billion in 2000 to nine billion in 2050. Meat production is expected to double in the same period, as demand grows from rising wealth. Pastures and fodder already use up 70% of all agricultural land, so increasing livestock production would require expanding agricultural acreage at the expense of rain forests and other natural lands. Officials at the United Nations Food and Agriculture Organization recently predicted that beef could become an extreme luxury item by 2050, like caviar, due to rising production costs.

Raising insects for food would avoid many of the problems associated with livestock. For instance, swine and humans are similar enough that they can share many diseases. Such co-infection can yield new disease strains that are lethal to humans, as happened during a swine fever outbreak in the Netherlands in the late 1990s. Because insects are so different from us, such risks are accordingly lower.

Insects are also cold-blooded, so they don't need as much feed as animals like pigs and cows, which 10 consume more energy to maintain their body temperatures. Ten pounds of feed yields one pound of beef, three pounds of pork, five pounds of chicken, and up to six pounds of insect meat.

Insects produce less waste, too. The proportion of livestock that is not edible after processing is 30% for pork, 35% for chicken, 45% for beef, and 65% for lamb. By contrast, only 20% of a cricket is inedible.

Raising insects requires relatively little water, especially as compared to the production of conventional meat (it takes more than 10 gallons of water, for instance, to produce about two pounds of beef). Insects also produce far less ammonia and other greenhouse gases per pound of body weight. Livestock is responsible for at least 10% of all greenhouse gas emissions.

Raising insects is more humane as well. Housing cattle, swine or chickens in high densities causes stress to the animals, but insects like mealworms and locusts naturally like to live in dense quarters. The insects can be crowded into vertical stacked trays or cages. Nor do bug farms have to be restricted to rural areas; they could sprout up anywhere, from a suburban strip mall to an apartment building. Enterprising gourmets could even keep a few trays of mealworms in the garage to ensure a fresh supply.

The first insect fare is likely to be incorporated subtly into dishes, as a replacement for meat in meatballs and sauces. It also can be mixed into prepared foods to boost their nutritional value—like putting mealworm paste into a quiche. And dry-roasted insects can be used as a replacement for nuts in baked goods like cookies and breads.

We continue to make progress in the Netherlands, where the ministry of agriculture is funding a 15 new $1.3 million research program to develop ways to raise edible insects on food waste, such as brewers' grain (a byproduct of beer brewing), soyhulls (the skin of the soybean), and apple pomace (the pulpy remains after the juice has been pressed out). Other research is focusing on how protein could be extracted from insects and used in processed foods.

Though it is true that intentionally eating insects is common only in developing countries, everyone already eats some amount of insects. The average person consumes about a pound of insects per year, mostly mixed into other foods. In the U.S., most processed foods contain small amounts of insects, within limits set by the Food and Drug Administration. For chocolate, the FDA limit is 60 insect fragments per 100 grams. Peanut butter can have up to 30 insect parts per 100 grams, and fruit juice can have five fruit-fly eggs and one or two larvae per 250 milliliters (just over a cup). We also use many insect products to dye our foods, such as the red dye cochineal in imitation crab sticks, Campari, and candies. So we're already some of the way there in making six-legged creatures a regular part of our diet.

Not long ago, foods like kiwis and sushi weren't widely known or available. It is quite likely that in 2020 we will look back in surprise at the era when our menus didn't include locusts, beetle larvae, dragonfly larvae, crickets, and other insect delights.

Critiquing "The Six-Legged Meat of the Future"

1. Earlier in this chapter, we noted that a problem faced by all proposal writers is "the need to overcome people's natural conservatism." Their readers' natural conservatism is a major constraint for coauthors Dicke and Van Huis ("Hey, I've never eaten bugs before! If four-legged meat was good enough for my parents, it's good enough for me!") How do the authors use the appeals of *logos*, *ethos*, and *pathos* to try to overcome this natural conservatism?

2. Although this journalistic piece does not have a tightly closed-form structure with transitions and *because* clauses marking each reason, it still provides a logical progression of separate reasons in support of eating insects. Convert this argument into a bulleted list of *because* clauses in support of the claim "Westerners should eat insects as a major source of protein."

3. Are you persuaded by this argument? Would you try some mealworm spaghetti or a handful of fried crickets? Why or why not?

Part Five
The Researched Argument

16 Finding and Evaluating Sources

17 Incorporating Sources into Your Own Argument

18 Citing and Documenting Sources

To the average passerby this overflowing trash is an ugly mess of soiled napkins, food boxes, plates, cups, and cans. Environmentalists see this eyesore as a complex but solvable problem. From an environmental perspective, fast-food restaurants need to use more recyclable containers; cities need to provide systems with recycling bins; and consumers need to understand their role in buying recyclable packaging and disposing of recyclable garbage. Environmental groups have found that over 30 percent of garbage could be recycled. How could you imagine using this photograph to support an argument directed to fast-food restaurants, to city planners working on a garbage policy, or to consumers?

Chapter 16
Finding and Evaluating Sources

Learning Objectives

In this chapter you will learn to:

16.1 Formulate a research question instead of a topic.

16.2 Think rhetorically about kinds of sources.

16.3 Find sources through field, library, or Web research.

16.4 Use rhetorical awareness to select and evaluate your sources and take purposeful notes.

Although the research paper is a common writing assignment in college, students are often baffled by their professor's expectations. The problem is that students often think of research writing as presenting information rather than creating an argument. One of our business-school colleagues calls these sorts of research papers "data dumps."

But a research paper shouldn't be a data dump. Like any other argument, it should use information to support a contestable claim. In academic settings (as opposed to arguments in many business or civic settings), a distinguishing feature of a researched argument is its formal documentation. By **documentation**, we mean the in-text citations and accompanying list of references that allow readers to identify and locate the researcher's sources for themselves while also establishing the writer's professionalism and *ethos.*

Fortunately, writing an argument as a formal research paper draws on the same argumentation skills you have already been using—the ability to pose a question at issue within a community, to formulate a contestable claim, and to support your claim with audience-based reasons and evidence. This chapter shows you how to find and evaluate sources. Chapter 17 then shows you how to incorporate your sources skillfully into your own prose using the academic conventions for ethical research. (Knowing and using these conventions will free you from any fears of plagiarism.) Finally, in Chapter 18 we explain the nitty-gritty details of in-text citations and end-of-paper lists of sources.

Formulating a Research Question Instead of a Topic

16.1 **Formulate a research question instead of a topic.**

The best way to use your research time efficiently is to pose a question rather than a topic. To appreciate this difference, suppose a friend asks you what your research paper is about. Consider the differences in the following responses:

Topic focus: I'm doing a paper on gender-specific children's toys.

Question focus: I'm researching the effects of gender-specific toys on children's intellectual development. Do boys' toys develop intellectual skills more than girls' toys do?

Topic focus: I'm doing a paper on eating disorders.

Question focus: I'm trying to sort out what the experts say is the best way to treat severe anorexia nervosa. Is inpatient treatment or outpatient treatment more effective?

As these scenarios suggest, a topic focus invites you to collect information without a clear point or purpose—an open road toward data dumping. In contrast, a question focus requires you to make an argument in which you support a claim with reasons and evidence. Your goal as a researcher is to pose an issue question about which reasonable persons may disagree. In many cases, you might not know where you stand yourself. Your research thus becomes a process of inquiry and clarification.

Thinking Rhetorically About Kinds of Sources

16.2 **Think rhetorically about kinds of sources.**

To be an effective researcher, you need to think rhetorically about the different kinds of sources.

Identifying Kinds of Sources Relevant to Your Question

At the beginning of your research process, think rhetorically about the conversation you will be joining and about the kinds of evidence you might use to support an argument. The brainstorming questions at the end of Chapter 4 on kinds of evidence (ranging from personal experience to library sources) can help you think of possible sources for your argument and help you discover different points of view on your question.

Approaching Sources Rhetorically

Whether you interview someone, listen to a speaker, or read a text, you need to analyze this source rhetorically, asking questions about the writer's or speaker's purpose, audience, genre, and angle of vision (explained in detail in Chapter 7 on analyzing arguments rhetorically). As a researcher, you often need to ascertain a text's genre even before you decide to select that text as a potential source for your paper. Your payoff for having a basic understanding of source types will be an increased ability to read sources rhetorically and to use them purposefully in your research writing.

To help you appreciate how rhetorical analysis can increase your skills as a researcher, peruse Table 16.1. The following explanations will help you understand the table's explanations of each source's degree of editorial review, stability, advocacy, and authority.

Table 16.1 A Rhetorical Overview of Sources

Genre of Source	Author and Angle of Vision	How to Recognize Them
Peer-Reviewed Scholarly Sources		
ARTICLES IN SCHOLARLY JOURNALS Examples: articles in *Journal of Abnormal Psychology* or *American Journal of Botany*	**Author:** Professors, industry researchers, independent scholars **Angle of vision:** Scholarly advancement of knowledge; presentation of research findings; development of new theories and applications	• Not sold on magazine racks • No commercial advertising • Academic style with documentation and bibliography • Cover often lists table of contents • Found through licensed online databases
SCHOLARLY BOOKS Example: *Shakespearean Negotiations: The Circulation of Social Identity in Renaissance England* by Stephen Greenblatt	**Author:** Professors, industry researchers, independent scholars **Angle of vision:** Scholarly advancement of knowledge; presentation of research findings; development of new theories and applications	• University press or other academic publisher on title page • Academic style with documentation and bibliography • Found in academic libraries; may be available as e-book
SCHOLARLY WEBSITES Example: http://seasia.museum.upenn.edu (Southeast Asian Archeology Scholarly website)	**Author:** Professors or institute scholars **Angle of vision:** Dissemination of research findings; informative access to primary sources	• Usually have a .edu web address or address of professional scholarly organization • Clearly identified with an academic institution • Material is usually peer reviewed, but may include reports on work-in-progress or links to primary sources
REFERENCE WORKS **Example:** *The Farmer's Almanac; New Dictionary of Cultural Literacy*	**Author:** Commissioned scholars **Angle of vision:** Balanced, factual overview	• Titles containing words such as *encyclopedia, dictionary, atlas,* and so forth • Found in library reference section or online
Public Affairs Sources		
NEWSPAPERS AND NEWS MAGAZINES Examples: *Time, Washington Post, Los Angeles Times*	**Author:** Staff writers and journalists; occasional freelance journalists **Angle of vision:** News reports aimed at balance and objectivity; editorial pages reflect perspective of editors; op-ed pieces reflect different perspectives	• Readily familiar by name, distinctive cover style • Widely available on newsstands, by subscription, and on the web • Ads aimed at broad, general audience
ARTICLES IN PUBLIC AFFAIRS PERIODICALS Examples: *Harper's, Commonweal, National Review*	**Author:** Staff writers, freelancers, scholars **Angle of vision:** Aims to deepen general public's understanding of issues; magazines often have political bias	• Long, well-researched articles reviewed by editors • Ads aimed at upscale professionals • Often have reviews of books, theater, film, and the arts • Often can be found in online databases or on the web

Genre of Source	Author and Angle of Vision	How to Recognize Them
ORGANIZATIONAL WHITE PAPERS Examples: "Congressional White Paper on a National Policy for the Environment" (on web) or "Reform Suggestions for Core Curriculum" (in-house document at a university)	**Author:** Organizational stakeholders; problem-solvers for a client **Angle of vision:** Informative document for client or argumentative paper for influencing policy or improving operations	• Desktop-published, internal documents aimed at problem solving; may also be written for clients • Internal documents generally not made available to the public • Sometimes posted to web or published in print
BLOGS Examples: dailykos.com (liberal blog site); michellemalkin.com (conservative blog site); theladysportswriter.blogspot.com (sports commentary)	**Author:** Anyone; some bloggers are practicing journalists **Angle of vision:** Varies from personal diaries to in-depth commentary on a subject or issues; wide range of views from conservative to liberal	• Usually published on time-stamped blog sites; most sites post responses from readers • Bloggers sometimes use pseudonyms • Often combines text with images or linked videos
NONFICTION BOOKS OF GENERAL INTEREST Example: *Cheap: The High Cost of Discount Culture* by Ellen Ruppell Shell (a journalism professor)	**Author:** Journalists, freelancers, scholars aiming at popular audience **Angle of vision:** Varies from informative to persuasive; often well researched and respected, but sometimes shoddy and aimed for quick sale	• Published by commercial presses for profit • Popular style; covers designed for marketing appeal • Usually documented in an informal rather than an academic style • May be available as an e-book
DOCUMENTARY FILMS Examples: Michael Moore, *Sicko*; Louie Psihoyos, *The Cove*	**Writer/Director:** Filmmakers, screenwriters trained in nonfiction documentaries **Angle of vision:** Varies from informative science documentaries to strong advocacy	• Specifically identified as "documentary" or "nonfiction" • Combines interviews and voice-overs with subject-matter footage
Advocacy Sources		
NEWSPAPER EDITORIALS, COMMENTARY, AND LETTERS TO THE EDITOR Examples: editorial page, letters to the editor, and op-ed pages of *Washington Post, Los Angeles Times, Wall Street Journal*, and some magazines	**Author:** Editorial writers; citizens writing letters to the editor; syndicated or guest columnists **Angle of vision:** Advocacy for certain positions or public policies	• Located in the editorial/op-ed sections of a newspaper • Editorials are often unsigned—they advocate positions held by owners or publishers of the newspaper • Letters and op-ed pieces are signed
EDITORIAL CARTOONS Examples: see www.cagle.com/politicalcartoons/	**Cartoonist:** Usually syndicated artists who specialize in cartoons **Angle of vision:** Varies from conservative to liberal	• Usually located in the op-ed section of newspapers • Occasionally political cartoonists are treated as comic strips (*Doonesbury*)
ADVOCACY ORGANIZATION WEBSITES, BLOGS, AND ADVERTISEMENTS Examples: NRA.org (National Rifle Association); csgv.org (Coalition to Stop Gun Violence)	**Author/Site Sponsor:** Advocacy organizations; staff writers/researchers; web developers; guest writers; often, it is difficult to identify individual writers **Angle of vision:** Strong advocacy for the site's viewpoint; often encourage donations through site	• .org in URL—denotes advocacy or nonprofit status • Sometimes doesn't announce advocacy clearly on home page • Facts/data selected and filtered by site's angle of vision • Often uses visuals for emotional appeals • Site often includes blogs (or links to blogs) that promote same angle of vision
Government Sources		
GOVERNMENT AGENCY WEBSITES Example: www.energy.gov (website of the U.S. Dept. of Energy)	**Author:** Development teams employed by agency; sponsoring agency is usually the author (corporate authorship); may include material by individual authors **Angle of vision:** Varies—informational sites publish data and objective documents; agency sites also advocate for agency's agenda	• .gov or .mil in URL—denotes government or military sites • Are often layered and complex with hundreds of links to other sites

(continued)

Genre of Source	Author and Angle of Vision	How to Recognize Them
LEGAL AND COURT DOCUMENTS	**Author:** Lawyers, judges, persons deposed for trials, trial testimony **Angle of vision:** Trial lawyers take strong advocacy positions; testifiers vow to tell the whole truth; judges defend decisions	• Legal briefs have distinctive formats • Court records can be accessed through www.pacer.gov (public access to court electronic records—requires user to establish an account)
POLITICAL AND LEGISLATIVE SPEECHES	**Author:** Politicians, political candidates, researchers, and aides **Angle of vision:** Reflects politics of speaker	• Widely available through newspapers, websites, YouTube videos, congressional records
Commercial Sources		
TRADE MAGAZINES Examples: *Advertising Age, Automotive Rebuilder, Farm Journal*	**Author:** Staff writers, industry specialists **Angle of vision:** Informative articles for practitioners; advocacy for the profession or trade	• Title indicating trade or profession • Articles on practical industry concerns • Ads geared toward a particular trade or profession
POPULAR NICHE MAGAZINES Examples: *Seventeen, People, Car and Driver, Golf Digest*	**Author:** Staff or freelance writers **Angle of vision:** Varies—focuses on interests of targeted audience; in some cases content and point of view are dictated by advertisers or the publisher's politics	• Glossy paper, extensive ads, lots of visuals • Popular; often distinctive style • Short, undocumented articles • Credentials of writer often not mentioned
COMMERCIAL WEBSITES AND ADVERTISEMENTS	**Author:** Development teams, in-house writers, contracted developers; advertising agencies **Angle of vision:** Varies from information to advocacy; promotes the viewpoint of the business	• .com or .biz in URL—denotes "commercial" or "business" • Advertisements or websites often promote corporate image as well as products • Frequent use of visuals as well as text
PERSONAL WEBSITES, BLOGS, OR CORRESPONDENCE	**Author:** Anyone can create a personal website or blog or write personal letters/e-mails **Angle of vision:** Varies from person to person	• Researcher using these sources is responsible for citing credentials of source or revealing bias of source

DEGREE OF EDITORIAL REVIEW

• Note that Table 16.1 begins with "peer-reviewed scholarly sources," which are published by nonprofit academic presses and written for specialized audiences. *Peer review* is a highly prized concept in academia. It refers to the rigorous and competitive selection process by which scholarly manuscripts get chosen for publication. When manuscripts are submitted to an academic publisher, the editor removes the names of the authors and sends the manuscripts to experienced scholars who judge the rigor and accuracy of the research and the significance and value of the argument. In contrast, the other types of sources listed in Table 16.1—many of which are published for profit—are not peer reviewed and may have little or no editorial review from the publisher. However, reputable publishers of books, magazines, and newspapers usually employ rigorous editors who oversee the production of books and freelance or commissioned magazine articles. Fortunately, it can be profitable for popular presses to publish superbly researched and argued intellectual material written for the general reader rather than for highly specialized scholars. These can be excellent sources for undergraduate research, but you need to separate the trash from the treasure.

DEGREE OF STABILITY

- Print sources (books, scholarly journals, magazines, newspapers), which can be stored in archives and retrieved many years later, are more stable than web-only material, which may change hourly. What complicates the distinction between "print" and "web only" is that many documents retrievable on the Web are also stable—either because they were originally print sources and have been made available online in pdf or html formats, or because they are produced by a reputable company as e-books, e-journals, or online newspapers that will be archived digitally. As a quick example of a stable versus nonstable source, suppose you wrote a letter to the editor that was published in a major newspaper. Your letter will be archived permanently, and it will be retrievable, just as you wrote it, long into the future. But if instead you posted a comment on a blog site, that comment (and the whole blog site) might disappear at any time.

For Writing and Discussion

Identifying Types of Sources

Your instructor will bring to class a variety of print sources—different kinds of books, scholarly journals, magazines, and so forth—and may also show you various kinds of sources retrieved online. Working individually or in small groups, decide to which category in Table 16.1 each piece belongs. Be prepared to justify your decisions based on the clues you used.

DEGREE OF ADVOCACY

- In Chapter 1 we explained how arguments combine truth seeking and persuasion. To illustrate these concepts, we charted a continuum from exploratory essays at one end of the continuum to outright propaganda at the other end (see Figure 1.5). To read a source rhetorically, you should try to determine where on this continuum your source resides. In Table 16.1, we identify as *advocacy sources* those sources that clearly announce their persuasive intentions. But other kinds of sources, such as an article in a public affairs magazine, a popular book, a legal brief, a documentary film, or a political speech, can have a strong advocacy stance.

DEGREE OF AUTHORITY

- Sometimes you turn to a specific genre because you just want the facts. Reputable newspapers are good sources for day-to-day reporting on "what happened." Other kinds of excellent fact-checking sources include encyclopedias, statistical abstracts, and other reference works that provide distilled background or overview information on many topics. For most sources, however, you need to be wary about the author's authority in a field and read rhetorically for angle of vision, accuracy of data, and cherry picking of sources. Be aware too that *Wikipedia* is not a reliable academic source. Although it is a fascinating cultural product that provides rapid access to overview information, it is often accused of inaccurate information, editorial bias, and shifting content because of constant revisions by its collaborative writers. Most instructors will not accept *Wikipedia* as a factual or informative source.

Finding Sources

16.3 Find sources through field, library, or Web research.

In the previous section, we explained differences among the kinds of sources you may uncover in a research project. In this section, we explain how to find these sources through field research (such as interviews and questionnaires), through using your campus's library resources (books, reference materials, and online databases for finding articles), and through web searches.

Conducting Interviews

Conducting interviews is a useful way not only to gather expert testimony and important data for use in your argument but also to learn about alternative views. To make interviews as productive as possible, we offer these suggestions.

- *Determine your purpose.* Consider why you are interviewing the person and what information he or she is uniquely able to provide.
- *Do background reading.* Find out as much as possible about the interviewee before the interview. Your knowledge of his or her background will help establish your credibility and build a bridge between you and your source. Also, equip yourself with a good foundational understanding of the issue so that you will sound informed and truly interested in the issue.
- *Formulate well-thought-out questions, but also be flexible.* Write out beforehand the questions you intend to ask, making sure that every question is related to the purpose of your interview. However, be prepared to move in unexpected directions if the interview opens up new territory. Sometimes unplanned topics can end up being the most illuminating and useful.
- *Arrive well prepared for the interview.* As part of your professional demeanor, be sure to have all the necessary supplies (notepaper, pens, pencils, perhaps a recording device if your interviewee is willing) with you.
- *Be prompt and courteous.* It is important to be punctual and respectful of your interviewee's time. In most cases, it is best to present yourself as a listener seeking clarity on an issue rather than an advocate of a particular position or an opponent. During the interview, play the believing role. Save the doubting role for later, when you are looking over your notes.
- *Take brief but clear notes.* Record the main ideas and be accurate with quotations. Ask for clarification of any points you don't understand.
- *Transcribe your notes soon after the interview.* Immediately after the interview, while your memory is still fresh, rewrite your notes more fully and completely.

When you use interview data in your writing, put quotation marks around any direct quotations. In most cases, you should also identify your source by name and indicate his or her title or credentials—whatever will convince the reader that this person's remarks are to be taken seriously.

Gathering Source Data from Surveys or Questionnaires

A well-constructed survey or questionnaire can provide lively, current data that give your audience a sense of the currency and importance of your views. To be effective and responsible, however, a survey or questionnaire needs to be carefully prepared and administered, as we suggest in the following guidelines.

- *Include both closed-response questions and open-response questions.* To gain useful information and avoid charges of bias, you will want to include a range of questions. *Closed-response questions* ask participants to check a box or number on a scale, and they yield quantitative data that you can report statistically, perhaps in tables or graphs. *Open-response questions* elicit varied responses and often short narratives in which participants offer their own input. These may contribute new insights to your perspective on the issue.

- *Make your survey or questionnaire clear and easy to complete.* Consider the number, order, wording, and layout of the questions in your questionnaire. Your questions should be clear and easy to answer. Neatness and an overall formal appearance of the questionnaire will also invite serious responses from your participants.

- *Explain the purpose of the questionnaire.* Respondents are usually more willing to participate if they know how the information gained from the questionnaire will benefit others. Therefore, it is a good idea to state at the beginning of the questionnaire how it will be used.

- *Seek a random sample of respondents in your distribution of the questionnaire.* Think out where and how you will distribute and collect your questionnaire to ensure a random sampling of respondents. For example, if a questionnaire about the university library went only to dorm residents, then you wouldn't learn how commuting students felt.

- *Convert questionnaires into usable data by tallying and summarizing responses.* Tallying the results and formulating summary statements of the information you gathered will yield material that might be used as evidence.

Finding Books and Reference Sources

To find the specialized resources provided by your campus library, your best initial research tool is your campus library's home page. This portal will lead you to two important resources: (1) the library's online catalog for its own holdings of books, periodicals, films, multimedia materials, reference works, and other resources, and (2) direct links to the many digital databases leased by the library. (We discuss these databases in the next section.) When searching for books related to your research question, particularly look for recent books that might have helpful indexes and bibliographies. Also be aware of your library's reference materials such as statistical abstracts, biographies, dictionaries, and encyclopedias.

In addition to checking your library's home page, make a personal visit to your library to learn its features and to meet your library's reference librarians, who are a researcher's best friends.

Using Licensed Databases to Find Articles in Scholarly Journals, Magazines, and News Sources

For many research projects, the most useful sources are articles that may be immediately available in your library's periodical collection or online through databases. In either case, you discover the existence of these articles by searching licensed databases leased by your library.

WHAT IS A LICENSED DATABASE?   Electronic databases of periodical sources are produced by for-profit companies that index the articles appearing in thousands of periodicals. You can search the database by author, title, subject, keyword, date, genre, and other characteristics. In most cases, the database contains an abstract of each article, and in many cases it contains the full text of the article, which you can download and print. These databases are referred to by several different generic names: *licensed databases* (our preferred term), *periodical databases*, or *subscription services*. Because access to these databases is restricted to fee-paying customers, they can't be searched through web search engines like Google. Most university libraries allow students to access these databases from a remote computer by using a password. You can therefore use the Internet to connect your computer to licensed databases as well as to the World Wide Web.

Although the methods of accessing licensed databases vary from institution to institution, we can offer some widely applicable guidelines. Most likely your library has access to one or more of the following databases:

- *Academic Search Complete (Ebsco):* Indexes nearly 8,000 periodicals, including full text of nearly 7,000 peer-reviewed journals. It features a mix of interdisciplinary scholarly journals, magazines, newspapers, and books.

- *Research Library Complete (ProQuest):* Similar to Academic Search Complete except that it includes trade publications and more business and industry materials.

- *LexisNexis Academic Universe:* Primarily a full-text database covering current events, business, and financial news; includes company profiles and legal, medical, and reference information.

- *JSTOR:* Offers full text of scholarly journal articles across many disciplines; you can limit searches to specific disciplines.

Generally, one of these databases is the default database chosen by your library for most article searches. Your reference librarian will be able to direct you to the most useful licensed database for your purpose.

Finding Cyberspace Sources: Searching the World Wide Web

Another valuable resource is the World Wide Web, but when using the web you need to be extra careful to evaluate your sources rhetorically. Web search engines search only the free-access, ever-changing portions of the Internet known as the World Wide Web. When you type keywords into a web search engine, it searches for matches in material made available on the web by all the users of the world's network of computers—government agencies, corporations, advocacy groups, information services, individuals with their own websites, and many others.

Because different web search engines search the web in different ways, your reference librarian can give you good advice on what works well for particular kinds of searches. On the web, an additional resource is NoodleTools.com, which offers lots of good advice for choosing the best search engine.

- The following example will quickly show you the difference between a licensed database search and a web search. When student Ivan Snook (see his proposal argument in Chapter 15) typed "women in combat roles" into Google, he received 5,800,000 hits. When he entered the same keywords into the licensed database *Academic Search Complete*, he received forty-four hits. When he limited the database search to full-text articles appearing in peer-reviewed journals, he received twenty hits. Clearly, the search tools are searching different fields. Google picks up, in addition to all the articles that someone may have posted on the web, all references to material appearing on advocacy websites, government publications, newspapers, blogs, chat rooms, student papers posted on the web, and so forth. In contrast, *Academic Search Complete* searches for articles primarily in scholarly journals and magazines.

Selecting and Evaluating Your Sources and Taking Purposeful Notes

16.4 Use rhetorical awareness to select and evaluate your sources and take purposeful notes.

So far, we have explained the importance of posing a good research question; understanding the different kinds of sources; and using purposeful strategies for conducting interviews, for designing questionnaires, and for searching libraries, licensed databases, and the web. In this final section, we explain how to read with rhetorical awareness, how to select and evaluate sources, and how to take purposeful notes. We also provide some additional advice for evaluating web sources.

Reading with Rhetorical Awareness

How you read a source may depend on where you are in the research process. Early in the process, when you are in the thesis-seeking, exploratory stage, your goal is to achieve a basic understanding about your research problem. You need to become aware of different points of view, learn what is unknown or controversial about your research question, see what values or assumptions are in conflict, and build up your store of background knowledge.

Given these goals, at the early stages of research you should select overview kinds of sources to get you into the conversation. In some cases, even an encyclopedia or specialized reference work can be a good start for getting general background information.

As you get deeper into your research, your questions become more focused, and the sources you read become more specialized. Once you formulate a thesis and plan a structure for your paper, you can determine more clearly the sources you need and read them with purpose and direction.

Table 16.2 Questions Asked by Rhetorical Readers

What was the source author's purpose in writing this piece?	What might be my purpose in using this piece in my own argument?
• Who is this author? What are his or her credentials and affiliations? • What audience is this person addressing? • What is the genre of this piece? (If you downloaded the piece from the World Wide Web, did it originally appear in print?) • If this piece appeared in print, what is the reputation and bias of the journal, magazine, or press? Was the piece peer reviewed? • If this piece appeared only on the web, who or what organization sponsors the website (check the home page)? What is the reputation and bias of the sponsor? • What is the author's thesis or purpose? • How does this author try to change his or her audience's view? • What is this writer's angle of vision or bias? • What is omitted or censored from this text? • How reliable and credible is this author? • What facts, data, and other evidence does this author use, and what are the sources of these data? • What are this author's underlying values, assumptions, and beliefs?	• How has this piece influenced or complicated my own thinking? • How does this piece relate to my research question? • How will my own intended audience react to this author? • How might I use this piece in my own argument? • Is it an opposing view that I might summarize? • Is it an alternative point of view that I might compare to other points of view? • Does it have facts and data that I might use? • Would a summary of all or part of this argument support or oppose one or more of my own points? • Could I use this author for testimony? (If so, how should I indicate this author's credentials?) • If I use this source, will I need to acknowledge the author's bias and angle of vision?

To read your sources rhetorically, you should keep two basic questions in mind:

1. What was the source author's purpose in writing this piece?
2. What might be my purpose in using this piece?

Table 16.2, which lists the questions that rhetorical readers typically ask, reinforces a point we've made throughout this text: All writing is produced from an angle of vision that privileges some ways of seeing and filters out other ways. You should guard against reading your sources as if they present hard, undisputed facts or universal truths. For example, if one of your sources says that "Saint John's wort [an herb] has been shown to be an effective treatment for depression," some of your readers might accept that statement as fact—but many wouldn't. Skeptical readers might ask whether the author is relying on published research, and if so, whether the studies have been peer-reviewed in reputable, scholarly journals. They would also want to know whether a trade association for herbal supplements sponsored the research and whether the author or the researchers had financial connections to companies that produce herbal remedies. Rather than settling the question about Saint John's wort as a treatment for depression, this author's assertion may open up a heated controversy about medical research.

Reading rhetorically is thus a way of thinking critically about your sources. It influences the way you evaluate sources, take notes, and shape your argument.

Evaluating Sources

When you read sources for your research project, you need to evaluate them as you go along. As you read each potential source, ask yourself questions about the author's reliability, credibility, angle of vision, political stance, and degree of advocacy.

RELIABILITY *Reliability* refers to the accuracy of factual data in a source. If you check a writer's "facts" against other sources, do you find that the facts are correct? Does the writer distort facts, take them out of context, or otherwise use them unreasonably? In some controversies, key data are highly disputed—for example, the frequency of date rape or the risk factors for many diseases. A reliable writer acknowledges these controversies and doesn't treat disputed data as fact. Furthermore, if you check out the sources used by a reliable writer, they'll reveal accurate and careful research—respected primary sources rather than hearsay or secondhand reports. Journalists of reputable newspapers (not tabloids) pride themselves on meticulously checking out their facts, as do editors of serious popular magazines. However, editing is often minimal for web sources, which can be notoriously unreliable. As you gain knowledge about your research question, you'll develop a good ear for writers who play fast and loose with data.

CREDIBILITY *Credibility* is similar to reliability but is based on internal rather than external factors. It refers to the reader's trust in the writer's honesty, goodwill, and trustworthiness and is apparent in the writer's tone, reasonableness, fairness in summarizing opposing views, and respect for different perspectives. (Authors who earn your trust have successfully appealed to *ethos*.) Audiences differ in how much credibility they will grant to certain authors. Nevertheless, a writer can achieve a reputation for credibility, even among bitter political opponents, by applying to issues a sense of moral courage, integrity, and consistency of principle.

ANGLE OF VISION By *angle of vision*, we mean the way that a piece of writing is shaped by its author's underlying values, assumptions, and beliefs, resulting in a text that reflects a certain perspective, worldview, or belief system. Of paramount importance are the underlying values or beliefs that the writer assumes his or her readers will share. You can get useful clues about a writer's angle of vision and intended audience by doing some quick research into the politics and reputation of the author on the Internet or by analyzing the genre, market niche, and political reputation of the publication in which the material appears.

POLITICAL STANCE Your awareness of angle of vision and political stance is especially important if you are doing research on contemporary cultural or political issues. In Table 16.3, we have categorized some well-known political commentators, publications, policy research institutes (commonly known as *think tanks*), and blogs across the political spectrum from left/liberal to right/conservative.

Although the terms *liberal* and *conservative* or *left* and *right* often have fuzzy meanings, they provide convenient shorthand for signaling a person's overall views about the proper role of government in relation to the economy and social values. Liberals, tending to sympathize with those potentially harmed by unfettered free markets (workers, consumers, plaintiffs, endangered species), are typically comfortable with government regulation of economic matters. Conservatives, who tend to sympathize with business interests, typically assert faith in free markets and favor a limited regulatory role for government. On social issues, conservatives tend to espouse traditional family values and advocate laws that would maintain these values (for example, promoting a constitutional amendment that would forbid abortions). Liberals, on the other hand, tend to espouse individual choice on many social matters. Some persons identify themselves as economic conservatives but social liberals; others side with workers' interests on economic issues but are conservative on social issues.

Table 16.3 Angles of Vision in U.S. Media and Think Tanks: A Sampling Across the Political Spectrum

Commentators				
Left	**Left Center**	**Center**	**Right Center**	**Right**
Barbara Ehrenreich	E. J. Dionne	David Ignatius	David Brooks	Charles Krauthammer
Naomi Klein	Leonard Pitts	Thomas Friedman	Peggy Noonan	Michelle Malkin
Michael Moore (film-maker)	Gail Collins	Kathleen Hall Jamieson	Jonah Goldberg	Glenn Beck (radio/TV)
Paul Krugman	Nicholas Kristof	Kevin Phillips	Andrew Sullivan	Rush Limbaugh (radio/TV)
Thom Hartman (radio)	Maureen Dowd	David Broder	George Will	Bill O'Reilly (radio/TV)
Rachel Maddow (television)	Mark Shields	William Saletan	Ruben Navarrette, Jr.	Kathleen Parker
	Frank Bruni	Mary Sanchez	Ross Douthat	Thomas Sowell
	Charles M. Blow		Paul Gigot	Avik Roy
	Froma Harrop			

Newspapers and Magazines**		
Left/Liberal	**Center**	**Right/Conservative**
The American Prospect	*Atlantic Monthly*	*American Spectator*
Harper's	*Business Week*	*Fortune*
Los Angeles Times	*Commentary*	*National Review*
Mother Jones	*Commonweal*	*Reader's Digest*
The Nation	*Foreign Affairs*	*Reason*
New York Times	*New Republic*	*Wall Street Journal*
New Yorker	*Slate*	*Washington Times*
Salon	*Washington Post*	*Weekly Standard*
Sojourners		*Breitbart News (far right)*

Blogs		
Liberal/Left	**Center**	**Right/Conservative**
americablog.com	donklephant.com	firstinthenation.us
crooksandliars.com	newmoderate.blogspot.com	instapundit.com
dailykos.com	politics-central.blogspot.com	littlegreenfootballs.com
digbysblog.blogspot.com	rantingbaldhippie.com	michellemalkin.com
firedoglake.com	stevesilver.net	polipundit.com
huffingtonpost.com	themoderatevoice.com	powerlineblog.com
mediamatters.com	washingtonindependent.com	sistertoldjah.com
talkingpointsmemo.com	watchingwashington.blogspot.com	redstate.com
wonkette.com		townhall.com

Think Tanks		
Left/Liberal	**Center**	**Right/Conservative**
Center for American Progress	The Brookings Institution	American Enterprise Institute
Center for Media and Democracy (sponsors Disinfopedia.org)	Carnegie Endowment for International Peace	Cato Institute (Libertarian)
Institute for Policy Studies	Council on Foreign Relations	Center for Strategic and International Studies
Open Society Institute (Soros Foundation)	Jamestown Foundation	Heritage Foundation (sponsors Townhall.com)
Progressive Policy Institute	National Bureau of Economic Research	Project for the New American Century
Urban Institute		

* For further information about the political leanings of publications or think tanks, ask your librarian about the Gale Directory of Publications and Broadcast Media or NIRA World Directory of Think Tanks.*

* Newspapers are categorized according to positions they take on their editorial page; any reputable newspaper strives for objectivity in news reporting and includes a variety of views on its op-ed pages. Magazines do not claim and are not expected to present similar breadth and objectivity.

Finally, many persons regard themselves as "centrists." In Table 16.3, the column labeled "Center" includes commentators who seek out common ground between the left and the right and who often believe that the best civic decisions are compromises between opposing views. Likewise, centrist publications and institutes often approach issues from multiple points of view, looking for the most workable solutions.

DEGREE OF ADVOCACY   By *degree of advocacy*, we mean the extent to which an author unabashedly takes a persuasive stance on a contested position as opposed to adopting a more neutral, objective, or exploratory stance. For example, publications affiliated with advocacy organizations (the Sierra Club, the National Rifle Association) will have a clear editorial bias. When a writer takes a strong stance on an issue, you need to weigh carefully the writer's selection of evidence, interpretation of data, and fairness to opposing views. Although no one can be completely neutral, it is always useful to seek out authors who offer a balanced assessment of the evidence. Evidence from a more detached and neutral writer may be more trusted by your readers than the arguments of a committed advocate.

Criteria for Evaluating a Web Source

When you evaluate a web source, we suggest that you ask five different kinds of questions about the site in which the source appeared, as listed in Table 16.4. These questions, developed by scholars and librarians as points to consider when you are evaluating websites, will help you determine the usefulness of a site or source for your own purposes.

Table 16.4 Criteria for Evaluating Websites

Criteria	Questions to Ask
1. Authority	• Is the document author or site sponsor clearly identified? • Does the site identify the occupation, position, education, experience, or other credentials of the author? • Does the home page or a clear link from the home page reveal the author's or sponsor's motivation for establishing the site? • Does the site provide contact information for the author or sponsor, such as an e-mail or organization address?
2. Objectivity or Clear Disclosure of Advocacy	• Is the site's purpose clear (for example, to inform, entertain, or persuade)? • Is the site explicit about declaring its point of view? • Does the site indicate whether the author is affiliated with a specific organization, institution, or association? • Does the site indicate whether it is directed toward a specific audience?
3. Coverage	• Are the topics covered by the site clear? • Does the site exhibit a suitable depth and comprehensiveness for its purpose? • Is sufficient evidence provided to support the ideas and opinions presented?
4. Accuracy	• Are the sources of information stated? • Do the facts appear to be accurate? • Can you verify this information by comparing this source with other sources in the field?
5. Currency	• Are dates included in the website? • Do the dates apply to the material itself, to its placement on the web, or to the time the site was last revised and updated? • Is the information current, or at least still relevant, for the site's purpose? For your purpose?

As a researcher, the first question you should ask about a potentially useful web source should be, "Who placed this piece on the web and why?" You can begin answering this question by analyzing the site's home page, where you will often find navigational buttons linking to "Mission," "About Us," or other identifying information about the site's sponsors. You can also get hints about the site's purpose by asking, "What kind of website is it?" Different kinds of websites have different purposes, often revealed by the domain identifier following the site name:

- **com, .co.,** *and* **.biz** *sites*: These are commercial sites designed to promote a business's image, attract customers, market products and services, and provide customer service. Their angle of vision is to promote the view of the corporation or business. Often, material has no identified author. (The sponsoring company is often cited as the author.)

- **org** *sites*: These are sites for nonprofit organizations or advocacy groups. Some sites provide accurate, balanced information related to the organization's mission work (Red Cross, World Vision), while others promote political views (Heritage Foundation) or advocate a cause (People for the Ethical Treatment of Animals).

- **edu** *sites*: These sites are associated with a college or university. Home pages aim to attract prospective students and donors and provide a portal into the site. Numerous subsites are devoted to research, pedagogy, libraries, and so forth. The angle of vision can vary from strong advocacy on issues (a student paper, an on-campus advocacy group) to the objective and scholarly (a university research site).

For Writing and Discussion

Analyzing the Rhetorical Elements of Two Websites

Individual task:

Using a web search engine, find a site opposing gun control (such as the National Rifle Association or Women Against Gun Control) and a site supporting gun control (such as National Gun Victims Action Council or the Brady Campaign). Peruse each of your chosen sites. Then write out your answers to the following questions:

1. What is the angle of vision and degree of advocacy of each of the sites? How does the selection of images, links to articles, and use of "facts" and "fact sheets" indicate an angle of vision?
2. Look for images of women on each of your sites. How do they construct women differently and imply differences in women's concerns about guns?
3. What range of underlying values does each of the sites appeal to? How do words and images create viewer awareness of these underlying values?
4. How does each of the sites use *logos, ethos,* and *pathos* to sway readers toward its point of view?

Group task:

Compare your answers to these questions with those of others in your class. How do your rhetorical observations intersect? Where do they differ?

- **gov** *or* **.mil** sites: These sites are sponsored by a government agency or military units. They can provide a range of basic data about government policy, bills in Congress, economic forecasts, census data, and so forth. Their angle of vision varies from objective (informational sites) to subjective (sites that promote the agency's agenda).

- **.net** *sites*: These sites were originally intended for networking businesses that provided Internet service or hosted Internet infrastructure. Recently the .net domain has expanded to include a wide range of commercial businesses and seems interchangeable with .com and .biz.

Because of a new rule by the agency that controls domain identifiers, people and organizations will be able to buy their own unique domain identifiers. Sites with unique identifiers are likely to be commercial sites because the identifiers cost thousands of dollars each.

Taking Purposeful Notes

By reading rhetorically and evaluating your sources as you proceed, you will make purposeful choices about the sources you will use in your researched argument. In this concluding section we offer advice on how to take notes about each of your sources. Many beginning researchers opt not to take notes—a serious mistake, in our view. Instead, they simply photocopy or print articles, perhaps using a highlighter to mark passages. This practice, which experienced researchers almost never use, reduces your ability to engage the ideas in a source and to find your own voice in a conversation. When you begin drafting your paper, you'll have no notes to refer to, no record of your thinking-in-progress. Your only recourse is to revisit all your sources, thumbing through them one at a time—a practice that leads to passive cutting and pasting (and possible plagiarism).

Good note taking includes recording bibliographic information for each source, recording information and ideas from each source, and responding to each source with your own ideas and exploratory writing.

RECORDING BIBLIOGRAPHIC INFORMATION To take good research notes, begin by making a bibliographic entry for each source, following the documentation format assigned by your instructor. Although you will be tempted to put off doing this mechanical task, there are two reasons to do it immediately:

- Doing it now, while the source is in front of you, will save you time in the long run. Otherwise, you'll have to try to retrieve the source, in a late-night panic, just before the paper is due.

- Doing it now will make you look at the source rhetorically. Is it a peer-reviewed journal article? A magazine article? An op-ed piece? A blog? Having to make the bibliographic entry forces you to identify the source's genre. Chapter 18 explains in detail how to make bibliographic entries for both the MLA format (called "Works Cited") and the APA format (called "References").

RECORDING IDEAS AND INFORMATION AND RESPONDING TO EACH SOURCE To take good research notes, follow the reading habits of summary and exploration discussed in Chapter 8, weaving back and forth between walking in the shoes of the source author and then standing back to believe and doubt what the source says. Think in terms of two categories of notes: informational and exploratory.

- *Your informational notes on each source:* Using the skills of summary writing explained in Chapter 8, summarize each source's argument and record useful information. To avoid the risk of plagiarism later, make sure that you put quotation marks around any passages that you copy word for word (be sure to copy exactly). When you summarize or paraphrase passages, be sure to put the ideas entirely into your own words. (For more on quoting, summarizing, and paraphrasing sources, see Chapter 17.)

- *Your own exploratory notes as you think of ideas:* Write down your own ideas as they occur to you. Speak back to the source. Record your thinking-in-progress as you mull over ways the source sparked your own thinking.

An approach that encourages both modes of writing is to keep a dialectic or double-entry journal. Divide a page in half; enter your informational notes on one side and your exploratory writing on the other. If you use a computer, you can put your informational notes in one font and your own exploratory writing in another.

Taking effective notes is different from the mechanical process of copying out passages or simply listing facts and information. Rather, make your notes purposeful by imagining how you might use a given source in your research paper. Table 16.5 shows the different functions that research sources might play in your argument and highlights appropriate note-taking strategies for each function.

Table 16.5 Strategies for Taking Notes According to Purpose

Function That Source Might Play in Your Argument	Strategies for Informational Notes	Strategies for Exploratory Notes
Provides background about your problem or issue	• Summarize the information. • Record specific facts and figures useful for background.	• Speculate on how much background your readers will need.
Gives an alternative view that you will mention briefly	• Summarize the source's argument in a couple of sentences; note its bias and perspective. • Identify brief quotations that sum up the source's perspective.	• Jot down ideas on how and why different sources disagree. • Begin making an idea map of alternative views.
Provides an alternative or opposing view that you might summarize fully and respond to	• Summarize the article fully and fairly (see Chapter 8 on summary writing). • Note the kinds of evidence used.	• Speculate about why you disagree with the source and whether you can refute the argument, concede to it, or compromise with it. • Explore what research you'll need to support your own argument.
Provides information or testimony that you might use as evidence	• Record the data or information. • If using authorities for testimony, quote short passages. • Note the credentials of the writer or person quoted.	• Record new ideas as they occur to you. • Continue to think purposefully about additional research you'll need.
Mentions information or testimony that counters your position or raises doubts about your argument	• Note counterevidence. • Note authorities who disagree with you.	• Speculate how you might respond to counterevidence.
Provides a theory or method that influences your approach to the issue	• Note credentials of the author. • Note passages that sparked ideas.	• Freewrite about how the source influences your method or approach.

Conclusion

This chapter has explained the need to establish a good research question; to understand the key differences among different kinds of sources; to use purposeful strategies for searching libraries, databases, and websites; and to use your rhetorical knowledge when you read and evaluate sources and take purposeful notes. It has also discussed briefly the special problems of evaluating a website. In the next chapter we focus on how to integrate research sources into your own prose.

Chapter 17

Incorporating Sources into Your Own Argument

Learning Objectives

In this chapter you will learn to:

17.1 Use your sources for your own purposes.

17.2 Summarize, paraphrase, and quote a source.

17.3 Punctuate quotations correctly.

17.4 Signal your use of sources through rhetorically effective attributive tags.

17.5 Avoid plagiarism.

Previous chapters taught you to pose a good research question, use online databases, search the web wisely, and evaluate your sources by reading them rhetorically. This chapter teaches you how to incorporate sources smoothly into your own argument.

Using Sources for Your Own Purposes

17.1 Use your sources for your own purposes.

To illustrate the purposeful use of sources, we will use the following short argument from the website of the American Council on Science and Health (ACSH)—an organization of doctors and scientists devoted to providing scientific information on health issues and to exposing health fads and myths. Please read the argument carefully in preparation for the discussions that follow.

Is Vegetarianism Healthier than Nonvegetarianism?

Many people become vegetarians because they believe, in error, that vegetarianism is uniquely conducive to good health. The findings of several large epidemiologic studies indeed suggest that the death and chronic-disease rates of vegetarians—primarily vegetarians who consume dairy products or both dairy products and eggs—are lower than those of meat eaters....

   The health of vegetarians may be better than that of nonvegetarians partly because of nondietary factors: Many vegetarians are health-conscious. They exercise regularly, maintain a desirable body weight, and abstain from smoking. Although most epidemiologists have attempted to take such factors into account in their analyses, it is possible that they did not adequately control their studies for nondietary effects.

   People who are vegetarians by choice may differ from the general population in other ways relevant to health. For example, in Western countries most vegetarians are more affluent than nonvegetarians and thus have better living conditions and more access to medical care.

   An authoritative review of vegetarianism and chronic diseases classified the evidence for various alleged health benefits of vegetarianism:

- The evidence is "strong" that vegetarians have (a) a lower risk of becoming alcoholic, constipated, or obese and (b) a lower risk of developing lung cancer.
- The evidence is "good" that vegetarians have a lower risk of developing adult-onset diabetes mellitus, coronary artery disease, hypertension, and gallstones.
- The evidence is "fair to poor" that vegetarianism decreases risk of breast cancer, colon cancer, diverticular disease, kidney-stone formation, osteoporosis, and tooth decay.

For some of the diseases mentioned above, the practice of vegetarianism itself probably is the main protective factor. For example, the low incidence of constipation among vegetarians is almost certainly due to their high intakes of fiber-rich foods. For other conditions, nondietary factors may be more important than diet. For example, the low incidence of lung cancer among vegetarians is attributable primarily to their extremely low rate of cigarette smoking. Diet is but one of many risk factors for most chronic diseases.

   How you might use this article in your own writing would depend on your research question and purpose. To illustrate, we'll show you three different hypothetical examples of writers who have reason to cite this article.

Writer 1: A Causal Argument Showing Alternative Approaches to Reducing Risk of Alcoholism

Writer 1 argues that vegetarianism may be an effective way to resist alcoholism. She uses just one statement from the ACSH article for her own purpose and then moves on to other sources.

Another approach to fighting alcoholism is through naturopathy, holistic   *Writer's claim*

medicine, and vegetarianism. Vegetarians generally have better health than the

Identification of source

Quotation from ACSH

rest of the population and particularly have, according to the American Council on Science and Health, "a lower risk of becoming alcoholic." This lower risk has been borne out by other studies showing that the benefits of the holistic health movement are particularly strong for persons with addictive tendencies....[goes on to other arguments and sources]

Writer 2: A Proposal Argument Advocating Vegetarianism

Writer 2 proposes that people should become vegetarians. Parts of his argument focus on the environmental costs and ethics of eating meat, but he also devotes one paragraph to the health benefits of vegetarianism. As support for this point he summarizes the ACSH article's material on health benefits.

Writer's claim

Identification of source

Summary of ACSH material

Not only will a vegetarian diet help stop cruelty to animals, but it is also good for your health. According to the American Council on Science and Health, vegetarians have longer life expectancy than nonvegetarians and suffer from fewer chronic diseases. The Council cites "strong" evidence from the scientific literature showing that vegetarians have reduced risk of lung cancer, obesity, constipation, and alcoholism. The Council also cites "good" evidence that vegetarians have a reduced risk of adult-onset diabetes, high blood pressure, gallstones, and hardening of the arteries. Although the evidence isn't nearly as strong, vegetarianism may also lower the risk of certain cancers, kidney stones, loss of bone density, and tooth decay.

Writer 3: An Evaluation Argument Looking Skeptically at Vegetarianism

Here, Writer 3 uses portions of the same article to make an opposite case from that of Writer 2. She focuses on those parts of the article that Writer 2 consciously excluded.

Writer's claim

Identification of source

Paraphrased points from ACSH

The link between vegetarianism and death rates is a classic instance of correlation rather than causation. While it is true that vegetarians have a longer life expectancy than nonvegetarians and suffer from fewer chronic diseases, the American Council on Science and Health has shown that the causes can mostly be explained by factors other than diet. As the Council suggests, vegetarians are apt to be more health conscious than nonvegetarians and thus get more exercise, stay slender, and avoid smoking. The Council points out that vegetarians also tend to be wealthier than nonvegetarians and see their doctors more regularly. In short, they live longer because they take better care of themselves, not because they avoid meat.

For Writing And Discussion

Using a Source for Different Purposes

Each of the hypothetical writers uses the short ACSH argument in different ways for different purposes. Working individually or in small groups, respond to the following questions. Be prepared to elaborate on and defend your answers.

1. How does each writer use the original article differently and why?
2. If you were the author of the article from the American Council on Science and Health, would you think that your article is used fairly and responsibly in each instance?
3. Suppose your goal were simply to summarize the argument from the American Council on Science and Health. Write a brief summary of the argument and then explain how your summary is different from the partial summaries by Writers 2 and 3.

Using Summary, Paraphrase, and Quotation

17.2 Summarize, paraphrase, and quote a source.

As a research writer, you need to incorporate sources gracefully into your own prose. Depending on your purpose, you might (1) summarize all or part of a source author's argument, (2) paraphrase a relevant portion of a source, or (3) quote small passages from the source directly. To avoid plagiarism, you'll need to reference the source with an in-text citation, put quotation marks around quoted passages, and convert paraphrases and summaries entirely into your own words. Table 17.1 gives you an overview of summary, paraphrase, and quotation as ways of incorporating sources into your own prose. With practice, you'll be able to use all these strategies smoothly and effectively.

Summarizing

Detailed instructions on how to write a summary of an article and incorporate it into your own prose are provided in Chapter 8. Summaries can be as short as a single sentence or as long as a paragraph. Make the summary as concise as possible so that you don't distract the reader from your own argument. In many cases, writers summarize only parts of a source, depending on what is relevant to their own argument. Writer 3's summary of the article by the American Council on Science and Health is a good example of a partial summary.

Paraphrasing

Unlike a summary, which is a condensation of a source's whole argument, a **paraphrase** translates a short passage from a source's words into the writer's own words. Writers often choose to paraphrase when the details of a source passage are particularly important or when the source is overly technical and needs to be simplified for the intended audience. When you paraphrase, be careful to

Table 17.1 Incorporating Sources into Your Own Prose

Strategy	What to Do	When to Use This Strategy
Summarize the source.	Condense a source writer's argument by keeping main ideas and omitting details (see Chapter 8).	• When the source writer's whole argument is relevant to your purpose • When the source writer presents an alternative or opposing view that you want to push against • When the source writer's argument can be used in support of your own argument
Paraphrase the source.	Reproduce an idea from a source writer but translate the idea entirely into your own words; a paraphrase should be approximately the same length as the original.	• When you want to incorporate factual information from a source or to use one specific idea from a source • When the source passage is overly complex or technical for your targeted audience • When you want to incorporate a source's point in your own voice without interrupting the flow of your argument
Quote short passages from the source using quotation marks.	Work brief quotations from the source smoothly into the grammar of your own sentences (see details in this chapter).	• When you need testimony from an authority (state the authority's credentials in an attributive tag, as explained in this chapter) • In summaries, when you want to reproduce a source's voice, particularly if the language is striking or memorable • In lieu of paraphrase when the source language is memorable
Quote long passages from the source using the block method. (Use this method sparingly.)	Use noticeably lengthy block quotations.	• When you intend to analyze or critique the quotation—the quotation is followed by your detailed analysis of its ideas or rhetorical features • When the flavor and language of testimonial evidence are important

avoid reproducing the original writer's grammatical structure and syntax. If you mirror the original sentence structure while replacing occasional words with synonyms or small structural changes, you will be doing what composition specialists call **patchwriting**—that is, patching some of your language onto someone else's writing.* Patchwriting is a form of academic dishonesty because you aren't fully composing your own sentences and are thus misrepresenting both your own work and that of the source writer. An acceptable paraphrase needs to be entirely in your own words. To understand patchwriting more fully, track the differences between unacceptable patchwriting and acceptable paraphrase in the following examples.

Original

- The evidence is "strong" that vegetarians have (a) a lower risk of becoming alcoholic, constipated, or obese and (b) a lower risk of developing lung cancer.
- The evidence is "good" that vegetarians have a lower risk of developing adult-onset diabetes mellitus, coronary artery disease, hypertension, and gallstones.

---

* We are indebted to the work of Rebecca Moore Howard and others who have led composition researchers to reexamine the use of sources and plagiarism from a cultural and rhetorical perspective. See especially Rebecca Moore Howard, Standing in the Shadow of Giants: Plagiarists, Authors, Collaborators (Stamford, CT: Ablex Pub., 1999).

Unacceptable Patchwriting

According to the American Council on Science and Health, there is strong evidence that vegetarians have a lower risk of becoming alcoholic, constipated, or obese. The evidence is also strong that they have a lower risk of lung cancer. The evidence is good that vegetarians are less apt to develop adult-onset diabetes, coronary artery disease, hypertension, or gallstones.

Identification of source

Note that phrases are taken word for word from the original

Acceptable Paraphrase

The Council summarizes "strong" evidence from the scientific literature showing that vegetarians have reduced risk of lung cancer, obesity, constipation, and alcoholism. The Council also cites "good" evidence that vegetarians have a reduced risk of adult-onset diabetes, high blood pressure, gallstones, or hardening of the arteries.

Identification of source

Doesn't follow original sentence structure

Quotes "strong" and "good" to indicate distinction made in original

Both the patchwriting example and the acceptable paraphrase reproduce the same ideas as the original in approximately the same number of words. But the writer of the acceptable paraphrase has been more careful to change the sentence structure substantially and not copy exact phrases. In contrast, the patchwritten version contains longer strings of borrowed language without quotation marks.

Among novice writers, the ease of copying web sources can lead to patchwriting. You may be tempted to copy and paste a web-based passage into your own draft and then revise it slightly by changing some of the words. Such patchwriting won't occur if you write in your own voice—that is, if you convert information from a source into your own words in order to make your own argument.

When you first practice paraphrasing, try paraphrasing a passage twice to avoid patchwriting:

- The first time, read the passage carefully and put it into your own words, looking at the source as little as possible.
- The second time, paraphrase your own paraphrase. Then recheck your final version against the original to make sure you have eliminated similar sentence structures or word-for-word strings.

We'll return to the problem of patchwriting in our discussion of plagiarism later in this chapter.

Quoting

Besides summary and paraphrase, writers often choose to quote directly in order to give the reader the flavor and style of the source author's prose or to make a memorable point in the source author's own voice. Be careful not to quote a passage that you don't fully understand. (Sometimes novice writers quote a passage because it sounds impressive.) When you quote, you must reproduce the source author's original words exactly without change, unless you indicate changes with ellipses or brackets. Also be careful to represent the author's intention and meaning fairly; don't change the author's meaning by taking quotations out of context.

Punctuating Quotations Correctly

17.3 Punctuate quotations correctly.

Because the mechanics of quoting offers its own challenges, we devote the following sections to it. These sections answer the nuts-and-bolts questions about how to punctuate quotations correctly. Additional explanations covering variations and specific cases can be found in any good handbook.

Quoting a Complete Sentence

In some cases, you will want to quote a complete sentence from your source. Typically, you will include an attributive tag that tells the reader who is being quoted. At the end of the quotation, you usually indicate its page number in parentheses. (For more information, see Chapter 18 on in-text citations.)

Original Passage

Many people become vegetarians because they believe, in error, that vegetarianism is uniquely conducive to good health. [found on page 359 of source]*

Writer's Quotation of This Passage

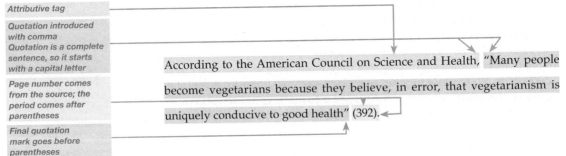

Attributive tag

Quotation introduced with comma
Quotation is a complete sentence, so it starts with a capital letter

Page number comes from the source; the period comes after parentheses

Final quotation mark goes before parentheses

According to the American Council on Science and Health, "Many people become vegetarians because they believe, in error, that vegetarianism is uniquely conducive to good health" (392).

Quoting Words and Phrases

Instead of quoting a complete sentence, you often want to quote only a few words or phrases from your source and insert them into your own sentence. In these cases, make sure that the grammatical structure of the quotation fits smoothly into the grammar of your own sentence.

Original Passage

The health of vegetarians may be better than that of nonvegetarians partly because of nondietary factors: Many vegetarians are health-conscious. They exercise regularly, maintain a desirable body weight, and abstain from smoking. [found on page 392]

---

* The cited page is from this text in its printed version. When quoting from print sources or other sources with stable page numbers, you indicate the page number as part of your citation. To illustrate how to punctuate page citations, we'll assume throughout this section that you found the American Council on Science and Health article in this textbook rather than on the web, in which case it would not be possible to cite page numbers.

Quoted Phrase Inserted into Writer's Own Sentence

The American Council on Science and Health argues that the cause of vegetarians' longer life may be "nondietary factors." The Council claims that vegetarians are more "health-conscious" than meat eaters and that they "exercise regularly, maintain a desirable body weight, and abstain from smoking" (392).

Attributive tag

Quotation marks show where quotation starts and ends

No comma or capital letter: Punctuation and capitalization determined by grammar of your own sentence

Period comes after parentheses containing page number

Modifying a Quotation

Occasionally you may need to alter a quotation to make it fit your own context. Sometimes the grammar of a desired quotation doesn't match the grammar of your own sentence. At other times, the meaning of a quoted word is unclear when it is removed from its original context. In these cases, use brackets to modify the quotation's grammar or to add a clarifying explanation. Place your changes or additions in brackets to indicate that the bracketed material is not part of the original wording. You should also use brackets to show a change in capitalization.

Original Passage

Many vegetarians are health-conscious. They exercise regularly, maintain a desirable body weight, and abstain from smoking. [found on page 359]

Quotations Modified with Brackets

The American Council on Science and Health hypothesizes that vegetarians maintain better health by "exercis[ing] regularly, maintain[ing] a desirable body weight, and abstain[ing] from smoking" (392).

Attributive tag

Brackets show change in quotation to fit grammar of writer's sentence

Page number from source

According to the American Council on Science and Health, "They [vegetarians] exercise regularly, maintain a desirable body weight, and abstain from smoking" (392).

Attributive tag

Brackets show that writer has added a word to explain what "they" stands for

Omitting Something from a Quoted Passage

Another way that writers modify quotations is to leave words out of the quoted passage. To indicate an omission, use three spaced periods called an **ellipsis** (. . .). Placement of the ellipsis depends on where the omitted material occurs. In the middle of a sentence, each of the periods should be preceded and followed by a space. When your ellipsis comes at the boundary between sentences, use an additional period to mark the end of the first sentence. When a parenthetical page number must follow the ellipsis, insert it before the final (fourth) period in the sequence.

Original Passage

People who are vegetarians by choice may differ from the general population in other ways relevant to health. For example, in Western countries most vegetarians are more affluent than nonvegetarians and thus have better living conditions and more access to medical care. [found on pages 359–360]

Quotations with Omitted Material Marked by Ellipses

Three spaced periods mark omitted words in middle of sentence; note the spaces between each period

Three periods form the ellipsis. (Omitted material comes before the end of the sentence)

This period ends the sentence

According to the American Council on Science and Health, "people who are vegetarians by choice may differ . . . in other ways relevant to health. For example, in Western countries most vegetarians are more affluent than nonvegetarians . . . " (392).

Quoting Something That Contains a Quotation

Occasionally a passage that you wish to quote will already contain quotation marks. If you insert the passage within your own quotation marks, change the original double marks (") into single marks (') to indicate the quotation within the quotation. The same procedure works whether the quotation marks are used for quoted words or for a title. Make sure that your attributive tag signals who is being quoted.

Original Passage

The evidence is "strong" that vegetarians have (a) a lower risk of becoming alcoholic, constipated, or obese and (b) a lower risk of developing lung cancer. [found on page 392]

Use of Single Quotation Marks to Identify a Quotation within a Quotation

Single quotation marks replace the double quotation marks in the original source

Double quotation marks enclose the material quoted from the source

According to the American Council on Science and Health, "The evidence is 'strong' that vegetarians have (a) a lower risk of becoming alcoholic, constipated, or obese and (b) a lower risk of developing lung cancer" (392).

Using a Block Quotation for a Long Passage

If you quote a long source passage that will take more than four lines in your own paper, use the block indentation method rather than quotation marks. Block quotations are generally introduced with an attributive tag followed by a colon. The indented block of text, rather than quotation marks, signals that the material is a direct quotation. Block quotations occur rarely in scholarly writing and are used primarily in cases where the writer intends to analyze the text being quoted. If you overuse block quotations, you simply produce a collage of other writers' voices.

Original Passage

The health of vegetarians may be better than that of nonvegetarians partly because of nondietary factors: Many vegetarians are health-conscious. They exercise regularly, maintain a desirable body weight, and abstain from smoking. Although most epidemiologists have attempted to take such factors into account in their analyses, it is possible that they did not adequately control their studies for nondietary effects. [found on page 359]

Block Quotation

The American Council on Science and Health suggests that vegetarians may be healthier than nonvegetarians not because of their diet but because of their more healthy lifestyle:

> *Block quotation introduced with a colon*

> Many vegetarians are health-conscious. They exercise regularly, maintain a desirable body weight, and abstain from smoking. Although most epidemiologists have attempted to take such factors into account in their analyses, it is possible that they did not adequately control their studies for nondietary effects. (392)

> *No quotation marks*

> *Block indented 1/2 inch on left*

> *Page number appears in parentheses. (Note that parentheses come after the closing period preceded by a space)*

Creating Rhetorically Effective Attributive Tags

17.4 Signal your use of sources through rhetorically effective attributive tags.

Throughout the previous examples we've been using attributive tags to indicate words or ideas taken from a source. *Attributive tags* are phrases such as "according to the American Council on Science and Health . . . ," "Smith claims that . . . ," or "the author continues . . . ." Such phrases signal to the reader that the material immediately following the tag is from the cited source. In this section we'll show you why attributive tags are often clearer and more powerful than other ways of signaling a source, such as a parenthetical citation. Particularly, attributive tags can also be used rhetorically to shape your reader's response to a source.

Attributive Tags versus Parenthetical Citations

Instead of attributive tags, writers sometimes indicate a source only by citing it in parentheses at the end of the borrowed material—a common practice in the social sciences and some other kinds of academic writing. However, the preferred practice when writing for nonspecialized audiences is to use attributive tags.

Less Preferred: Indicating Source through Parenthetical Citation

Vegetarians are apt to be more health-conscious than nonvegetarians (American Council on Science and Health).*

More Preferred: Indicating Source through Attributive Tag

According to the American Council on Science and Health, vegetarians are apt to be more health-conscious than nonvegetarians.

A disadvantage of the parenthetical method is that it requires readers to wait until the end of the source material before the source is identified. Attributive tags, in contrast, identify the source the moment it is first used, thus marking more clearly the beginning of borrowed material. Another disadvantage of the parenthetical method is that it tends to treat the borrowed material as "fact" rather than as the view of the source author. In contrast, attributive tags call attention to the source's angle of vision. An attributive tag reminds the reader to put on the glasses of the source author—to see the borrowed material as shaped by the source author's biases and perspectives.

Creating Attributive Tags to Shape Reader Response

Attributive tags can be used not only to identify a source but also to shape your readers' attitudes toward the source. For example, if you wanted your readers to respect the expertise of a source, you might say, "According to noted chemist Marjorie Casper . . . ." If you wanted your readers to discount Casper's views, you might say, "According to Marjorie Casper, an industrial chemist on the payroll of a major corporate polluter . . . ."

When you compose an initial tag, you can add to it any combination of the kinds of information in Table 17.2, depending on your purpose, your audience's values, and your sense of what the audience already knows about the source. Our

Table 17.2 Modifying Attributive Tags to Shape Reader Response

Add to Attributive Tags	Examples
Author's credentials or relevant specialty (enhances credibility)	Civil engineer David Rockwood, a noted authority on stream flow in rivers
Author's lack of credentials (decreases credibility)	City Council member Dilbert Weasel, a local politician with no expertise in international affairs
Author's political or social views	Left-wing columnist Alexander Cockburn [has negative feeling]; Alexander Cockburn, a longtime champion of labor [has positive feeling]

---

* This parenthetical citation is in MLA form, and it assumes that the source was found on the web. If this had been a print source rather than a web source, a page number would also have been given as follows: (American Council on Science and Health 43). APA form also indicates the date of the source: (American Council on Science and Health, 2002, p. 43). We explain MLA and APA styles for citing and documenting sources in Chapter 18.

Table 17.2 Continued

Add to Attributive Tags	Examples
Title of source if it provides context	In her book *Fasting Girls: The History of Anorexia Nervosa,* Joan Jacobs Brumberg shows that [establishes credentials for comments on eating disorders]
Publisher of source if it adds prestige or otherwise shapes audience response	Dr. Carl Patrona, in an article published in the prestigious *New England Journal of Medicine*
Historical or cultural information about a source that provides context or background	In his 1960s book popularizing the hippie movement, Charles Reich claims that
Indication of source's purpose or angle of vision	Feminist author Naomi Wolfe, writing a blistering attack on the beauty industry, argues that

point here is that you can use attributive tags rhetorically to help your readers understand the significance and context of a source when you first introduce it and to guide your readers' attitudes toward the source.

Avoiding Plagiarism

17.5 Avoid plagiarism.

In Chapter 18, we proceed to the nuts and bolts of citing and documenting sources—a skill that will enhance your *ethos* as a skilled researcher and as a person of integrity. Unethical use of sources—called **plagiarism**—is a major concern not only for writing teachers but for teachers in all disciplines. To combat plagiarism, many instructors across the curriculum use plagiarism-detection software like turnitin.com. Their purpose, of course, is to discourage students from cheating. But sometimes students who have no intention of cheating can fall into producing papers that look like cheating. That is, they produce papers that might be accused of plagiarism even though the students had no intention of deceiving their readers.* Our goal in this section is to explain the concept of plagiarism more fully and to sum up the strategies for avoiding it.

Why Some Kinds of Plagiarism May Occur Unwittingly

To understand how unwitting plagiarism might occur, consider Table 17.3, where the middle column—"Misuse of Sources"—shows common mistakes of novice writers. Everyone agrees that the behaviors in the "Fraud" column constitute deliberate cheating and deserve appropriate punishment. Everyone also agrees that good scholarly work meets the criteria in the "Ethical Use of Sources" column. Novice researchers, however, may find themselves unwittingly in the middle column until they learn the academic conventions for using research sources.

---

* See Rebecca Moore Howard, *Standing in the Shadow of Giants: Plagiarists, Authors, Collaborators* (Stamford, CT: Ablex Pub., 1999).

Table 17.3 Plagiarism and the Ethical Use of Sources

	Plagiarism		Ethical Use of Sources
Fraud	Misuse of Sources (*Common Mistakes Made by New Researchers*)		
The writer	The writer		The writer
• buys a paper from a paper mill • submits someone else's work as his own • copies chunks of text from sources with obvious intention of not being detected • fabricates data or makes up evidence • intends to deceive	• copies passages directly from a source and references the source with an in-text citation, but fails to use quotation marks or block indentation • in attempting to paraphrase a source, makes some changes, but follows too closely the wording of the original (patchwriting) • fails to indicate the sources of some ideas or data (often is unsure what needs to be cited or has lost track of sources through poor note taking) • in general, misunderstands the conventions for using sources in academic writing		• writes paper entirely in her own words and uses exact quotations from sources • indicates all quotations with quotation marks or block indentation • indicates her use of all sources through attribution, in-text citation, and an end-of-paper list of works cited or references

You might appreciate these conventions more fully if you recognize how they have evolved from Western notions of intellectual property and patent law associated with the rise of modern science in the seventeenth and eighteenth centuries. A person not only could own a house or a horse, but also could own an idea and the words used to express that idea. You can see these cultural conventions at work—in the form of laws or professional codes of ethics—whenever a book author is disgraced for lifting words or ideas from another author or whenever an artist or entrepreneur is sued for stealing song lyrics, publishing another person's photographs without permission, or infringing on some inventor's patent.

This understanding of plagiarism may seem odd in some non-Western cultures where collectivism is valued more than individualism. In these cultures, words written or spoken by ancestors, elders, or other authority figures may be regarded with reverence and shared with others without attribution. In these cultures, it might also be disrespectful to paraphrase certain passages or to document them in a way that would suggest the audience didn't recognize the ancient wisdom.

However, such collectivist conventions won't work in research communities committed to building new knowledge. In the academic world, the conventions separating ethical from unethical use of sources are essential if research findings are to win the community's confidence. Effective research can occur only within ethical and responsible research communities, where people do not fabricate data and where current researchers respect and acknowledge the work of those who have gone before them.

Strategies for Avoiding Plagiarism

Table 17.4 will help you review the strategies for using source material ethically and avoiding plagiarism.

Table 17.4 Avoiding Plagiarism or the Appearance of Plagiarism

What to Do	Why to Do It
At the beginning	
Read your college's policy on plagiarism; listen to your teachers' statements regarding plagiarism in class or read about them on course syllabi.	Understanding policies on plagiarism and academic integrity will help you research and write ethically.
Pose a research question rather than a topic area.	Your thesis statement is your contestable answer to your thesis question. Arguing your own thesis gives you a voice, establishes your *ethos*, and urges you to write ethically.
At the note-taking stage	
Create a bibliographic entry for each source.	This action makes it easy to create an end-of-paper bibliography and encourages rhetorical reading.
When you copy a passage into your notes, copy it word for word and enclose it within quotation marks.	It is important to distinguish a source's words from your own words.
When you enter summaries or paraphrases into your notes, avoid patchwriting.	If your notes contain any strings of a source's original wording, you might later assume that these words are your own.
Distinguish your informational notes from your personal exploratory notes.	Keeping these kinds of notes separate will help you identify borrowed ideas when it's time to incorporate the source material into your paper.
When writing your draft	
Except for exact quotations, write the paper entirely in your own words.	This strategy keeps you from patchwriting when you summarize or paraphrase.
Indicate all quotations with quotation marks or block indentation. Use ellipses or brackets to make changes to fit your own grammar.	Be careful to represent the author fairly; don't change meaning by taking quotations out of context.
Never cut and paste a web passage directly into your draft. Paste it into a separate note file and put quotation marks around it.	Pasted passages are direct invitations to patchwrite.
Inside your text, use attributive tags or parenthetical citations to identify all sources. List all sources alphabetically in a concluding Works Cited or References list.	This strategy makes it easy for readers to know when you are using a source and where to find it.
Cite with attributive tags or parenthetical citations all quotations, paraphrases, summaries, and any other references to specific sources.	These are the most common in-text citations in a research paper.
Use in-text citations to indicate sources for all visuals and media such as graphs, maps, photographs, films, videos, broadcasts, and recordings.	The rules for citing words and ideas apply equally to visuals and media cited in your paper.
Use in-text citations for all ideas and facts that are not common knowledge.	Although you don't need to cite widely accepted and noncontroversial facts and information, it is better to cite them if you are unsure.

For Writing and Discussion

Avoiding Plagiarism

Individual task:

Reread the original article from the American Council on Science and Health (at the start of this chapter) and Writer 3's use of this source in her paragraph about how nondietary habits may explain why vegetarians are healthier than nonvegetarians. Then read the paragraph below by Writer 4, who makes the same argument as Writer 3 but crosses the line from ethical to nonethical use of sources. Imagine that Writer 4 says in dismay, "How can this be plagiarism? I cited my source." Write a message to Writer 4 explaining how this passage falls into the category of plagiarism.

Writer 4's Argument (Example of Plagiarism)

According to the American Council on Science and Health, the health of vegetarians may be better than that of nonvegetarians partly because of nondietary factors. People who eat only vegetables tend to be very conscious of their health. They exercise regularly, avoid getting fat, and don't smoke. Scientists who examined the data may not have adequately controlled for these nondietary effects. Also, in Western countries, most vegetarians are more affluent than nonvegetarians and thus have better living conditions and more access to medical care.

Group task:

Working in small groups or as a class, respond to the following questions.

1. Share with one another your messages to Writer 4.
2. Explore the possible causes of Writer 4's difficulty. Psychologically or cognitively, what may have caused Writer 4 to misuse the source? How might this writer's note-taking process or composing process have differed from that of Writer 3? In other words, what happened to get this writer into trouble?

Conclusion

This chapter has shown you how to use sources for your own purposes; how to summarize, paraphrase, and quote a source; how to signal your use of sources through rhetorically effective attributive tags; and how to punctuate quotations correctly. It has also explained how to use sources ethically to avoid plagiarism and create a professional *ethos*. In the next chapter we will provide guidelines and formats for citing and documenting your sources.

Chapter 18
Citing and Documenting Sources

Learning Objectives

In this chapter you will learn to:

18.1 Understand the correspondence between in-text citations and the end-of-paper list of cited works.

18.2 Cite and document your sources using the style and format of the Modern Language Association (MLA).

18.3 Cite and document your sources using the style and format of the American Psychological Association (APA).

The previous chapter showed you how to use sources ethically, incorporating them into your own prose so as to further your argument as well as to avoid plagiarism.

The Correspondence between In-Text Citations and the End-of-Paper List of Cited Works

18.1 Understand the correspondence between in-text citations and the end-of-paper list of cited works.

The most common forms of documentation use what are called in-text citations that match an end-of-paper list of cited works (as opposed to footnotes or endnotes). An **in-text citation** identifies a source in the body of the paper at the point where it is summarized, paraphrased, quoted, inserted, or otherwise referred to.

At the end of your paper you include a list—alphabetized by author (or by title if there is no named author)—of all the works you cited. Both the Modern Language Association (MLA) system, used primarily in the humanities, and the American Psychological Association (APA) system, used primarily in the social sciences, follow this procedure. In MLA, your end-of-paper list is titled **Works Cited.** In APA it is titled **References.**

Whenever you place an in-text citation in the body of your paper, your reader knows to turn to the Works Cited or References list at the end of the paper to get the full bibliographic information. The key to the system's logic is this:

- Every source in Works Cited or References must be mentioned in the body of the paper.
- Conversely, every source mentioned in the body of the paper must be included in the end-of-paper list.
- The first word in each entry of the Works Cited or References list (usually an author's last name) must also appear in the in-text citation. In other words, there must be a one-to-one correspondence between the first word in each entry in the end-of-paper list and the name used to identify the source in the body of the paper.

Suppose a reader sees this phrase in your paper: "According to Debra Goldstein . . . ." The reader should be able to turn to your Works Cited list and find an alphabetized entry beginning with "Goldstein, Debra." Similarly, suppose that in looking over your Works Cited list, your reader sees an article by "Guillen, Manuel." This means that the name "Guillen" has to appear in your paper in one of two ways:

- As an attributive tag: Economics professor Manuel Guillen argues that . . . .
- As a parenthetical citation, often following a quotation: " . . . changes in fiscal policy" (Guillen 49).

Because this one-to-one correspondence is so important, let's illustrate it with some complete examples using the MLA formatting style:

If the body of your paper has this:	Then the Works Cited list must have this:
According to linguist Deborah Tannen, political debate in America leaves out the complex middle ground where most solutions must be developed.	Tannen, Deborah . *The Argument Culture: Moving from Debate to Dialogue*. Random House, 1998.
In the 1980s, cigarette advertising revealed a noticeable pattern of racial stereotyping (Pollay et al.).	Pollay, Richard W., et al. "Separate, but Not Equal: Racial Segmentation in Cigarette Advertising." *Journal of Advertising*, vol. 21, no. 1, 1992, pp. 45–57.
On its website, the Children's Movement of California offers advice to parents on how to talk with children about alcohol and drugs ("Talking").	"Talking with Kids about Drugs and Alcohol." *Children's Movement of California*, www.childrennow.org/parenting-resources/drugs-alcohol. Accessed 12 Apr. 2018.

How to format an MLA in-text citation and a Works Cited list entry is the subject of the next section. The APA system is similar except that it emphasizes the date of publication in both the in-text citation and the References entry. APA formatting is discussed in the final section of this chapter.

MLA Style

18.2 Cite and document your sources using the style and format of the Modern Language Association.

An in-text citation and its corresponding Works Cited entry are linked in a chicken-and-egg system: You can't cite a source in the text without first knowing how the source's entry will be alphabetized in the Works Cited list. However, because most Works Cited entries are alphabetized by the first author's last name, for convenience we start with in-text citations.

In-Text Citations in MLA Style

A typical in-text citation contains two elements: (1) the last name of the author and (2) the page number of the quoted or paraphrased passage. However, in some cases a work is identified by something other than an author's last name, and sometimes no page number is required. Let's begin with the most common cases.

Typically, an in-text citation uses one of these two methods:

- **Parenthetical method.** Place the author's last name and the page number in parentheses immediately after the material being cited.

  The Spanish tried to reduce the status of Filipina women, who had been

  able to do business, get divorced, and sometimes become village chiefs

  (Karnow 41).

- **Attributive tag method.** Place the author's name in an attributive tag at the beginning of the source material and the page number in parentheses at the end.

  According to Karnow, the Spanish tried to reduce the status of Filipina

  women, who had been able to do business, get divorced, and sometimes

  become village chiefs (41).

Once you have cited an author and it is clear that the same author's material is being used, you need cite only the page numbers in parentheses in subsequent citations. A reader who wishes to look up the source will find the bibliographic information in the Works Cited section by looking for the entry under "Karnow."

Let's now turn to the variations. Table 18.1 identifies the typical variations and shows again the one-to-one connection between the in-text citation and the Works Cited list.

When to Use Page Numbers in In-Text Citations   When the materials you are citing are available in print or in PDF format, you can provide accurate page numbers for parenthetical citations. If you are working with web sources or HTML files, however, do not use the page numbers obtained from a printout because they will not be consistent from printer to printer. If the item has numbered paragraphs, cite them with the abbreviation *par.* or *pars.*—for example, "(Jones, pars. 22–24)." In the absence of reliable page numbers for the original material, MLA

Table 18.1 In-Text Citations in MLA Style

Type of Source	Works Cited Entry at End of Paper *(Construct the entry while taking notes on each source.)*	In-Text Citation in Body of Paper *(Use the first word of the Works Cited entry in parentheses or an attributive tag; add page number at end of quoted or paraphrased passage.)*
One author	Pollan, Michael. *The Omnivore's Dilemma: A Natural History of Four Meals.* Penguin, 2006.	. . . (Pollan 256). OR According to Pollan, . . . (256).
Two authors	Lewis, Robin, and Michael Dart. *The New Rules of Retail: Competing in the World's Toughest Marketplace.* Macmillan, 2010.	. . . retail" (Lewis and Dart 52). OR Lewis and Dart have argued that "advertisers . . . retail" (52). *For the in-text citation, cite the specific page number rather than the whole range of pages given in the Works Cited entry.*
More than two authors	Pollay, Richard W., et al. "Separate, but Not Equal: Racial Segmentation in Cigarette Advertising." *Journal of Advertising,* vol. 21, no. 1, 1992, pp. 45-57.	. . . race" (Pollay et al. 52) OR Pollay et al. have argued that "advertisers . . . race" (52). *For the in-text citation, cite the specific page number rather than the whole range of pages given in the Works Cited entry.*
Author has more than one work in Works Cited list	Dombrowski, Daniel A. *Babies and Beasts: The Argument from Marginal Cases.* U of Illinois P, *1997.* ---. *The Philosophy of Vegetarianism.* U of Massachusetts P, 1984. *Note that the second Dombrowski entry uses three hyphens in place of the author's name.*	. . . (Dombrowski, *Babies* 207). . . . (Dombrowski, *Philosophy* 328). OR According to Dombrowski, . . . *(Babies* 207). Dombrowski claims that . . . *(Philosophy* 328). *Because author has more than one work in Works Cited, include a short version of the title to distinguish between entries.*
Corporate author	American Red Cross. *Standard First Aid.* Mosby Lifeline, 1993.	. . . (American Red Cross 102). OR Snake bite instructions from the American Red Cross show that . . . (102).
No named author (Work is therefore alphabetized by title.)	"Body Piercing. Ouch!" *Menstuff,* www.menstuff .org/issues/byissue/bodypiercing.html. Accessed 12 Apr. 2018.	. . . ("Body"). OR According to the National Men's Resource Center, . . . ("Body"). • *Add "Body" in parentheses to show that work is alphabetized under "Body," not "National."* • *No page numbers are shown because website pages aren't stable. The website does not provide a date on which "Body Piercing. Ouch!" was posted. When a website does not provide a date of posting or publication, add the access date as the last item in the Works Cited entry.*
Indirect citation of a source that you found in another source *Suppose you want to use a quotation from Peter Singer that you found in a book by Daniel Dombrowski. Include Dombrowski but not Singer in Works Cited.*	Dombrowski, Daniel A. *Babies and Beasts: The Argument from Marginal Cases.* U of Illinois P, 1997.	Animal rights activist Peter Singer argues that . . . (qtd. in Dombrowski 429). • *Singer is used for the attributive tag, but the in-text citation is to Dombrowski.* • *"qtd. in" stands for "quoted in."*

says to omit page references from the parenthetical citation. Table 18.1 summarizes the use of page numbers in in-text citations.

Include a page number in the in-text citation:	Do not include a page number:
If the source has stable page numbers (print source or PDF version of print source): • If you quote something • If you paraphrase a specific passage • If you refer to data or details from a specific page or range of pages in the source	• If you are referring to the argument of the whole source instead of a specific page or passage • If the source does not have stable page numbers (articles on websites, HTML text, and so forth)

Works Cited List in MLA Style

In the MLA system, you place a complete Works Cited list at the end of the paper. The list includes all the sources that you mention in your paper. However, it does *not* include works you read but did not use. Entries in the Works Cited list follow these general guidelines:

- Entries are arranged alphabetically by author's last name, or by title if there is no author.

- If there is more than one entry per author, the works are arranged alphabetically by title. For the second and all additional entries, type three hyphens and a period in place of the author's name.

Dombrowski, Daniel A. *Babies and Beasts: The Argument from Marginal Cases.* U of Illinois P, 1997.

—. *The Philosophy of Vegetarianism.* U of Massachusetts P, 1984.

You can see a complete, properly formatted Works Cited list on the last pages of Ivan Snook's paper (see Chapter 15).

The remaining pages in this section show examples of MLA citation formats for different kinds of sources and provide explanations and illustrations as needed.

MLA Works Cited Citation Models

The *MLA Handbook* provides a set of guidelines to help you format your Works Cited list correctly. You can also visit the MLA's help center online at https://style.mla.org.

The following templates will help you compile the information you need for your MLA Works Cited list and format your entries correctly. Take note of the punctuation following each element, and use the same punctuation in your entries.

- **Author** can contain other identifying information, such as "editor," "translator," "actor," or "director."

- **Title of source** requires you to use italics and quotation marks correctly. Italicize the titles of books, magazines, newspapers, journals, websites, films, albums/CDs, and TV series. Use quotation marks for titles that are part of larger works. Specifically, place article titles, essay titles, episode titles, song titles, and titles of web posts in quotation marks. When a source is untitled, provide a generic description of it, neither italicized nor in quotation marks. When you document an e-mail, use its subject line as the title.

- **Container** is a generic term that is intended to capture any type of print or digital medium. A container may be a book, magazine, scholarly journal, TV series, website, comic book, any type of social media (Twitter, Facebook), and so on. One container can be nested in a larger container. For example, one blog may be part of a network of blogs. A scholarly journal (the first container) may be retrieved from a larger container—for example, an academic database such as Academic Search Complete (the second container). When a container is nested in a larger container, both containers should be documented, with a period separating the two containers.

- **Other contributors** are people who have played a role in the creation of the source. Other contributions include "adapted by," "directed by," "illustrated by," "performance by," and "introduction by."

- **Version** is the version you are citing (for example, the second edition of a work).

- **Number** refers to identifying numbers when a publication is too long to be printed in one book (for example, "vol. 2"). With periodicals, the number is the volume number and the issue number, separated by a comma.

- **Publication date** should be as specific as possible. Provide month, date, and year whenever possible. For books, usually the year alone is sufficient.

- **Location** usually refers to page numbers in a print work and to a URL or DOI in an online source. Whenever possible, DOIs are preferred to URLs because DOIs are more stable. Note that "http://" and "https://" are not included in URLs. If a publication date is not provided for a URL, complete the Works Cited entry by listing the date you accessed the URL.

Print Source

Author.	Herrera-Sobek, Maria.
Title of source.	"Border Aesthetics: The Politics of Mexican Immigration in Film and Art."
Title of container,	*Western Humanities Review,*
Other contributors,	
Version,	
Number,	vol. 60, no. 2,
Publisher,	
Publication date,	2006,
Location.	pp. 60-71.

Online Source

Author.	Gourlay, Alexander S.
Title of source.	"An Emergency Online Glossary of Terms, Names, and Concepts in Blake."
Title of container,	*The William Blake Archive,*
Other contributors,	

Version,

Number,

Publisher,

Publication date,

Location.   www.blakearchive.org/exist/blake/archive/glossary.xq?chunk.
                         id=glossary&toc.depth=1&toc.id=0. Accessed 14 Apr. 2018.

Print Articles in Scholarly Journals   All scholarly journal entries include both volume number and issue number, regardless of how the journal is paginated.

One author

Herrera-Sobek, Maria. "Border Aesthetics: The Politics of Mexican Immigration in Film and Art." *Western Humanities Review,* vol. 60, no. 2, 2006, pp. 60–71.

Two authors

Kwon, Ohbyung, and Yixing Wen. "An Empirical Study of the Factors Affecting Social Network Service Use." *Computers in Human Behavior,* vol. 26, no. 2, Mar. 2010, pp. 254–63.

Three or more authors

List the first author, and use "*et al.*" (meaning "and others") to replace all but the first author. Your Works Cited entry and the parenthetical citation should match. Do not italicize *et al.* in your Works Cited entry or in-text citation.

Pollay, Richard W., et al. "Separate, but Not Equal: Racial Segmentation in Cigarette Advertising." *Journal of Advertising,* vol. 21, no. 1, 1992, pp. 45–57.

Print Articles in Magazines and Newspapers   If no author is identified, begin the entry with the title or headline. Distinguish between news stories and editorials by putting the word "Editorial" after the title of an editorial and "Letter to the editor" when appropriate. If a magazine comes out weekly or biweekly, include the complete date ("27 Sept. 2013"). If it comes out monthly, then state the month only ("Sept. 2013"). Indicate reviews by clearly indicating the key identifying information of the work being reviewed.

Note: If the article begins on one page but continues in another part of the magazine or newspaper, add "+" to the number of the first page to indicate the nonsequential pages: pp. 45+.

Magazine article with named author

Snyder, Rachel L. "A Daughter of Cambodia Remembers: Loung Ung's Journey." *Ms.,* Aug.–Sept. 2001, pp. 62–67.

Magazine article without named author

"Sacred Geese." *The Economist,* 1 June 2013, pp. 24–25.

Review of book, film, or performance

Schwarz, Benjamin. "A Bit of Bunting: A New History of the British Empire Elevates Expediency to Principle." Review of *Ornamentalism: How the British Saw Their Empire,* by David Cannadine. *The Atlantic,* Nov. 2001, pp. 126–35.

Kaufman, Stanley. "Polishing a Gem." Review of *The Blue Angel,* directed by Josef von Sternberg. *New Republic,* 30 July 2001, pp. 28–29.

Lahr, John. "Nobody's Darling: Fascism and the Drama of Human Connection in *Ashes to Ashes.*" Review of *Ashes to Ashes,* by Harold Pinter, The Roundabout Theater Co. Gramercy Theater, New York. *The New Yorker,* 22 Feb. 1999, pp. 182–83.

Newspaper article

Page numbers in newspapers are typically indicated by a section letter or number as well as a page number. The "+" indicates that the article continues on one or more pages later in the newspaper.

Dougherty, Conor. "The Latest Urban Trend: Less Elbow Room." *The Wall Street Journal,* 4 June 2013, pp. A1+.

Newspaper editorial

"Dr. Frankenstein on the Hill." Editorial. *The New York Times,* 18 May 2002, p. A22.

Letter to the editor of a magazine or newspaper

Tomsovic, Kevin. Letter to the editor. *The New Yorker,* 13 July 1998, p. 7.

Print Books

One author

Pollan, Michael. *The Omnivore's Dilemma: A Natural History of Four Meals.* Penguin, 2006.

Two authors

Dombrowski, Daniel A., and Robert J. Deltete. *A Brief, Liberal, Catholic Defense of Abortion.* U of Illinois P, 2000.

Lewis, Robin, and Michael Dart. *The New Rules of Retail: Competing in the World's Toughest Marketplace.* Macmillan, 2010.

Three or more authors

List the first author, and use *"et al."* (meaning "and others") to replace all but the first author. Your Works Cited entry and the parenthetical citation should match. Do not italicize *et al.*

Belenky, Mary, et al. *Women's Ways of Knowing: The Development of Self, Voice, and Mind.* Basic Books, 1986.

Second, later, or revised edition

Montagu, Ashley. *Touching: The Human Significance of the Skin.* 3rd ed., Perennial, 1986.

In place of "3rd ed.," you can include abbreviations for other kinds of editions: "Rev. ed." (for "revised edition") or "Abr. ed." (for "abridged edition").

Republished book (for example, a paperback published after the original hardback edition or a modern edition of an older work)

Hill, Christopher. *The World Turned Upside Down: Radical Ideas During the English Revolution.* 1972. Penguin, 1991.

Wollstonecraft, Mary. *A Vindication of the Rights of Woman, with Strictures on Political and Moral Subjects.* 1792. Tuttle, 1995.

The date immediately following the title is the original publication date of the work.

Multivolume work

Churchill, Winston S. *A History of the English-Speaking Peoples.* Dodd, Mead, 1956–58. 4 vols.

Churchill, Winston S. *The Great Democracies.* Dodd, Mead, 1957. *A History of the English-Speaking Peoples,* vol. 4, Dodd, Mead, 1956–58. 4 vols.

Use the first method when you cite the whole work; use the second method when you cite one individually titled volume of the work.

Article in familiar reference work

"Mau Mau." *The New Encyclopaedia Britannica.* 15th ed., 2008, p. 808.

Article in less familiar reference work

Hirsch, E. D., et al. "Kyoto Protocol." *The New Dictionary of Cultural Literacy,* Houghton Mifflin, 2002, pp. 256-57.

Translation

De Beauvoir, Simone. *The Second Sex.* Translated by H. M. Parshley, 1949. Bantam, 1961.

Illustrated book

Jacques, Brian. *The Great Redwall Feast.* Illustrated by Christopher Denise, Philomel, 1996.

Graphic novel

Miyazaki, Hayao. *Nausicaa of the Valley of Wind.* Viz, 1995–97. 4 vols.

Corporate author (a commission, committee, or other group)

American Red Cross. *Standard First Aid.* Mosby Lifeline, 1993.

No author listed

The Complete Cartoons of The New Yorker. Black Dog & Leventhal, 2004.

Whole anthology

O'Connell, David F., and Charles N. Alexander, editors. *Self Recovery: Treating Addictions Using Transcendental Meditation and Maharishi Ayur-Veda.* Haworth, 1994.

Anthology article

Royer, Ann. "The Role of the Transcendental Meditation Technique in Promoting Smoking Cessation: A Longitudinal Study." *Self Recovery: Treating Addictions Using Transcendental Meditation and Maharishi Ayur-Veda,* edited by David F. O'Connell and Charles N. Alexander, Haworth, 1994, pp. 221–39.

Articles or Books from an Online Database

Article from online database

Matsbuba, Kyle. "Searching for Self and Relationships Online." *CyberPyschology and Behavior,* vol. 9, no. 3, June 2006. *Academic Search Complete,* doi:10.1089/cpb.2006.9.275.

To see where each element in this citation was found, see Figure 18.1, which shows the online database screen from which the Matsuba article was accessed. For articles in databases, you will need to use two containers. The first container is the scholarly journal and its identifying information. The second container is the academic database and its DOI or URL.

Article from a scholarly e-journal

Welch, John R., and Ramon Riley. "Reclaiming Land and Spirit in the Western Apache Homeland." *American Indian Quarterly,* vol. 25, no. 4, 2001, pp. 5–14. *JSTOR,* www.jstor.org/stable/1185999?seq=1#.

Figure 18.1 Article downloaded from an online database, with elements identified for an MLA-style citation

Matsuba, M. Kyle. "Searching for Self and Relationships Online." *CyberPsychology and Behavior*, vol. 9, no. 3, 2006, pp. 275–84. *Academic Search Complete*, doi:10.1089/cpb.2006.9.275.

Broadcast transcript from website

Conan, Neal. "Arab Media." *NPR Talk of the Nation*, guest appearance by Shibley Telhami, 2002, http://www.npr.org/programs/totn/transcripts/2004/may/040504.conan.html. Transcript.

"Transcript" at the end of the entry indicates a text (not audio) version.

E-book from online database

Hanley, Wayne. *The Genesis of Napoleonic Propaganda, 1796–1799.* Columbia UP, 2002. *Gutenberg-e*, www.gutenberg-e.org/haw01. Accessed 12 Apr. 2018.

Paine, Thomas. *Rights of Man.* 1791. *Bibliomania*, www.bibliomania.com/2/1/327/2414/frameset.html. Accessed 12 Apr. 2018.

Information about the original print version, including a translator if relevant and available, should be provided. Access date should be provided for any sources that are not dated.

E-book on Kindle, iPad, or other e-reader

According to MLA, a book is a book whether you read it in print or on an e-reader (such as a Kindle, Nook, or iPad).

Boyle, T. C. *When the Killing's Done.* Viking Penguin, 2011.

Other Internet Sources

Article on website

Saucedo, Robert. "A Bad Idea for a Movie." *theeagle.com,* 13 Mar. 2012, www.theeagle
.com/entertainment/a-bad-idea-for-a-movie/article_00454e59-7d77-5bc3-9e56
-8eec8ca488ee.html.

Date of access is not required because the article is dated (13 Mar. 2012). Break URLs onto a new line only after a piece of punctuation, such as a hyphen, slash, or period.

Entire website

Agatho. *Mysterious Matters,* 2007–18, mysteriousmatters.typepad.com. Accessed 14 Apr. 2018.

Documents within a website

Gourlay, Alexander S. "An Emergency Online Glossary of Terms, Names, and Concepts in Blake." *The William Blake Archive,* www.blakearchive.org/exist/blake/archive/
glossary.xq?chunk.id=glossary&toc.depth=1&toc.id=0. Accessed 14 Apr. 2018.

"Body Piercing. Ouch!" *Menstuff,* www.menstuff.org/issues/byissue/bodypiercing
.html. Accessed 12 Apr. 2018.

Article from a newspaper or newswire site

Brennan, Charlie. "Boulder Scientists over the Moon at Chance to Work on Lunar Dust." *Daily Camera Boulder News,* 3 Oct. 2015, www.dailycamera.com/news/
boulder/ci_28913824/boulder-scientists-over-moon-at-chance-work-lunar.

"Great Lakes: Rwanda Backed Dissident Troops in DRC-UN Panel." *IRIN,* 21 July 2004, www.irinnews.org/report/50763/great-lakes-rwanda-backed-dissident
-troops-drc-un-panel.

Broadcast transcript from a website

Woodruff, Judy, et al. "Experts Analyze Supreme Court Free Speech Rulings." *PBS NewsHour,* 25 June 2007, www.pbs.org/newshour/bb/law-jan-june07
-freespeech_06-25. Transcript.

"Transcript" at the end of the entry indicates a text (not audio) version.

Blog posting

Dyer, Bob, and Ella Barnes. "The 'Greening' of the Arctic." *Greenversations: The Official*
　　Blog of the U.S. Environmental Protection Agency, 7 Oct. 2008, blog.epa.gov/
　　blog/2008/10/07/the-greening-of-the-artic.

To see where each element of this citation comes from, refer to Figure 18.2.

Tweet

Identify a short untitled message, such as a tweet, by reproducing its full text,
without changes, in place of a title. Enclose the text in quotation marks, and
include not only date but also time.

@persiankiwi. "We have report of large street battles in east & west of Tehran now
　　- #Iranelection." *Twitter,* 23 June 2009, 11:15 a.m., twitter.com/persiankiwi/
　　status/2298106072.

Figure 18.2　An item published on the web, with elements identified for an MLA-style citation

Dyer, Bob, and Ella Barnes. "The 'Greening' of the Arctic." *Greenversations: The Official*
　　Blog of the U.S. Environmental Protection Agency, 7 Oct. 2008, blog.epa.gov/
　　blog/2008/10/07/the-greening-of-the-artic.

Podcast

"The Long and Winding Road: DNA Evidence for Human Migration." *Scientific American Science Talk,* 7 July 2008, www.scientificamerican.com/podcast/episode/fe166e6b-f88f-3538-2702d97555f62442.

Web video

"Immigration, World Poverty, and Gumballs." *YouTube,* 10 Sept. 2010, www.youtube.com/watch?v=LPjzfGChGlE.

Note that the date is the date on which the video was uploaded to YouTube.

Home page

Center for Africana Studies. Home page. School of Advanced International Study, Johns Hopkins University, krieger.jhu.edu/africana. Accessed 12 Apr. 2018.

E-mail

Start with the sender's name. The title is the subject line.

Rubino, Susanna. "Reasons for Unemployment." Received by Matthew Rollins, 12 Dec. 2018.

Miscellaneous Sources

Episode of television or radio program

"Lie Like a Rug." *NYPD Blue,* directed by Steven Bochco and David Milch, ABC, 6 Nov. 2001.

Ashbrook, Tom. "Turf Wars and the American Lawn." *On Point,* National Public Radio, 22 July 2008, onpoint.wbur.org/2008/07/22/turf-wars-and-american-lawns.

Film or video recording

Use the first format to cite a film on DVD. Use the second format (which uses a second container) if you watched the film via a rental service such as Netflix or Hulu.

Shakespeare in Love. Directed by John Madden, performances by Joseph Fiennes and Gwyneth Paltrow, screenplay by Marc Norman and Tom Stoppard. Universal Miramax, 1998.

Shakespeare in Love. Directed by John Madden, performances by Joseph Fiennes and Gwyneth Paltrow, screenplay by Marc Norman and Tom Stoppard. Universal Miramax, 1998. *Netflix,* 9 Mar. 2010.

Song on a CD

Dylan, Bob. "Rainy Day Women #12." *Blonde on Blonde,* Columbia, 1966.

The song title is "Rainy Day Women #12." The CD title is *Blonde on Blonde.* If you are citing the CD, use the following:

Dylan, Bob. Blonde on Blonde, Columbia, 1966.

Cartoon or advertisement (print)

Trudeau, Garry. "Doonesbury." *Seattle Times,* 19 Nov. 2001, p. B4.

Banana Republic. Advertisement. *Details,* Oct. 2001, p. 37.

Cartoon (online)

Sipress, David. "Anger Management Therapy." *The New Yorker,* 14 Mar. 2016, www
.newyorker.com/cartoons/daily-cartoon/monday-march-14th-anger-management.

Interview

Castellucci, Marion. Personal interview, 7 Oct. 2018.

Lecture, speech, or conference presentation

Sharples, Mike. "Authors of the Future." Conference of European Teachers of Academic Writing, 20 June 2001, University of Groningen, Groningen, Netherlands.

Government publications

When a work's publisher and author are separate organizations, give both names,
starting the entry with the author.

When an organization or institution is both publisher and author, begin the
entry with the title.

When an entry starts with a government agency as the author, begin with the
name of the largest entity, followed by a comma, followed by smaller organizational units within the agency, arranged from largest to smallest and separated
by commas.

New York State, Committee on State Prisons. *Investigation of the New York State Prisons.*
Arno Press, 1974.

Foreign Direct Investment, the Service Sector, and International Banking. Centre on Trans-
national Corporations, United Nations, 1987.

Great Britain, Ministry of Agriculture, Fisheries, and Food. *Our Countryside, the Future:
A Fair Deal for Rural England.* Her Majesty's Stationery Office, 2000.

MLA-Style Research Paper

As an illustration of a student research paper written in MLA style, see Ivan
Snook's argument about women in combat roles in Chapter 15.

APA Style

**18.3 Cite and document your sources using the style and format of the
American Psychological Association.**

In many respects, the APA style and the MLA style are similar, and their basic
logic is the same. In the APA system, the list where readers can find full bibliographic information is titled "References"; as in MLA format, it includes only the

sources cited in the body of the paper. The distinguishing features of APA citation style are summarized in Table 18.2 and highlighted in the following sections.

In-Text Citations in APA Style

A typical APA-style in-text citation contains three elements: (1) the last name of the author, (2) the date of the publication, and (3) the page number of the quoted or paraphrased passage. Table 18.2 identifies some typical variations and shows again the one-to-one connection between the in-text citation and the References list.

References List in APA Style

The APA References list at the end of a paper presents entries alphabetically by author's last name. If you cite more than one item for an author, repeat the author's name each time and arrange the items in chronological order, beginning with the earliest. In cases where two works by an author appeared in the same year, arrange

Table 18.2 In-Text Citations in APA Style

Type of Source	References Entry at End of Paper	In-Text Citation in Body of Paper
One author	Pollan, M. (2006). *The omnivore's dilemma: A natural history of four meals*. New York, NY: Penguin.	. . . (Pollan, 2006, p. 256). OR According to Pollan (2006), . . . (p. 256).
Two authors	Kwon, O., & Wen, Y. (2010). An empirical study of the factors affecting social network service use. *Computers in Human Behavior, 26*, 254–263. doi:10.1016 /j.chb.2009.04.011	. . . (Kwon & Wen, 2010, p. 262). OR Kwon and Wen (2010) claim that . . . (p. 262).
Three to seven authors	Pollay, R. W., Lee, J. S., & Carter-Whitney, D. (1992). Separate, but not equal: Racial segmentation in cigarette advertising. *Journal of Advertising, 21*(1), 45–57.	. . . race" (Pollay, Lee, & Carter-Whitney, 1992, p. 52). OR Pollay, Lee, and Carter-Whitney have argued that "advertisers . . . race" (1992, p. 52). *For subsequent citations, use Pollay et al. For a quotation, use the specific page number, not the whole range of pages.*
Author has more than one work in References list	Dombrowski, D. A. (1984). *The philosophy of vegetarianism*. Amherst: University of Massachusetts Press. Dombrowski, D. A. (1997). *Babies and beasts: The argument from marginal cases*. Urbana: University of Illinois Press.	. . . (Dombrowski, 1984, p. 207). . . . (Dombrowski, 1997, p. 328). OR Dombrowski (1984) claims that . . . (p. 207). According to Dombrowski (1997), . . . (p. 328).
Indirect citation of a source that you found in another source *You use a quotation from Peter Singer from a book by Dombrowski. Include Dombrowski, not Singer, in References.*	Dombrowski, D. A. (1997). *Babies and beasts: The argument from marginal cases*. Urbana: University of Illinois Press.	Animal rights activist Peter Singer argues that . . . (as cited in Dombrowski, 1997, p. 429). *Singer is used for the attributive tag, but the in-text citation is to Dombrowski.*

them in the list alphabetically by title, and then add a lowercase "a" or "b" (etc.) after the date so that you can distinguish between them in the in-text citations:

Smith, R. (1999a). *Body image in non-Western cultures, 1750–present*. London, England: Bonanza Press.

Smith, R. (1999b). Eating disorders reconsidered. *Journal of Appetite Studies, 45,* 295–300.

A formatted References list appears with the student paper in Chapter 13.

APA References Citation Models

Print Articles in Scholarly Journals

General Format for Print Article in Scholarly Journal

Author. (Year of Publication). Article title. *Journal Title, volume number*(issue number), page numbers. doi:xx.xxxx/x.xxxx.xx

If there is one, include the **DOI** (digital object identifier), a code that is uniquely assigned to many journal articles in numeric or URL form. Note the style for capitalizing article titles and for italicizing the volume number.

One author

Herrera-Sobek, M. (2006). Border aesthetics: The politics of Mexican immigration in film and art. *Western Humanities Review, 60,* 60–71. doi:10.1016/j.chb.2009.04.011

Two to seven authors

McElroy, B. W., & Lubich, B. H. (2013). Predictors of course outcomes: Early indicators of delay in online classrooms. *Distance Education, 34*(1). http://dx.doi.org/10.1080/01587919.2013.770433

When a source has more than seven authors, list the first six and the last one by name, separated by an ellipsis (. . .) to indicate the authors whose names have been omitted.

Scholarly journal that restarts page numbering with each issue

Pollay, R. W., Lee, J. S., & Carter-Whitney, D. (1992). Separate, but not equal: Racial segmentation in cigarette advertising. *Journal of Advertising, 21*(1), 45–57.

Note that the issue number and the parentheses are *not* italicized, but the volume number is.

Print Articles in Magazines and Newspapers

General Format for Print Article in Magazine or Newspaper

Author. (Year, Month Day). Article title. *Periodical Title, volume number,* page numbers.

If page numbers are discontinuous, identify every page, separating numbers with a comma.

Magazine article with named author

Hall, S. S. (2001, March 11). Prescription for profit. *The New York Times Magazine*, 40–45, 59, 91–92, 100.

Magazine article without named author

Sacred geese. (2013, June 1). *The Economist*, 24–25.

Review of book or film

Schwarz, B. (2001, November). A bit of bunting: A new history of the British empire elevates expediency to principle [Review of the book *Ornamentalism: How the British saw their empire*, by D. Cannadine]. *Atlantic Monthly, 288*, 126–135.

Kaufman, S. (2001, July 30). Polishing a gem [Review of the motion picture *The blue angel*]. *New Republic, 225*, 28–29.

Newspaper article

Dougherty, C. (2013, June 4). The latest urban trend: Less elbow room. *The Wall Street Journal*, pp. A1, A12.

Newspaper editorial

Nearing a climate legacy [Editorial]. (2014, June 3). *The New York Times*, p. A22.

Letter to the editor of a magazine or newspaper

Harvey, J. (2014, April 21). The lives of Paul de Man [Letter to the editor]. *The New Yorker*, 7.

Print Books

General Format for Print Books

Author. (Year of publication). *Book title: Subtitle.* City, State [abbreviated]: Name of Publisher.

Brumberg, J. J. (1997). *The body project: An intimate history of American girls.* New York, NY: Vintage.

If the publisher's name indicates the state in which it is located, list the city but omit the state.

Reid, H., & Taylor, B. (2010). *Recovering the commons: Democracy, place, and global justice.* Champaign: University of Illinois Press.

Second, later, or revised edition

Montagu, A. (1986). *Touching: The human significance of the skin* (3rd ed.). New York, NY: Perennial Press.

Republished book (for example, a paperback published after the original hardback edition or a modern edition of an older work)

Wollstonecraft, M. (1995). *A vindication of the rights of woman, with strictures on political and moral subjects*. Rutland, VT: Tuttle. (Original work published 1792)

The in-text citation should read: (Wollstonecraft, 1792/1995).

Multivolume work

Churchill, W. S. (1956–1958). *A history of the English-speaking peoples* (Vols. 1–4). New York, NY: Dodd, Mead.

This is the citation for all the volumes together. The in-text citation should read: (Churchill, 1956–1958).

Churchill, W. S. (1957). *A history of the English-speaking peoples: Vol. 4. The great democracies*. New York, NY: Dodd, Mead.

This is the citation for a specific volume. The in-text citation should read: (Churchill, 1957).

Article in reference work

Hirsch, E. D., Kett, J. F., & Trefil, J. (2002). Kyoto Protocol. In *The new dictionary of cultural literacy*. Boston, MA: Houghton Mifflin.

Translation

De Beauvoir, S. (1961). *The second sex* (H. M. Parshley, Trans.). New York, NY: Bantam Books. (Original work published 1949)
The in-text citation should read: (De Beauvoir, 1949/1961).

Corporate author (a commission, committee, or other group)

American Red Cross. (1993). *Standard first aid*. St. Louis, MO: Mosby Lifeline.

Anonymous author

Complete cartoons of The New Yorker. (2004). New York, NY: Penguin Books.

The in-text citation is (*Complete Cartoons*, 2004).

Whole anthology

O'Connell, D. F., & Alexander, C. N. (Eds.). (1994). *Self recovery: Treating addictions using transcendental meditation and Maharishi Ayur-Veda*. New York, NY: Haworth Press.

Anthology article

Royer, A. (1994). The role of the transcendental meditation technique in promoting smoking cessation: A longitudinal study. In D. F. O'Connell & C. N. Alexander (Eds.), *Self recovery: Treating addictions using transcendental meditation and Maharishi Ayur-Veda* (pp. 221–239). New York, NY: Haworth Press.

Articles or Books from an Online Database

Article from database with digital object identifier (DOI)

Scharrer, E., Daniel, K. D., Lin, K.-M., & Liu, Z. (2006). Working hard or hardly
working? Gender, humor, and the performance of domestic chores in television commercials. *Mass Communication and Society, 9*(2), 215–238. doi:10.1207/
s15327825mcs0902_5

Omit the database name. If an article or other document has been assigned a
digital object identifier (DOI), include the DOI at the end. Do not put a period
after the DOI.

Article from database without DOI

Highland, R. A., & Dabney, D. A. (2009). Using Adlerian theory to shed light on drug
dealer motivations. *Applied Psychology in Criminal Justice, 5*(2), 109–138. Retrieved
from http://www.apcj.org

Omit the database name. Instead, use a search engine to locate the publication's home page, and cite that URL. If you need to break a URL at the end
of a line, do not use a hyphen. Instead, break it *before* a punctuation mark or
after http://.

Other Internet Sources

General Format for Web Documents

Author, editor, director, narrator, performer, compiler, or producer of the work, if available. (Year, Month Day of posting). *Title of web document, italicized as indicated below.*
Retrieved from Name of website if different from author or title: URL of home page

Barrett, J. (2007, January 17). *MySpace is a natural monopoly.* Retrieved from ECommerce
Times website: http://www.ecommercetimes.com

Marks, J. (n.d.). "Overview: Letter from the president." Retrieved June 3, 2014, from
the Search for Common Ground website: http://www.sfcg.org

Entire website

BlogPulse. (n.d.). Retrieved September 3, 2014, from the Intelliseek website: http://
www.intelliseek.com

Article from a newspaper site

Bounds, A. (2007, June 26). Thinking like scientists. *Daily Camera* [Boulder]. Retrieved
from http://www.dailycamera.com

Article from a scholarly e-journal

Welch, J. R., & Riley, R. (2001). Reclaiming land and spirit in the western Apache homeland. *American Indian Quarterly, 25,* 5–14. Retrieved from http://muse.jhu.edu/
journals/american_indian_quarterly

Reference material

Cicada. (2004). In *Encyclopaedia Britannica*. Retrieved from http://www.britannica.com

E-book

Hoffman, F. W. (1981). *The literature of rock: 1954–1978*. Retrieved from http://www
.netlibrary.com

E-mail, interviews, and personal correspondence
Cite personal correspondence in the body of your text, but not in the References
list: "Daffinrud (personal communication, December 12, 2018) claims that. . . . "

Blog posting

Goddard, A. L. (2014, May 31). Maya Angelou's words were a comfort to abducted aid
worker [Blog post]. Retrieved from annegoddard.tumblr.com

Social media posting

Storm King Art Center. (2013, May 30). Rattlesnake figure (aluminum) by Thomas
Houseago [Facebook update]. Retrieved from http://www.facebook.com/
StormKingArtCenter

Web video

Beck, R. (2006, November 2). *Immigration gumballs* [Video file]. Retrieved from http://
www.youtube.com/watch?v=n7WJeqxuOfQ
Note that the date is the day on which the video was uploaded.

Podcast

Funke, E. (Host). (2007, June 26). ArtScene [Audio podcast]. *National Public Radio*.
Retrieved from http://www.npr.org

Miscellaneous Sources

Television program

Bochco, S., & Milch, D. (Directors). (2001, November 6). Lie like a rug [Television series
episode]. In *NYPD blue*. New York, NY: American Broadcasting Company.

Film

Madden, J. (Director). (1998). *Shakespeare in love* [Motion picture]. United States: Universal Miramax.

Sound recording

Dylan, B. (1966). Rainy day women #12. On *Blonde on blonde* [Record]. New York, NY:
Columbia.

Government publications

U.S. Department of Health and Human Services. (2012). *Preventing tobacco use among youth and young adults: A report of the Surgeon General.* Retrieved from http://www.surgeongeneral.gov/library/reports/preventing-youth-tobacco-use/index.html#Full Report

APA-Style Research Paper

An example of a paper in APA style is shown at the end of Chapter 13.

Conclusion

This chapter has shown you the nuts and bolts of citing and documenting sources in both the MLA and APA styles. It has explained the logic of parenthetical citation systems, showing you how to match sources cited in your text with those in your concluding bibliography. It has also shown you the documentation formats for a wide range of sources in both MLA and APA styles.

Appendix
Informal Fallacies

This appendix introduces you to **informal fallacies**, which form a compendium of ways that arguments can go wrong. Informal fallacies (as opposed to *formal fallacies*) serve as warning signs alerting readers to possibly illegitimate arguments. Whereas formal logic is a kind of mathematics concerned with logical certainty, informal logic is concerned with probable persuasiveness within everyday arguments. Certain argumentative moves—unless we recognize them as informal fallacies—can make flawed arguments seem deceptively persuasive, especially to unwary audiences. In this appendix, we first look at the difference between formal and informal logic. We then provide an overview of the most commonly encountered informal fallacies.

The Difference Between Formal and Informal Logic

In real-world disagreements, we seldom encounter arguments that are conclusive. Rather, arguments are, to various degrees, persuasive or nonpersuasive. In the pure world of formal logic, however, it is possible to have completely conclusive arguments. Logicians first look for the form of an argument. If the form is valid, then the conclusion is logically certain. They next ask whether the premises are true. If the premises are true, then the conclusion is necessarily true. For example, here is a validly constructed Aristotelean syllogism with a true major premise, a true minor premise, and a necessarily true conclusion:

Valid Syllogism with True Premises

Major premise: All ducks are feathered animals.

Minor premise: Quacko is a duck.

Conclusion: Therefore Quacko is a feathered animal.

This syllogism is said to be valid because it follows a correct form. Moreover, because both premises are true, then the conclusion is guaranteed to be true. However, if the syllogism follows an incorrect form (and is therefore invalid), we can't determine whether the conclusion is true.

Invalid Syllogism with True Premises

Major premise: All ducks are feathered animals.

Minor premise: Clucko is a feathered animal.

Conclusion: Therefore Clucko is a duck.

In the valid syllogism, the conclusion is guaranteed (Quacko is a feathered animal) because the minor premise states that Quacko is a duck and the major premise places ducks within the larger class of feathered animals. But in the invalid syllogism, the conclusion is not guaranteed. We know that Clucko is a feathered animal, but we can't know whether he is a duck. He may be a duck, but he may also be a buzzard or a chicken. The invalid syllogism thus commits a *formal fallacy* in that its form doesn't guarantee the truth of its conclusion even if the initial premises are true.

From the perspective of real-world argumentation, formal logic isn't very helpful because it focuses mostly on the form of the argument and not on its content. For example, the following argument is logically valid even though the premises and conclusion are obviously untrue:

Valid Syllogism with Untrue Premises

Major premise: The blood of insects can be used to lubricate lawn-mower engines.

Minor premise: Vampires are insects.

Conclusion: Therefore the blood of vampires can be used to lubricate lawn-mower engines.

Even though this syllogism meets the formal requirements for validity, its argument is ludicrous.

In this appendix, therefore, we are concerned with informal rather than formal fallacies because informal fallacies are embedded within real-world arguments addressing contestable issues of truth and value. Disputants argue about issues because these issues can't be resolved with mathematical certainty; any contestable claim always leaves room for doubt and alternative points of view. Disputants can create only more or less persuasive arguments, never conclusive arguments.

An Overview of Informal Fallacies

The study of informal fallacies is a murky business. Informal fallacies identify some kind of disconnect between evidence and reason or between reason and claim, but they do not contain formal flaws that make an argument's conclusions illegitimate. In other words, finding an informal fallacy in an argument does not necessarily make the argument wrong, although it might make it weaker. Detecting the presence of an informal fallacy often depends on the rhetorical situation, particularly the audience. Sometimes we may even disagree whether a fallacy is present in a given argument. It's much easier, for example, to find informal fallacies in a hostile argument than in a friendly one simply because we are likely to expand or narrow the fallacy's descriptors according to our own biases. In evaluating arguments with informal fallacies, we usually find that arguments are "more or less" fallacious, and determining the degree of fallaciousness is a matter of judgment.

In arranging the fallacies, we have, for convenience, put them into three categories derived from classical rhetoric: *pathos*, *ethos*, and *logos*. Fallacies of *pathos* rest on flaws in the way an argument appeals to the audience's emotions and values. Fallacies of *ethos* rest on flaws in the way the argument appeals to the character of opponents or of sources and witnesses within an argument. Fallacies of *logos* rest on flaws in the relationship among statements in an argument.

Fallacies of *Pathos*

ARGUMENT TO THE PEOPLE (APPEALING TO STIRRING SYMBOLS)   This is perhaps the most generic example of a *pathos* fallacy. Arguments to the people appeal to the fundamental beliefs, biases, and prejudices of the audience in order to sway opinion through a feeling of solidarity among those of the group. Thus a "Support Our Troops" bumper sticker, often including the American flag, creates an initial feeling of solidarity among almost all citizens. (Who doesn't support our troops?) But the car owner may have the deeper intention of implying "support our president" or "support the war in _____." The stirring symbol of the flag and the desire shared by most people to support our troops is used fallaciously to urge support of a particular political act or political figure. Arguments to the people often use visual rhetoric, as in the soaring eagle used in Walmart corporate ads or images of happy families in advertisements for consumer products.

APPEAL TO IGNORANCE   This fallacy tries to persuade an audience that a claim is true because it hasn't been proven false or that a claim is false because it hasn't been proven true: "Jones must have used steroids to get those bulging biceps because he can't prove that he hasn't used steroids." Appeals to ignorance are particularly common in the murky field of pseudoscience: "UFOs (ghosts, abominable snowmen) do exist because science hasn't proved that they don't exist." Sometimes, however, it is hard to draw a line between a fallacious appeal to ignorance and a legitimate appeal to precaution: "Genetically modified organisms may be dangerous to our health because science hasn't proved that they are safe."

APPEAL TO POPULARITY—BANDWAGON   To board the bandwagon means (to use a more contemporary metaphor) to board the bus or train of what's popular. Appeals to popularity are fallacious because the popularity of something is irrelevant to its actual merits: "Living together before marriage is the right thing to do because most couples are now doing it." Bandwagon appeals are common in advertising where the claim that a product is popular substitutes for evidence of the product's excellence. There are times, however, when popularity may indeed be relevant: "Global warming is probably caused by human activity because a preponderance of scientists now hold this position." (Here we assume that scientists haven't simply climbed on a bandwagon but instead have formed their opinions based on research data and well-vetted, peer-reviewed papers.)

APPEAL TO PITY   Here the arguer appeals to the audience's sympathetic feelings in order to support a claim that should be decided on more relevant or objective grounds: "Honorable judge, I should not be fined $200 for speeding because I was distraught from hearing news of my brother's illness and was rushing to see him in the hospital." Here the argument is fallacious because the arguer's reason, while evoking sympathy, is not a relevant justification for speeding (as it might have been, for instance, if the arguer had been rushing an injured person to the emergency room). In many cases, however, an arguer can legitimately appeal to pity, as in the case of fund-raising for victims of a tsunami or other disaster.

RED HERRING   This fallacy's funny name derives from the practice of using a red herring (a highly odiferous fish) to throw dogs off a scent that they are supposed to be tracking. It refers to the practice of throwing an audience off track by raising an unrelated or irrelevant point. "Debating a gas tax increase is valuable, but I really think there should be an overhaul of the tax code." Here the arguer, apparently uncomfortable with the gas-tax issue, diverts the conversation to the emotionally charged issue of a revised tax code. A conversant who noted how the argument has gotten off track might say, "Stop talking, everyone. The tax code question is a red herring; let's get back to the topic of a gas tax increase."

Fallacies of *Ethos*

APPEAL TO FALSE AUTHORITY   Arguers appeal to false authority when they use famous people (often movie stars or other celebrities) to testify on issues about which these persons have no special competence: "Joe Quarterback says Gooey Oil keeps his old tractor running sharp; therefore, Gooey Oil is a good oil." Real evidence about the quality of Gooey Oil would include technical data about the product rather than testimony from an actor or hired celebrity. However, the distinction between a false authority and a legitimate authority can become blurred. For example, in the early years of advertising for drugs that treat erectile dysfunction, Viagra hired former senator and presidential hopeful Bob Dole to help market the drug. (You can see his commercials on YouTube.) As a famous person rather than a doctor, Dole would seem to be a false authority. But Dole was also widely known to have survived prostate cancer, and he may well have used Viagra. To the extent a person is an expert in a field, he or she is no longer a false authority.

AD HOMINEM   Literally, *ad hominem* means "to the person." An *ad hominem* argument is directed at the character of an opponent rather than at the quality of the opponent's reasoning. Ideally, arguments are supposed to be *ad rem* ("to the thing"), that is, addressed to the specifics of the case itself. Thus an *ad rem* critique of a politician would focus on her voting record, the consistency and cogency of her public statements, her responsiveness to constituents, and so forth. An *ad hominem* argument would shift attention from her record to features of her personality, life circumstances, or the company she keeps: "Senator Sweetwater's views on the gas tax should be discounted because her husband works for a huge oil company" or "Senator Sweetwater supports tax cuts for the wealthy because she is very wealthy herself and stands to gain." But not all *ad hominem* arguments are *ad hominem* fallacies. For example, when questioning expert witnesses who give damaging testimony, lawyers often make an issue of their honesty, credibility, or personal investment in an outcome.

POISONING THE WELL   This fallacy is closely related to *ad hominem*. Arguers poison the well when they discredit an opponent or an opposing view in advance: "Before I yield the floor to the next speaker, I must remind you that her argument will hurt working people."

STRAW MAN   The straw man fallacy occurs when you oversimplify an opponent's argument to make it easier to refute or ridicule. Rather than summarizing an opposing view fairly and completely, you make up the argument you wish your opponent had made because it is so much easier to knock over, like knocking over a straw man or scarecrow in a corn field. See Chapter 6 for an example of a straw man argument.

Fallacies of *Logos*

HASTY GENERALIZATION   This fallacy occurs when someone makes a broad generalization based on too little evidence. Generally, persuasive evidence needs to meet the STAR criteria (sufficiency, typicality, accuracy, and relevance) discussed in Chapter 4. But what constitutes a sufficient amount of evidence? The generally accepted standards of sufficiency in any given field are difficult to determine. The Food and Drug Administration (FDA), for example, generally requires extensive testing of a drug before certifying it as "safe." However, if people are harmed by a new drug, their lawyers often accuse the FDA of having made a hasty generalization—that is, of concluding that a drug is safe without going through enough trials. At the same time, patients eager to have access to a new drug may lobby the FDA to quit "dragging its feet" and allow the drug to be released to the market. Hence, the point at which a hasty generalization passes into the realm of a prudent generalization is nearly always uncertain and contested.

PART FOR THE WHOLE   Sometimes called by its Latin name *pars pro toto*, this fallacy is closely related to hasty generalization. In this fallacy, arguers pick out a part of the whole or a sample of the whole (often not a typical or representative part or sample) and then claim that what is true of the part is true for the whole. If, say, individuals wanted to get rid of the National Endowment for the Arts (NEA), they might focus on several controversial programs funded by the NEA and use them as justification for wiping out all NEA programs. The flip side of this fallacy occurs when an arguer picks only the best examples to make a case and conveniently forgets about examples that may weaken the case.

POST HOC, ERGO PROPTER HOC   The Latin name of this fallacy means "after this, therefore because of this." The fallacy occurs when a sequential relationship is mistaken for a causal relationship. (See Chapter 13, where we discuss this fallacy in more depth.) For example, you may be guilty of this fallacy if you say, "Cramming for a test really helps because last week I crammed for my psychology test and I got an A on it." When two events occur frequently in conjunction with each other, we've got a good case for a causal relationship. But until we can show how one causes the other and until we have ruled out other causes, we cannot be certain that a causal relationship is occurring. For example, the A on your psych test may have been caused by something other than your cramming. Maybe the exam was easier, or perhaps you were luckier or more mentally alert. It is often difficult to tell when a *post hoc* fallacy occurs. When the New York City police department changed its policing tactics in the early 1990s, the crime rate plummeted. But did the new policing tactics cause the drop in the crime rate? Many experts suggested other causes, including economist Steven Levitt, who attributes the declining crime rate to the legalization of abortion in the 1970s (and hence to a decline in unwanted children who might grow up to be criminals).

BEGGING THE QUESTION—CIRCULAR REASONING   Arguers beg the question when they provide a reason that simply restates the claim in different words. Here is an example: "Abortion is murder because it is the intentional taking of the life of a human being." Because "murder" is defined as "the intentional taking of the life of a human being," the argument is circular. It is tantamount to saying, "Abortion is murder because it is murder." In the abortion debate, the crucial issue is whether a fetus is a "human being" in the legal sense. So in this case the arguer has fallaciously begged the question by assuming from the start that the fetus is a legal human being. The argument is similar to saying, "That person is obese because he is too fat."

FALSE DILEMMA—EITHER/OR This fallacy occurs when an arguer oversimplifies a complex issue so that only two choices appear possible. Often one of the choices is made to seem unacceptable, so the only remaining option is the other choice. "It's my way or the highway" is a typical example of a false dilemma. Here is a more subtle one: "Either we allow embryonic stem cell research, or we condemn people with diabetes, Parkinson's disease, or spinal injuries to a life without a cure." Clearly, there may be other options, including other approaches to curing these diseases. A good historical example of the false dilemma fallacy is found in sociologist Kai Erikson's analysis of President Truman's decision to drop the A-bomb on Hiroshima. His analysis suggests that the Truman administration prematurely reduced numerous options to just two: either drop the bomb on a major city, or sustain unacceptable losses in a land invasion of Japan. Erikson, however, shows there were other alternatives.

SLIPPERY SLOPE The slippery slope fallacy is based on the fear that once we put a foot on a slippery slope heading in the wrong direction, we're doomed to slide right out of sight. The controlling metaphor is of a slick mountainside without places to hold on rather than of a staircase with numerous stopping places. Slippery-slope arguments are frequently encountered when individuals request exceptions to bureaucratic rules: "Look, Blotnik, no one feels worse about your injury and your need for knee surgery than I do. But I still can't let you turn this paper in late. If I were to let you do it, then I'd have to let everyone turn in papers late." Slippery-slope arguments can be very persuasive—and often rightfully so because every slippery-slope argument isn't necessarily a slippery-slope fallacy. Some slopes really are slippery. The slippery slope becomes a fallacy when we forget that we can often dig a foothold into the slope and stop. For example, we can define procedures for exceptions to rules so that Blotnik can turn in his paper late without allowing everyone to turn in a paper late.

FALSE ANALOGY In Chapter 12 on definition and resemblance arguments, we explained that no analogy is perfect. Any two things being compared are similar in some ways and different in other ways. Whether an analogy is persuasive or false often depends on the audience's initial degree of skepticism. For example, gun-rights advocates opposed to gun control may find the following argument persuasive: "Banning guns because gun accidents can kill people is like banning cars because car accidents can kill people." Supporters of gun control are likely to call this argument a false analogy by pointing out dissimilarities between cars and guns. (For example, they might say that banning cars would be far more disruptive to our society than banning guns would be. Or they might create their own counter-analogy: "But we do ban certain kinds of cars (those that produce too much pollution); therefore we should ban certain kinds of guns that produce too many deaths (certain kinds of handguns or automatic weapons)." Just when a persuasive analogy turns into a false analogy is difficult to say.

NON SEQUITUR The name of this fallacy means "it does not follow." *Non sequitur* is a catchall term for any claim that doesn't follow from its premises or is supported by irrelevant premises. Sometimes the arguer seems to make an inexplicably illogical leap: "Genetically modified foods should be outlawed because they are not natural." (Should anything that is not natural be outlawed? In what way are genetically modified foods not natural?) At other times there may be a gap in the chain of reasons: "Violent video games have some social value because the army uses them for recruiting." (There may be an important idea emerging here, but too many logical steps are missing.) At still other times an arguer may support a claim with irrelevant reasons: "I should not receive a C in this course because I currently have a 3.8 GPA." In effect, almost any fallacy could be called a *non sequitur* because fallacious reasoning always indicates some kind of disconnect between the reasons and the claim.

LOADED LABEL OR DEFINITION Sometimes arguers try to influence their audience's view of something by creating a loaded label or definition. For example, people who oppose the "estate tax" (which calls to mind rich people with estates) have relabeled it the "death tax" to give it a negative connotation without any markers of class or wealth. Or to take another example, proponents of organic foods might create definitions like the following: "Organic foods are safe and healthy foods grown without any pesticides, herbicides, or other unhealthy additives." "Safe" and "healthy" are evaluative terms used fallaciously in what purports to be a definition. The intended implication is that nonorganic foods are neither safe nor healthy.

For Writing and Discussion

Persuasive or Fallacious?

Individual task:

For each of the following arguments, explain the extent to which you find the argument persuasive or fallacious. If any argument seems doomed because of one or more of the fallacies discussed in this appendix, identify the relevant fallacies and explain how they render the argument nonpersuasive. Remember that it is often hard to determine the exact point where fallacious reasoning begins to kick in, especially when you consider different kinds of audiences. So, in each case, consider also variations in audience. For which audiences would any particular argument appear potentially fallacious? Which audiences would be more likely to consider the argument persuasive?

1. Either we invest more money in improving our mental health care system or our society will experience more frequent outbursts of violence in mass shootings.
2. Smoking must cause lung cancer because a much higher percentage of smokers get lung cancer than do nonsmokers.
3. Smoking does not cause cancer because my grandfather smoked two packs per day for fifty years and died in his sleep at age ninety.
4. Society has an obligation to provide housing for the homeless because people without adequate shelter have a right to the resources of the community.
5. Based on my observations of the two renters in our neighborhood, I have concluded that people who own their own homes take better care of them than those who rent. [This arguer provided detailed evidence about the house-caring practices of the two renters and of the homeowners in the neighborhood.]
6. Intelligent design must qualify as a scientific theory because hundreds of scientists endorse it.

(continued)

7. If we pass legislation requiring mandatory registration of handguns, we'll open the door to eventual confiscation of hunting rifles.
8. Those who support gun control are wrong because they believe that no one should have the right to defend himself or herself in any situation.
9. The United States is now suffering from an epidemic of opioid abuse. Therefore, doctors should drastically reduce their prescription of painkillers.
10. We should question Mr. Robin Albertson's endorsement of charter schools because he is one of the major shareholders in a corporation that develops curricula used in these schools.

Group task:
Share your analyses with classmates.

PART SIX
An Anthology of Arguments

This photo shows a trainer and a dog visiting a nursing home. Such animal-assisted therapy has gained popularity as a treatment for depression and loneliness, especially in long-term care facilities for elderly people who have been removed from their familiar living situations, possessions, and pets of their own. Some studies in psychology and nursing have shown that regular contact with animals has as many mental and physical benefits as contact with people. However, this helpful intervention is in danger of being reduced or eliminated by potential cuts in medical insurance and Medicaid. What appeals does this photo make, and what claim might it support about animal-assisted therapy?

Overview of the Anthology

Part Six, an anthology of engaging arguments addressing a variety of contemporary and classic issues, invites you to apply your rhetorical understanding of argument as inquiry and persuasion. In reading and analyzing these arguments, you will encounter multiple stakeholders' perspectives and practice your new skills of conducting inquiry, examining the construction and rhetorical effectiveness of arguments, and joining argumentative conversations. You can particularly apply the following skills:

- From Chapter 7, writing a rhetorical analysis of an argument
- From Chapter 8, summarizing an argument and using dialectic thinking to place it in conversation with two or more arguments with alternative points of view
- From Chapter 9, analyzing and creating your own multimodal arguments using visual components
- From Chapters 11-15, analyzing arguments using insights from the claim types

Choices for a Sustainable World

The 2017 Global Change Research Program's *Climate Science Special Report*, which is the combined work of thirteen U.S. federal agencies, concludes that human activities are primarily responsible for climate change and that the world is already feeling its effects, from rising global temperatures to more extreme weather events. Much of the public debate has now shifted from arguing about causes of global warming to arguing about potential consequences and solutions. The dominant question is no longer whether climate change is happening, but rather what actions we should take to mitigate its impact. What choices should we make as a society? What actions should we expect of our government? What life choices should we make as ethical members of society when we consider how our individual actions affect both our close neighbors and those who live around the globe?

On a national scale, the idea of a carbon tax to curb or even reverse the damage of carbon pollution has been presented by conservatives and liberals alike, yet the subject is still controversial. How should such a tax be levied? What should be done with the proceeds? Should it be returned to the American people via a dividend, or should it be reinvested in energy-efficient technologies and research? Will it incentivize a reduction in the use of fossil fuels?

At the community level, concerns over plastic's contribution to pollution (from microplastics in our waterways, soil, animal life, and human bodies to massive contamination such as the Great Pacific Garbage Patch) have led many communities to consider reducing or even banning the use of plastic bags. Yet concerns persist about what might take the place of those bags and whether the ban would have any impact on the environment.

Finally, what can an individual, ethical consumer and citizen do? Is it enough to make more environmentally sound decisions in our everyday lives? What must be sacrificed, and what concessions must we make as we continue to live on this planet? The readings in this unit invite you into the debates sparked by these increasingly urgent questions.

Curbing Climate Change Has a Dollar Value — Here's How and Why We Measure It

JOSEPH ALDY

Joseph Aldy is Associate Professor of Public Policy at Harvard University, specializing in climate change policy and energy policy. He previously served as Special Assistant to the President for Energy and Environment under President Barack Obama. This essay was posted on March 12, 2017, on The Conversation, *an open-access site for academic and research news and commentary.*

President Trump is expected to issue an executive order soon to reverse Obama-era rules to cut carbon pollution, including a moratorium on leasing public lands for coal mining and a plan to reduce carbon emissions from power plants.

Trump and his appointees argue that these steps will bring coal miners' jobs back (although coal industry job losses reflect competition from cheap natural gas, not regulations that have yet to take effect). But they ignore the fact that mitigating climate change will produce large economic gains.

While burning fossil fuels produces benefits, such as powering the electric grid and fueling cars, it also generates widespread costs to society—including damages from climate change that affect people around the world now and in the future. Public policies that reduce carbon pollution deliver benefits by avoiding these damages.

Since the Reagan administration, federal agencies have been required to enact only regulations whose potential benefits to society justify or outweigh their potential costs. To quantify benefits from acting to curb climate change, the U.S. government developed a formal measure in 2009 of the value of reducing carbon pollution, which is referred to as the social cost of carbon, or SCC. Currently, federal agencies use an SCC figure of about US\$40 per ton in today's dollars.

Now the Trump administration and critics in Congress may reduce this figure or even stop using it. EPA Administrator Scott Pruitt's recent comment that carbon dioxide is not "a primary contributor" to climate change suggests that Pruitt may challenge the agency's 2009 finding that carbon emissions are pollutants and threaten human health.

As an economist for the White House, I was a member of the working group that developed the first government-wide SCC estimate. We can always improve our processes for estimating and using the SCC, but getting rid of it would be a mistake. A well-functioning democracy needs transparency about the economic benefits of investments driven by public policy—as well as the benefits we give up when we walk away from making these investments.

The value of avoiding hurricanes and wildfires

Scientists widely agree that carbon dioxide emissions, primarily from burning fossil fuels, pose significant risks to Earth's climate. Intuitively, it makes sense that reducing carbon emissions benefits society by reducing risks of flooding, wildfires, storms and other impacts associated with severe climate change.

We can estimate the benefits of many goods and services, from pop music to recreation, from the prices people pay for them in markets. But valuing environmental benefits is not so simple. Americans can't go to the store and buy a stable climate.

Carbon pollution drives global warming that causes many different impacts on the natural and built environment and human health. Because carbon emissions have such broad and diverse impacts, scholars have developed models to characterize the economic benefits (or costs) of reducing them.

10   Current U.S. government practice draws from three peer-reviewed integrated assessment models. An integrated assessment model represents a chain of events, starting with economic activities that involve fossil fuel combustion. This generates carbon emissions, which contribute to climate change.

And climate change causes outcomes that can be measured in monetary terms. For example, rising carbon pollution will increase the likelihood of lower agricultural yields, threaten public health through heat stress, and damage infrastructure through floods and intense storms.

Thousands of scenarios

The social cost of carbon represents the damages of one ton of carbon dioxide emitted into the air. To estimate it, economists run models that forecast varying levels of carbon dioxide emissions. They can then model and compare two forecasts—one with slightly higher emissions than the other. The difference in total climate change damages represents the social cost of carbon.

Carbon pollution can remain in the atmosphere for up to 200 years, so these models are run over a century or more in order to account for long-term damages that carbon emissions impose on society.

SCC estimates are based on chains of events that include many uncertainties—for example, how many tons of carbon will be emitted in a given year, the amount of warming that will result, and how severely this warming will exacerbate risks like floods and heat waves. Since we cannot predict any single scenario with certainty, the U.S. government has modeled hundreds of thousands of different scenarios to produce its SCC estimates.

15   Some model scenarios, based on admittedly extreme assumptions, produce negative SCC estimates—that is, they find that carbon pollution is good for the planet. But the vast majority of scenarios show that carbon pollution is bad for the planet, and that on average, every ton of carbon dioxide emitted into the atmosphere imposes damages equal to about $40 in today's dollars.

Balancing costs and benefits of regulations

The federal government began calculating a social cost of carbon after the U.S. Court of Appeals for the Ninth Circuit ruled in 2007 that the Department of Transportation had to account for climate benefits from its regulations to improve automobile fuel economy. Environmental groups and a dozen states challenged the regulations, in part because the Bush administration had valued the benefits of cutting carbon dioxide emissions at zero.

In response, the Obama administration created a working group in 2009 with officials from 12 agencies to develop the federal government's first official SCC estimate. Our initial figure of $25 for 2010 was updated in 2013, 2015, and 2016, reflecting updates in the underlying models.

Agencies have used these estimates in benefit-cost analyses for scores of federal regulations, including the Environmental Protection Agency's Clean Power Plan, the Department of Transportation's medium and heavy-duty vehicle fuel economy standards, and the Department of Energy's minimum efficiency standard for refrigerators and freezers. Some of these studies were required only by executive order, but others were required by law. Unless the authorizing statutes are amended, the Trump administration will have to produce analyses accounting for carbon pollution reduction benefits if it wants to issue new regulations that can withstand legal challenges.

The Trump administration could continue to use SCC estimates in regulatory evaluations, but water them down. For example, some scholars have called for focusing only on domestic benefits—as opposed to total global benefits—of reducing carbon pollution in the United States. Emitting a ton of carbon imposes damages in the United States and around the world, just as a ton emitted in Beijing imposes damages on the United States and other countries around the world. Considering only the domestic impacts of carbon pollution could lower the SCC by three-quarters.

But if the United States ignores the benefits of reducing carbon pollution that other countries enjoy, then those other countries may follow suit and consider only how cutting emissions will benefit them internally. This approach ignores the strategic value that serves as the primary motivation for countries to work together to combat climate change. The world would achieve much greater emissions reductions and greater net economic benefits if countries implement policies based on the global social cost of carbon instead of a domestic-only SCC. 20

As climate change science and economics continue to evolve, our tools for estimating benefits from reducing carbon pollution will need to evolve and improve. In January the National Academies of Sciences published a report that lays out an extensive research agenda for improving the estimation and use of the social cost of carbon.

The federal government has used benefit-cost analysis to calculate society's bottom line from regulations for decades. So far, the Trump administration appears to be focused solely on costs—an approach that maximizes the corporate bottom line, but leaves the public out of the equation.

The Conservative Case for a Carbon Tax and Dividends

JAMES A. BAKER

James A. Baker served as Secretary of State under President George H. W. Bush. This column, which appeared in the Dallas Morning News *on February 15, 2017, is excerpted from a policy proposal by the Climate Leadership Council, a group composed of corporations and conservatives who have served in past Republican administrations.*

Mounting evidence of climate change is growing too strong to ignore. While the extent to which climate change is due to man-made causes can be questioned, the risks associated with future warming are too big and should be hedged. At least we need an insurance policy.

For too long, many Republicans have looked the other way, forfeiting the policy initiative to those who favor growth-inhibiting command-and-control regulations, and fostering a needless climate divide between the GOP and the scientific, business, military, religious, civic, and international mainstream. Now that the Republican Party controls the White House and Congress, it has the opportunity and responsibility to promote a climate plan that showcases the full power of enduring conservative convictions.

Any climate solution should be based on sound economic analysis and embody the principles of free markets and limited government. As this paper argues, such a plan could strengthen our economy, benefit working-class Americans, reduce regulations, protect our natural heritage, and consolidate a new era of Republican leadership. These benefits accrue regardless of one's views on climate science.

The four pillars of a carbon dividends plan

1. **The first pillar is a gradually increasing tax on carbon dioxide emissions** to be implemented at the refinery or the first point where fossil fuels enter the economy, meaning the mine, well, or port. Economists are nearly unanimous in their belief that a carbon tax is the most efficient and effective way to reduce carbon emissions. A sensible carbon tax might begin at $40 a ton and increase steadily over time, sending a powerful signal to businesses and consumers, while generating revenue to reward Americans for decreasing their collective carbon footprint.

5   2. **All the proceeds from this carbon tax would be returned to the American people** on an equal and quarterly basis via dividend checks, direct deposits, or contributions to their individual retirement accounts. In the example above, a family of four would receive approximately $2,000 in carbon dividend payments in the first year. This amount would grow over time as the carbon tax rate increases, creating a positive feedback loop: the more the climate is protected, the greater the individual dividend payments to all Americans. The Social Security Administration should administer this program, with eligibility for dividends based on a valid Social Security number.

3. **Border adjustments for the carbon content of both imports and exports** would protect American competitiveness and punish free-riding by other nations, encouraging them to adopt carbon dioxide pricing of their own. Exports to countries without comparable carbon pricing systems would receive rebates for carbon taxes paid, while imports from such countries would face fees on the carbon content of their products. Proceeds from such fees would benefit the American people in the form of larger carbon

dividends. Other trade remedies could also be used to encourage our trading partners to adopt comparable carbon pricing.

4. **Eliminate regulations that are no longer necessary** upon the enactment of a rising carbon tax whose longevity is secured by the popularity of dividends. Much of the Environmental Protection Agency's regulatory authority over carbon dioxide emissions would be phased out, including an outright repeal of the Clean Power Plan. Robust carbon taxes would also make possible an end to federal and state tort liability for emitters. To build and sustain a bipartisan consensus for a regulatory rollback of this magnitude, the initial carbon tax rate should be set to exceed the emissions reductions of current regulations.

Putting a Price on Carbon is a Fine Idea. It's Not the End-All Be-All

DAVID ROBERTS

David Roberts is a Seattle-based writer and blogger on energy and environment for Vox.com, a website that "explains the news." This commentary was published on Vox on April 22, 2016.

What is the most important policy tool for fighting climate change? Ask just about any economist and the answer will be the same: a price on carbon emissions.

Not only is there a robust consensus among economists, but they have been remarkably successful in spreading the gospel to the wider world as well. Climate activists, wonks, funders, politicians, progressives, and even conservatives (the few who take climate seriously) all sing from the same hymnal. It has become conventional wisdom that a price on carbon is the *sine qua non* of serious climate policy.

But it is worth keeping carbon pricing in perspective. It has become invested with such symbolic significance that it is inspiring some unhelpful purism on policy and magical thinking on politics.

Slowing climate change will require a suite of policies, regulatory reforms, and investments. Carbon pricing will be an important part of that portfolio. But only a part. It is not the only legitimate climate policy, the one true sign of seriousness on global warming, or a substitute for the difficult and painstaking political work that will be required to transition to a sustainable energy system.

I have no interest in a carbon-pricing backlash. But maybe a sidelash—a reality check. 5

This post will be a two-parter. Tomorrow I'm going to get into politics, how it shapes carbon taxes, and what's to be done with the revenue.

But first, I want to take a step back. In this post, I'll have a quick look at why carbon pricing has become so central to climate economics and raise some questions about its primacy in policy and political circles.

First, a word on cap-and-trade versus carbon tax

The most straightforward form of carbon pricing is a carbon tax, which, in its simplest version, imposes a fee on every ton of carbon that enters the economy ("upstream," on fossil fuel producers and importers, as opposed to "downstream," on fossil fuel consumers).

But taxes are not the only "price-based instrument" used to control pollution. In the 1980s and 90s, a new policy called cap-and-trade started to catch on. Rather than imposing a fee, it caps the total amount of a pollutant and issues tradable permits under that (declining) cap. The market for those permits sets the price of the pollutant.

10   Cap-and-trade was successfully used by the Environmental Protection Agency to control, for example, the pollutants that cause acid rain. A national carbon cap-and-trade bill failed in 2010, but the policy has taken hold regionally in the Northeast, California, and numerous other places around the world.

Depending on how they are structured, the economic impacts of the two policies are equivalent. They raise the price of fossil fuels. There are interesting debates to be had about their relative merits, but that's for another post.

For now, I'm mostly going to focus on a carbon tax, because (a) many of the same considerations apply to both policies; (b) cap-and-trade has fallen out of favor in the US, both among conservatives, who are convinced it's secretly a tax, and liberals, who are angry it isn't a tax; and (c) it's just simpler.

Why economists love carbon taxes

Ever since the early 20th century, mainstream economists have had a favorite policy for dealing with pollution. It's called a Pigouvian tax, after British economist Arthur Pigou.

The idea is simple. Sometimes markets produce negative impacts that are not accounted for in market prices. The market participants who produce the impacts do not pay for them; society absorbs the costs. (Air pollution is a good example.) These "externalities," costs external to markets, are considered a form of market failure.

15   The most efficient remedy for this kind of failure is to price the externality into the market via a Pigouvian tax. A tax raises the prices of polluting products to reflect their true costs. Markets respond accordingly.

Theoretically, if the tax is set at the correct social cost of the externality, the market becomes *more* efficient, with better information; it inexorably finds the "right" level of pollution, based on full costs and benefits. In this way, markets, not meddling regulators, will find the economically optimal way to address pollution.

When it comes to climate change, economists have turned en masse to this familiar tool; thus the carbon tax. If carbon emissions are causing damage, the solution is to tax them at the level of that damage. The market will do the rest.

This has an undeniable logic, and has captured the wonk imagination. Many environmentalists are thrilled at the idea of a green policy that passes muster with real economists and even some conservatives.

And for various reasons (some legitimate, some deeply muddled), a carbon tax has come to be seen by the green left as a simpler, more virtuous, more authentic alternative to cap-and-trade.

But three things about the case for carbon taxes give me pause.   20

(1) Skepticism toward activist government is baked in the cake

In the early 1990s, Bill Clinton declared that "the era of big government is over." The idea was that Democrats had abandoned their vestigial socialist tendencies, their knee-jerk preference for more regulations and more spending, and embraced the power of markets.

They would pursue liberal goals, based on liberal values, they said, but use the power of markets to keep costs down. This was an alleged "third way" between heartless conservatism and spendthrift liberalism.

This kind of thinking is sometimes referred to as "neoliberalism," tracing back to Charles Peters's original 1983 manifesto in *Washington Monthly*. The term has been mangled and overused lately, to the point that it probably ought to be abandoned, but it does seem to apply here.

The broader (and especially younger) left has, of late, rejected neoliberalism with great vigor. It has seen that markets are not always great at solving social problems, that market-based policies are often a veneer for steering public money into private hands, and that markets, unrestrained by vigorous progressive governance, generate huge inequalities of wealth and opportunity. That's part of what the Sanders insurgency is about.

So the new left fixation on a carbon tax is at least facially peculiar, since, it   25
seems to me, the policy issues from classically neoliberal instincts. It is a way of achieving a social goal (less carbon) while minimizing interference in markets.

The impetus for minimizing interference is a deep-seated belief that attempts to meddle in markets via industrial policy, "command and control" regulations, and targeted spending tend to backfire, distorting the economy and slowing growth. A (politically conservative) skepticism toward activist government is baked into the neoliberal cake.

Reinforcing that skepticism is not a wise long-term strategy for climate hawks, because I can guarantee that climate change is eventually going to require activist government. No market-based policy is going to equitably resettle the residents of Miami.

Of course, it's entirely possible to support carbon taxes without buying into the larger neoliberal worldview. And, hell, maybe some climate hawks really do have that kind of faith in markets. But I get the sense that lots of carbon tax enthusiasts, especially on the left, haven't really thought through all the implications.

(2) There are no free markets

Even if you accept the premise that free, competitive markets are always or almost always better at allocating resources than legislators or regulators, it's questionable just how far that gets you on energy policy.

30   Carbon taxes are meant to remedy one market failure: unpriced carbon emissions. But those familiar with US energy markets will attest that they are ridden with such failures. They bear virtually no resemblance to idealized neoclassical markets.

The US electricity sector, for instance, is a Rube Goldberg contraption of overlapping jurisdictions, regulated monopolies, and quasi-markets. Coal, oil, and gas are extracted from public land and transported over public right-of-ways, leaving behind an array of local pollutants. At every stage from extraction/production to transportation to consumption, all forms of energy are heavily regulated and dependent on public subsidies and public infrastructure.

In fact, there are so many market failures in energy, one almost wonders whether beginning with an idealized market and working backward through its "failures" is a fruitful way to approach policy thinking. Hmm.

Unpriced carbon is a market failure, if you want to look at it that way. But real-life markets, not just in energy but in transportation and agriculture, are failures all the way down—irrational behaviors, asymmetrical information, barriers to entry, monopoly control, and more. Then layer on top of that complicated regulatory systems, legacy policies and infrastructure, and the distorting influence of status quo interests, and you've got quite a mess.

One can look at the task ahead as painstakingly correcting an almost endless series of market failures. Or one can look at it as actively shaping and designing new markets to produce better social outcomes.

35   Either way, the "set it and forget it" schemes of hardcore tax advocates are a fantasy. It's a blunt-force tool. It will do wonders in some sectors (driving coal out of electricity) but very little in others (driving oil out of transportation). It will not do all the necessary work in any sector. Different markets are different; they have their own idiosyncrasies, their own failures.

Believing a single tool will accomplish everything requires seeing the economy as a frictionless machine, a spreadsheet, not what it is: a path-dependent accretion of past decisions and sunk costs, to be tweaked and unwound.

One other thing: The neoclassical model of a perfectly efficient economy depends on full employment, which hasn't been the case in the US for a very long time. Resources are being left slack, capital is cheap, and deficit spending is likely to boost growth. But when it comes to carbon and clean energy, many economists default to the knee-jerk stance that government spending is distortionary and only price-based instruments are legitimate.

(3) Marginally reducing carbon emissions is one thing; mounting a high-speed Industrial Revolution is another

It is somewhat misleading to describe the goal of climate change mitigation as "reducing carbon emissions." Reducing carbon emissions is easy; lots of policies can do that.

We need to reduce emissions a *lot*—to zero, or close to it—as fast as possible. That's going to require more than changes at the margins. It's going to require phasing out virtually our entire installed industrial base and replacing it with new, low-carbon technologies and practices. It's going to require an explosion of innovation and building, the likes of which hasn't been seen since the Industrial Revolution—only much, much faster, constrained by a tight carbon budget.

We know price-based policies like Pigouvian taxes (and cap-and-trade programs) can efficiently generate marginal changes. Economists don't just love them because of theory; they work, especially in bounded markets where demand is elastic or substitution is cheap. The economic literature on that score is copious.

But carbon isn't just one pollutant from one product category. It's the whole economy. The whole *world* economy. Can price-based policies drive economy-wide energy transitions?

History doesn't seem to offer any examples. Large-scale energy transitions of the past have generally been driven by industrial policy and technology innovation; none have been driven by increases in the prices of existing energy sources. (Vaclav Smil is the go-to scholar on this.)

In a recent critical review of the new book from economist Nicholas Stern, Alex Trembath puts it nicely:

"History reveals that prices and scarcity have rarely, if ever, driven large-scale energy transitions. We transitioned away from whale oil after discovering much more abundant and useful petroleum-derived kerosene, not because we were running out of whales. Electricity and the internal combustion engine emerged after decades of technological toiling and created whole new uses for energy. War, perhaps the most state-directed of all enterprises, accelerated the diffusion of several key energy technologies, most notably the internal combustion engine, jet turbines, and nuclear reactors. Today, hydraulic fracturing in shale emerged from government-funded labs and has diffused because of its usefulness in cost-effectively accessing previously hard-to-reach natural gas deposits. This is the work that governments have done since Alexander Hamilton invented industrial policy, not as a corrective to proliferating market failures, but as foundational and continuous policy to create and shape markets themselves."

Note the difference in perspective: not gingerly correcting markets, striving to return them to their edemic state of perfect efficiency, but *creating and shaping* markets that work better to achieve outcomes chosen (ideally) through democratic deliberation.

It has been proactive government, developing and diffusing technologies, sculpting markets through regulations and investments, that has sparked industrial shifts in the past.

Maybe we can engineer such a transition, faster than all the previous transitions, using a price-based instrument as our primary tool. But that is a *very* big gamble, not something we can confidently predict based on economic theory. At the very least, it seems novel and uncertain enough that we might not want to put all our eggs in that basket.

It is entirely possible to share all the reservations I describe above and still support putting a price on carbon. (I do!) It is, after all, one way of proactively shaping markets.

But it is dangerous to believe that a carbon price, or any single market-based policy, will do the work for us, rendering other efforts superfluous or unnecessary. There's a lot of messy, frustrating work ahead, involving any number of political compromises and kludged, suboptimal policies. No way around it.

50   Creating a whole new world is hard. Tax or no tax, our children and their children will still be working at it. And they will need every tool they can get their hands on.

Our Human Right Not to Be Poisoned

JULIAN CRIBB

Julian Cribb is an Australian science communicator and author of several books, including The Coming Famine (2010), Poisoned Planet (2014), *and* Surviving the 21st Century (2017). *This article, based on his keynote address to the Cleanup 2015 Conference in Melbourne, was printed in the journal* Australasian Science *in December 2015.*

Earth, and all life on it, is being saturated with anthropogenic chemicals and wastes in an event unlike anything in the previous four billion years of our planet's story. Each moment of our lives, from conception to death, we are exposed to thousands of substances, some lethal, many toxic, and most of them unknown in their effects on our health or on the natural world.

This has mainly happened in barely the space of a single lifetime. Collectively humanity manufactures around 144,000 different chemicals, and the US Department of Health and Human Services estimates that 1000–2000 new ones are released each year. Many of these are untested for safety.

These are the mere tip of the iceberg. Each year we also generate:

- 150 million tonnes of nitrogen and 11 million tonnes of phosphorus, mainly from farming, burning fossil fuels, and waste disposal;
- 400 million tonnes of hazardous wastes, including 50 million tonnes of old computers and phones;
- 15 billion tonnes of coal, oil, and gas, contributing the lion's share of 50 billion tonnes of carbon dioxide gas;
- 72 billion tonnes of minerals, metals, and materials;
- up to 100 billion tonnes of rock, soil, tailings, overburden, and slags from mining; and
- 75 billion tonnes of topsoil, mainly from farming and development.

These substances move constantly in both space and time. They travel on the wind, in water, attached to soil, in dust, in plastic particles, in wildlife, in food and traded goods, and in (and on) people. They combine and recombine with one another, and with naturally occurring substances, giving rise to generations of new compounds—some more toxic, others less, and many completely unknown. They leapfrog around the planet in cycles of absorption and rerelease known as the "grasshopper effect."

Many of these substances, especially heavy metals, last for generations, creat-   5
ing a cumulative toxic load in the environment—and in ourselves. Their effects are, even now, being passed on to future generations of people through our genes.

Tests show that most people in modern societies now carry a lifelong chemical burden (tinyurl.com/mooul6r), that unborn babies are contaminated with industrial chemicals (tinyurl.com/ ndyls8b), and that mothers' milk in 68 countries is contaminated with pesticides and other noxious substances (tinyurl.com/ oj3mwgl). Around 4000–6000 chemicals—mostly pesticides, preservatives, additives, and dyes—are regularly used in the growing, processing, and packaging of our food.

The World Health Organization and UN Environment Program have estimated that one in 12 people die from these environmental toxins, and around 86 million are maimed each year (tinyurl.com/o96pbo6). This toll is greater than for HIV, malaria, or car crashes. One in five cancers—about two million fatalities per year—are attributable to our exposure to carcinogens in our living environment (tinyurl.com/njkzkmf). Medical scientists have warned of a silent pandemic of childhood brain damage caused by the global release of neurotoxins due to human activity, and health officials have cautioned that reproductive and gender disorders caused by endocrine-disrupting chemicals are on the rise worldwide.

Above all, health researchers are concerned at the potential impact of billions of mixtures of thousands of different substances combining in our diet and living environment, which they now increasingly link to conditions including developmental disorders, sexual dysfunction, obesity, cancers, heart disease, and nerve and brain diseases including autism, depression, Parkinson's, and Alzheimer's.

Current human life expectancy figures are based on historical data, and on medical successes gained with vaccines, antibiotics, and sound public health. The impact of the toxic flood may be temporarily masked by this success, but many scientists fear this will not last long because "lifestyle" diseases and society's toxic burden are on the rise.

We cannot afford to wait until death rates rise. We must act now to prevent   10
them from doing so.

The Stockholm Convention has so far banned just 19 out of our 144,000 chemicals, and appears powerless to stem the global flood of new releases, especially as the bulk of the world's chemical output is now shifting to poorly regulated Third World locations. From Minamata to Bhopal to Tianjin, a string of toxic disasters has demonstrated the futility of legal action against individual companies to stem global contamination. However, blaming industry and calling for tougher regulation will not solve the problem of the poisoned planet.

We need a smarter way to protect society and all future generations from the toxic flood. This starts with recognizing that we are the ones who generate the market signals that lead to the mass production and ill-considered release of toxins. Every act of consumption on a crowded planet has chemical consequences. Every dollar we spend sends a signal to a string of industries to produce, use, or emit a mass of chemicals. Those innocent signals, in all likelihood, are now killing more people per year than in World War II.

In a sense we are all getting away with murder. This uncomfortable thought is essential if modern society is to take effective action to clean up the Earth and protect our children in the future. If we have given rise to the problem by demanding goods that are produced using toxic substances or with toxic processes, then we alone have the power to correct it. It is already clear that governments do not have the capacity or the will to regulate a global toxic flood. Regulation is important, but if we rely on rules alone to protect our children, the evidence indicates they will not succeed.

In a globalized world only we, the people, are powerful enough—as consumers—to send the market signals to industry to cease toxic emissions. And to properly reward it for producing clean, safe, healthy products or services. For the first time in history we have the means to share a universal understanding of a common threat and what we can each do to mitigate it.

15   Through the Internet and social media, concerned citizens and parents are already mobilizing around the world—reaching out to one another across cultural, ethnic, religious, linguistic, and economic borders. Concerned citizens and parents are joining hands at lightspeed to cleanse our poisoned planet. This is an expression of people power and global democracy like never before.

Many exciting new technologies and approaches are being trialed to clean up our planet, like green chemistry, industrial ecology, product stewardship, and zero waste. But we have to find ways to encourage industry to adopt, and the most effective of these are consumer-generated market signals.

Far from being harmful to industry, this universal demand for clean, safe products will open fresh markets, create more jobs, build new companies, and generate greater prosperity and better health.

There are many ways in which we can all contribute to detoxifying our world:

- form a partnership of concerned citizens, industries, and regulators;
- demand a new human right not to be poisoned;
- eliminate coal, oil, gas, and fossil fuels as the primary sources of most contamination;
- eliminate toxins from the food chain through regulation;
- institute worldwide preventative healthcare to replace the "get-sick-and-treat-with-more-chemicals" approach);
- incorporate the teaching of ethics with chemistry in order to train young scientists, like doctors, to "first, do no harm";
- educate children to choose non-toxic products;
- reward industry by buying green;

- implement zero waste, green chemistry, and product stewardship in our consumption patterns, lives, and occupations; and
- test all new chemical products for health and environmental safety.

Every person in the world has a right to life, liberty, personal security, marriage and family, equality, work, education, freedom of belief, and freedom from torture. These rights are available to each of us under the Universal Declaration on Human Rights. It is more than a little disturbing that there is no human right not to be poisoned—a privilege enjoyed by all our ancestors until recent times.

Unless and until we have such a right, there will probably never again be a   20
day in history when we and our children are free from man-made poisons.

I Stopped Wearing Leather . . .

ALEX HALLATT

Alex Hallatt is a cartoonist and children's author best known for his comic strip, Arctic Circle, *which has run in syndication since 2006. His work frequently engages with scientific and environmental questions of the day. This cartoon was published on April 2, 2017.*

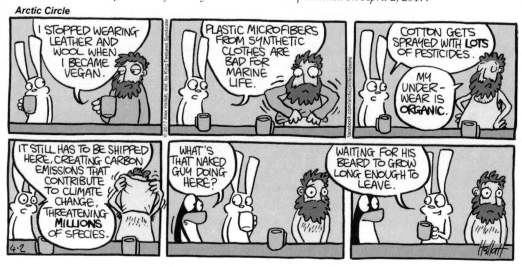

The Question I Get Asked the Most

BILL MCKIBBEN

Bill McKibben is an author and environmental activist whose 1989 book, The End of Nature, *was the first book on climate change for a general audience. He went on to found 350.org, a website and grassroots climate change movement that has organized over 20,000 rallies around the world and helped to launch the fossil fuel divestment movement.*

His most recent book is Oil and Honey: The Education of an Unlikely Activist *(2013). This commentary appeared in the Spring 2017 issue of* Communities.

The questions come after talks, on Twitter, in the days' incoming tide of email—sometimes even in old-fashioned letters that arrive in envelopes. The most common one by far is also the simplest: What can I do? I bet I've been asked it 10,000 times by now and—like a climate scientist predicting the temperature—I'm pretty sure I'm erring on the low side.

It's the right question or almost: It implies an eagerness to act and action is what we need. But my answer to it has changed over the years, as the science of global warming has shifted. I find, in fact, that I'm now saying almost the opposite of what I said three decades ago.

Then—when I was 27 and writing the first book on climate change—I was fairly self-obsessed (perhaps age appropriately). And it looked like we had some time: No climate scientist in the late 1980s thought that by 2016 we'd already be seeing massive Arctic ice melt. So it made sense for everyone to think about the changes they could make in their own lives that, over time, would add up to significant change. In *The End of Nature*, I described how my wife and I had tried to "prune and snip our desires," how instead of taking long vacation trips by car we rode our bikes in the road, how we grew more of our own food, how we "tried not to think about how much we'd like a baby."

Some of these changes we've maintained—we still ride our bikes, and I haven't been on a vacation in a very long time. Some we modified—thank God we decided to have a child, who turned out to be the joy of our life. And some I've abandoned: I've spent much of the last decade in frenetic travel, much of it on airplanes. That's because, over time, it became clear to me that there's a problem with the question "What can I do?"

5   The problem is the word "I." By ourselves, there's not much we can do. Yes, my roof is covered with solar panels and I drive a plug-in car that draws its power from those panels, and yes our hot water is heated by the sun, and yes we eat low on the food chain and close to home. I'm glad we do all those things, and I think everyone should do them, and I no longer try to fool myself that they will solve climate change.

Because the science has changed and with it our understanding of the necessary politics and economics of survival. Climate change is coming far faster than people anticipated even a couple of decades ago. 2016 smashed the temperature records set in 2015, which smashed the records set in 2014; some of the world's largest physical features (giant coral reefs, vast river deltas) are starting to die off or disappear. Drought does damage daily; hundred-year floods come every other spring. In the last two years we've seen the highest wind speeds ever recorded in many of the world's ocean basins. In Basra, Iraq—not far from the Garden of Eden—the temperature hit 129 Fahrenheit last summer, the highest reliably recorded temperature ever and right at the limit of human tolerance. July and August 2016 were not just the hottest months ever recorded, they were, according to most climatologists, the hottest months in the entire history of human civilization. The most common phrase I hear from scientists is "faster than antici-pated." Sometime in the last few years we left behind the Holocene, the 10,000-year period of benign climatic stability that marked the rise of human civilization. We're in something new now—something new and frightening.

Against all that, one's Prius is a gesture. A lovely gesture and one that every-one should emulate, but a gesture. Ditto riding the bike or eating vegan or what-ever one's particular point of pride. North Americans are very used to thinking of themselves as individuals, but as individuals we are powerless to alter the trajectory of climate change in a meaningful manner. The 5 or 10 percent of us who will be moved to really act (and that's all who ever act on any subject) can't cut the carbon in the atmosphere by more than 5 or 10 percent by those actions.

No, the right question is "What can we do to make a difference?"

Because if individual action can't alter the momentum of global warming, movements may still do the trick. Movements are how people organize themselves to gain power—enough power, in this case, to perhaps overcome the financial might of the fossil fuel industry. Movements are what can put a price on carbon, force politicians to keep fossil fuel in the ground, demand subsidies so that solar panels go up on almost every roof, not just yours. Movements are what take 5 or 10 percent of people and make them decisive—because in a world where apathy rules, 5 or 10 percent is an enormous number. Ask the Tea Party. Ask the civil rights movement.

The other side knows this, which is why it ridicules our movements at all times. When, for instance, 400,000 people march on New York City, I know that I will get a stream of ugly tweets and emails about how—saints preserve us—it takes gasoline to get to New York City. Indeed it does. If you live in a society that has dismantled its train system, then lots of people will need to drive and take the bus, and it will be the most useful gallons they burn in the course of the year. Because that's what pushes systems to change.

When brave people go to jail, cynics email me to ask how much gas the paddy wagon requires. When brave people head out in kayaks to block the biggest drill-ing rigs on earth, I always know I'll be reading dozens of tweets from clever and deadened souls asking "don't you know the plastic for those kayaks requires oil?" Yes, we know—and we've decided it's well worth it. We're not trying to be saints; we're trying to be effective.

We're not going to be forced into a monkish retreat from society—we need to engage this fight with all the tools of the moment. We're trying to change the world we live in and if we succeed then those who come after will have plenty of time to figure out other ways to inhabit it. Along the way those who have shifted their lives can provide inspiration, which is crucial. But they don't by themselves provide a solution. Naomi Klein once described visiting an "amazing" community farm in Brooklyn's Red Hook that had been flooded by Hurricane Sandy. "They were doing everything right, when it comes to climate," she said. "Growing organic, localizing their food system, sequestering carbon, not using fossil fuel inputs—all the good stuff." Then came the storm. "They lost their entire fall harvest and they're pretty sure their soil is now contaminated, because the water that flooded them was so polluted. It's important to build local alternatives, we have to do it, but unless we are really going after the source of the problem"—namely, the fossil fuel industry and its lock on Washington—"we are going to get inundated."

Like Klein, I find that the people who have made some of those personal changes are usually also deeply involved in movement-building. Local farmers, even after a long day pulling weeds, find the energy to make it to the demonstration, often because they know their efforts out in the field aren't enough, even to guarantee a climate that will allow them to continue their efforts. No, the people calling environmentalists hypocrites for living in the real world are people who want no change at all. Their goal is simply to shame us and hence to quiet us. So we won't make them feel bad or disrupt the powers that be.

It won't work, unless we let it. Movements take care of their own: They provide bail money and they push each other's ideas around the web. They join forces across issues: Black Lives Matter endorsing fossil fuel divestment, climate justice activists fighting deportations. They recognize that together we might just have enough strength to get it done. So when people ask me what can I do, I now say the same thing every time: "The most important thing an individual can do is not be an individual. Join together—that's why we have movements like 350.org or Green for All, like Black Lives Matter or Occupy. If there's not a fight where you live, find people to support, from Standing Rock to the Pacific islands. Job one is to organize and jobs two and three."

15   And if you have some time left over after that, then by all means make sure your light bulbs are all LEDs and your kale comes from close to home.

Ecologically Relevant Data Are Policy-Relevant Data

CHELSEA M. ROCHMAN

Chelsea M. Rochman holds a Ph.D. in ecology and is on the faculty of the University of Toronto. This perspective was published in the June 3, 2016, issue of Science.

History tells us that the motivation for new environmental policy is much stronger when there is demonstrated ecological impact. Multinational agreements to stop the use of DDT followed the precipitous decline of predatory bird populations. Similarly, decisions to regulate emissions to prevent acid rain followed widespread degradation of aquatic habitats. Ideally, environmental policy should be catalyzed by scientific evidence rather than environmental catastrophe. As scientists, we can do our part by providing evidence that is relevant to the natural environment. On page 1213 of this issue, Lönnstedt and Eklöv (1) take an important step forward in this regard by reporting ecologically relevant evidence on a growing environmental issue: microplastic pollution.

Plastic can remain in the environment for hundreds to thousands of years. Moreover, its production and global consumption outpace waste management (2).

The mismanagement of plastic waste is now coming back to haunt us as marine and freshwater debris. Much of this debris is microplastics: plastic fragments < 5 mm in all dimensions that are either manufactured that way (plastic microbeads in many personal care products) or are broken-down bits of larger pieces of debris. Microplastic fragments float on the surface of every major ocean (3); microbeads are found in freshwater lakes (4); plastic fibers shed from clothing are coming down with rain (5); and a medley of plastic particles have been found in commercial sea salt (6), fish (7), and oysters (8).

Hundreds of studies have demonstrated global microplastic contamination, but few have investigated its impacts on animal populations, communities, and ecosystems. This pattern is not unique. For many chemical contaminants in the environment, widespread contamination is documented, yet little is known about their ecological impacts (9). A recent systematic review found that evidence of ecological impacts of microplastic debris is not lacking because there are none, but because scientists are not asking questions about impacts at biological levels above the individual organism (10). Most studies investigate suborganismal effects such as cell death, organ damage, or changes in gene expression in animals exposed to quick and unrealistically large doses of microplastics (10). These studies are critical for understanding physiological mechanisms but tell us little about ecological impacts that may be occurring in nature now (11).

To increase understanding of ecological impacts, Lönnstedt and Eklöv exposed fish to concentrations of polystyrene microplastics comparable to those found in nature. They studied European perch (Perca fluviatilis) at the sensitive embryonic and larval stages and exposed them to microplastics similar in size to those found in ocean samples. Most importantly, they asked ecologically relevant questions about survival and recruitment in their laboratory populations.

The results show that exposure of embryos to microplastics decreases hatching success. Moreover, exposed 2-week-old larvae were much less able to escape predation, leading to reduced survival. In another recent study, Sussarellu et al. exposed reproductively active oysters to an environmentally relevant concentration of polystyrene microplastics and found similar results: decreases in egg production and motile sperm, leading to reduced larval yield (12). Such ecologically relevant impacts, including compromised reproduction, reduced survival, and changes in predator–prey interactions, may translate to population- or community-level impacts.

Lönnstedt and Eklöv's study marks an important step toward understanding ecological impacts of microplastics. Future work should ask questions about multigenerational impacts, changes in biodiversity indices, community structure, and ecosystem function. Ideally, such studies will guide mitigation efforts—for example, by determining the types of microplastics that may be most hazardous and by identifying the most sensitive populations, species, and/or ecosystems. With such data in hand, practitioners can shift their energy toward prevention and avoid the need for costly recovery and restoration.

References and Notes

O. M. Lönnstedt, P. Eklöv, *Science* 352, 1213 (2016).

J. Jambeck et al., *Science* 347, 768 (2015).

E. van Sebille et al., *Environ. Res. Lett.* 10, 124006 (2015).

M. Eriksen et al., *Mar. Pollut. Bull.* 77, 177 (2013).

R. Dris et al., *Mar. Pollut. Bull.* 104, 290 (2016).

D. Yang et al., *Environ. Sci. Technol.* 49, 13622 (2015).

C. Rochman et al., *Sci. Rep.* 5, 14340 (2015).

L. Van Cauwenberghe, C. Janssen, *Environ. Pollut.* 193, 65 (2014).

E. Johnston, M. Mayer-Pinto, T. Crowe, *J. Appl. Ecol.* 52, 140 (2015).

C. Rochman et al., *Ecology* 97, 302 (2016).

P. Chapman, *Environ. Int.* 33, 492 (2007).

R. Sussarellu et al., *Proc. Natl. Acad. Sci. U.S.A.* 113, 2430 (2016).

Acknowledgments: I thank K. L. Law, D. L. Mahler, and A. J. Underwood for comments and the David H. Smith Conservation Research Fellowship Program for support.

Banning Plastic Bags is Great for the World, Right? Not So Fast

BEN ADLER

Ben Adler reports on climate-change policy for Grist *and on news literacy for* Columbia Journalism Review. *This analysis was posted to* Wired *on June 10, 2016.*

Like cigarettes, plastic bags have recently gone from a tolerated nuisance to a widely despised and discouraged vice.

Last month, the New York City Council passed a 5-cent-per-bag fee on single-use bags handed out by most retailers. Two weeks ago, the Massachusetts State Senate passed a measure that would ban plastic bags from being dispensed by many retail businesses and require a charge of 10 cents or more for a recycled paper or reusable bag. The Massachusetts proposal may not become law this year, but it's the latest sign that the plastic bag industry is losing this war. Already in Massachusetts, 32 towns and cities have passed bag bans or fees. So have at least 88 localities in California, including the cities of Los Angeles and San Francisco, plus cities and towns in more than a dozen other states and more than a dozen other countries.

The adverse impacts of plastic bags are undeniable: When they're not piling up in landfills, they're blocking storm drains, littering streets, getting stuck in trees, and contaminating oceans, where fish, seabirds, and other marine animals eat them or get tangled up in them. As longtime plastic bag adversary Ian Frazier recently reported in *The New Yorker*, "In 2014, plastic grocery bags were the seventh most common item collected during the Ocean Conservancy's International Coastal Cleanup, behind smaller debris such as cigarette butts, plastic straws, and bottle caps." The New York City Sanitation Department collects more than 1,700 tons of single-use carry-out bags every week, and has to spend $12.5 million a year to dispose of them.

Bag bans cut this litter off at the source: In San Jose, California, a plastic bag ban   5 led to an 89 percent reduction in the number of plastic bags winding up in the city's storm drains. Fees have a smaller, but still significant, effect. Washington, DC's government estimates that its 5-cent bag tax has led to a 60 percent reduction in the number of these bags being used, although that figure is contested by other sources.

Is plastic really worse than paper?

But advocates of these laws and journalists who cover the issue often neglect to ask what will replace plastic bags and what the environmental impact of that replacement will be. People still need bags to bring home their groceries. And the most common substitute, paper bags, may be just as bad or worse, depending on the environmental problem you're most concerned about.

That's leading to a split in the anti-bag movement. Some bills, like in Massachusetts, try to reduce the use of paper bags as well as plastic, but still favor paper. Others, like in New York City, treat all single-use bags equally. Even then, the question remains as to whether single-use bags are necessarily always worse than reusable ones.

Studies of bags' environmental impacts over their life cycle have reached widely varying conclusions. Some are funded by plastic industry groups, like the ironically named American Progressive Bag Alliance. Even studies conducted with the purest of intentions depend on any number of assumptions. How many plastic bags are replaced by one cotton tote bag? If a plastic bag is reused in the home as the garbage bag in a bathroom waste bin, does that reduce its footprint by eliminating the need for another small plastic garbage bag?

If your chief concern is climate change, things get even muddier. One of the most comprehensive research papers on the environmental impact of bags, published in 2007 by an Australian state government agency, found that paper bags have a higher carbon footprint than plastic. That's primarily because more energy is required to produce and transport paper bags.

"People look at [paper] and say it's degradable, therefore it's much better   10 for the environment, but it's not in terms of climate change impact," says David Tyler, a professor of chemistry at the University of Oregon who has examined the research on the environmental impact of bag use. The reasons for paper's higher carbon footprint are complex, but can mostly be understood as stemming from the fact that paper bags are much thicker than plastic bags. "Very broadly, carbon footprints are proportional to mass of an object," says Tyler. For example, because paper bags take up so much more space, more trucks are needed to ship paper bags to a store than to ship plastic bags.

Looking beyond climate change

Still, many environmentalists argue that plastic is worse than paper. Climate change, they say, isn't the only form of environmental degradation to worry about. "Paper does have its own environmental consequences in terms of how much energy it takes to generate," acknowledges Emily Norton, director of the Massachusetts Sierra Club. "The big difference is that paper does biodegrade eventually. Plastic is a toxin that stays in the environment, marine animals ingest it, and it enters their bodies and then ours."

Some social justice activists who work in low-income urban neighborhoods or communities of color also argue that plastic bags are a particular scourge. "A lot of the waste ends up in our communities," says Elizabeth Yeampierre, executive director of UPROSE, an environmental and social justice-oriented community organization in Brooklyn. "Plastic bags not only destroy the physical infrastructure," she says, referring to the way they clog up storm drains and other systems, "they contribute to emissions." And she points out that marine plastic pollution is a threat to low-income people who fish for their dinner: "So many frontline communities depend on food coming from the ocean." That's why her group supported New York City's bag fee even though it's more of a burden on lower-income citizens. A single mom, or someone working two jobs, is more likely to have to do her shopping in a rush on the way home from work than to go out specifically with a tote bag in hand. But for UPROSE, that concern is outweighed by the negative impacts of plastic bags on disadvantaged communities.

Increasingly, environmentalists are pushing for laws that include fees for all single-use bags, and that require paper bags to be made with recycled content, which could lower their carbon footprint. The measure now under consideration in Massachusetts, for example, would mandate that single-use paper bags contain at least 40 percent recycled fiber. That's the percentage the Massachusetts Sierra Club has advocated for at the state level and when lobbying for municipal bag rules.

It's complicated

But what if reusable bags aren't good either? As the Australian study noted, a cotton bag has major environmental impacts of its own. Only 2.4 percent of the world's cropland is planted with cotton, yet it accounts for 24 percent of the global market for insecticides and 11 percent for pesticides, the World Wildlife Fund reports. A pound of cotton requires more than 5,000 gallons of water on average, a thirst far greater than that of any vegetable and even most meats. And cotton, unlike paper, is not currently recycled in most places.

15   The Australian study concluded that the best option appears to be a reusable bag, but one made from recycled plastic, not cotton. "A substantial shift to more durable bags would deliver environmental gains through reductions in greenhouse gases, energy and water use, resource depletion and litter," the study concluded.

"The shift from one single-use bag to another single-use bag may improve one environmental outcome, but be offset by another environmental impact."

But studies conducted in Australia or Europe have limited applicability in the US, particularly when you're considering climate impact, because every country has a different energy mix. In fact, every region of the US has a different energy mix.

"There's no easy answer," says Eric Goldstein, New York City environment director for the Natural Resources Defense Council, which backed NYC's bag fee. "There are so very many variables. Here's just one tiny example: Does the paper for paper bags come from a recycled paper mill on Staten Island or a virgin forest in northern Canada? As far as I know, nobody has done the definitive analysis, which would necessarily need to have a large number of caveats and qualifications. Also, this question is something like asking, 'Would you prefer to get a parking ticket or a tax assessment?' It depends on the specifics, but it's better to avoid both wherever possible." Goldstein is confident that if people switch to reusable bags, even cotton ones, and use them consistently, that will ultimately be better for the environment.

The ideal city bag policy would probably involve charging for paper and plastic single-use bags, as New York City has decided to do, while giving out reusable recycled-plastic bags to those who need them, especially to low-income communities and seniors. (The crunchy rich should already have more than enough tote bags from PBS and Whole Foods.)

The larger takeaway is that no bag is free of environmental impact, whether   20
that's contributing to climate change, ocean pollution, water scarcity, or pesticide use. The instinct to favor reusable bags springs from an understandable urge to reduce our chronic overconsumption, but the bags we use are not the big problem.

"Eat one less meat dish a week—that's what will have a real impact on the environment," says Tyler. "It's what we put in the bag at the grocery store that really matters."

Plastic Bag Ban: Let's Not Get Carried Away

SUN SENTINEL EDITORIAL BOARD

This editorial appeared in the March 25, 2017, edition of the Sun-Sentinel, *a daily newspaper in Broward County, Florida.*

Plastic bags are everywhere in our lives. We grab one in the morning to pack our lunch. We slip our hands in them to pick up dog doo. We use them to line garbage cans, separate dirty laundry in the luggage, and carry things from here to there.

If you doubt the convenience of grocery store plastic bags, try going a month without using one.

But plastic bags also are dangerous for the environment. They take considerable energy to manufacture and a thousand years to disintegrate. And they're so light, breezes easily lift them up and litter them along highways, waterways, and in trees. The Florida Department of Environmental Protection says plastic bags "can harm land and marine life, interfere with landfill operations, clog flood control systems, and breed mosquitoes."

Because of the damage they cause, Coral Gables this week expects to become the first Florida city to ban plastic bags. Exceptions would be made for bags from dry cleaners, newspapers, pharmacies, and veterinarians, plus bigger bags that hold garbage or yard waste, and those designed for dog waste.

5   You can understand the frustration of Coral Gables city commissioners, who like those in many other Florida communities, have faced nothing but obstacles from Tallahassee in addressing plastic bag pollution.

But while the city's goal is good, we believe the proposed ban goes too far, too fast.

Experience elsewhere suggests bans create backlash. If you want to change behavior, a better middle ground is to charge a tax—say, 5 or 10 cents each—on plastic bags dispensed by stores or vendors.

Chicago, for example, repealed its plastic bag ban because of consumer pushback, opting instead for a checkout tax. Santa Fe, New Mexico, found its ban led people to switch to paper bags, and so imposed a 10-cent tax on those. A 5-cent tax in Washington, D.C., has cut in half the use of plastic bags. And in Ireland, a 20-cent tax on plastic bags led to a 95 percent drop in use.

While the world is crimping the use of plastic bags, the same cannot be said for Tallahassee, where lawmakers continue to turn a blind eye.

10   While California enacted a statewide ban in 2015—a step too far, in our opinion—Florida took the opposite tack in 2008 by banning communities from banning the distribution of plastic bags.

In imposing the ban on plastic bag bans, state lawmakers said they first wanted to study the environmental hazards. But that study was completed in 2010 and they've yet to adopt a single one of its recommendations. Yet the ban on bans remains.

You can only shake your head at how state lawmakers beat their chests for state's rights, yet believe they know better than local leaders what's best for their communities.

The state's argument is that a patchwork of local regulations is bad for businesses with multiple outlets. You can understand that. If Publix can dispense plastic bags in Fort Lauderdale, but not Coral Gables, that's a complication. It's the same argument heard from Uber, whose drivers cross county lines and want a single statewide standard for insurance coverage and background checks.

But what happens when state lawmakers refuse to listen to local communities?

15   The state's standoff with Coral Gables started last year, after "The City Beautiful" banned the use of Styrofoam, or polystyrene. A month later, the Legislature banned Styrofoam bans and made the law retroactive to January. When the city refused to back down, the Florida Retail Federation sued. A circuit court this month sided with the city—not only on Styrofoam, but on the state's

plastic bag pre-emption, too. While an appeal is likely, the city quickly moved to pass a plastic bag ban two weeks ago. The final reading is Tuesday.

Meanwhile, a Senate committee last week passed a bill that would let coastal communities—of less than 100,000 population—temporarily ban plastic bags during a two-year pilot program. The legislation wouldn't allow a tax, though. And the communities would have to collect a lot of data.

This is the third year that mostly Democratic lawmakers have sought a pilot program. But the bill faces four committee stops in the Senate, which everyone knows is the kiss of death.

The voice of opposition comes from the Florida Retail Federation, whose argument is unpersuasive.

Samantha Padgett, the federation's general counsel, says it's not that a ban would create a financial burden on retailers. It's that customers like plastic bags.

"They enjoy the convenience, the ease of the plastic bag," she said. "It's   20 durable, reusable. If it gets wet, it's not a problem. It allows them to carry their material and it has so many second uses—pet waste bags, garbage can liners, a lunch bag even."

Padgett rightly notes that plastic bags are no worse for the environment than paper bags, which also leave a big energy footprint in their manufacture and disposal.

"It's not necessarily about choosing one material over another, but making sure we have an adequate recycling structure in place, adequate disposal," she said.

And therein lies the problem. An adequate recycling structure is not in place, no matter the collection bins at so many grocery stores. Customers fail or forget to return their used plastic bags, just as they fail or forget to bring the reusable fiber bags they had every intention of using.

Florida lawmakers should learn from others and let cities attempt to change consumer behavior.

If not a ban, at least let cities pass a tax on plastic bags.   25

For if these lawmakers ever participated in a coastal clean-up, they'd know the problem won't be solved by sticking their heads in the sand.

For Writing and Discussion
Choices for a Sustainable World

1. Many of the readings in this unit describe the effects of climate change and environmental pollution that we are already experiencing. What examples did you find surprising, impactful, or new? What examples were already familiar to you from experience, education, or media coverage? As a reader, do you find it more powerful to recognize a current or familiar example of an issue, or to be presented with a possible future impact?

2. The readings on carbon taxes focus on the role of government and corporations, rather than individual action, when it comes to mitigating the effects of climate change. What do you believe to be the responsibilities of these entities in protecting our environment? What are our responsibilities as consumers and citizens? Now, using the debate over plastic bags, write a one-paragraph position statement on who should be responsible for regulating plastic bag use (if at all), and what action should be taken.

3. Bill McKibben's essay is in part a response to critics who dismiss environmental activists as hypocrites because their protests and other actions use fossil fuels. He argues that individual action is not enough—that movements are needed even though these movements consume resources in the service of a greater good. What other oversimplified critiques of complicated issues have you encountered? How would you respond to a critic who might be inclined to dismiss your entire argument based on a small concession or a necessary compromise?

4. Keep a log of your own consumption of resources (water, energy, or fossil fuel use; trash, compost, or recycling generated; etc.) over a 24-hour period. Multiply that number by the population of a community of which you are a member, such as your campus, your hometown, or your nation. What observations can you make about that community's use of resources as well as its ability to reduce or mitigate the effects of that consumption? Do you believe your patterns of and attitudes toward consumption are typical of the larger community's? If not, what has influenced your behaviors positively or negatively?

Writing Assignment

Rhetorical Analysis

The groups of readings in this unit often begin with a shared goal—for example, finding a way to reduce carbon consumption. Yet each reading is composed in a different rhetorical context and is often targeted to different audiences. Write a thesis-driven rhetorical analysis in which you examine the rhetorical effectiveness of one of the arguments in this unit. Identify the target audience, briefly summarize the argument, and present your thesis highlighting two or more rhetorical features that you believe contribute to the effectiveness or ineffectiveness of the argument. You may wish to refer to Chapter 7 on analyzing arguments rhetorically to generate ideas for your analysis.

Post-Fact, Post-Truth Society?

Dealing with Misinformation, Fake News, and Misconceptions

In recent years, the phrases *fake news*, *alternative facts*, and *post-truth* appear frequently in public discourse, encompassing layers of complex ideas. But what does a phrase like *fake news* actually mean? Sometimes *fake news* is simply a hoax without factual basis. But more often the term captures an array of problems (distortions, lies, misrepresentations, and sharply contrastive angles of vision). After all, a distortion or misrepresentation of an event is not a complete fake or lie. Some pieces of "fake" news have a basis in reality while others do not. Analyzing the truth or falseness of news requires all one's rhetorical skills.

From the perspective or rhetorical theory, all stories are told from an angle of vision: The story-teller selects and arranges the details so that some parts of underlying reality get "seen" while other parts are unseen. (See Chapter 4 on framing of evidence.) But in recent years the charges of fake news have become so frequent that social commentators fear a profound unsettling of our society's confidence in the news media. Have "facts" become thoroughly disconnected from any process of verification? Do today's citizens reject any possibility of objective truth, making what really happened or what really exists entirely a matter of social consensus and therefore determined by who has the power to impose their view of reality on others? Have questions like these been with us for centuries, as evidenced by the sensationalized news reporting of other periods and the biases revealed in history books? Or has the expansion of social media and the infosphere radically changed our access to and comprehension of public information?

Many people would argue that our access to and mental processing of news about social, political, economic, and scientific information has been complicated by the proliferation of sources: no longer mainly television, radio, and print publications but also social media feeds, social media platforms for disseminating information (think Twitter and Facebook), and all kinds of Internet news sites, which compete with traditional journalism. Furthermore, many of these news sources reflect a strong partisan stance, ranging from the Alt-right to the Far Left on the political spectrum.

If news consumption was not muddied enough, analysts point to a number of social and psychological problems affecting our ability to be informed citizens and to argue effectively to sustain democracy. Clearly, our attraction to sensationalism, our desire for entertainment, and our choice of convenience over responsibility affect how we respond to news. In his influential book *Amusing Ourselves to Death: Public Discourse in the Age of Show Business* (1984) scholar Neil Postman echoes novelist Aldous Huxley's dystopian vision of people relinquishing their independence, freedom, and critical thinking through their embrace of technology and their love of entertainment. Clicking on click bait, retweeting sensational postings, forwarding social media memes, and indulging our curiosity for the bizarre instead of active thinking bring us closer to actualizing Huxley's and Postman's fears. Other analysts point to the power of desirability bias (our tendency to grant authority to what we want to believe) and our immersion in our own beliefs and worldviews as we cling to values that we consider sacred and absolute. These attitudes lead us to live in echo chambers instead of seeking out a variety of news sources. Even if we do want to consider multiple perspectives, we are challenged by the effort and time it takes to seek them out and to evaluate their authority, accuracy, and context.

Our consumption of news about science is particularly affected by these problems. Indeed, misunderstandings about what science is and how it builds knowledge have become vulnerable to postmodernism's post-truth stance, to the politicizing of science, and to science's dependence on and allegiance to its sources of financial backing.

The readings in this unit approach these problems from a range of perspectives, countries, and publications. Several of the readings strive to clarify, contextualize, and historicize the problems with news production and consumption. Others argue for solutions to equip individuals to be more savvy, vigilant news consumers—information-literate rhetorical readers, if you will. Several readings address the larger societal issue of digital ethics and the responsibility of monitoring systems. Finally, several readings explore how science is entangled in misinformation and misconceptions. At the core, these readings suggest the question: How does our ability to detect shoddy coverage and fake news and to listen to diverse perspectives nurture ethical communication in the public sphere?

The Real History of Fake News

DAVID UBERTI

David Uberti holds a B.A. and M.A. in journalism from Northwestern University and Columbia University, respectively. He is currently a media reporter for Gizmodo Media Group and a freelance feature writer for Guardian News & Media. He wrote this piece when he was a staff writer for Columbia Journalism Review. *This journal strives to be "the intellectual leader in the rapidly changing world of journalism." It is known for its "fast-turn analysis" and "deep reporting" ("Mission Statement"). The* CJR *published this article on December 15, 2016.*

In an 1807 letter to John Norvell, a young go-getter who had asked how to best run a newspaper, Thomas Jefferson penned what today would make for a fiery Medium post condemning fake news.

"It is a melancholy truth, that a suppression of the press could not more compleatly [sic] deprive the nation of its benefits, than is done by its abandoned prostitution to falsehood," the sitting president wrote. "Nothing can now be believed which is seen in a newspaper. Truth itself becomes suspicious by being put into that polluted vehicle."

That vehicle grew into a commercial powerhouse in the 19th century and a self-reverential political institution, "the media," by the mid-20th. But the pollution has been described in increasingly dire terms in recent months. PolitiFact named fake news its 2016 "Lie of the Year," while chagrined Democrats have warned about its threat to an honest public debate. The pope compared consumption of fake news to eating feces. And many of the wise men and women of journalism have chimed in almost uniformly: Come to us for the real stuff.

"Whatever its other cultural and social merits, our digital ecosystem seems to have evolved into a near-perfect environment for fake news to thrive," *New York Times* CEO Mark Thompson said in a speech to the Detroit Economic Club on Monday.

A little bit of brake-tapping may be in order: It's worth remembering, in the 5 middle of the great fake news panic of 2016, America's very long tradition of news-related hoaxes. A thumbnail history shows marked similarities to today's fakery in editorial motive or public gullibility, not to mention the blurred lines between deliberate and accidental flimflam. It also suggests that the recent fixation on fake news has more to do with macro-level trends than any new brand of faux content.

Macedonian teenagers who earn extra scratch by concocting conspiracies are indeed new entrants to the American information diet. Social networks allow smut to hurtle through the public imagination—and into pizza parlors—at breakneck speed. People at or near the top of the incoming administration have shared fake news casually. And it's appearing in news organizations' own programmatic ads.

But put aside the immediate election-related PTSD and the rampant self-loathing by journalists, which has led to cravings for a third-party, perhaps Russian-speaking, fall guy. The broader issue driving the paranoia is the tardy realization among mainstream media that they no longer hold the sole power to shape and drive the news agenda. Broadsides against fake news amount to a rearguard action from an industry fending off competitors who don't play by the same rules, or maybe don't even know they exist.

"The existence of an independent, powerful, widely respected news media establishment is an historical anomaly," Georgetown Professor Jonathan Ladd wrote in his 2011 book, *Why Americans Hate the Media and How it Matters*. "Prior to the twentieth century, such an institution had never existed in American history." Fake news is but one symptom of that shift back to historical norms, and recent hyperventilating mimics reactions from eras past.

Take Jefferson's generation. Our country's earliest political combat played out in the pages of competing partisan publications often subsidized by government printing contracts and typically unbothered by reporting as we know it. Innuendo and character assassination were standard, and it was difficult to discern content solely meant to deceive from political bomb-throwing that served deception as a side dish. Then, like now, the greybeards grumbled about how the media actually inhibited the fact-based debate it was supposed to lead.

10   "I will add," Jefferson continued in 1807, "that the man who never looks into a newspaper is better informed than he who reads them; inasmuch as he who knows nothing is nearer to truth than he whose mind is filled with falsehoods & errors."

Decades later, when Alexis de Tocqueville penned his seminal political analysis, *Democracy in America*, he also assailed the day's content producers as men "with a scanty education and a vulgar turn of mind" who played on readers' passions. "What [citizens] seek in a newspaper is a knowledge of facts," de Tocqueville wrote, "and it is only by altering or distorting those facts that a journalist can contribute to the support of his own views." His concerns weren't for passive failures of journalism, but active manipulation of the truth for political ends.

While circulation in those days was relatively low—high publishing costs, low literacy rates—proliferation of multiple titles in each major city provided a menu of worldviews that's similar to today. The infant republic nevertheless managed to survive the fake news scourge of early 19th-century newspapermen. "The large number of news outlets, the heterogeneity of the coverage, the low public esteem toward the press, and the obvious partisan leanings of publishers limited the power of the press to be influential," political scientist Darrell M. West wrote in his 2001 book, *The Rise and Fall of the Media Establishment*.

With the growth of the penny press in the 1830s, some newspapers adopted advertising-centric business models that required much larger audiences than highbrow partisan opinions would attract. So the motivation to mislead shifted slightly more toward commercially minded sensationalism, spurring some of the most memorable media fakes in American history.

In 1835, *The New York Sun* ran a six-part series, "Great Astronomical Discoveries Lately Made," which detailed the supposed discovery of life on the Moon. The hoax landed in part because the Sun's circulation was huge by standards of the day, and the too-good-to-be-true story supposedly enticed many new readers to fork over their pennies as well.

Edgar Allan Poe, who weeks before had published his own moon hoax in the *Southern Literary Messenger*, quickly criticized the *Sun* story's unbelievability—and the public's gullibility. "Not one person in 10 discredited it," Poe recounted years later. He went on to chastise the *Sun*'s fake news story for what he saw as low production value:

15

> Immediately upon completion of the 'Moon story'. . . I wrote an examina-
> tion of its claims to credit, showing distinctly its fictitious character, but was
> astonished at finding that I could obtain few listeners, so really eager were all
> to be deceived, so magical were the charms of a style that served as a vehicle
> of an exceedingly clumsy invention. . . . Indeed, however rich the imagination
> displayed in this fiction, it wanted much of the force that might have been
> given to it by a more scrupulous attention to analogy and fact.

Many other newspapers were skeptical of the *Sun*'s moon story. But public back-lash was muted in part because of the lack of widely accepted standards for the content appearing in readers' news feeds, not unlike today. Objective journalism had yet to settle in, and there were no clear dividing lines between reporting, opinions, and nonsense. The public's credulity—potentially embellished by Poe and other contemporaneous accounts—became part of the legend, particularly given elites' apprehension of Jacksonian populism.

These historic purveyors of fake news were by no means obscure publica-tions from the 19th-century equivalent of the digital gutter. In 1874, the widely read *New York Herald* published a more than 10,000-word account of how ani-mals had broken out of the Central Park Zoo, rampaged through Manhattan, and killed dozens. The Herald reported that many of the escaped animals were still at large as of press time, and the city's mayor had installed a strict curfew until they could be corralled. A disclaimer, tucked away at the bottom of the story, admitted that "the entire story given above is a pure fabrication. Not one word of it is true."

Many readers must have missed it. The hoax quickly spread through real-life social networks, as historian Hampton Sides described in his 2014 book, *In the Kingdom of Ice: The Grand and Terrible Polar Voyage of the USS Jeannette*:

> Alarmed citizens made for the city's piers in hopes of escaping by small boat or
> ferry. Many thousands of people, heeding the mayor's 'proclamation,' stayed
> inside all day, awaiting word that the crisis had passed. Still others loaded their
> rifles and marched into the park to hunt for rogue animals.

Even as the late-19th and early-20th centuries saw the early stages of the shift toward a more professionalized media, corruption of the information that reached readers remained common. In his 1897 book critiquing American news coverage of the Cuban War of Independence, *Facts and Fakes about Cuba*, George Bronson Rea outlined the stages of embellishment between minor news events outside of Havana to seemingly fictionalized front-page stories in New York. Cuban sources wanted to turn public opinion against Spain, while American correspondents were eager to sell newspapers.

20   "But the truth is a hard thing to suppress," Rea wrote, "and will sooner or later come to light to act as a boomerang on the perpetrators of such outrageous 'fakes,' whose only aim is to draw this country into a war with Spain to attain their own selfish ends."

There are fewer glaring examples of fake news stretching toward the mid-20th century, as journalistic norms—as we conceive of them today—began to emerge. Commercial monopolies, coupled with lack of political partisanship, gave news organizations daylight to professionalize and police themselves. But that's not to say this golden era was free from myths.

Indeed, many uncorrected stories concern the news media itself, which could provide clues as to why today's notion of fake news seems to have so much cultural currency. As American University Professor W. Joseph Campbell debunks in his book, *Getting It Wrong: Ten of the Greatest Misreported Stories in American Journalism*, a remark by Walter Cronkite wasn't *actually* the first domino to fall en route to ending the Vietnam War. *The Washington Post* didn't *really* bring down Nixon. (Media coverage and public opinion toward the war had already gone south; Nixon was felled by subpoena-wielding authorities and a wide array of other constitutional processes.)

"They're neat and tidy, easy to remember, fun to tell, and media centric," Campbell says in an interview. "They serve to elevate media actors. There is an aspirational component to these myths that help keep them alive."

The opposite force could be at play in today's fake news debate. Public trust of the media has been in decline for decades, though the situation now feels particularly cataclysmic with the atomization of media consumption, partisan criticism from all corners, and the ascension of Donald Trump to the White House. Just as Watergate gave the media a bright story to tell about itself, fake news provides a catchall symbol—and a scapegoat—for journalists grappling with their diminished institutional power.

25   It's telling that the most compelling reporting on fake news has focused on distribution networks—what's new—even if those stories have yet to prove they've exacerbated the problem en masse. In the meantime, let's retire the dreaded moniker in favor of more precise choices: misinformation, deception, lies. Just as the media has employed "fake news" to discredit competitors for public attention, political celebrities and partisan publications have used it to discredit the press wholesale. As hard as it is to admit, that's an increasingly unfair fight.

How to Spot Fake News

EUGENE KIELY AND LORI ROBERTSON

Eugene Kiely, a journalist with more than twenty years of experience writing about government and politics, has worked for USA TODAY *and the* Philadelphia Inquirer *and is currently the director of FactCheck.org. Lori Robertson, currently the managing editor at FactCheck.org, worked previously for* American Journalism Review. *FactCheck.org is affiliated with the Annenberg Public Policy Center of the University of Pennsylvania and describes itself as "a nonpartisan, nonprofit 'consumer advocate' for voters" that seeks "to apply the best practices of both journalism and scholarship" so that the American public will have accurate information. This piece was posted to this website on November 8, 2016.*

Fake news is nothing new. But bogus stories can reach more people more quickly via social media than what good old-fashioned viral emails could accomplish in years past.

Concern about the phenomenon led Facebook and Google to announce that they'll crack down on fake news sites, restricting their ability to garner ad revenue. Perhaps that could dissipate the amount of malarkey online, though news consumers themselves are the best defense against the spread of misinformation.

Not all of the misinformation being passed along online is complete fiction, though some of it is. Snopes.com has been exposing false viral claims since the mid 1990s, whether that's fabricated messages, distortions containing bits of truth and everything in between. Founder David Mikkelson warned in a Nov. 17 article not to lump everything into the "fake news" category. "The fictions and fabrications that comprise fake news are but a subset of the larger *bad news* phenomenon, which also encompasses many forms of shoddy, unresearched, error-filled, and deliberately misleading reporting that do a disservice to everyone," he wrote.

A lot of these viral claims aren't "news" at all, but fiction, satire, and efforts to fool readers into thinking they're for real.

We've long encouraged readers to be skeptical of viral claims, and make good   5 use of the delete key when a chain email hits their inboxes. In December 2007, we launched our Ask FactCheck feature, where we answer readers' questions, the vast majority of which concern viral emails, social media memes, and the like. Our first story was about a made-up email that claimed then-House Speaker Nancy Pelosi wanted to put a "windfall" tax on all stock profits of 100 percent and give the money to, the email claimed, "the 12 Million Illegal Immigrants and other unemployed minorities." We called it "a malicious fabrication"—that's "fake news" in today's parlance.

In 2008, we tried to get readers to rid their inboxes of this kind of garbage. We described a list of red flags—we called them Key Characteristics of Bogusness— that were clear tip-offs that a chain email wasn't legitimate. Among them: an anonymous author; excessive exclamation points, capital letters, and misspellings;

entreaties that "This is NOT a hoax!"; and links to sourcing that does not support or completely contradicts the claims being made.

Those all still hold true, but fake stories—as in, completely made-up "news"—has grown more sophisticated, often presented on a site designed to look (sort of) like a legitimate news organization. Still, we find it's easy to figure out what's real and what's imaginary if you're armed with some critical thinking and fact-checking tools of the trade.

Here's our advice on how to spot a fake:

Consider the source.

In recent months, we've fact-checked fake news from abcnews.com.co (not the actual URL for ABC News), WTOE 5 News (whose "about" page says it's "a fantasy news website"), and the Boston Tribune (whose "contact us" page lists only a gmail address). Earlier this year, we debunked the claim that the Obamas were buying a vacation home in Dubai, a made-up missive that came from WhatDoesItMean.com, which describes itself as "One Of The Top Ranked Websites In The World for New World Order, Conspiracy Theories and Alternative News" and further says on its site that most of what it publishes is fiction.

10   Clearly, some of these sites do provide a "fantasy news" or satire warning, like WTOE 5, which published the bogus headline, "Pope Francis Shocks World, Endorses Donald Trump for President, Releases Statement." Others aren't so upfront, like the Boston Tribune, which doesn't provide any information on its mission, staff members, or physical location—further signs that maybe this site isn't a legitimate news organization. The site, in fact, changed its name from Associated Media Coverage, after its work had been debunked by fact-checking organizations.

Snopes.com, which has been writing about viral claims and online rumors since the mid-1990s, maintains a list of known fake news websites, several of which have emerged in the past two years.

Read beyond the headline.

If a provocative headline drew your attention, read a little further before you decide to pass along the shocking information. Even in legitimate news stories, the headline doesn't always tell the whole story. But fake news, particularly efforts to be satirical, can include several revealing signs in the text. That abcnews.com.co story that we checked, headlined "Obama Signs Executive Order Banning The Pledge Of Allegiance In Schools Nationwide," went on to quote "Fappy the Anti-Masturbation Dolphin." We have to assume that the many readers who asked us whether this viral rumor was true hadn't read the full story.

Check the author.

Another tell-tale sign of a fake story is often the byline. The pledge of allegiance story on abcnews.com.co was supposedly written by "Jimmy Rustling." Who is he? Well, his author page claims he is a "doctor" who won "fourteen Peabody awards and a handful of Pulitzer Prizes." Pretty impressive, if true. But it's not. No one by the name of "Rustling" has won a Pulitzer or Peabody award. The photo accompanying Rustling's bio is also displayed on another bogus story on a different site, but this time under the byline "Darius Rubics." The Dubai story was written by "Sorcha Faal, and as reported to her Western Subscribers." The Pope Francis story has no byline at all.

What's the support?

Many times these bogus stories will cite official—or official-sounding—sources, but once you look into it, the source doesn't back up the claim. For instance, the Boston Tribune site wrongly claimed that President Obama's mother-in-law was going to get a lifetime government pension for having babysat her grand-daughters in the White House, citing "the Civil Service Retirement Act" and providing a link. But the link to a government benefits website doesn't support the claim at all.

The banning-the-pledge story cites the number of an actual executive 15 order—you can look it up. It doesn't have anything to do with the Pledge of Allegiance.

Another viral claim we checked a year ago was a graphic purporting to show crime statistics on the percentage of whites killed by blacks and other murder statistics by race. Then-presidential candidate Donald Trump retweeted it, tell-ing Fox News commentator Bill O'Reilly that it came "from sources that are very credible." But almost every figure in the image was wrong—FBI crime data is publicly available—and the supposed source given for the data, "Crime Statistics Bureau – San Francisco," doesn't exist.

Recently, we've received several questions about a fake news story on the admittedly satirical site Nevada County Scooper, which wrote that Vice President-elect Mike Pence, in a "surprise announcement," credited gay conversion therapy for saving his marriage. Clearly such a "surprise announcement" would garner media coverage beyond a website you've never heard of. In fact, if you Google this, the first link that comes up is a Snopes.com article revealing that this is fake news.

Check the date.

Some false stories aren't completely fake, but rather distortions of real events. These mendacious claims can take a legitimate news story and twist what it says—or even claim that something that happened long ago is related to current events.

Since Trump was elected president, we've received many inquiries from read-ers wanting to know whether Ford had moved car production from Mexico to Ohio, because of Trump's election. Readers cited various blog items that quoted from and linked to a CNN Money article titled "Ford shifts truck production from Mexico to Ohio." But that story is from August 2015, clearly not evidence of Ford making any move due to the outcome of the election. (A reminder again to check the support for these claims.)

20   One deceptive website didn't credit CNN, but instead took CNN's 2015 story and slapped a new headline and publication date on it, claiming, "Since Donald Trump Won The Presidency . . . Ford Shifts Truck Production From Mexico To Ohio." Not only is that a bogus headline, but the deception involves copyright infringement.

If this Ford story sounds familiar, that's because the CNN article has been distorted before.

In October 2015, Trump wrongly boasted that Ford had changed its plans to build new plants in Mexico, and instead would build a plant in Ohio. Trump took credit for Ford's alleged change of heart and tweeted a link to a story on a blog called Prntly.com, which cited the CNN Money story. But Ford hadn't changed its plans at all, and Trump deserved no credit.

In fact, the CNN article was about the transfer of some pickup assembly work from Mexico to Ohio, a move that was announced by Ford in March 2014. The plans for new plants in Mexico were still on, Ford said. "Ford has not spoken with Mr. Trump, nor have we made any changes to our plans," Ford said in a statement.

Is this some kind of joke?

Remember, there is such a thing as satire. Normally, it's clearly labeled as such, and sometimes it's even funny. Andy Borowitz has been writing a satirical news column, the Borowitz Report, since 2001, and it has appeared in the *New Yorker* since 2012. But not everyone gets the jokes. We've fielded several questions on whether Borowitz's work is true.

25   Among the headlines our readers have flagged: "Putin Appears with Trump in Flurry of Swing-State Rallies" and "Trump Threatens to Skip Remaining Debates If Hillary Is There." When we told readers these were satirical columns, some indicated that they suspected the details were far-fetched but wanted to be sure.

And then there's the more debatable forms of satire, designed to pull one over on the reader. That "Fappy the Anti-Masturbation Dolphin" story? That's the work of online hoaxer Paul Horner, whose "greatest coup," as described by the *Washington Post* in 2014, was when Fox News mentioned, as fact, a fake piece titled, "Obama uses own money to open Muslim museum amid government shut-down." Horner told the *Post* after the election that he was concerned his hoaxes aimed at Trump supporters may have helped the campaign.

The posts by Horner and others—whether termed satire or simply "fake news"—are designed to encourage clicks and generate money for the creator through ad revenue. Horner told the *Washington Post* he makes a living off his posts. Asked why his material gets so many views, Horner responded, "They just keep passing stuff around. Nobody fact-checks anything anymore."

Check your biases.

We know this is difficult. Confirmation bias leads people to put more stock in information that confirms their beliefs and discount information that doesn't. But the next time you're automatically appalled at some Facebook post concerning, say, a politician you oppose, take a moment to check it out.

Try this simple test: What other stories have been posted to the "news" website that is the source of the story that just popped up in your Facebook feed? You may be predisposed to believe that Obama bought a house in Dubai, but how about a story on the same site that carries this headline: "Antarctica 'Guardians' Retaliate Against America With Massive New Zealand Earthquake." That, too, was written by the prolific "Sorcha Faal, and as reported to her Western Subscribers."

We're encouraged by some of the responses we get from readers, who—like   30 the ones uncertain of Borowitz's columns—express doubt in the outrageous, and just want to be sure their skepticism is justified. But we are equally discouraged when we see debunked claims gain new life.

We've seen the resurgence of a fake quote from Donald Trump since the election—a viral image that circulated last year claims Trump told *People* magazine in 1998: "If I were to run, I'd run as a Republican. They're the dumbest group of voters in the country. They believe anything on Fox News. I could lie and they'd still eat it up. I bet my numbers would be terrific." We found no such quote in *People*'s archives from 1998, or any other year. And a public relations representative for the magazine confirmed that. *People*'s Julie Farin told us in an email last year: "We combed through every Trump story in our archive. We couldn't find anything remotely like this quote—and no interview at all in 1998."

Comedian Amy Schumer may have contributed to the revival of this fake meme. She put it on Instagram, adding at the end of a lengthy message, "Yes this quote is fake but it doesn't matter."

Consult the experts.

We know you're busy, and some of this debunking takes time. But we get paid to do this kind of work. Between FactCheck.org, Snopes.com, the *Washington Post* Fact Checker, and PolitiFact.com, it's likely at least one has already fact-checked the latest viral claim to pop up in your news feed.

FactCheck.org was among a network of independent fact-checkers who signed an open letter to Facebook's Mark Zuckerberg suggesting that Facebook "start an open conversation on the principles that could underpin a more accurate news ecosystem on its News Feed." We hope that conversation happens, but news readers themselves remain the first line of defense against fake news.

On our Viral Spiral page, we list some of the claims we get asked about the   35 most; all of our Ask FactChecks can be found here. And if you encounter a new claim you'd like us to investigate, email us at editor@factcheck.org.

Warning!! This Newspaper May Contain Traces of Journalism

KARSTEN SCHLEY

Karsten Schley is a German cartoonist from Hamburg. He has illustrated seven books, and he publishes his cartoons with agencies in Germany, England, and Italy. This cartoon appeared on the website for cartoonstock.com.

The Cure for Fake News Is Worse Than the Disease; Stop Being Trump's Twitter Fool

JACK SHAFER

Jack Shafer has written columns for Reuters and Slate *and has had his writing published in numerous high-profile venues—among them* The New Republic, Foreign Affairs, The New York Times Magazine, *and* The Wall Street Journal. *He currently serves as* Politico's *senior media writer. These editorials appeared on November 22, 2016, in* Politico, *a web and print magazine that strives to present insightful, provocative, non-partisan analysis of and arguments on current issues.*

The Cure for Fake News Is Worse Than the Disease

Since the election, our fussing over "fake news" has ballooned into a full-blown moral panic. A moral panic is the term sociologists give what the rest of us call a mass freak-out, and they are often typified by media-boosted scare campaigns that identify the "social deviants" (drug users, prostitutes, juvenile delinquents, gamblers, criminals, etc.) who are violating the norms practiced by regular people. Unchecked moral panics tend to do more damage than the deviants themselves if authorities and leaders—"moral entrepreneurs," to use the lingo—overreact to whatever harm those deviants might be causing.

The good news about moral panics is that they burn so hot that they tend to quickly run out of fuel as the culture's attention drifts to other subjects. But the fake news moral panic looks to have legs, which means that somebody is likely to get hurt before it abates. Already, otherwise intelligent and calm observers are cheering plans set forth by Facebook's Mark Zuckerberg to censor users' news feeds in a fashion that will eliminate fake news. Do we really want Facebook exercising this sort of top-down power to determine what is true or false? Wouldn't we be revolted if one company owned all the newsstands and decided what was proper and improper reading fare?

Once established to crush fake news, the Facebook mechanism could be repurposed to crush other types of information that might cause moral panic. This cure for fake news is worse than the disease.

As we applaud Facebook's decision to blue-pencil the News Feed, we need to ask why fake news exists and—as I previously wrote—why it has existed for centuries. The audience for fake news resembles the crowds who pay money to attend magic shows. Magic-show patrons know going in that some of what they're going to see is genuine. But they also know that a good portion of what they're going to see is going to look real but be phony. Like a woman sawed in half. Or an act of levitation. Being shown something fantastical that is almost true brings delight to almost everybody. People *like* to be fooled.

Stop Being Trump's Twitter Fool

The magic show audience—like fake-news consumers—willingly suspends disbelief to be entertained or titillated. They are a willing party to their own (temporary) deception, and no societal safeguards are likely to protect them from seeking that which they want. The supermarket tabloids used to specialize in this sort of bunk, publishing stories about UFOs, Elvis sightings, and other malarkey, but they've largely gotten out of that market for sensational and often "truish" stories about celebrities.

From an economist's viewpoint, fake news is mostly a *demand side* problem. If readers weren't so determined to click sexy headlines that lead them to websites of dubious or unknown reputation, and do it again and again, and often sharing the link, fake news would soon be extinct. But its prevalence indicates that the market is only providing the cheap and stupid thrill some readers desire. Rather than tweaking its algorithms, Facebook might be better off trying to change human nature.

Almost every genre of news has been invaded by fake news, but some subject areas appear to be more or less immune to its charms. Fake news about sports or business is extremely rare. Oh, the sports and business pages aren't fake-free. Hoaxes and baseless rumors get published, but sports and business readers tend to be knowledgeable and discerning about their interests. A fake story about a stock price or a baseball score is quickly resisted by savvy readers who demand that it must be corrected or retracted. They chase down the works of pranksters and hoaxers like white blood cells in pursuit of infectious disease. Fake weather news seems rare, too, for the same reason. The same for fake traffic reports.

Fake political news thrives because intense media coverage causes nearly everybody to develop some sort of interest in political topics during a campaign year. But not everybody acquires the expertise to equal their baseline interest in politics. This makes them easy to fool and easy prey for, say, a bogus story about anti-Trump protesters getting paid and bused in to demonstrate against the president-elect. The anti-Trump protester story gained extra velocity because it confirmed the biases and expectations of its readers. How many low-political-interest Clinton voters shared the story, I wonder? Few, I would guess, in part because they didn't want the story to be true.

5   Not all fake news fits into this bias pattern, but, in general, the pattern holds. The more outrageous and partisan a fake bundle is, the greater the chance it will be reshared, go viral, and break into the mainstream.

Fake news is too important to be left to the Facebook remedy—Mark Zuckerberg is no arbiter of truth. First, we need to learn to live with a certain level of background fake news without overreacting. Next, we need to instruct readers on how to spot and avoid fake news, which many publications are already doing. A few years ago, Factcheck.org showed readers how to identify bogus email claims. Snopes does yeoman work in this area, as does BuzzFeed. Software wizards should be encouraged to create filters and tools, such as browser extensions, that sniff out bogusity.

But no matter what measures we take, fake news will persist because human nature persists: People throw their money away on get-rich schemes, play three-card monte, correspond with Nigerian scamsters and get fleeced, even though they know better. Deep in the brain exists a hungry lobe that loves to be deceived. We may never end fake news, but arresting the current moral panic is a simple matter of applying small doses of reason to our media diet.

Sign the Statement: Truth-Seeking, Democracy, and Freedom of Thought and Expression

ROBERT P. GEORGE AND CORNEL WEST

This online position statement, published March 14, 2017, on the website for the James Madison Program in American Ideals and Institutions at Princeton University, is a response to a violent student outburst at Middlebury College related to a controversial speaker. This statement was authored by two well-known public intellectuals and professors, Cornel West and Robert P. George. Cornel West, a famous African American thinker and writer, has been a professor of philosophy, theology, and African American studies, teaching at Harvard University and Princeton University, among other places. Of the twenty books he has authored, two of the best known are Race Matters *and* Democracy Matters. *As a public intellectual, West is an activist democrat. In contrast, Robert P. George, a professor of law and philosophy at Princeton University who holds an endowed chair and serves as director of the James Madison Program, is known for his leadership and prolific political writing and activism as a Roman Catholic conservative. The disparate political and religious perspectives of these men lend weight to this declaration of the importance of respectful open communication to counter narrow-mindedness and intolerance in public discourse.*

The pursuit of knowledge and the maintenance of a free and democratic society require the cultivation and practice of the virtues of intellectual humility, openness of mind, and, above all, love of truth. These virtues will manifest themselves and be strengthened by one's willingness to listen attentively and respectfully to intelligent people who challenge one's beliefs and who represent causes one disagrees with and points of view one does not share.

That's why all of us should seek respectfully to engage with people who challenge our views. And we should oppose efforts to silence those with whom we disagree—especially on college and university campuses. As John Stuart Mill taught, a recognition of the possibility that we may be in error is a good reason to listen to and honestly consider—and not merely to tolerate grudgingly—points of view that we do not share, and even perspectives that we find shocking or scandalous. What's more, as Mill noted, even if one happens to be right about this or that disputed matter, seriously and respectfully engaging people who disagree will deepen one's understanding of the truth and sharpen one's ability to defend it.

None of us is infallible. Whether you are a person of the left, the right, or the center, there are reasonable people of goodwill who do not share your fundamental convictions. This does not mean that all opinions are equally valid or that all speakers are equally worth listening to. It certainly does not mean that there is no truth to be discovered. Nor does it mean that you are necessarily wrong. But they are not necessarily wrong either. So someone who has not fallen into the idolatry of worshiping his or her own opinions and loving them above truth itself will want to listen to people who see things differently in order to learn what considerations—evidence, reasons, arguments—led them to a place different from where one happens, at least for now, to find oneself.

All of us should be willing—even eager—to engage with anyone who is prepared to do business in the currency of truth-seeking discourse by offering reasons, marshaling evidence, and making arguments. The more important the subject under discussion, the more willing we should be to listen and engage—especially if the person with whom we are in conversation will challenge our deeply held—even our most cherished and identity-forming—beliefs.

5   It is all-too-common these days for people to try to immunize from criticism opinions that happen to be dominant in their particular communities. Sometimes this is done by questioning the motives and thus stigmatizing those who dissent from prevailing opinions; or by disrupting their presentations; or by demanding that they be excluded from campus or, if they have already been invited, disinvited. Sometimes students and faculty members turn their backs on speakers whose opinions they don't like or simply walk out and refuse to listen to those whose convictions offend their values. Of course, the right to peacefully protest, including on campuses, is sacrosanct. But before exercising that right, each of us should ask: Might it not be better to listen respectfully and try to learn from a speaker with whom I disagree? Might it better serve the cause of truth-seeking to engage the speaker in frank civil discussion?

Our willingness to listen to and respectfully engage those with whom we disagree (especially about matters of profound importance) contributes vitally to the maintenance of a milieu in which people feel free to speak their minds, consider unpopular positions, and explore lines of argument that may undercut established ways of thinking. Such an ethos protects us against dogmatism and groupthink, both of which are toxic to the health of academic communities and to the functioning of democracies.

Fake News and a 400-Year-Old Problem: We Need to Resolve the "Post-Truth" Crisis

LUCIANO FLORIDI

Luciano Floridi is Professor of Philosophy and Ethics of Information at the University of Oxford in Great Britain. He serves on various government and industry advisory boards for ethics and the infosphere. He has written a number of books on digital, ethical problems, among them The Philosophy of Information, The Ethics of Information, *and most recently* The Fourth Revolution—How the Infosphere Is Reshaping Human Reality. *This editorial appeared on November 29, 2016, in* The Guardian, *a daily center-left-leaning British newspaper.*

The Internet echo chamber satiates our appetite for pleasant lies and reassuring falsehoods and has become the defining challenge of the 21st century

The Internet age made big promises to us: a new period of hope and opportunity, connection and empathy, expression and democracy. Yet the digital medium has aged badly because we allowed it to grow chaotically and carelessly, lowering our guard against the deterioration and pollution of our infosphere.

We sought only what we wanted—entertainment, cheaper goods, free news and gossip—and not the deeper understanding, dialogue, or education that would have served us better.

The appetite for populism is not a new problem. In the ferocious newspaper battles of 1890s New York, the emerging sensational style of journalism in Joseph Pulitzer's *New York World* and William Randolph Hearst's *New York Journal* was dubbed "yellow journalism" by those concerned with maintaining standards, adherence to accuracy, and an informed public debate. We now have the same problem with online misinformation.

Humans have always been prejudiced and intolerant of different views. Francis Bacon's philosophical masterwork *Novum Organum*, published in 1620, analyses four kinds of idols or false notions that "are now in possession of the human understanding, and have taken deep root therein."

One of them, the "idols of the cave," refers to our conceptual biases and sus-   5
ceptibility to external influences. "Everyone . . . has a cave or den of his own, which refracts and discolors the light of nature, owing either to his own proper and peculiar nature; or to his education and conversation with others; or to the reading of books, and the authority of those whom he esteems and admires; or to the differences of impressions, accordingly as they take place in a mind preoccupied and predisposed or in a mind indifferent and settled; or the like." It is at least a 400-year-old problem.

Likewise, the appetite for shallow gossip, pleasant lies and reassuring falsehoods has always been significant. The difference is that the Internet allows that appetite to be fed a bottomless supply of semantic junk, transforming Bacon's caves into echo chambers. In that way, we have always been "post-truth."

These kinds of digital, ethical problems represent a defining challenge of the 21st century. They include breaches of privacy, of security and safety, of ownership and intellectual property rights, of trust, of fundamental human rights, as well as the possibility of exploitation, discrimination, inequality, manipulation, propaganda, populism, racism, violence and hate speech. How should we even begin to weigh the human cost of these problems? Consider the political responsibilities of newspapers' websites in distorting discussions around the UK's Brexit decision, or the false news disseminated by the "alt-right," a loose affiliation of people with far-right views, during the campaign waged by President-elect Donald Trump.

So far, the strategy for technology companies has been to deal with the ethical impact of their products retrospectively. Some are finally taking more significant action against online misinformation: Facebook, for example, is currently working on methods for stronger detection and verification of fake news, and on ways to provide warning labels on false content—yet only now that the U.S. presidential election is over.

But this is not good enough. The Silicon Valley mantra of "fail often, fail fast" is a poor strategy when it comes to the ethical and cultural impacts of these businesses. It is equivalent to "too little, too late," and has very high, long-term costs of global significance, in preventable or mitigable harms, wasted resources, missed opportunities, lack of participation, misguided caution and lower resilience.

10   A lack of proactive ethics foresight thwarts decision making, undermines management practices and damages strategies for digital innovation. In short, it is very expensive. Amazon's same-day delivery service, for example, systematically tends to exclude predominantly black neighborhoods in the 27 metropolitan areas where it was available, Bloomberg found. It would have been preventable with an ethical impact analysis that could have considered the discriminatory impact of simple, algorithmic decisions.

The near instantaneous spread of digital information means that some of the costs of misinformation may be hard to reverse, especially when confidence and trust are undermined. The tech industry can and must do better to ensure the Internet meets its potential to support individuals' well-being and social good.

We need an ethical infosphere to save the world and ourselves from ourselves, but restoring that infosphere requires a gigantic, ecological effort. We must rebuild trust through credibility, transparency and accountability—and a high degree of patience, coordination and determination.

There are some reasons to be cheerful. In April 2016, the British government agreed with the recommendation of the House of Commons' Science and Technology Committee that the government should establish a Council of Data Ethics. Such an open and independent advisory forum would bring all stakeholders together to participate in the dialogue, decision-making, and implementation of solutions to common ethical problems brought about by the information revolution.

In September 2016, Amazon, DeepMind, Facebook, IBM, Microsoft, and Google (whom I advised on the right to be forgotten) established a new ethical body called the Partnership on Artificial Intelligence to Benefit People and Society. The Royal Society, the British Academy, and the Alan Turing Institute, the national institute for data science, are working on regulatory frameworks for managing personal data, and in May 2018, Europe's new General Data Protection Regulation will come into effect, strengthening the rights of individuals and their personal information. All these initiatives show a growing interest in how online platforms can be held more responsible for the content they provide, not unlike newspapers.

15   We need to shape and guide the future of the digital, and stop making it up as we go along. It is time to work on an innovative blueprint for a better kind of infosphere.

Teaching Writing in a Post-Truth Era

PETER WAYNE MOE

Peter Wayne Moe holds a doctorate from the University of Pittsburgh in composition, literacy, pedagogy, and rhetoric. He serves as Assistant Professor of English and Director of Campus Writing at Seattle Pacific University and publishes in many venues. This argument appeared in a shorter version as a guest essay in The Seattle Times *on February 28, 2017.*

Back in December, President-Elect Donald Trump declared to have had "a massive landslide victory" in the election. Fact checkers at the Associated Press, Politi-Fact, CNN, and others were quick to point out his problematic use of "landslide" (though Chris Wallace, who was interviewing Trump, let it slide). NPR's Arnie Seipel's research showed that Trump's margin of victory places him 46th in the 58 presidential elections, well behind Reagan's 489 electoral votes in 1980 and his 525 electoral votes in 1984. And never mind that Hillary Clinton led the popular vote by 2.8 million. Hardly a landslide, let alone a massive one.

Although he's far from the only politician to stretch the truth, Trump's disregard for facts also showed up in his claims regarding the size of his inauguration crowds and with his administration's groundless claims of voter fraud. Journalists run through this cycle of checking the president's facts again and again, not only because of the good work journalists do, but also because we're living in a post-truth era where facts just don't seem to matter.

In a recent episode of *This American Life*, Ira Glass argues that "facts seem less meaningless than they ever have." He points, among other things, to the continued skepticism of President Obama's birthplace and that 30 percent of the country thinks he's Muslim. Coupled with the rise of fake news, it becomes harder and harder to have a discussion, to talk about the problems facing our country, to move forward in any way when we can't even agree upon the facts upon which the discussion rests.

As a teacher of writing, all this bothers me greatly. If facts don't count for anything, then how is public discourse possible? How do I teach my students to write when it's becoming increasingly difficult to make a claim grounded in fact? What's a writing teacher to do?

First, our writing classrooms need to make information literacy a cornerstone 5 of the curriculum. Last November, researchers at Stanford released a report showing that 80 percent of middle-school students cannot distinguish between real and fake news and are clueless as to what "sponsored content" means on a news website.

This is a problem of information literacy, and it reaches beyond just the middle school. Our students—at all levels—need to learn to write and read well. They need to learn how to gather reliable sources, how to evaluate those sources, how to make use of those sources in fair, ethical, and generous yet critical ways. There's a push from news outlets to teach the public these skills, and many schools are now including information literacy in their curriculum.

The college writing course needs to be at the forefront of such teaching, and the library needs to have a role, too. Students need to learn the difference between Google and a library database, between BuzzFeed and Politico, between a blog and fact-checked reporting. Whatever our students are reading, we must couch that reading within larger discussions of information literacy.

We must also redeem rhetoric. Writing professor Victor Villanueva defines rhetoric as "the conscious use of language" and all of us—teachers and students, citizens and politicians—need to become more conscious of how we use language. Such awareness comes through the study of rhetoric, the art of persuasion. John Locke called rhetoric "that powerful instrument of error and deceit" and, judging from this past election, he's right.

But there's more to rhetoric than manipulation. Aristotle said the study of rhetoric is useful for four reasons. First, the public needs to know how an argument works. Only then they can respond to faulty claims so that truth can prevail.

10   Second, Aristotle knows that "there are people whom one cannot instruct." Rhetoric gives the ability to reach these people. If students are to have any hope of changing public policy, of persuading others who so vehemently and ignorantly disagree, they need more resources at their disposal than facts alone—because, as we've seen this past year, facts don't always work.

Third, training in rhetoric enables students to more fully understand the issues at hand. To make a smart and sound argument, the student must know how opponents will likely be making theirs; rhetoric allows for a deeper knowledge of what's going on.

And fourth, Aristotle says rhetoric is vital because a person needs to be able to "defend himself with speech and reason." I cannot help but read that as a call to arms, as Aristotle giving his students the tools they need to enter into public discussions, fraught as they are. Aristotle finishes with this: a person "can confer the greatest of benefits by a right use of these [rhetorical arts], and inflict the greatest of injuries by using them wrongly."

We regularly see plenty of instances of the misuse of rhetoric. It's imperative that we teach our students to respond with thoughtful, careful, and nuanced reading and writing that engages fully and substantively the issues at hand. When facts don't matter, information literacy and rhetoric do all the more.

Why Aren't People Listening to Scientists?

MARCUS DU SAUTOY

Marcus du Sautoy's titles as Simonyi Professor for the Public Understanding of Science and Professor of Mathematics at Oxford University indicate his professional range. He has won awards for his mathematical scholarship, but he is also well-known in Britain for communicating about mathematics and science to the public through numerous BBC television programs, a TED talk, and his books and articles about science and mathematics, among them The Music of the Spheres, Symmetry: A Journey into the Patterns of Nature, The Number Mysteries: A Mathematical Odyssey Through Everyday Life, *and* What We Can't Know. *He has written for* The Times [of London] The Daily Telegraph, *and* The Guardian *in Britain, and he has been published in other major international newspapers. He published this article as an opinion-editorial in* The Los Angeles Times *on April 23, 2017.*

Who would you trust more: a politician or a scientist? Even in our age of skepticism, I think more people would vote for the scientist. And yet politicians who challenge well-tested scientific theories are getting unprecedented traction of late. The whole concept of the expert is under extraordinary attack on both sides of the Atlantic.

To be fair, science often goes against intuition. As kids, we build up models in our heads to explain the world around us. The Earth appears to be flat. The sun appears to go around the Earth. Humans appear to be very different from mice. Only a careful presentation of evidence counters these intuitive stories.

Take the mouse genome. It contains nearly the same amount of base pairs—the ladder rungs of the double helix—as the human genome, about 3.1 billion. Only 5% of these base pairs are responsible for coding the proteins that make us what we are. The other 95% is junk. Of the important stuff, 85% of human genes are, on average, identical to those of the mouse.

If you are still reading this, you have already experienced one of the problems with countering intuition: It takes time to lay out evidence, and the evidence can be complicated. Although you don't need a doctorate to understand the science, you do need time and a willingness to invest it in something other than the instantaneous news hits we've become accustomed to.

But even people who do put in the effort seem all too ready to dismiss scientific evidence. It's not that they don't believe the facts presented to them, exactly. It's that they question whether those facts are relevant to their own situation.

Why, for example, are people rejecting the idea that vaccines are essential to preventing the spread of disease? The science is pretty clear. Every virus has something called a "reproduction number," which represents the quantity of secondary infections produced by an infected individual in an unvaccinated population. Typically, influenza has a reproduction number of around two to three. Smallpox had a reproduction number of five to seven. Given the smallpox rate, epidemiologists predicted that inoculating 80% of the world population would successfully eradicate the virus. They were right.

We are currently experiencing a worrying growth in cases of measles. According to the World Health Organization, there were 134,200 measles deaths in 2015—about 367 deaths every day, or 15 deaths every hour. We have a vaccine for measles. But because of its high reproduction number—14 to 18—measles will be eradicated only if we inoculate 95% of the population. A few irresponsible doctors have spread rumors that the measles, mumps, and rubella vaccine is linked to autism. Their original study, published in *The Lancet*, was rescinded and repudiated, and thousands of scientists have come out to explain why the rumors are not true. Yet the fear persists.

Our approach as a society to countering deadly diseases hinges on what is called "herd immunity." The concept requires us to think collectively, for the good of humanity, rather than individually. Think individually, and you might argue that there is a risk involved in taking any vaccine. But while there is a risk, it is often tiny. Herein lies one of the primary reasons for the dismissal of the expert, in my view: Rejectionists don't believe that the scientist has their best interests at heart.

Perhaps it is up to scientists to better understand this psychology and take it into account when we present our conclusions. But scientists don't always speak with one voice. Indeed, robust argument over the interpretation of data is a critical part of practicing science. Any new model must undergo questioning. This can be confusing to a public and government that want clear, definitive answers.

10   The public's desire for certainty presents one of the biggest challenges for the scientific community, since tension between the known and unknown animates much of what we do. We are sure that our model of the cosmos is correct, while at the same time recognizing that new revelations could require that we reconsider it. We grow confident in a theory if it is confirmed every time we test it, and yet, as the great philosopher of science Karl Popper pointed out, a theory is considered scientific only if it can be falsified—that is, if it has the potential to be challenged.

But while new evidence may reveal that a model is awry, such revelations do not throw all of science into question. The discovery of a new subatomic particle doesn't challenge our understanding of biology or gravity. That science is constantly improving does not mean it is always wrong.

Scientists could help bridge the gulf in understanding by engaging more with the public, particularly when it comes to research that will have a big impact on society. In fact, this should be part of our job descriptions. Not one-way lecturing, but a genuine exchange. We need to show our work, as a teacher of mine used to say—to not just present but elucidate the evidence for climate change, for evolution, for all of the scientific theories we have developed to explain our place in the universe. People don't want experts telling them how it is. They want to understand how we arrived at our conclusions.

This weekend, many scientists around the world gathered to take a stand against the attack on science. Though it feels good to march, protests signs alone won't convince. Only a sustained dialogue with the public will do that.

The Hermeneutics of Bunk: How a Physicist Gave Postmodernism a Black Eye

JEFF HESTER

Jeff Hester holds a Ph.D. in space physics and astronomy from Rice University and currently teaches at the California Institute of Technology. His international reputation as an astrophysicist derives from his work on the Hubble Space Telescope Wide Field and

*Planetary Camera, his famous space photo "Pillars of Creation," a Hubble image, and his
speaking and writing. This article, which examines and exposes "the postmodern critique
of science," appeared in the journal* Astronomy *for July 2017. "Hermeneutics" means
"methods and principles of interpretation" and "bunk" refers to "ridiculous nonsense,"
shortened from the verb to debunk.*

How a physicist gave postmodernism a black eye.

For anyone who pays attention to popular accounts of physics and cosmology,
quantum gravity is a thing. How could it not be? Quantum gravity is the place
where the two pillars of modern physics—quantum mechanics and relativity—
collide head-on at the very instant of the Big Bang. The two theories, each triumphant in its own realm, just don't play well together. If you are looking for
fundamental challenges to our ideas about the universe, quantum gravity isn't a
bad place to start.

A bit over two decades ago, quantum gravity also proved to be the perfect
honey trap for a bunch of academics with a taste for nonsense and an envious
bone to pick with science.

In 1994, NYU physicist Alan Sokal ran across a book by biologist Paul Gross
and mathematician Norman Levitt. In *Higher Superstition: The Academic Left and Its
Quarrels with Science,* Gross and Levitt raised an alarm about those in the new field
of "cultural studies" who were declaring that scientific knowledge, and at some
level reality itself, is nothing but a social construct. Unsure whether he should
take Gross and Levitt at face value, Sokal went to the library and dove into the
literature that they were criticizing. When he came up for air, he was much more
familiar with the postmodernist critique of science. He was also appalled at the
depth of its ignorance about the subject.

Most scientists respond to such nonsense with a muttered, "good grief," but
Sokal felt compelled to do more. He decided to give postmodernists a first-hand
demonstration of the destructive testing of ideas that tie science to a reality that
cuts across all cultural divides.

Sokal had a hypothesis: Those applying postmodernism to science couldn't   5
tell the difference between sense and nonsense if you rubbed their noses in it. He
predicted that the cultural science studies crowd would publish just about anything, so long as it sounded good and supported their ideological agenda. To test
that prediction, Sokal wrote a heavily footnoted and deliciously absurd 39-page
parody entitled, "Transgressing the Boundaries: Toward a Transformative Hermeneutics of Quantum Gravity."

The paper is worth reading just for a belly laugh. It promises "emancipatory
mathematics" at the foundation of "a future post-modern and liberatory science."
"Physical 'reality,'" it declares, "is at bottom a social and linguistic concept." He
embraces the notion, seriously proposed by some, that logic itself is invalidated
by "contamination of the social." When he showed it to friends, Sokal says, "the
scientists would figure out quickly that either it was a parody or I had gone off
my rocker."

Sokal submitted his paper to a trendy journal called *Social Text*. Understanding the importance of ego, he freely and glowingly cited work by several of the journal's editors. For their part, the folks at *Social Text* were thrilled to receive Sokal's manuscript. Here at last was a physicist who was "on their side"! After minor revisions, the paper was accepted and scheduled to appear in an upcoming special "Science Wars" edition.

The bait had been taken, but the trap had yet to be sprung. That came with a piece by Sokal in *Lingua Franca* that appeared just after *Social Text* hit the stands, exposing "Transgressing the Boundaries" as the hoax it was.

Parody sometimes succeeds where reasoned discourse fails. Sokal's little joke burst free of the ivory tower on May 18, 1996, when *The New York Times* ran a front-page article entitled, "Postmodern Gravity Deconstructed, Slyly." The Sokal Hoax became a hot topic of conversation around the world!

10   Reactions to Sokal's article were, shall we say, mixed. The editors of *Social Text* were not amused, to put it mildly, and they decried Sokal's unethical behavior. One insisted that the original paper was not a hoax at all, but that fearing reprisal from the scientific hegemony, Sokal had "folded his intellectual resolve." It was lost on them that had they showed the paper to anyone who knew anything about science or mathematics, the hoax would have been spotted instantly.

As most scientists did: When I heard about it, I busted a gut!

I still laugh, but the Sokal Hoax carries a serious message. In addition to diluting intellectual rigor, the postmodern assault on science undermines the very notion of truth and robs scientists and scholars of their ability to speak truth to power. As conservative columnist George Will correctly observed, "the epistemology that Sokal attacked precludes serious discussion of knowable realities." Today, from climate change denial, to the anti-vaccine movement, to the nonsensical notion of "alternative facts," that blade is wielded on both sides of the political aisle.

Sokal gets the last word. Quoting from his 1996 *Lingua Franca* article, "Anyone who believes that the laws of physics are mere social conventions is invited to try transgressing those conventions from the windows of my apartment. (I live on the 21st floor.)"

Blinded by Science: Modern-Day Hucksters Are Cashing In on Vulnerable Patients

TIMOTHY CAULFIELD

At the University of Alberta, Canada, Timothy Caulfield is Professor in the Faculty of Law and the School of Public Health. He is Research Director of the Health Law Institute. His interdisciplinary research projects have focused on stem cell research, patient safety, and obesity policy, among other topics. In addition to winning academic awards in health sciences and policy, he is the author of several books on health issues for a popular audience:

The Cure for Everything: Untangling the Twisted Messages about Health, Fitness, and Happiness *and* Is Gwyneth Paltrow Wrong About Everything?: When Celebrity Culture and Science Clash. *Although he published this article in* The Walrus *in 2011, Caulfield's concept of "scienceploitation" to describe how science and its studies are misrepresented and monetized to the detriment of public health, research in science, and the public's understanding of that research make this article continue to be relevant and thought-provoking.* The Walrus, *a general interest Canadian magazine in the vein of* Harper's Monthly, *says that it strives "to educate and [its] journalism is edited and fact checked to the highest standards" (Mission Statement).*

Earlier this year, I was invited to speak at an international biomedical conference held in a Latin American country better known for its vacation locales than for the quality of its healthcare system or its scientific research. My talk addressed the marketing of unproven stem cell therapies by clinics around the world. This growing industry, often called stem cell tourism, is fueled by Internet advertising and social media–driven word of mouth. It appeals to desperate patients who travel to providers in China, India, South and Central America, Russia, and the Caribbean to receive treatments with no chance of success.

International scientific organizations, patient advocacy groups, and, in a few notable cases, national governments have roundly condemned these therapies. Last year, for instance, the Costa Rican ministry of health closed one of the world's best-known clinics. But despite such action, the industry continues to flourish, generating false hope, robbing families of their resources, and potentially compromising legitimate stem cell science. An organization in China claims to have treated more than 8,000 patients with such incurable conditions as autism, amyotrophic lateral sclerosis (Lou Gehrig's disease), spinal cord injury, and cerebral palsy. The cost of such unproven procedures is substantial, averaging around $30,000 per session.

At the conference, I spoke about this problem with passion and clarity—or at least I thought so. The audience, which included clinicians and policy-makers, was not impressed. Afterwards, my host, a respected physician, took me for dinner. During the ride to the restaurant, she explained why my talk had met with such a chilly reaction. She (and, I suspect, many of the other participants) provides stem cell therapies for a variety of serious ailments. She swears they work. As we wove through the city's chaotic nighttime traffic, she recounted numerous successes, including patients who had regained movement in paralyzed limbs. I didn't doubt her sincerity; she gave the impression of a caring clinician, not a huckster peddling snake oil.

When I returned to Canada, I contacted a friend who is an eminent stem cell researcher. "Is there any chance this stuff works?" I asked. I know the relevant literature fairly well, but I wanted to make sure I hadn't missed some recent breakthrough. My friend's response didn't surprise me: "That clinician is full of it. Ask for the evidence."

While stem cell tourism, which is likely generating hundreds of millions of 5 dollars, is a worrisome development, it's part of a much broader trend:

capitalizing on newsworthy scientific advances as marketing opportunities. Call it "scienceploitation"—the exploitation of both good science and vulnerable patients. Threads of the phenomenon can be found in the ongoing debates about the efficacy of Italian doctor Paolo Zamboni's liberation treatment for multiple sclerosis and in questions about the value of alternative medicine like homeopathy. Some scientific hoaxes have led to a dangerous clouding of the facts, as in the fraudulent British research that engendered the myth that vaccines cause autism.

These are tough issues. But true scienceploitation constitutes a different and insidious concern. While the ideas may be real, the therapies are unfounded. Just as science fiction bends and stretches the truth in the service of entertainment, science marketing does so with the goal of profit. This has been going on for centuries. Scientific breakthroughs stir the public imagination, become part of popular culture, and then get packaged and sold by opportunists. Research on magnetism resulted in the sale of products promising magical restorative properties, curing everything from gout to constipation to paralysis. According to one advertisement from the late nineteenth century, "There need not be a sick person in America . . . if our Magneto-Conservative Underwear would become a part of the wardrobe of every lady and gentleman, as also of infants and children." More dangerous was the excitement over atomic physics in the early 1900s. The work of scientists such as Marie Curie in the field of radiology garnered considerable public interest, which led to an array of radioactive products, including skin creams, toothpaste, bath salts, and pills. A market even arose for radium water, which was said to "revitalize" and "energize." Not surprisingly, these inventions resulted in dire outcomes: "The Radium Water Worked Fine Until His Jaw Came Off," read one *Wall Street Journal* headline.

Today the best examples of science spin can be found in more frivolous corners of health care: anti-aging products and wrinkle creams. These lotions and tonics borrow language and imagery from groundbreaking areas of science. Skin creams are "nanotech encapsulated" and "genetically guided." There are even innumerable stem cell–based elixirs. Of course, this is nothing but scientific babble. When it comes to anti-aging and wrinkle prevention, there is little we can do, other than stay out of the sun and quit smoking. If there were a pill or product that actually reversed the aging process, we'd know. But, strangely, whether or not a treatment works doesn't seem to matter to consumers. A joint study published in *European Advances in Consumer Research* found that perceived effectiveness had little impact on women's use of skin care products. The failure of a skin cream actually enhances one's motivation to use it; one doesn't interpret a lack of results as proof of a sham product, but rather as a call to try harder.

Still, the reason for the science-based marketing strategy is obvious. The language creates a veneer of legitimacy, and allows manufacturers to leverage the media excitement associated with promising research. And there is evidence that this tactic works. A 2008 Yale University study found that people were more likely to believe a bad or illogical explanation for human behavior if it included a reference to scientific information. (The study used fake brain scan data to explain psychological phenomena in areas such as attention and perception.) This worked even if the purported data was completely irrelevant to the claim. The mere presence of scientific-sounding language caused participants to believe the nonsensical account of a phenomenon.

We want to be wrinkle-free, and we know it's a lost cause, but the term "stem cells" injects hope. Stem cells, after all, represent cutting-edge science. Who knows—perhaps this will be the cure that works.

Research on stem cells, which have the potential to develop into many cell   10
types in the body, is an extraordinarily promising field. One day, likely decades from now, it may result in therapies for conditions such as heart disease and spinal injuries. But at the moment, with a few notable exceptions, none are ready for clinical use. Blood stem cell transplants have long been used to treat a few diseases that affect the blood and the immune system, including some types of leukemia. And stem cells are used in skin grafts and corneal transplants. But that's it. As yet, no other stem cell therapies have been scientifically verified. Despite claims to the contrary by clinics around the world, no cures exist for autism, ALS, MS, spinal injuries, or Alzheimer's.

A few early-stage clinical trials are under way; the best-known and most scrutinized is one by the American biopharmaceutical company Geron. Its purpose is to test the possible therapeutic benefits of embryonic stem cells in individuals with recent spinal injuries. This is a Phase I trial, meaning that the primary objective is to test safety, not effectiveness. It has taken years for Geron to reach this stage, and to date the company has only recruited two test subjects. It is far from certain that the trial will succeed, and even if it did the treatment wouldn't be available to the public for years. Geron would still need to move to Phase II and III trials and then, if all went well, seek regulatory approval. A similar process would be involved in the development of any stem cell therapy. Each disease will likely require a unique cell type and a unique cell delivery system. You can't just inject stem cells into the body and hope they work, which seems to be the basic therapeutic approach of most stem cell tourism clinics.

Several patients have reportedly developed tumors from unproven stem cell therapies. In one case, a boy with a neurodegenerative disorder received injections of fetal stem cells at a clinic in Russia. He later developed life-threatening brain tumors. Deaths have also been attributed to these therapies. At Europe's largest stem cell treatment center, the XCell-Center, in Düsseldorf, Germany, an eighteen-month-old died in 2010 after having stem cells injected directly into his brain. The government shut it down in May.

As noted earlier, these bogus treatments are rarely cheap. Not long ago, I followed a website dedicated to raising money to send an infant girl with an incurable neurological disorder to China for stem cell therapy. The site, created by the child's parents, requested donations and posted a public countdown for the trip. Its home page displayed a box with the number of days, hours, minutes, and seconds left until the family left for China for the treatment. As the page explained, the parents wanted their little girl to be able to "walk, talk, and see."

Such stories are heartbreaking—and infuriating. Much of the money raised from friends, family, and well-intentioned strangers likely ended up in the pockets of providers who either knowingly deceived the public about the value of the treatment—fraud of the cruelest sort—or willfully ignored what peer-reviewed literature says about the state of the science.

How do legitimate and promising, if still nascent, areas of science become so quickly transformed into illegitimate products and services? Greed forms the primary motive, but there are other factors at play, including demand. Christen Rachul, my colleague at the University of Alberta, recently finished an analysis of thirty patient and caregiver blogs that discuss unproven stem cell treatments. She found desperation to be a common theme. As one blog stated, "While China is certainly not our first choice, it is our only choice for now. We will go anywhere and do anything to give our children a chance at life."

15   Rachul's research also revealed that many patients are angry at their home countries for not supporting specific treatments. "We need therapies in our own cities and towns. It is deplorable and inhumane that we must put ourselves in harm's way," wrote one blogger. Another, an American patient, was even more pointed: "At least China is doing something in the fight against this awful disease. Ya hear that usa—they are doing, not sitting on there [sic] ass hoping!" Individuals who travel to these clinics also view themselves as leaders helping to further biomedical research. One patient put it thusly: "Basically this is the clinical trial on humans they won't do in the west. We are pioneers. We have replaced the mouse model. (Your [sic] welcome, all you naysayer's out there.)"

Another force that facilitates scienceploitation is the media. The popular press loves stories about miracle cures and last chances, and pseudo-scientific remedies largely attract positive attention. Last year, I co-authored a study, published in the journal *Nature Biotechnology*, that examined 445 newspaper articles on the stem cell tourism industry. Most were optimistic in tone and portrayed the treatments as effective; they were framed as human-interest stories and driven by patient testimonials. Risk and scientific fact received little space. Sample headlines included: "Young Holly's Brave Stem-Cell Quest"; "Hope for Harvey in Fight Against Palsy"; "El Paso Teen Gets Stem Cell Treatment in China in Hopes of Seeing"; and "Trip to Mexico a Last Resort." If you are a desperate patient looking for hope, these kinds of stories tell you where it may be found.

Then there's hype. The scientific community faces unprecedented pressure to justify research in practical terms, whether for clinical benefit or commercial gain. Researchers hear one loud and consistent message, one that emanates from funding agencies, universities, and government: produce. The competition for funding is stiff, so it helps if the work appears innovative and relevant. Incremental advances are reported as major breakthroughs, and many stories about successful animal studies include enthusiastic projections of imminent clinical applications. This past May, my local newspaper, the *Edmonton Journal*, ran the following headline on the front page: "Preemie Twins Fight for Breath: Stem-Cell Research Holds Promise for Tiny, Damaged Lungs." The story was about legitimate, promising research on the potential regeneration of damaged lungs. But the work has yet to be tested on anything but rats. Still, the lead researcher, Bernard Thébaud, a highly respected scientist, is quoted as saying he hopes to treat patients "in five years' time."

The public hears this message: If it works in animals, it will work in humans, although this is often—usually—untrue. Successful animal studies translate to successful human clinical trials only about 10 percent of the time. And this rate is for the highly referenced and most influential animal studies; if you include all animal studies, the number would likely be much lower. The public expectations that form the basis of the market for pseudo-scientific products arise from hype, which happens even though true medical breakthroughs are fantastically rare. Science is a slow, incremental plod—two steps forward, one and a half steps back.

Skepticism is good, and it lies at the heart of the best scientific inquiry, the starting point that produces the most convincing data and the surest path to true, robust health care advances. History tells us that the likelihood of a new, effective, and widely applicable treatment appearing during the early days of a new sphere of research is minuscule, hovering around zero. So healthy skepticism must remain the default. We should not, however, allow this disposition to slide into cynicism about the value of research. History also promises that genuine benefits will emerge, even if they are more modest than first envisioned. While magnetic underwear and radium water proved to be shams, we now have magnetic resonance imaging and effective radiation therapy. The same pattern will unfold with genetics, stem cells, nanotechnology, or any other new and stimulating field of science permeates the zeitgeist. There will be few, if any, miracle cures. But growth in knowledge, whatever the outcome, is certain.

For Writing and Discussion
Dealing with Misinformation, Fake News, and Misconceptions

1. A number of the readings in this unit explore how news and information get distorted, focusing on different causes of these distortions. How do David Uberti, Jack Shafer, Eugene Kiely and Lori Robertson, Luciano Floridi, Karsten Schley, and Peter Wayne Moe interpret these causes? What assumptions underlie their arguments? Which of the proposed solutions for combating the unethical and irresponsible spreading of misinformation and outright falsities do you think offer the most promise?

2. Think about your own consumption of news and your favorite sources. Do you rely on social media or Internet news sites? Which of the signs of fake news identified by Eugene Kiely and Lori Robertson have you encountered? What examples of bogus stories, fake news, viral emails, and sensational social media memes have you read? Based on the guidelines and advice that Kiely and Robertson and Peter Wayne Moe offer and suggestions for reading with rhetorical awareness and evaluating sources for reliability, credibility, and angle of vision in Chapter 16, what changes would you consider making in your own engagement with news to become a better rhetorical reader of news?

3. Choose a current event and trace its coverage in news sources from different locations on the political spectrum (from sources far on the Right such as Breitbart News and Blaze to centrist sources such as BBC News and the *New York Times* to Left sources such as Vox and farther left such as Alternet). Look particularly at how the angle of vision influences the choice of language (loaded words, emotional appeals), the selection of material to be covered, the degree of advocacy, and the overtness of bias (emphases and omissions). Use one of these sites for fact-checking to determine what has been misrepresented and distorted: Politfact.com, FactCheck.org, Snopes.com. As you discuss your findings with your classmates, also share which of the readings in this unit particularly helped you in the assessment of your sources.

4. Cornel West and Robert P. George approach the problems of misinformation and siloed communication from a different tack than the other readings in this unit. What are their underlying assumptions, their main claim, and the reasoning they use to support their argument? Based on your study of argument as a process of inquiry and a search for the best solution to problems and on your experience as a college student, how important do you think it is that citizens endorse this statement? What argument of your own would you construct in favor of this statement or questioning it?

5. Marcus du Sautoy (mathematics and science communication), Timothy Caulfield (public health, policy, and the law), and Jeff Hester (astrophysics) identify different problems with the way science as knowledge-making is communicated to the public. According to these writers, what distortions, misunderstandings, and misinformation confuse the way science is reported and interpreted? What actions do these writers argue that scientists and the public should take?

Writing Assignment

Researched Proposal Speech on Understanding and Evaluating Scientific Claims

In April 2017, scientists and supporters of science gathered in cities all around the world for the March for Science. Advocates for science praised the contributions that science makes to the quality of life—designing livable cities, developing vaccines and life-saving health treatments, exploring alternative energy, and so forth. In writing, voices for science reminded readers that in the United States, government funding for the National Institute of Health, the Environmental Protection Agency, and grants for science in universities are at stake. Some marchers carried banners saying such things as "Fact: The World Is Running Out of Alternatives" and "Make America Think Again." However, as these edgy banners illustrate and Marcus du Sautoy, Jeff Hester, and Timothy Caulfield argue, many forces have damaged the public's understanding of science. After researching science reporting and its reception, write a proposal speech in which you argue for the most needed steps to prepare nonscientists to evaluate scientific claims.

Public Health

Since the 1980s, public health officials have watched with alarm as the average American's weight has climbed. Currently, one in three American adults and one in six children and adolescents are categorized as obese by the Centers for Disease Control and Prevention. One study predicts that by 2030, nearly half of the adult population of the United States will be dangerously overweight. The consequences of this trend include millions of potential cases of diabetes, stroke, and heart disease, adding to rising medical care costs. Public health officials, politicians, and concerned citizens have thus been engaged in conversation about how to slow or reverse this trend.

For children, a natural place to start has been the National School Lunch Program. Many children consume one or even two meals per day at school, and nutrition has been linked not only to healthy weights for kids and healthy outcomes as they age, but also to their ability to focus in school and thus their academic success. The passage of the Healthy, Hunger-Free Kids Act in 2010, championed by First Lady Michelle Obama, set higher nutritional standards for school lunches. But the changes to the school lunch program have been met with resistance by parents and school officials, who argue that the program cannot achieve its goals if kids won't eat the healthier food on offer.

Attention is also increasingly being paid to the role of sugar as a potential culprit in the obesity crisis. For decades, health officials urged Americans to reduce their fat intake, but the low-fat alternatives often contained significant amounts of sugar. Now, the World Health Organization and the American Heart Association, among others, are calling on Americans to reduce the amount of added sugars in their diet. One way that local and national governments are attempting to reduce sugar intake is the "soda tax," which would levy an additional tax on sugared beverages. This tax has been successful in other countries. For example, in Mexico, consumption of sugary drinks dropped by 12 percent in the first year the soda tax was levied. However, others argue that using a tax to enforce healthy behaviors is symptomatic of a "nanny state"; they believe that individuals should have the choice to consume or not consume added sugars. Similar arguments have arisen with respect to food stamps: Should food-stamp recipients be prohibited from purchasing sugary drinks and other junk foods with these publicly provided benefits?

What these conversations have in common is the role of government in incentivizing personal health decisions. Do the obesity epidemic's threats to the common good and the public purse outweigh our rights as individuals to make decisions about food, even if those decisions are detrimental to our own health? Is it more effective to encourage positive behaviors or to penalize negative ones? Especially when our children's health is at stake, these are urgent questions.

Keep Up Fight against Childhood Obesity

DEMOCRAT AND CHRONICLE EDITORIAL BOARD

This editorial appeared in the May 10, 2017 edition of the Democrat and Chronicle, *a daily newspaper in Rochester, New York.*

As childhood obesity continues to vex this nation, we should be forging ahead with solutions, not standing pat like a tablespoon of chilled lard. The health of our children—our future as a nation—depends on it.

Seventeen percent of children and adolescents are obese in the United States, according to the Centers for Disease Control. Given the fact that children can consume up to 50 percent of their daily calories at school, it's critical that school lunches contain nutritious options.

Yet the fight against childhood obesity hit a snag recently when new Agriculture Secretary Sonny Perdue signed a proclamation that relaxes nutritional standards for whole grains, salt, and milk in the coming school year. The previous, stricter nutritional target was part of the Healthy Hunger-Free Kids Act of 2010 that implemented school lunch standards across the board in 2012.

Hitting the brakes on nutritional standards was the wrong move. Thankfully, despite the move to relax the nutritional standards for school lunches, there are things families and school districts can do to combat childhood obesity.

5   Parents can help build healthy eating habits by preparing healthier meals and serving water with meals instead of drinks with added sugar. And plenty of fruits and vegetables should always be on the menu. The 2010 Dietary Guidelines for Americans offers nutrition advice while the CDC's healthy recipes page offers meal ideas.

As the *Democrat and Chronicle* has reported, fewer Monroe County students are buying school lunches. Along with price, taste has played a role in the drop, and some kids who are buying lunches are tossing food away, a point mentioned by the Secretary of Agriculture when relaxing the nutrition standards.

Schools need to get a little creative to get kids to eat their veggies and whole grains. Area districts might consider taking a page from Pennsylvania's Mt. Lebanon School District, which has held taste-testing events with families to try new offerings, and sends recipe cards home with kids. Districts should consider a little extra time for lunch, too: a Harvard University study shows students with limited time will leave the thing they like least on the plate and scarf down what they like best (which tends to be the least healthful). But, given more time to eat, they'll get around to the healthful stuff.

Childhood obesity is a national problem that must be taken seriously. We can start by making sure families and schools are working together to build healthy eating habits in our youth.

Fed or Fed Up? Why We Support Easing School Lunch Rules

SAN DIEGO UNION-TRIBUNE EDITORIAL BOARD

This brief editorial was published on May 5, 2017 in the San Diego Union-Tribune, *a daily newspaper in San Diego, California.*

The Trump administration's decision to relax some of the school lunch rules involving sodium intake, whole grain content, and milk approved in 2012, following the provisions of a 2010 law adopted at the behest of then-First Lady Michelle Obama, drew fire from some health experts. An American Heart Association official warned that "there could be serious health consequences" for students.

But in explaining the decision to give school districts the option to not meet strict standards, Secretary of Agriculture Sonny Perdue made a crucial point: "If kids aren't eating the food, and it's ending up in the trash, they aren't getting any nutrition—thus undermining the intent of the program." Patricia Montague, CEO of the School Nutrition Association, agreed with the decision: "We have been wanting flexibility so that schools can serve meals that are both nutritious and palatable. We don't want kids wasting their meals by throwing them away."

The evidence that the lunch rules backfired is considerable. A 2013 study estimated that 1.1 million students had stopped buying school lunches in the 2012–13 school year, the first year-to-year decline after nearly a decade of steady increases. Another 2013 study pegged the annual cost of wasted food at school cafeterias at $1.24 billion. Anyone who doubts student antipathy to school food should search #ThanksMichelleObama on Twitter for a look at photos of lunches that left kids fed up instead of fed.

Good intentions don't always pay off with good results. Having a healthy school lunch menu achieves nothing if the lunch goes uneaten.

Tips for Parents—Ideas to Help Children Maintain a Healthy Weight

CENTERS FOR DISEASE CONTROL AND PREVENTION

This Q&A page was posted on the website of the Division of Nutrition, Physical Activity, and Obesity of the Centers for Disease Control and Prevention in 2017. The CDC is a government agency whose mission is to "protect America from health, safety, and security threats, both foreign and in the U.S." It conducts scientific research, provides health information, and responds to health threats when they arise.

You've probably read about it in newspapers and seen it on the news: in the United States, the number of obese children and teens has continued to rise over the past two decades.[1] You may wonder: Why are doctors and scientists troubled by this trend? And as parents or other concerned adults, you may also ask: What steps can we take to help prevent obesity in our children? This page provides answers to some of the questions you may have and provides you with resources to help you keep your family healthy.

Why Is Childhood Obesity Considered a Health Problem?

Doctors and scientists are concerned about the rise of obesity in children and youth because obesity may lead to the following health problems:

- Heart disease, caused by:
  - high cholesterol and/or
  - high blood pressure
- Type 2 diabetes
- Asthma
- Sleep apnea
- Social discrimination

Childhood obesity is associated with various health-related consequences. Obese children and adolescents may experience immediate health consequences and may be at risk for weight-related health problems in adulthood.

Psychosocial Risks

Some consequences of childhood and adolescent overweight are psychosocial. Obese children and adolescents are targets of early and systematic social discrimination.[2] The psychological stress of social stigmatization can cause low self-esteem which, in turn, can hinder academic and social functioning, and persist into adulthood.[3]

Cardiovascular Disease Risks

5   Obese children and teens have been found to have risk factors for cardiovascular disease (CVD), including high cholesterol levels, high blood pressure, and abnormal glucose tolerance. In a population-based sample of 5- to 17-year-olds, almost 60 percent of overweight children had at least one CVD risk factor while 25 percent of overweight children had two or more CVD risk factors.[2]

Additional Health Risks

Less common health conditions associated with increased weight include asthma, hepatic steatosis, sleep apnea, and Type 2 diabetes.

- Asthma is a disease of the lungs in which the airways become blocked or narrowed, causing breathing difficulty. Studies have identified an association between childhood overweight and asthma.[4, 5]

- Hepatic steatosis is the fatty degeneration of the liver caused by a high concentration of liver enzymes. Weight reduction causes liver enzymes to normalize.[2]

- Sleep apnea is a less common complication of [being] overweight for children and adolescents. Sleep apnea is a sleep-associated breathing disorder defined as the cessation of breathing during sleep that lasts for at least 10 seconds. Sleep apnea is characterized by loud snoring and labored breathing. During sleep apnea, oxygen levels in the blood can fall dramatically. One study estimated that sleep apnea occurs in about 7 percent of overweight children.[6]

- Type 2 diabetes is increasingly being reported among children and adolescents who are overweight.[7] While diabetes and glucose intolerance, a precursor of diabetes, are common health effects of adult obesity, only in recent years has Type 2 diabetes begun to emerge as a health-related problem among children and adolescents. Onset of diabetes in children and adolescents can result in advanced complications such as CVD and kidney failure.[8]

In addition, studies have shown that obese children and teens are more likely to become obese as adults.[9, 10]

What Can I Do as a Parent or Guardian to Help Prevent Childhood Overweight and Obesity?

To help your child maintain a healthy weight, balance the calories your child consumes from foods and beverages with the calories your child uses through physical activity and normal growth.

Remember that the goal for overweight and obese children and teens is to reduce the rate of weight gain while allowing normal growth and development. Children and teens should NOT be placed on a weight reduction diet without the consultation of a health care provider.

Balancing Calories: Help Kids Develop Healthy Eating Habits

One part of balancing calories is to eat foods that provide adequate nutrition and an appropriate number of calories. You can help children learn to be aware of what they eat by developing healthy eating habits, looking for ways to make favorite dishes healthier, and reducing calorie-rich temptations.

Encourage Healthy Eating Habits.   There's no great secret to healthy eating. To help your children and family develop healthy eating habits:

- Provide plenty of vegetables, fruits, and whole-grain products.
- Include low-fat or non-fat milk or dairy products.
- Choose lean meats, poultry, fish, lentils, and beans for protein.
- Serve reasonably sized portions.
- Encourage your family to drink lots of water.
- Limit sugar-sweetened beverages.
- Limit consumption of sugar and saturated fat.

Remember that small changes every day can lead to a recipe for success!

For more information about nutrition, visit ChooseMyPlate.gov and the Dietary Guidelines for Americans 2010.

Look for Ways to Make Favorite Dishes Healthier. The recipes that you may prepare regularly, and that your family enjoys, with just a few changes can be healthier and just as satisfying.

15 **Remove Calorie-Rich Temptations!** Although everything can be enjoyed in moderation, reducing the calorie-rich temptations of high-fat and high-sugar, or salty snacks can also help your children develop healthy eating habits. Instead only allow your children to eat them sometimes, so that they truly will be treats! Here are examples of easy-to-prepare, low-fat and low-sugar treats that are 100 calories or less:

- A medium-size apple
- A medium-size banana
- 1 cup blueberries
- 1 cup grapes
- 1 cup carrots, broccoli, or bell peppers with 2 tbsp. hummus

Balancing Calories: Help Kids Stay Active

Another part of balancing calories is to engage in an appropriate amount of physical activity and avoid too much sedentary time. In addition to being fun for children and teens, regular physical activity has many health benefits, including:

- Strengthening bones
- Decreasing blood pressure
- Reducing stress and anxiety
- Increasing self-esteem
- Helping with weight management

Help Kids Stay Active. Children and teens should participate in at least 60 minutes of moderate intensity physical activity most days of the week, preferably daily.[11] Remember that children imitate adults. Start adding physical activity to your own daily routine and encourage your child to join you.

Some examples of moderate intensity physical activity include:

- Brisk walking
- Playing tag
- Jumping rope
- Playing soccer
- Swimming
- Dancing

Reduce Sedentary Time. In addition to encouraging physical activity, help children avoid too much sedentary time. Although quiet time for reading and homework is fine, limit the time your children watch television, play video games, or surf the web to no more than 2 hours per day. Additionally, the American Academy of Pediatrics (AAP) does not recommend television viewing for children age 2 or younger.[12] Instead, encourage your children to find fun activities to do with family members or on their own that simply involve more activity.

References

1. Ogden CL, Carroll MD, Curtin LR, McDowell MA, Tabak CJ, Flegal KM. Prevalence of overweight and obesity in the United States, 1999-2004. *JAMA* 2006;295(13):1549–1555.

2. Dietz W. Health consequences of obesity in youth: Childhood predictors of adult disease. *Pediatrics* 1998;101:518–525.

3. Swartz MB and Puhl R. Childhood obesity: a societal problem to solve. *Obesity Reviews* 2003; 4(1):57–71.

4. Rodriguez MA, Winkleby MA, Ahn D, Sundquist J, Kraemer HC. Identification of populations subgroups of children and adolescents with high asthma prevalence: findings from the Third National Health and Nutrition Examination Survey. *Arch Pediatr Adolesc Med* 2002;156:269–275.

5. Luder E, Melnik TA, Dimaio M. Association of being overweight with greater asthma symptoms in inner city black and Hispanic children. *J Pediatr* 1998;132:699–703.

6. Mallory GB, Fiser DH, Jackson R. Sleep-associated breathing disorders in morbidly obese children and adolescents. *J Pediatr* 1989;115:892–897.

7. Fagot-Campagna A, Narayan KMV, Imperatore G. Type 2 diabetes in children: exemplifies the growing problem of chronic diseases [Editorial]. *BMJ* 2001;322:377–378.

8. Must A, Anderson SE. Effects of obesity on morbidity in children and adolescents. *Nutr Clin Care* 2003;6:1;4–11.

9. Whitaker RC, Wright JA, Pepe MS, Seidel KD, Dietz WH. Predicting obesity in young adulthood from childhood and parental obesity. *N Engl J Med* 1997; 37(13):869–873.

10. Serdula MK, Ivery D, Coates RJ, Freedman DS. Williamson DF. Byers T. Do obese children become obese adults? A review of the literature. *Prev Med* 1993;22:167–177.

11. http://www.aap.org/family/tv1.htm, accessed 12/18/06.

12. This physical activity recommendation is from the *Dietary Guidelines for Americans 2010.*

We Need to Call American Breakfast What It Often Is: Dessert

JULIA BELLUZ AND JAVIER ZARRACINA

Julia Belluz is a senior health correspondent and self-described "evidence enthusiast" writing for Vox.com. The infographic was created by Javier Zarracina, graphics editor for the site. This essay and infographic were posted to Vox.com, a website that "explains the news," on July 11, 2016.

In America, breakfast is often nothing more than disguised dessert, as this tweet from author and researcher Alan Levinovitz reminded us: Dessert translations of breakfast foods: muffin = cupcake; smoothie = milkshake; granola = streusel top; yogurt = ice cream; waffle = cookie.

Look no further than the menu at IHOP, where dessert for breakfast reigns. You can find such items as New York cheesecake pancakes or raspberry white chocolate chip pancakes, which come with a whopping 83 grams (nearly 21 teaspoons) of sugar. Remember that the government recommends no more than 12 teaspoons of sugar per person per day (though the average American consumes 23.)

But you don't need to go to IHOP to get a day's worth of sugar in your morning meal. The muffins that greet us in the bakery aisle and at the coffee shop can contain about 37 grams of sugar—or a little more than 9 teaspoons.

And yogurt? The fermented dairy product has the patina of a health food, thanks to its protein and beneficial bacteria.

5   Yet companies like Yoplait and Chobani have built yogurt empires in America by saturating their products with sugar. Yoplait recently lowered the sugar in its classic 6-ounce strawberry yogurt from 26 grams to 18 grams (4.5 teaspoons), but that's still more than the 15 grams you'll get in a standard brownie.

And if you believe granola is any healthier, think again.

A fascinating story from *The New York Times*'s Upshot blog looked at the results of a poll that asked nutritionists about their perceptions of the healthfulness of popular foods and compared their answers with those of the general public.

"No food elicited a greater difference of opinion between experts and the public than granola bars," wrote *Times* reporters Kevin Quealy and Margot Sanger Katz. "About 70 percent of Americans called it healthy, but less than 30 percent of nutritionists did."

Granola didn't fare much better. Less than half of the nutritionists described the crunchy food, made popular by hippies, as healthy.

10   The main reason nutritionists worry about granola: Most of it is deceptively high in calories and sugar, particularly in the quantities people are likely to eat. According to CSPI, many granola brands pack at least 200 calories in each serving—and servings are usually listed as half a cup. (For some brands, a serving

is only a quarter-cup—or a measly 4 tablespoons.) Many people eat much more than that in one sitting, which means you could be getting 600 calories or more from one bowl.

Let's not forget cereal, which continues to find new ways to hide lots of sugar behind healthy-sounding labels.

Numerous reports from health advocates like the Environmental Working Group have pointed out the gratuitous amount of sugar in the usual suspects like Lucky Charms and Honey Smacks.

But then you have Cheerios Protein, a variation on the classic but with added protein. "A serving of Cheerios Protein, with its four teaspoons of sugar, has much more sugar than a typical cereal marketed to kids, such as Trix or Frosted Flakes," said Michael Jacobson, president of CSPI, in a statement. "They really ought to call the product Cheerios Sugar." Meanwhile, a serving of Honey Nut Cheerios contains more sugar than three Chips Ahoy cookies.

Crushed-up cookies in a bowl: That's how many cereals really should be viewed.

Breakfast doesn't have to be dessert

There are many cereals that look and taste nothing like dessert—with plenty of   15
fiber to fill you up and little or no added sugar, as food policy and nutrition researcher Marion Nestle has noted. (A helpful ranking of cereals according to their healthfulness is available from the Food Advertising to Children and Teens Score project.)

Similarly, some yogurts are far healthier than others. I've written about Siggi's, an Icelandic yogurt that was created in response to the overly sweet options on offer in US supermarkets. Every serving has about 100 calories and 25 to 50 percent less sugar than mainstream brands. Plain yogurts from any brand are a safe bet, and it's always a good idea to steer clear of yogurts with names like Key lime pie and Philly cheesecake.

Eggs, particularly when served with vegetables, are a dependable, nutrient-rich option. They're also satiating, thanks to their protein and fat. A less satiating breakfast is going to be low fat, low protein, and high sugar—like a low-fat muffin.

Or maybe you want to try something completely different. Though sweet foods (or egg-based meals) have become synonymous with breakfast in the US, people in some countries branch out much further.

In Japan, for example, breakfast will often include a hearty mix of fish, rice, and miso soup. Lots of filling protein, vitamins, and minerals, with no cookies in a bowl or sugar-loaded dairy.

And don't forget: Not everyone necessarily has to eat breakfast. That's a myth   20
that was mostly cooked up by the makers of sugary desserts—I mean, breakfasts—outlined here.

BREAKFAST FOOD	DESSERT EQUIVALENT
Dunkin Donuts banana chocolate chip muffin (1 serving)	**Starbucks vanilla buttercream cupcake**
Sugar: 46 grams	Sugar: 34 grams
510 calories	400 calories
Chobani Blueberry Fruit On The Bottom yogurt (1 serving)	**Breyers French Vanilla ice cream (1/2 cup)**
Sugar: 15 grams	Sugar: 14 grams
130 calories	140 calories
IHOP New York cheesecake pancakes (1 serving)	**Cheesecake Factory chocolate tower truffle cake**
Sugar: 55 grams	Sugar: 51 grams
940 calories	1,679 calories
Quaker Oats & Honey natural granola (1 cup)	**5 Oreo cookies**
Sugar: 26 grams	Sugar: 23 grams
420 calories	266 calories
General Mills Nature Valley Sweet & Salty Nut granola bars, peanut (1 bar)	**Oh Henry! candy bar (fun size)**
Sugar: 12 grams	Sugar: 14 grams
170 calories	120 calories

Vox

I've Heard All the Arguments against a Sugar Tax. I'm Still Calling for One in Australia

SARAH WILSON

Sarah Wilson is an author, TV host, blogger, and director of the website IQuitSugar.com. *She is also a former editor of Australian* Cosmopolitan. *This commentary was posted on April 19, 2016, to* The Guardian, *a London-based newspaper that also produces digital editions in the United States and Australia.*

Since launching the campaign for a tax on sugary soft drinks in Australia last week, the pushback has been interesting to view from my social dashboard.

I'm used to pushback, it's almost to be expected when your business encourages people to cut back on a highly addictive, emotionally seductive, economically explosive substance that they rather like the taste of: sugar.

But the cries that by calling for a sugar tax I'm pushing a "tax on the poor" particularly intrigues me. Mostly because I know where they come from—Big Soda's songsheet.

I'm now familiar with their full aria. It goes like this.

"Yeah, OK, we admit soft drink is not that great for you."   5

Big Soda likes to say this a bit. It's a great tactic. This conglomeration of vested interests that regularly release illicitly sponsored studies that exonerate their products then, next breath, trawl out the "everything in moderation" argument. They suggest we can drink their cans of fizzy water with 10 teaspoons of added sugar, but we really need to be burning off those calories with a good run or bike ride. *Calories in, calories out, people!*

Which would be a super argument if there were a skerrick of science to it. The body doesn't work this way. We're a little more complex. Indeed, we are consuming no more calories than we did 70 years ago, doing more exercise, and yet obesity has skyrocketed. Um, at the same rate as our sugar consumption.

No matter. Their equation is lovely and simple and it sticks with the public, especially when they throw hundreds of millions at "educating" us on it, via vested studies that are illicitly funded. Yes, they call it education.

(No surprise, then, that we hear "you should be spending your energy on education, not taxes" on the online forums. Same songsheet.)

Next, Big Soda like to push the "personal responsibility" line.   10

Says Coca-Cola's CEO: "Americans need to be more active and take greater responsibility for their diets." The American Beverage Association has said similar.

But again, zilch science. The specifics of sugar's impact on our health are such that we can't do "self-control." It's addictive and it's the only food molecule on the planet that switches off our appetite hormones. That is, we have no "off switch" for sugar. Why so? Back when we had to hunt down our calories, and sugar was a scarcity (a few bitter berries and beehives here and there), it made sense to have a unique capacity to binge on it because, wait for it, sugar is the best source of fat on the planet.

It also made sense to not burn off these sugar calories in their sourcing. That would just be silly. Ergo, so is the "you just need to go for a jog" argument.

Plus, sugar is now force-fed to us by the food industry. More than 80% of products in supermarkets contain (mostly) hidden, added sugar. Which is my point.

15   Most Australians have no *choice* about how much sugar they eat because they don't even know they're eating it. Once addicted to the stuff, they have no *choice* in being able to eat it moderately.

There is absolutely no personal responsibility argument when there's no choice.

We're also warned by the personal responsibly proponents that taxes like this are a tax on the poor. A confounding line to take. But then desperate times . . .

Sure, more poor folk drink Coke. Of course, Big Soda knows this; they throw most of their sugar advertising revenue at poor areas. The simple equation would be you drink more fizzy sugar water, you pay more tax (assuming Big Soda on-passes the tax to consumers).

But the science shows the burden of a sugar tax on consumers is "almost negligible." A senior research fellow at Monash University Centre for Health Economics told journalists last week: "Low-income individuals would reduce consumption the most and they would be the most to benefit in terms of weight reduction."

20   A coalition of Australian scientists and stakeholders, including Deakin University, the University of Queensland, and the Cancer Council, last week drew on science to show that an Australian sugar tax would prevent 4,400 heart attacks and 1,100 strokes, and save the health care system $609m over 25 years.

Sugar is the new tobacco. For every 10% increase in the price of cigarettes, we see a 4% decrease in consumption. Mexico implemented a 10% "soda tax" in 2014; in just one year consumption had decreased by 12%.

Granted, consumers might switch to sugary flavored milks and fruit juices (most of which are owned by the Big Soda giants and contain just as much added sugar as soft drinks). But a soda tax could lead to a broader sugar tax. Or other initiatives.

It's a start. And when you consider that Australian kids get almost 30% of their sugar from soft drinks, that they consume on average 1.2 cans a day, and that up to half of our kids are overweight or obese, well, it's a very good start.

And in the process we have a conversation. I call *this* education.

25   The UK government recently announced their sugar tax on sugary drinks. Mexico, France, and Hungary have one. These governments saw through the personal responsibility palaver.

When I put our completed petition to Scott Morrison in coming weeks I'll be flagging this with him. And reminding him of Malcolm Turnbull's oft-said line, "If you want people to do less of something, you put up the tax."

Soda Tax Is Nanny-State Overreach

HARTFORD COURANT EDITORIAL BOARD

This brief editorial was printed on February 27, 2015, in the Hartford Courant, *Connecticut's largest daily newspaper.*

There's no question that childhood obesity continues to be a problem in the United States. The medical conditions to which it is linked, from diabetes to coronary heart disease, are well known. According to the Centers for Disease Control and Prevention, 18 percent of American children under 12, and 21 percent of adolescents, are obese.

But a new state tax on sugary drinks is not the way to fight obesity. Other steps will likely be more effective and involve less nanny-state intrusion into private choices.

Last year, a similar national tax was proposed by U.S. Rep. Rosa DeLauro, D-3rd District. This year's state version, introduced by Rep. Juan R. Candelaria, D-New Haven, is flawed for many of the same reasons.

The state bill would impose a tax of 1 cent per ounce on carbonated soft drinks that are high in sugar, although exactly what "high" means has yet to be determined. Money collected from the tax would go toward anti-obesity programs, its advocates say.

"The science is a slam dunk on this," said Roberta R. Friedman of UConn's   5 Rudd Center on Food Policy and Obesity, and the truth of that is self-evident. Of course kids—adults, too—would be healthier if they weren't addicted to soft drinks and other junk food.

In fact, a federal advisory committee has just suggested that consumers strictly limit the amount of sugar they consume.

But science isn't the issue. The question is: Once the door is opened, where do we stop?

High-calorie foods in general, along with a sedentary lifestyle, are the major causes of obesity. Singling out just some of the likely suspects doesn't make much sense.

Drinking spring water instead of cola is fine, but using it to wash down pizza or doughnuts doesn't equal a healthy diet.

A new tax, whether at the federal or state level, is not the answer. Educating   10 consumers, getting fresh fruits and vegetables into cities, making healthier choices more attractive to young people, and reducing the availability of sodas in schools are far better approaches.

More Jobs Lost to Soda Taxes!

SIGNE WILKINSON

Signe Wilkinson is an editorial cartoonist with the Philadelphia Daily News, *and her work also appears in syndication nationally. She was the first female cartoonist to win the Pulitzer Prize for Editorial Cartooning. This cartoon was published on March 1, 2017.*

Are We Subsidizing a Public Health Crisis by Allowing the Poor to Buy Soda with Food Stamps?

LOS ANGELES TIMES EDITORIAL BOARD

This editorial was printed in the March 29, 2017 edition of the Los Angeles Times.

A major study of the grocery-buying habits of millions of Americans released late last year found that people using food stamps generally make the same unhealthy food choices as everyone else in America. Too many sweets, salty snacks, and prepared desserts. Junk food, in other words.

But when it came to soda and its sugary ilk, the results were more surprising, and not in a good way. According to the USDA-funded study, shoppers using food stamps spent a larger share of their budget—9.25% to be exact—on sugar-sweetened beverages than other shoppers. Even more startling: Food-stamp shoppers bought more soda than any other single grocery item.

The new data revived an old debate about banning soda from the $71 billion food-stamp program. In February, the House Agriculture Committee held a hearing to gather testimony about the pros and cons of such a restriction. It does seem counterproductive to spend billions of taxpayer dollars in an effort to improve the nutrition of low-income Americans on a product with little or no nutritional value. It is called the Supplemental Nutrition Assistance Program, after all. What's worse is that soda has been identified by public health experts as one of the prime culprits in soaring U.S. obesity and Type 2 diabetes rates.

The study and committee debate, however, raised some of the same uncomfortable issues that have caused the proposal to languish in the past. On the conservative side, folks have worried that this type of nanny-state regulation will lead to other heavy-handed health-related restrictions (enforced exercise, perhaps). Liberals, meanwhile, have been concerned that it is patronizing and punitive to tell people how to spend their government benefits. Add in the opposition from the beverage industry lobby and it's no surprise this idea hasn't gotten very far when it's been proposed in the past. In recent years, a handful of states and cities, including New York City, have tried to impose such a requirement, but were blocked by the U.S. Department of Agriculture.

The difference now is that the attitude toward soda has rapidly soured as   5
more evidence has poured in that beverages with added sugars are making people fat and sick. The USDA has issued dietary guidelines warning people to limit their consumption of food with added sugars, the largest sources of which are sweetened beverages. This belief helped San Francisco, Philadelphia, and a handful of other cities push through new taxes on soda. A handful more are considering their own soda levies, and it wouldn't be a surprise to see an effort to adopt a statewide soda tax in California before too long.

We know that there are detrimental health effects of drinking lots of soda, but we don't know if barring SNAP recipients from spending their benefits on soda will really improve their health. It's worth finding out by undertaking a limited pilot program, regardless of the qualms we may have about imposing restraints on the poor that better-off Americans don't face. The assumption is that those billions of dollars not going to buy Coke or Red Bull will be spent on healthier food. But that may not be the case. What if consumption of other sugary items, like ice cream and pudding, increases? Or if SNAP recipients simply transferred their sweet drink habit ounce-for-ounce to more expensive and still sugar-laden fruit juice? Or if they spent their non-SNAP money on soda? Before making a permanent change, we need to know if it would improve nutrition or be pointlessly punitive.

But it is a good step to take to gather data. And the argument that it would be too hard on grocers to carve out sugary drinks doesn't hold water. As the study shows, modern grocery check stand technology is sophisticated enough to easily separate out purchases by UPC code. Indeed, SNAP already comes with restrictions on alcohol, tobacco, and hot foods, among other things. Grocers don't have a problem sorting them out. The Women, Infant, and Children food-assistance program is even more prescriptive, permitting only specific items to be purchased: milk, cheese, cereal, and formula, for example, but absolutely nothing with added sugar or artificial sweetener. Ideally, a pilot program would also find ways to improve access to safe drinking water. One of the reasons that low-income people may choose sweetened beverages is that their drinking water isn't reliable.

Denying poor people the ability to use food aid to buy a Coke on a hot day may raise some unsettling questions. Yet the findings in the USDA's study about excessive soda consumption shouldn't be ignored.

For Writing and Discussion

Public Health

1. Several of the readings in this unit use health statistics in making their case. How did the author's choice of statistic, and language used in framing it, influence your views or contribute to the success of the essay overall?
2. The arguments in this unit may strike close to home with you, based as they are on school lunches (which you may have consumed) and sugar or soda (which you may still consume). Read one of the essays in this unit as both a believer and a doubter. Working in small groups, discuss the following questions: What are the underlying assumptions (warrants) that one must hold in order to accept the author's argument? What beliefs and values would enable one to doubt the author's argument?
3. Think of another public health issue you have seen discussed in the media, engaged with on social media, or experienced personally. How is your issue linked to the debates in this unit? Which authors seem to share underlying values and assumptions with the stakeholders in your issue? Where do you stand on the issue, and why?
4. If a soda tax were implemented as some authors in this anthology unit advocate, how would the revenues be distributed? Do some brief research on the programs that have been funded by "sin taxes" around the country or the world (other sugar taxes, cigarette or alcohol taxes, even lotteries). What programs, in your view, should be funded by these proceeds? Should the recipient programs be related to the taxed item, or should the revenues be up for grabs by any program benefiting the public?

Writing Assignment

Multimodal Argument: A Storyboard or Cartoon

Many of the arguments presented in this unit speak from an outsider's perspective—that is, as someone who is not a member of the population of school lunch eaters or sugar consumers. Construct a visual argument in the form of a cartoon or storyboard of at least four frames in which you respond as one of the consumers being discussed. For instance, you might draw a cartoon illustrating a kid encountering the food on the school lunch line. Or your cartoon might tell the story of a food stamp recipient responding to a proposed soda tax or the exclusion of soda from goods that can be purchased with food stamps. You may wish to consult Chapter 9, "Making Visual and Multimodal Arguments," for tips on constructing a visual argument.

Challenges in Education

Conflicts and challenges are rocking America's educational system, kindergarten through college, school classrooms to university campuses. Adding fuel to the conflicts are social and political divisions, from free-market values to egalitarian values, which hold different assumptions about education. How can education in the United States best prepare students to compete in the global community? Researchers, scholars, and analysts are noting that parts of this generation are less educated than their parents. Stanford University scholar-teacher Linda Darling-Hammond writes that "[s]tates that would not spend $10,000 a year to ensure adequate education for young children of color spend $30,000 a year to keep them in jail" (*The Flat World and Education: How America's Commitment to Equity Will Determine Our Future*, Teachers College, 2010, p. 24).

U.S. students' mediocre rankings on national and international K-12 tests (sometimes referred to as the *achievement gap*) go hand in hand with the enormous *opportunity gap* (differences in access to quality education), intensifying the debate over what reforms would improve our schools. Critics are asking questions about access to pre-K education; testing; teacher training and accountability; digital technology in schools; and the effect of gender, racial, and sexual-orientation prejudice on student performance. Related to the big questions about reform are two current educational policy debates, discussed in the readings in this chapter.

One major area of controversy concerns charter schools and vouchers, which affect individual choice and funding for schools as well as individual choice regarding which school to attend. Charter schools are mostly publicly funded schools that have considerable autonomy in their curriculum and management. The school-voucher program allows parents to use the public money allotted for their child's public education to pay for alternatives to public school. Opponents contend that both programs weaken public education. Another area of potential reform concerns school discipline policies and practices. Some researchers and schools have chosen to examine the racial disciplinary gaps seen in the implementation of strict zero-tolerance policies: Why are students of color punished more frequently and harshly for behavior and rule-breaking than white students are? Are detentions, suspensions, and expulsions effective disciplinary policies? Do these policies lead students to acquire criminal records? Would restorative justice, a relationship-building method based on accountability and communication, be more socially just and effective? How do students' safety, the learning environment, and order in schools factor into this disciplinary issue?

We also see many challenges at the university level. In addition to concerns about the cost of college and its value, another question about the purpose of college has received much public attention: How much should the college experience allow for exposure to diversity, conflict, and complexity versus how much should universities and colleges prioritize sheltering students emotionally, intellectually, and physically? Controversies surround recent cases of sexual assault and harassment on college campuses, as well as violent protests over students' freedom to invite controversial speakers to campus and to express their political views. In light of these conflicts, several readings in this chapter examine assumptions about colleges' role in preparing students to become adults and responsible citizens. Other readings explore the problem of controversial speakers on campus and instructors' use of trigger warnings, which are heads-up messages about disturbing content in readings, films, and other course materials.

Rethinking School Discipline

RACHEL M. COHEN

Rachel M. Cohen is a fellow at The American Prospect, *a progressive quarterly political magazine. A liberal journalist, she writes regularly on education issues and politics. On a freelance basis, she has also contributed articles to leading publications such as* Slate, In These Times, *and* The Daily Beast. *This article was published in the Fall 2016 issue of* The American Prospect.

On a Friday morning in early September, all the middle school students at Hampstead Hill Academy, a pre-K–8 school in Baltimore, filed into the gym. The Ravens were playing on Sunday, which meant that students could take a day off from wearing their navy-blue collared uniforms if they wanted to dress in purple in support of the city's football team.

The roughly 240 students sat on the gym floor, forming a big circle. Each week, all sixth-, seventh-, and eighth-graders come together for this half-hour event—to formally recognize the good deeds of their peers and teachers, to offer apologies to those they had wronged, and to share upcoming personal announcements. Matthew Cobb, an eighth-grade science teacher, helped facilitate the morning's community circle. Encouraging students to make eye contact with one another and to project their voices, it was an exercise in public speaking as much as it was in relationship-building.

Matthew Hornbeck, the school's principal, has been leading Hampstead Hill for 14 years. For the past nine, he and his staff have actively incorporated "restorative justice" into their school's culture, a model that involves holding structured conversations to facilitate relationships and reconciliation. While Hampstead Hill still has suspensions and detentions, Hornbeck says restorative justice has dramatically reduced the need for them. Hampstead Hill holds school-wide circles, class-wide circles, and when someone misbehaves, teachers hold circles that include the offending student, the victim, and anyone else who may have been affected. "It's not a silver bullet, it's not going to save the world, but it's a huge piece of the puzzle and I think principals would be crazy not to check it out and take it seriously," Hornbeck says. "It's not a fad."

Every teacher at Hampstead Hill is required to lead at least three class-wide circles per week. These don't take very long, perhaps 10 to 12 minutes, but the idea is to regularly create the space for students to share their feelings, ask each other questions, and build trust.

Later that Friday morning, Mr. Cobb led a restorative circle for the 20 students in his science class. The day's question was a silly one: *Would you eat a worm sandwich if you could meet your favorite TV star or musician?* One by one, each student went around the room and answered the question. "No way," Nyya told her classmates. "It would depend on how much time I'd have with the stars, but I would probably do it if I could meet the Dolan twins," said Hannah. Taras said he'd eat a worm sandwich if Drake were waiting for him at the end.

"I would eat a worm sandwich to meet who, class?" Mr. Cobb asked his students.

"Beyoncé!!!!" they all yelled back, laughing.

In the era of Black Lives Matter,   the movement that has spotlighted racist policies afflicting black Americans, a new national focus on school discipline disparities has taken hold. Activists point to staggering statistics—for instance, that the number of high school students suspended or expelled over the course of a school year increased roughly 40 percent between 1972 and 2009, while the racial disciplinary gaps also widened. During the 2013–2014 school year, the Department of Education's Office of Civil Rights reported that black students were 3.8 times more likely than white students to receive an out-of-school suspension. Similar disparities held true even for black preschoolers. Advocates have pressured school officials and policy-makers to end these suspensions, expulsions, and school-based arrests, which they say push too many students into the criminal justice system—a process commonly referred to as the "school-to-prison pipeline."

Many districts have responded to the calls for change. By the 2015–2016 school year, 23 of the 100 largest school districts in the United States had implemented policy reforms requiring limits to the use of suspension and/or the implementation of non-punitive approaches to discipline, according to Matthew Steinberg, an education researcher and assistant professor at the University of Pennsylvania. Some cities have banned certain types of suspensions, while others have reduced the length of suspensions, or curtailed the types of penalties students could receive for lower-level offenses.

When it comes to exemplary models of discipline reform, Hampstead Hill stands tall. Yet the racially integrated public charter is rather unusual in its ability to devote meaningful resources to implementing restorative justice. The school employs a full-time psychologist, social worker, guidance counselor, family therapist, and a director of restorative practice. Many cash-strapped schools have none of these, but are still being asked to revamp their policies, and fast.

Much of the liberal and education establishment has thrown its weight behind school discipline reform. In February, Democratic presidential candidate Hillary Clinton took the stage in Harlem to discuss societal barriers facing African Americans—among them, the school-to-prison pipeline.

"We've seen a significant increase in police involvement in school discipline, especially in schools with majority-black students," she declared. "We're seeing an over-reliance on suspensions and expulsions." Investments in school districts, Clinton said, will help leaders reform their school discipline practices. She pledged to commit $2 billion to the effort, and promised to push the Office of Civil Rights to intervene if schools and states refuse to change their ways.

Five months after Clinton's Harlem speech, the Democratic Party platform adopted at its convention included language to end the school-to-prison pipeline, and to oppose discipline policies that disproportionately affect students of color and students with disabilities. Embraced by the highest echelons of Democratic politics, the battle against the school-to-prison pipeline has traveled a long way since researchers first coined the term back in 2003.

But challenges remain for progressive reformers. Research has well established that removing students from class has negative impacts on their academic achievement, and there's broad recognition that suspensions and expulsions do very little on their own to address the underlying issues that cause most students to misbehave. However, good evidence on potential alternatives is fairly thin, and the linkages between school discipline and the criminal justice system are also less clear than advocates tend to acknowledge. While there's a lot of energy to move forward, to do *something* about the glaring racial inequities, this same pressure threatens to produce policy change that could inadvertently hurt other students, teachers, and schools. Tackling such deep structural inequities as segregation and resource allocation is likely necessary to really address school discipline disparities—lest we face yet another instance of educators being asked to throw local solutions at systemic problems.

15   **Long before Hillary Clinton**   gave her speech on the school-to-prison pipeline, activists, lawyers, and researchers were figuring out how to raise public awareness about the harms of punitive school discipline.

"It's been incredible to hear the Democratic candidate speak specifically about the school-to-prison pipeline. That really didn't just come out of the year; it was through a movement that has been built over the past decade and a half," says Judith Browne Dianis, the executive director of Advancement Project, a civil-rights group.

Critics describe the school-to-prison pipeline as the policies and practices that push American public school students—particularly students of color and students with disabilities—out of school and into the juvenile and criminal justice systems. The American Civil Liberties Union says the pipeline begins with over-crowded classrooms, unqualified teachers, and a dearth of funding and supports like school counselors and special education resources.

Advocates point to "zero tolerance" policies—which automatically impose predetermined punishments for certain types of student misconduct—as another major factor contributing to the school-to-prison pipeline. Judith Kafka, an education historian and author of *The History of "Zero Tolerance" in American Public Schooling*, traces the phrase "zero tolerance" back to a U.S. Customs Service antidrug program from the 1980s, which was soon adopted by states and districts for school discipline. The idea was elevated into federal law in 1994, when Bill Clinton signed the Gun-Free Schools Act, requiring schools to expel for one year any student found with a gun. Since 1994, most jurisdictions have passed additional zero-tolerance policies that extend well beyond those mandated by federal law.

By 1997, the National Center for Education Statistics reported that 94 percent of all schools had zero-tolerance policies for weapons or firearms, 87 percent had them for alcohol, and 79 percent had them for tobacco. Critics say that these nondiscretionary policies are regularly used in response to low-level, nonviolent student misconduct. And the greater the number of suspended and expelled students there are, they say, the greater the likelihood there is that unsupervised young people will engage in negative behaviors, leading them ultimately to the criminal justice system.

The school-to-prison pipeline is also linked to the growth of police assigned to work in schools—known euphemistically as "school resource officers." According to the Vera Institute of Justice, a research and policy nonprofit, between the 1996–1997 and 2007–2008 school years, the number of public high schools with full-time law enforcement and security guards tripled. Advocates say this has yielded an increase in school-based arrests, many of them for nonviolent offenses.   20

Monique Dixon, deputy director of policy at the NAACP Legal Defense Fund, ideally wants to see no police in schools, because they're too often used to handle disciplinary problems traditionally managed by school administrators. But, Dixon says, if they *are* going to be in schools, then they should be evaluated annually on their effectiveness, based on clear data on who is getting arrested, the reasons why, and what available alternatives could have been used. One analysis of federal data revealed that more than 70 percent of students involved in school-based arrests or referred to law enforcement in 2010 were black or Hispanic.

More than four decades of research has shown that black students are suspended at two to three times the rate of white students. These disparities have been consistently found in all sorts of studies, across and within school districts.

In 2008, an American Psychological Association task force released a literature review on zero tolerance, concluding that not only do such practices fail to make schools safer or improve student behavior, but they also actually increase the likelihood that students will act out in the future.

"In the 1980s and 1990s, there was a sense that our schools were becoming more violent," says Russell Skiba, a long-time researcher on school discipline issues, and the lead author of the American Psychological Association report. "A careful examination of the data, though, showed there never really was an increase in youth violence in schools. But it made for a good sound bite for policymakers to say we'd be tough on school crime." When better data emerged in the late 1990s and early 2000s, Skiba says it became clear that zero tolerance was ineffective.

25   After the release of the American Psychological Association's report, along with the advent of scandalous news stories featuring students expelled for infractions like bringing nail clippers to school, more focus was directed at finding alternatives to zero tolerance. Citing districts like Oakland and Indianapolis, which have revised their codes of conduct to emphasize more preventative approaches to school discipline, Skiba says there's been tremendous interest in reforming punitive policies over the past three years.

The 2014–2015 school year   marked the first time white students no longer comprised a majority of the nation's public school students. And after Eric Garner, Michael Brown, and Tamir Rice were killed by police officers in 2014, followed by subsequent police killings in 2015 and 2016, an increasing number of activists and political leaders began drawing connections between the disproportionate discipline black youth face in school and the unequal treatment of black adults by law enforcement.

This national focus on racism prompted attention from teachers unions, too. In the summer of 2015, the National Education Association passed a resolution committing the nation's largest labor union to fighting institutional racism. The NEA pledged to provide support for programs that end the school-to-prison pipeline, and expand professional development opportunities that emphasize "cultural competence, diversity, and social justice."

The American Federation of Teachers also took action following the death of 25-year-old Freddie Gray, forming a Racial Equity Task Force to outline how the union could move schools away from zero-tolerance policies, reform discipline practices, and create more supportive environments for youth, especially young black men.

Individual districts prioritizing school discipline reform, like Denver and Baltimore, also began to attract national attention. In 2007, Baltimore hired a new school CEO, Andres Alonso, who worked to overhaul the district's discipline policies. He scaled back the scope of offenses that could warrant out-of-school suspensions and expanded the number of non-punitive discipline measures to keep kids in class. The results were dramatic: During the 2009–2010 school year, Baltimore issued fewer than 10,000 suspensions, a decrease of more than 50 percent from 2004.

30   The federal government took notice. In 2014, then–Education Secretary Arne Duncan and then–Attorney General Eric Holder came to Baltimore to unveil the first-ever set of national school discipline guidelines, calling on districts to

"rethink" their policies. The joint guidance from the U.S. Justice and Education departments instructed schools nationwide to examine their discipline data and to end racial disparities.

The government's rethink was also informed by a key report, the "Breaking Schools' Rules" study, released in 2011 by the Council of State Governments and Texas A&M University. This study tracked school records for all Texas seventh-graders in 2000, 2001, and 2002, and analyzed each student's grades for at least a six-year period, comparing this information to the state juvenile justice database.

"That particular study made it crystal clear, it gave a clear vision of what the school-to-prison pipeline really looked like," a Department of Education official says. "It made clear that when a child is suspended or expelled from school, their risk of involvement with the juvenile justice system goes up, as does their likeli-hood of dropping out of school, and repeating a year."

The discipline policy shifts by a range of governments have yielded real change: In 2014, California became the first state in the nation to ban "willful defiance" suspensions for its youngest students—a category of misconduct that includes refusing to remove a hat, to wear the school uniform, or to turn off a cell phone. Consequently, the number of California students suspended at least once during the 2014–2015 school year declined by 12.8 percent from the previous year. Similarly, in Chicago, out-of-school suspensions fell by 65 percent between the 2012–2013 and 2014–2015 school years after the district revised its policies, while New York City, after a policy shift, issued 31 percent fewer suspensions in the first half of the 2015–2016 school year than it did in 2014.

In July 2015, the White House convened a "Rethink Discipline" conference, highlighting progress made by the school districts of Oakland, Los Angeles, Broward County (Florida), and others. This past June, Education Secretary John King went to the National Charter Schools Conference in Nashville to urge char-ter school leaders to "rethink" their discipline policies. And this September, the Departments of Justice and Education released the first-ever federal guidance for districts that employ school police officers.

In terms of concrete alternatives, advocates point to models that focus   35
on improving relationships within the school building. Supporters of these approaches—that have names like "Social and Emotional Learning" and "Positive Behavioral Interventions and Supports"—say that teaching students positive social skills can help prevent or eliminate such risky behaviors as drug use, violence, bullying, and dropping out.

Another popular reform, backed by teachers unions and civil-rights groups, aims to train educators on ways to overcome any racial biases they may harbor. Many worry that middle-class white educators in particular lack the cultural understanding that could help them work more compassionately with poor black and brown students.

The last major alternative is restorative justice, the kind of climate-based improvement program that Matthew Hornbeck has been building in his school over the past nine years. The amount of high-quality research on the effectiveness of restorative justice is limited, but academics at the Johns Hopkins School of Education are currently engaged in a rigorous evaluation of schools implementing the model. Cities aren't waiting around, though: From Chicago to Los Angeles to New York City, many districts have already moved to implement restorative justice pilot programs.

Kathy Evans, an education professor at Eastern Mennonite University, helped start the nation's first graduate program focused on training teachers to use restorative justice. "It's not just that I think restorative justice is more effective, it's that I think suspensions and expulsions hurt a lot of kids," she says. "They experience suspensions or expulsions not as a deterrent, but as just one more message that 'You're not worthy,' 'You're not important,' and 'You don't matter.'"

"I think reform really comes down to leadership, and how well we've managed to get information in the hands of leaders that are willing to take on this challenge," a Department of Education official told me. "And it is a challenge. You have had educators who for so many years may not have been trained to manage classrooms without the use of exclusionary discipline, and have become reliant on their ability to send children out of the classroom."

40   **But even as districts turn** away from the harsh disciplinary policies of recent decades, few studies exist on alternative approaches. This is partly because so many reforms are only just emerging, and it will take time for academics to evaluate their impacts. However, some researchers also question how much we can really conclude based on the studies we currently have.

There is, for instance, little evidence that black students and white students within the same school receive different kinds of school discipline. In 2011, Josh Kinsler, an education economist at the University of Georgia, ran a study that looked at roughly 500,000 students across 1,000 elementary, middle, and high schools in North Carolina. He found that within schools, black and white students were treated similarly, but that student disciplinary outcomes varied significantly across schools.

Another recent study released by the University of Chicago Consortium on School Research echoes some of these findings: Researchers found that the specific Chicago public school students attended was a much stronger predictor of whether they would be suspended or expelled than any individual student characteristic, including race or gender. Chicago schools with high rates of suspensions and expulsions served extremely vulnerable, segregated populations, while those with low levels of exclusionary discipline did not.

There are also limitations to the "Breaking Schools' Rules" study, which produced correlational, not causal, findings. "The Texas study . . . would fail the Department of Education's own research evaluation tool," says Kinsler, referring to a rubric for high-quality research by the Institute of Education Sciences.

Nevertheless, the immediate challenge for school leaders is figuring out how to balance the harm a disruptive student would face from losing more class time with their responsibility to effectively teach the rest of the class. We already know that those students who arrive at school with the most serious challenges, those who need the most instructional support, are also among those who are most likely to be suspended.

Academics with the Civil Rights Project at UCLA say that softening disci- plinary practices would be minimal and manageable, and that resolving unequal discipline is necessary to reduce the racial achievement gap. They point to the Denver Public Schools, a district that has made concerted efforts to reduce suspensions and expulsions. Researchers found that at the same time that Denver's punitive discipline went down, the district showed "a steady and substantial increase" in the percentage of students scoring proficient or higher in nearly every subject for six consecutive years. Another recent study found that the impact of Chicago shortening the length of suspensions for more serious misconduct from ten days to five did not seriously disrupt or harm other students.

"We summarily reject this narrative that if you just identify the kids that don't deserve to be in school then everyone else is going to thrive," says Kesi Foster, a coordinator with the Urban Youth Collaborative, a youth-led group focused on the school-to-prison pipeline in New York City. "Communities thrive when [people] see that everyone in the community is valued and supported. This theory that some people are disposable is what has led to mass incarceration and continues to ensnare young black people."

Robust agreement in favor of exploring less-punitive disciplinary measures has not prevented the emergence of controversy, however, especially as elected officials and districts move to implement broad policy changes quickly.

When the federal government released its school discipline guidelines at the start of 2014, the American Federation of Teachers praised the effort, but warned that new policies would succeed only if additional resources were made available.

It's been difficult for teachers like Kimberly Colbert, an English teacher in Saint Paul, who feels passionate about social justice and reducing exclusionary discipline. Colbert has taught for 21 years, and has helped lead her local union to push for reductions in suspensions and expulsions. In their recent round of collective bargaining, her union negotiated increased funding for restorative justice pilots. "We're looking at racism, we're calling it out, and we're trying to interrupt it," she says.

Colbert remains hopeful about change, but also worried that the expectation to fix everything will fall, as usual, on the shoulders of under-supported teachers. She notes that not every public school has a librarian or a school nurse, and Minnesota has one of the highest student-to-counselor ratios in the United States. Last year, a series of violent school incidents in Saint Paul served as harsh reminders of the daunting challenges that persist. In October, a student showed up to one Saint Paul high school with a loaded handgun in his backpack. Two months later, a student at Colbert's own school slammed a teacher against a concrete wall, choked him unconscious, and ultimately gave him a traumatic brain injury.

A few months later, at a third Saint Paul school, two students assaulted a teacher, punching him in the face, and throwing him to the ground.

"It was really difficult for everybody," recalls Colbert. "We don't want to see our colleagues hurt, we don't want to be hurt, and at the same time we understand that we have students who get angry and have needs."

These concerns extend beyond Saint Paul. Several years into various efforts across the country to scale back suspensions and expulsions, more and more teachers are saying they feel they are being put in untenable situations.

In 2013, the teachers unions in California initially opposed the statewide "willful defiance" suspension ban, which many felt went too far in limiting teachers' discretion. "Some legislators don't understand, they haven't been in the environment, so when they say let's eliminate all suspensions and expulsions, we've had to work to make sure the teacher still has authority in the classroom," says Jeff Freitas, the secretary treasurer for the California Federation of Teachers. "And we need doctors, mental-health specialists—you're going to take away this [disciplinary] tool without providing strategies? That's been our struggle."

Teachers aren't the only ones worried about losing their discretion. Mark Cannizzaro, the executive vice president for the Council of School Supervisors and Administrators, the union representing New York City principals, says that while the renewed focus on school discipline has been very welcome, his members worry about the degree to which school leaders are losing their authority. He cites a new rule the city's education department implemented last year, requiring principals to seek permission to suspend students for infractions related to "defying the lawful authority of school personnel." Local political leaders are also considering a citywide ban on suspensions for students in kindergarten through second grade. Both Cannizzaro's union and the New York City teachers union have raised objections to this proposal.

55   "The school leader is the person who knows the community, knows the circumstances, and that person is in the best position to make that discipline call," says Cannizzarro. "You can't legislate every type of social interaction into a code of conduct. We agree that suspensions should be extremely rare, but there are cases where something egregious happens, and there are often few other tools in a principal's toolkit."

Kenneth Trump, the president of National School Safety and Security Services, a school safety consulting firm, says the push to ban all suspensions is just zero tolerance by another name.

"Suffice to say that suspending and expelling students from school certainly is not a real solution to the underlying negative behaviors and problems of individual students," he says. "That said, there are very legitimate cases when student misconduct poses a serious threat to other students and even the student demonstrating the unsafe behaviors."

Trump also thinks the public should be more critical of districts that tout dramatic drops in school suspensions. "Have school officials reduced negative behaviors or have they just reduced their discipline numbers? Rarely does behavior change overnight, nor do even the most successful programs have dramatic drops of 30, 50, or greater percent in one year," he says.

Reports have been surfacing of teachers who say they feel they can't discipline out-of-control students because their district wants to "keep their numbers down." Relatedly, many educators are saying they feel unsupported, and even unsafe, as they try to keep up with new school discipline policies.

Los Angeles was the first city in California to ban suspensions for "willful defiance" and was also hailed for its commitment to roll out restorative justice pilots. But last fall, *The Los Angeles Times* reported that teachers at only about a third of the district's 900 campuses had been trained in restorative justice, and that the district was failing to budget sufficient funds for its implementation. The report cited one Los Angeles middle school where teachers felt overwhelmed by their inability to respond to students who pushed, threatened, and cursed at them. Two teachers took leaves of absence as a result.

Change always brings resistance, but finding ways to sustain support from teachers and school administrators will matter greatly moving forward. That means figuring out how to engage local stakeholders so they don't feel that a series of unfunded mandates are descending upon them.

One challenge will be to find the dollars necessary to invest in non-punitive policies and practices. To be sure, as some advocates point out, when districts need to expand the number of school police officers or implement expensive testing programs, somehow there seems to be far less anguish scraping up the funds. Redirecting school budget line items to better reflect progressive priorities will no doubt be a critical aspect of discipline reform.

But to truly overcome racial disproportionality in school discipline, leaders will need to do more than just shuffle local dollars around. It will require more than just sending individual teachers to anti-racism trainings. Important though those things are, the evidence suggests that systemic problems like the concentration of racially and economically segregated schools must also be addressed if the real, if narrower, issue of racial school discipline disparities is to be resolved.

Restorative Justice: The Zero-Tolerance-Policy Overcorrection

RICHARD ULLMAN

Richard Ullman teaches social studies at Cuba-Rushford High School, New York. In this editorial, published in Education Week *on September 13, 2016, he brings his years of teaching to bear on the practical problems with school disciplinary policies.* Education Week *newspaper covers K-12 education nationally.*

The rise of "soft discipline" hurts students

Why can't Johnny read? Or, assuming he can, why isn't Johnny closing the achievement gap?

It's politically fashionable to blame his tenure-protected teacher. But might it have more to do with the pathologically disruptive classmate who, given infinite "second chances" by detached policymakers and feckless administrators, never gets removed from Johnny's classroom?

Thanks, in part, to an increasingly popular behavior-management approach known as "restorative justice," soft discipline is on the rise in public schools at the same time that education reformers are demanding higher standards and teacher accountability.

Restorative justice emphasizes correction and counseling over punishment, and seeks to replace strict zero-tolerance discipline policies with collaborative opportunities for restitution. Its primary goal is to keep students in school rather than suspending or expelling them.

5 Detractors argue that these programs are long on coddling but lacking in consequences, and that they make it a priority to warehouse students who've repeatedly demonstrated they can't be educated in a conventional classroom setting. We're not talking here about the kid who forgot his pencil.

So while many districts proudly point to a reduction in student-removal numbers, critics point out that fewer suspensions don't mean fewer infractions.

The concept of restorative justice has merit. Indeed, I've been practicing elements of it throughout my 27-year teaching career. When students in my classroom do something disruptive, I chastise the behavior and give them the opportunity to backtrack and apologize. "Fix it," I say. "Make it right." Almost without exception, they do. Justice restored.

Alas, in a profession where ideologically motivated reforms abound, restorative justice in many districts has recklessly morphed into de facto "no student removal" policies that are every bit as flawed as the inflexible zero-tolerance policies they were designed to replace.

The process by which this happens is all too familiar to teachers.

10 Far removed from the pedagogical trenches, federal and state education departments craft behavior-management guidelines designed to vastly reduce suspensions and expulsions, and keep even the most dangerous and defiant students in the least-restrictive educational environment possible.

Then, at the district level, administrators oversee policy specifics based on their idealistic vision of how they wish schools could function, as well as a tendency to blame most classroom misbehavior on teachers who aren't sufficiently "engaging" students. Factor in the costs associated with alternative placement and the fact that many states make graduation rates the primary instrument for administrative evaluations, and even the most dangerous and defiant students aren't going anywhere.

But administrators and other insulated "experts" aren't the ones doing the heavy lifting in the now more dysfunctional classroom they helped create.

Ultimately, teachers—and only teachers—are left to raise the academic bar while education policymakers lower or, in some cases, virtually eliminate discipline standards.

Wow, that's some powerful union those teachers have.

It should be mentioned that restorative justice is a reaction in part to statistics that indicate higher suspension and expulsion figures for minority students. The elephant in the classroom is race, and a phenomenon generally referred to as the school-to-prison pipeline. Students removed from schools do have a higher likelihood of ending up in the juvenile and adult criminal-justice system.

However, while all educators must be mindful of biases and pushing out kids   15
considered at risk, it bears emphasizing that the biggest victims of warehousing miscreants are the large numbers of nondisruptive, genuinely teachable students who tend to come from the same home environments as their poorly behaved classmates.

Teachers, especially in high-poverty areas, are some of the most tolerant, patient, social-justice-oriented humanitarians in any profession. But just how many times should the student who spews obscenities be sent back to class with no reprisals? Just how much instructional time has to be sacrificed to hold yet another assembly on why yet another schoolwide brawl occurred?

Education reformers often argue that you can't have great schools without great teachers. That's probably true. But, given the numerous factors—especially related to discipline—over which teachers have minimal control, is it possible to have great teachers and still have "failing" schools?

Take It From a New Orleans Charter School Teacher: Parents Don't Always Get School Choice Right

CASSADY ROSENBLUM

Cassady Rosenblum wrote this op-ed piece for the Los Angeles Times, *which published it on July 10, 2017. She is a graduate student in investigative reporting at the UC Berkeley School of Journalism. She did her undergraduate work in international relations at Wellesley College and then taught in public high schools in New Orleans. In this piece, she writes about that experience.*

"Cohen—isn't that a ghetto school?" the mom filling out her son's application to a New Orleans high school asked me.

It was July of 2015, and we were sitting across from each other at an open enrollment fair at Dillard University, where it seemed as if the whole city had shown up to choose charter schools for their children. I was there as a volunteer to help parents sift through their options and fill out school applications. I struggled to figure out how to answer this woman's question.

As a teacher at Cohen College Prep, I knew it to be one of her son's best options, boasting the highest college acceptance rate of any open-enrollment high school in the city. But in my duties as a volunteer that day, I was prohibited from giving any opinion that could influence her decision.

"Cohen earned a B last year, according to the state," I finally responded weakly.

5   "Hmm," she said, turning to her son whose future we were trying to determine. "What do you think?"

"I want to go to Lake Area," he said. "They say it's fun there."

My stomach sank. I had taught at Lake Area too. Despite the Herculean efforts of many of my old colleagues, Lake Area traditionally bounced between a C and a D. I knew firsthand that this child would not receive the same quality of education there as he would at Cohen.

Saying nothing, I checked to see how many seats Lake Area had left. It was full.

"Sorry," I said. "Lake Area was a popular choice this year."

10   It had been that way for the past few years. Despite its poor rankings, Lake Area consistently remained one of parents' top choices. Cohen, meanwhile, struggled each year to persuade parents to send their students there. When I signed on as a civics teacher in 2015, 71% of the graduating class had enrolled in a four-year college, compared with 55% of Lake Area's. But while class sizes ballooned at Lake Area, Cohen was under-enrolled by several hundred students.

How could a D school be a top-five pick with parents while a B school ranked near the bottom of the barrel? Here was the free-market theory of parent choice played out like Milton Friedman and Los Angeles' new school board member, Nick Melvoin, imagined—except parents weren't always choosing the best schools.

Why?

The answer is a cautionary tale for Los Angeles, where the new school board, sworn in on Friday, has made it clear that it will make parent choice a priority.

During my three years teaching in New Orleans, I heard hundreds of reasons why parents chose the schools they did. Some, at Lake Area, liked the brand-new building. In a city where Hurricane Katrina had pulverized the majority of the city, appearances mattered. The sleek glass angles of Lake Area were a source of pride, whereas the bleak concrete of Cohen suggested a history of hardship many preferred to forget.

15   Other parents cared about safety, and rightly so. Whereas Cohen had existed as a neighborhood school for years (a conversion, as we would call it in L.A.), Lake Area was a start-up. That meant that Cohen had decades to acquire a reputation for being a rough school, while Lake Area began with a spotless record. Although I witnessed far more fights at Lake Area than I ever did at Cohen—where new leadership had created a much calmer, better-run school—parents' institutional memories were slow to change.

Other families cared deeply about sports, choosing schools based on athletics rather than academics. For some students and their parents, getting a sports scholarship was the best ticket to college they felt they had. Considering the fact that, prior to Katrina, 62% of New Orleans students attended what today would be considered an F school, it wasn't an irrational premise. Just outdated.

Over and over again, I watched parents make choices that weren't academically sound—a giant wrinkle for parent-choice theory. While I've been thrilled to see New Orleans parents choosing more A and B schools in recent years, thousands of students remain enrolled in lower-performing schools while seats at better schools remain open. Students who could have gone to college may never get the chance.

The lesson for Los Angeles is that parent choice is not a perfect substitute for quality. It's imperative that the school board make student performance—not choice—the focal point of its decisions, especially when weighing which schools to open and which to close.

It's hardly an enviable task, especially when faced with rows of emotional parents armed with speaker cards, and school data still so murky.

California's Department of Education could help ease the shift by releasing the new state test data to an impartial institution like Stanford's Center on Research for Educational Outcomes. CREDO's last study comparing charter student performance with traditional student performance in L.A. uses data from five years ago that does not reflect the new Common Core tests that Los Angeles has since adopted. 20

The California Charter School Association has a complementary role to play. If an institution such as CREDO indeed shows that students in charter schools are doing better, skeptics will continue to argue it is because charter schools exclude vulnerable populations, who are harder to educate. The California Charter School Assn. could preemptively silence such a debate by welcoming equity and transparency bills. With hope, the group's newfound support for SB 1360, which would make it harder for charter schools to cherry pick students and expel those who aren't excelling, harbingers a new direction for the organization, which traditionally has lobbied against such legislation.

I watched thousands of students in New Orleans receive a subpar education because policymakers oversubscribed to the free-market notion that parents will fix the schools if only you let them vote with their feet. Los Angles can avoid the same mistake—but only if it stops emphasizing "parent choice" and starts emphasizing quality.

Educators Try to Keep Public Education away from School Vouchers and Charter Schools

PAUL FELL

Paul Fell is an editorial cartoonist who formerly worked for the Lincoln (Nebraska) Journal *and who now runs his own freelance business, Paul Fell Cartoons, selling his cartoons nationally and internationally. In his earlier careers, Fell worked as a coach, high-school art teacher, and college art professor. His cartoons often focus on education, sports, and politics. He drew this cartoon in 2016.*

Why Managed Competition Is Better Than a Free Market for Schooling

DOUGLAS N. HARRIS

At Tulane University, Douglas N. Harris is Director of the Education Research Program at the Murphy Institute; Associate Professor of Economics; and Director of the Education Research Alliance for New Orleans. In these capacities, he researches the impact of desegregation, school choice, privatization, and other policies on student educational outcomes. He also serves as a government consultant. This researched policy recommendation was appeared on the website for the Brown Center on Education Policy at the Brookings Institution, a think tank known for its independent research into social problems and its impact on policymakers.

Introduction

President Donald Trump and Secretary Betsy DeVos's support for school choice, and especially private school vouchers, have brought to the forefront a long-standing debate, one nearly as old as the country. On one hand, opponents argue that schooling is a public good that should be governed by public means, especially the democratic accountability of school districts. Voucher supporters counter that we value individual freedom and that those on the front lines, families and school leaders, should make decisions that they believe are in the best interests of children.

I believe this apparent conflict between public and private goals is exaggerated. Specifically, I argue that a "managed competition" approach would place more decisions in the hands of families and school leaders while providing certain roles for government. This approach would best support our values for individual freedom and public goals, such as democratic citizenship, social cohesion, and equitable access to quality schools.1

Schooling Is a Prime Example of Market Failure

The roots of my argument may be somewhat surprising. Vouchers are often justified on the basis of free market economics, but this represents a simplistic view of the situation. In reality, the economics case against vouchers is stronger than the argument for it.

Economics tells us that markets work best when consumers have good information and many options to choose from, and when the decisions made by one family do not affect others. None of these conditions holds in schooling. Families expect many different things from schools, almost all of which are hard to measure and turn into practical information. We measure math, reading, and other skills with standardized tests because these are the skills we agree schools should provide—and we happen to be able to measure them reasonably well. But measuring creativity, social skills, citizenship, art, and music skills is much more difficult.

Unfortunately, geography also stands in the way of free markets. We use most   5
services only occasionally—haircuts, car repairs, and doctor visits. This is important because it allows us to worry less about distance. People often drive hours to get to the best doctor, but we have to get students to school every day, and families want schools to be accessible so they can avoid long commutes, attend sporting events and parent-teacher conferences, and pick up their children when they are sick. Except in high-density urban areas, families will have few options to choose from.

An additional condition for efficient free markets is that transactions between one consumer and producer do not affect other people. This also fails to hold with schools. Again, schooling is inherently public. One of the most widely accepted facts about education is that results depend not only on schools and families, but on peers and classmates. All parents worry about who their children interact with, and for good reason. The problem is that this gives incentives to schools to compete not on instructional quality, but on the types of students they can attract and retain, similar to country clubs. This is not a sound basis for competition. It is a zero-sum game.

Further, in almost no other market do we compel families to use a product or service. This means that, no matter how bad schools are in a given city or town, they will always draw a large number of consumers. Parents have to send their children somewhere. Since school buildings are only so large, most schools do not seek to expand, the better schools will not necessarily expand to meet high demand. This means the market will allow low-performing schools to continue operating.

The concern with markets is not just about efficiency, however. A key public goal of education is to level the playing field and provide opportunity to all children. But due to the fact that families pay so much attention to the kinds of students schools attract, private schools have a strong incentive to use admission requirements. In a free market, then, the most vulnerable students are likely to end up with the fewest good options—not only because of geography and limited competition among schools, but because they are discouraged or excluded from entering the schools most successful in attracting strong students.

While thinking of schooling as a market can seem cold-hearted and detached from the caring environments we wish our classrooms to be, there is no denying that schooling is a market and acts like one. Indeed, it is precisely the unusual features of schooling described above that make it hard to think about it as a market. Of course, we should not just rely on theory to understand the problems with the schooling market. The same conclusion arises when we consider the evidence.

The Evidence for a Scaled-Up Voucher Program Is Very Weak

10   There is now a large and growing base of evidence about the effects of market-based school reforms, especially charter schools and vouchers, on student outcomes. I start with vouchers, which take a free market approach.

There are so many studies of vouchers that it is not necessary to rely on reviews across studies. In particular, one recent survey of evidence from the University of Arkansas showed that the average effect of U.S.–based voucher programs on student achievement is essentially zero.[2]

Scaled-up voucher programs like those previously advocated by Secretary DeVos show the worst effects. There have recently been four statewide voucher programs: Florida, Indiana, Louisiana, and Ohio. The Florida study[3] is inconclusive, and the others show large *negative* effects. In some respects, the Louisiana results[4] are more convincing because the results have been corroborated by two different sets of researchers and students were assigned to vouchers by lottery— the most rigorous way to evaluate vouchers. In terms of providing convincing results, the Indiana[5] and Ohio[6] programs are somewhere in between, but these show negative results as well.

To see large negative effects is worrisome and highly unusual—many programs do not work in education, but few seem to make things worse. And all but one of these statewide program studies were released after the review showed no effect on achievement.

Voucher supporters argue that the results have been worse in the recent statewide programs because they have been "heavily regulated," by which they mean the requirements that students be tested, that these results be made publicly available, and that schools must let in any student who is eligible for the voucher. The fact that this fairly minimal oversight is considered controversial or heavy-handed, however, only reinforces that private schools are designed to be exclusive and have little interest in external accountability.

Voucher supporters have also argued that the Louisiana and Ohio results   15
look worse than they are because the tests have higher stakes for the traditional
public schools in these studies, which serve as the comparison group. In this case,
the scores of the public school students in the voucher studies may be inflated
and make the results for private schools look worse than they are. This probably
explains at least part of these unusual effects, but since earlier studies of vouchers
were based on tests more like those used by private schools, this raises questions
about why the earlier results that used difference tests still seem to show no effects
on achievement.[7]

Only a handful of studies have examined the long-term effects of vouchers
on measures like high school graduation and college entry. While a study of New
York City[8] shows no average effect on college-going, studies from Milwaukee[9]
and Washington, D.C.,[10] do show positive effects. There is not yet any evidence
available on the long-term effects of the statewide program like those now being
pursued across the country.

The Evidence for Managed Competition Is Strong— and Getting Stronger

My argument is that a system of managed competition is much more likely than
vouchers and tax credits to produce measureable results for all children. The evidence on charter schools is most relevant to the managed competition argument
because charter schools have more government involvement. We also know much
more about charter schools than vouchers, and the results are more promising.

While statewide voucher programs generate negative effects, statewide
charter programs typically yield positive effects on achievement. The best and
broadest-scale study covering lasting consequences in a number of states has also
found positive long-term effects on high school graduation and college-going.[11]

The charter systems in many states started off with somewhat poor results,
but there is a clear and consistent pattern of improvement over time.[12] This is not
especially surprising since charter schools were being created from scratch, while
vouchers were being used mainly to send children to long-established private
schools. As the charter sector developed, and as the government shut down low-
performing charter schools, the results have gotten consistently better.

One of the advantages of managed competition is that it still leaves power in   20
the hands of families, creating competition among schools. Research consistently
shows that, whether we are talking about charter schools[13] or vouchers,[14] competition does seem to improve student outcomes in traditional public schools.

We have also learned a great deal about how to make charter policies work
better. Here, the case of my hometown of New Orleans becomes especially relevant. I have studied this for many years now through my role as the founding
director of the Education Research Alliance for New Orleans at Tulane University.

In the wake of Hurricane Katrina, New Orleans experienced the most sweeping school reforms of any city in the country, if not the world. Our schools are now
run almost entirely by charter schools and charter management organizations.

But New Orleans was, for several years after Katrina, perhaps the freest schooling market the country has ever seen. For reasons we might predict from the unusual nature of the schooling market, this period is widely seen as problematic:

- Rather than families choosing schools, schools were choosing students, sometimes called "cream-skimming."[15]
- The enrollment process was time-consuming, chaotic, and created considerable uncertainty for families and schools. Schools did not know how many students would show up until just before classes started.[16]
- Student mobility and discipline incidents increased dramatically.[17]
- Many of the schools that initially opened soon failed.[18]

When the government stepped in to solve these problems, schools improved on almost every available metric. Achievement, high school graduation, and college entry continued to get better. Discipline incidents and student mobility, both of which had spiked during the free market period, began to drop when the state stepped in. Government oversight produced better outcomes with fewer unintended consequences than the market alone. This suggests at the very least that the government did not hinder improvement—and still left most of the key decisions to families and school leaders.

Managed Competition Defined

25   While I have focused so far on charter schools, this is not meant to be a charter proposal, and certainly I am not arguing that an all-charter system is best. Rather, the unique features of schooling combined with evidence on vouchers and charter schools point toward a general approach—managed competition—that will provide all families with real and better options. Managed competition includes five key elements:

Accountability: It is important that some agency actively ensure that schools are of high quality, that families have good options to choose from, and that tax dollars are used wisely. With charter schools, this occurs through the charter authorization process, performance-based contracts, and, as a last resort, taking over low-performing schools. As the federal Every Student Succeeds Act recognizes, performance frameworks should be based on a wide variety of measures, not just student test scores.

Accessibility: Given the unusual features of the schooling market, school choice is no guarantee at all that families will have real options. Broad access requires oversight of enrollment, discipline, and transportation policies to prevent intended, as well as unintended, exclusion of students.

Transparency: Markets do not function without good information, and markets themselves often fail to provide that on their own. In addition to requiring data gathering and reporting, the government also needs to ensure that charter boards post their meetings publicly, provide audited financial statements, and ensure that publicly funded schools do not fall prey to conflicts of interest.

Coordination: Some problems that may emerge (e.g., creating a supply of quality teachers) may be more easily solved through coordination by a government body that has some degree of authority.

Enforcement: The rules and information necessary to make the market function   30 are obviously of little use if they are not enforced. Moreover, the government needs to carry out its most basic function: protecting and enforcing students' civil rights.

   This managed competition approach provides many advantages. It shifts control down to those who are closest to students—their families and school leaders. It helps ensure that families have good options to choose from. It also creates healthy pressures on all schools to improve and meet students' needs. Paul Hill and others have made similar observations.[19]

   One possible response by those supporting free markets is that the complexity of schooling means that families will have better information than governments. This is partially correct. Families have information that others do not, but the government is arguably the only feasible source for some of the information that parents want, especially if parents want to compare schools as they are making choices. A system of managed competition, which combines both sources of information, is likely to yield the best results, and allow the government to carry out its fiduciary role to hold schools accountable for public funds.

   More generally, managed competition provides the advantages of markets while avoiding the disadvantages.

School Districts and State Governments Still Have Important Roles to Play

This proposal for managed competition is admittedly vague. There are many variations on the managed competition theme that could be effective. The above functions could be carried out by various combinations of state and local government agencies and nonprofits.

   The role of school districts is perhaps most noteworthy given that these   35 agencies still operate the vast majority of publicly funded schools for more than a century. I believe districts still have important roles to play. There is a reason that local school districts have continued to operate for more than a century and that most families still like their public schools. They help build local neighborhoods and communities—the public aspect of schooling. They take advantage of economies of scale, which allows them to reduce administrative costs and push more funding into the classroom. There is something to be said as well for local democratic control in deciding the right mix of schools and providers to make available.

This does not mean school districts should be the main agency carrying out the five main functions of government. Having school districts serve as authorizer of independent schools is unlikely to help, given that such schools, such as charters, would then compete with existing traditional public schools. But making district schools available as an option for families helps address many concerns, including the possibility that the market alone will not serve some students well, and that the market leaves families with considerable uncertainty about what schools their children will be able to get into when they move to a new neighborhood. This means that school districts can be an important part of the managed competition mix.

It is difficult to imagine that these various roles for government under managed competition could be carried out at the state or federal levels; there are far too many schools to execute all these functions effectively. This means that some other local government agency would need to perform most of the key tasks. But again, there are many ways to design such systems, and we probably need different approaches in different locations. In many places, where traditional public schools are working well, a district-focused system may make sense. In others, where they are performing poorly, a more significant shift to managed competition will likely make more sense.

Market Reform Works Better in Urban Locations

There is another important pattern in the evidence that may be more important than anything discussed thus far. While there are no achievement effects on average from vouchers, the more positive effects that have sometimes emerged with longer-term outcomes are all in urban locations: Milwaukee, New York City, and Washington, D.C. Indeed, this is exactly where we would expect a free market to work best, where traditional public schools appear least effective and where population density and transportation networks give more choice to families.

We see the same pattern with charter schools. A nationwide study of charter schools by Stanford researchers finds positive effects in urban areas and negative effects in rural areas, further reinforcing the conclusion that a broad-scale free market program will not succeed.[20] Other studies of the effects of private schools (even aside from voucher programs) also suggest that their effects, where they arise, are concentrated in urban areas.[21]

40   An important implication of this pattern is that all of these types of market-based reforms, whether charter or voucher, seem to have more limited prospects in suburban and rural locations. This means that, for the vast majority of the country, we will need a different approach, and probably a strong reliance on traditional school districts.

Conclusion

Schooling is a highly unusual market. It is hard to identify other markets with such complex, hard-to-measure outcomes. It is hard to identify other markets where we have to travel to a specific location every day, limiting options and choice. It is hard to identify other markets where the value of the service is so dependent on who else is in the building. This is why schooling is one of the clearest imaginable economic cases of market failure. If there is any market that would benefit from a role for government, it is the market for schooling.

The evidence to date should also make us cautious about broad-scale vouchers and tax credits involving almost no government oversight. While voucher programs have produced some modest positive results in small-scale pilot programs with low-income and minority children in urban areas, they have failed when taken to scale in the way that some policymakers are now pursuing.

A system of managed competition, with varying designs in different types of locations, can provide the accountability, accessibility, transparency, coordination, and enforcement necessary to make this very unusual market work for all children.

Endnotes

1. For a broader discussion of various goals of education and how they apply to schools and school choice, see Henry M. Levin (2002). A Comprehensive Framework for Evaluating Educational Vouchers. *Educational Evaluation and Policy Analysis* 24(3): pp. 159–174.

2. To be precise, the estimates are slightly positive but not statistically different from zero. See M. Danish Shakeel, Kaitlin P. Anderson, & Patrick J. Wolf (2016). *The Participant Effects of Private School Vouchers across the Globe: A Meta-Analytic and Systematic Review*. EDRE Working Paper 2016-07. University of Arkansas. Downloaded January 10, 2017, from http://www.uaedreform. org/downloads/2016/05/the-participant-effects-of-private-school-vouchers-across-the-globe-a-meta-analytic-and-systematic-review-2.pdf

3. David N. Figlio (2011). *Evaluation of the Florida Tax Credit Scholarship Program Participation, Compliance and Test Scores in 2009–10*. Downloaded January 10, 2017, from https://www.floridaschoolchoice.org/pdf/FTC_Research_2009-10_report.pdf.

4. Jonathon Mills and Patrick Wolf (2016). *How Has the Louisiana Voucher Program Affected Students*. Tulane University: Education Research Alliance for New Orleans. Downloaded January 20, 2017, from http://educationresearchalliancenola.org/files/publications/ERA-Policy-Brief-Public-Private-School-Choice-160218.pdf. This research has since been published in the journal *Educational Evaluation and Policy Analysis*.

5. Mark Berends and R. Joseph Waddington (forthcoming). School Choice in Indianapolis: Effects of Charter, Magnet, Private, and Traditional Public Schools. *Education Finance and Policy*.

6. David Figlio (2016). *Evaluation of Ohio's EdChoice Scholarship Program: Selection, Competition, and Performance Effects*. Fordham Institute. Downloaded January 20, 2017, from https://edexcellence.net/publications/ evaluation-of-ohio%E2%80%99s-edchoice-scholarship-program-selection-competition-and-performance.

7. One possible reason earlier voucher studies find no effects on achievement is that they are not held accountable for them, but this also reflects a lack of transparency even to the families who choose private schools. It is also worth noting that the Florida statewide study found no conclusive evidence of effects even though private schools in that case were allowed to the test of their choice.

8. Matthew M. Chingos and Paul Peterson (2013). The Impact of School Vouchers on College Enrollment. *Education Next* 13(3), 59–64. Downloaded January 10, 2017, from http://educationnext.org/files/ednext_XIII_3_chingos.pdf. This study has been widely misinterpreted because the authors focused on the positive effects of just one subgroup (African Americans). Such interpretations are widely rejected by education researchers because, if you separate students into enough groups, someone is likely to experience a result by chance. Moreover, there were apparently large negative effects on other students that were not emphasized in the study.

9. Cowen, Joshua M., David J. Fleming, John F. Witte, Patrick J. Wolf, and Brian Kisida (2013). School Vouchers and Student Attainment: Evidence from a State-Mandated Study of Milwaukee's Parental Choice Program. *Policy Studies Journal* 41(1): 147–167.

10. Patrick Wolf, Babette Gutmann, Michael Puma, Brian Kisida, Lou Rizzo, Nada Eissa, and Matthew Carr (2010). *Evaluation of the DC Opportunity Scholarship Program: Final Report*. Downloaded January 20, 2017, from https://ies. ed.gov/ncee/pubs/20104018/pdf/20104018.pdf.

11. Kevin Booker, Tim Sass, Brian Gill, and Ron Zimmer (2011). The Effects of Charter High Schools on Educational Attainment. *Journal of Labor Economics* 29: 377–415.

12. This can be seen in two ways. First, a study in Texas documents improvements over time in charter performance within the state: Patrick L. Baude, Marcus Casey, Eric A. Hanushek, and Steven G. Rivkin (2014). The Evolution of Charter School Quality. Downloaded January 20, 2017, from http://harris.uchicago.edu/sites/default/files/Rivkin.paper_.pdf. The same conclusion can be seen by comparing the periodic CREDO studies over time. The CREDO studies include the majority of the nation's charter schools.

13. Julian Betts (2010). *The Competitive Effects of Charter Schools on Traditional Public Schools*. In Mark Berrends, Matthew Springer, Dale Ballou, and Herbert Walberg, *Handbook of Research on School Choice* (pp.195–208). New York: Routledge.

14. David Figlio (2016). Ibid.

15. Huriya Jabbar (2015). *How Do School Leaders Respond to Competition?* Tulane University: Education Research Alliance for New Orleans. Downloaded January 10, 2017, from http://educationresearchalliancenola.org/publications/ how-do-school-leaders-respond-to-competition.

16. Harris, D., Valant, J., & Gross, B. (2015). The New Orleans OneApp. *Education Next*. http://educationnext.org/ new-orleans-oneapp/

17. These results are based on internal calculations that have not been released.

18. Whitney Bross and Douglas N. Harris (2016). *The Effects of Performance-Based School Closure on Charter Takeover on Student Performance*. Tulane University: Education Research Alliance for New Orleans. Downloaded January 20, 2017, from http://educationresearchalliancenola.org/files/publications/Bross-Harris-Liu-The-Effects-of-Performance- Based-School-Closure-and-Charter-Takeover-on-Student-Performance.pdf.

19. The managed competition approach I am proposing is similar in many ways to Hill's portfolio model—indeed, the New Orleans system closely resembles his recommendations. What I am proposing is less specific, places greater emphasis on the potentially positive role for school districts, even in urban areas. See, for example, Paul Hill and Christine Campbell (2011). *Growing Number of Districts Seek Bold Change With Portfolio Strategy*. University of Washington: Center for Reinventing Public Education.

20. This conclusion is based on the author's compilation of results across state-specific studies by the Center for Research on Educational Outcomes at Stanford University.

21. Derek Neal (1997). The Effects of Catholic Secondary Schooling on Educational Achievement. *Journal of Labor Economics* 15(1), 98–123.

Separate but Unequal

RACHEL LAM

Dr. Rachel Lam is an American research scientist currently working in Singapore at the National Institute of Education at Nanyang Technological University. She writes and speaks internationally, often on her research with elementary school children on collaborative learning and complex problem solving. This short editorial appeared in the May 2017 edition of Sojourners, *whose mission is "to articulate the biblical call to social justice, to inspire hope and build a movement to transform individuals, communities, the church, and the world" ("Our Mission").*

Betsy DeVos's plan for U.S. education is at odds with Christian values.

Education is a fundamental good and a fundamental human right. It is basic to determining social justice. Betsy DeVos, the new Secretary of Education under President Trump, has championed three major policies that further the oppression of children of color, children with special needs, and children who live in poverty. As a matter of faith, Christians should call to account those who promote injustice—especially from positions of power. "Woe to those who make unjust laws," railed the prophet Isaiah, "to deprive the poor of their rights and withhold justice from the oppressed of my people."

In the debate between egalitarian and libertarian approaches to education policy, DeVos is an extreme libertarian. She's a proponent of privatizing education and letting market forces and philanthropy sort out any inequalities. Privatized education favors children of the dominant culture and the financially elite. It drives public funding toward specialized schools and programs, such as charter schools, and away from regular public schools. DeVos claims that this promotes individual freedom and allows Christian schools to be better supported. In reality, it promotes an unfair distribution of educational resources across the few while disadvantaging the many. Michigan, where DeVos has long been active, leads the country in for-profit charter schools, while student performance has plummeted.

DeVos has indicated that she might remove federal regulations that guarantee a "free and appropriate education" for children with special needs. She argues that these protections should be regulated at the state level, providing local governments with more "freedom of choice." Practically speaking, this would increase the chances that children will be denied access to needed resources at local levels and create unfair distribution of assets. Strong federal regulations hold local education systems accountable to the children they are to educate. Without these protections, the most vulnerable children in our communities suffer.

DeVos advocates voucher programs and "school-choice" legislation that provide tax incentives for parents to send children to non-public schools. However, these programs undercut access to quality education for the majority. Voucher programs siphon funds away from public education and increase the gap between high-performing and low-performing schools. Children without strong parental support or who have disabilities or behavioral issues are removed from private schools, despite their vouchers, or are never accepted in the first place because private schools have little incentive to educate these students. The highest achieving students benefit most from attending the high-performing schools, leaving the children most in need in poorer quality schools with fewer resources.

5　DeVos displays a gross ignorance of the systemic oppression of children of color, the obstacles of families who grow up in poverty, and the needs of children who are atypical in development. The moral duty of the education secretary is to make decisions that best serve *all* children.

Educational opportunity should be equal with respect to existing social structures. Equal opportunity means that resources are available and appropriate for a child's unique gifts, needs, abilities, and experiences. Children who are underserved, overburdened, or unsafe in their communities must be given access to opportunities that allow them to reach their potential as much as children who are well-resourced, able-bodied, and otherwise privileged.

Models such as those DeVos manufactured in Michigan—structured to increase private wealth above all else and favoring certain people's children over others—are not the way forward, nor worthy of Christian support.

The goal of education reform should not be to remove a few children from failing schools, but to create opportunity for every child. All children should be able to learn and develop into well-functioning members of society.

How Canceling Controversial Speakers Hurts Students

RAFAEL WALKER

Rafael Walker holds a Ph.D. in English from the University of Pennsylvania and is currently a visiting assistant professor at the University of Maryland, Baltimore County. His scholarly work focuses on nineteenth- and twentieth-century American literature. This article appeared in The Chronicle of Higher Education *on February 8, 2017, in response to the riots at the University of California at Berkeley regarding a controversial right-wing speaker. He has written several articles for this publication, which appears online and in print weekly.* The Chronicle *serves as a major forum for the discussion of controversial issues in education.*

The riot at the University of California at Berkeley last week that forced campus officials there to cancel a scheduled talk from the controversial conservative Milo Yiannopoulos is the most recent testament to how pressing the problem of campus speakers has become for colleges and universities across the country. Higher-education administrators everywhere have had to wrestle with the question of how to respond to the wishes of their many constituents to invite controversial speakers.

Berkeley officials made a concerted effort to allow the speech to take place, but surprising numbers of administrators elsewhere have settled the matter by rescinding the invitation. Over the last few years, a host of elite institutions—Brandeis University, New York University, and Williams College among them—have rescinded invitations to high-profile, contentious speakers. In almost every case, the disinvited speaker was a leading light from the political right.

Understandably, colleges want to make students feel safe on their campuses, now more than ever. The hateful rhetoric suffusing the nation's most recent presidential election and the profoundly anti-immigration agenda of the Trump administration have put many people on edge and made academic leaders feel their roles as protectors even more acutely than before.

As admirable as their intentions are, however, we have to wonder whether the gains that administrators make in sheltering students from potentially hurtful speech come at too great a cost to academic freedom. When academe gets in the business of suppressing voices that it doesn't like and limiting students to only those views that it broadly sanctions—no matter how popular those views are in the culture at large—is free speech safe anywhere? Moreover, do we do our undergraduates any favors by shielding them from the "deplorable" views of the big bad conservatives beyond the ivory tower?

5   In so intensely regulating the speakers permitted to visit campuses, college leaders risk making their institutions just the sort of liberal echo chambers that abetted the ascent of a president at odds with virtually every principle that academe espouses—openness, complexity, and civility, to name only a few. If students are denied the opportunity to see for themselves that the world is full of people who don't think as they do, don't believe what they do, and might even dislike them for nothing more than their demographics, they will be inestimably less equipped for the demands of democratic citizenship.

The well-intentioned efforts of their colleges to curate what they hear holds out to them the false promise of a world in which they never come into contact with ideas diametrically opposed to their own. In so doing, colleges leave students far less capable of combating those ideas. Not only do they miss out on vital practice in responding to uncongenial viewpoints (e.g., arguments against abortion, same-sex marriage, government regulation of the economy), but they are also deprived of the chance to cultivate one of the faculties most essential to persuasion—empathy.

Our nation is diverse in so many respects, and, while many valuable advantages accompany this rich diversity, it confronts us with a number of hard challenges. In order for diversity to work, we have to be able to listen to and understand one another. Students who have not been asked frequently enough to look at the world through eyes not their own will have a far more difficult time making the empathic leap from their limited points of view into another's. They will remain interpersonally handicapped, better trained to scream and brandish signs at their opponents than to sit down with them and possibly win a new convert.

We cannot ignore, however, the real dilemma that administrators confront when faced with the prospect of a controversial speaker. Most administrators are academics and ought to respect the sacrosanct right of academic freedom, but they are also business leaders charged with protecting a brand. Consider Williams College's recent brush with this issue. A provocative student group wanted to bring the conservative writer John Derbyshire to campus, not because all its members supported his views but because at least some of them planned to refute those views. However, they should have taken a moment to anticipate the kind of press to which the event, as planned, would have inevitably given rise: "Williams to Host Notorious Racist" is not a headline that any college president wants to find himself having to explain to alumni.

Canceling the speech, however, was a missed teaching opportunity for the leaders at Williams. The students' idealistic hearts were in the right place: They aimed to get all the ideas out in the open, in the hope that, in Darwinian fashion, only the fittest would survive. But their approach was way off. This was fundamentally a framing issue that faculty and administrators should have worked with students to overcome rather than dismissing the proposal out of hand.

No, it would not have done for a student group to bring a speaker of Derbyshire's stature with the intent to engage him on their own. No matter how intelligent Williams's student body is, this simply wouldn't have been a fair fight. Surely a less objectionable alternative would have been to stage the event as a debate rather than a lecture; in so doing, the students might have brought in any number of pundits from the swelled ranks of the liberal intelligentsia to oppose Derbyshire's message.

Just as students could stand to become more business-savvy and shrewd in dealing with the speaker conundrum, administrators could stand to become more academic, remembering the ideals that make higher-education institutions what they are. Forbidding speakers who offend or who do not share our views simply isn't a viable response. It turns colleges into hypocrites and opens them to not-entirely-baseless charges of liberal bias. More important, it stunts students' development by decreasing the opportunities they have to stretch themselves beyond their comfort zones and learn to navigate the precarious waters of fundamental disagreement. Beyond such high-minded concerns, a more pragmatic benefit of working with students on framing these controversial events is that doing so would provide them an excellent occasion to sharpen their rhetorical and marketing skills, preparing them to think like the professionals we hope they will become.

If colleges do anything to prepare future generations for effective citizenship, it will not be through the bubbles they erect around their campuses to keep out the waves of fear and hate flooding "the real world." As much as we shun the divisive rhetoric and illiberal executive orders threatening everything we stand for, no good can come from attempts to conceal these realities from our students, no matter how painful direct exposure might feel in the short term. If, finally, we want students to engage the wide world and insert themselves into it meaningfully, we have to let them.

I'm Not Giving Students "Trigger Warnings"

GINA BARRECA

Gina Barreca is Professor of English at the University of Connecticut, but she is best known as a columnist for The Hartford Courant, *a blogger for* Psychology Today, *a guest on high-profile television shows, and a contributor to other major publications such as* The New York Times, The Chicago Tribune, *and* The Chronicle of Higher Education. *In her journalism and her books, she writes about gender, feminist issues, and politics, and she is known for her spirited humor. Her most recent book is*

If You Lean In, Will Men Just Look Down Your Blouse? (2016). This op-ed piece discussing the controversial issue of trigger warnings appeared in The Seattle Times *on June 12, 2016.*

No to trigger warnings: Students need exposure to things that challenge them, says Gina Barreca

The day I'm forced to offer "trigger warnings" before teaching is the day I stop teaching. To insist that I, or any other teacher, warn students that the material in a class might upset them defeats the purpose of education. Colleges and universities must remain institutions that inflame curiosity and, by their very existence, disturb those who enter their gates.

But if trigger warnings become a perfunctory, sanctioned, and unopposed knee-jerk reaction—however well-meaning—to precisely the kind of discomfort, dissatisfaction, disruption, and disturbance of the peace that is the mission of authentic education, then I'll call it quits. If that day arrives, I'll be done with classrooms and will hold lessons in my house, or in the woods or on the city streets. Education is not designed to reassure; its job is not to soothe but to disturb—otherwise intellect and emotion both remain inert and unmoved. If you protect the unexplored intellectual and psychological landscapes within yourself, you end up with a wilderness.

In his poem "Andrea del Sarto," Victorian poet Robert Browning wrote, "Ah, but a man's reach should exceed his grasp, or else what's a heaven for?" But instead, are we encouraging today's students to insist that everything be modified in order to be in reach? If somebody can't get it, it should be taken off the shelves?

Put it this way: If you're afraid of cats and you're assigned "Winnie-the-Pooh," do you need a Tigger warning?

5   I believe it's a sign not of fragility but of immaturity to stick your fingers in your ears and say "nyah nyah nyah" if you're hearing something you don't like. If you spend your life putting your fingers across your eyes and looking between them because you worry about something disturbing, you're going to miss most of what's going on.

Like shutting the window to the sound of distant thunder or shutting your eyes to the sight of a beggar on the street, trigger warnings encourage you to interrupt or suppress responses before you encounter any representation, action, idea, or emotion you suspect might make you uncomfortable. By doing so, trigger warnings inhibit a reaction to the essential ingredient of any great work of art—or any moment of human connection, for that matter—that might arouse pity, empathy, sympathy, or connection.

The New Yorker's May 30 article, "The Big Uneasy," quoted a student from Oberlin who wanted "Antigone" to come with a trigger warning because, he argued, trigger warnings are "like ingredient lists on food." The Oberlin student went on to explain, "People should have the right to know and consent to what they are putting into their minds, just as they have the right to know and consent what they are putting into their bodies."

Greek drama is not Greek yogurt; college professors are not food tasters. Such a comparison reduces university students to the ultimate consumers.

Trigger warnings are the intellectual equivalent of refusing vaccinations: They are misguidedly seen as a way of protecting the young. As my colleague Kristina Dolce argues, the anti-vaccine crowd and the trigger-warning crowd both employ "fear of exposure" rhetoric, believing that exposure leads to contamination. But as Kristina argues, "Vaccines, like great works of art, make one more resilient, not less."

Here's a personal example: My mother died of a miserable illness when I was   10 a kid. Had I spent my life avoiding dying female protagonists, I'd have stayed away from the Bible, Bambi, and all the Brontës.

In trying to protect myself, I would have missed out on what I would now call "my life."

You can cry out about what you don't know, but you can't argue against it. Only those who understand something and have experience with it can wrestle with it, grapple with it, and if appropriate, undermine the authority of it. Trigger warnings are a version of a kind of intellectual eugenics. There's something sterile, unproductive, and grossly contorted about the process. Their fiercest advocates are poorly equipped not only because they are dealing with their own intolerance but also because what they're learning to cherish is ignorance.

You can't lead if you don't know what's in front of you or what's behind you. You can't lead if you're afraid to look around.

I Use Trigger Warnings—But I'm Not Mollycoddling My Students

ONNI GUST

Dr. Onni Gust is Assistant Professor, Faculty of Arts in the Department of History at the University of Nottingham. She writes and teaches on British history of the eighteenth and nineteenth centuries, culture, and Empire. She is particularly focused on gender issues, queer theory, sexuality studies, race, and post-colonialism, applying these theories to historical contexts. She has led collaborative historical projects with school teachers. This editorial defending the value of trigger warnings appeared in the British online and print newspaper The Guardian *on June 14, 2016, as a Higher Education Network feature.*

Critics claim trigger warnings stifle debate, but they do the opposite. They give students a chance to pause, then focus on something tricky.

I vividly remember switching on *Monsters Inc.*, thinking it would entertain my two-year-old nephew. As the shadow of the monster loomed over a sleeping child, my nephew sat rooted to the spot, wide-eyed, barely breathing. I switched off the film and scrambled around for another form of amusement more appropriate for toddlers. Together, we exhaled.

I teach the history of the idea of monstrosity in the eighteenth-century British Empire, its relationship to deformity, disability and gender nonconformity. Unlike with two-year-olds, I do not let my students avoid difficult or disturbing topics. We read and talk about sexual assault, racism, mutilation, and violence against women. I expect my students to think critically and carefully about the subject matter.

But before we can begin learning, the most important thing that I need each of my students to do is to breathe. The harder they need to think, the deeper they need to breathe. A stuffy classroom can be the death of a debate and critical thinking requires copious amounts of oxygen. I use trigger warnings because they help students to stop for a moment and breathe, which helps them to think.

Disturbing content

A trigger warning (or content note) alerts readers or viewers to violent and disturbing content, which could be sexual assault, racist violence, transphobic or homophobic slurs. There are various ways of issuing a warning, for example in a lecture I might state that the next slide has a reference to mutilation, or I might add a note in parenthesis on the reading list where a text includes graphic description of sexual violence.

5   A trigger warning does not give permission for students to skip class, avoid a topic or choose alternative readings. What it does do is signal to survivors of abuse or trauma that they need to keep breathing. It reminds them to be particularly aware of the skills and coping strategies that they have developed and to switch them on.

Trigger warnings are necessary adjustments for students who hold in their bodies one of the most prevalent but also most disabling of wounds—trauma. Like adjustments for dyslexia, they do not solve the challenges of being different, they simply make it easier to navigate the difficulty of living in a world that assumes certain norms.

Yet if you read the recent debates on trigger warnings you would think that they banned all reading or intellectual engagement. Trigger warnings have become the sign of a generation wrapped in cotton wool; "infantilized" as Stephen Fry recently claimed, or "coddled" according to President Obama. They are represented as the weakening of the stiff upper lip, and thereby the undoing of the "manly" fabric of society. They are seen as the ultimate form of censorship, often ranted about in the same breath as no-platforming and safe spaces.

In fact, trigger warnings are the opposite of this so-called infantilization—they tell students to hold themselves. They implicitly demand that students assess their own needs and take responsibility for them.

Make no assumptions

Trigger warnings also remind me, as a teacher, to think carefully about how I present material, to ask myself why I am including a particular image or text and to what purpose. Having "triggers" in mind forces me think about the potential diversity of experiences in my classroom, not to make assumptions about my students' lives and to think carefully about the language I use and the framing of the topic.

Equally, trigger warnings remind students who may not have suffered a   10 trauma or may never have faced prejudice and abuse, that these experiences happen. They tell students that they are sitting in a class with people with different life experiences and they cannot take for granted that their personal story is the norm.

For me, trigger warnings are a fundamental part of feminist teaching because they help create a community of learners who acknowledge difference. Overall, trigger warnings remind everybody, regardless of their personal history, to keep breathing, and to think carefully and compassionately about what they are learning. They indicate that learning is, and should be, challenging and that learning is, and should be, for everyone.

For Writing and Discussion
Challenges in Education

1. Rachel M. Cohen and Richard Ullman enter the public debate over restorative justice as a disciplinary policy from different perspectives. What stakeholders do they mention in their arguments? What are Cohen's and Ullman's claims, reasons, assumptions, and evidence? How would you outline a case for restorative justice and one challenging it? What assumptions about human nature and students underlie zero-tolerance and restorative-justice disciplinary policies? After reading these articles, what additional questions do you have about each of these approaches to school discipline?

2. The issues of who should choose which schools children attend and who should pay for education are complex, with many social and individual repercussions. In the different genres of op-ed piece, researched policy recommendation, short editorial, and editorial cartoon, Cassady Rosenblum, Douglas N. Harris, Rachel Lam, and Paul Fell tackle the public school–charter school-voucher program controversy from different perspectives. How does each writer frame the controversy? Summarize the main argument of each writer. Based on these readings and your own school experience prior to college, what questions do you think the public should be asking about this educational controversy?

(continued)

3. Rafael Walker, Cornel West and Robert P. George (in the "Post-Truth, Post-Fact" anthology chapter), Gina Barreca, and Onni Gust in their articles about exposure in college to disturbing ideas and content base their arguments on fundamental assumptions about the purpose and process of education. What are these assumptions? What reasoning and evidence do you find most compelling? If you were entering one of these subconversations, what position would you take regarding tolerance of difference and exposure to emotionally difficult content and why? Thinking of your own educational experience and learning style, which approach to disturbing content do you support—that is, how (if at all) do you think instructors should inform students about material that includes violent, racist, homophobic, or graphic sexual content?

4. Arguments about education reform can range from academic and government studies involving statistics to views that have been nurtured through professional and personal experience. Several writers of the arguments in this chapter (particularly Ullman, Rosenblum, Barreca, and Gust) draw heavily on their personal experience as teachers for their reasoning and evidence. If handled well, this evidence can enhance the writer's *ethos* by building credibility and authority. It can also tap readers' emotions and values (appeals to *pathos*). Cite examples of this use of evidence that you find particularly persuasive. What other stakeholders and views do you think the public needs to hear to make informed decisions on these education issues?

Writing Assignment

A Researched Evaluation Argument on an Educational Policy

As part of a student task force, you have been asked to evaluate a school policy related to one of these issues: the adoption of restorative-justice disciplinary methods in your former high school, the expansion of charter-school options in your home state, your university's position on extending invitations to controversial speakers, or your university's adoption of a campus-wide policy on trigger warnings. After researching both the rhetorical context of your institution and the issue, develop criteria by which you will evaluate this policy. Is it an effective educational policy for this educational context? Which criteria will you choose? Which policies are likely to yield the most positive results? You might consider such consequences as reducing the opportunity gap in America's schools, promoting student safety, promoting learning, and preparing students for post-college life.

Self-Driving Cars

To many people, streets full of self-driving cars seem like a far-off sci-fi fantasy. But car enthusiasts, technology buffs, and market watchers see self-driving cars as the next transportation wave—one that is already washing ashore and may become a tsunami in the next decade. Google is already testing more than a hundred self-driving cars that have logged more than three million miles in cities and highways across the United States. Tesla already has cars that can drive autonomously on highways. Many experts believe that fully autonomous cars will be available commercially by 2020 and that the economic and cultural impacts of self-driving cars will be fully apparent by 2030, perhaps even sooner.

We use the tsunami metaphor purposefully. As the readings in this unit make clear, self-driving cars will not only change our driving experience but also will have tsunami-like effects on jobs, the economy, the environment, the design of cities, and the ways we spend our time and money. Many of these issues involve causal and evaluative arguments: What will be the consequences of self-driving cars? Will these consequences be good or bad? The readings in this unit provide a stimulating dialog among commentators who are essentially optimistic about the benefits of self-driving cars and those who fear this brave new world. Here are some of the specific questions and issues raised in this unit:

- Will self-driving cars work in real-world conditions (rain, snow, electricity outages)?
- Will they reduce driving accidents, making our streets and highways safer?
- How will they be programmed to make ethical choices (swerve to save the passengers or not swerve to save little children on the sidewalk)?
- What impact will they have on people who make their living as drivers (truck drivers, bus drivers, taxi or Uber drivers, and so forth)?
- If an "Internet of moving things" creates a network of computer-controlled cars, what will be the effects on traffic congestion, parking, and commuting time?
- If you could summon a self-driving car at any time, would you need to own your own car?
- If self-driving cars are proven to be safer and more efficient than human-driven cars, should laws prevent humans from driving?
- Overall, what effect will self-driving cars have on our car-buying habits, on the automobile industry, on highway construction, on tax revenues, on the environment, on the design of cities, and on our way of life?

Self-Driving Cars Will Improve Our Cities, If They Don't Ruin Them

ROBIN CHASE

Robin Chase, a co-founder of Zipcar, is a transportation entrepreneur who has been listed in Time's *"100 Most Influential People" and* Business Week's *"Top 10 Designers." She has served on the board of the Massachusetts Department of Transportation and the National Advisory Council for Innovation & Entrepreneurship for the U.S. Department of Commerce. She is also the author of books and articles on transportation issues, has delivered a widely viewed TED talk, and frequently appears in the media as a visionary who brings market innovations to bear on such global issues as climate change, income inequality, and urban design. This article appeared in the online magazine* Backchannel *on August 10, 2016.*

If we take action, we can build a dream transportation system around self-driving cars. If we don't, we'll create a nightmare.

Ten years ago I found myself standing outside the Automotive Hall of Fame in Dearborn, Michigan. I looked out over acres of glinting windshields in a packed parking lot. I'd reached this spot by driving from Ann Arbor on the I-94, where the highway sometimes reaches 12 lanes across, in a little over an hour. Public transit would have taken me three and a half hours. What would Henry Ford think, one hundred years after the birth of the car? Pride or horror? It took 50 years to transition from the horse to the car. Surely few could have imagined the impact the car would have as it tore through cities, countries, and economies worldwide. Today, average Americans spend almost two of their eight hours at work paying off their car, which they need to get to that job. Last year in the United States, more than 38,000 people died and 4.4 million were seriously injured due to motorized transport. Farther afield, in Singapore, 12 percent of the island nation's scarce land is devoted to car infrastructure. In Delhi, 2.2 million children have irreversible lung damage because of poor air quality.

Incredibly, we might actually get a chance at a do-over—of our cities, our fossil fuel dependence, and the social contract with labor—thanks to the impending advent of autonomous cars. Yes, their arrival is inevitable, but how they will impact us is yet to be determined.

Most of what has been written about self-driving or automated vehicles (often abbreviated as AVs) focuses on subjects like their technical aspects, the regulatory battles to license them, or the fascinating but remote dilemma of a self-driving car being forced to choose between holding its course and hitting grandma, or swerving into a troop of boy scouts. There's relatively little discussion of the speed and scope of change, the impacts that go well beyond the auto industry, or the roadmap to unlocking the enormous upside potential if we actively guide the trajectory of their adoption.

We're at a fork on that roadmap. One direction leads to a productive new century where cities are more sustainable, livable, equitable, and just.

But if we take the wrong turn, we're at a dead end. Cities are already complex and chaotic places in which to live and work. If we allow the introduction of automated vehicles to be guided by existing regulations we'll end up with more congestion, millions of unemployed drivers, and a huge deficit in how we fund our transportation infrastructure. We will also miss an opportunity to fix transportation's hereto intractable reliance on liquid fossil fuels (and their associated pollution). 5

Right now, we're not even alert to how crucial the choices are. In fact, we're falling asleep at the wheel. Most people in charge of shaping cities—mayors, transportation planners, developers, and lawmakers—haven't realized what is about to hit them and the speed at which it is coming. They continue to build as if the future is like the present.

Instead, cities and countries must actively shape the introduction of AVs. We are getting access to this technical marvel at the precise moment when cities are full and bursting from the urbanizing of our planet, when we absolutely need to transition rapidly from fossil fuels, and when it is imperative to improve people's access to opportunity: jobs, education, health services. We have the ability to eliminate congestion, transform the livability of cities, make it possible to travel quickly and safely from A to B for the price of a bus ticket, improve the quality of our air, and make a significant dent in reducing CO_2 emissions. We might also find ourselves with the political support to transform social benefits, and rebalance corporate and labor taxation, but these will be second-order effects. Every one of these possibilities requires policymakers and communities to take an active role.

The advent of autonomous vehicles couldn't have happened at a better time. Or a worse one. Here's how to steer towards the better outcome.

Step 1: Wake Up, This Is Happening

I used to think that self-driving cars belonged in some distant sci-fi future. Indeed, car manufacturers used to preach that AVs were at least 20 years off. But in 2010 Google announced that it had a car that was safely self-driving around San Francisco. Wha-at? With no special roadside infrastructure or city retrofitting? This was just 6 short years after not a single autonomous car had been able to complete a course in the middle of the desert set by DARPA (the U.S. military agency that financed the Internet). How is it possible the technology advanced so quickly? While I might drive 600,000 miles in my lifetime, a fleet of cars can accumulate that amount of experience in weeks, sharing the learning with each other. They are doing so now, for multiple companies: dozens of cars are now driving all-day shifts in Mountain View, Austin, Ann Arbor, Wuhu, China, and Singapore. In the last few years, a hundred Google cars have completed 2 million miles of on-road travel without injuries or fatalities, and are simulating and learning from 3 million virtual miles of driving every day. Tesla has 50,000 vehicles, sold to the public, that are driving autonomously on highways right now, collecting millions of more miles of real-world driving experience (albeit with one fatality).

10   This gives companies like Google, Tesla, GM, Ford, Toyota, BMW, and Nissan the confidence to promise commercial sales of fully autonomous cars by 2020. . . .

Once those vehicles go on sale, the pace of adoption and transition will exceed any proposed speed limit, driven by compelling economics on both the demand side (us) and supply side (taxi, transit, shuttle services). Companies that are currently paying drivers can shed one of their most significant costs—Uber, for instance, can't wait for self-driving cars and has invested in its own technology to make it happen. It's only one of many players who will switch to autonomous as soon as they can. There will also be big savings for the trucking industry, so it's no surprise that startups like Otto (founded by ex-Googlers) are already testing mammoth road carriers that drive themselves.

Consumers also can't wait — just look at how quickly Tesla owners have taken the company's "autopilot" features beyond prescribed limits. And there are millions who will appreciate new services that, without the cost of drivers, will give them speedy, reliable, on-demand travel.

Once it starts, there will hardly be time to shape how AVs are used. But we must.

Step 2: Recognize the High Cost of Doing Nothing

Simply eliminating the drivers from cars, and keeping everything else about our system the same, will be a disaster. Picture zombie cars—those with no one in them—clogging our cities and our roads, because it will be cheaper to keep them moving than to pay for expensive urban parking, and cheaper to bring retail to a customer than to pay rent on a retail store. While the number of vehicle miles driven skyrockets, our transportation infrastructure revenues, dependent on the gas tax, parking, fees, and fines, will disappear. Unemployment will spike as professional drivers will be laid off in droves. It will be a nightmare of pollution, congestion, and social unrest. Let's break it down.

15   **Congestion.**   The traffic alone will make people curse the technologists who brought AVs to our streets. Right now, our "congested" roads and cities are mostly filled by individuals driving alone in their cars (75 percent of all trips). Just imagine our streets and your frustration when 50 percent of the cars have no people in them at all.

When we don't have to drive them, we'll use our cars more. My 2004 Prius costs me about $1.50 for an hour of run time. It will be cheaper to have my car double-park or circle blocks rather than pay for a parking meter or, heaven forbid, pay for parking in a downtown garage. It'll also be cheaper to have my car pick up pizza or drop off dry cleaning than to tip a delivery person. Endless double-parking and block circling already happens in places where the cost of a human driver is either very cheap (think Delhi) or expense is irrelevant (think about luxury black cars in New York City).

Unemployment.   There are 3.5 million freight and delivery truck drivers in the United States. There are 665,000 bus drivers. In New York City alone, there are 90,000 registered taxi and livery drivers—not counting Uber and Lyft drivers. If US car manufacturers miss out on this transition, or if we use vehicles more efficiently, there are 5.5 million people manufacturing and designing cars, and 1.65 million people working at dealerships. All of these jobs are at high risk.

Lost Tax Revenue.   The Center for Automotive Research found that taxes associated with motor vehicle manufacturing and use amounted to $206 billion a year. Major sources of revenue for city, state, and country transportation infrastructure—fuel taxes, parking revenue, parking and speeding fines, driver registrations—will disappear if we go with electric AVs. These vehicles won't pay for parking when it's cheaper to drive themselves back home and park for free. They won't violate posted traffic speeds or get parking tickets. Machine learning will make sure that every AV can recognize a speed trap. We'll also lose the income taxes from employees made redundant, and of course all the income they would have spent in the economy.

Step 3: Seize the Opportunity

But there is so much opportunity to love! If we steer toward it, and plan for it, we will get benefits that once seemed as distant and unlikely as those science fiction scenarios I mentioned earlier.

Shared Cars.   For starters, getting away from our wasteful model of car owner-   20
ship totally eliminates the congestion problem. If we share rides in shared cars, we will only need 10 percent of the cars we have today. That also makes a huge dent in our pollution problem. Just as Zipcar, Uber, and Lyft have demonstrated, wireless technology and smartphones have taken almost all the hassle out of sharing. AV technology removes all of it.

I feel pretty confident about this estimate. It's from an excellent study by the International Transport Forum at the OECD that used actual origins, destinations, and timing for trips in the city of Lisbon. This is in line with numbers I've heard from a modeler at Google, a transport planner for the Bay Area, and taxi studies in Singapore and New York City. I can even see how this happens. A bold mayor will be the first mover, welcoming a discrete pilot within city limits. A hundred cars will shepherd tourists, students, late-shift workers, and the curious. No one will die. It'll be cheap and convenient.

After all, these first vehicles won't be cheap, so unlike personal cars, which are idle 95 percent of the time, these will be intensively used—rather like Zip-cars (the company I co-founded) or taxis. Today, 50 percent of all Uber and Lyft rides in San Francisco are shared—meaning that passenger-strangers going in the same general direction are sharing the trip and enjoying a reduced fare. If I use Zipcar's economics (like self-driving cars, Zipcar doesn't pay for drivers), the company is profitable earning about $70 per car per day. The cost of "fuel-ing" and maintaining electric cars is one-tenth that of regular combustion engine cars, and the parking would be cheaper since most vehicles could be stored in distant locations the little time they are not in use. When we take trips in shared cars, the cost of inner-city travel will be the same as bus fare and the trip time will rival personal car travel (especially once you remember you never have to find parking).

There will be operational problems in this pilot city and they'll be fixed. Another 400 cars will be added. These cars market themselves. Everyone sees one. Everyone knows someone who has taken one. Second cars are sold as people realize it is cheaper, faster, better to use the shared electric AVs. And then many people, if not most, will sell their primary car, as well.

Yes, I can already hear the car lovers out there bleating their horns at the very concept of sharing their beloved vehicles with people outside the family "People love driving!" they'll insist. "Cars are important status symbols!"

25   No one is forcing you to make the switch. You will be able to drive your own car for years to come. And some minority of people will miss what was once a fun part of their lives. (People loved smoking, too.) But the vast majority of us will reap massive benefits. We will be able to admire the scenery instead of worrying about threading our way through traffic. We will get to punch away at our smartphones and get things done while in motion—safely. We will rent or own housing that is 25 percent cheaper because it won't include parking. We will never squander time refueling, washing, or maintaining a car, will never care about whether and how expensive parking is at our destination, will walk or bike for most short trips because we'll want to, and we will certainly appreciate pocketing the thousands of dollars we would have spent on our cars. That money will go toward purchases that will surely be more beneficial to the local economy.

The very landscape of our cities will change.   On-street and almost all off-street parking, including parking garages, will be unnecessary and we'll get rid of them. Communities and local governments can come up with criteria and priorities for how to repurpose that newly available public space: wider sidewalks, more street trees and plantings, bike lanes, street furniture. Progressive cities will make use of old parking lots, garages, and gas stations to fix what was lacking: affordable housing, green space, grocery stores, schools. Proactive cities will know their priorities neighborhood by neighborhood, as well as their criteria for action, before the transition begins.

We'll have a better taxation system.   The old way of collecting taxes to pay for transportation infrastructure will be gutted. With only 10 percent of the vehicles, and electric ones at that, we can kiss goodbye to gas taxes, parking revenues, driver's licenses, and traffic fines. We'll also lose 60 to 80 percent of the toll revenue (shared trips, fewer cars), car registrations, and inspections. This reality makes me feel joy—because whatever replaces our current means of transportation taxation is bound to be better. Our current system for raising money to pay for our transportation infrastructure in the United States has been broken for years. The federal gas tax has been stalled at 18.4 cents a gallon since 1993. The United States has the second lowest gas tax rate in the world. Our fuel prices are half those experienced by Europeans. Our roads, bridges, train stations, and airports are decrepit, as noted by visitors from Europe and Asia. With the impending rapid adoption of AVs, our hand is forced. It would be unfair to let these new vehicles use publicly financed infrastructure for free.

The new system will build on what we've learned from our 100-year history of driving, creating needed disincentives and incentives. A tax on gasoline was first introduced in 1919. It was a delightfully simple solution but it didn't disincentivize things that we now know to be very costly: air pollution, congestion, and vehicle size (seventy-five percent of cars today have only one person in them, congesting roads and requiring larger areas for parking). Vehicle registration can assign cars to the right tax category based on fuel type and footprint, then we can apply the appropriate rates based on such factors as distance traveled and peak usage times. We'd also need to make it really expensive to be a zombie car (those empty cars running errands for their owners).

Our energy grid will expand, while the climate benefits. As we move BTUs from fossil fuel gasoline to electricity, the incremental energy will come from renewables. Of course this will only happen if we demand that it be so, with state-based regulations. But we should, since installing new wind and solar capacity will mean jobs, to design, manufacture, install, and then maintain this new additional capacity. And, we have to because every nation has pledged to have zero emissions by 2050. There's also a second-order benefit: savings in military spending and wars avoided by weaning ourselves from fossil fuel dependency for passenger vehicles.

We'll rethink labor security and how we tax income. The unemployment of 30 professional drivers outlined in our hellish scenario will come about no matter what happens. And it won't only be drivers who lose jobs. As personal car owners switch from owning a vehicle they use just 5 percent of the time and costs them 18 percent of their income to being driven for a fraction of that price, we'll see lay-offs in repairs and maintenance, and car insurance, as well as car design and manufacturing (5.5 million jobs nationwide), sales (1.65 million work in dealerships), and distribution/logistics.

But once again, innovative planning will turn the problem into an opportunity for positive transformation. The cost and inaccessibility to transport has been found to be the largest barrier keeping people in poverty. Shared AVs have the potential to transform access to opportunity—jobs, education, health care, leisure. We'll also have way fewer traffic deaths and injuries (up to 90 percent, so over 30,000 lives saved in the United States every year); greener and more livable cities; clean air; reduced CO_2 emissions; more disposable income; and more money spent locally. This goes a long way towards compensating for those lost jobs.

I'm not suggesting we abandon those workers stranded by the transformation. In the short run, we will cushion and support these workers who did nothing to merit the loss of their income and profession. I'm no expert on labor theory, but I do know that in a future where all sorts of automation will replace jobs, we need to make it easy and safe to have a diversified stream of income, a key to individual resilience. Easy: to hire and work part-time. Safe: all benefits—social security, paid vacation, catastrophic insurance, health care—follow a worker regardless of the number of hours he or she works. And we must eliminate loopholes that allow employers to pretend that such benefits are applicable only to full-time labor, no matter how configured.

A Capitalism Do-Over. Productivity gains once were the harbinger of improved standards of living, and improved quality of life, but automation brings jobless productivity gains. Self-driving cars will be the ultimate example of this: AVs will probably be productively employed and generating revenue about 65 percent of the time, compared to our personal car's 5 percent. No one can deny that enormous productivity gains are being enjoyed. But with so few associated workers, enjoyed by whom?

As an entrepreneur, I appreciate the hours and years of effort that has gone into building these AVs: the new IP, the many years and huge costs without any revenue to show for it. But I also understand that this is a massive market (trillions of dollars worldwide seems plausible), and the marginal cost of running the software for each of those trips will be close to zero. We need to make sure we distribute this new wealth, by closing corporate tax loopholes and taxing wealth and platforms more effectively.

35 **As we lose more jobs, the necessity for change opens up the possibility of a fairer system, one that minimizes income inequality.** A Bureau of Labor Statistics study projected an 83 percent probability of job loss by automation for workers earning less than $20 an hour, and a 34 percent probability for jobs between $20–40 an hour. In the new automated world, does it really make sense to be taxing labor at all? It makes much more sense to be taxing the new technical platforms that are generating the profits, and taxing the wealth of the small number of talented and lucky people who founded and financed these new jobless wonders.

In a world where machines do most of the work, it is time for a universal basic income. This will distribute the gains from productivity, and give more people the opportunity to focus on purposeful, passion-driven work, allowing for the next generation of ideas and technologies to emerge faster.

How we deal with the job loss caused by AVs will be a signature model for how we respond to automation throughout the economy. Even more, it may be the flood that sweeps clean a system that no longer serves the people.

Remember, *this is going to happen.* While one city, or one state, or one country might try to slow it down, there are many others that will step forward to lead the way. No matter how protracted the fight and the transition, we are going to end up choosing self-driving cars so that we can avoid the 38,000 traffic deaths in the United States, the 1.25 million deaths worldwide, and the tens of millions of serious injuries, with all their associated suffering and medical costs. That in itself is a worthy reason for adoption. But with the right planning, we will expand that upside to include better cities, a livable planet, and a future that serves us all. In the future, when some entrepreneur looks out over Dearborn, Michigan, or New York City, I want them to reflect with gladness on how one hundred years earlier, people had seized on the opportunities offered by the autonomous car to rein in the tyranny of single occupancy vehicles and domination of cars in cities, to distribute the fruits of automation, and to address climate change.

All by keeping our hands off the wheel.

Self-Driving Trucks Are Going to Hit Us Like a Human-Driven Truck

SCOTT SANTENS

Scott Santens is an influential writer and blogger who explores the impact of technology on income inequality and employment. He is an advocate of universal basic income for all. His ideas and opinions have been published in the Huffington Post, TechCrunch, The Boston Globe, Atlantic Monthly, Forbes, Vox, *and* Politico. *He has a Bachelor of Science degree in psychology from the University of Washington and currently lives in New Orleans. This article appeared in* medium.com *on May 14, 2015.*

The imminent need for basic income in recognition of our machine-driven future

Late last year, I took a road trip with my partner from our home in New Orleans, Louisiana, to Orlando, Florida, and as we drove by town after town, we got to talking about the potential effects self-driving vehicle technology would have not only on truckers themselves, but on all the local economies dependent on trucker salaries. Once one starts wondering about this kind of one-two punch to America's gut, one sees the prospects aren't pretty.

We are facing the decimation of entire small town economies, a disruption the likes of which we haven't seen since the construction of the interstate highway system itself bypassed entire towns. If you think this may be a bit of hyperbole . . . let me back up a bit and start with this:

This is a map of the most common job in each US state in 2014.

SOURCE: NPR

It should be clear at a glance just how dependent the American economy is on truck drivers. According to the American Trucker Association, there are 3.5 million professional truck drivers in the United States, and an additional 5.2 million people employed within the truck-driving industry who don't drive the trucks. That's 8.7 million trucking-related jobs.

5   We can't stop there though, because the incomes received by these 8.2 million people create the jobs of others. Those 3.5 million truck drivers driving all over the country stop regularly to eat, drink, rest, and sleep. Entire businesses have been built around serving their wants and needs. Think restaurants and motels as just two examples. So now we're talking about millions more whose employment depends on the employment of truck drivers. But we still can't even stop there.

Those working in these restaurants and motels along truck-driving routes are also consumers within their own local economies. Think about what a server spends her paycheck and tips on in her own community, and what a motel maid spends from her earnings in the same community. That spending creates other paychecks in turn. So now we're not only talking about millions more who depend on those who depend on truck drivers, but we're also talking about entire small town communities full of people who depend on all of the above in more rural areas. With any amount of reduced consumer spending, these local economies will shrink.

One further important detail to consider is that truck drivers are well paid. They provide a middle class income of about $40,000 per year. That's a higher income than just about half (46%) of all tax filers, including those of married households. They are also greatly comprised of those without college educations. Truck driving is just about the last job in the country to provide a solid middle-class salary without requiring a post-secondary degree. Truckers are essentially the last remnant of an increasingly impoverished population once gainfully employed in manufacturing before those middle-income jobs were mostly all shipped overseas.

If we now step back and look at the big national picture, we are potentially looking at well over 10 million American workers and their families whose incomes depend entirely or at least partially on the incomes of truck drivers, all of whom markedly comprise what is left of the American middle class.

So as long as the outlook for US trucking is rosy, we're fine, right?

The Short-Term Job Outlook of the American Trucker

10   The trucking industry expects to see 21 percent more truck driving jobs by 2020. They also expect to see an increasing shortfall in drivers, with over 100,000 jobs open and unable to find drivers to fill them. Higher demand than supply of truckers also points to higher pay, so for at least the next five years, the future is looking great for truck drivers. The only thing that could put a damper on this would be if the demand for truck drivers were to say . . . drive off a sharp cliff.

That cliff is the self-driving truck.

The technology already exists to enable trucks to drive themselves. Google shocked the world when it announced its self-driving car it had already driven over 100,000 miles without accident. These cars have since driven over 1.7 million miles and have only been involved in 11 accidents, all caused by humans and not the computers. And this is *mostly within* metropolitan areas.

"And as you might expect, we see more accidents per mile driven on city streets than on freeways; we were hit 8 times in many fewer miles of city driving."—Chris Urmson, director of Google's self-driving car program

So according to Google's experience, the greater danger lies within cities and not freeways, and driving *between* cities involves even fewer technological barriers than within them. Therefore, it's probably pretty safe to say driverless freeway travel is even closer to our future horizon of driverless transportation. How much closer? It has *already* happened.

On May 6, 2015, the first self-driving truck hit the American road in the state   15
of Nevada.

Self-driving trucks are no longer the future. They are the present. They're here.

"AU 010." License plates are rarely an object of attention, but this one's special—the funky number is the giveaway. That's why Daimler bigwig Wolfgang Bernhard and Nevada governor Brian Sandoval are sharing a stage, mugging for the phalanx of cameras, together holding the metal rectangle that will, in just a minute, be slapped onto the world's first officially recognized self-driving truck.

According to Daimler, these trucks will be in a decade-long testing phase, racking up over a million miles before being deemed fit for adoption, but the technology isn't even anything all that new. There's no laser-radar or LIDAR like in Google's self-driving car. It's just ordinary radar and cameras. The hardware itself is already yesterday's news. They're just the first ones to throw them into a truck and allow truckers to sit back and enjoy the ride, while the truck itself does all the driving.

If the truck needs help, it'll alert the driver. If the driver doesn't respond, it'll slowly pull over and wait for further instructions. This is nothing fancy. This is not a truck version of KITT from Knight Rider. This is just an example of a company and a state government getting out of the way of technology and letting it do what it was built to do—**enable us to do more with less**. In the case of self-driving trucks, one big improvement in particular is fewer accidents.

In 2012 in the United States, 330,000 large trucks were involved in crashes that   20 killed nearly 4,000 people, most of them in passenger cars. About 90 percent of those were caused by driver error.

That's like one and a half 9/11s yearly. Human-driven trucks kill people. Robot trucks will kill far fewer people, if any, because machines don't get tired. Machines don't get distracted. Machines don't look at phones instead of the road. Machines don't drink alcohol or do any kind of drugs or involve any number of things that somehow contribute to the total number of accidents every year involving trucks. For this same reasoning, pilots too are bound to be removed from airplanes.

Humans are dangerous behind the wheel of anything.

Robot trucks also don't need salaries—salaries that stand to go up because fewer and fewer people want to be truckers. A company can buy a fleet of self-driving trucks and never pay another human salary for driving. The only costs will be upkeep of the machinery. No more need for health insurance either. Self-driving trucks will also never need to stop to rest, for any reason. Routes will take less time to complete.

All of this means the replacement of truckers is inevitable. It is not a matter of "if," it's only a matter of "when." So the question then becomes, how long until millions of truckers are freshly unemployed and what happens to them and all the rest of us as a result?

The Long-Term Job Outlook of the American Trucker

25   First, let's look at the potential time horizons for self-driving cars. Tesla intends to release a software update *next month* that will turn on "autopilot" mode, immediately allowing all Tesla Model S drivers to be driven between "San Francisco and Seattle without the driver doing anything," in Elon Musk's own words. The cars actually already have the technology to even drive from "parking lot to parking lot," but that ability will remain unactivated by software.

Tesla-driven humans won't be able to legally let their cars do all the driving, but who are we kidding? There will be Teslas driving themselves, saving lives in the process, and governments will need to catch up to make that driving legal. This process is already here in 2015. So when will the process end? When will self-driving cars conquer our roads?

According to Morgan Stanley, complete autonomous capability will be here **by 2022**, followed by massive market penetration **by 2026** and the cars we know and love today then entirely extinct in another 20 years thereafter.

Granted, this is only one estimate of many and it's all educated guesswork. So here are some other estimates:

- Navigant Research: "**By 2035**, sales of autonomous vehicles will reach 95.4 million annually, representing 75% of all light-duty vehicle sales."
- IHS Automotive: "There should be nearly 54 million self-driving cars in use globally **by 2035**."
- ABI Research: "Half of new vehicles shipping in North America to have driverless, robotic capabilities **by 2032**."
- Nissan: "**In 2020** we're talking more autonomous drive capability. It's going to be an evolutionary process and 2020 will be the first year to truly see some of these capabilities start to be introduced in the vehicle."

Take all of these estimates together, and we're looking at a window of massive disruption starting somewhere between 2020 and 2030.

There is no turning the wheel in prevention of driving off this cliff either. 30
Capitalism itself has the wheel now, and what the market wants, the market gets.
Competition will make sure of it. Tesla and Google are not the only companies
looking to develop autonomous vehicles. There are others.

A company named **Veeo Systems** is developing vehicles as small as 2-seaters
to as large as 70-seat buses, and will be testing them in 30 US cities by the end of
2016.

*At 25 to 40 percent cheaper, the cost to ride the driverless public transit vehicles
will be significantly less expensive than traditional buses and trains. . . . The vehicles are
electric, rechargeable, and could cost as low as $1 to $3 to run per day.*

Apple is also developing its own self-driving car.

The project is code-named Titan and the vehicle design resembles a minivan, the
Wall Street Journal reported. . . . Apple already has technology that may lend itself
to an electric car and expertise managing a vast supply chain. The company has
long researched battery technology for use in its iPhones, iPads, and Macs. The
mapping system it debuted in 2012 can be used for navigation. . . .

And Uber is developing its own self-driving car.

Uber said it will develop "key long-term technologies that advance Uber's mission of bringing safe, reliable transportation to everyone, everywhere," including
driverless cars, vehicle safety, and mapping services.

It's this last one that fully intends to transform the transportation landscape. 35
Uber is going all-in on self-driving vehicles to the point it wants to entirely eliminate car ownership as a 20th century relic.

Travis Kalanick, the CEO and founder of Uber, said at a conference last year
that he'd replace human Uber drivers with a fleet of self-driving cars in a second.
"You're not just paying for the car—you're paying for the other dude in the car,"
he said. "When there's no other dude in the car, the cost of taking an Uber anywhere becomes cheaper than owning a vehicle." That, he said, will "bring the cost
below the cost of ownership for everybody, and then **car ownership goes away**."

That's the potential of self-driving cars—**the outright extinction of car
ownership**. And with that, the elimination of entire industries built up around
the existence of car ownership like mechanics, car washes, parking, valets, body
shops, rental companies, car insurance, car loans, and on and on. Even hugely
expensive and capital intensive mass-transit infrastructure projects like street-
cars and light rail can be dropped in favor of vastly cheaper on demand robotic
"transportation clouds," and all those construction and maintenance jobs right
along with it.

Big players are already in the game. There are huge savings to be found, huge
profits to be created. Higher quality and safety is assured. Driverless vehicles are
coming, and they are coming fast.

But again, what about **trucks** specifically?

40   Any realistic time horizon for self-driving trucks needs to look at horizons for cars and shift those even further towards the present. Trucks only need to be self-driven on highways. They do not need warehouse-to-store autonomy to be disruptive. City-to-city is sufficient. At the same time, trucks are almost entirely corporate driven. There are market forces above and beyond private cars operating for trucks. If there are savings to be found in eliminating truckers from drivers seats, *which there are*, these savings will be sought. It's actually really easy to find these savings right now.

Wirelessly linked truck platoons are as simple as having a human driver drive a truck, with multiple trucks without drivers following closely behind. This not only saves on gas money (7 percent for only two trucks together), but can immediately eliminate half of all truckers if, for example, 2-truck convoys became the norm. There's no real technical obstacles to this option. It's a very simple use of present technology.

Basically, the only real barrier to the immediate adoption of self-driven trucks is purely legal in nature, not technical or economic. With self-driving vehicles currently only road legal in a few states, many more states need to follow suit unless autonomous vehicles are made legal at the national level. And Sergey Brin of Google has estimated this could happen as soon as 2017. Therefore . . .

The answer to the big question of "When?" for self-driving trucks is that they can essentially hit our economy at any time.

The Eve of Massive Social and Economic Disruption

Main Street USA has already taken a big hit, and increasingly so, over the past few decades. Manufacturing has been shipped overseas to areas where labor is far cheaper because costs of living are far cheaper. Companies like Walmart have spread everywhere, concentrating a reduced labor force into one-stop shopping facilities requiring fewer total workers than what was needed with smaller, more numerous, and more widely spread Mom & Pop type stores. Companies like Amazon have even further concentrated this even further reduced labor force into automated warehouse centers capable of obviating stores entirely and shipping directly to consumers.

45   All of the above means fewer ways of securing employment in fewer places, while commerce has become more geographically concentrated and access to money has become increasingly shifted away from the bottom and middle of the income spectrum towards the top.

This is what happens when good-paying jobs are eliminated, and that money not spent on wages and salaries instead stays in the hands of owners of capital, or is given in smaller amounts to lower-paid employees in lower-wage jobs. Inequality grows more and more extreme and our land of opportunity vanishes. **Economic growth slows to a crawl**.

This is where we're at and this is what we face as we look towards a quickly approaching horizon of **over 3 million unemployed truckers** *and millions more* unemployed service industry workers in small towns all over the country dependent on truckers as consumers of their services.

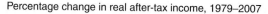

Percentage change in real after-tax income, 1979–2007

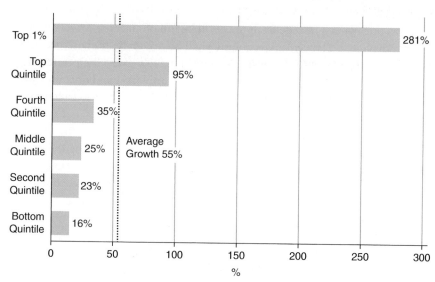

SOURCE: Mother Jones

The removal of truckers from freeways will have an effect on today's towns similar to the effects the freeways themselves had on towns decades ago that had sprung up around bypassed stretches of early highways. When the construction of the interstate highway system replaced Route 66, things changed as drivers drove right on past these once thriving towns. The result was **ghost towns** like Glenrio, Texas.

With self-driving cars and trucks, here again we face the prospect of town after town being zipped past by people (if even present) choosing to instead just sleep in their computer-driven vehicles. Except this time, there is no new highway being made for businesses to relocate closer to and new towns to emerge along. This time, as is true of the effect of technology on jobs, it's different. This time, there's no need for entire towns to even exist *at all*.

The Road Left to Take

As close as 2025—that is in a mere 10 years—our advancing state of technology will begin disrupting our economy in ways we can't even yet imagine. Human labor is increasingly unnecessary and even economically unviable compared to machine labor. And yet we still insist on money to pay for what our machines are making for us. As long as this remains true, we must begin providing ourselves the money required to purchase what the machines are producing.

Without a **technological dividend**, the engine that is our economy will seize, or we will fight against technological progress itself in the same way some once destroyed their machine replacements. Without non-work income,

50

we will actually fight to keep from being replaced by the technology we built to replace us.

Just as our roads a decade from now will be full of machine drivers instead of human drivers, a 21st century economy shall be driven by human *consumers*, not human workers, and these consumers must be freely given their purchasing power. If we refuse, if we don't provide ourselves **a universal and unconditional basic income** soon, the future is going to hit us like a truck—a truck driven solely by ourselves.

To allow this to happen would be truly foolish, for what is the entire purpose of technology but to free us to pursue all we wish to pursue? Fearing the loss of jobs shouldn't be a fear at all. It should be welcomed. It should be freeing.

No one should be asking what we're going to do *if* computers *take* our jobs.

55   **We should all be asking what we *get* to do once *freed* from them.**

Five Reasons You Should Embrace Self-Driving Cars

DREW HENDRICKS

Drew Hendricks is the CEO of a San Francisco public relations agency as well as a social media consultant. He is also a freelance writer focusing on technology, social media, and environmental issues. He has written for many major publications, such as Forbes, Entrepreneur, *and* National Geographic. *This article originally appeared in startupgrind.com.*

2016 has been an exciting year so far for technologies that, until recently, have been confined to the world of science fiction dreams. Whether it's 3D printing revolutionizing the health care industry or the widespread commercial availability of VR technology, we're continuing to witness amazing innovations that even just a few years ago seemed like distant possibilities at best.

Another technological advancement causing widespread wonder is self-driving cars. We may not have arrived at a Jetsons-like future of flying automated vehicles just yet, but the self-driving car is getting closer and closer to becoming a widespread, viable method of transportation. And, while many are skeptical about the future of driverless and self-driving cars on the road, there's actually a good deal of data and research to support the idea that self-driving cars may actually be better for our future.

With that in mind, here are five reasons to embrace self-driving cars:

1. Our roads will be safer

It's tough at first to wrap our minds around the fact that a car operated by computers could somehow be safer, but think of it this way: how many car accidents have been caused by some sort of human error, be it speeding, driving recklessly, inattentiveness, or worse, impaired driving? Turns out that an over-whelming majority of accidents have been caused by humans. In fact, a study by the National Highway Traffic Safety Administration (NHTSA) revealed that 94 percent of accidents were caused by the drivers themselves.

Self-driving cars, on the other hand, are purely analytical, relying on cameras, radar, and other sensors to navigate. There's no emotion involved, and certainly no distractions like cell phones or impairing factors like alcohol to affect driving performance. The computers in a smart car simply react quicker than our minds can and aren't susceptible to the many potential mistakes we can make on the road. As a result, a future full of self-driving cars will be a safer one.

2. We'll be more productive

More and more businesses are operating remotely these days, or are at least allow-ing people to work from home more often, and for good reasons, not the least of which is increased productivity. On average, Americans spend 26 minutes com-muting to work each day. That's almost an hour each day, and it largely goes wasted. In 2014, Americans spent an astonishing cumulative total of 29.6 billion hours commuting. Imagine what we could do with all that time back.

While many already commute on buses or trains, a whole lot of people still travel to work in their own cars. A self-driving car would allow them to get some work done, knock a few emails out, or even get a little extra sleep if they have to wake up early to get to work. Many people find themselves tempted to look at their phones while driving anyway, so why not at least do it safely in a self-driving car?

3. We can save money

Cars can be very expensive investments, even if you're not in the luxury sports car tax bracket. Indeed, AAA reports that the average annual amount spent on a car in America is close to $9,000. Some of these things you can't avoid, like licensing and registration fees, but other costs can be eliminated or at least reduced with the help of self-driving cars.

Because self-driving cars are safer, they'll cut down on any accident-induced costs, which means insurance premiums won't skyrocket either. Additionally, self-driving cars don't sustain the same kind of wear and tear as human-piloted vehicles. They don't floor the gas pedal or slam the brakes unless an emergency is detected, making for better upkeep, slower depreciation, and even better fuel efficiency. These little things can quickly add up, meaning that self-driving cars, while more expensive up front, can easily put money back in your pocket in the long term.

4. We'll move more efficiently

We've already talked about the benefits self-driving cars will have on the fuel economy of your vehicle, but the improved efficiency of travel thanks to self-driving cars stretches far beyond that benefit. For one, since self-driving cars are connected to the Internet, their navigation will use GPS programs like Google

Maps to automatically generate the quickest possible route. The deliberative architecture in self-driving cars' software means the car is also intelligent enough to detect delays and accidents before you arrive at them, so it can reroute the vehicle's path without running into any impediments.

Speaking of delays, if we really reach a future where the road is occupied only by self-driving vehicles, even stops at traffic lights and intersections will become a thing of the past. With sensors and scheduling nodes at traffic intersections, along with the ability of cars to communicate back and forth, it's possible that in the future we could see a perfectly efficient roadway featuring only autonomous intersections, in which the car would never have to stop until it reached its destination.

5. The environment will thank us

Self-driving cars could be of huge benefit to the environment. According to the Union of Concerned Scientists, transportation, in general, was responsible for over half of the carbon monoxide and nitrogen oxide air pollution as well as a quarter of the hydrocarbons emitted into our atmosphere. While many self-driving cars might still emit these same materials, their improved efficiency would be a huge step forward toward a cleaner future.

Part of the reason cars cause so much air pollution is traffic gridlock in highly congested areas. The efficiency of self-driving cars, in addition to the possibility of a future without any gridlock or traffic stops, will cut down on these emissions. If future manufacturers of self-driving cars follow Google's precedent and make electric vehicles, the positive impact on the environment could be even greater. It's worth the benefits to the environment alone to embrace the future of self-driving cars.

Would You Buy a Self-Driving Future from These Guys?

THE EDITORIAL BOARD OF THE NEW YORK TIMES

The kairotic moment for the following editorial from the New York Times *editorial board (October 14, 2017) was a Pew Research Center survey showing widespread public reservations about self-driving cars and about an automated future dominated by robots.*

When the owner of an automated Tesla was killed in a crash last year, the carmaker's founder, Elon Musk, urged journalists to peer into the future.

"If, in writing some article that's negative, you effectively dissuade people from using an autonomous vehicle," Mr. Musk said, "you're killing people."

Scary. But self-driving vehicle proponents like Mr. Musk envision a world where those cars would all but eliminate traffic accidents, unleash our productivity, and allow the old and disabled to travel freely.

Most Americans look at that future, though, and say — not so fast.

While companies like Alphabet, General Motors, and Tesla are investing bil- 5
lions of dollars to turn lofty goals for driverless cars into reality, the Pew Research
Center found that most people surveyed did not want to ride in them and were
not sure whether the vehicles would make roads safer or more dangerous
(39 percent vs. 30 percent). And 87 percent favored requiring that a person always
be behind the wheel, ready to take control if something goes wrong.

It might be tempting for corporate executives and proponents to dismiss
these concerns as part of humanity's aversion to change and argue that this resistance will soften once people see the benefits of self-driving technologies. That
would be a mistake.

People have good reason to doubt grand promises about world-changing
technology. They have lost countless hours to unreliable software and had their
personal data hacked. They have been let down by companies that hid safety
defects (General Motors and Takata) or lied about emissions (Volkswagen).

Further, experts warn that the hype around automated cars is belied by the
struggles these machines have in the rain, or when tree branches hang too low, or
on bridges or on roads with faded lane markings.

Yet, members of Congress, encouraged to do so by auto and tech lobbyists,
have proposed bipartisan bills that would let industry roll out automated cars
more quickly by exempting them from existing safety regulations, like those that
govern the performance of steering wheels, airbags, and brakes, and by directing
the Department of Transportation to come up with new rules instead.

Lawmakers have to do better than that if they care about what the public is 10
saying. A bill passed by the House last month would let manufacturers sell up
to 25,000 automated cars a year without meeting all federal safety standards,
and up to 100,000 cars after three years. The companies would not even have to
establish that their cars are as safe as conventional vehicles before the number of
exemptions increased.

A bill approved by the Senate Commerce Committee is a bit better. It would
require a safety evaluation before raising the cap on exemptions. It would also
limit the total number to 80,000.

A larger problem with both bills is that they would do nothing to increase the
size of the budget or staff of the National Highway Traffic Safety Administration,
which is responsible for overseeing the industry and will have to write new rules
for self-driving cars.

The agency has been underfunded for years and has struggled to investigate
auto defects and improve safety standards. Worse still, President Trump has proposed cutting the agency's operations and research budget by $24 million, or 7.5
percent, in the 2018 fiscal year.

Today, the agency is woefully unprepared to regulate self-driving cars, particularly at the scale proponents hope to see down the line. More electrical engineers, programmers, and cybersecurity specialists who can evaluate such cars
have to be hired.

15   Among other challenges, the agency has to come up with standards for what happens when a highly automated car has to hand control back to a human driver. The results could be devastating if drivers are distracted because they place too much trust in their cars.

    The National Transportation Safety Board ruled that one reason the Tesla, a Model S operating in its Autopilot mode, crashed into a tractor-trailer illegally crossing in front of it was "overreliance on automation."

    States and cities that wish to regulate self-driving cars will also be disappointed. The House and Senate bills, as a further boon to industry, would prohibit such action. Unaddressed, though, is the fact that those governments still would largely retain oversight of traffic laws and would be forced to answer their own complicated questions: When an automated car violates traffic rules, should a police officer write a ticket for the owner or the carmaker? Should states require automakers to carry liability insurance, as they do for drivers? California last week proposed rules attempting to answer some of these questions.

    There's no doubt that a driverless future would profoundly change society, even in ways we're not even considering yet. People might stop buying cars because services like Uber, once its cars are automated, would be cheaper to use. That could cause mass unemployment for taxi drivers and greatly reduce car sales, potentially hurting the economy. It would also make parking garages and parking spaces superfluous, freeing up valuable real estate.

    More people might decide to live, say, 100 miles from their workplaces because algorithms would make traffic flow more smoothly and allow people to nap, work or watch Netflix while commuting.

20   Cities could be forced to put up barriers separating cars from pedestrians, who might feel emboldened to walk into traffic believing that cars would automatically stop for them.

    Yet Mr. Musk's point about the hazards of human drivers is well taken: If automated cars make the roads safer — as seatbelts, airbags, and other innovations have done — millions of lives may be saved. More than 37,000 people were killed in crashes in the United States last year alone.

    Automakers, lawmakers and regulators need to do more to perfect this technology, and reassure the public. There is a lot riding on that work.

For Writing and Discussion

Self-Driving Cars

1. In this unit, perhaps the most consistently optimistic view of self-driving cars is that of Dave Hendricks. Review Hendricks's five reasons for embracing self-driving cars. Then explore how other authors in this unit might cast doubts on Hendricks's optimism, either by disagreeing with him or by raising reservations or uncertainties. Look at each of his reasons in turn.

2. In your discussion of ways that some authors might cast doubt on Hendricks's optimism, where did you encounter disagreements about the consequences of self-driving cars (disagreements about facts or truth)? For example, do writers agree that self-driving cars will make our roads safer? Where did you encounter disagreements about values? For example, do all writers agree that the predicted loss of jobs by truck drivers and Uber or taxi drivers is a bad thing?

3. Make a pro–con list of the benefits to society of self-driving trucks. Then do a rhetorical analysis of Scott Santens's argument (see Chapter 7 on rhetorical analysis). Most readers would agree that Santens makes a powerful case that self-driving trucks will bring economic disaster to truckers and to the communities and businesses that depend on them. How does Santens's argument appeal to *logos, ethos,* and *pathos*? What positive views of self-driving trucks remain largely "invisible" in Santens's argument?

4. Robin Chase seems optimistic that self-driving cars will eventually improve our cities, but she realistically describes the "nightmare" we will create if we don't have effective planning and government action. Do you share Chase's basic optimism about our transition to self-driving cars (an optimism also shared by Hendricks), or do see a nightmare coming? Or do you see self-driving cars as a passing fad that will never fully catch on?

5. Many people imagine self-driving cars as co-existing with human drivers. Drivers might turn the self-driving features of their cars on or off just as they now turn cruise control on or off. Based on the readings in this , do you think it will be possible long term for self-driving cars to share the road with human drivers?

Writing Assignment

A Researched Argument on a Subissue Related to Self-Driving Cars

Choose a subissue connected to disagreements about fact or value in this collection of arguments on self-driving cars. For example, you might be interested in subissues such as these: Scott Santens's claim that self-driving trucks and other kinds of robots will put so many people out of work that we need to consider a universal basic income; concerns raised by several authors about legal and ethical issues (Who is responsible if an autonomous car gets in an accident? How will cars be programmed to handle ethical decisions?); or issues related to government regulation or city planning. Once you have chosen a subissue, research it in depth, determine a targeted audience whose views you want to change, and write a documented argument, addressed to that audience, that makes and supports a contestable claim.

Immigration in the Twenty-First Century

As some of the readings in this section point out, we are accustomed to discussing immigration as a political issue, but not always as a humanitarian issue. Politicians debate immigration policy or strategies for stopping the flow of illegal immigrants across our borders. But abstract policy may seem difficult to apply when we see compelling photos of refugees desperate to escape war, violence, or crushing poverty—people who go to extreme lengths to reach foreign shores, only to be turned back or to find themselves stuck in the limbo of refugee camps. Our hearts may reach out to them, but we may also fear them because some of the countries being fled are hotspots for terrorism.

For those immigrants who already reside within our borders, shifting federal immigration policies and enforcement priorities are sources of tension and concern. Some U.S. citizens want to support federal immigration laws while others seek to create "sanctuary cities" that protect illegal aliens from deportment. As the first reading in this unit from the Washington Post demonstrates, even though there is no legal definition of "sanctuary city," many cities and counties enact policies that limit cooperation with federal requests to detain individuals. Advocates for sanctuary cities claim that such policies encourage trust in local law enforcement by immigrant communities and therefore increase public safety. Those opposed say that local law enforcement is hampering the federal government's ability to detain and deport dangerous individuals. Some immigrants may be refugees from harsh conditions in their home countries, but formal refugee status is quite difficult to obtain.

The readings in this unit ask you to consider the issues and challenges of immigration in a country that prides itself on its immigrant origins but sometimes has trouble welcoming people with unfamiliar appearances, languages, and practices. How well is the United States accommodating its immigrant populations? Are we doing enough to protect Americans from those who might cause harm? Should we be opening our doors wider to the citizens of other countries who are suffering? When determining policy, what or whose concerns should take precedence?

Fact Checker: The White House's Claim that "Sanctuary" Cities Are Violating the Law

MICHELLE YE HEE LEE

Michelle Ye Hee Lee is a reporter for the Washington Post's *"Fact Checker" column. The rating system is based on what the* Post *calls the "Pinocchio Test," where one Pinocchio is "mostly true," and four Pinocchios is a "whopper." The rare claim that is found to be completely yet unexpectedly true receives the Geppetto Checkmark. This analysis was published on April 28, 2017.*

> *"That means, according to Congress, a city that prohibits its officials from providing information to federal immigration authorities—a sanctuary city—is violating the law. Sanctuary cities, like San Francisco, block their jails from turning over criminal aliens to federal authorities for deportation."*
>
> — White House statement in response to judge's ruling on President Trump's executive order on "sanctuary" jurisdictions, April 25, 2017

Claims about "sanctuary" cities often get muddled, so this claim caught our attention. It was a part of the White House's response to a district court judge's decision to halt President Trump's executive order from taking effect, pending litigation.

The statement referred to a section in the U.S. Code that the executive order used in order to pull federal funding from jurisdictions that are not cooperating with federal immigration efforts.

The White House claimed that under that section in the law, "a city that prohibits its officials from providing information to federal immigration authorities—a sanctuary city—is violating the law." The statement then pointed to sanctuary cities, such as San Francisco, that "block their jails from turning over criminal aliens to federal authorities for deportation."

(Note: Re the phrase "criminal aliens," the act of being in the United States without permission is not a criminal violation of the law, but a civil infraction. But people who have illegally entered the country or falsified documents have violated criminal law. And not everyone held in local jails are convicted criminals, and instead may be charged with crimes.)

There are some things going on here that obfuscate the narrow focus of the law, and whether "sanctuary" cities are violating it. Let's dig in.

The Facts

The debate over "sanctuary" policies gets confusing for one simple reason: There's no official definition for "sanctuary" in immigration policy or law. In general, it refers to rules restricting state and local governments from alerting federal authorities about people who may be in the country illegally.

The administration argues that sanctuary cities are violating federal law because they run afoul of section 1373(a) of title 8 of the U.S. code. That section prohibits local and state governments from enacting laws or policies that limit the governments from exchanging immigration and citizenship information with the department of homeland security.

10   For example, say you're an employee of a city government and you found out someone who applied for benefits was an undocumented immigrant. If you want to report that person's immigration status to Immigration and Customs Enforcement (ICE), the government cannot forbid you from doing so without violating Section 1373. But the federal government also could not force the city government to report that person's information to ICE. (The District of Columbia would be an exception because it is controlled by the federal government.)

This is one interpretation of the term "sanctuary." Another involves "immigration detainers." These are the cities that fit the description in the next part of the White House statement: "Sanctuary cities, like San Francisco, block their jails from turning over criminal aliens to federal authorities for deportation." But Section 1373 does not explicitly address immigration detainers, and that's not clear in the White House statement.

ICE can issue a detainer, which is a request to be notified when a noncitizen detainee is being released at state or local levels. It's voluntary for agencies to comply with an ICE detainer.

If they comply, they notify ICE and hold noncitizens, typically for up to 48 hours, beyond the time they otherwise would have been released. During that time, ICE can take custody and figure out whether the person should be deported. If ICE doesn't take action, the local or state agency is required to release them.

"Sanctuary" is commonly used to describe jurisdictions that decline to do this, whether out of fear it might silence victims or potential witnesses, or because they don't have enough resources to cooperate. But some do cooperate with ICE in certain cases, such as when ICE obtained a warrant, or for offenders deemed to be a public safety threat.

15   There are 165 to 608 local and state governments with "sanctuary" policies. It's unclear how many cities have policies that violate Section 1373.

In 2016, the Department of Justice inspector general took a sample of 10 out of 140 jurisdictions that receive federal grant funds to see if they are violating Section 1373. All 10 jurisdictions had policies that limited cooperation with detainer requests, but the inspector general found that Section 1373 does not specifically address detainers.

These jurisdictions did not have explicit policies limiting communication with the federal government on immigration and citizenship, so they were not in clear violation of Section 1373. Still, the inspector general raised concerns that some local policies on detainer requests affected communication between the governments and ICE, and therefore were "inconsistent with at least the intent of Section 1373."

The bottom line: The White House claims in broad terms that sanctuary cities are violating the law under Section 1373, but the law narrowly applies to an unknown number of jurisdictions. The White House lumps together cities that violate Section 1373 and cities that "block their jails from turning over criminal aliens to federal authorities for deportation" (i.e., decline detainer requests), even though Section 1373 does not clearly apply to the latter.

Legal experts say the administration is interpreting Section 1373 more broadly to apply to both types of sanctuary cities. Some experts argue that Section 1373 may be unconstitutional, as it violates the 10th Amendment's anti-commandeering doctrine. The executive order would have given the Homeland Security secretary authority to designate any jurisdiction as "sanctuary."

This discrepancy is one of the main issues under litigation. The judge halted   20
the executive order upon finding that the administration may use it as "a weapon" against any city it deems a sanctuary city, without actually defining what "sanctuary" means. When reached for comment, the White House referred us to the Department of Justice, which said it could not comment on ongoing litigation but pointed to the government's argument in its legal brief.

[*Update*: On May 22, 2017, Attorney General Jeff Sessions issued a memo that defined sanctuary jurisdictions as ones that "willfully refuse to comply with" Section 1373. However, Sessions also warned that the Department of Justice may seek to "tailor" grants, or to impose additional immigration enforcement conditions on jurisdictions receiving federal grant funds. That means the Justice Department could try to tie grant requirements or the definition of "sanctuary" to whether local jurisdictions comply with immigration detainers.]

The Pinocchio Test

This issue gets confusing because it has to do with a technical, legal issues over a term —"sanctuary" —that has no technical or legal definition. In the absence of an official definition, the White House is adopting a broad interpretation of the term and whether the cities are violating the specific section of the U.S. Code.

But there is a difference between cities that clearly limit information-sharing on immigration and citizenship with the federal government (which Section 1373 is about) and cities that do not comply with immigration detainers (which Section 1373 is not about). The White House lumps both types of cities into one statement, obfuscating what's really going on. We award Two Pinocchios for the lack of context.

Stop Immigration Processing as Leverage against Sanctuaries?

KENT LUNDGREN

Kent Lundgren is a past chairman of the National Association of Former Border Patrol Officers and a board member of the Center for Immigration Studies, which published this proposal on February 3, 2017. The Center is an independent, nonpartisan research organization that believes that "debates about immigration policy that are well-informed and grounded in objective data will lead to better immigration policies."

Across the country, local governments are declaring themselves so-called "sanctuaries" for deportable aliens. They refuse to cooperate with immigration enforcement. They refuse to honor detainers placed against dangerous aliens in their jails, releasing them instead back to the community rather than turn them over to federal authorities to be removed from the country. They forbid employees to notify immigration authorities of illegal aliens in our midst, even those drawing public benefits to which they are not, by law, entitled. Their law enforcement officers are not allowed to assist federal officers in enforcement actions against illegal aliens, against whom immigration laws may be used to good effect. In short, those entities resist federal exercise of authority over aliens in this country.

The following proposal starts from the position that the federal government has a duty to control the presence of aliens in this country and that it must bring the practice of sanctuary to an end. Justifying that position (although it seems to the writer perfectly clear) is beyond the scope of this proposal, so no attempt will be made to do so here. The writer does, however, comment that the sanctuary practice has ramifications beyond immigration law and must, for the sake of the Republic, be stopped without further delay. Secession, as an idea, was put to bed in 1865.

How best to dissuade the local governments from their chosen path? The proposal has been made to cut off federal funds to those cities. Good: a first step. But many of them have already said they are willing to forego that money for the sake of protecting alien lawbreakers.

Another likely proposal would have the federal government arrest and prosecute officials responsible for adopting or executing such policies. Title 8 US Code, Sec. 1324(a)(1)(A)(iii), which deals with harboring, concealing, or shielding from detection illegal aliens, and Title 18 US Code, Sec. 371, which covers conspiracy to commit a violation of U.S. law, are the relevant federal statutes. While the writer finds the vision of the sheriff, mayor, and city council being led off in irons entertaining, he concedes that it should be a last resort.

5   What is lacking in this two-step continuum of persuasion is an intermediate step. One is available.

We posit that if those governments choose not to cooperate in enforcing immigration laws then, by their intransigence, they have placed themselves and those they govern (who put them in place, after all) beyond the services and benefits offered by our immigration laws. This idea is not without approximate parallel in law. Some countries refuse to take back their citizens who have been ordered deported from the United States. In such cases, Title 8 USC, Sec. 1253(d) provides that the US Secretary of State shall direct US consuls in that country to cease issuing visas to citizens of that country.

The U.S. Citizenship and Immigration Services (USCIS) is a branch of the Department of Homeland Security charged with receiving, adjudicating, and delivering the benefits of immigration and naturalization laws. *Therefore, the writer proposes that the White House direct USCIS to suspend the adjudication of any applications or petitions received from a business or resident in a sanctuary entity.*

We will not attempt here to get into the "how-to" of that process. Those are details to be worked out by USCIS and other personnel charged with making it happen, but it would not be difficult.

What that will mean in practical terms is this: USCIS will accept applications as always, but they will go, in date order, into a "pending adjudication" file. Once the dispute between the federal government and the local entity is resolved the decision process will begin again, with oldest cases being first.

What will the effect be on the public? Employers in sanctuary cities will be   10 unable to get approval to bring foreign employees to this country. Alien employees already here legally will be unable to have their status extended or changed. Aliens who are temporarily here for any purpose, such as students, professional athletes and performers, businessmen, or tourists will be unable to extend their stay or change their status. They will have to leave when their authorized stay expires. Families will be unable to file petitions to have alien relatives admitted to the United States. Permanent alien residents who are eligible to naturalize will have to wait until this unpleasantness is settled.

This entire continuum should be extended to schools (colleges or otherwise) that accept federal funds or alien students of any category and which declare themselves sanctuaries. Their status as educators does not render them immune from the law or persuasive action.

This is intended to be, in a blunt phrase, political arm-twisting. Local governments have shown themselves willing to loot the public treasury and endanger the public over the issue. Now we will see how much inconvenience, loss of revenue, or even emotional pain the public is willing to accept for the sake of the principle of "sanctuary"—a concept which does not exist in law.

Convicted of the Gospel

DARLENE NICGORSKI

Darlene Nicgorski is a former nun who was convicted of sheltering refugees from El Salvador and Guatemala in the early 1980s. She was a leader in the Sanctuary movement of that era. This piece was published in the September–October 2016 issue of Sojourners *magazine, which describes itself as sitting "at the intersection of faith, politics, and culture."*

On May 1, 1986, a federal jury found nine church activists guilty of conspiracy to violate U.S. immigration laws for assisting Central American refugees. At our sentencing, I faced a possible 25-year prison sentence.

The "sanctuary trial" drew national attention; millions of Americans learned about the plight of Central American refugees and the church-led sanctuary movement to aid them. After a seven-month trial and our conviction, the judge suspended our sentence and gave us five years of probation.

In the 1980s, our case hinged on the fact that we knew that those arriving over the southern border were refugees from brutal wars in Guatemala and El Salvador. I had worked in Guatemala and in Guatemalan camps in southern

Mexico. We placed refugees in communities of faith where people met them as real people and learned why they had fled. We defied U.S. immigration laws in order to protect life. We also challenged the Reagan administration's support of brutal regimes in Guatemala and El Salvador.

Today, most of the non-Mexican undocumented immigrants coming over the border are from Guatemala, El Salvador, and Honduras. Many are unaccompanied minors or single adults with children. Many have legitimate asylum cases, but don't have adequate legal representation.

5   The new sanctuary movement is addressing four key areas: First, assisting migrants when they arrive with basic needs and legal help. Diocesan Migrant Refugee Services in El Paso, Texas, is the largest provider of "Know Your Rights" information to refugees, particularly those staying in community-run hospitality houses along the border. Without the assistance of volunteers, usually church-affiliated, migrants would be on their own—or worse, detained in for-profit prisons.

The Austin-based nonprofit Grassroots Leadership provides research and documentation on the growth of the for-profit prison system—a field dominated by Corrections Corporation of America and the GEO Group. U.S. policies that pay Mexico to catch refugees before they enter the United States and the use of for-profit prisons (with the financial incentive to keep them full) keep U.S. citizens separated from refugees, making it harder to know them as individual people.

Second, organizing for humane immigration reform and to win just legal treatment for immigrants, especially those who are undocumented and their families. Two years ago President Obama attempted to move immigration reform forward through his executive actions on Deferred Action for Parents of Americans (DAPA) and Deferred Action for Childhood Arrivals (DACA). In June, the deadlocked Supreme Court vote on DAPA ended Obama's immigration reform efforts by upholding a lower-court injunction. This is devastating for more than 16 million people in "mixed status" families living in the United States. Immigration attorneys agree that this should not affect the status of more than 800,000 young Dreamers protected by Obama's 2012 DACA action. However, since DACA is the result of an executive action rather than a law passed by Congress, the incoming president could rescind it.

Third, protecting immigrants from deportation. Several denominations have taken strong action in support of immigrants' needs. In June, the Presbyterian Church (USA) reaffirmed its commitment to the "the ministry of sanctuary" and for "those congregations that have supported and offered sanctuary to immigrants threatened with deportation."

Fourth, meeting people *before* they migrate and learning the complexities of why they leave. In 2015, I joined a pilgrimage to Honduras and Guatemala developed specifically to help U.S. citizens understand the factors that compel migration. Some U.S. policies set in place to protect multinational corporations contribute to conditions that compel migration.

10   In the 1980s, there were more than 500 sanctuary churches and synagogues, at least 19 sanctuary cities, 20 sanctuary universities, and one sanctuary state, New Mexico. How will we encounter the divine in the face of refugees today? What risks will we take in order to protect their lives?

Enforcement in Sanctuary Cities Should Be Feds' Job, Not Local Police

LUPE VALDEZ, ED GONZALEZ, AND JAVIER SALAZAR

Lupe Valdez is sheriff of Dallas County, Ed Gonzalez is sheriff of Harris County, and Javier Salazar is sheriff of Bexar County, all in Texas. Their commentary appeared in the Dallas Morning News *on April 14, 2017.*

We believe locally elected sheriffs know the needs of their communities better than state and national leaders who are currently trying to tie our hands.

Our communities each have unique public safety and law enforcement needs that should not be undermined by the state's unfunded mandates in Senate Bill 4. The bill would punish local government entities for not enforcing federal immigration laws.

If passed, SB 4 would coerce local law enforcement to dedicate often scarce resources such as jail-space, on-duty time of officers, and local tax dollars to a job that is supposed to be done by the federal government and paid for with federal dollars. While it is in the interest of federal agencies to let local law enforcement do its job, the costs will be entirely passed onto you, the local taxpayers. Federal enforcement should not be paid for with our local taxes. Our communities' tax dollars should be used to invest in our local priorities and programs. It is at the local level that we are aware of the most pressing issues facing each of our communities in Texas.

A law enforcement official's foremost priority is to protect and serve our local communities, which we have done while maintaining cooperation with U.S. Immigration and Customs Enforcement. The author of SB 4, state Sen. Charles Perry, R-Lubbock, has accused our local departments of "perpetuating instability" because we are not focused on new and controversial federal immigration mandates.

The reality is that SB 4 would perpetuate instability by making it impossible for us to effectively direct and manage our deputies. Immigrants are significantly less likely to commit crimes than other population groups. In fact, FBI crime statistics have found that labeled "sanctuary" cities experience lower rates of all crime types, including homicides. Further, we rely on all members of our community, regardless of race, religion, or national origin, to report crime. We cannot drive crime victims and witnesses into the shadows without undermining local public safety.

SB 4 provides zero support to local officials. In addition to opening up law enforcement departments and officers to costly litigation, the bill would force local taxpayers to shoulder the cost of ICE detainers. In 2016 alone, Texas county compliance with ICE detainers cost local taxpayers $61 million. Despite the federal government's promises, they have reimbursed only a tiny fraction of the costs to local communities and counties. Ultimately, it is our local taxpayers who will pay even more for this unfunded state mandate. SB 4 robs our communities of local tax dollars while hampering our ability to allocate our scarce resources to protect our communities from the largest threats facing our neighborhoods.

SB 4 fundamentally functions with the assumption that the state government knows what is best for our local communities. It ignores our familiarity with our own cities and counties, and how to keep them safe. Our government is designed to balance the power of federal officials with state and local authority.

This bill is a result of anti-immigrant grandstanding and will strip local law enforcement of our designated power and ability to protect and serve our communities. We ask that the Texas House reject SB 4 and any initiative to force local law enforcement to carry out the responsibilities of the federal government.

Coming Soon to a House Like Yours

JEFF DANZIGER

Jeff Danziger is a political cartoonist whose work appears in The Wall Street Journal, Forbes, The New Yorker, *and other magazines and newspapers around the globe. He has received the Herblock Prize and the Thomas Nast Prize for his work. This cartoon was published on February 15, 2017.*

Foreword to Tackling the Global Refugee Crisis: From Shirking to Sharing Responsibility

SALIL SHETTY, AMNESTY INTERNATIONAL

Salil Shetty is a human rights activist and Secretary General of Amnesty International. This foreword is the introduction to a 42-page report and proposal, published in late 2016, that maps the hotspots for refugees and provides a blueprint for host nations to share the burden of resettlement more equitably while treating refugees more humanely.

On 19 September 2016 the United Nations (UN) General Assembly collectively, and spectacularly, failed the 21 million refugees of this world. The "High-level Summit to address large movements of refugees and migrants" was to address the global refugee crisis, a crisis in which, daily, millions fleeing war and persecution in countries like Syria, South Sudan, Myanmar, and Iraq suffer intolerable misery and human rights violations. World leaders at the General Assembly agreed [on] an Outcome document that said they would help, but agreed [on] no actual plan. Empty words that change nothing.

No amount of post-Summit spin can or should be allowed to give comfort to the world's leaders. Collectively they failed. Agreeing to cooperate to address the refugee crisis, while eschewing any specific action, is not progress. Deferring a global plan on refugees to 2018 is not progress. Removing the only tangible target—to resettle 10% of refugees annually—is not progress. Not all states failed, however. A few countries, such as Canada which has accepted 30,000 refugees in the past year, have shown leadership. But the majority spent the months leading to the Summit ensuring no progress could be made.

The UN Summit had a reasonable aim: to share responsibility for the world's refugees among states. There are 193 countries in the world. And 21 million refugees. More than half of these refugees—nearly 12 million people—are living in just 10 of these 193 countries. This is inherently unsustainable. Countries hosting such high numbers of refugees cannot provide for them. Many refugees are living in grinding poverty without access to basic services and without hope for the future. Not surprisingly, many are desperate to move elsewhere. And some are willing to risk dangerous journeys to try and find a better life.

If all—or most—countries were to take a fair share of responsibility for hosting refugees then no one country would be overwhelmed. A "fair share" can be based on reasonable criteria such as national wealth, population size, and unemployment rate—common-sense criteria which acknowledge that people arriving as refugees will, at first, have an impact on the local population and resources.

No doubt this solution will be condemned by some as too simplistic. But not by those countries that are hosting hundreds of thousands of refugees. Those who

5

do not want to take a fair share will find objections and cite reasons why it is unworkable. But that is a failure of leadership. It is also morally bankrupt and intellectually shoddy to fail to face up to reality. There are 21 million refugees, and they need a place to live safely. The current "formula," accepted by many world leaders, is geographic proximity to war-torn countries, regardless of the capacity of such neighboring countries. It is hard to imagine a less useful basis for addressing any problem. But that is the basis on which many of the world's leaders are operating.

When we break the global refugee crisis down by the numbers, the inequality in the response of states is stark. This is because the problem is not the number of refugees but that the vast majority (86% according to figures from UNHCR, the UN refugee agency) are hosted in low- and middle-income countries.

Meanwhile, many of the world's wealthiest nations host the fewest and do the least. For example, the UK has accepted approximately 8,000 Syrians since 2011, while Jordan—with a population almost 10 times smaller than the UK and just 1.2% of its GDP—hosts over 656,000 Syrian refugees. The total refugee and asylum-seeker population in Australia is 58,000 compared to 740,000 in Ethiopia. Such unequal sharing of responsibility is at the root of the global refugee crisis and the many problems faced by refugees.

An initiative by President Obama, which followed the failed UN Summit, increased pledges from 18 countries to admit 360,000 refugees globally. But 360,000 has to be seen in the context of more than 21 million refugees worldwide, 1.2 million of whom UNHCR considers vulnerable and desperately in need of resettlement. In truth, we are almost nowhere in terms of real responsibility sharing.

It is not simply a matter of sending aid money. Rich countries cannot pay to keep people "over there." The result is that people who have fled war are now enduring dehumanizing living conditions and dying of entirely treatable diseases. They escaped bombs to die of infections, diarrhea, or pneumonia. Children are not attending school, with devastating consequences for the rest of their lives.

10   In any event, humanitarian appeals to support major refugee crises, such as Syria, are consistently, and severely, underfunded. As of mid-2016, governments around the world had pledged less than 48% of the amount needed by aid agencies to support refugees from Syria.

More money is vital, but so also is the need to move refugees from places like Lebanon that are overwhelmed. When we look at it from the perspective of individuals affected, the refugee crisis seems enormous, but viewed with a global lens it is solvable. Twenty-one million people represent just 0.3% of the world's population. Finding a safe place for them to live is not only possible but it can be done without any one country having to take in very large numbers.

Around 30 countries currently run some kind of refugee resettlement program, and the number of places offered annually falls far short of the needs identified by UNHCR. With only around 30 countries currently operating such programs, there is real scope for positive change. Make it 60 or 90, the situation will improve—and we are not yet up to half the countries in the world. If we can increase the number of countries resettling refugees from 30 to 90, we could make a significant impact on the crisis. More importantly, the lives of the refugees would be significantly improved.

So why is this kind of responsibility-sharing not happening? While we know some countries such as Germany and Canada have tried to meet the challenge—the prevailing narrative in many countries is xenophobic, anti-migration, and driven by fear and concerns about security. The public in some countries are subjected almost daily to misinformation. In other countries the scale of the global refugee crisis is not known. In yet others, the feeling of powerlessness leads people to turn away. We need to change this, shift it to a narrative of generosity and positivity, one in which we can ensure security and help refugees—we do not need to make a choice. People can be moved to be part of a shared, fair, worldwide solution. And leaders should be making this case, not pandering to their own political ambitions.

The cost of failing to act is that we condemn millions to endure lives of unrelenting misery. The most vulnerable will not survive. Quietly, and in their thousands, vulnerable refugees trapped in unsustainable situations will die because they cannot get the help they need. They will die because some countries took in just a few hundred, leaving others with a million.

Of course there are challenges. Yes, not every one of the 193 countries is a safe place and we would exclude countries facing UN sanctions over human rights violations and those in active conflict. But if our starting point is 12 million people in just 10 countries, then the scope to improve the situation is vast.

15

Responsibility-sharing will remain an empty commitment without some kind of criteria or basis, a global system making clear how that can be done. We are proposing that basic common-sense criteria relevant to a country's capacity be used to host refugees: its wealth, population, and unemployment rate are the main criteria. Other factors may be relevant (population density, for example, and whether a country has a large number of existing asylum claims). No formula will be perfect, none should be overly complex. The purpose would be to give an indicative and relative number so that all participating countries would have a basis against which to assess their fair share and see what the fair share of others looks like.

In the face of brutal wars, we can feel like powerless bystanders, overwhelmed by the horror inflicted on our fellow human beings and the seeming impossibility of doing anything about it. But finding a formula to ensure just 0.3% of the world can go somewhere safe—this we can do. And we must.

We Must Remain Vigilant through Responsible Refugee Policies

STEVEN P. BUCCI

Steven P. Bucci, Ph.D., has served as an Army Special Forces officer and Pentagon official. He is a visiting research fellow at the Heritage Foundation, whose mission is to "formulate and promote conservative public policies." This commentary was posted on its website on December 2, 2015.

Refugees continue to flood out of Syria at a breathtaking pace. According to the United Nations, parts of Europe are now facing the worst migration crisis since World War II. President Barack Obama recently requested that Congress double the funding to house refugees here in the United States. However, given the threat that ISIS poses to the United States, as well as the recent revelation that one of the Paris attackers entered France as a refugee, many have expressed concerns that the refugees need to be properly vetted before entering the United States.

The concern over the potential dangers accrued by letting some individuals into the United States is real. It is not insurmountable, but it is also not trivial. America has long been a refuge to those seeking a new life, but to ensure that this dream continues to be a reality, a thorough vetting process must be instituted for refugees fleeing areas prone to extremism.

The challenges that exist in vetting individuals from these regions are significant. It is extremely difficult to vet personnel from war-torn areas where there has been a complete breakdown of governmental authority and control. Syria clearly is in this category.

It is harder still in Arabic-speaking cultures. Some of this is simply because we as English speakers have a terrible time with accurate name identification from which all this vetting begins. Whether it is simply spelling due to transliteration errors or family and locational "attachments" to names, we are often in error. Anyone who waves this off is dangerously optimistic.

5   Secondly, we have failed at this before. I personally sat through numerous meetings with Iraqi expatriates and have a particularly painful memory of leading Ahmed Chalabi in the secretary of defense's office in the months leading up to the invasion of Iraq. People who had extensive "vetting" were determined to be our friends and allies. These assessments proved to be terribly wrong. Even our best regional experts and social scientists are still Americans and see things through an American lens, which has proven to be faulty when trying to sort out opaque motivations of members of Middle Eastern cultures. There are other examples of failures as well.

The Islamist extremists of ISIS and al-Qaeda have become more radicalized, more determined to harm the United States, and more convinced that they need to do it here to be really effective.

The attack in Garland, Texas, this May is a perfect example. Their motivation to "do something" here in our homeland is enormous. Several thousand refugees who may have ill feelings toward a world that allowed them to lose their homes and country would be a lucrative recruitment target.

America has always been a haven for the dispossessed, and I pray she will always be so. But we must be cautious. The effort in these cases must be over the top in the vetting process. We must enlist all elements of the U.S. government and our allies to do everything we can to ensure that no already radicalized individuals slip through.

Anyone who gives you the old "we got this" line is not being entirely realistic. The Department of State, the Department of Homeland Security, and the intelligence community must prove to Congress that their vetting process is rigorous, extensive, redundant, and ongoing. There also needs to be a detailed handoff to both the FBI and local law enforcement as these folks are settled. Anything less than that would be an abrogation of Congress's oversight responsibilities.

A more effective vetting process must be established for Syrian refugees com-   10
ing to the United States. The extensive vetting we do for visa applicants is a good starting point. From there, every list and database available to the entire U.S. government, particularly the intelligence community, must be checked. I would also recommend screening any refugee applicant against the lists of our allies, particularly the U.K., Israel, Jordan, and other NATO countries, before any final determination is made.

America cannot isolate itself, and we must remain the beacon of freedom we have always been, but in this particular situation, we must go way beyond due diligence. The safety of our citizens deserves nothing less.

Facing Responsibility:
The Face of a Refugee Child

RICH STEARNS

Rich Stearns is the president of World Vision U.S., a global Christian humanitarian organization working to end poverty and injustice. This piece was published on the organization's blog on March 15, 2017.

How does God get your attention about something that matters?

For me, God tends to use people, specifically children, to shake me out of complacency. One child's story can simplify a complicated crisis and bring into sharp focus what's most important. Statistics and rhetoric fall away when I'm staring into the face of a suffering child. All I want to do is find a way to help.

This is how it was when I met Haya, a 10-year-old Syrian refugee in Jordan, in 2013.

At the time, the Syrian civil war was in its second year—one of several Middle East countries in upheaval following the Arab Spring. Honestly, I wasn't focused on this crisis; World Vision was responding, but there were plenty of other ministry priorities demanding my attention. Now the conflict was escalating, with refugees pouring into neighboring countries. A colleague asked me to go and see the refugee crisis for myself, so after some meetings in London I tacked on a visit to Jordan.

5   At ground level, the scene was disturbing. I toured Za'atari refugee camp, a sprawling mass of tents stretching as far as the eye could see, surrounded by barbed wire. This was home (if you can call it that) to nearly 100,000 people—so many that another camp, Azraq, was being built nearby for the expected influx of refugees. These were people who had left middle-class lives to flee with little more than the clothes on their backs. They had survived bombings and sniper attacks only to suffer the miseries of hunger, thirst, sickness, and hopelessness.

The need was eminently clear. But even if World Vision scaled up our response, I thought, would our supporters care? A man-made crisis doesn't trigger the kind of generous outpouring a natural disaster does. And this war was mind-numbingly complex, causing most Americans to give up and tune out. To top it all off, the refugees were largely Muslim—a group increasingly distrusted in the Western world.

Then I met Haya. Her father had gone missing in the war, and she and her mother and brother had taken refuge in Irbid, Jordan. This bright girl wasn't in school, but she attended a remedial education class run by World Vision. And evidently, when she was told that the president of an organization was coming to visit, she thought very carefully about what she was going to say to me.

Haya poured her feelings into a song and a letter. "Syria is crying out for her children," she sang. "Her children were her candles, and they have faded out." In her letter, she was more direct, and she aimed for a much wider audience than me. "I am calling on you—the people of the other world. Have you ever thought of the children of Syria?"

Her words hit me on a visceral level. Looking at Haya, I realized: *This is the face of a refugee.*

10   Meeting Haya was a turning point for me. No matter how hard it would be to draw Americans' attention and compassion to the Syrian refugee crisis, I knew I had to try. I had to find a way. And I would use Haya's face and words hundreds of times over the next few years as I spoke at churches and Christian conferences: "Have you ever thought of the children of Syria?"

This wasn't the first time a child had changed me.

In 1998, as a brand-new, wet-behind-the-ears president of World Vision U.S., I took my first trip to Uganda, ground zero of the AIDS pandemic. That's where I met a young boy with the same name as me, Richard. He was an orphan living in a meager thatch hut with his brothers. Their parents, who had succumbed to AIDS, lay buried in graves marked by crude piles of stones outside. I had been told that there were 12 million children like Richard across AIDS-ravaged Africa. Sitting in that hut, my mind reeled at the enormity of the crisis.

I asked Richard if he had a Bible, and he brought out his treasured book. "I love to read the book of John," he told me, "because it says that Jesus loves the children."

At the time, Americans regarded AIDS as a shameful sexually transmitted disease, and Christians were somewhere on the spectrum between uncaring and downright hostile toward its victims. It would not be easy to change hearts and mobilize support for AIDS orphans, but in that moment with Richard, I knew I had to try. I had to find a way. I would preach what Richard made plain to me— that Jesus loves these children.

With AIDS, we were successful; World Vision launched an initiative that   15 engaged hundreds of U.S. churches and connected sponsors with tens of thousands of AIDS-affected children across Africa. We helped turn the tide of that vicious disease. And it all started with the face of a child.

I hope someday I can report the same generous response to the Syrian refugee crisis.

Is God trying to get your attention with a hurting child? She may not be physically in front of you. Maybe she stares at you from a magazine or your computer screen. Don't look away. That child can tell you what you most need to know about a faraway, complicated crisis—simply that precious children Jesus loves are suffering.

Look at that face, and find a way to help.

For Writing and Discussion

Immigration in the Twenty-First Century

1. Do some brief research into the reasons why someone might choose to or be forced to emigrate from his or her home country. Consider economic, environmental, political, and social factors. What would a humane immigration policy look like, in your view? Should there be different rules for different categories of immigrants?

2. The authors in this unit provide different scenarios for those immigrants who may be protected by sanctuary cities or who may be refugees, and they use different terms to describe these individuals. What is the rhetorical effect of these competing definitions and the language employed? How might the intended audience for each piece feel more or less sympathetic toward specific groups of immigrants?

3. Read Steven Bucci's essay "We Must Remain Vigilant . . . " as both a believer and a doubter. Working in small groups or as a class, discuss the following questions: What are the warrants for believing his argument—that is, what other beliefs or values must one hold in order to accept his contentions about the consequences of allowing refugees in the United States from countries like Syria? What beliefs and values would enable one to doubt Bucci's argument?

4. What activities or privileges do citizens of the United States take for granted that might be difficult or impossible for illegal immigrants or their children? How might these barriers perpetuate or even create some of the problems stemming from illegal immigration in the United States?

Writing Assignment

White Paper Summarizing the Arguments about a Policy Proposal

Although not all of the readings in this unit deal specifically with U.S. immigration laws and policies, the people discussed in these readings are affected by those policies on a daily basis. Research one recent proposal to change federal or state immigration laws (such as the current vetting program for refugees, or a specific element of comprehensive reform such as the E-Verify system or the H-2A Seasonal Agricultural Worker program) and read about it in three to five sources. Identify and characterize the stakeholders in the debate: Who are they? What do they stand to gain or lose? Then analyze the arguments used by these stakeholders. What are their strengths and weaknesses? Finally, write a white paper in which you summarize the proposal and the arguments for and against it for a citizen wanting to be better informed. You might find the following resources helpful as a starting place: the Federation for American Immigration Reform, the National Immigration Law Center, or the League of Women Voters Immigration Study.

Argument Classics

In this unit, we present three arguments that have been particularly effective at influencing public opinion, presenting uncomfortable truths to their audiences, and demonstrating powerful strategies of persuasion. Each of these arguments has made a difference in the world, either because it has persuaded people of the justice of its claims or has evoked powerful resistance and counterargument. Richly suitable for classroom analysis, each of these classic arguments can move students and teachers alike to introspection and to agreement or dissent.

A Modest Proposal: For Preventing the Children of Poor People in Ireland, from Being a Burden on Their Parents or Country, and for Making Them Beneficial to the Public

JONATHAN SWIFT

"A Modest Proposal," by Jonathan Swift—a political journalist, satirist, clergyman in the Anglican Church, and Dean of St. Patrick's Cathedral in Dublin—was first published as a pamphlet in 1729. It remains one of the most famous satirical arguments in western literature. In this argument, which has the problem–solution structure of a practical proposal, Swift addresses the ruling classes in both England and Ireland, attacking the political and economic policies, including bans on Irish industries and imports, that are starving the lower classes in Ireland. Satire is a rhetorical vehicle of exposure and critique with the intent of rendering its object ridiculous or shocking in order to inspire reform. One of the main tools of satire is verbal irony, in which the speaker means something quite different from what is actually said. In this satirical argument, Swift, speaking in the persona of what critics have variously identified as an eighteenth-century humanitarian or an economist, proposes a solution to the suffering of the Irish poor—a solution that pretends to be rational and pragmatic. Note how the speaker gives the problem presence, offers a pragmatic (but ironic) solution, justifies his solution with reasons and evidence, and engages with opposing views.

It is a melancholy object to those who walk through this great town or travel in the country, when they see the streets, the roads, and cabin doors, crowded with beggars of the female sex, followed by three, four, or six children, all in rags and importuning every passenger for an alms. These mothers, instead of being able to work for their honest livelihood, are forced to employ all their time in strolling to beg sustenance for their helpless infants: who as they grow up either turn thieves for want of work, or leave their dear native country to fight for the Pretender in Spain, or sell themselves to the Barbadoes.

I think it is agreed by all parties that this prodigious number of children in the arms, or on the backs, or at the heels of their mothers, and frequently of their fathers, is in the present deplorable state of the kingdom a very great additional grievance; and, therefore, whoever could find out a fair, cheap, and easy method of making these children sound, useful members of the commonwealth, would deserve so well of the public as to have his statue set up for a preserver of the nation.

But my intention is very far from being confined to provide only for the children of professed beggars; it is of a much greater extent, and shall take in the whole number of infants at a certain age who are born of parents in effect as little able to support them as those who demand our charity in the streets.

As to my own part, having turned my thoughts for many years upon this important subject, and maturely weighed the several schemes of other projectors, I have always found them grossly mistaken in the computation. It is true, a child just dropped from its dam may be supported by her milk for a solar year, with little other nourishment; at most not above the value of 2s., which the mother may certainly get, or the value in scraps, by her lawful occupation of begging; and it is exactly at one year old that I propose to provide for them in such a manner as instead of being a charge upon their parents or the parish, or wanting food and raiment for the rest of their lives, they shall on the contrary contribute to the feeding, and partly to the clothing, of many thousands.

5   There is likewise another great advantage in my scheme, that it will prevent those voluntary abortions, and that horrid practice of women murdering their bastard children, alas! too frequent among us! sacrificing the poor innocent babes I doubt more to avoid the expense than the shame, which would move tears and pity in the most savage and inhuman breast.

The number of souls in this kingdom being usually reckoned one million and a half, of these I calculate there may be about two hundred thousand couple whose wives are breeders; from which number I subtract thirty thousand couples who are able to maintain their own children, although I apprehend there cannot be so many, under the present distresses of the kingdom; but this being granted, there will remain an hundred and seventy thousand breeders. I again subtract fifty thousand for those women who miscarry, or whose children die by accident or disease within the year. There only remains one hundred and twenty thousand children of poor parents annually born. The question therefore is, how this number shall be reared and provided for, which, as I have already said, under the present situation of affairs, is utterly impossible by all the methods hitherto proposed. For we can neither employ them in handicraft or agriculture; we neither build houses (I mean in the country) nor cultivate land: they can very seldom pick up a livelihood by stealing, till they arrive at six years old, except where they are of towardly parts, although I confess they learn the rudiments much earlier, during which time, they can however be properly looked upon only as probationers, as I have been informed by a principal gentleman in the county of Cavan, who protested to me that he never knew above one or two instances under the age of six, even in a part of the kingdom so renowned for the quickest proficiency in that art.

I am assured by our merchants, that a boy or a girl before twelve years old is no salable commodity; and even when they come to this age they will not yield above three pounds, or three pounds and half-a-crown at most on the exchange; which cannot turn to account either to the parents or kingdom, the charge of nutriment and rags having been at least four times that value.

I shall now therefore humbly propose my own thoughts, which I hope will not be liable to the least objection.

I have been assured by a very knowing American of my acquaintance in London, that a young healthy child well nursed is at a year old a most delicious, nourishing, and wholesome food, whether stewed, roasted, baked, or boiled; and I make no doubt that it will equally serve in a fricassee or a ragout.

I do therefore humbly offer it to public consideration that of the hundred and twenty thousand children already computed, twenty thousand may be reserved for breed, whereof only one-fourth part to be males; which is more than we allow to sheep, black cattle or swine; and my reason is, that these children are seldom the fruits of marriage, a circumstance not much regarded by our savages, therefore one male will be sufficient to serve four females. That the remaining hundred thousand may, at a year old, be offered in the sale to the persons of quality and fortune through the kingdom; always advising the mother to let them suck plentifully in the last month, so as to render them plump and fat for a good table. A child will make two dishes at an entertainment for friends; and when the family dines alone, the fore or hind quarter will make a reasonable dish, and seasoned with a little pepper or salt will be very good boiled on the fourth day, especially in winter.

I have reckoned upon a medium that a child just born will weigh 12 pounds, and in a solar year, if tolerably nursed, increaseth to 28 pounds.

I grant this food will be somewhat dear, and therefore very proper for landlords, who, as they have already devoured most of the parents, seem to have the best title to the children.

Infant's flesh will be in season throughout the year, but more plentiful in March, and a little before and after; for we are told by a grave author, an eminent French physician, that fish being a prolific diet, there are more children born in Roman Catholic countries about nine months after Lent than at any other season; therefore, reckoning a year after Lent, the markets will be more glutted than usual, because the number of popish infants is at least three to one in this kingdom: and therefore it will have one other collateral advantage, by lessening the number of papists among us.

I have already computed the charge of nursing a beggar's child (in which list I reckon all cottagers, laborers, and four-fifths of the farmers) to be about two shillings per annum, rags included; and I believe no gentleman would repine to give ten shillings for the carcass of a good fat child, which, as I have said, will make four dishes of excellent nutritive meat, when he hath only some particular friend or his own family to dine with him. Thus the squire will learn to be a good landlord, and grow popular among his tenants; the mother will have eight shillings net profit, and be fit for work till she produces another child.

15   Those who are more thrifty (as I must confess the times require) may flay the carcass; the skin of which artificially dressed will make admirable gloves for ladies, and summer boots for fine gentlemen.

As to our city of Dublin, shambles may be appointed for this purpose in the most convenient parts of it, and butchers we may be assured will not be wanting; although I rather recommend buying the children alive, and dressing them hot from the knife, as we do roasting pigs.

A very worthy person, a true lover of his country, and whose virtues I highly esteem, was lately pleased in discoursing on this matter to offer a refinement upon my scheme. He said that many gentlemen of this kingdom, having of late destroyed their deer, he conceived that the want of venison might be well supplied by the bodies of young lads and maidens, not exceeding fourteen years of age nor under twelve; so great a number of both sexes in every country being now ready to starve for want of work and service; and these to be disposed of by their parents, if alive, or otherwise by their nearest relations. But with due deference to so excellent a friend and so deserving a patriot, I cannot be altogether in his sentiments; for as to the males, my American acquaintance assured me, from frequent experience, that their flesh was generally tough and lean, like that of our schoolboys by continual exercise, and their taste disagreeable; and to fatten them would not answer the charge. Then as to the females, it would, I think, with humble submission be a loss to the public, because they soon would become breeders themselves; and besides, it is not improbable that some scrupulous people might be apt to censure such a practice (although indeed very unjustly), as a little bordering upon cruelty; which, I confess, hath always been with me the strongest objection against any project, however so well intended.

But in order to justify my friend, he confessed that this expedient was put into his head by the famous Psalmanazar, a native of the island Formosa, who came from thence to London above twenty years ago, and in conversation told my friend, that in his country when any young person happened to be put to death, the executioner sold the carcass to persons of quality as a prime dainty; and that in his time the body of a plump girl of fifteen, who was crucified for an attempt to poison the emperor, was sold to his imperial majesty's prime minister of state, and other great mandarins of the court, in joints from the gibbet, at four hundred crowns. Neither indeed can I deny, that if the same use were made of several plump young girls in this town, who without one single groat to their fortunes cannot stir abroad without a chair, and appear at playhouse and assemblies in foreign fineries which they never will pay for, the kingdom would not be the worse.

Some persons of a desponding spirit are in great concern about that vast number of poor people, who are aged, diseased, or maimed, and I have been desired to employ my thoughts what course may be taken to ease the nation of so grievous an encumbrance. But I am not in the least pain upon that matter, because it is very well known that they are every day dying and rotting by cold and famine, and filth and vermin, as fast as can be reasonably expected. And as to the young laborers, they are now in as hopeful a condition; they cannot get work, and consequently pine away for want of nourishment, to a degree that if at any time they are accidentally hired to common labor, they have not strength to perform it; and thus the country and themselves are happily delivered from the evils to come.

I have too long digressed, and therefore shall return to my subject. I think the   20
advantages by the proposal which I have made are obvious and many, as well as of the highest importance.

For first, as I have already observed, it would greatly lessen the number of papists, with whom we are yearly overrun, being the principal breeders of the nation as well as our most dangerous enemies; and who stay at home on purpose with a design to deliver the kingdom to the Pretender, hoping to take their advantage by the absence of so many good protestants, who have chosen rather to leave their country than stay at home and pay tithes against their conscience to an episcopal curate.

Secondly, The poorer tenants will have something valuable of their own, which by law may be made liable to distress and help to pay their landlord's rent, their corn and cattle being already seized, and money a thing unknown.

Thirdly, Whereas the maintenance of an hundred thousand children, from two years old and upward, cannot be computed at less than ten shillings a-piece per annum, the nation's stock will be thereby increased fifty thousand pounds per annum, beside the profit of a new dish introduced to the tables of all gentlemen of fortune in the kingdom who have any refinement in taste. And the money will circulate among ourselves, the goods being entirely of our own growth and manufacture.

Fourthly, The constant breeders, beside the gain of eight shillings sterling per annum by the sale of their children, will be rid of the charge of maintaining them after the first year.

Fifthly, This food would likewise bring great custom to taverns; where the   25
vintners will certainly be so prudent as to procure the best receipts for dressing it to perfection, and consequently have their houses frequented by all the fine gentlemen, who justly value themselves upon their knowledge in good eating: and a skilful cook, who understands how to oblige his guests, will contrive to make it as expensive as they please.

Sixthly, This would be a great inducement to marriage, which all wise nations have either encouraged by rewards or enforced by laws and penalties. It would increase the care and tenderness of mothers toward their children, when they were sure of a settlement for life to the poor babes, provided in some sort by the public, to their annual profit instead of expense. We should see an honest emulation among the married women, which of them could bring the fattest child to the market. Men would become as fond of their wives during the time of their pregnancy as they are now of their mares in foal, their cows in calf, their sows when they are ready to farrow; nor offer to beat or kick them (as is too frequent a practice) for fear of a miscarriage.

Many other advantages might be enumerated. For instance, the addition of some thousand carcasses in our exportation of barreled beef, the propagation of swine's flesh, and improvement in the art of making good bacon, so much wanted among us by the great destruction of pigs, too frequent at our tables; which are no way comparable in taste or magnificence to a well-grown, fat, yearling child, which roasted whole will make a considerable figure at a lord mayor's feast or any other public entertainment. But this and many others I omit, being studious of brevity.

Supposing that one thousand families in this city, would be constant customers for infants flesh, besides others who might have it at merry meetings, particularly at weddings and christenings, I compute that Dublin would take off annually about twenty thousand carcasses; and the rest of the kingdom (where probably they will be sold somewhat cheaper) the remaining eighty thousand.

I can think of no one objection, that will possibly be raised against this proposal, unless it should be urged, that the number of people will be thereby much lessened in the kingdom. This I freely own, and 'twas indeed one principal design in offering it to the world. I desire the reader will observe, that I calculate my remedy for this one individual Kingdom of Ireland, and for no other that ever was, is, or, I think, ever can be upon Earth. Therefore let no man talk to me of other expedients: Of taxing our absentees at five shillings a pound: Of using neither cloaths, nor household furniture, except what is of our own growth and manufacture: Of utterly rejecting the materials and instruments that promote foreign luxury: Of curing the expensiveness of pride, vanity, idleness, and gaming in our women: Of introducing a vein of parsimony, prudence and temperance: Of learning to love our country, wherein we differ even from Laplanders, and the inhabitants of Topinamboo: Of quitting our animosities and factions, nor acting any longer like the Jews, who were murdering one another at the very moment their city was taken: Of being a little cautious not to sell our country and consciences for nothing: Of teaching landlords to have at least one degree of mercy towards their tenants. Lastly, of putting a spirit of honesty, industry, and skill into our shopkeepers, who, if a resolution could now be taken to buy only our native goods, would immediately unite to cheat and exact upon us in the price, the measure, and the goodness, nor could ever yet be brought to make one fair proposal of just dealing, though often and earnestly invited to it.

30   Therefore I repeat, let no man talk to me of these and the like expedients, 'till he hath at least some glympse of hope, that there will ever be some hearty and sincere attempt to put them into practice.

But, as to my self, having been wearied out for many years with offering vain, idle, visionary thoughts, and at length utterly despairing of success, I fortunately fell upon this proposal, which, as it is wholly new, so it hath something solid and real, of no expence and little trouble, full in our own power, and whereby we can incur no danger in disobliging England. For this kind of commodity will not bear exportation, and flesh being of too tender a consistence, to admit a long continuance in salt, although perhaps I could name a country, which would be glad to eat up our whole nation without it.

After all, I am not so violently bent upon my own opinion as to reject any offer proposed by wise men, which shall be found equally innocent, cheap, easy, and effectual. But before something of that kind shall be advanced in contradiction to my scheme, and offering a better, I desire the author or authors will be pleased maturely to consider two points. First, as things now stand, how they will be able to find food and raiment for an hundred thousand useless mouths and backs. And secondly, there being a round million of creatures in human figure throughout this kingdom, whose whole subsistence put into a common stock would leave them in debt two millions of pounds sterling, adding those who are beggars by profession to the bulk of farmers, cottagers, and laborers, with their wives and children who are beggars in effect: I desire those politicians who dislike my overture, and may perhaps be so bold as to attempt an answer, that they will first ask the parents of these mortals, whether they would not at this day think it a great happiness to have been sold for food, at a year old in the manner I prescribe, and thereby have avoided such a perpetual scene of misfortunes as they have since gone through by the oppression of landlords, the impossibility of paying rent without money or trade, the want of common sustenance, with neither house nor clothes to cover them from the inclemencies of the weather, and the most inevitable prospect of entailing the like or greater miseries upon their breed for ever.

I profess, in the sincerity of my heart, that I have not the least personal interest in endeavoring to promote this necessary work, having no other motive than the public good of my country, by advancing our trade, providing for infants, relieving the poor, and giving some pleasure to the rich. I have no children by which I can propose to get a single penny; the youngest being nine years old, and my wife past child-bearing.

The Declaration of Sentiments and Resolutions Seneca Falls Conference (1848)

ELIZABETH CADY STANTON

Elizabeth Cady Stanton was a prolific writer, courageous activist, and leader of the women's rights movement in the United States for the latter half of the nineteenth century. She advocated for women's legal and political rights, including suffrage, property rights, and the right to divorce. She envisioned a reconstruction of society to include women's public and professional equality. Stanton had been radicalized by her work in her father's law office and her participation in the anti-slavery movement. In 1848, she authored The Declaration of Sentiments, *a bold document modeled after* The Declaration of Independence, *and read it at the first convention on women's rights at Seneca Falls, New York, on July 20, 1848. About three hundred people attended the convention, and one hundred initially signed the document. After the Civil War, Stanton and Susan B. Anthony formed the National Woman's Suffrage Association and edited a weekly paper,* The Revolution, *to promote women's rights, an effort that eventually led to the passage of the Nineteenth Amendment in 1920, finally giving women the right to vote.*

Declaration of Sentiments

When in the course of human events, it becomes necessary for one portion of the family of man to assume among the people of the earth a position different from that which they have hitherto occupied, but one to which the laws of nature and nature's God entitle them, a decent respect to the opinions of mankind requires that they should declare the causes that impel them to such a course.

We hold these truths to be self-evident: that all men and women are created equal; that they are endowed by their Creator with certain inalienable rights; that among these are life, liberty, and the pursuit of happiness; that to secure these rights governments are instituted, deriving their just powers from the consent of the governed. Whenever any form of government becomes destructive of these ends, it is the right of those who suffer from it to refuse allegiance to it, and to insist upon the institution of a new government, laying its foundation on such principles, and organizing its powers in such form, as to them shall seem most likely to effect their safety and happiness. Prudence, indeed, will dictate that governments long established should not be changed for light and transient causes; and accordingly all experience hath shown that mankind are more disposed to suffer while evils are sufferable, than to right themselves by abolishing the forms to which they accustomed. But when a long train of abuses and usurpations, pursuing invariably the same object, evinces a design to reduce them under absolute despotism, it is their duty to throw off such government, and to provide new guards for their future security. Such has been the patient sufferance of women under this government, and such is now the necessity which constrains them to demand the equal station to which they are entitled.

The history of mankind is a history of repeated injuries and usurpations on the part of man toward woman, having in direct object the establishment of an absolute tyranny over her. To prove this, let facts be submitted to a candid world.

He has never permitted her to exercise her inalienable right to the elective franchise.

5   He has compelled her to submit to laws, in the formation of which she had no voice.

He has withheld from her rights which are given to the most ignorant and degraded men—both native and foreigner.

Having deprived her of this first right of a citizen, the elective franchise, thereby leaving her without representation in the halls of legislation, he has oppressed her on all sides.

He has made her, if married, in the eye of the law, civilly dead.

He has taken from her all right in property, even to wages she earns.

He has made her, morally, an irresponsible being, as she can commit many   10
crimes with impunity, provided they can be done in the presence of her husband. In the covenant of marriage, she is compelled to promise obedience to her husband, he becoming, to all intents and purposes, her master—the law giving him power to deprive her of her liberty, and to administer chastisement.

He has so framed the laws of divorce, as to what shall be the proper causes, and in case of separation, to who, the guardianship of the children shall be given, as to be wholly regardless of the happiness of women—the law, in all cases, going upon a false supposition of the supremacy of man, giving all power into his hands.

After depriving her of all rights as a married woman, if single, and the owner of property, he has taxed her to support a government which recognizes her only when her property can be made profitable to it.

He has monopolized nearly all the profitable employments, and from those she is permitted to follow, she receives but a scanty remuneration. He closes against her all the avenues to wealth and distinction which he considers most honorable to himself. As a teacher of theology, medicine, or law, she is not known.

He has denied her the facilities for obtaining a thorough education, all colleges being closed against her.

He allows her in Church, as well as State, but a subordinate position, claiming   15
Apostolic authority for her exclusion from the ministry, and, with some exceptions, from any public participation in the affairs of the Church.

He has created a false public sentiment by giving to the world a different code of morals for men and women, by which moral delinquencies which exclude women from society, are not only tolerated, but deemed of little account in man.

He has usurped the prerogative of Jehovah himself, claiming it as his right to assign for her a sphere of action, when that belongs to her conscience and to her God.

He has endeavored, in every way that he could, to destroy her confidence in her own powers, to lessen her self-respect and to make her willing to lead a dependent and abject life.

Now, in view of this entire disfranchisement of one-half the people of this country, their social and religious degradation—in view of the unjust laws above mentioned, and because women do feel themselves aggrieved, oppressed and fraudulently deprived of their most sacred rights, we insist that they have immediate admission to all the rights and privileges which belong to them as citizens of the United States.

20   In entering upon the great work before us, we anticipate no small amount of misconception, misrepresentation, and ridicule; but we shall use every instrumentality within our power to effect our object. We shall employ agents, circulate tracts, petition the State and National legislatures, and endeavor to enlist the pulpit and the press in our behalf. We hope this Convention will be followed by a series of Conventions embracing every part of the county.

Resolutions

Whereas, The great precept of nature is conceded to be, that "man shall pursue his own true and substantial happiness." Blackstone in his Commentaries remarks, that this law of Nature being coeval with mankind, and dictated by God himself, is of course superior in obligation to any other. It is binding over all the globe, in all countries and at all times; no human laws are of any validity if contrary to this, and such of them as are valid, derive their force, and all their validity, and all their authority mediately and immediately from this original; therefore,

Resolved, That all laws which prevent woman from occupying such a station in society as her conscience shall dictate, or which place her in a position inferior to that of man, are contrary to the great precept of nature, and therefore of no force or authority.

Resolved, That woman is man's equal—was intended to be so by the Creator, and the highest good of the race demands that she should be recognized as such.

Resolved, That the women of this country ought to be enlightened in regard to the laws under which they live, that they may no longer publish their degradation by declaring themselves satisfied with their present position, nor their ignorance, by asserting that they have all the rights they want.

25   Resolved, That inasmuch as man, while claiming for himself intellectual superiority, does accord to woman moral superiority, it is pre-eminently his duty to encourage her to speak and teach, as she has an opportunity, in all religious assemblies.

Resolved, That the same amount of virtue, delicacy, and refinement of behavior that is required of woman in the social state, should also be required of man, and the same transgressions should be visited with equal severity on both man and woman.

Resolved, That the objection of indelicacy and impropriety, which is so often brought against woman when she addresses a public audience, comes with a very ill-grace from those who encourage, by their attendance, her appearance on the stage, in the concert, or in feats of circus.

Resolved, That woman has too long rested satisfied in the circumscribed limits which corrupt customs and a perverted application of the Scriptures have marked out for her, and that it is time she should move in the enlarged sphere which her great Creator has assigned her.

Resolved, That it is the duty of women of this country to secure to themselves their sacred right to the elective franchise.

Resolved, That the equality of human rights results necessarily from the fact   30
of the identity of the race in capabilities and responsibilities.

Resolved, That the speedy success of our cause depends upon the zealous and untiring efforts of both men and women, for the overthrow of the monopoly of the pulpit, and for the securing to women an equal participation with men in the various trades, professions, and commerce.

Resolved, therefore, That, being invested by the creator with the same capabilities, and the same consciousness of responsibility for their exercise, it is demonstrably the right and duty of woman, equally with man, to promote every righteous cause by every righteous means; and especially in regard to the great subjects of morals and religion, it is self-evidently her right to participate with her brother in teaching them, both in private and in public, by writing and by speaking, by any instrumentalities proper to be used, and in any assemblies proper to be held; and this being a self-evident truth growing out of the divinely implanted principles of human nature, any custom or authority adverse to it, whether modern or wearing the hoary sanction of antiquity, is to be regarded as a self-evident falsehood, and at war with mankind.

The Morality of Birth Control

MARGARET SANGER

Margaret Sanger was a nurse who became a birth-control activist, believing that the ability to limit family size would free working-class women from the economic and physical burden of unwanted pregnancy. In 1921, Sanger founded the American Birth Control League, which is now known as the Planned Parenthood Federation of America. As a courageous proponent of sex education and the distribution of contraceptives, Sanger ran afoul of the 1873 Federal Comstock Law, which made it a crime to "import or distribute any device, medicine, or information designed to prevent conception or induce abortion, or to mention in print the names of sexually transmitted infections." "The Morality of Birth Control" was originally scheduled to be delivered at the close of the First American Birth Control Conference on November 12, 1921, but police raided the Town Hall and arrested Sanger. The speech was then delivered a week later at the Park Theatre in New York City on November 18, 1921. In arguing for the morality of birth control, Sanger also, in the last section of the speech, argues for eugenics (a social movement advocating improvement of the human genetic stock through selective breeding)—a position that generated controversy even among supporters of the birth control movement. Sanger's speech reveals the historical complexity of an era in which women's liberation, sexual freedom, eugenics, poverty eradication, and racism were intermixed.

The meeting tonight is a postponement of one which was to have taken place at the Town Hall last Sunday evening. It was to be a culmination of a three day conference, two of which were held at the Hotel Plaza, in discussing the Birth Control subject in its various and manifold aspects.

The one issue upon which there seems to be most uncertainty and disagreement exists in the moral side of the subject of Birth Control. It seemed only natural for us to call together scientists, educators, members of the medical profession and the theologians of all denominations to ask their opinion upon this uncertain and important phase of the controversy. Letters were sent to the most eminent men and women in the world. We asked in this letter, the following questions:

1. Is over-population a menace to the peace of the world?

2. Would the legal dissemination of scientific Birth Control information through the medium of clinics by the medical profession be the most logical method of checking the problem of over-population?

3. Would knowledge of Birth Control change the moral attitude of men and women toward the marriage bond or lower the moral standards of the youth of the country?

4. Do you believe that knowledge which enables parents to limit the families will make for human happiness, and raise the moral, social and intellectual standards of population?

We sent such a letter not only to those who, we thought, might agree with us, but we sent it also to our known opponents. Most of these people answered. Every one who answered did so with sincerity and courtesy, with the exception of one group whose reply to this important question as demonstrated at the Town Hall last Sunday evening was a disgrace to liberty-loving people, and to all traditions we hold dear in the United States. I believed that the discussion of the moral issue was one which did not solely belong to theologians and to scientists, but belonged to the people. And because I believed that the people of this country may and can discuss this subject with dignity and with intelligence I desired to bring them together, and to discuss it in the open.

When one speaks of moral[s], one refers to human conduct. This implies action of many kinds, which in turn depends upon the mind and the brain. So that in speaking of morals one must remember that there is a direct connection between morality and brain development. Conduct is said to be action in pursuit of ends, and if this is so, then we must hold the irresponsibility and recklessness in our action is immoral, while responsibility and forethought put into action for the benefit of the individual and the race becomes in the highest sense the finest kind of morality.

5   We know that every advance that woman has made in the last half century has been made with opposition, all of which has been based upon the grounds

of immorality. When women fought for higher education, it was said that this would cause her to become immoral and she would lose her place in the sanctity of the home. When women asked for the franchise it was said that this would lower her standard of morals, that it was not fit that she should meet with and mix with the members of the opposite sex, but we notice that there was no objection to her meeting with the same members of the opposite sex when she went to church.

The church has ever opposed the progress of woman on the ground that her freedom would lead to immorality. We ask the church to have more confidence in women. We ask the opponents of this movement to reverse the methods of the church, which aims to keep women moral by keeping them in fear and in ignorance, and to inculcate into them a higher and truer morality based upon knowledge. And ours is the morality of knowledge. If we cannot trust woman with the knowledge of her own body, then I claim that two thousand years of Christian teaching has proved to be a failure.

We stand on the principle that Birth Control should be available to every adult man and woman. We believe that every adult man and woman should be taught the responsibility and the right use of knowledge. We claim that woman should have the right over her own body and to say if she shall or if she shall not be a mother, as she sees fit. We further claim that the first right of a child is to be desired. While the second right is that it should be conceived in love, and the third, that it should have a heritage of sound health.

Upon these principles the Birth Control movement in America stands. When it comes to discussing the methods of Birth Control, that is far more difficult. There are laws in this country which forbid the imparting of practical information to the mothers of the land. We claim that every mother in this country, either sick or well, has the right to the best, the safest, the most scientific information. This information should be disseminated directly to the mothers through clinics by members of the medical profession, registered nurses and registered midwives.

Our first step is to have the backing of the medical profession so that our laws may be changed, so that motherhood may be the function of dignity and choice, rather than one of ignorance and chance. Conscious control of offspring is now becoming the ideal and the custom in all civilized countries. Those who oppose it claim that however desirable it may be on economic or social grounds, it may be abused and the morals of the youth of the country may be lowered. Such people should be reminded that there are two points to be considered. First, that such control is the inevitable advance in civilization. Every civilization involves an increasing forethought for others, even for those yet unborn. The reckless abandonment of the impulse of the moment[,] and the careless regard for the consequences, is not morality. The selfish gratification of temporary desire at the expense of suffering to lives that will come may seem very beautiful to some, but it is not our conception of civilization, [n]or is it our concept of morality.

10   In the second place, it is not only inevitable, but it is right to control the size of the family for by this control and adjustment we can raise the level and the standards of the human race. While Nature's way of reducing her numbers is controlled by disease, famine and war, primitive man has achieved the same results by infanticide, exposure of infants, the abandonment of children, and by abortion. But such ways of controlling population [are] no longer possible for us. We have attained high standards of life, and along the lines of science must we conduct such control. We must begin farther back and control the beginnings of life. We must control conception. This is a better method, it is a more civilized method, for it involves not only greater forethought for others, but finally a higher sanction for the value of life itself.

Society is divided into three groups. Those intelligent and wealthy members of the upper classes who have obtained knowledge of Birth Control and exercise it in regulating the size of their families. They have already benefited by this knowledge, and are today considered the most respectable and moral members of the community. They have only children when they desire, and all society points to them as types that should perpetuate their kind.

The second group is equally intelligent and responsible. They desire to control the size of their families, but are unable to obtain knowledge or to put such available knowledge into practice.

The third are those irresponsible and reckless ones having little regard for the consequence of their acts, or whose religious scruples prevent their exercising control over their numbers. Many of this group are diseased, feeble-minded, and are of the pauper element dependent entirely upon the normal and fit members of society for their support. There is no doubt in the minds of all thinking people that the procreation of this group should be stopped. For if they are not able to support and care for themselves, they should certainly not be allowed to bring offspring into this world for others to look after. We do not believe that filling the earth with misery, poverty and disease is moral. And it is our desire and intention to carry on our crusade until the perpetuation of such conditions has ceased.

We desire to stop at its source the disease, poverty and feeble-mindedness and insanity which exist today, for these lower the standards of civilization and make for race deterioration. We know that the masses of people are growing wiser and are using their own minds to decide their individual conduct. The more people of this kind we have, the less immorality shall exist. For the more responsible people grow, the higher do they and shall they attain real morality.

For Writing and Discussion

Argument Classics

1. Each of the arguments in this unit is trying to persuade its audience toward the writer's position or angle of vision on a major problem. Working in small groups or as a class, explore your answers to the following questions for one of the arguments selected by your instructor:
   a. What is the question or problem addressed by the writer?
   b. What is the writer's position or angle of vision?
   c. What reasons and evidence does the writer use? What are the writer's underlying assumptions and values?
   d. What positions or views is the writer pushing against or opposing?
   e. What is at stake?
2. How effective is the argument for you? What might have made it effective for its original targeted audience?

Writing Assignment

Rhetorical Analysis

Write a thesis-driven rhetorical analysis of one of the classic arguments chosen by your professor. Follow the instructions and guidelines for a rhetorical analysis essay as explained in Chapter 7, especially Table 7.2, Questions for Rhetorical Analysis.

Credits

Text Credits

Chapter 1   Page 4 © June Johnson.

Chapter 3   Page 46 Reprinted by permission from Carmen Tieu; p.50 Reprinted by permission from Carmen Tieu; p.51 Reprinted by permission from Carmen Tieu.

Chapter 4   Page 57 Surowiecki, James. "The Pay Is Too Damn Low" The New Yorker. Used with permission from Chris Calhoun Agency.

Chapter 5   Page 70 Buchanan, Bobbie "Don't Hang Up, That's My Mom Calling" New York Times (2003, December 07), op-ed.

Chapter 6   Page 92 Reprinted by permission from Trudie Makens; p.108 Reprinted by permission from Lauren Shinozuka; p.95 Oh, How I Will Miss the Plastic Bag; Alexander Chancellor. The Spectator, Oct. 10, 2015; Retrieved from https://spectator.com. au/2015/10/oh-how-i-will-miss-the-plastic-bag/.

Chapter 7   Page 112 Rev. Jim Ball, Ph.D., "It's Kairos Time for Climate Change: Time to Act," Creation Care: A Christian Environmental Quarterly (Summer 2008), 28; p.112 Sierra Club, "Global Warming Policy Solutions," 2008, http://www.sierraclub. org/; p. 113 Lopez, Kathryn Jean, "Egg Heads" 1998 National Review, Inc., Reprinted by permission; p.121 From The Boston Globe, April 11, © 2008. Boston Globe Media Partners. All rights reserved. Used by permission and protected by the Copyright Laws of the United States. The printing, copying, redistribution, or retransmission of this Content without express written permission is prohibited.

Chapter 8   Page 132 Schmitt, John, and Janelle Jones, 2012 "Low-Wage Workers Are Older and Better Educated than Ever." Washington, DC: Center for Economic and Policy Research.; p.132 Reprinted by permission from Trudie Makens; p.133 Reprinted by permission from Trudie Makens; p.134 Reprinted by permission from Trudie Makens; p.136 Surowiecki, James. "The Pay Is Too Damn Low" The New Yorker. Used with permission from Chris Calhoun Agency.; p.139 Reprinted by permission from Trudie Makens; p.143 Reprinted by permission from Trudie Makens; p.144 Reprinted by permission from Trudie Makens; p.148 Michael Saltsman (2013), "To Help the Poor, Move Beyond 'Minimum' Gestures" Huffington Post. Used with permission.; p.161 Reprinted by permission from Trudie Makens.

Chapter 9   Page 186 Based on U.S. Census Bureau, 2010.; p.181 U.S. Energy Information Administration. Data accessed from: https:// www.eia.gov/totalenergy/data/monthly/#consumption; p.199 Data from United States Energy Information Administration; p.200 Adapted from United States Energy Information Administration; p.184 Data from United States Energy Information Administration; p.186 Data from United States Energy Information Administration; p.187 Data from United States Energy Information Administration.

Chapter 10   Page 199 Reproduced with permission from Colleen Fontana.; p.205 Reprinted by permission from Monica Allen.

Chapter 11   Page 219 Hutchinson, Alex, "Your Daily Multivitamin May Be Hurting You - The debate is on: just useless, or truly dangerous?". Used with permission from Outside Magazine.

Chapter 12   Page 245 Reprinted by permission from Alex Mullen; p.248 Mark Oppenheimer (2017). How Do We Define Adulthood?; Los Angeles Times, March 13, 2017; Used with permission.

Chapter 13   Page 251 Data from Dr. Pieter Tans, NOAA/ESRL; p.274 Data from NASA Goddard Institute for Space Studies Surface Temperature Analysis.; p.275 Carlos Macias. The Credit Card Company Made Me Do It! —The Credit Card Industry's Role in Causing Student Debt.; p.273 © Pearson Education; p.267 What Causes Math Anxiety? By Jess Goncalves. Used with permission.

Chapter 14   Page 302 Reprinted by permission from Lorena Mendoza-Flores; p.302 Daar, Judith and Erez Aloni, "Three Genetic Parents—For One Healthy Baby" LA Times. Used with permission.; p.303 Aquila, Samuel, "The 'Therapeutic Cloning' of Human Embryos". © 2017 National Review. Used with permission.; p.299 Used with permission from Hadley Reeder.

Chapter 15   Page 324 Used with permission from Megan Johnson.; p.358 Reprinted by permission from Ivan Snook; p.338 Dicke, Marcel and Arnold Van Huis, "The Six-Legged Meat of the Future" Wall Street Journal. Retrived from: https://www.wsj.com/ articles/SB10001424052748703293204576106072340020728.

Chapter 17   Page 361 Reprinted with permission of American Council on Science and Health. For more information visit acsh.org.

Chapter 18   Page 385 Reprinted by permission from EBSCO Host.; p.420 U.S. Environmental Protection Agency.

Anthology 1   Page 411 David Roberts (2016). Putting a Price on Carbon in a Fine Idea. It's Not the End-All Be-All, Vox, Apr. 22, 2016; Source url: http://www.vox.com/2016/4/22/11446232/ price-on-carbon-fine. Used with permission.; p.407 Joseph Aldy, Curbing Climate Change Has a Dollar Value—Here's How and Why We Measure It, The Conversation, Mar. 12, 1017; Retrieved from: https://theconversation.com/curbing-climate-change-has-a-dollar-value-heres-how-and-why-we-measure-it-70882; p.416 Julian Cribb (2015). Our Human Right Not to be Poisoned, Australasian Science, Dec. 2015, pp. 38-39. Reproduced from Australasian Science (www.austscience.com).; p.419 Bill McKibben (2017). The Question I Get Asked the Most, Communities, no. 174 (Spring 2017), pp. 10-11 Used with permission.; p.422 Republished with permission of American Association for the Advancement of Science (AAAS) from Ecologically Relevant Data Are Policy-Relevant Data, Chelsea M Rochman, Science, Vol. 352, no. 6290 (June 2, 2016), p. 1172 Permission conveyed through Copyright Clearance Center, Inc; p.427 Plastic Bag Ban: Let's Not Get Carried Away, Sun Sentinel,

Photo Credits

Chapter 1 Page 7 CartoonStock Ltd; p.1 blickwinkel/Alamy Stock Photo; p.6 Original cover by Science for the People organization. Modified for the web by Melanie McCalmont; p.7 Mikael Karlsson/Alamy Stock Photo.

Chapter 2 Page 28 Deborah Thompson/Alamy Stock Photo;

Chapter 4 Page 66 Ivan Sgualdini/Shutterstock; p.67 June Johnson Bube.

Chapter 5 Page 84 Bullit Marquez/AP Images; p.85 Men Can Stop Rape; p.79 Chief Seattle's Letter or Speech to the President (1852).

Chapter 7 Page 103 jim West/Alamy Stock Photo.

Chapter 8 Page 130 © Employment Policies Institute EPI; p.131 CartoonStock Ltd.

Chapter 9 Page 169 Peter Byrne/AP Images; p.179 The Advertising Council; p.182 U.S. National Library of Medicine; p.191 TxtResponsibly.org; p.192 Milt Priggee/Cagle Cartoons, Inc.; p.175 The Advertising Council; p.171 Alex Milan Tracy/Anadolu Agency/Getty Images; p.171 padu_foto/Shutterstock; p.171 Huguette Roe/Shutterstock; p.171 Pavel L Photo and Video/Shutterstock; p.171 Moreno Soppelsa/Shutterstock; p.172 Aleksej Orel/123RF; p.177 Kris Saknussemm; p.169 June Johnson Bube; p.169 June Johnson Bube; p.169 June Johnson Bube; p.169 June Johnson; p.170 June Johnson; p.170 June Johnson Bube; p.170 June Johnson Bube; p.170 June Johnson Bube; p.172 June Johnson Bube; p.174 Kris Saknussemm.

Chapter 10 Page 195 Jim West/Alamy Stock Photo; p.195 Gila Photography/Shutterstock; p.195 Felipe Chacon/EFE/Newscom.

Chapter 11 Page 211 Kathy deWitt/Alamy Stock Photo.

Chapter 12 Page 229 Randy Bish/Cagle Cartoons, Inc.; p.222 Tina's Groove used with the permission of Rina Piccolo, King Features Syndicate and the Cartoonist Group. All rights reserved.

Chapter 13 Page 259 Free the Captives.

Chapter 14 Page 281 NEILL BLOMKAMP FILM COMPANY/AF archive/Alamy Stock Photo; p.314 John Bean.

Chapter 15 Page 307 Devito/Verdi,Sal Devito,Executive Creative Director; p.311 FLPA/Alamy Stock Photo; p.319 Jane E Bube; p.335 Kathryn Gilje/Save-Bees.org; p.337 Peter Essick/Aurora Photos/Alamy Stock Photo; p.337 Simon Belcher/Alamy Stock Photo; p.338 Gavriel Jecan/Photodisc/Getty Images.

Chapter 16 Page 341 June Johnson.

Anthology 1 Page 405 June Johnson; p. 419 Arctic Circle used with the permission of Alex Hallatt, King Features Syndicate and the Cartoonist Group. All rights reserved.

Anthology 2 Page 442 CartoonStock Ltd.

Anthology 3 Page 474 Signe Wilkinson Editorial Cartoon used with the permission of Signe Wilkinson, the Washington Post Writers Group and the Cartoonist Group. All rights reserved.; p.470 Javier Zarracina, Vox.com, and Vox Media, Inc.

Anthology 4 Page 492 CartoonStock Ltd.

Anthology 5 Page 557 From Mother Jones, September 18 © 2013 Foundation for National Progress. All rights reserved. Used by permission and protected by the Copyright Laws of the United States. The printing, copying, redistribution, or retransmission of this Content without express written permission is prohibited.

Anthology 6 Page 540 Jeff Danziger Editorial Cartoon used with the permission of Jeff Danziger and the Cartoonist Group. All rights reserved.

Index